PETRO-ECONOMICS

PETRO-ECONOMICS

Dr. A.N. Sarkar

POWERING ENERGY...
PENTAGON ENERGY PRESS

Pertro-Economics / Dr. A.N. Sarkar
Includes Preface, index

ISBN 978-81-8274-421-9

First Edition 2009

Published by
PENTAGON ENERGY PRESS
An Imprint of
PENTAGON PRESS
206, Peacock Lane, Shahpur Jat,
New Delhi-110049
Phones: 011-64706243, 26491568
Telefax: 011-26490600
email: rajan@pentagon-press.com
website: www.pentagon-press.com

Printed at
Syndicate Binders
A-20, Hosiery Complex, Noida Phase-II Extn., Noida-201305, U.P.

Preface

The modern industrial world is extensively energy-intensive and energy-driven. Oil and natural gas are two important precursors to fuel the energy sector for meeting spiraling demands of energy, power, transport, commercial, domestic and industrial sectors, predominantly the petrochemical-based and allied industries. In recent years, macro-trends are being experienced in the global scene in petroleum industry, especially in the sphere of oil, natural gas, refining, long-distance transportation and petro-retailing. Other notable changes are also taking place in restructuring, reforms initiatives and introduction of compilation, consolidation and above all in sustainable conservation and environmental security aspects.

Fossil fuels, such as oil and natural gas, meeting nearly 85 per cent of the global energy demand, constitute the backbone of many petrochemical-based and allied industries—prominently in energy, domestic, industrial and transport sectors. The demand for these resources is presently high from the developed economy; but the projected demand in the next decade is predicted to be even higher from the developing economies; especially from Brazil, Russia, India and China (i.e. BRIC's). In past 4 or 5 decades, the demand-supply equilibrium has been artificially disrupted off-and-on by creating a divide across OPEC and Non-OPEC oil producing, exporting and importing countries. A phenomenon of this kind is largely attributable to such factor as geo-politics, causing both trade distortions as well as regional and economic imbalances in the supply-chain and consumption scenario.

Anticipated worldwide economic growth in the first decade of the 21st century will lead to concomitant increases in energy demand and carbon emissions. In the developing world in particular, the global tendencies toward over-dependency syndrome are going to be pronounced. Over the next two decades, the total world energy consumption is expected to increase by more than 50 per cent. By 2020, energy demand in the developing world will be more than double, which will roughly equal to those of the industrialized nations as of now.

Transportation is the primary driver of increased oil demand, while increased natural gas consumption will largely be for power generation, domestic requirement and for meeting greater industrial requirements. US consumption represents roughly half of that for the industrialized world and US fuel source consumption closely mirrors world patterns. Developing Asia, Central America, and South America will see the greatest increase in requirements for natural gas; they are even expected to triple their demand over the next twenty years.

The main consumers of oil continue to be the industrialized countries of the Organization for Economic Cooperation and Development (OECD), particularly the US, Europe and Japan, which together consume about half of the world's annual oil output. However, consumption in emerging market regions is expanding at a faster pace (especially in China and India) as, going by their GDP trend analysis, these countries will grow rapidly as their use of energy in transportation, industry and residential sectors expands phenomenally. The transportation sector accounts for about two-thirds of the oil consumed in the United States and around half of the oil used in the world.

World marketed energy consumption is projected to grow by 57 per cent between 2004 and 2030, according to the reference case projection from the International Energy Outlook 2007 (IEO, 2007) released by the Energy Information Administration (EIA). The IEO-2007 shows the most rapid growth in energy demand for nations outside the Organization for Economic Cooperation and Development (OECD), especially in non-OECD Asia, where strong projected economic growth drives the increase in energy use.

Global energy demand grows despite the relatively high world oil and natural gas prices in the reference case. However, rising oil prices dampen growth in demand for petroleum and other liquids fuels after 2015 and, as a result, reducing their share of overall energy use from 38 per cent in 2004 to a projected 34 per cent in 2030. In contrast, the energy shares of natural gas, coal, and renewable energy sources are expected to grow over this period. Liquids consumption is still expected to grow strongly, however, reaching 118 million barrels per day in 2030. The United States, China, and India together account for nearly half of the projected growth in world liquids use.

To meet the increment in world liquids demand in the IEO-2007 reference case, supply in 2030 is projected to be 35 million barrels oil equivalent per day higher than the 2004 level of 83 million barrels per day. Conventional resources account for about 27 million barrels per day of this increase, with a projected 21 million barrels per day increase in production by members of the Organization of Petroleum Exporting Countries (OPEC) and 6 million barrels per day increase in non-OPEC countries. Production from unconventional resources (including biofuels), coal-to-liquids (CTL) and gas-to-liquids) increases by nearly 8 million barrels per day and accounts for nearly 9 per cent of total world liquids supply in 2030.

An analysis of global Hydrocarbon business environment would reveal that the world oil consumption has gone up by almost 3-folds from the level of 312.50 million barrels per day in 1965 to 807.57 million barrels per day in 2004. Of this, the consumption of North America accounts for nearly 30 per cent. Compared to this, the overall demand from Asia and Pacific region is proximately one-fourth of the global demand.

To meet the growing oil demands, mainly for industrial and transport segments, global oil production has perfectly matched the global consumption trend over the years 1965-2004. The global production has gone up to 807.57 million barrels/ day in 2004, compared to 312.50 million barrels/ day in 1965 to keep pace with growing demands. Of the global production, the major contributors have been the Middle-east countries with 245.71 million barrels/ day production figure in 2004.

On individual country-basis, among the top 10 major oil-producing countries, Saudi Arabia (9.93 mbpd), USA (8.44 mbpd) and Russia (8.44 mbpd) ranks 1st, 2nd and 3rd position respectively. The USA (490.8 m. tones/year) and Russia (520.8 m.tonnes/year) are the major contributors of Natural gas. Similarly; Saudi Arabia, United States and Russia are the best (in the given order) amongst 10 top oil producers of the world.

Because of high demand placed and projected by the USA, EU and some of the Asian countries like India, China, as well as Brazil and Russia, the projected demands for oil can go up to the level of 120 mbpd in 2030 from 75 mbpd in 2000. The projected Natural gas demands of the OECD countries put together (2449 billion cubic metres) are nearly 50 per cent of the global demands (5047 billion cubic metres) of Natural gas resources.

In the International Energy Outlook, 2005 (IEO, 2005), world demand for crude oil grows from 77 million barrels per day in 2002 to 103 million barrels per day in 2015 and to just over 119 million barrels per day in 2025. Much of the growth in oil consumption is projected for the emerging Asian nations, where strong economic growth results in a robust increase in oil demand. Emerging Asia (including China and India) accounts for 45 per cent of the total world's increased production in oil-use over the forecast period (i.e. 2005-25).

In the International Energy Outlook (IEO, 2005) forecast, growth in the world oil demand averages 1.9 per cent per year over the forecast period. Most of the world's incremental oil demand is projected for use in the transportation sector, where there are currently no competitive alternatives to petroleum; however, several of the technologies associated with non-conventional liquids (gas to liquids, coal to liquids and energy crops that can be sued to produce ethanol and bio-diesel) could reduce the pressure on conventional oil supply from the transportation sector. Of the projected increase in oil use over 2002 to 2025 period, 61 per cent will occur in the transportation sector. The industrial sector also accounts for a fairly large share of the projected increase in the world oil consumption: 28 per cent of the increase is expected to be for industrial sector uses, mostly for industries relying upon chemical and petrochemical processes.

On a regional basis, two parts of the world account for most of the projected growth in the world oil demand: emerging Asia and North America. Outside North America, oil consumption in the mature market economy regions grows much more slowly—by about 0.3 per cent per year—in both Western Europe and mature market of Asia, reflecting expectations of slow growth or declines in population and economic growth over the next two decades.

In the emerging economies, strong expansion of oil-use is projected, as robust economic growth fuels demand for oil to buttress burgeoning industrial sectors and rapidly expanding transportation use. The fastest growth in oil demand is projected for the emerging Asian economies, at an average rate of 3.5 per cent per year over the forecast period. From 2002 to 2025, the consumption of petroleum is projected to increase on average by 2.1 per cent per year in the Middle-East, 2.5 per cent per year in Central and South America; and 2.7 per cent per year in Africa.

Economic development in Asia will be crucial to long-term growth in oil markets. China, India and the other nations of emerging Asia are expected to experience combined economic growth of 5.5 per cent per year between 2002 and 2025, the highest rate of growth in the world. This robust expansion in GDP translates to 3.5 per cent annual increase in regional oil use. The projected evolution of Asian oil demand could strengthen economic ties between the Middle-East and Asia, as Asian nations rely more and more on Middle-East oil supplies.

The total energy consumption in India is 352 million tonnes of oil equivalent (MTOE). Oil and natural gas constitutes 43 per cent of the energy busket (oil-35% and gas-8%). Coal remains the dominant fuel at 55 per cent of the primary consumption at present. Oil and natural gas have been constantly replacing coal as a primary commercial source of energy. The sector-wise order of predominance in the consumption of oil and natural gas is as follows: transport, domestic, industry and agriculture in that order.

India is both a major energy producer and consumer. India currently ranks as the world's eleventh greatest energy producer, accounting for about 2.4 per cent of the world's total annual energy production, and as the world's sixth greatest energy consumer, accounting for about 3.3 per cent of the world's total annual energy consumption. Despite its large annual energy production, India is a net energy importer, mostly due to the large imbalance between oil production and consumption.

India's proved oil reserves were estimated (as of January 2005) at about 5 billion barrels, or about 4.5 per cent of the world total. Most of these reserves lie offshore near Mumbai and onshore in Assam state. However, exploration is still happening, and India's off-shore and on-shore basins may contain as much as 11 billion barrels. India presently ranks as the 25th greatest producer of crude oil, accounting for about 1 per cent of the world's annual crude oil production. About 30 per cent of India's energy needs are met by oil, and more than 60 per cent of that oil is imported. A strong growth in oil demand has resulted in India's annual petroleum consumption increasing by more than 75 per cent from what it was a decade ago, and petroleum consumption is projected to climb to about 3 million barrels per day by 2010. India is currently the world's sixth greatest oil consumer, accounting for about 2.9 per cent of world's total annual petroleum consumption.

India's natural gas reserves were estimated (as of January 2005) at about 29-32 trillion cubic feet (tcf), or about 0.5 per cent of the world total. Most of these reserves lie offshore northwest of Mumbai in the Arabian Sea and onshore in Gujarat state. India does not yet rank in the top 20 of the world's greatest natural gas consumers, but that will soon change. Natural gas has experienced the fastest rate of increase of any fuel in India's primary energy supply; demand is growing at about 4.8 per cent per year and is forecast to rise to 1.2 tcf per year by 2010 and 1.6 tcf per year by 2015.

India's consumption of petroleum products has been growing at the rate of 5.6 per cent per annum during past 30 years (1975-76 to 2004-05). It has grown at the rate of 5.5 per cent per annum during last three decades (1975-76 to 2004-05). The proved reserve to production (R/P) ratio is about 22 at present. India now imports 72.2 per cent the domestic consumption and the country's import is growing rapidly. India's import dependence is projected to rise to 75 per cent of the total consumption during 11th Plan. The demand vis-à-vis production gap of oil & natural gas is met through import of these commodities. To meet the energy requirement in India the sources other than petroleum and natural gas include: coal, nuclear, solar, hydro-, hydel-thermal, biomas, biofuel, solar, and wind energy.

India's Gross import bill of petroleum products, valued at Rs.131756 crore during 2004-05, was almost four times as much as the export bill, valued at Rs. 28386 crore. The quantum of sale of Petroleum products during 2002-05 by the public sector companies/ govt. undertakings was 5 times higher than the private sector enterprises during the given period.

The challenges facing the petroleum and natural gas sectors in India is multifold; the prominent among them being: (a) ensuring uninterrupted and sustained supply of oil and natural gas from domestic and competitive global market amidst rising prices; (b) demand-supply management of petroleum products in the growing economy; (c) rational pricing of petroleum products and natural gas under expanding petro-retail routes; also ensuring accessibility in the remote areas under deregulated market environment;(d) removal of entry barriers for private players in distribution and retail businesses for creating competitive retail markets; (e) evolving and streamlining improved regulations of upstream and downstream sector; (f) improving administration of LPG and kerosene subsidy; (g) environmental management through product upgradation; (h) addressing the issue concerning energy security and evolving appropriate short-term and long-term strategic policy to ensure energy security compatible with the developed economy.

One major reason for confidently projecting higher—but of course erratic—oil prices are: world oil demand on a 'demographic' base has almost unlimited upward potential, and higher oil prices themselves drive oil demand upward. It is no surprise, then, to find that the "10-year trend rate" of 1.3 per cent annual growth of world oil demand has almost certainly disappeared as oil prices have responded to much more buoyant demand, and have themselves generated faster economic growth, mostly outside the OECD bloc, that itself underpins world oil demand and therefore prices. Understanding the mechanisms in play is vital to making accurate and realistic forecasts for future demand through the coming 4-5 years, and beyond.

The Book, inter alia, highlights some of the major issues concerning the Geopolitics of Oil Trading and its overall impact on Global Economy. Hence, an attempt has been particularly made to discuss the various aspects and dimensions of geo-politics in oil-trading in the global business scene seeking to suggest future strategies and options to minimize the negative impact of geo-politics on the global economy by resorting to certain positive policy interventions—both at the regional as well as global levels.

In a state of super-competitiveness in oil & natural gas trading together with a wide-ranging petro-products the scope of e-Business especially in monitoring and control of information flow linking upstream, mid-stream and down-stream activities, inclusive of Petro-retailing, has been vital not only to compete but also for survival and future growth. Appropriately a chapter on E-Business has been included to broad-base the concept of Petro-economics.

Cheap Oil is seen by the decision-making elite in the richer nations as the 'passport to economic growth'. This is a pure fantasy. Only 'extreme' oil prices (probably above $150/barrel) will abort or cancel the global economy expansionary impacts of higher oil prices.

Since about 1995 'demand shock' has begun to operate in the world economy for a number of economic, social or 'secular' and technical reasons, leading to considerably higher underlying growth rates of world oil demand. Current 'trend growth rates' for world energy and world oil demand are about 2.25 per cent for oil and about 2.5 per cent for energy on an annual basis. Cheap oil and energy remains the essential base of conventional economic development and social progress anyplace in the world. This in turn is a powerful motor for continued and strong demand growth for fossil energy, worldwide. Upward potential for personal consumption of fossil fuels is essentially unlimited in this context.

Conventional or classic economic growth is enabled and facilitated at the world or 'composite' level by rising oil prices to high price levels. This also underpins, or even increases world demand for fossil energy supplies, indicating that concerted international action is needed to plan for the effects of persistent underestimates of real demand growth trends.

India's oil development policy has treaded the path of experimentation with a national vision of providing energy to the development process of the country. Oil policy is of special significance to the growing Indian economy on the following counts: (i) Oil is an essential ingredient in the country's development process; (ii) They did not have the requisite capital and technology to explore oil in the beginning of the development era; (iii) India is not endowed with oil resources as much as it would require for its domestic consumption; (iv) India took considerable time to open up its economy for private investment and to foreign market; and eventually did so under a set of delicate market conditions; and (v) Oil sector being intertwined with the other sectors of economy, any major constraints in the sectoral achievement would directly hits the other sectors of the economy.

In the given scenario, a sound knowledge in different facets of Petro-economics is a *sine quo non* for the industries dealing with exploration, production, refining, transport and marketing of oil and natural gas. Evolution and application of the concept of Petro-economics, following the first-ever major 'oil shock' in the early 1970's has gained strategic significance and tremendous momentum from the first decade of the 21 st century on the following grounds: (i) integration of National energy security with Global energy security environment; (ii) growing concerns on dwindling oil and natural gas reserves to cater to the growing economy in the developing world with much greater projected future demand for oil and natural gas; (iii) segmentation of the global oil and natural gas market on geo-political basis, compounded by the overwhelming ramifications of regional economic unions; (iv) Price structuring and attendant accounting problems of oil and natural gas in terms of upstream, midstream, downstream and marketing/retailing activities associated with crudes, refined oil and natural gas (including LNG) products; (v) Benchmarking the quality standards of petro-products with branding and customization for reaching out the global market; (vi) Activating reforms process to allow free-flow of petro-products and services in the hyper-competitive global market. With this backdrop and thematic approaches in mind it was thought appropriate to attempt a book on Petro-Economics, focusing on the following broad objectives:

(a) To develop a broad understanding about the genesis, exploration, production, refining, transportation and marketing of petroleum and natural gas—both from technological and management angles;
(b) Familiarities in broad terms with general economic principles and accounting procedure for efficiently run and manage petro-businesses, covering major upstream, midstream and downstream activities;
(c) Familiarities with national and global issues concerning energy securities and exposure to national policies conducive to oil and natural gas trading under deregulated market environment;
(d) Implications of geopolitics and allied issues in global petro-businesses; and
(e) Role of E-commence and petro-informatics in oil trading/petro-retailing.

Within this overall conceptual framework, the book on Petro-economics is specially designed to cover 14 chapters, encompassing the following themes:

- Introduction to Oil and Natural Gas
- World Energy Scene and Contribution of Oil and Gas in Energy-Mix
- Oil and Natural Gas Exploration, Drilling and Production
- Pipelines: Mid-stream Sector
- Management and Evaluation of Assets
- Transportation of Oil and Natural Gas
- Economics of Crude Oil
- Refinery Economics
- Petroleum Marketing and Trading
- Petro-Retailing
- Financial and Accounting System of Oil and Natural Gas
- International Hydrocarbon Economic Environment
- Geo-Politics of Oil Trading: Scanning Global Business Scene
- E-Business in Oil and Natural Gas Trading

For orienting the readers towards the real world situation of petro-businesses, some selective and illustrative case studies have been suitably incorporated.

The author believes that the book will be of immense value to the professionals of petrochemical industries, planners, research scholars and the students at large in the Petroleum, Natural Gas and Energy Sector.

Dr. A.N.Sarkar

Contents

Preface v

1. **Introduction to Oil and Natural Gas** **1**
   - Genesis and Technology Options of Oil Exploration 1
     - Genesis 1
     - Reserves and Resources 1
     - Origin of Oil 2
       - A. Biogenic theory 2
       - B. Abiogenic theory of origin of oil 3
     - History of Oil Production 3
     - Classification of Oil 5
       - Types of Crude Oil according to the U.S. Environmental Protection Agency 5
     - A Brief History of Oil and Gas Industry 6
     - History of Oil Prices 8
     - Origin of Petroleum and Processes of Extraction 8
       - Fault trap 9
       - Anticline 9
       - Salt dome 9
   - Profile of Petroleum Operations 11
     - The Basic Element of a Product in a System 12
     - Well Completion 12
     - Fluid Separation and Treatment 12
     - Treatment of Emulsion and Contaminants 13
     - Treatment Processes 13
     - Electrical Dehydration 13
     - Crude Oil desalting System 13
     - Fluid Separation and Treatment 14
     - Natural Gas Treatment 15
       - Prevention of Hydrate 15
       - Dehydration of Natural Gas 15
       - Measurement of Oil and Gas 15
     - Simple Distillation 17

Downstream Processing 17
Crude Oil Quality 18
Other Refinery Inputs 19
Production Tests 19
Drill Stem Test (DST) 20
Conventional Testing 20
Production Logging 20
Crude Oil Storage 21
EOR/IOR: Artificial Lift 21
Positive Displacement Pumps 22
Classification of Wells 22
Safety Systems in Oil and Gas well and Association Surface Equipment 23
Classification 23
1. Subsurface Controlled Subsurface Safety Valves (SCSSV) 23
2. Surface Safety Systems Surface Safety Valve 23
Natural Gas—The Fuel of the 21st Century 23
A Brief History of Oil Companies 24
Evolution of NOCs 25
Development of NOCs in Second Half of 12th Century 26
Indian Oil Corporation Limited (Indian Oil) 28
Indian Downstream Major 28
Drivers of Change 29
New Paradigm In Oil Industries 30

2. Global Energy Scene and Contribution of Oil and Natural Gas 35
Projection of Global Energy Demand: IEA vs. IEO 35
IEA Projections of Global Energy Demand 38
Global Energy Demand Perspective 38
India's Overall Production, Consumption and Projected Demand of Energy: Overview of India's Oil and Gas Sector 40
Petroleum 41
Natural Gas 42
Coal 43
Electricity 43
Carbon Emissions Information 45
Fossil Fuels 45
Non-Fossil Fuels 46
Nuclear 46
Hydro 46
Non-conventional Renewable 46
Oil Demand Shock and World Oil Price Trend 47
Demographic Demand and Oil prices 47
Impact of Oil Shocks on Demographic Demand 48
The Real Impact of Higher Oil Prices on Global Economic Growth 48
Global Economy Growth is Vital for Future Oil Production 49
Oil Demand is Driven by Higher Prices—Demand Shock 50

Higher Oil prices Change vs. Future Demand Trends 51
Demand Shock can Trigger Price Hike 51
Future Perspectives 52
India's position in Global Primary Energy Consumption 53
Energy Distribution between Developed and Developing Countries 53
Indian Energy Scenario 53
Energy Supply Scenario 54
  Coal Supply 54
  Natural Gas Supply 55
  Electrical Energy Supply 56
  Nuclear Power Supply 56
  Hydro-Power Supply 56
Projected Demand of Final Energy Consumption 56
Energy Needs of Growing Indian Economy 56
Plan-wise Outlay 57
Future Supply vs. Demand of Conventional Oil 57
Tapping Non-conventional Oil Resources 58
Competitive Market Position 58
Fear of Shortage 59
Uncertainty and Price 60
Capacity Issues 60
Short-Term Oil Market 61
Geo-Politics and Oil 62
Long-term Outlook 62
Oil Supply Security 63
Global scenario in Natural Gas 63
Availability and Utilization of Natural Gas in India 63
Utilization of Natural Gas 64
Natural Gas Allocation and Supply Scenario 64
Import of Natural Gas through Transnational Pipelines 65
  (a) Iran-Pakistan-India (IPI) Pipeline Project 65
  (b) Myanmar-Bangladesh-India Gas Pipeline Project 66
  (c) Turkmenistan-Afghanistan-Pakistan (TAP) pipeline 67
Liquefied Natural Gas (LNG) 67
LNG Imports to India 67
Gas Pricing 68
Regulatory Framework of Gas Industry 69
Hydrocarbon Vision-2025 69
Objectives for the Hydrocarbon Sector 69
Exploration and Production Sector 70
Medium Term Objectives 70
  Long-Term 71
Natural Gas 71
  Medium-Term Objective 71
  Long-Term Strategy 71
  Tariff and Pricing 72
  Medium Term 72

Restructuring and Divestment 72
New Exploration Licensing Policy (NELP): The Backdrop 73
 Why NELP? 73
Salient Achievement under NELP 74
Conclusions 75

3. Oil and Natural Gas Exploration, Drilling and Production (Upstream Sector) 77
Introduction 77
Regulated Industry 78
Exploration and Production 79
Off-shore Drilling Operations 81
Drilling for Oil 82
Types of Rigs 82
Preparing to Drill 83
Setting the Rig 83
Drilling Operation 86
Recovery Processes 88
Production and Sales 89
Future Outlook 89
Exploration and Development in the Ninth Plan: The Indian Scene 90
Increasing Role of Technology in finding Oil 91
Seismic Exploration 91
 Onshore Seismic Exploration 93
 Offshore Seismic Exploration 93
 2-D Seismic Interpretation 94
 Computer Assisted Exploration 94
 3-D Seismic Imaging 95
Exploration Techniques for Petroleum 96
 Surface Geology 96
 Direct Indications 97
 Surface Data 97
 Oil Seeps 98
 Well Cuttings 98
 Cores 98
 Electric Logs 99
 Drill Stem Tests 99
 Geophysical Surveys 99
 Geochemical Surveys 100
 Maps and Cross-Sections 100
 Contour Maps 100
 Geologic Maps 100
 Cross-Sections 101
Formation Evaluation 101
Enhanced Oil Recovery (EOR) 101
EOR Production by Country 102
 Thermal Methods 102

Solvent Flooding 102
Chemical Methods 102
Future of Oil 103
Historical Perspective Oil Industry in Indian Context 104
Crude Oil Reserves 108
Strategy of 10th Plan (2002-07) for E&P Activities 112
Target and Strategy for Oil Production during 11th Plan 113
Future Vision and Strategy 114
Oil and Gas Demand Supply Scenario 114
Enhancing Oil and Gas Production 114
New Exploration Licensing Policy (NELP) 115
Improved Oil Recovery/Enhanced Oil Recovery Projects 115
Oil and Gas from Abroad 116
Alternate Sources of Oil and Gas 116
Coal-Bed Methane 116

4. Management and Evaluation of Upstream Assets 119
Scope of Asset Management 119
Asset Management Objectives 120
(a) What are Asset Management Objectives? 120
(b) Why are they Important? 120
(c) Why must we Balance Internal and External Factors in Setting Objectives? 120
(d) What are the Consequences of not Setting Asset Management Objectives? 121
Asset Management Processes 122
Preparation of Asset Management Plans 122
Factors Affecting Asset Value 123
Asset Life-Cycle 123
Key Decisions 123
Decision Check Points and Decision Criteria 124
(a) Strategic Fit 124
(b) Economic Fit 125
(c) Work Quality 125
(d) Technology 125
(e) Reality Check 125
(f) Financial Considerations 125
(g) Risks 125
Key Tools used in Asset Management 125
Quality Assurance 126
Work Accomplishment between Major Decisions 127
Decision-making by the Business Unit 127
Quality Assurance Checks 129
Performance Measurement 129
Key Performance Indicators 130
Explore Phase Measures 130
Key Performance Indicators 131
Develop Phase Measures 131

Quality Indicators 131
Operating Indicators 131
Key Performance Indicators 131
Disposal Phase Measures 131
Portfolio Management 132
Risk Profile of Portfolio 134
Limitations to Portfolio Matrix and Way to Overcome 134
Knowledge Management Perspective of Asset Management 135
Role of Technology in Asset Management 135
Oil and Gas Properties 136
Operating Costs 138
Discounted Cash-flow Analysis 139
Discount Rate Components 140
Master Limited Partnerships 143
Pipelines and Natural Gas 146
Rate Determination 147
Revenue Requirement 147
Cost of Service 148
Rate Base 148
Deferred Taxes and the Cost of Capital 148
Test Year 149
Rate Design 149
Book Value Multiples 149
Cash-Flow Multiples 149
Foreign Operations 150
Country Risk Factor 150
Valuation of Foreign Oil and Gas Reserves 150
Foreign Exchange Laws 151
Optimization of Upstream Technologies for Upgrading and Implementation 151
Continuous Improvement through Post-Auditing 155
Summary 155

5. Mid-Stream Sector: Pipelines **158**
Pipeline Transportation 158
Perspectives in Indian Pipeline Systems Development 159
Cairn India Initiative in Rajasthan-Gujarat Pipeline 159
Petronet Initiative 160
Other Issues of Pipeline Transportation 161
Pipeline Route Selection 161
Design Optimization 161
Clearances Required 162
Agencies According Approval 162
Governance Issues 162
Processing Facilities Required at the Oil Field for Oil 163
A. Well Treatment 163
B. Gathering Systems 163

C. Gas-Plant Processing 163
Sulfur Removal 164
Pipeline Transportation 164
Oil and Gas Pipelines: Comparison 164
Pipeline Transportation Operations 165
Configuration of Cross-Country Pipeline 165
Import Through Pipelines: pros and cons 169
The Future Role of Cross-Border Pipelines 169
The Size of Gas Reserves 170
The Problems of Negotiating Export Contracts 170
Security of Supply 170
The Problems of Long-distance Transportation 171
The Problems of Cross-Border Pipelines 172
CASE STUDY 172
Crude Oil and Product Pipelines in India 173
IOC's Petroleum Pipelines under Operation in the Country 173
Pipelines Operations 175
Offshore Terminals 176
Tank Farms 176
Pump Stations 176
Pipeline Maintenance 176
Stations Maintenance 176
Mainline Maintenance 176
Corrosion Monitoring 176
Online Inspection 177
Pipeline Repairs and Rehabilitation 177
Pipeline Materials Management 177
New Pipeline Project Implementation 177
Tank Wagons 178
Tank Trucks 178
Product Tankers 178

6. Transportation of Oil and Natural Gas 179
Introduction 179
A. Supply Plan Management in Oil Industry 181
Oil Industry Supply Chain Management 181
Supply Plan Management 182
B. Transportation of Petroleum Products 183
Integrated Transport operation 184
Players in Petroleum Transportation 184
Transportation in Oil Industry : A Multi-Modal Operation 184
Modes of Transportation 185
Transportation by Railways 185
Transportation by Roads 186
Ocean transportation 186
Handling at Ports 187
Crude Oil and Gas Shipping 187

A. Terminal Management 187
B. Shipping 190
Size of Vessels 190
Types of Ship 191
Dry Trade 191
Wet Trade 191
Tonnage 191
Tanker Chartering 192
Voyage Charter 192
Time Charter 192
Bareboat Charter 192
Trip-Time Charter 193
Contract of Affreightment (COA) 193
Freight Market 193
INCHOE Terms 193
Bill of Lading 194
World Scale 194
Shipping of Liquefied Natural Gas 194
Trade in LNG 194
Natural Gas Pipelines in India 196
Pipeline Transportation 197
LPG Transportation by Road and Rail 198
Transportation of LPG by Pipeline: Jamnaar-Loni Pipeline 199
CNG Marketing 199
Sectoral Use of Petroleum Products 199
Market Segments and Transportation Legs 199
Marketing of Transportation Fuels in India 200
Structural Shifts Envisaged in Transportation of Petroleum Products 201
Import through Pipelines: pros and cons 201

7. Economics of Crude Oil 203
Introduction 203
Basic Petroleum Supply Chain Economics 203
Crude Oil is a Composite Product 203
Crude Oil is Quality-Specific 204
How Crude Oil is converted in the Refinery Process? 204
Separation: Heavy on the Bottom, Light on the Top 205
Conversion: Cracking and Rearranging Molecules to add Value 205
Sources and Availability 206
Crude Oil Pricing and Evaluation 208
Pricing 208
Physical Market 208
Players in the Physical Market 209
Paper Market 211
Fundaments of Physical Market 211
Tradable and non-tradable Crude 212
Formula Price 213

Benchmark Crude 214
OSP of NOCs 214
Crude Oil Evaluation 215
Value of Crude 215
Price of Crude 215
Price of Products 216
Gross Refinery Margin (GRM) 216
    Drivers of High Refining Margin 216
Evaluation Methodology 216
GPW 216
Landed Cost of Crude 216
Pecking Order 217
Platts & Argus 217
Trade and Transportation 217
    Oil Trade—The Balancing Flow 217
Tanker—The Most Economic Transport Mode 218
Taxation 218
OPEC's Role in Price Structuring 219
    OPEC vis-à-vis World Oil Market 219
World Oil Production and Exportable Surplus 220
    OPEC Reserves 221
OPEC's Oil Policy 221
OPEC's Production Cut and Compliance 223
The Impacts of OPEC Policy 224
India's OPEC Policy 225
Policy Direction for India 227
Areas of Action for Indian Refineries 227
Crude Oil of Indian Origin 228
Summary 229

8. Refinery Economics 230
Introduction 230
Historic Backdrop of Refining: Global Scene 232
Refining Techniques and Processes 232
The Product Lines 233
    Crude oil 233
    Gases 233
    Light Gasoline 233
    Naphtha 233
    Middle Distillates 234
    Residual Fuel Oils 234
Changing Patterns of Demand and Consumption 234
Refinery Process and Technology 236
Primary Separation 236
Atmospheric Distillation 237
    CDU Process Objective 238
Vacuum Distillation 240

Conversion Process 242
Conversion for Upgradation of Product Quality 242
Catalytic Reforming 242
Feed Naphtha Quality and Pre-treatment 243
Chemistry of Naphtha Hydro Treatment 243
Pre-Process Disposition of the Pre-treatment Process 244
Platforming Process 244
Reactions In Catalytic Reforming 244
Types of Process Configurations 245
Isomerization 245
Isomerization Process Objective 245
Main Reactions 246
Advanced Recycle Technologies 247
Ipsorb 247
Deisopentanizer 247
Hexorb 248
Reactor-Regenerator Section 248
Fluidic Catalytic Cracking Process (FCC) 248
Reactor-Riser 248
Reactor 249
Regenerator 251
Fractionation Section 251
Hydrocracking 252
Process Principles 252
Process Configurations 253
Reaction Chemistry 254
Catalysts 254
Catalytic Reforming Process 256
Lube Oil Manufacture 256
Sulphur Recovery Unit 257
Reaction Chemistry 257
Sour Water Stripping 258
Product Specifications 258
Process Control Basics 260
Process Definition 260
Process Parameters 260
Control Functions 260
Process Control 261
Control of Parameters 261
Refining Capacity and Capacity Utilisation 268
Expansion of Existing Refineries 268
Guidelines for Laying Petroleum Product Pipelines 269
Auto Fuel Policy 269
Schedule for Introducing Improved Quality Fuels as per Auto Fuel Policy 269
Refining Capacity Additions during Tenth Plan 270

Refining Capacity Addition during the Eleventh/Twelfth Plan 270
Market share and Infrastructure 271
Liberalization in Indian Oil Industries 272
Paradigm Shift in Business Process 274
Crude Oil Pipelines in India 275
Product Pipelines 275
Refinery Cost Elements 276
Elements of Crude Costs 276
Crude Cost Elements: 277
Operating Cost Elements 278
Crude Freight Cost 278
Elements of Refining Cost 281
Refinery Profitability/Margins 281
Refining Profitability under APM 282
Need and Importance of Refining Margin 282
Pooling Mechanism 282
Special Products 283
Fixation of Retention Price per Ton of Crude 'Throughput' for each Refinery 283
Refinery Profitability/Margins under Free Market Scenario 283
Crude Distilation Unit (CDU) 285
Measures for Improving Refinery Profitability 288
(A) Optimising Existing Operations 288
(B) Technological Upgradations 290
(C) Planning for Economics of Scale 290
(D) Optimization of Refinery Configuration 290
(E) Backward and Forward Integration 290
(F) Human Resource Development 290
Refining Strategy and Operations 292
How to Run an Individual Refinery 293

9. Strategy for Petroleum and Natural Gas Trading 296
Crude Oil Marketing 296
OPEC's Role In International Oil Trading 297
Trading Petroleum Products 298
Natural Gas Marketing 302
LPG Marketing by Public Sector Oil Marketing Companies (OMCs) 303
Marketing of Mini-LPG Cylinders by OMCs 303
Promoting LPG as Auto-Fuel 303
Parallel Marketing of LPG 304
Marketing of Transportation Fuels 304
Refined and Petro-chemical Product Marketing 305
Trading of Oil and Natural Gas 305
Import and Export of Petroleum 306
Supply Strategy 308
Demand Profile 309
Transportation: Mechanism of Pipeline Nominations 311

Pipeline Economics 313
LNG Transportation Policy of GOI (FOB) 313
LNG Transportation Policy 314
Rationale for FOB 314
LNG Carriage Cost—Indian Flag vs. Foreign Flag 314
TERI Report 315
Asian Gas Market Overview 316
Importance of Natural Gas in Asia's Energy Supply Chain 316
Asia's Natural Gas Supply and Demand 316
Global and Regional Lng Supplies Continue to Expand 317
Downward Pressure on Lng Prices: A Feature of the Next Decade? 318
OTC Energy and Oil Derivative Markets 319
The OTC Oil Derivatives Market 320
Futures and Options Contracts and Markets 321
Commodity Futures and Options 323
Contracts and Markets 323
Comparison of Forward and Futures Contracts 325
Commodity Futures Exchanges 325
Electronic Trading 327
Regulations 327
Foreign Direct Investment 328
Policies and Procedures 329
Natural Gas Futures Market: A Case Study
"The SMC Report—Natural Gas Futures Advisory Report" 329
SMC Reports: Natural Gas Price Forecasting and Advisory Services 330
Navigating the Natural Gas Futures Market 330

10. Petro-Retailing 331
Understanding Petroleum Retail Business 331
Retailing Concept 332
Strength of Retailing 332
Retailing is Selling 333
Retail Function Involves 333
The Effect of Retailing 333
Social Consequences 333
Economic Consequences 333
Establishing a New Retail Outlet 334
Site Selection Criteria 334
Market Intelligence (MI) 335
Franchising Models in the Petroleum Industry 335
The Wheel of Retailing 338
Commodity vs. Brand Retailing 338
Basic difference between Brand and Product 340
Special Nature of Petro-retail 341
A.T. Kearney Report on Petro-retailing 342
Research Findings 342
Linked Retailing 343

Convenience Stores 343
Food Services 343
Ancillary Services 343
Indian Experience in Petro-Retailing 344
Petro-Retailing: A Chronology of the Evolution of Concept 345
Oil Industrial Structure in India 346
A Deregulation Overview of Petro-retail Business 346
Strong Brands Drive Revenue Growth 347
Findings of A.T. Kearney Report 347
Know your Consumer 347
The Petroleum Shopper in India 349
Routine Chore Doer 349
Time Poor 349
Trust Seeker 349
Prestige Seeker 350
Build the Offer 351
1. Fuel-based Differentiation 351
2. Value-added Products and Services-based Differentiation 352
BPCL's Additional Value Propositions 353
3. Price-based Differentiation 355
Key Success Factors for Price-based Differentiation Strategies 355
4. Consumer Experience-based Differentiation 356
Indian Oil's Initiatives 356
Conclusions 357
Gas Station Canopy 358
Project Overview 359

11. Financial and Accounting Systems for Oil and Natural Gas (Petro-Accounting) 363

Generally Accepted Accounting Principles 363
Accounting Concepts: The Basic Elements 364
Accrual vs. Cash 365
Reserve Recognition Accounting 367
Full-Cost and Successful Efforts Accounting 368
Successful Efforts Accounting 368
Ceiling Test 369
Cost Depletion and Percentage Depletion 372
Oil and Natural Gas Accounting: Broad Principles 373
SE vs. FC 374
Financial Statements 375
Income Statements 375
The Historical Development of Accounting Standards on Deferred Tax 377
Methods of Computation 377
Bases of Calculation 378
Introduction to Full-cost Accounting 378
Drilling Costs 378

Exploratory Drilling Costs 379
Development Drilling Costs 380
Stratigraphic 'Test Wells' 381
Full-Cost Accounting 382
Measurement and Sale of Oil and Gas 383
Oil Measurement and Sale 383
Gas Measurement and Sale 383
Recording Oil Revenue 385
ISI-Developed Integrated Oil and Gas Accounting Software 385
Crude Oil Exchanges 386
Crude Oil Pricing 387
Pricing of Physical Crude Oil Trades 388
Crude Oil as an Input Cost to Refiners 388
Oil and Gas Revenue: A Case of ATP Oil and Gas Corporation 388
Results of Operations 389
Capital Resources and Liquidity 390
Recording Gas Revenue 391
Natural Gas Processing 391
Timing of Revenue Recognition 392
Revenue from Oil 392
Allocation of Oil and Gas 392
Gross Refining Margin 393
Internal Factors 393
External Factors 393
Operating Cost of the Refinery 393
Net Margin 394
Components of Gross Refining Margin 394
Attachment 1: Gross Margin 395
Attachment 2: Sample Working of Netback Calculations 395
Accounting for International Operations 396
Petroleum Fiscal Systems 396
Contractual Systems 397
Government Involvement in Operations 398
Production Sharing Contracts 398
Signature and Production Bonuses 399
Payment of Royalties 399
Sliding Scale Royalty 400
Government Participation 400
Cost Recovery 400
Profit Oil 401
Service Contracts 401
Joint Operating Agreements 402
Recoverable versus Non-recoverable Costs 402
Financial Accounting Issues 403
Financial Accounting versus Contract Accounting 403
International Accounting Standards 403
Comparing Financial Statements 404

Reserve Ratios 405

Reserve Replacement Ratio 405

Reserve Cost Ratios 406

Finding Costs Ratios 406

Reserve Value Ratios 407

Gas Pipeline Accounting 409

General Regulations 409

Transportation Services 410

Revenue Accounting 411

Kelkar Committee on Price Structure and Pricing Policy 411

Sankar Committee on Gas Pricing 413

Domestic Price Structure of Natural Gas 414

Producer Price of Gas 414

Components of Producer Price 414

Consumer Price 414

Gas Purchase from JVCs 414

Gas Pool Account 415

Price Build-up for Gas Transporter 415

Price Build-up for End Consumers 415

Consumer Price 415

Transmission Charges 416

Panna-Mukta and Tapti 417

Price Applicable for Gas Produced under pre-NELP Exploratory Fields 417

Price Applicable for Gas Produced under NELP Blocks 418

Increase in Gas Costs 418

LNG Pricing 418

Planning and Measuring Financial Performance 420

Internal Rate of Return/Return on Investment 420

Tracking of Sales 421

Gap Analysis 421

Sales Maximization vs. Profit Maximization 424

Petroleum Accounting Management System (PAMS) 425

PAMS Module 425

Financial Modules 425

Accounts Payable 426

Accounts Receivable 426

12. International Hydrocarbon Economic Environment 430

Global Oil Production 430

Global Oil Consumption 431

The Future of Oil 432

E-Commerce—The Impact on Both Upstream and Down Stream Industries 432

The Upstream Industry 433

Electronic Trading 435

Downstream Industry—Refining and Marketing 435

Environmental Issues 435
Exploring Alternative Fuels 435
Domestic Hydrocarbon Economic Environment 436
Structure of Indian Oil and Gas Economy 436
Indian Oil Industry in a Growing Economy 437
Importance of Oil and Gas for National Economy 438
Oil and Gas in Meeting Energy Requirement 438
Global Facet of Indian Oil Industry 438
Reforms in Indian Economy 439
Oil Securities for India: Issues and Concerns 441
Phased Deregulation of India's Hydrocarbon Sector 441
Mergers and Consolidation in Indian Oil and Gas Sector 442
Trend and Structure of Oil and Gas Economy 443
Structure of Oil and Gas Economy 443
Oil Majors 443
Other Integrated Companies 443
Independents 443
Emerging Forces for Change during the 1990s 444
Structure and Forces Prior to the 1990s 444
1. Developing Strategic Assets 451
2. Technology Leadership Approach 451
3. Reputation and Goodwill 452
4. Evolving new Industrial Architecture 452
Trends of Oil and Gas Economy 452
1. Globalization 453
2. Economic Development 453
3. Factors that Shape Decisions of Sellers and Buyers 454
Evolving Phases in Indian Oil Industries 455
1. Indian Oil Industries—Its Global Facet 455
2. Reform in Oil Industry—A Historical Perspective 455
3. Phased Deregulation of India's Hydrocarbon Sector 456
4. Self-Reliance 457
Conclusions 458

13. Geo-Politics of Oil Trading: Scanning the Global Business Scene 459
Global energy in Perspective 459
World Oil Production and Consumption 460
OPECand Non-OPEC Fact Sheet 463
Oil dependence and National Security 465
Developing Natural Gas Resources 466
Peak Oil: An Overview 466
Developing World Energy Use 467
Geopolitics: The Great Unknown 468
The Seven Sisters 469
OPEC 469
Context 469

The First Major Oil-Shock 469
The Second Oil-Shock 470
Oil Counter-Shock 470
The Middle-East in the Global Oil Balance 471
The Iraq Episode 472
Energy Dominates Growth Debate in South Africa 473
Geo-Politics of Oil and Natural Gas 473
Geopolitics of EU Energy Supply 474
The Geopolitics of Oil in Central Asia 475
Russia and the Caspian Basin 476
Africa 476
North America 477
Venezuela 477
Saudi Arabia and the Gulf Producers 478
Energy Scenario in South Asia 478
The World Oil Crisis: Implications for Global Security and the Middle-East 480
China's Middle-East Strategy 481
India Joins the Scramble for Oil and Natural Gas 482
India's Energy Security Pact with Russia 483
Diplomacy over Oil-bids with Iran and Pakistan 483
A Hemisphere of Energy Security Environment in NAFTA Region 484
Transferring the World's Wealth 484
How Oil Shapes Foreign Policy? 485
Role of IEA 486
Geopolitics of Natural Gas 488
Conclusions 489

14. E-Commerce Applications in Oil and Natural Gas Industries (Petro-Informatics) 492

Principles of E-Business 492
Emerging Technology Related E-Business 494
Model of E-business 499
E-Business in Oil and Gas 500
A. Upstream Sector Impact and E-business Opportunity 500
B. Downstream Sector Impact and E-business Opportunities 502
E-Markets 504
E-Markets in Oil and Gas 505
E-Market Outlook 506
Winners are VAC's 506
Losers are VAC's 506
Trade/Exchange 506
E-Trading in Oil and Gas 507
External trends that push E-Trading 507
Internal trends that push E-Trading: 507
Trading Outlook 509
Market Trends 509

Sun and Cyberonix eGasStation Architecture 509
The e-GasStation Architecture 510
Sun's Role in e-GasStation Implementations 511
Business Models/Benefits 511
Unique Features of the e-GasStation Architecture 512
Next-Generation Services 512
E-Business Applications used by Oil Giants 513
BP Amoco Experience in E-Business in Oil Trading 517
ERP and E-Business 519
E-Business by a Lead Oil Company 519
Future Trends 520
Conclusions 521

Index 525

CHAPTER I

Introduction to Oil and Natural Gas

GENESIS AND TECHNOLOGY OPTIONS OF OIL EXPLORATION

Genesis

Petroleum (from Greek Petra—rock and elaion—oil or Latin oleum—oil), crude oil, sometimes colloquially called black gold or "Texas Tea", is a thick, dark brown or greenish liquid. Petroleum exists in the upper strata of some areas of the Earth's crust. It consists of a complex mixture of various hydrocarbons, largely of the alkane series, but may vary much in appearance, composition, and purity. Petroleum is used mostly, for producing fuel oil, which is an important "primary energy" source. It is also the raw material for many chemical products, including solvents, fertilizers, pesticides, and plastics. Finding Petroleum is not a single activity. It involves a series of steps: identifying a prospect, testing the rock, drilling a well, determining whether the find is commercially viable and estimating the dimensions of the reservoir with further drilling. Production wells are then installed and gathering pipelines are assembled to transport the oil to central points for further shipment. The upstream sector involves the most investment risk because of the high capital has expenditures and great uncertainty that oil will be found. On the other hand, it historically provided greater rewards in terms of profit and return on investment than other segments of the industry. Recent technological advances have reduced the uncertainties and contributed to the more efficient use of capital, enhancing the industry's success, even in a low-price environment.

Reserves and Resources

Oil reserves are the estimated quantities of crude oil that are claimed to be recoverable under existing economic and operating conditions (U.S. Energy Information Agency, 2007). The total amount of oil in an oil reservoir is known as oil in place. However, because of reservoir characteristics and limitations in petroleum extraction technologies only a fraction of this oil can be brought to the surface, and it is only this producible fraction that is considered to be *reserves*. The ratio of reserves to oil in place for a given field is often referred to as the *recovery factor*. The recovery factor of a field may change over time based on operating history and in response to changes in technology and economics. The recovery factor may also rise over time if additional investment is made in enhanced oil recovery techniques such as gas injection or water-flooding (BP Global Review, 2008). Because the geology of the subsurface cannot be examined directly, indirect techniques must be used to estimate the size and recoverability of the resource. While new technologies have increased the accuracy of these techniques, significant uncertainties still remain. In general, most early estimates of the reserves of an oil field are conservative and tend to grow with time. This phenomenon is called *reserves growth.*

"Proved reserves" are estimates of the amount of oil recoverable from known reservoirs under current economic and operating conditions. Total global proved reserves have been estimated at approximately 1 trillion barrels since the late 1980's, because additions to reserves from new discoveries and from revisions to previous estimates have approximately matched the annual volume of oil produced (or withdrawn). Proved oil reserves reflect only a fraction of the oil that a reservoir may hold, and say nothing of reservoirs that have not yet been evaluated. Historically, only some 30 percent of the total oil in a reservoir—the "original oil-in-place"—was recoverable. As pressure declines in the reservoir, the oil becomes costlier and costlier to produce until further production becomes uneconomic, as discussed in the section on oil production. However recent advances now allow greater recovery from old reservoirs. "Recoverable resources" is a broader category, encompassing estimates of both proved and Undiscovered volumes that would be economically extractable under specified price-cost relationships and technological conditions. By definition, there is a lower level of certainty attached to resource estimates than to proved reserve estimates.

Origin of Oil

A. Biogenic Theory

Most geologists view crude oil, like coal and natural gas, as the product of compression and heating of ancient vegetation over geological time scales. According to this theory, it is formed from the decayed remains of prehistoric marine animals and terrestrial plants. Over many centuries this organic matter, mixed with mud, is buried under thick sedimentary layers of material. The resulting high levels of heat and pressure cause the remains to metamorphose, first into a waxy material known as kerogen, and then into liquid and gaseous hydrocarbons in a process known as catagenesis. These then migrate through adjacent rock layers until they become trapped underground in porous rocks called reservoirs, forming an oil field, from which the liquid can be extracted by drilling and pumping. Three conditions must be present for oil reservoirs to form: a rich source rock, a migration conduit, and a trap (seal) that forms the reservoir. Over the years, the organisms decayed in the sedimentary layers. In these layers, there was little or no oxygen present. So, microorganisms broke the remains into carbon-rich compounds that formed organic layers. The organic material mixed with the sediments, forming fine-grained shale, or source rock.

As new sedimentary layers were deposited, they exerted intense pressure and heat on the source rock. The heat and pressure distilled the organic material into crude oil and natural gas. The oil flowed from the source rock and accumulated in thicker, more porous limestone or sandstone, called reservoir rock. Movement in the Earth trapped the oil and natural gas in the reservoir or rocks between layers of impermeable rock or cap rock such as granite or marble.

B. Abiogenic Theory of Origin of Oil

The idea of abiogenic petroleum origin was championed in the Western world by Thomas Gold based on thoughts from Russia, mainly on studies of Nikolai Kudryavtsev. The idea proposes that large amounts of carbon exist naturally in the planet, some in the form of hydrocarbons. Hydrocarbons are less dense than aqueous pore fluids, and migrate upward through deep fracture networks. Thermophilic, rock-dwelling microbial life-forms are in part responsible for the biomarkers found in petroleum. However, their role in the formation, alteration, or contamination of the various hydrocarbon deposits is not yet understood. As with any petroleum, the idea goes, these hydrocarbons would migrate upwards with methane, sometimes bearing helium and nitrogen and heavy metals. Oiamondoids are common in oil and gas and its nature probably is related to natural diamonds that come from earth's mantle. The proponents of abiogenic petroleum claim that reserves are never exhausted because they are filled from below.

This idea was verified in 1999, when an oil basin named "Eugene Island 330" off the coast of Louisiana went from being a relatively depleted reserve to suddenly refilling with pure oil, causing production to quickly raise back up to levels competing with when drilling began. Further evidence, such as the existence of hydrocarbons on planetary bodies (e.g. methane on Titan) where life has not been found, supports this theory. Also, the implications of this theory are what have been used to find most of the recent reserves world-wide. Traditional biotic theory only predicts oil in certain rock at a certain depth, but the abiotic theory allows for much more. Reserves in much of Canada, l(an, Kazakhstan, the coast of Vietnam, and virtually all the oil in Russia were found either at depths or in source rock that are incompatible with traditional techniques.

History of Oil Production

The first oil wells were drilled in China in the 4th century or earlier. They had depth of up to 800 feet and were drilled using bits attached to bamboo poles. The oil was burned to evaporate brine and produce salt. By the 10th century, extensive bamboo pipelines connected oil wells with salt springs. Ancient Persian tablets indicate the medicinal and lighting uses of petroleum in the upper echelons of their society. In the 8th century, the streets of the newly-constructed Baghdad were paved with tar, derived from easily-accessible petroleum from natural fields in the region.

In the 9th century, oil fields were exploited in Baku, Azerbaijan, to produce naphtha. These fields were described by the geographer Masudi in the 10th century, and by Marco Polo in the 13th century, who described the output of those wells as hundreds of shiploads. The modern history of oil began in 1853, with the discovery of the process of oil distillation. Crude oil was distilled into kerosene by Ignacy Lukasiewicz, a Polish scientist. The first "rock oil" ("petroleum") mine was created in Bobrka, near Krosno in southern Poland in the following year and the first refinery (actually a distillery) was built in Ulaszowice, also by Lukasiewicz.

These discoveries rapidly spread around the world, and Meerzoeff built the first Russian refinery in the mature oil fields at Baku in 1861. At that time Baku produced about 90% of the world's oil. The first commercial oil well drilled in North America was in Oil Springs, Ontario, Canada in 1858, dug by James Miller Williams. The American petroleum industry began with Edwin Drake's discovery of oil in 1859, near Titusville, Pennsylvania. The industry grew slowly in the 1800s, driven by the demand for kerosene and oil lamps. It became a major national concern in the early part of the 20th century; the introduction of the internal combustion engine provided a demand that has largely sustained the industry to this day. Early "local" finds like those in Pennsylvania and Ontario were quickly exhausted, leading to "oil booms" in Texas, Oklahoma, and California.

By 1910, significant oil fields had been discovered in Canada (specifically, in the province of Alberta), the Dutch East Indies (1885, in Sumatra), Persia (1908, in Masjed Solei man), Peru, Venezuela, and Mexico, and were being developed at an industrial level. Even until the mid-(1950s), coal was still the world's foremost fuel, but oil quickly took over. Following the 1973 energy crisis and the 1979 energy crisis, there was significant media coverage of oil supply levels. This brought to light the concern that oil is a limited resource that will eventually run out, at least as an economically viable energy source. Some argue that technology will continue to allow for the production of cheap hydrocarbons and that the earth has vast sources of unconventional petroleum reserves in the form of tar sands, bitumen fields and oil shale that will allow for petroleum use to continue" for an extremely long period in the future.

Today, about 90% of vehicular fuel needs are met by oil. Petroleum also makes up 40% of tota1 energy consumption in the United States, but is responsible for only 2% of electricity generation. Petroleum's worth as a portable, dense energy source powering the vast majority of vehicles and as the base of many industrial chemicals makes it one of the world's most important commodities. Oil demand is highly dependent on global macroeconomic conditions, so this is also an important determinant of price. Some economists claim that high oil prices have a large negative impact on the global growth. This means that the relationship between the oil price and global growth is not particularly stable although a high oil price is often thought of as being a late cycle phenomenon.

The New York Mercantile Exchange (NYMEX) trades crude oil (including futures contracts) and provides the basis of US crude oil pricing via WTI (West Texas Intermediate). Other exchanges also trade crude oil futures, e.g. the International Petroleum Exchange (IPE) in London trades contracts in Brent crude. Even individuals can now trade crude oil through online trading sites margin account or their banks through structured products indexed on the Commodities markets.

Classification of Oil

The oil industry classifies "crude" by the location of its origin (e.g., "West Texas Intermediate, WTI" or "Brent") and often by its relative weight (API gravity) or viscosity ("light", "intermediate" or "heavy"); refiners may also refer to it as "sweet", which means it contains relatively little sulfur, or as "sour", which means it contains substantial amounts of sulfur and requires more refining in order to meet current product specifications. OPEC attempts to keep the price of the OPEC Basket between upper and lower limits, by increasing and decreasing production. This makes the measure important for market analysts. The OPEC Basket, including a mix of light and heavy crudes, is heavier than both Brent and WTI.

Brent Blend is comprised of 15 oils from fields in the Brent and Ninian systems in the East Shetland Basin of the North Sea. The brent crude Oil is landed at Sullom Voe in the Shetlands. Oil production from other parts of the world is often compared to the price of this brent oil, which forms a benchmark for the oil price. Brent Crude Oil is one of the major classifications of oil consisting of Brent Crude, Brent Sweet Light Crude, Oseberg and Forties. Brent Crude oil is produced or sourced from the North Sea. Brent blend is a fairly light crude oil, though not as light as West Texas Intermediate (WTI). It contains approx 0.37% of sulfur, classifying it as Sweet Crude, yet again not as sweet as WTI. Brent blend is ideal for production of Gasoline. It is most often refined in Northwest Europe, but when the market oil prices are favorable for export, it can also be refined also in the United States or the Mediterranean region (http://www.oilgasarticles.com/articles/7/1/Classification-of-Oil/Page1.html).

Types of Crude Oil according to the U.S. Environmental Protection Agency

The petroleum industry often characterizes crude oils according to their geographical source, e.g., Alaska North Slope Crude. Oils from different geographical areas have unique properties; they can vary in consistency from a light volatile fluid to a semi-solid. Classification of crude oil types by geographical source is generally not a useful classification scheme for response personnel because they offer little information about general toxicity, physical state, and changes that occur with time and weathering. These characteristics are primary considerations in oil spill response. The classification scheme provided below is more useful in a response scenario (http://wetestit.com/Crude_101.htm).

Class A: Light, Volatile Oils. These oils are highly fluid, often clear, spread rapidly on solid or water surfaces, have a strong odor, a high evaporation rate, and are usually flammable. They penetrate porous surfaces such as dirt and sand,

and may be persistent in such a matrix. They do not tend to adhere to surfaces; flushing with water generally removes them. Class A oils may be highly toxic to humans, fish, and other biota. Most refined products and many of the highest quality light crudes can be included in this class.

Class B: Non-Sticky Oils. These oils have a waxy or oily feel. Class B oils are less toxic and adhere more firmly to surfaces than Class A oils, although they can be removed from surfaces by vigorous flushing. As temperatures rise, their tendency to penetrate porous substrates increases and they can be persistent. Evaporation of volatiles may lead to a Class C or D residue. Medium to heavy paraffin-based oils fall into this class.

Class C: Heavy, Sticky Oils. Class C oils are characteristically viscous, sticky or tarry, and brown or black. Flushing with water will not readily remove this material from surfaces, but the oil does not readily penetrate porous surfaces. The density of Class C oils may be near that of water and they often sink. Weathering or evaporation of volatiles may produce solid or tarry Class D oil. Toxicity is low, but wildlife can be smothered or drowned when contaminated. This class includes residual fuel oils and medium to heavy crudes.

Class D: Nonfluid Oils. Class D oils are relatively non-toxic, do not penetrate porous substrates, and are usually black or dark brown in color. When heated, Class D oils may melt and coat surfaces making cleanup very difficult. Residual oils, heavy crude oils, some high paraffin oils, and some weathered oils fall into this class.

These classifications are dynamic for spilled oils; weather conditions and water temperature greatly influence the behavior of oil and refined petroleum products in the environment. For example, as volatiles evaporate from Class B oil, it may become Class C oil. If a significant temperature drop occurs (e.g., at night), a Class C oil may solidify and resemble a Class D oil. Upon warming, the Class D oil may revert back to Class C oil.

A Brief History of Oil and Gas Industry

The discovery and use of oil and natural gas has a long and fascinating history spanning thousands of years. The development of oil and gas has evolved over time and its numerous uses have also expanded and become an integral part of the global economy. The petro-product demand in the early years of discovery was mainly limited to kerosene only. The use of oil eventually replaced coal as the world's primary source of energy to feed industrial power production activities in the early twentieth century. Just as oil and gas drives today's world economy, the control and accessibility of oil and gas played a major role in both World Wars and still remains the critical fuel source that fuels industry, transportation and the domestic utilities.

The petroleum-based industry expanded mostly in the 20th century as new industrial and domestic uses of oil and natural gas started gaining momentum. The invention of the automobile and mass transport systems (including cargo operations) was responsible for much of the industry's meteoric growth in the later part of the century (BERA: http://www.loc.gov/rr/business/BERA/issue5/history.html).

When Marco Polo in 1264 visited the Persian city of *'Baku'*, on the shores of the Caspian Sea in modern Azerbaijan, he saw oil being collected from seeps. He wrote that "on the confines toward Geirgine there is a fountain from which oil springs in great abundance, inasmuch as a hundred shiploads might be taken from it at one time." In addition to oil seeps, Marco Polo also saw spectacular mud volcanos, sourced by natural gas seeping through ponds, and a flaming hillside, the "Eternal Fires of the Apsheron Peninsula", where condensate and natural gas seeping through fractured shales has burned, and been worshipped, for centuries.

Shallow pits were dug at the *Baku* seeps in ancient times to facilitate collecting oil, and hand-dug holes up to 35 meters (115 feet) deep were in use by 1594. These holes were essentially oil wells, which makes Baku the first true field. Apparently 116 of these wells in 1830 produced 3,840 metric tons (about 710 to 720 barrels) of oil. Later, Russian engineer F.N. Semyenov used a cable tools to drill an oil well on the Apsheron Peninula, ten years before Colonel Drake's famous well in Pennsylvania. Also, offshore drilling started up at Baku at Bibi-Eibat field near the end of the 19th century, about the same time that the "first" offshore oil well was drilled in 1896 at Summerland field on the California Coast (http://www.geocities.com/mudsmeller/history.html).

Early in the 20th century, World War-I strained the industry's ability to cope with the supply of fuel, prompting the decade of the 1920s to be dedicated to great U.S. oil discovery. In that decade, many U.S. companies also began exploring for foreign oil in the Middle East, South America, Africa, and the Far East. The onset of World War-II in 1937 once again tested the industry's ability to supply oil. During World War II, drilling operations began in the U.S. waters on offshore structures that resembled the offshore drilling platforms of today. Rest of the world also followed that suit in later years. During and following World War II, major global. Oil companies also increased foreign exploration in a big way, especially in the Persian Gulf region. Following World War-II, in addition to oil, natural gas was recognized to be a major source of fuel for industry and domestic consumption. It was also during the post-war period that natural gas transmission pipelines were constructed, linking remote producing areas to large population centers and petro-chemical industries.

The petroleum industry includes the global processes of exploration, extraction, refining, transporting (often by oil tankers and pipelines), and marketing petroleum products. The largest volume products of the industry are fuel oil and gasoline (petrol). Petroleum is also the raw material for many chemical products, including pharmaceuticals, solvents, fertilizers, pesticides, and plastics. The industry is usually divided into three major components: upstream, midstream and downstream. Midstream operations are usually included in the downstream category (http://en.wikipedia.org/wiki/Petroleum_industry).

In 1960, the Organization of Petroleum Exporting Countries (OPEC) was formed. Although OPEC was ineffective during its first decade of existence, its oil embargo of 1973-74, coupled with an increase in the price of crude oil created an energy crisis particularly for the developed and the developing economies in the U.S, Europe and Asia resulting in shortages of petroleum products. The developed nations, in particular, for the first time became aware of the myriad of problems and issues resulting from its dependence on foreign oil. The world oil supply was again disrupted in 1990s, with Iraq's invasion of Kuwait and subsequently consequential to Asia Economic crisis. Although the crisis was short-lived and in two phases, it once more brought to the forefront the world's growing dependence on foreign oil, and the need for sustained development of alternative fuel sources (e.g. solar, hydro, hydro-thermal, wind, biogas, bio-fuel etc.).

History of Oil Prices

The following Para describes a chronological sequence of events outlining a brief history of oil prices (http://www.swiftenergy.com/SFY/Investor-Info/Industry-Outlook/2001/HistO&G/oilpricehist.htm):

1880-99: The Standard Oil monopoly controlled prices for years, but prices rose as reserves in the Northeast declined.

1901: The Spindletop well in Texas expanded the industry outside the Northeast, but supply exceeded demand, reducing prices.

1908-20: Mass production of the Model T created demand for oil with increasing prices.

1933: Texas' dominance over oil production allowed the Texas Railroad Commission to stabilize prices for decades.

1939-45: World War II brought further stabilization of prices through government price controls.

1950-70: U.S. economic growth fueled by oil led to somewhat higher prices.

1973-79: With U.S. oil reserves in decline, OPEC dominated the market and greatly increased oil prices.

1980-91: OPEC's power declined and so did prices, until the 1990-91 Gulf War shot them upward again.

Origin of Petroleum and Processes of Extraction

Most crude oil and natural gas originate from plant and animal life that thrived millions of years ago in swamps and oceans. These organic materials were deposited with mud and silt from streams and rivers. The sediments eventually hardened to form sedimentary rock. Heat and pressure transformed the soft parts of the plants and animals into solid, liquid or gaseous hydrocarbons known as fossil fuels—coal, crude oil or natural gas (http://www.capp.ca/default.asp?V_DOC_ID=25).

The most widely accepted hypothesis of the origin of oil and gas is the organic theory involving humification and fosilification. This theory holds that petroleum (hydrocarbons) is formed from organic material including marine plants and animals that lived millions of years ago in low-lying areas-normally in the oceans of the world. These plant and animal remains were deposited throughout the years, along with layer after layer of eroded particles of igneous rock. The weight and pressure of the overlying layers caused the eroded rock particles to form sedimentary rock. The weight and pressure of overlying layers-and other not fully understood factors, such as chemical and bacterial processes changed, and still change, the organic material into oil and gas.

After formation, oil and gas move upward through the layers of sedimentary rock due to pressure and the natural tendency of oil and gas to rise through water (salt water is normally contained in the pore space of sedimentary rock). The petroleum migrates upward through porous and permeable rock formations until it becomes trapped by an impervious layer of rock. The impervious rock that prevents further movement of the oil and gas is called a 'trap'.

Some of the common types of traps are as follows (Gallun et al, 2004):

Fault trap

A trap formed when the movement of the earth's crust causes different rock strata to offset or shear off. In a fault trap, a nonporous rock formation that has shifted stops the movement of oil or gas within an offsetting formation that allows petroleum to migrate.

Anticline

A trap formed by the folding of the earth's crust into a dome. This upward folding is caused by pressures developed from the earth's molten core. An impervious or nonporous layer of rock overlying the anticline traps the oil or gas in the anticline structure. Most of the earth's oil and gas reserves are found in anticlines.

Salt dome

A trap created by a bed of nonporous salt pushing upward through overlying formations. Faults, in which oil and gas are trapped, are created along the sides of the upthrusted salt dome.

In order for an oil or gas reservoir to have been formed, four conditions must have been present:

- A source of petroleum, i.e ., remains of land and sea life
- Conditions such as heat and pressure resulting in the transformation of the organic material into petroleum
- Porous and permeable rock through which the petroleum was able to migrate after formation
- An impervious rock formation that acts as a trap or cap rock, permitting petroleum to collect.

Assuming these four conditions are present, the reservoir rock itself must have porosity and permeability. Porosity is the measure of the pore space, *i.e.*, openings in a rock in which petroleum can exist. The greater the porosity, the more fluid (petroleum) the rock can hold. Permeability measures the "connectability" of the pores, which determines the ability of the petroleum to flow through the rock from one pore space to another.

High porosity is often accompanied by high permeability (Figs. 1.2 and 1.3).

To be commercially productive, a petroleum reservoir must have adequate

Fig. 1.1: Types of Traps

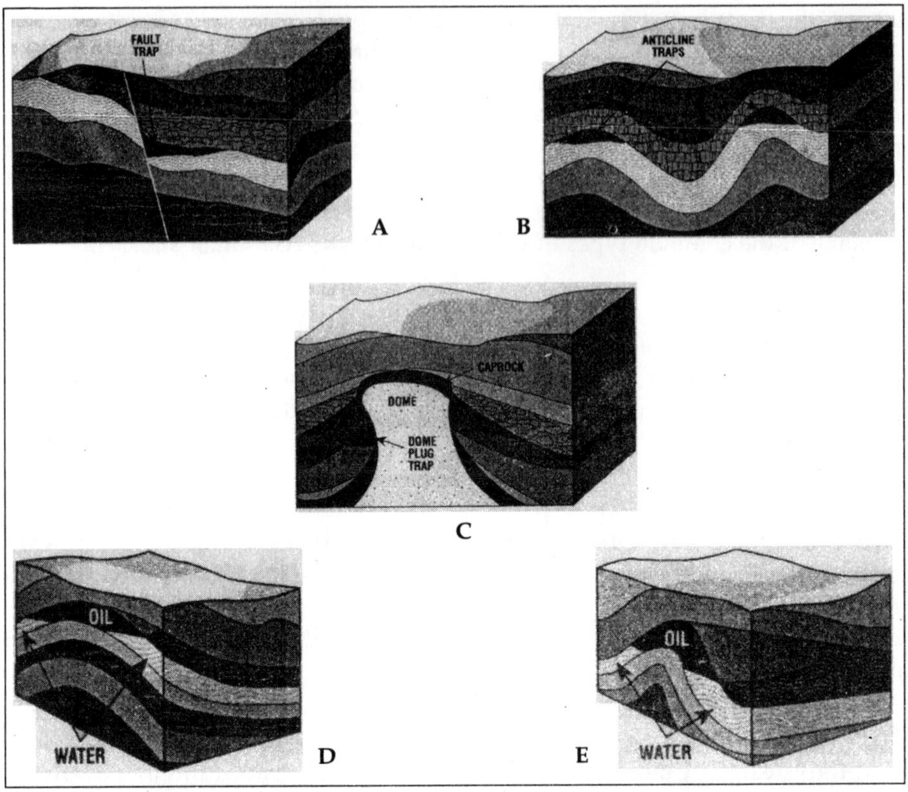

Fig. 1.2: Porosity

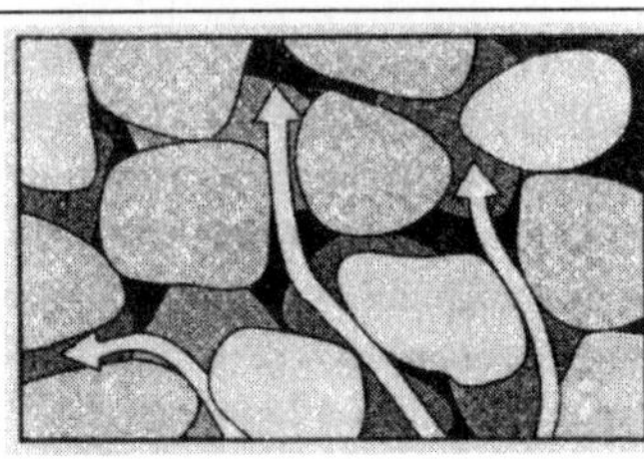

Fig. 1.3: Permeability

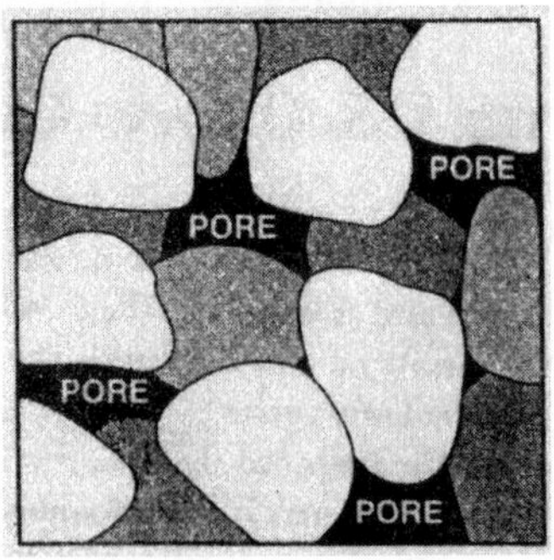

porosity and permeability, and also have a sufficient physical area of rock that contains hydrocarbons (oil and natural gas). In other words, the reservoir must contain enough oil and natural gas to, when produced and sold, cover attendant costs and provide a profit for the producing company. If an oil and gas reservoir has low permeability, procedures exist to increase the flow of oil or gas through the formation to the well bore. One method used to increase the flow from a "tight" formation is *fracturing*. This method usually involves introducing sand mixed with water or oil into the formation under high pressure to open or clean channels between the pores.

PROFILE OF PETROLEUM OPERATIONS

Today's oil and gas companies are broadly involved in four different types of operational functions:

- Exploration and Production
- Transportation
- Refining and Gas Processing
- Marketing and Distribution

An integrated oil company is one involved in E&P activities as well as at least one of the other segments listed above. An independent oil company is one involved primarily in Exploration and Production (E&P) activities. Hence, the oil industry is uniquely characterized by:

- A high level of risk
- A long time span before a return on investment is received
- A lack of correlation between the magnitude of expenditures and the value of any resulting reserves.
- A high level of regulation
- Complex tax rules
- Specialized financial accounting rules
- Complex International operation
- Geopolitics

These characteristics are most evident in the E&P functions of oil and gas companies needing holistic strategic planning leading to development and expansion of operations at economy of scale. Exploration and production procedures and processes are essentially the same for any type of oil and Gas Company.

Most oil, initially, is produced by "natural lift" production methods: the pressure underground is high enough to force the oil to the surface. Reservoirs in the Middle East tend to be long-lived on "natural lift," that is, the reservoir pressure continues over time to be great enough to force the oil out. The underground pressure in older reservoirs, however, eventually dissipates, and oil no longer flows to the surface naturally. It must be pumped out by means of an "artificial lift"—a pump powered by gas or electricity. The majority of the oil reservoirs in the United States are produced using some kind of artificial lift. Over time, these "primary" production methods become ineffective, and continued production requires the use of additional "secondary" production methods. One common method uses water to displace oil, using a method called "water flood," which forces the oil to the drilled shaft or "well bore." Finally, producers may need to turn to "tertiary" or "enhanced" oil recovery methods. These techniques are often centered on increasing the oil's flow characteristics through the use of steam, carbon dioxide and other gases or chemicals. A Production system is essentially a system that transports reservoir fluids to the surface and separates it into oil, gas and water. The oil and gas streams are treated, if necessary and transported from the field. Any water produced is also treated and prepared for disposal or reinjection to the production reservoir.

The Basic Element of a Product in a System

1. Wells/Well heads/Well Completion
2. Flow lines
3. Production Manifold
4. Separators and process equipment
5. Metering vessels
6. Storage vessels

Well Completion

The well completion is the most important part of the operation in well's life, which covers virtually every operation between the actual drilling and putting the well on stream and is dependent upon and effects the productivity and down hole equipment and associated problems.

A well when completed consists of three strings:

1. Conductor casing
2. Surface casing
3. Production string or oil string

The elements of a single well are constituted of:

(a) the production casing or liner
(b) the tubing string
(c) the production packer
(d) the well head and tubing hanger and
(e) the Christmas tree.

Fluid Separation and Treatment

Hydrocarbon wells produce multiple fluids of gas, oil and water in different ratios. The various phases require different methods for processing and measurement. It is therefore necessary to separate them through separate piping and process equipment.

A set of Equipment used for Separation Process are as follows:

1. Oil and gas Separators
2. Stage separators
3. Trap
4. Water separators and Knock-Out Vessel
5. Flash Chamber
6. Expansion vessel
7. Emulsifiers

8. Coalescers (Mist extractors)
9. Scrubbers
10. Filters

Types of Separators:

1. Vertical
2. Horizontal
3. Spherical
4. Gun Barrel
5. Heater Treater

Treatment of Emulsion and Contaminants

Before produced crude can be sent to storage for delivery to a pipeline and ultimate delivery to a refinery, it must meet pipe line requirements of virtual elimination of salt water, free water and all basic sediments less than 0.2%. The removal of water, breaking of emulsions and removal of sulphur are therefore a major part of production operations in many cases.

Water produced with oil (salt water or fresh water) contains different types and concentrations of salts, and mix due to agitation, in reservoir flow, tubing and flow line flows and valves, orifices, chokes, fittings, pressure and temperature reduction.

Colloidal materials produced with oil (clay, asphalts) act as emulsifying agent by forming film around water or oil droplets. We must treat emulsion to obtain oil free of water and water free of oil.

Treatment Processes

The treatment process entails the following steps:

1. Gravity separation of produced fluids by settling
2. Chemicals are added to improve coalescence
3. Heat added to improve coalescence and gravity separation
4. Mechanical coalescer
5. Electrostatic coalescer

Free water knock outs can reduce heater loads. Pressure vessel installed ahead of emulsion treating system removes 60-90% of free water. Chemical addition facilitates more water removal.

Electrical Dehydration

Emulsion is passed through two high voltage electrodes. As water droplet approach the electrode plates, they accept the charge of the closest plate and are repelled towards the plate of opposite charge. This results in collision of oppositely charged droplets as they move back and forth.

Crude Oil desalting System

Salt is produced with crude oil in the form of brine which beyond a stipulated limit is unacceptable to refineries and should not be more that 10 ppb. The most common removal t4echnique is to dilute the original brine in the well stream with fresher water. Salt content of the remaining water after separation and dehydration is brought to an acceptable level. The fluid flows through the master valve and flow line. The high pressure gas wells may require a series of two master valves and two wing valves (one on each side of the outlet), to contend with high pressure requirement and greater safety requirements. A choke valve regulates the rate of flow and reduces the well head pressure to the lower flow-line pressure (on down-stream side). In wells, flowing during a routine production test, bottom-hole pressure is measured and recorded with a wire-line retrievable down-hole gauge.

At the same time liquid flow rate is measured at the surface in the stock tank after the gas has separated from the oil. Gas from the separator is measured by a flow meter installed in the gas line, and volumetric rates are reported at standard conditions of pressure and temperature (14.7 psia and 60 f). The separator is regulated by two controls: the liquid level controller (LLC) and separator pressure controller (PC). The liquid level in the separator is regulated by a controller connected to a float that monitors the liquid level in the separator, compares with preset levels, and activates the valve to increase the opening when the liquid level is too high or decrease it when the liquid level drops.

Separator pressure is controlled by a back pressure valve in gas line. The valve is activated by a pressure regulator, which decreases the valve opening when separator pressure drops below a preset value or increases it when the pressure exceeds this value. Production from several wells passes through the flow lines to production manifold. By a suitable valve arrangement in manifold it is possible to direct the flow in either of the separators. In the separators the produced fluid is split into liquid and gas streams, which are metered and transferred for further treatment. The manifold valves isolate production from any individual well into two collecting pipes, called headers or collectors.

In a production system one separator serves for continuous handling of production (production separator) and the header pipe connected to it is called a production header and the second header pipe known as test header connected to a second separator known as test separator. The production of each well can be directed through the production header and onto the production separator or it can be diverted through the test header to the test separator. Check valves are installed between the well and the manifold. Such valves prevent backflow through the manifold from high to low pressure wells. The design of a multi well production system should always allow flow from any well to any separator unless the additional costs do not justify the additional flexibility.

Fluid Separation and Treatment

Hydrocarbon wells produce multiple fluids of gas, oil and water in different ratios. The various phases require different methods for processing and measurement. It is therefore necessary to separate them through separate piping and process equipment.

Equipment Used For Separation Process:

1. Oil and gas Separators
2. Stage separators

3. Trap
4. Water separators and Knock-Out Vessel
5. Flash Chamber

Several acceptable methods of produced salt water removal are available:

1. Mechanical Coalescer
2. Heater treater
3. Electrostat coalescing

Natural Gas Treatment

The natural gas must be removed from the crude oil, water condensate etc. Secondly, the gas must be processed to remove condensable and recoverable hydrocarbon vapour. The gas must be treated to remove condensable water vapour which might cause hydrate formation and to remove other undesirable components, such as hydrogen sulfide or carbon dioxide.

Prevention of Hydrate

A hydrate is a hydrocarbon and water compound, resembling ice formed under reduced temperature and pressure, in gas gathering compression and transmission facilities. Hydrates may pack solidly in gas lines in partially or completely block flow lines. The moisture helps formation of hydrates in the lines immediately after the chokes due to immense cooling effect and sudden fall of pressure. Hydrate inhibitors are injected in the lines to prevent the formation of hydrates.

Dehydration of Natural Gas

In dehydration of natural gas, ideally desiccants used in dehydration of Natural gas are drying agents that attract or absorb water. Common liquid desiccants used are Diethylene Glycol (DEG) and Tri-ethylene Glycol (TEG).

Measurement of Oil and Gas

In oil/gas production systems most common meters that are used for measurement include:

1. Differential Pressure Elements:
    - Orifice meters
2. Mechanical Sensing elements:
    - Positive displacement meters
    - Turbine meters
3. Fluid sensing elements.

A turbine meter consists of a bladed rotor suspended in a fluid stream with its axis of rotation perpendicular to the flow direction. Rotor is driven by liquid or gas impinging on the blades and its angular velocity is proportional to the fluid velocity/volume flow rate.

The unmanned offshore installations are required to produce oil and gas locally with a few well slots and then transfer it to a main processing installation (manned platform) from where the oil and gas is fed into the trunk lines going to the shore terminals and treatment facilities.

The main systems in place on the unmanned installations, as described briefly here, are as follows:

1. Manifolds
2. Test Separator
3. Fuel and instrument gas skid
4. Sump system
5. Drainage system
6. Gas lift system
7. Autocon panel
8. Generator
9. Crane
10. Davit and monorail
11. Solar panels
12. Telemetry system
13. Fog horn
14. Navigational lights
15. Crude injection system
16. Chemical injection system
17. HVAC Unit and Bunk House
18. Switch Gear
19. Barge Bumpers
20. Helideck
21. ESD/FSD system
22. Fire and gas detection system
23. Fire suppression system
24. Life rafts
25. Fire water pump
26. Boat landing
27. Battery bank

Autocon panel: A pneumatically operated shut down system, which incorporates we!!/fire shut down to protect platform in general and separator shutdown to protect separator equipment.

Manifold: It consists of two headers (group and test headers) and set of valves to facilitate diversion of individual wells to test separator for testing purposes. Another manifold for gas lift lines for the wells on gas lift is also available.

Test Separator: It is a pressure vessel used for testing the individual wells for assessing the well behavior, the flow rates of oil, gas and water are measured individually at regular intervals.

Fuel and instrument gas skid: It consists of K.O. Pot, cooler, filter drier, scrubber and volume bottle. Gas for instrument purposes tapped from the main line through a K.O. Pot. It is cooled, filtered and dried to a quality suitable for use in pneumatic instruments and as fuel gas. For pneumatic starting of Fire Water Pump and Generator, pressurized gas from volume bottle is utilized.

Fire Water Pump: It is a diesel engine driven submersible pump. These are provided with manual, hydraulic and pneumatic auto start system. These are to start in auto in case of FSD to provide water to sprinklers for the suppression of fire. This pump is also used for line flushing.

Generator: This is for supplying power to various platform utilities like lighting, crude injection pump, monorail hoists, and sump pump, charging of batteries, HV AC and telemetry system.

Pedestal crane: It is installed on the platform to enable loading/unloading of tools, equipment, and supplies from OSV s, wire line and well servicing operations.

Davit and Monorail Hoist: Davit is provided for launching the life rafts into the sea for abandoning the platform in case of an emergency. Mono rail hoists are provided for general maintenance of fire water pumps, generators etc.

Life raft: Two number of inflatable life raft are provided as a life saving equipment for abandoning the platform in case of emergency.

Fire and gas detection system: gas detectors are installed throughout the platform to detect and alarm high gas concentration and to initiate platform shut down if concentration goes beyond the allowable limits (60% LEL). For fire detection fixed temperature thermal detectors are provided in enclosures. Fusible plug loops are provided in the open process area. Thermal detectors will initiate the release of Halon in the enclosures for extinguishing the fire (at 60 degree Centigrade). Fusible plugs which melt at 85 Degree Centigrade releases the pressure in fire loops initiating the platform shutdown and starting of fire suppression system (Fire Water Pump and sprinklers)

Fire Suppression System: Suppression of fire is by manualmatic or by a combination of both. Auto system consists of halon discharge for enclosures and deluge system for outside areas. Manual system consists of water/foam hose reels, skid mounted dry chemical powder system and portable DCP/CO_2 extinguishers. Foam water and DCP hose reels are located at different strategic locations like heli-deck, main deck and cellar deck.

Telemetry/telecontrol system: system is for monitoring of various parameters from a remote process complex. Facilities for opening and closing of wells from the remote process complex are also provided.

Simple Distillation

The core refining process is simple distillation, illustrated in a stylized fashion at the light. Because crude oil is made up of a mixture of hydrocarbons, this first and basic refining process is aimed at separating the crude oil into its "fractions," the broad categories of its component hydrocarbons. Crude oil is heated and put into a still—a distillation column—and different products boil off and can be recovered at different temperatures. The lighter products u liquid petroleum gases (LPG), naphtha, and so-called "straight run" gasoline—are recovered at the lowest temperatures. Middle distillates n jet fuel, kerosene, and distillates (such as home heating oil and diesel fuel) come next. Finally, the heaviest products (residuum or residual fuel oil) are recovered, sometimes at temperatures over 1000°F.

Downstream Processing

Additional processing follows crude distillation, "downstream" (or closer to the refinery gate and the consumer) of the distillation process. Downstream processing is grouped together in this discussion, but encompasses a variety of highly complex units designed for very different upgrading processes. Some change the molecular structure of the input with chemical reactions, some in the presence of a catalyst, and some with thermal reactions. In general, these processes are designed to take heavy, low-valued feedstock—often itself the output from an earlier process and change it into lighter, higher-valued output. A catalytic cracker, for instance, uses the gas oil (heavy distillate) output from crude distillation as its feedstock and produces additional finished distillates (heating oil and diesel) and gasoline.

Sulfur removal is accomplished in a hydrotreater. A reforming unit produces higher octane components for gasoline from lower octane feedstock that was recovered in the distillation process. A coker uses the heaviest output of distillation, the residue or residuum, to produce a lighter feedstock for further processing, as well as petroleum coke.

Crude Oil Quality

The physical characteristics of crude oils differ. Crude oil with a similar mix of physical and chemical characteristics, usually produced from a given reservoir, field or sometimes even a region, constitutes a crude oil "stream." Some crude oils also have a higher sulfur content, an undesirable characteristic with respect to both processing and product quality. For pricing purposes, crude oils of similar quality are often compared to a single representative crude oil, a "benchmark," of the quality class. The quality of the crude oil dictates the level of processing and re-processing necessary to achieve the optimal mix of product output. Hence, price and price differentials between crude oils also reflect the relative ease of refining.

A premium crude oil like West Texas Intermediate, the U.S. benchmark, has a relatively high natural yield of desirable naphtha and straight-run gasoline. Another premium crude oil, Nigeria's Bonny Light, has a high natural yield of middle distillates. By contrast, almost half of the simple distillation yield from Saudi Arabia's Arabian Light, the historical benchmark crude, is a heavy residue ("residuum") that must be reprocessed or sold at a discount to crude oil. Even West Texas Intermediate and Bonny Light have a yield of about one-third residuum after the simple distillation process.

In addition to gravity and sulfur content, the type of hydrocarbon molecules and other natural characteristics may affect the cost of processing or restrict a crude oil's suitability for specific uses. The presence of heavy metals, contaminants for the processing and for the finished product, is one example. The molecular structure of a crude oil also dictates whether a crude stream can be used for the manufacture of specialty products, such as lubricating oils or of petrochemical feedstocks.

Refiners therefore strive to run the optimal mix (or "slate") of crudes through their refineries, depending on the refinery's equipment, the desired output mix, and the relative price of available crudes. In recent years, refiners have confronted two opposite forces—consumers' and government mandates that increasingly required light products of higher quality (the most difficult to produce) and crude oil supply that was increasingly heavier, with higher sulfur content (the most difficult to refine).

Other Refinery Inputs

In addition to crude oil that runs through a simple distillation, a variety of other specialized inputs, usually to downstream units, enhance the refiner's capability to make the desired mix of products. Among these products might be unfinished (partly refined) oil, or imported residual fuel oil used as input to a vacuum distillation unit. The supply pattern for "reformulated gasoline" or RFG, the mandated low-pollution product first required in 1995, includes an important share of blending components that are classified as refinery inputs. These blending components include oxygenates but consist mainly of products that could be classified' as finished gasoline in other jurisdictions or products that require little additional blending to be classified as finished gasoline.

Production Tests

Production tests are carried out to know the producing potential of the formation. It gives valuable information, e.g. formation evaluation, reservoir pressure, pressure gradients, well bore damage, transmissibility, and or permeability, radius of investigation, depletion, distance to barrier, type of fluid, productivity index, etc.

There are different methods to carryout formation testing. They can be briefly described as follows:

- Wire-line formation testers,
- Drill stem testing
- Conventional testing

Wire-line testing: Formation testers are lowered with the help of able and provide fluid samples and pressure recordings. They give almost all the information required for realistic formation evaluation in quickest time. But they can not be substituted for conventional testing and DST's. The accurate positioning of the tool is done with the help of S.P. or Gamma ray log run along with the tool. A hydraulic system activates a backup shoe which pushes the tool against the borehole wall and causes the selling of a relatively small circular packer. The control and recording equipments is on surface. An initial shut in pressure is recorded and then the sample chamber is opened to flow. The following pressure is continuously recorded.

There are two types of wire-line formation tester:

1. **The Formation Internal Tester (FIT):** FIT provides a safe, economical, fast and reliable method for testing of a potential producing zone in open as well as in cased hole. It can recover only one sample and only one static measurement can be made in one trip.
2. **The Repeat Formation Tester (RFT):** It is possible with RFT to make an

unlimited number of static pressure measurements and in addition, two formation fluid samples can be taken per trip.

Drill Stem Test (DST)

It is a method of knowing exactly about the producing potential of a formation by removing the hydrostatic pressure of drilling completion fluid from the formation and allowing the formation fluids to flow. There are two types of DST Tests:

(i) Open Hole DST
(ii) Cased Hole DST

Conventional Testing

After the well is completed, perforated, it is activated and generally flowed through tubing. The following studies are carried out:

- Stabilized flow rate measurement
- Reservoir studies
- Productivity test
- Productivity index
- Specific productivity index
- Inflow performance test
- Indicator diagram flow often flow study
- Isohronal studies
- Pressure building studies
- Multiple rate testing
- Fall off test, etc.

Production Logging

Any log which gives useful information in a cased well may be called cased hole log/production log.

Following are the logs:

- Cement bond log
- Fluid density log
- Temperature log
- Collar isocater log
- Casing caliper log
- TrauJ log
- Gamma ray and neutron log
- Flow meter log
- Pulse neutron log

These logs are useful in a cased well in detecting and solving various problems encountered during the production history of the well. These problems may occur just after the casing cementation or in the later part of the production.

Following are the problems generally encountered in a cased well:

- Channeling behind casing

- Zone of lost circulation
- Tubing/casing I packer leakage
- Zone of entry of oil water gas
- Quality of cementation
- Casing damage
- Log depth correlation
- Collar location

These logs are also useful in monitoring reservoir performance i.e. calculate which zone is producing how much oil/water/gas.

Crude Oil Storage

(a) Land Storage Individual land production properties require storage of crude until sufficient quantities are accumulated to deliver the oil to a pipeline. Oil field storage has progressed from earthen pits and wooden tanks to modern welded production tanks. Construction, strapping bagging and maintains are important of storage systems tanks for crude oil. The tank battery is point of custody transfer to the pipeline and in today's operation, a custody transfer (LACT) systems. It is therefore important that in the terminal point for equipment and operations, that is to be installed and maintained with great care. Loss of valuable liquids and gases and resulting economic less can occur if storage is not given proper attention.

Oil is stored in steel tanks which are constructed either of bolted or welded steel. It is usually provided with inlet and outlet for oil, bottom drain system, manhole etc.

Number of tanks in oil field is usually dependent on production. It should usually hold 3 to 7 days production. Tanks are calibrated and calibration table prepared Volumes of oil is measured with reference to level of oil in tank.

(b) Offshore storage: Most offshore storage has been handled by installing tanks platforms. However, because of high production rates and larger volumes to be handled design of large offshore surface, sub-sea and underwater storage systems has developed.

EOR/IOR: Artificial Lift

When reservoir pressure is insufficient to sustain the flow of oil to the surface at adequate rates, natural flow must be added by artificial life, when self flow of sea. Two basic form of artificial lift available are continuous gas lift and bottom hole pumping. Both methods supplement the natural drive energy of the reservoir and increase the flow by reducing back pressure at the well bore caused by flowing fluids in the tubing. The rate pressure, relationship of a well is used for investigating the need to introduce artificial lift, selecting the most suitable lift system, and determining its size and capacity.

The following two basic forms of continuous artificial lifts are recognized:

1. **Downhole/Bottom hole pumping** is accomplished by operating a pump at the bottom of the well. Downhole pumps boost the transfer of liquid from the bottom hole to the well head, eliminating back pressure caused by the fluids flowing in the tubing.

2. **Gas lift** is accomplished by injecting gas into the lower part of the production tubing. Injection of gas into the production string aerates the flowing fluid, reducing the pressure gradient and lowering back pressure at the information. For both lift methods, the production rate is increased by reducing well bore flowing pressure. As artificial lift consumes significant amount of generated energy, "it is introduced only after all adjustments in a natural flow systems are exhausted.

Wells with low productivity and low reservoir pressure require batch gas lift instead of continuous gas lift. Batch lift includes intermittent gas lift, plum or lift and chamber lift.

Oil Well Pumping pumps are generally classified according to the principle used to transform driving forces into the pressure.

Positive Displacement Pumps

(i) **Sucker Rod Pump (SRP):** A positive displacement pump that compresses liquid by the reciprocating motion of a piston. Which is actuated by a string of sucker rod that extend from the bottom hole pump to the pumping unit at the surface.

(ii) **Reciprocating Hydraulic Pump:** A positive displacement pump with a reciprocating piston, which is actuated by a reciprocating hydraulic motor coupled and assembled with the pump. The down hole motor is driven by a power fluid injected at high pressure from the surface.

Dynamic displacement pumps developed pressure by a sequence of accelerations building up kinetic energy and decelerations of the pumped liquid and the kinetic energy is transformed into potential energy.

They are of two types:

(i) **Centrifugal submersible pump:** a dynamic displacement multistage centrifugal turbine pump coupled by a short shaft to a down-hole electric motor. The motor is supplied with electrical power by cable extending to the surface. High discharge multistage centrifugal pumps to knock out high volume of water to produce left over oil.

(ii) **Jet pump:** an injector type dynamic displacement pump operated by a stream of high pressure power fluid that converts gas into jet in the nozzle of the pump. Downstream from the nozzle the high velocity low-pressure jet is mixed with the well's fluid. The stream of the mixture is then expanded in a diffuser, and as the flow velocity drops, the pressure is built up.

Classification of Wells

1. Geological/Geophysical information Wells:
   (a) *Key Wells*: For obtaining stratigraphic information in a new sedimentary basin.
   (b) *Parametric Wells*: For studying structure at depth and getting necessary data on characteristic and other Geophysical data and Geological information.

2. **Structural Wells**: For obtaining specific information of structure like folding, faulting etc.
3. **Exploratory Wild Cat Wells**: Structural/stratigraphic prospecting in any area where oil and gas deposit have not been discovered.
4. **Exploratory Test Well**: For Knowing stratigraphic and structural traps.
5. **Exploratory Step Out Well**: For determination of the pool discovered by test well wild cat well.
6. **Explicatory Off Set Well**: For obtaining all relevant information regarding reservoir rocks and fluid parameters in 'B' Category.
7. **Development Well**: Exploitation Production, injection wells.
8. **Special Well**: Like killing, blowout well, under ground storage of gas, disposal or water of oil field well.

Safety Systems in Oil and Gas well and Association Surface Equipment

Every oil or gas well capable of flowing from reservoir pressure can give rise sometimes to uncontrolled flow which an eliminate profit, destroy installations. Contaminate the environment etc. Automatic devices are available that are designed to stop uncontrolled flow and their use in mandatory in all offshore operations and many land areas.

Those are not fool proof and their effectiveness depends on proper installation, maintenance and trained operation.

Classification

(a) Subsurface devices installed in the tubing to stop well flow in case of well head or surface line breaks. They include surface and subsurface controlled valves installed in the tubing, bottom-hole chokes and regulators to control flow into the tubing and injection chock valves used when squeezing liquids into the formation.

1. *Subsurface Controlled Subsurface Safety Valves (SCSSV)*

Which were originally called storm checks are installed in tubing 200 to 300 feet below the surface and in offshore wells below the modline. Change in well flow pressure and fluid velocity course pressure difference that close them such as Ball type, Flapper type, sleeve type and Poppet type. Bellous control valves closure. These systems respond to either fire or pressure clergies in platform installation. They can also be closed manually if a disaster is impending and it is necessary to abandon the platform.

2. *Surface Safety Systems Surface Safety Valve*

The purpose of all the complex control panels, manifolds; pilots and related equipment is to hold this valve open for normal flow of fluids, under normal operation conditions and allow it to close instantly if a line broke or any other deviation from the normal occurs on the platform.

Natural Gas—The Fuel of the 21st Century

Natural gas will overtake coal as a global energy source early in the 21st century. This development reflects the tripling of proven gas reserves and the expansion of European and other markets for gas over the period since 1975. Gas thus entered the 21st century with a reserves-to-production ratio in excess of 60 years, with the implication that the expansion of production in the early decades will continue to be limited by demand, rather than by resources. Reserves in already discovered and producing fields could in themselves serve to keep global gas production growing at 3% or more a year until 2025, demand permitting, but additionally the continuation of additional discoveries is a certain prospect. This arises from the geographically broadening base of gas exploration activities and the continuing opportunities for the more intensive exploitation of existing gas-rich provinces, including some hitherto thought to be fully mature, including the Gulf of Mexico and the North Sea. The mid-point of the range of estimated additional reserves indicates a volume about one and-a-half times that of currently declared proven reserves. Proven reserves plus only half the estimated additional reserves are thus sufficient to support a conventional gas production curve which grows until at least 2050 (http://www.world-petroleum.org/docs/cook.doc).

Odell (2004) predicted how the 200-year curve of conventional gas supplý from 1940 to 2140 will be complemented by an additional production curve for non-conventional natural gas. This latter curve emerges from a conservative assumption of ultimately recoverable reserves of 650Gtoe from coal-bed methane, tight formation gas, gas from fractured shales and ultra-deep gas. It does, however, exclude the possibility of any recovery from gas hydrates, the volumes of which have been estimated to be up to 20 times larger than all other non-conventional gas resources taken together. Large-scale non-conventional gas production is indicated to start in the 2020s and to become the more important component in the total gas supply before 2070. Its production will continue to grow to the end of the 21st century. In 2100 gas is predicated to supply about 50% of the world's carbon energy production and, over the 21st century as a whole, about 43% of the cumulative total.

Gas will undoubtedly be the fuel of the 21st century (as coal was of the 19th century and oil of the 20th), even given the limiting assumptions on the exploitation of gas resources specified above. These limitations, however, do inhibit the ability of the gas supply to grow sufficiently after 2060 to sustain a 2% a year expansion in overall non-renewable energy use. There is, however, a prospect by then for additional gas supplies from the initial exploitation of gas from hydrates. A further 60 years of continuing scientific advances and engineering capabilities would seem likely to provide enough time to achieve the recovery at least a small part of that massive potential source of energy, in the form of the world's preferred carbon fuel for both commercial and environmental reasons. It thus seems more likely than not to be brought to the market—assuming, of course, that the gas can then still compete with the alternative, renewable energy sources (Odell, 2004).

A Brief History of Oil Companies

The 20th century began with the creation of the first major government-owned oil company and is ending in a wave of privatizations. To many observers, national oil companies (NOCs) seemed to be a creation of the post-embargo world of the 1970s. In fact, as shown on Fig. 1.4 (Treat, 1994) they have been around far longer.

Fig. 1.4: Creation of National Oil Companies

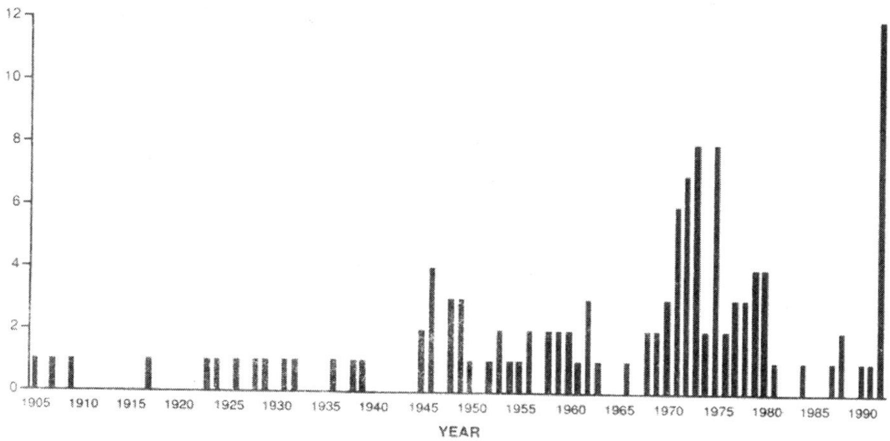

Evolution of NOCs

The development of national oil companies went through four distinct states during the first half of this century.

- **Pre-World War I:** The conversion of the British Navy from coal-to oil prompted the creation of the first major national oil company, British Petroleum (BP). BP began its life as Anglo-Iranian, a private company.
- **Russian Oil Turns Red.** The Russian Revolution of 1917 triggered creation of the second major national oil company, the Soviet Oil Ministry and its affiliated production, refining and distribution associations, as the Bolshevik government nationalized the private oil companies operating within their territory.
- **The First Postcolonial Wave:** The history of national oil companies in the producing areas of the developing world ironically begins in Argentina-one of the leaders of today's privatization movement. Yacimentos Petroliferos Fiscales (YPF) was founded in 1922.
  Initially, it operated in competition with private companies such as Shell, Exxon (then called Standard Oil of New Jersey) and Astra. However, in 1935, YPF was given exclusive rights to new exploration and development in Argentina. Until the establishment of Petroleos Mexicanos (Pemex) in March 1937, YPF remained the solitary example of a national oil company in the developing world for 15 years.
- **World War II: A** war fought in part about oil and access to it, triggered two very different responses. The Axis powers of Germany, Austria and Japan, plus sympathizer Spain, all created national oil monopolies. In contrast, the Allies tended to rely more on the national mobilization of private company resources without changing actual ownership.

It was also during the first half of this century that the management structure of oil companies evolved to reflect their growing complexity and increasing geographic scope. During this time, oil companies moved from highly centralized organizations to companies with multidivisional structures.

Development of NOCs in Second Half of 12th Century

Creation of national oil companies during the second half of this century can be divided into five distinct eras (Treat, 1994):

- *European Recovery:* In the aftermath of World War II, ENI was created in 1953 by the charismatic, visionary, and controversial Enrico Mattei, who built a major international oil company on the domestic Italian base of Agip.
- *Catching the Second Postcolonial Wave:* Following the creation of ENI, a second round of nationalism was touched-off in earnest. Petrobras was established in Mexico in 1953 and Sasol in South Africa in 1955.

EGPC was created in Egypt in 1957, following Nasser's revolution. ONGC was formed in India in the same year. Venezuela created CVP in 1960. OGDC was formed in Pakistan in 1961, and Algeria created Sonatrach in 1963. Iraq's INOC was formed in 1964, and Petroperu was created in Peru in 1968.

- *The New World Economic Order:* The Arab oil embargo is inevitably linked in peoples' minds with the nationalizations that followed, but actually the trend started before that. It was, in fact, Libya's Colonel Khaddafi who set off the third wave of nationalizations in the second half of the twentieth century.

After his seizure of power from King Idris in 1969, the controversial colonel set his mind to redistributing the growing revenues from oil production in Libya. He did that by creating Libya's National Oil Company in 1970. Prior to the 1973 embargo, a diverse group of countries nationalized as well. Trinidad did in 1970, Nigeria and Abu Dhabi in 1971, Norway and Saudi Arabia in 1972, and Iran the following year.

- *The Post-embargo National oil Company Explosion: OPEC*'s success in raising and sustaining oil prices in the aftermath of the 1973 embargo led to the creation of the NOCs in over a dozen countries including the Philippines (1973), Qatar (also 1973), Australia in 1974 (although they changed their mind in 1975), Malaysia (1974), Canada (1976), Ecuador (1976), France (Elf in 1976), Kuwait (1976), New Zealand (1978), and Gabon (1979).

In 1974, there was even a short-lived attempt to create a U.S. national oil company, but it was handily defeated in Congress, in part due to an astute decision by one opponent to call the proposed project "FOGCO," the Federal Oil and Gas Corporation. The breakup of the Soviet Union spawned the creation of a dozen NOCs as the newly independent former Soviet Union republics rushed to create their own oil companies.

- **Oil *Stocks of the Third Kind:*** Throughout most of the past 100 years, the trend was toward ever greater government ownership in the oil industry. However, in the century's final decades, a powerful countercurrent has developed. Once again, the British led the way. It was Britain that created the first major government-owned oil company, and it is Britain that is leading the privatization charge by abolishing the British National Oil Corporation and returning BP and Britoil to private ownership.

The move began in the early 1980s. The British Treasury needed money and Prime Minister Margaret Thatcher wanted to take a bold step toward bolstering the role of the private sector in the British economy. Few anticipated the momentous impact her proposals would soon have on the structure of the world's oil industry. Soon thereafter, New Zealand privatized Petrocorp, and the dynamic Carlos Menem of Argentina announced the privatization of both YPF and Gas Del Estado.

Within the space of half dozen years, the nationalization trend quickly accelerated and spread, involving in varying degrees: Repsol, Total, Elf, Singapore Petroleum, OMV, Petrocanada, and more recently, Petroperu and ENI. And an even larger number of companies were "commercialized," transformed from government bureaucracies into more market-oriented companies. Examples include: Pemex, Saudi Aramco, KPC, PTT, Petronas, CPC, and many of the oil companies of Eastern Europe and the former Soviet Union. In essence, they are taking a middle course between being a traditional national oil company and one that is privately owned. Despite the ever–growing trends, the national oil companies continue to dominate the world's petroleum reserves and plays a dominant role in the downstream market as could be seen from Figs 1.5 and 1.6 respectively.

Yet too often national oil companies are thought to be indistinguishable from their governments. That impression is not surprising since the national government

Fig 1.5: Historic Oil Production 1970-92

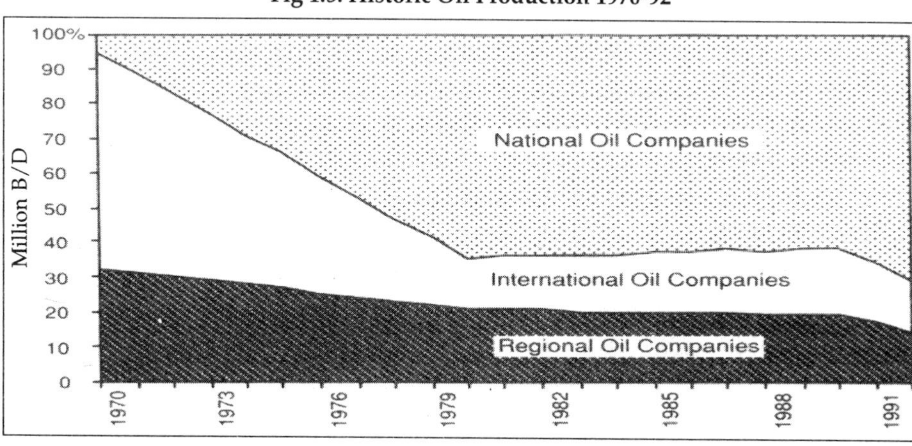

Source: Petro-companies, Oil and Gas Journal, BAH Analysis.

Fig. 1.6: Historic Refining Capacity 1970-92

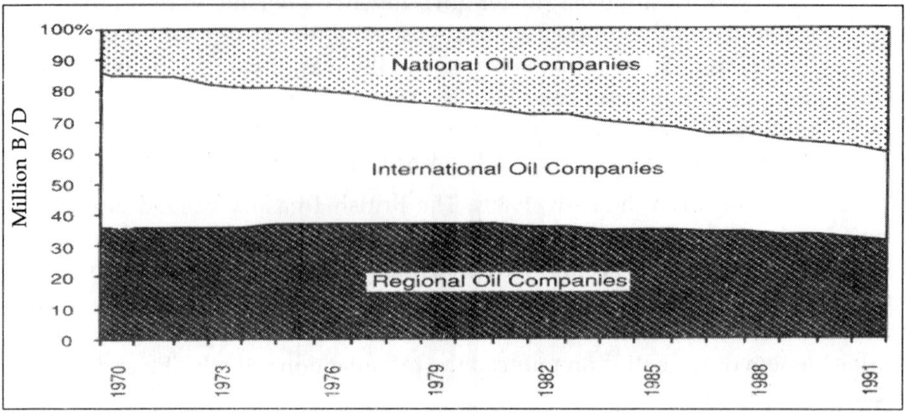

Source: Petro-companies, Oil and Gas Journal, BAH Analysis.

is their primary and often exclusive shareholder. But today NOCs from Venezuela to Taiwan are asserting their own identifies and are striving to become full-fledged partners with the independent oil companies of the world. Obviously, this fact will be an important part of our discussion. After all, this book is about the process of transformation which oil companies-whatever their ownership must undertake in today's changing petroleum markets.

Indian Oil Corporation Limited (Indian Oil)

Indian Oil Corporation Ltd. (IndianOil) is India's largest commercial enterprise, with a sales turnover of Rs. 2,47,479 crore (US $ 61.70 billion) and profits of Rs. 6,963 crore (US $ 1.74 billion) for the year 2007-08. IndianOil is also the highest ranked Indian company in the prestigious Fortune 'Global 500' listing, having moved up 19 places to the 116th position in 2008. It is also the 18th largest petroleum company in the world.

Indian Downstream Major

Beginning in 1959 as Indian Oil Company Ltd., Indian Oil Corporation Ltd. was formed in 1964 with the merger of Indian Refineries Ltd. (established 1958). IndianOil and its subsidiaries account for 49% petroleum products market share, 40.4% refining capacity and 69% downstream sector pipelines capacity in India.

For the year 2007-08, the IndianOil group sold 59.29 million tonnes of petroleum products, including 1.74 million tonnes of natural gas, and exported 3.33 million tonnes of petroleum products.

The IndianOil Group of companies owns and operates 10 of India's 19 refineries with a combined refining capacity of 60.2 million metric tonnes per annum (MMTPA, i.e. 1.2 million barrels per day). These include two refineries of subsidiary Chennai Petroleum Corporation Ltd. (CPCL) and one of Bongaigaon Refinery and Petrochemicals Limited (BRPL).

The Corporation's cross-country network of crude oil and product pipelines, spanning about 9,300 km and the largest in the country, meets the vital energy needs of the consumers in an efficient, economical and environment-friendly manner.

IndianOil is investing Rs. 43,393 crore (US $10.8 billion) during the period 2007-12 in augmentation of refining and pipeline capacities, expansion of marketing infrastructure and product quality upgradation as well as in integration and diversification projects (http://www.iocl.com/AboutUs/Profile.aspx).

Drivers of Change

A fundamental transformation of oil markets is presently underway. This change affects all companies, large and small; regional, national, and international. It is driven by the convergence of nine forces (Treat, 1996):

- *Intensification of Global Competition:* The entry of new players and the breakdown of market barriers have intensified global competition in petroleum markets worldwide.
- *Volatility of Oil Prices:* The growing competition, coupled with the decline in OPEC's ability to control prices, have led to an unprecedented volatility of oil prices.
- *Deintegration:* The decoupling of upstream resources from downstream outlets, and the subsequent robust growth of both spot and derivative markets, has further de-integrated the oil industry. In spite of the well publicized downstream moves by several large national oil companies, such as PDVSA's purchase of CITGO and its subsequent absorption of Champlin, KPC's expansion in Europe, and Saudi Arabia's joint venture with Texaco, the industry remains far less integrated today than it was two decades ago.
- *New Technology:* Throughout history, new technology has lowered commodity production costs and expanded our geographic and geologic horizons. Oil is no exception. Recent innovations which are driving down the costs of exploration and production include: 3-D seismic, horizontal drilling, coiled tube drilling and tension leg platforms.
- *Communications revolution:* The global telecommunications revolution has dramatically reduced the cost of information processing, making decentralization far more feasible.
- *Political transformation and the breakdown of national frontiers:* Recent profound political transformations have opened many previously closed economies to foreign investment and private ownership.
- *Growing Global Environmental Awareness:* This factor has also had a profound impact on the oil industry. Restricted access to resources, particularly in North America, has accelerated the globalization *efforts* of North American oil companies. Increased costs of exploration, production, refining, transportation and marketing-especially in North America and Europe-has required major changes in the formulation of key petroleum products. And increased regulation worldwide has forced companies to

spend more on compliance. In response to these forces, oil companies are fundamentally reevaluating their businesses.

- ***Ownership and Governance:*** As previously mentioned, the entire question of ownership and governance is being revisited. In stark contrast to what happened at the beginning of the century, there is now a marked reversal of the trend towards greater government ownership. However, ownership of the upstream remains overwhelmingly under government controls. Of the 50 largest petroleum companies in the world, 31 are reported to be state-owned. And, in spite of the downstream moves by several large national companies discussed earlier, the industry remains less integrated today those two decades ago.
- ***Deregulation:*** Oil and gas have enjoyed (or suffered, depending on your point of view) regulation for over 50 years. The regulations often took the form of price controls and restrictions on competition. They also limited inter-fuel competition, for example, by limiting the ability of oil companies from entering the power generation business. In the past decade, governments throughout the world have begun eliminating those barriers. In recent years, oil and gas companies such as Enron have entered the power generation business. And throughout the world, price controls and import restrictions are being eliminated or at least relaxed.

New Paradigm in Oil Industries

Companies are adapting their corporate strategies to the realities of the new marketplace. Their primary goals are improved profitability and the achievement of sustainable competitive advantage.

Some of key characteristics of this transformation include:

- Greater concern with creating shareholder value rather than growth in physical terms. In the case of state-owned companies, the increasing emphasis is on sustaining income for government shareholders.
- Recognizing the importance of segment profitability because deep spot markets now permit the decoupling of the upstream from the downstream. Some companies are even separating exploration from production and refining from marketing.
- Cutting both capital and operating costs: although the results of this effort are only beginning to show up in annual reports.
- Divesting unprofitable and nonessential assets: Companies have left such non-core businesses as minerals, office products, and hotels. They are also selling or swapping poorly performing oil or gas assets.
- Identifying and building core capabilities, while outsourcing non-core functions (drilling, payroll processing, land development, etc.).
- Reallocating investments towards more profitable sectors: For example, major U.S. oil companies are shifting their exploration and production funds away from the United States and toward overseas prospects.
- Reducing the scope of operations: companies are concentrating on more profitable geographies or niches.

- Redesigning their business processes and organizational structure to reduce costs and increase flexibility. Examples abound from the radical restructuring of companies such as BP and Pemex to the evolutionary changes in companies such as Amoco and Chevron.
- Increasing productivity improvements from technology investments: The falling cost of communications has made decentralization far more feasible. Lower computing costs and the growing client/server environment, have helped enormously as well. The ability to integrate data from a variety of sources has been dramatically improved by the use of 3-D seismic techniques. In addition, improved financial systems can now give business unit managers the information they need to run their businesses more profitably because they provide those managers with a better understanding of their costs.

In all these approaches, the key to success is recognizing that strategy should drive the design of key business processes, and that the company's organizational structure should facilitate-not impede-those processes as illustrated in Booz Allen's Performance Wheel (Fig. 1.7).

While the realignment of oil company structures that has occurred over the past five years is new to the industry, other businesses have been restructuring for decades. The fact that oil companies have lagged behind other industries in restructuring is nothing new. For nearly a century, oil companies have been a "lagging indicator" of what is going on in the rest of business.

The reasons for this are both cultural and technical. The engineering and technical backgrounds of oil company executives and the perceived value of tight

Fig. 1.7: The Booz Allen Performance Wheel

vertical integration led most oil companies to initially create organizational structures that were hierarchical and highly functional. As a result, the oil industry was among the last of the major industrial sectors to move to a multidivisional structure during the interwar period. After World War II, oil companies restructured again to accommodate the growth of their allied chemical businesses, and the growing geographic reach of their operations. However, most companies (Shell was an exception) retained a high degree of central control until recently.

The last five years have seen an explosion or organizational restructurings. The most noteworthy change has been the move toward business units, breaking the old divisional structures down to a lower level, and substituting financial oversight for direct operational control. The first pace of global and regional production-sharing contracts, strategic alliances, merger and acquisitions etc. is making the oil industry hyper-competitive in recent times. The transformation process continues, but there are two big obstacles to change. First is the failure of companies to properly adjust business processes to the new organizational structure. The second hurdle is the entrenched resistance of corporate cultures; particularly at the middle management level, where executives are not yet comfortable with the new order.

Looking to the future vision, the International Energy Agency (IEA)—has predicted that oil production could peak as soon as 2012 and that we could need 125 million barrels per day (bpd) by 2025—levels are currently hovering around the 85 million (bpd), just one million above worldwide consumption levels. Adding to the strain are the new economic tigers like China, India, Brazil and Russia. In fact, China and India are forecast to account for 45 percent of the increase in global energy demand by 2030 (O&G-Next Generation of Oil & Gas: http://www.ngoilgas.com/pastissue/article.asp?art=272498&issue=236).

Though there is a link between long-term strategic investment decision and performance in oil exploration, development and the various industrial downstream activities that are followed by oil companies, there could be a lot of instances to show that the performance cannot be strictly linked to the quantum of investment to determine the spending prudence in economic terms on account of innovations that are constantly taking place. Booz Allen Hamilton's annual study of the world's 1,000 largest corporate R&D budgets uncovers a small group of high-leverage innovators who outperform their oil industries (http://www.strategy-business.com/resiliencereport/resilience/rr00039). The Global Innovation 1000 study is the most comprehensive effort to date to assess the influence of R&D on corporate performance. Last year, our in-depth analysis—studying the 1,000 companies that reported the most spending on research and development around the world in 2004—demonstrated that there is no simple relationship between the level of R&D spending and corporate performance. This year, the data reinforced that conclusion and extended it, with a new understanding of innovation practices and additional metrics (such as the number and quality of patents). Among the specific findings:

- Deep pockets can be dry wells: Analysis of the 2005 Global Innovation 1000 confirms the major finding from our initial study last year: Money simply cannot buy effective innovation. There are no significant statistical relationships between R&D spending and the primary measures of financial or corporate success: sales and earnings growth, gross and operating profitability, market capitalization growth, and total shareholder returns. Gross profits as a percentage of sales is the single performance variable with a statistical relationship to R&D spending.

- Less than 10 percent of companies are high-leverage innovators: Compared with others in their industries, only 94 of the companies in the Global Innovation 1000 produced significantly better performance per R&D dollar over a sustained period.
- Companies are getting better at squeezing benefits from R&D spending: R&D spending by the Global Innovation 1000 rose last year by more than $20 billion, but revenues rose more.
- Bigger can be better, even if it doesn't boost breakthroughs: Scale provides advantages to R&D spenders. For the largest 500 companies, ranked by revenue and indexed by industry, median R&D spending was only 3.5 percent of sales in 2005, compared with 7.6 percent for the 500 smallest firms.
- Patents generally don't drive profits: Boosting R&D spending can increase the number of patents that a company controls, but there is no statistical relationship between the number or even the quality of patents and overall financial performance.
- Masters of the innovation value chain have an edge: The high-leverage innovators and the companies with best overall performance distinguish themselves not by the money they spend, but by the capabilities they demonstrate in ideation, project selection, development, or commercialization.

Conventional wisdom often seems to view R&D as a predictable 'black box' that automatically translates today's innovation investments into tomorrow's profits, even if nobody quite understands how it works. The principal findings from the above-mentioned study may undermine some people's faith in innovation as a financial savior; however, they comport with the real-world experience of most corporate decision makers, as well as with the lessons of business history. Innovation often does lead to higher performance, but the process may not be automatic or one leading to other. Many companies' R&D efforts are not strictly directed towards either quantitative and/ or qualitative performance along with long-term financial and economic viability. In the process, money is seemingly wasted in "reinventing wheels" that others have already rolled out. Many of the innovative ideas may also get stuck in developmental bottlenecks of various kinds, and promising innovations, in that sense, never get to market places because of flawed understanding of customers' needs, and poor marketing and investment planning.

REFERENCES

Atmanand (2004), Growth and Deregulation of Indian Oil Industry. Excel Books, New Delhi.

GAIL (2004), Natural Gas in India. GAIL-Infraline, I.Infraline.com

Gallun, R.A.; C.J. Wright; L.M. Nichols & J.W. Stevenson. (2004), Fundamentals of Oil & Gas Accounting, Pennwell Pub.

H.K.Abdel-AAL, B.A. Bakr. and M.A.Al Sahlawi (1992), Petroleum Economics & Engineering, Marcel Deckker Inc.

Odell, Peter R. (2004), Why Carbon Fuels will dominate the 21st Century's Global Energy Economy. Multi-science Publishing Co. Ltd.

O&G-Next Generation of Oil & Gas: http://www.ngoilgas.com/pastissue/article.asp?art=272498&issue=236

Patra, D.C. (2004), Oil Industry in India. Mittal Publication, New Delhi.

Treat, John Elting (1994), Creating High Performance International Petroleum Company: Dinosaurs can fly. Penn Well Publishing Co., Oklahoma, USA.

U.S. Energy Information Agency (2007), Retrieved on 2008-04-17.

Websites

BERA: http://www.loc.gov/rr/business/BERA/issue5/history.html

http://www.geocities.com/mudsmeller/history.html

http://www.world-petroleum.org/docs/cook.doc

http://www.iocl.com/AboutUs/Profile.aspx

http://www.strategy-business.com/resiliencereport/resilience/rr00039

http://www.oilgasarticles.com/articles/7/1/Classification-of-Oil/Page1.html

http://wetestit.com/Crude_101.htm

http://en.wikipedia.org/wiki/Petroleum_industry

http://www.oilgasarticles.com/articles/7/1/Classification-of-Oil/Page1.html

http://www.capp.ca/default.asp?V_DOC_ID=25

CHAPTER II

Global Energy Scene and Contribution of Oil and Natural Gas

Projection of Global Energy Demand: IEA vs. IEO

The International Energy Agency (IEA, 2007) provides projections comparable with those in *IEO2007* in its *World Energy Outlook 2006*. Because IEA releases projections only for the years 2015 and 2030, two time periods are compared here—2004 to 2015 and 2015 to 2030. In the 2004 to 2015 projection period, both *IEO2007* and IEA expect world energy demand to increase by an average of 2.1 percent per year (Table 1). Not surprisingly, both outlooks project much faster growth in energy demand among the non-OECD nations than in the OECD, with non-OECD energy use growing three times as rapidly. There are, however, some regional differences. IEA's expectations for demand growth in OECD Asia, for instance, are much higher than those in *IEO2007*, and the projected 1.4 percent annual growth rate projected by IEA for the region exceeds the 1.3 percent rate in the *IEO2007* high economic growth case. In the non-OECD regions, both outlooks have similar projections for growth in Europe and Eurasia. *IEO2007* projects 1.6-percent average annual growth in energy use between 2004 and 2015, and IEA projects 1.4 percent annual growth. IEA projects much slower growth than *IEO2007* over the 2004 to 2015 period for China and other non-OECD Asia, as well as for Africa and Central and South America. In each case, IEA's projected growth rates are lower than those in the *IEO2007* low economic growth case. On the other hand, IEA's projected 4.2 percent annual growth in Middle Eastern energy use over the same period is much higher than the projection of 3.1 percent per year in the *IEO2007* reference case and, in fact, exceeds the projected growth rate in the *IEO2007* high macroeconomic growth case. In the later years of the projections, *IEO2007* and IEA generally agree, with worldwide energy demand rowing by 1.5 percent per year between 2015 and 2030 in the *IEO2007* reference case and by 1.3 percent per year in the IEA projection (Table 2.1).

Table 2.1: Comparison of IEO2007 and IEA World Energy Consumption Growth Rates by Region, 2015-30 (Average Annual Percent Growth)

Region	IEO2007			IEA
	Low Growth	Reference	High Growth	
OECD	0.6	0.9	1.2	1.2
North America	0.9	1.2	1.5	1.3
United States	0.7	1.0	1.3	1.2
Europe	0.3	0.5	0.8	0.8
Asia	0.7	1.0	1.3	1.4
Non-OECD	2.9	3.2	3.6	3.0
Europe and Eurasia	1.2	1.6	2.0	1.4
China	4.2	4.5	4.9	4.0
Other Non-OECD Asia	3.0	3.3	3.6	2.8
Middle East	2.7	3.1	3.4	4.2
Africa	2.8	3.1	3.4	2.1
Central and South America	2.8	3.1	3.4	2.4
Total World	1.8	2.1	2.4	2.1

Source: *IEO2007*: Energy Information Administration (EIA), System for the Analysis of Global Energy Markets (2007). IEA: International Energy Agency, *World Energy Outlook 2006* (Paris, France, November 2006), pp. 492-527.

Both outloo'cs anticipate similar regional growth over the 2015 to 2030 period. The largest regional difference between the two projections—and the only instance in which IEA regional growth projections fall outside the range defined by the *IEO2007* low and high macroeconomic growth cases—is for China. The IEA growth projection for energy use in China from 2015 to 2030 is lower than the *IEO2007* low macroeconomic growth case projection. The projections vary not only with respect to levels of total energy demand but also with respect to the mix of primary energy inputs. In the 2004 to 2015 period, IEA expects slightly higher growth in fossil fuel use and slower growth in the use of non-fossil fuels than does *IEO2007* (Table 2.2).

Table 2.2: Comparison of IEO2007 and IEA World Energy Consumption Growth Rates by Fuel, 2004-15 (Average Annual Percent Growth)

Region	IEO2007			IEA
	Low Growth	Reference	High Growth	
OECD	0.4	0.8	1.2	0.6
North America	0.6	1.1	1.5	0.8
United States	0.6	1.0	1.5	0.7
Europe	-0.1	0.3	0.6	0.4
Asia	0.4	0.8	1.2	0.6

Non-OECD	1.6	2.1	2.6	1.8
Europe and Eurasia	0.6	1.2	1.7	0.8
China	2.3	2.7	3.2	2.0
Other Non-OECD Asia	1.9	2.4	2.9	2.1
Middle East	1.3	1.7	2.2	2.1
Africa	1.3	1.8	2.2	1.8
Central and South America	1.4	1.8	2.3	2.0
Total World	1.1	1.5	2.0	1.3

Source: *IEO2007*: Energy Information Administration (EIA), System for the Analysis of Global Energy Markets (2007). IEA: International Energy Agency, *World Energy Outlook 2006* (Paris, France, November 2006), pp. 492-527.

For both renewables and nuclear power consumption, the growth rates projected by IEA are slower than those in the *IEO2007* low economic growth case. For renewables, the differences may be explained by the fact that IEA renewables projections include estimates for traditional, non-marketed biomass and the *IEO2007* projections do not. Traditional biomass is a substantial portion of the renewable energy base and is not expected, in most regions, to expand as nations migrate away from non-marketed to commercial energy use over the projection period—in contrast to hydroelectric power and other marketed renewable energy sources captured in the *IEO2007* projection. For nuclear power, there are only small differences in projected growth rates between the *IEO2007* high macroeconomic growth and reference cases and no difference between the reference case and the low macroeconomic growth case. This is because the projections include only a limited number of plants, which are already planned or under construction, with expected completion dates before 2015 that analysts largely agree are achievable. For the period from 2015 to 2030, *IEO2007* and IEA are largely in agreement. The only exception is nuclear power, for which the IEA growth projection falls below that in the *IEO2007* low macroeconomic growth case (Table 2.3).

Table 2.3: Comparison of IEO2007 and IEA World Energy Consumption Growth Rates by Fuel, 2015-30 (Average Annual Percent Growth)

Fuel	IEO2007			IEA
	Low Growth	Reference	High Growth	
Liquids	1.2	1.5	1.9	1.7
Natural Gas	2.0	2.4	2.7	2.5
Coal	2.2	2.6	2.9	2.7
Nuclear	1.5	1.5	1.6	1.2
Renewable/Other	2.1	2.3	2.6	2.0
Total	1.8	2.1	2.4	2.1

Note: In the IEA projections, Renewable/Other includes traditional biomass.

Source: *IEO2007*: Energy Information Administration (EIA), System for the Analysis of Global Energy Markets (2007). IEA: International Energy Agency, *World Energy Outlook 2006* (Paris, France, November 2006), pp. 492-527.

IEA Projections of Global Energy Demand

The International Energy Agency (IEA, 2007) summarizes the issues of energy security facing the world as insufficient and secure supplies at affordable prices. The broad issues encompass the following strategic areas pertaining to Global Energy Demand:

- environmental harm caused by consuming too much fossil-fuel energy:
- the need to diversify production and consumption both by geographical location and fuel type.;
- the impact of rising oil and gas demand increasing the vulnerability of consumers to disruption and price shock. The IEA's principal concerns are environmental and economic.

Other observers of the world energy scene have raised political risks in the following manner:

- heightened competition over depleting energy sources;
- the new scramble for Africa's oil and gas;
- the security of supplies from the Middle-East and instability of their governments' dependency on "petrodollars";
- the future of Iraq, with the second largest world oil reserves;
- energy-rich countries using energy supply and price as a political weapon.

Despite national differences f approach, the trend in European Union countries in recent years has been to open up their gas and electricity utilities to competition, promoting cheaper gas and electricity.

Global Energy Demand Perspective

World marketed energy consumption is projected to grow by 57 percent between 2004 and 2030, according to the reference case projection from the International Energy Outlook 2007 (IEO, 2007) released today by the Energy Information Administration (EIA). The IEO2007 shows the most rapid growth in energy demand for nations outside the Organization for Economic Cooperation and Development (OECD), especially in non-OECD Asia, where strong projected economic growth drives the increase in energy use as given in Figure 2.1 (www.eia.doe.gov/neic/press283gifs/fig1.gif).

Global energy demand grows despite the relatively high world oil and natural gas prices in the reference case. However, rising oil prices dampen growth in demand for petroleum and other liquids fuels after 2015 and, as a result, reducing their share of overall energy use from 38 percent in 2004 to a projected 34 percent in 2030. In contrast, the energy shares of natural gas, coal, and renewable energy sources are expected to grow over this period. Liquids consumption is still expected to grow strongly, however, reaching 118 million barrels per day in 2030. The United States, China, and India together account for nearly half of the projected growth in world liquids use.

To meet the increment in world liquids demand in the IEO-2007 reference case, supply in 2030 is projected to be 35 million barrels oil equivalent per day higher than the 2004 level of 83 million barrels per day (Fig. 2.1). Conventional resources

Fig. 2.1: Global Energy Demand Outlook—2030

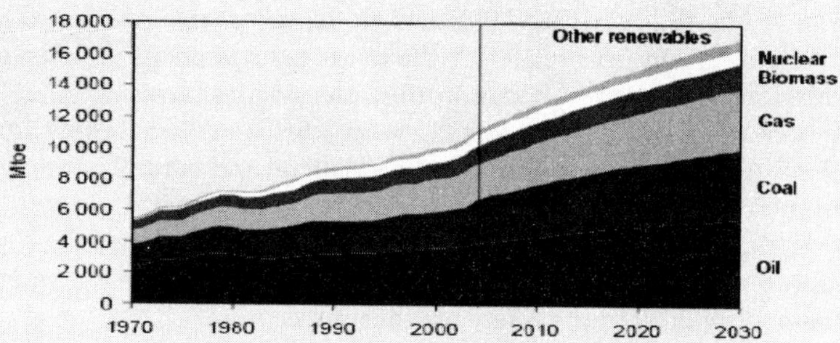

Global demand grows by more than half over the next quarter of a century, with coal use rising most in absolute terms

account for about 27 million barrels per day of this increase, with a projected 21 million barrels per day increase in production by members of the Organization of Petroleum Exporting Countries (OPEC) and 6 million barrels per day increase in non-OPEC countries. Production from unconventional resources (including biofuels, coal-to-liquids (CTL) and gas-to-liquids) increases by nearly 8 million barrels per day and accounts for nearly 9 percent of total world liquids supply in 2030 (Fig 1: www.eia.doe.gov/neic/press283gifs/fig2.gif).

Other report of EIA highlights the following projection of Energy Supply vis-à-vis demand during 2004-20 (Table 2.4).

Table 2.4: Global Energy Supply vis-à-vis Demand Scenario (2004-20)

Item	2004		2010		2020		2004-20 Growth Rate (%)
	Million KLOE	%	Million KLOE	%	Million KLOE	%	
Total Supply	129.1	100	147.2	100	173.9	100	2.1
Indigenous	12.2	9	39.5	27	45.6	26	18.3
Imported	116.9	91	107.7	73	128.3	74	0.5
Coal	43.5	34	44.2	30	64.3	37	2.9
Petroleum	63.5	49	63.8	43	56.3	32	-0.5
Natural Gas	0.8	1	0.7	0	0.7	0	-1.2
LNG	9.9	8	18.2	12	29.0	17	7.9
Pumped Storage Hydro	1.0	1	1.0	1	0.9	1	-0.6
Nuclear Power	9.8	8	14.3	10	12.0	7	1.3
Renewable Energy	0.6	0	5.0	3	10.7	6	17.4
Domestic Consumption	107.6	100	123.9	100	146.3	100	2.1
Coal	10.8	10	130.0	11	15.9	11	2.1
Petroleum	42.2	39	41.8	34	36.8	25	-0.5
Natural Gas	2.4	2	3.0	2	3.3	2	1.9
Electricity	51.5	48	61.1	49	79.5	54	2.9
Renewable Energy	0.6	1	5.0	4	10.7	7	17.4

Source: IEO, Paris 2007.

Coal consumption, which grows an average annual rate of 2.2 percent, is the fastest-growing energy source worldwide in the IEO2007 reference case projection, which assumes that existing laws and policies remain in effect through 2030 notwithstanding concerns related to the rising level of energy-related greenhouse gas emissions. World coal consumption increased sharply from 2003 to 2004, largely because of a 17 percent increase—on a British thermal unit (Btu) basis—in non-OECD Asia (mainly China and India). With oil and natural gas prices expected to continue rising, coal is an attractive fuel for nations with access to ample coal resources, especially in coal-rich countries like China, India, and the United States. These three countries combined account for 86 percent of the increment in world coal demand by 2030 in the reference case projection.

Higher fossil fuel prices, energy security concerns, improved reactor designs, and environmental considerations are expected to improve prospects for nuclear power capacity in many parts of the world, and a number of countries are expected to build new nuclear power plants. World nuclear capacity is projected to raise from 368 gigawatts in 2004 to 481 gigawatts in 2030. Declines in nuclear capacity are projected only in OECD Europe, where several countries (including Germany and Belgium) have either plans or mandates to phase out nuclear power, and where some old reactors are expected to be retired and not replaced.

In the IEO2007 reference case, which does not include specific policies to limit greenhouse gas emissions, energy-related carbon dioxide emissions are projected to rise from 26.9 billion metric tons in 2004 to 33.9 billion metric tons in 2015, and 42.9 billion metric tons in 2030. From 2003 to 2004, carbon dioxide emissions from the non-OECD countries grew by almost 10 percent, while emissions in the OECD countries grew by less than 2 percent. The result of the large increase in non-OECD emissions was that 2004 marked the first time in history that emissions from the non-OECD exceeded those from the OECD countries. Further, because of the expectation that non-OECD countries will rely on fossil fuels to supply much of their future energy demand growth, carbon dioxide emissions from the non-OECD countries in 2030 are projected to exceed those from the OECD by 57 percent.

India's Overall Production, Consumption and Projected Demand of Energy

Overview of India's Oil and Gas Sector

India is the fifth largest energy consumer in the world with primary commercial energy consumption in 2004 of 375.8 Million Metric Tonnes of Equivalent (MMTOE) (Source: BP statistical survey, 2005). In 2004, the consumption of oil and gas formed a major percentage in the world energy consumption basket. In India, however, coal dominated the consumption basket. Energy consumption grew at an average compounded annual growth rate (CAGR) of 3.8 per cent in the period 1999-2005 with the GDP growing at CAGR of 6.3 per cent resulting into a very attractive GDP elasticity of little above 0.6.

The significance of the Indian Oil and Gas Sector can be gauged from the following facts (http://www.pwc.com/extweb/pwcpublications.nsf/docid/5EBE732379E5428ECA257184005E7A2B/$file/oil_gas.pdf):

- Largest contributor to the national exchequer in 2004-05 with taxes amounting to US$ 27 billion.
- Oil and Gas constituted 40 per cent of primary energy source in 2004.
- India is sixth largest crude oil consumer in the world with consumption at 119.3 MMT in 2004.
- Petroleum, Oil Lubricants (PoL) imports is 28 per cent (Source: PwC Analysis) of the total imports of India and PoL exports is 8 per cent of total exports for 2004-05.
- All five Indian companies appearing on the Fortune 500 list operate in the Oil and Gas sector.
- India is Ninth largest crude oil importer in the world.
- India ranks sixth in refining capacity in the world with capacity at 2.5 million barrels of oil per day in 2004 which is 3 per cent of the world's refining capacity.
- Reliance Industries Ltd (RIL) in India is the third largest refinery in the world with a capacity of 33 MMTPA.

India is both a major energy producer and consumer. India currently ranks as the world's eleventh greatest energy producer, accounting for about 2.4% of the world's total annual energy production, and as the world's sixth greatest energy consumer, accounting for about 3.3% of the world's total annual energy consumption. Despite its large annual energy production, India is a net energy importer, mostly due to the large imbalance between oil production and consumption. An historical summary of India's Total Primary Energy Production (TPEP) and Consumption (TPEC) is shown in Table 2.5.

Table 2.5: India's TPEP and TPEC, 1993-2003 (in Quads)

	1993	1994	1995	1996	1997	1998	1999	2000	2001	2002	2003
TPEP	7.49	8.00	9.48	8.75	9.17	9.37	9.58	9.83	10.23	9.99	10.15
TPEC	9.24	9.97	11.49	11.14	11.76	12.17	12.74	13.50	13.85	13.79	14.03

Note: 1 Quad = 1 quadrillion Btu.
Source: DOE/EIA.

The overall projection of India's total primary energy requirement from various non-renewable and renewable sources, as estimated by the Planning Commission, Government of India, is given in Table 2.6. It may be seen that coal and Oil and Natural Gas constitute nearly 85% of the Primary Energy Requirement of India as in 2003-04 (WEC, 2006).

Petroleum

India's proved oil reserves are estimated (as of January 2005) at about 5 billion barrels, or about 4.5% of the world total. Most of these reserves lie offshore near Mumbai and onshore in Assam state. However, exploration is still happening, and India's off-shore and on-shore basins may contain as much as 11 billion barrels. India presently ranks as the 25th greatest producer of crude oil, accounting for about 1% of the world's annual crude oil production. About 30% of India's energy

Table 2.6: India Primary Energy Requirements Scenario
7% Growth Per-Year (Million TOE)

Year	Hydro	Nuclear	Coal	Oil	Gas	TPES
2003-04	7	5	167	119	29	327
	(2.1%)	(1.5%)	(51.1%)	(36.4%)	(8.9)	(100%)
2006-07	9	7	200	124	35	375
2011-12	15	15	253	151	49	483
2016-17	19	29	322	188	67	625
2021-22	24	54	393	234	92	797
2026-27	34	79	517	294	127	1051
2031-32	43	115	641	370	175	1344
	(3.2%)	(8.6%)	(47.7%)	(27.5%)	(13%)	(100%)
Growth Rates 2032 (%)	6.7	12.2	4.9	4.1	7	5.2

Source: Pradeep Chaturvedi, Chairman, Safety and Quality Forum, Institute of Engineers, India; "An integrated policy for India": page-32, Table-1: Draft Report of the Expert Committee on Integrated Energy Policy—Planning Commission, Government of India, December 2005; World Energy in 2006, WEC.

needs are met by oil, and more than 60% of that oil is imported. A strong growth in oil demand has resulted in India's annual petroleum consumption increasing by more than 75% from what it was a decade ago, and petroleum consumption is projected to climb to about 3 million barrels per day by 2010. India is currently the world's sixth greatest oil consumer, accounting for about 2.9% of world's total annual petroleum consumption. An historical summary of petroleum production and consumption in India is shown in Table 2.7.

Table 2.7: Petroleum Production and Consumption in India, 1993-2003
(in thousands of barrels per day)

	1993	1994	1995	1996	1997	1998	1999	2000	2001	2002	2003
Production (total)*	578	651	770	751	780	761	765	770	782	813	815
Production (Crude Oil only)	534	590	703	651	675	661	653	646	642	665	660
Consumption	1,311	1,413	1,575	1,681	1,765	1,844	2,031	2,127	2,184	2,263	2,320

*includes crude oil, natural gas plant liquids, other liquids, and refinery processing gain.
Source: DOE/EIA.

Natural Gas

India's natural gas reserves are currently estimated (as of January 2005) at about 29-32 trillion cubic feet (tcf), or about 0.5% of the world total. Most of these reserves lie offshore northwest of Mumbai in the Arabian Sea and onshore in Gujarat state. India does not yet rank in the top 20 of the world's greatest natural gas consumers, but that will soon change. Natural gas has experienced the fastest rate of increase of any fuel in India's primary energy supply; demand is growing at about 4.8%

per year and is forecast to rise to 1.2 tcf per year by 2010 and 1.6 tcf per year by 2015. An historical summary of natural gas production and consumption in India is shown in Table 2.8.

Table 2.8: Dry Natural Gas Production and Consumption in India, 1993-2003 (in tcf)

	1993	1994	1995	1996	1997	1998	1999	2000	2001	2002	2003
Production	0.53	0.59	0.63	0.70	0.72	0.76	0.75	0.79	0.85	0.88	0.96
Consumption	0.53	0.59	0.63	0.70	0.72	0.76	0.75	0.79	0.85	0.88	0.96

Note: "dry" gas means gas with condensates removed.
Source: DOE/EIA, 2003.

Coal

India's has huge proven coal reserves, estimated (as of January 2005) at more than 90 billion tons, or about 10% of the world's total. Most of these reserves are relatively high ash bituminous coal and are located in Bihar, West Bengal, and Madhya Pradesh states. At the current level of production and consumption, India's coal reserves would last more than two hundred years. India is currently the third-largest coal-producing country in the world (behind China and the United States), and accounts for about 8.5% of the world's annual coal production. India is also currently the third-largest coal consuming country (behind the China and the United States), and accounts for nearly 9% of the world's total annual coal consumption. More than half of India's energy needs are met by coal, and about 70% of India's electricity generation is now fueled by coal. The annual demand for coal has been steadily increasing over the past decade, and is now nearly 50% greater than it was a decade ago. Even though India is able to satisfy most of its country's coal demand through domestic production, less than 5% of its reserves is coking coal used by the steel industry. As a result, India's steel industry imports coking coal, mainly from Australia and New Zealand, to meet about 25% of its annual needs. An historical summary of coal production and consumption in India is shown in Table 2.9.

Table 2.9: Coal Production and Consumption in India, 1996-2005 (in millions of short tons)

	1996	1997	1998	1999	2000	2001	2002	2003	2004	2005
Production	295.56	311.96	323.63	319.93	326.58	337.94	352.60	367.29	389.20	412.95
Anthracite	n/a	n/a	n/a	n/a	n/a	n/a	n/a	n/a	n/a	n/a
Bituminous	273.41	289.32	300.40	296.51	304.10	313.69	327.79	341.27	361.24	382.61
Lignite	22.15	22.64	22.23	23.42	22.48	24.25	24.81	26.02	27.96	24.34
Consumption	332.2	358.5	362.9	375.4	406.1	413.6	430.6	430.6	N/A	N/A

n/a—not applicable; N/A—not available.
Note: components may not add to total due to rounding.
Source: Ministry of Coal and Mines, Government of India.

Electricity

India is presently the sixth-greatest electricity generating country and accounts for about 4% of the world's total annual electricity generation. India is also currently ranked sixth in annual electricity consumption, accounting for about 3.5% of the world's total annual electricity consumption. Overall, India's need for power is growing at a prodigious rate; annual electricity generation and consumption in India have increased by about 64% in the past decade, and its projected rate of increase (estimated at as much as 8-10% annually, through the year 2020) for electricity consumption is one of the highest in the world. An historical summary of electricity generation and consumption in India is shown in Table 2.10.

Table 2.10: Electricity Generation and Consumption in India, 1995-2005 (in billions of kilowatt-hours)

Year	1995	1996	1997	1998	1999	2000	2001	2002	2003	2004	2005
Net Generation	396.0	412.6	441.1	470.7	504.3	529.1	548.0	563.5	556.8	558.33	587.37
hydroelectric	71.9	68.2	73.9	82.2	79.9	73.7	73.0	63.5	68.5	73.77	84.50
nuclear	6.5	7.4	10.4	10.6	11.4	14.1	18.2	17.8	16.4	17.77	16.84
geo/solar/wind/biomass	0.5	0.8	0.9	1.0	2.3	2.9	3.9	4.1	4.2	n/a	n/a
conventional thermal	317.2	336.1	355.8	376.8	410.7	438.5	453.0	478.2	467.7	466.82	486.03
Net Consumption	369.8	385.2	411.6	439.0	470.1	493.4	510.9	525.4	519.0	n/a	n/a
Imports	1.7	1.6	1.6	1.5	1.4	1.5	1.5	1.5	1.4	1.4	1.4
Exports	0.1	0.1	0.1	0.2	0.3	0.2	0.3	0.2	0.2	0.2	0.2

n/a—not applicable.
Note: Generation components may not add to total due to rounding.
Source: DOE/EIA and Government of India.

India is currently ranked fifth in the world in terms of total installed electricity generating capacity, and accounts for about 3.5% of the world total. Hydroelectric capacity represents about one-fourth of India's total installed capacity, and overall, India is currently ranked sixth-largest in the world in that category (accounting for about 3.7% of the world's installed hydroelectric generating capacity). There is a large amount of hydroelectric capacity in construction and planning stages, and in particular, hydropower development in the Brahmaputra river basin in eastern India is expected to result in six large power plants, which will add nearly 30,000 megawatts (MWe) of generating capacity. The largest of these will be the 11,000 MWe Dihang Upper project, which, when completed in about 2012, would become the world's third-largest power plant. An historical summary of installed electricity generating capacity in India is shown in Table 2.11.

Table 2.11: Installed Electricity Generation Capacity in India (in thousands of megawatts)

	1997	2002	2003	2004	2005
Hydroelectric	21.65	26.26	26.76	29.50	30.94
Nuclear	2.22	2.72	2.72	2.72	2.77
Geothermal/Solar/ Wind/Biomass	1.27	1.51	1.74	1.87	3.81
Conventional Thermal	59.64	74.55	76.65	77.97	80.90
Total Capacity	85.79	105.05	107.88	112.06	118.42

Note: Components may not add to total due to rounding.
Source: Government of India.

Carbon Emissions Information

Lowering energy intensity of GDP growth through higher energy efficiency is key to meeting India's energy challenge and ensuring its energy security. India's energy intensity vis-à-vis GDP growth has been falling and is about half what is used to be in early 70s. Energy consumption, per unit of GDP in purchasing power parity terms is only 0.19 kilogram oil equivalent per dollar as compared to 0.21 of the world average. But there is a still room for improvement and can be brought down further significantly with current commercially available technologies. Despite of a reasonable growth in GDP and dependence on fossil fuels to meet the Energy needs of India, carbon dioxide emission per capita in India is still low, i.e., around 1 tonne against the world average of about 4 tonnes and of about 19 tonnes in case of some developed countries (According to IEA). A historical summary of CO_2 emissions from fossil fuel use in India is shown in Table 2.12.

Table 2.12: Fossil Fuel-related CO_2 Emissions in India, 1990-2002

Component	1990	1995	1998	1999	2000	2001	2002	% change
90-02								
CO_2/TPES								
(t CO_2 per Tj)	38.87	42.88	43.77	44.29	45.00	44.90	45.10	16.0%
CO_2/GDP								
(kg CO_2 per 1995US$)	2.16	2.23	2.09	2.06	2.07	1.99	1.97	-8.8%
CO_2/GDP								
(kg CO_2 per 1995US$ PPP)	0.45	0.47	0.44	0.43	0.43	0.42	0.41	-8.9%
CO_2/Population								
(t CO_2 per capita)	0.70	0.85	0.90	0.93	0.96	0.95	0.97	38.6%

Source: Planning Commission, GOI.

A composite position of Primary energy and electricity resources, exploiting fossil fuels, nuclear, and renewable sources are illustrated in Table 2.13.

Assumptions for Potential Calculations are as given below:

Fossil Fuels

1. Complete Source is used for calculating electricity potential with a thermal efficiency of 0.36.
2. Calorific Values: Coal: 4,200 kcal/kg, Hydrocarbon: 10,200 kcal/kg.
3. Ministry of Petroleum and Natural Gas has set strategic goals for the next two decades (2001-20) of 'doubling reserve accretion' to 12 BT (Oil + Oil equivalent gas) and 'improving recovery factor' to the order of 40%. Considering the fact that exploration is a dynamic process and India is one of the les explored countries, reference assumes that cumulative availability of hydrocarbons up to 2052 will be 12 BT.

Table 2.13: Primary Energy and Electricity Resources

	Amount	Thermal energy			Electricity potential
		EJ	TWh	GWYr	GWe-Yr
Fossil					
Coal	38-BT	667	185,279	21,151	7,614
Hydrocarbon	12-BT	511	141,946	16,204	5,833
Non-Fossil					
Nuclear					
Uranium-Metal	61,000-T				
In PHWRs		28.9	7,992	913	328
In Fast breeders		3,699	1,027,616	117,308	42,231
Thorium-Metal	2,25,000-T				
In Breeders		13,622	3,783,886	431,950	155,502
Renewable					
Hydro	150-GWe	6.0	1,679	192	69
Non-conventional renewable	100-GWe	2.9	803	92	33

Source: Planning Commission, GOI.

Non-Fossil Fuels

Thermal energy is the equivalent fossil energy required to produce electricity with a thermal efficiency of 0.36.

Nuclear

1. PHWR burn-up = 6,700 MWd/T of U-oxide, thermal efficiency 0.29.
2. It has been assumed that complete fission of 1kg of fissile material gives 1000 MWd of thermal energy. Fast reactor thermal efficiency is assumed to be 42%. Fast breeders can use 60% of the Uranium. This is an indicative number. Actual value will be determined as one proceeds with the programme and gets some experience. Even if it is half of this value the scenario presented does not change.
3. Breeders can use 60% Thorium with thermal efficiency 42%. At this stage, types of reactors wherein thorium will be used are yet to be decided. The numbers are only indicative.

Hydro

1. Name plate capacity is 150 GWe.
2. Estimated hydro-potential of 600 billion kWh and name plate capacity of 150,000 MWe gives a capacity factor of 0.46.

Non-conventional Renewable

1. Includes: Wind 45 GWe, Small Hydro 15 GWe, Biomass Power/Co-generation 19.5 GWe and Waste to Energy 1.7 GWe etc.
2. Capacity factor of 0.33 has been assumed for potential calculations.

Oil Demand Shock and World Oil Price Trend

The standard comment by fit-to-print business and economy 'experts' on oil price and the economy is that "High oil prices hurt economic growth". This slogan can be expected whenever the 'Talk' button is pushed. Slogans are of course comforting, and easy to remember but this slogan—now an article of faith and even a reason for 'Regime change' put forward by American Neo-Conservatives and their camp followers—is totally undermined by real world, and real economy trends. It could be imagined that architects of the New Economy based on Cheap Oil have at least understood one fact of oil demand/oil price relationships through the last 25 years: demand tends to rise when prices rise, and tends to fall when prices fall. Keeping demand growth low can keep a lid or cap on price rises, so keeping the price low can or may or might be a way to keep demand from growing.

The world-wide economic mechanism tending to maintain annual oil demand growth at low levels when oil prices are low is complex and ramifying. The components of this simple fact of world economic history notably include the world average per capita or 'demographic' demand for oil, which reached its most recent peak when oil prices reached their most recent all-time high. In 1979 world average demand on a per capita basis hit 5.53 barrels/year. Since the mid-1980s it is around 4.5 barrels/person/year. Because of this fact, any argument that higher oil prices—unless prices rise to perhaps $75 or $100/barrel—will or can result in a fall of world oil demand is doomed to failure when tested by real world and real economy data. The major reason for 'price inelasticity', or in fact 'reverse elasticity' that is demand tending to rise with rising prices, is that world economic growth tends to increase when oil prices rise.

Demographic Demand and Oil Prices

World annual average per capita or 'demographic' oil demand increased, regularly but erratically, through the 1970s (from about 4.7 barrels/capita/year in 1970) to attain a peak of a little more than 5.5 barrels/capita/year (bcy) in 1979. Since that time, the demographic rate 'bottomed' in the low oil price period of 1986-99, and of late slowly started to increase again. Table 2.14 shows how demographic demand has varied since 1979:

Table 2.14: Demographic Demand and Oil Price through 1979-2003

Year	1979	1985	1990	1995	2003
World population Millions*	4342	4810	5236	5640	6300
World oil demand Daily average Mbd**	65.9	58.3	66.7	69.5	78
Demographic demand Barrels/capita	5.53	4.42	4.64	4.49	4.52
Year oil price range in 2003 dollars/barrel §	53-103	45-52	21-39	19-25	25-45 †

*Population data/UN Population Information Network (PIN).

** Year average oil demand BP Statistical Review, OECD IEA.

§ Year oil price data/ Platts Oilgram, OPEC Bulletin, 'Oil Economists Handbook' Elsevier Press Dollar purchasing parity correction utilizing price deflator of California Energy Commission 'Delphi Series' and OECD data.

† Estimated price range for 2003.

World annual average per capita or 'demographic' oil demand is a key indicator, which also has oil price forecasting applications. Demographic demand has regularly but erratically increased through the long period 1965-2007, from about 3.5 bcy in 1965, through a peak during the 'inter-shock period' of 1975-79, and slowly growing again, with rising oil and energy prices, since about 1998.

Impact of Oil Shocks on Demographic Demand

The term 'oil shock' can have many meanings, but here we utilize what would be the essential element of the term—very large price changes in a short period of time. On this base, there have been at least 4 'oil shocks' since 1973, that is 3 upward price shocks (1973-74, 1979-1981 and 1998-1999), and 1 downward price shock (1985-86). None of these price shocks had an immediate and large impact on demographic demand. The only 'price elastic' response that can be attributed to oil shocks would be the consistent, and large cumulative falls in demographic oil demand through 1980-85, with the demand rate of 4.42 bcy in 1985 being the lowest in the entire 1979-2003 period. Troubling yet further any supposed 'price elastic' response or trigger for this fall is the fact that demographic demand had begun to fall by 1977-78.

Three essential points have to be mentioned. In the 1973-79 period, after a 295% oil price rise in nominal terms through 1973-74, there was almost no effective reduction in the demographic demand rate. The price rise impact through 1973-74 can be called a 'pause', rather than a major inflexion or change of trend. After 1979-81, with oil prices briefly attaining $103-per-barrel (in dollars of 2003) in that period, the decline in the demographic rate began to accelerate. What is most notable, however, is that the demographic rate continued to fall after prices had fallen well below the highs of the 1979-81 periods. As the table above shows, the 1995 demographic rate was almost unchanged from that of 1985, but oil prices had been more than halved in real terms. Perhaps most important to note is the third point: since 1999, and the 'price shock' of 1998-99 (about 230% price rise in nominal terms), the demographic demand rate has continued to rise, if only slowly.

The Real Impact of Higher Oil Prices on Global Economic Growth

The real impact of higher oil prices, certainly up to the range of about $60/barrel, is to increase economic growth at the global, or composite worldwide level. This is the main reason why demographic oil demand in the 1975-79 period, with the barrel oil price in the range of about $40-$65 in 2003 dollars, was significantly higher than it is today. It should be clearly understood that if the demographic rate in 2003 was the same as 1979, then world oil demand in 2003 would be 95.4 Million barrels per day. Relative to real demand at this time (about 78 Mbd) the additional capacity needed would be close to two times Saudi exports, more than three times Russia's export offer, or well above 5 times Venezuela's current export capacity. There is no certainty at all that the world oil supply would meet this demand (Andrew McKillop, 2008).

Higher oil prices operate to stimulate first the world economy, outside the OECD countries, and then lead to increased growth inside the OECD. This is through the income or revenue effect on oil exporter countries, and then on metals, minerals and agro commodity exporter countries, most of them Low Income (GNP per capita below $400/year). Almost all such countries have very high marginal propensity to consume. That is any increase in revenues, due to prices of their export products increasing in line with the oil price, is very rapidly spent on purchasing manufactured goods and services of all kinds. In the 1973-81 period, in which oil price rises before inflation were of 405%, the New Industrial Countries (NICs) of that period—notably Taiwan, South Korea and Singapore—experienced very large and rapid increases in solvent demand for their export goods. The NICs as a group or bloc of economies rapidly expanded their oil imports and increased their oil consumption as prices increased in 1974-81, because demand for their export goods had increased, due to the global economic impacts of higher oil and 'real resource' prices. This has very strong implication for oil demand of today's emerging and giant NICs with large populations and immense internal markets—China, India, Brazil, Pakistan and Iran. For the much smaller NICs of the 1975-85 periods their oil import trends through 1974-81 show dramatic growth only slightly impacted by the major price rises of the period. In general terms (Table 2.15) the NICs Taiwan, South Korea and Singapore increased their oil demand by about 60% to 80% in volume terms in this period of a 405% increase in nominal prices.

Table 2.15: Asian Tiger Export Demand Driven Adjustment to Oil-Shock

	Oil Consumption Thousand barrels/day							
	1975	**1976**	**1977**	**1978**	**1979**	**1980**	**1981**	
Singapore	141	165	165	170	183	181	208	Increase 1975-81 : 47.5%
South Korea	278	310	371	426	480	475	497	Increase 1975-81 : 78.8%
Taiwan ROC	214	271	304	353	358	388	359	Increase 1975-81 : 67.8%

Source: BP Statistical Review of World Energy, various editions.

Global Economy Growth is Vital for Future Oil Production

This macroeconomic mechanism of higher revenues for fast spending poorer countries quickly levering up world economic growth (the very simplest type of Keynesianism, but at the global level) is rapidly and easily triggered by rising oil and other 'real resource' prices. This flatly contradicts the arguments by authorized 'experts' who opine that higher oil prices 'hurt poorer countries the most'. What is more important is to consider how the investment need for assuring future world oil, gas, coal and renewable energy supplies will be met without higher oil prices and faster global economy growth. Some idea of that need has recently been spelled out by ExxonMobil and by the IEA, which released its 'World Energy Investment Outlook' report for 2003 in November 2003, forecasting a need to spend an average of US dollars 103 Billion per year, for oil, and 105 Billion USD per year for gas, through to 2030. ExxonMobil has indicated (most recently in September 2003) that safeguarding existing oil and gas production capacity itself requires the finding and development of 36 Million barrels/day of replacement capacity by 2015 (https://www.oilmarketreport.org/textbase/speech/2003/va_nice.pdf).

Without strong economic growth it is unrealistic to expect that any 'energy transition' can occur, for example as predicated by the Kyoto Treaty. More critically it is also unrealistic to expect that world oil supply can be increased at the rates required or stated as 'feasible' in such publications as the OECD IEA's 'World Energy Outlook', that is a net annual average increase of about 2.25 Mbd through 2003-2020 (raising capacity to about 115 Mbd), over an above all replacement of capacity lost through depletion. These gigantic investment needs are very obviously dependent on strong and sustained economic growth. Without much higher and firmer oil prices it is unlikely that global economic growth can be significantly increased from current, low average annual rates for many key economies.

Oil Demand is Driven by Higher Prices—Demand Shock

There is almost unlimited upward potential for world oil demand, and the price factor must be integrated in any forward analysis at the global or composite worldwide level. Current world oil demand trends extend down from 25.6 bcy for the USA to well below 0.2 bcy in rural areas of low income developing countries (LDCs). While it is totally impossible that this could happen, the world's current 6.3 Bn population consuming oil at US per capita rates would generate a demand of around 445 Million barrels/day (Mbd). At the other extreme, at 0.2 bcy world total oil demand would be telescoped to less than 3.5 Mbd. The current 4.5 bcy world average is around one-third the average in European Union countries, but more than 4 times per capita average consumption in India, and over 3 times that of China—which will soon become the world's biggest industrial economy. Annual increase of the world's population (which is continuing to fall as a percentage rate, and in absolute numbers) is now running at about 85-90 Million. At a demographic demand rate of 4.5 bcy the 'latent' or potential annual growth in world oil demand is itself about 1.1 Mbd, assuming no change in the energy economy, no fuel substitution, and also no economic growth (Table 2.16).

Table 2.16: Demographic Rate of Oil Demand, 2002-03

Country/Region	bcy	World demand at this rate
USA	25.6	445 Mbd
Italy	12.4	215 Mbd
China	1.45	25 Mbd
Rural areas, LDCs	0.2	3.45 Mbd
Real world	4.5	78 Mbd
World annual population growth Annual 'latent demand' increase	85 Million	1.06 Mbd

Source: BP Amoco Statistical Review of World Energy, various editions.

The BP Amoco Statistical Review in its 2003 edition notes the 'surprising growth' of world energy demand since 2001 and 2002—about 2.6% annual compared with a so-called "10-year trend rate" of about 1.3% annual for oil alone. Through the 1975-79 periods, with oil prices in today's dollars in the $38-$55/bbl range, world oil demand growth easily achieved 4% annual, and most OECD countries achieved annual economy growth rates of about 3.75%, on a real GDP base. It is therefore easy to suggest the "10-year trend rate" of 1.3% annual growth was an aberration—and that one of its determinants was cheap oil and gas in the 1986-99 periods. Another was the continually falling rates of economic growth in the OECD countries, whose average annual economy growth rates fell by about 50% over the period 1975-1995, and are now below 2%, on a real GDP base.

The BP Statistical Review 2008 reported that the World primary energy consumption increased by 2.4% in 2007—down from 2.7% in 2006, but still the fifth consecutive year of above-average growth. The Asia-Pacific region accounted for two-thirds of global energy consumption growth, rising by an above-average 5% even though consumption in Japan declined by 0.9%. North American consumption rebounded after a weak year in 2006, rising by 1.6%—double the 10-yearaverage. Chinese growth of 7.7% was the weakest since 2002, although still above the10-year average (as was China's economic growth). China again accounted for half of global energy consumption growth. Indian consumption grew by 6.8%, the third-largest volumetric increment after China and the US.EU energy consumption declined by 2.2%, with Germany registering the world's largest decline in energy consumption (BP Statistical Review, 2008).

Higher Oil Prices Change vs. Future Demand Trends

One major reason for confidently projecting higher—but of course erratic—oil prices are: world oil demand on a 'demographic' base has almost unlimited upward potential, and higher oil prices themselves drive oil demand upward. It is no surprise, then, to find that the "10-year trend rate" of 1.3% annual growth of world oil demand has almost certainly disappeared as oil prices have responded to much more buoyant demand, and have themselves generated faster economic growth, mostly outside the OECD bloc, that itself underpins world oil demand and therefore prices. Understanding the mechanisms in play is vital to making accurate and realistic forecasts for future demand through the coming 4-5 years, and beyond. This can be appreciated from the chart below (Fig. 2.2), comparing the actual trend rate of demand growth, and official forecasts from elsewhere.

Demand Shock can Trigger Price Hike

As the above chart indicates, world oil demand can increase by as much as 7.25 Mbd in the next 54-60 months. By comparison, in the 72 month period of 1995-2001 world oil demand increase by only 6.7 Mbd (from a year average 69.2 to 75.9 Mbd). Under these conditions of world demand growth the 'Iraqi wild card' becomes the most probable deciding factor in future price trends, certainly on the 2 to 3 year horizon through 2005-06. The unpreparedness in official circles for this 'demand shock' can be judged by the fact that the 11 July 2003 issue of the IEA's 'Oil Market Report' forecasts that world oil demand by July 2004 will increase by no more than 1 Mbd, to 79.08 Mbd. This unrealistic forecast utilizes a growth rate of 1.28%, which is even less than that which BP Amoco claimed as the '10-year trend rate' for the period of about 1989-99. The reason or reasons why the OECD IEA would imagine that the rate of world oil demand growth should decline by nearly 50% in one year is not explained in the above cited report, and is certainly

Fig. 2.2: Comparison of the Real Demand Growth Trend Rate and Official Forecasts

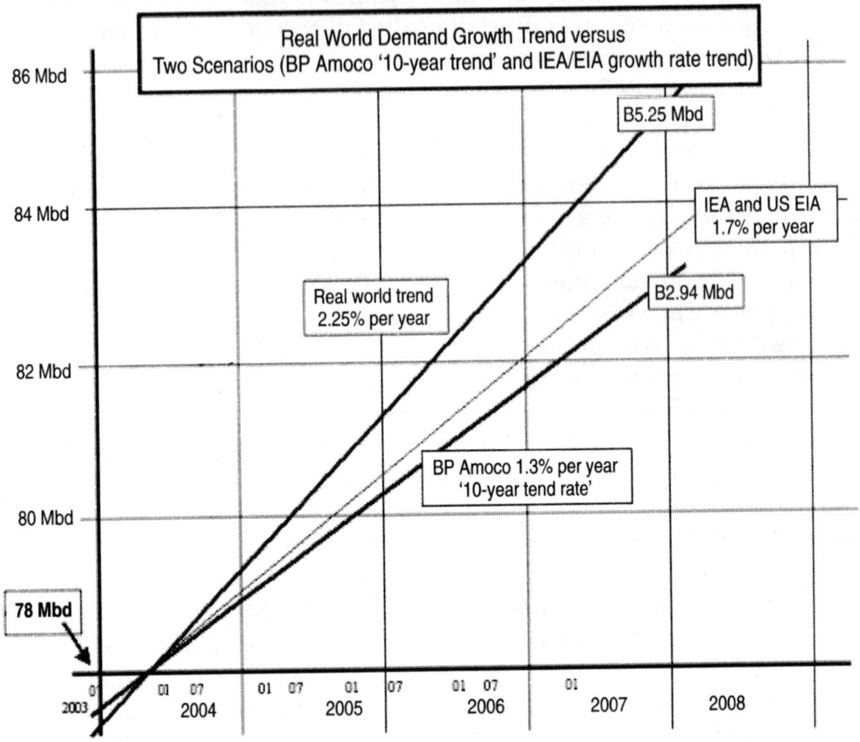

not integrated in the Nov 2003 'World Investment Outlook' Report (http://www.iea.org/dbtw-wpd/Textbase/speech/2004/haug/CSLF.pdf).

The implications of underestimated growth combined with overoptimistic, and in fact fantasy beliefs about how much oil Iraq can be forced or persuaded to produce and move to export terminals, can be compared to any previous upward price Oil Shock. That is supply reductions or cuts in the face of steady or increasing demand. The actual shortfall needed to enable upward price bidding to overcome the effects of all attempts to 'inform' the market of large new supply potentials and possibilities is rather small—about 3% to 5%, or around 3.5 Mbd shortfall through a few months. On the base of the growth trends shown in the chart above, and persistent underestimates of demand growth by official and/or respected market analyzing entities, the period in which prices can break out of the range below about $35-per-barrel, and increase to at least $50 or $60-per-barrel, is likely approaching very fast.

Future Perspectives

Cheap Oil is seen by the decision-making elite in the richer nations as the 'passport to economic growth'. This is a pure fantasy. Only 'extreme' oil prices (probably above $150/barrel) will abort or cancel the global economy expansionary impacts of higher oil prices. Since about 1995 'demand shock' has begun to operate in the world economy for a number of economic, social or 'secular' and technical reasons, leading to considerably higher underlying growth rates of world oil demand. Current 'trend growth rates' for world energy and world oil demand are about 2.25% for oil and about 2.5% for energy on an annual basis. Cheap oil and energy remains the essential base of conventional economic development and social progress anyplace in the world. This in turn is a powerful motor for continued and strong demand growth for fossil energy, worldwide. Upward potential for personal consumption of fossil fuels is essentially unlimited in this context. Conventional or classic economic growth is enabled and facilitated at the world or 'composite' level by rising oil prices to high price levels. This also underpins, or even increases world demand for fossil energy supplies, indicating that concerted international action is needed to plan for the effects of persistent underestimates of real demand growth trends.

India's Position in Global Primary Energy Consumption

World oil and gas reserves are estimated at just 45 years and 65 years respectively. Coal is likely to last a little over 200 years. The primary energy consumption for few of the developed and developing countries is shown in Table 2.17. It may be seen that India's absolute primary energy consumption is only 1/29th of the world, 1/7th of USA, 1/1.6th time of Japan but 1.1, 1.3, 1.5 times that of Canada, France and U.K respectively.

Energy Distribution between Developed and Developing Countries

Although 80 percent of the world's population lies in the developing countries (a fourfold population increase in the past 25 years), their energy consumption amounts to only 40 percent of the world total energy consumption. The high standards of living in the developed countries are attributable to high-energy consumption levels. Also, the rapid population growth in the developing countries has kept the per capita energy consumption low compared with that of highly industrialized developed countries.

The world average energy consumption per person is equivalent to 2.2 tonnes of coal. In industrialized countries, people use four to five times more than the world average and nine times more than the average for the developing countries. An American uses 32 times more commercial energy than an Indian.

Indian Energy Scenario

Coal dominates the energy mix in India, contributing to 55% of the total primary energy production. Over the years, there has been a marked increase in the share of natural gas in primary energy production from 10% in 1994 to 13% in 1999. There has been a decline in the share of oil in primary energy production from 20% to 17% during the same period.

Table 2.17: Primary Energy Consumption by Fuel, 2003

(In Million tonnes oil equivalent)

Country	Oil	Natural Gas	Coal	Nuclear Energy	Hydro electric	Total
USA	914.3	566.8	573.9	181.9	60.9	2297.8
Canada	96.4	78.7	31.0	16.8	68.6	291.4
France	94.2	39.4	12.4	99.8	14.8	260.6
Russian Federation	124.7	365.2	111.3	34.0	35.6	670.8
United Kingdom	76.8	85.7	39.1	20.1	1.3	223.2
China	275.2	29.5	799.7	9.8	64.0	1178.3
India	113.3	27.1	185.3	4.1	15.6	345.3
Japan	248.7	68.9	112.2	52.2	22.8	504.8
Malaysia	23.9	25.6	3.2	-	1.7	54.4
Pakistan	17.0	19.0	2.7	0.4	5.6	44.8
Singapore	34.1	4.8	-	-	-	38.9
Total World	3636.6	2331.9	2578.4	598.8	595.4	9741.1

Source: BP Statistical Review of World Energy, 2004, Bureau of Energy Supply; Ministry of Petroleum and Natural Gas, GOI.

Fig. 2.3: Energy Distribution between Developed and Developing Countries

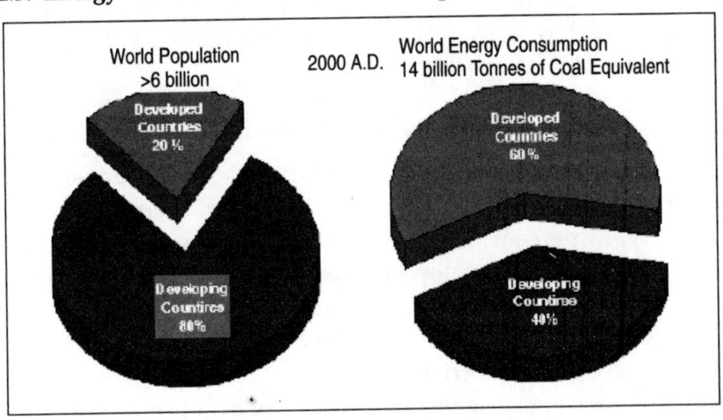

Energy Supply Scenario

Coal Supply

India has huge coal reserves, at least 84,396 million tonnes of proven recoverable reserves (at the end of 2003). This account for almost 8.6% of the world reserves and it may last for about 230 years at the current Reserve to Production (R/P) ratio. In contrast, the world's proven coal reserves are expected to last only for 192 years at the current R/P ratio.

Reserves/Production (R/P) ratio—If the reserves remaining at the end of the year are divided by the production in that year, the result is the length of time that the remaining reserves would last if production were to continue at that level.

India is the fourth largest producer of coal and lignite in the world. Coal production is concentrated in these states (Andhra Pradesh, Uttar Pradesh, Bihar, Madhya Pradesh, Maharashtra, Orissa, Jharkhand, and West Bengal).

Oil Supply: The following table 2.18 indicates the quantum of import bills of oil and the corresponding value thereof during 1996-2005: whereas the quantum of import has risen by 3 folds, the payment liability in terms of cash-outflow has increased by 8 folds.

Table 2.18: The Quantum of Oil Import vis-à-vis the Cash Out-flow
(The ever rising import bill)

Year	Quantity (MMT)	Value (Rs. Crore)
1996-97	33.90	18,337
1997-98	34.49	15,872
1998-99	39.81	19,907
1999-2000	57.80	40,028
2000-01	74.10	65,932
2001-02	84.90	8,116
2002-03	90	85,042
2003-04	95	93,159
2004-05*	100	1,30,000

* Estimated.
Source: Bureau of Energy Supply; Ministry of Petroleum and Natural Gas.

Oil accounts for about 36 % of India's total energy consumption. India today is one of the top ten oil-guzzling nations in the world and will soon overtake Korea as the third largest consumer of oil in Asia after China and Japan. The country's annual crude oil production is peaked at about 32 million tonne as against the current peak demand of about 110 million tonne. In the current scenario, India's oil consumption by end of 2007 is expected to reach 136 million tonne (MT), of which domestic production will be only 34 MT. India will have to pay an oil bill of roughly $50 billion, assuming a weighted average price of $50 per barrel of crude. In 2003-04, against total export of $64 billion, oil imports accounted for $21 billion. India imports 70% of its crude needs mainly from gulf nations. The majority of India's roughly 5.4 billion barrels in oil reserves are located in the Bombay High, upper Assam, Cambay, Krishna-Godavari Basins. In terms of sector wise petroleum product consumption, transport accounts for 42% followed by domestic and industry with 24% and 24% respectively. India spent more than Rs.1, 10,000 crore on oil imports at the end of 2004.

Natural Gas Supply

Natural gas accounts for about 8.9 per cent of energy consumption in the country. The current demand for natural gas is about 96 million cubic metres per day (mcmd) as against availability of 67 mcmd. By 2007, the demand is expected to be around 200 mcmd. Natural gas reserves are estimated at 660 billion cubic meters.

Electrical Energy Supply

The all India installed capacity of electric power generating stations under utilities was 1,12,581 MW as on 31st May 2004, consisting of 28,860 MW-hydro, 77,931 MW—thermal and 2,720 MW—nuclear and 1,869 MW—wind (Ministry of Power).

The gross generation of power in the year 2002-03 stood at 531 billion units (kWh).

Nuclear Power Supply

Nuclear Power contributes to about 2.4 per cent of electricity generated in India. India has ten nuclear power reactors at five nuclear power stations producing electricity. More nuclear reactors have also been approved for construction.

Hydro-Power Supply

India is endowed with a vast and viable hydro potential for power generation of which only 15% has been harnessed so far. The share of hydropower in the country's total generated units has steadily decreased and it presently stands at 25% as on 31st May 2004. It is assessed that exploitable potential at 60% load factor is 84,000 MW.

Projected Demand of Final Energy Consumption

Final energy consumption is the actual energy demand at the user end. This is the difference between primary energy consumption and the losses that takes place in transport, transmission and distribution and refinement. The actual final energy consumption (past and projected) is given in Table 2.19.

Table 2.19. Demand for Commercial Energy for Final Consumption (BAU Scenario)

Source	Units	1994-95	2001-02	2006-07	2011-12
Electricity	Billion Units	289.36	480.08	712.67	1067.88
Coal	Million Tonnes	76.67	109.01	134.99	173.47
Lignite	Million Tonnes	4.85	11.69	16.02	19.70
Natural Gas	Million Cubic Meters	9880	15730	18291	20853
Oil Products	Million Tonnes	63.55	99.89	139.95	196.47

Source: Planning Commission, *BAU: Business as Usual.*

Energy Needs of Growing Indian Economy

Economic growth is desirable for developing countries, and energy is essential for economic growth. However, the relationship between economic growth and increased energy demand is not always a straightforward linear one. For example, under present conditions, 6% increase in India's Gross Domestic Product (GDP) would impose an increased demand of 9% on its energy sector.

In this context, the ratio of energy demand to GDP is a useful indicator. A high ratio reflects energy dependence and a strong influence of energy on GDP growth. The developed countries, by focusing on energy efficiency and lower energy-intensive routes, maintain their energy to GDP ratios at values of less than 1. The ratios for developing countries are much higher.

Plan-wise Outlay

The overall position concerning sector-wise energy consumption and plan-wise financial outlays in the energy sector by the Government of India (Planning Commission) are shown in Figs. 2.4 and 2.5 respectively.

Future Supply vs. Demand of Conventional Oil

There is uncertainty in estimates of future supply vs. demand of conventional oil and the scope for replacing cheap oil with other alternative energy sources. The oil shocks of 1970s made the entire world quite conscious of depleting resources. Most oil explored and produced by the world so far and will be produced over the next 20 years is termed "conventional" oil, which flows at high rates from giant oilfields. There is also "non-conventional" oil, viz. heavy oil, tar, sand oil and shale oil, oil obtained by enhanced recovery. But, such oil represents a small and relatively expensive fraction of total production and can be produced only at slow rates.

Fig. 2.4: Sector-wise Energy Consumption (1999-2000)

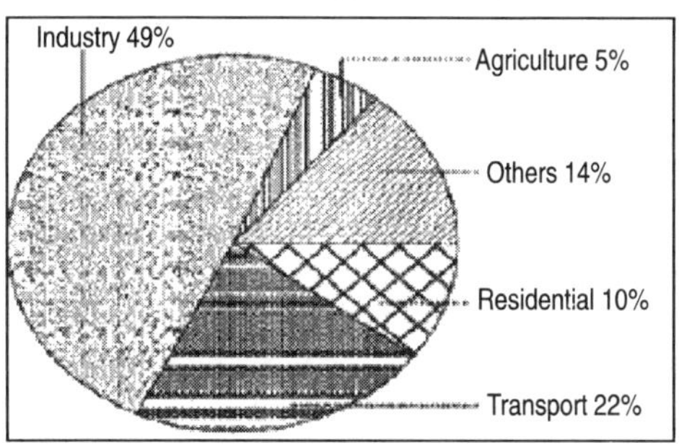

Source: Planning Commission, New Delhi.

Fig. 2.5: Expenditure towards Energy Sector

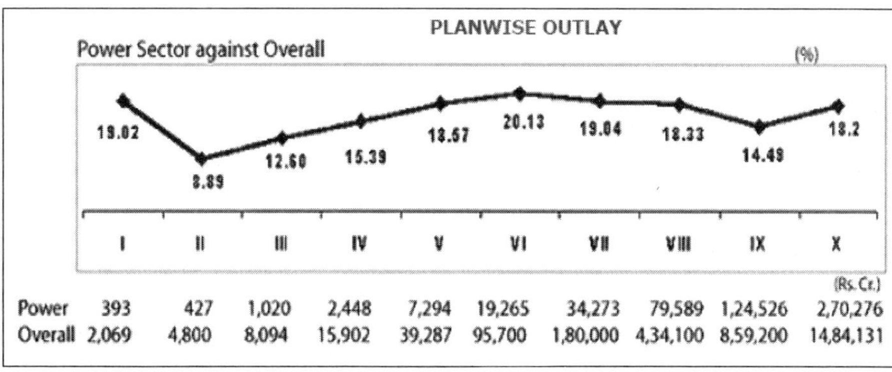

(Rs. Cr.)

	I	II	III	IV	V	VI	VII	VIII	IX	X
Power	393	427	1,020	2,448	7,294	19,265	34,273	79,589	1,24,526	2,70,276
Overall	2,069	4,800	8,094	15,902	39,287	95,700	1,80,000	4,34,100	8,59,200	14,84,131

Depleting Global Reserves

The current annual consumption of the world is just over 26 bn b of conventional oil but only finding 6 bn b of new oil to replace, thereby creating an annual deficit of 20 bn b in its demand-supply scenario. Most of the oil remaining to be found will be discovered in even smaller fields in existing basins. Deep water resources could have a global potential of about 100 bn b, of which 25 bn b have already been found (Petroleum Review, 1998).

The main finds of various studies report that "insufficient oil reserves" is a stark reality. Major points are summarized here:

- Four fifths of world oil output comes from fields discovered before 1973 (Laherrere, 1997).
- A study of 528 major oilfields worldwide shows that more had overestimated reserves than underestimated ones (Laherrere, 1997).
- It now seems unlikely that the world contains any really major, i.e., more than 15 bn b– undetected petroleum provinces (Jennings, 1996).
- The last giant oilfield was discovered in 1986.
- Political oil reserves amount to between 200 and 300 bn b—readily included in official reserve-estimates (Campbell, 1995).
- Proven oil developed—the 'easy' oil—is now (in 1991) 50 per cent deputed.
- The world has not been replacing production since 1970 and in the past decade (in 1980s) the shortfall has been growing (Odell, 1997). And the nineties have not been any better.

Tapping Non-conventional Oil Resources

Oil supply from outside Middle East OPEC countries is expected to decline. Oil supply from Middle East producers in projected to peak at around 2013. Since the total conventional oil supply will not be able to fully match demand, additional supplies of liquid fuels are expected to become available from non-conventional sources. The share of OECD is expected to increase to about 54% in the overall supply. Non-Conventional oil is expected to contribute to just over 8% to total oil supplies by 2030. This represents production of 9.9 million barrels per day—a sharp increase over the 1.1 million barrels per day availability of 2000. The increase results mainly from technological improvements that reduce the cost of extracting and upgrading non-conventional resources. Gas-to-liquid (GTL) plants will make growing contribution to non-conventional oil supplies. GTL production is projected to rise from 43 K barrels per day to 300 k barrels per day by 2030. The greater part of future non-conventional oil will come from Canadian Oil sands and Venezuelan extra heavy bituminous crude. It is estimated that these two regions contains 580 billion barrels of recoverable reserves—more than the entire reserves of conventional crude oil in the Middle-East.

Competitive Market Position

The global oil market remains relatively tight. More importantly, the level of oil inventories around the world is low. While inventories of crude oil have climbed back into normal ranges in volumetric terms, product inventories remain low. This follows developments in the world oil market in the last few years since the early 1990s.ln the last few years, OPEC has been careful not to oversupply the market. In particular, following the collapse of the price of oil in 1998-99, the organization's aim has been to prevent an unbridled increase in global oil stocks. In this effort, the group has been helped by shareholder pressure on managers of private oil companies. Forced to.concentrate on the short-term performance of their companies' stock, managers reduce costs in every way possible to increase immediate profits. One cost cutting strategy is to keep inventories as low as possible, lowering both working capital and the costs of maintaining stocks. Analysts in 2004 had been giving serious consideration to the 1 990s trend of inventory reduction. Some were even discussing the pros and cons of 'zero stock' oil companies. In brief, the market fundamentals indicate a tight supply-demand balance, reduced level of global oil inventories and decreasing OPEC spare production capacity. They imply a diminishing back-up supply and less reassurance for the global oil industry operations and oil market trade.

Fear of Shortage

Despite tight balances, oil supplies have been sufficient to meet world demand. The market, however, has remained fearful of a possible shortage of crude oil or petroleum products. Transitory factors have also influenced the market. For example, seasonal variations have accentuated market anxiety. During the spring of 2004 (as in previous years), there was fear of a shortage of gasoline at the start of summer driving season in the Northern Hemisphere, especially in the United States. Since mid-summer 2004, there has been fear of a shortage of middle distillates and heating oil at the start of winter. Gasoline shortage did not occur and heating oil shortage was not evident in the winter 2004. Refineries are running at maximum capacity and their output will be sufficient especially if the winter in the Northern Hemisphere remains mild. Nevertheless, the fear of shortage persists in the global oil market.

Market fear is aggravated by bombing, terrorism, social strife, Oil Company and government disagreements, domestic and global politics and other events in different parts of the world. Sources of fear include:

- The military campaign in Afghanistan followed by Iraq, the fall of Sadam Hussein's regime and the subsequent looting, terrorism, armed conflict and sabotage of oil installations in that country;
- The terrorist attack near Saudi Arabia's petrochemical plants and clashes with and arrests of terrorists in different parts of that country as well as in the USA, U.K. India and elsewhere in the world;
- Political instability in Venezuela, where oil industry strikes interrupted exports late in 2002; Protests and clashes in the on-shore oil producing areas of Nigeria;
- The saga of OAO Yukos, which filed for bankruptcy in the face of disputed tax claims by a Russian government that later took possession of and sold the company's main producing subsidiary;
- Concerns voiced by some analysts about shrinkage of the spare oil

production capacity of OPEC and whether it is sufficient to replace a possible supply disruption anywhere in the world. Some analysts have even raised questions about the size of reserves and the present and future production capability of OPEC's member countries, including Saudi Arabia.

These questions have further increased market anxiety and have deepened fears about shortage and an impending global energy crisis.

Uncertainty and Price

In 2004, crude oil prices averaged $ 36 per barrel, with prices turning upward throughout the year and well into 2005. Although OPEC production quotas (excluding Iraq) were raised form 23.5 million barrels per day in April 2004 to 28 million barrels per day in July 2005, world oil prices generally continued to rise. In June 2005, crude oil futures prices exceeded $ 60 per barrel, a record high price in nominal dollar.

Several factors have worked to keep world crude oil prices high in the near terms. First, world petroleum demand grew at a robust 3.4% (2.5 million barrels per day) in 2004, reflecting dramatic increases in China's demand for oil generated power and oil based transportation fuels, as well as a rebound in U.S. oil demand. Second, oil prices typically are sensitive to any incremental tightening of supply during periods of high economic growth. On the supply side, there was very little spare upstream capacity and the spare downstream capacity was not always properly configured to produce the required slate of products. World oil inventories, in terms of 'days of supply' were unusually low. Next, geopolitical tensions in major oil producing countries, including the continuing war in Iraq and uncertain prospects for a return to normalcy in Iraq's oil sector, and potential unrest in Nigeria and Venezuela contributed to the volatility in world oil markets.

Oil prices have been highly volatile over the past 25 years and periods of price volatility can be expected in future, principally because of unforeseen political and economic circumstances. It is well recognized that tensions in Middle East, for example, could give rise to serious disruptions of normal oil production and trading patterns. On the other hand, market forces can playa significant role in restoring balance over an extended period. High real prices deter consumption and encourage the emergence of significant competition from large marginal sources of oil, which currently are uneconomical to produce and other energy supplies. Persistently low prices have the opposite effects.

Limits to long-term oil price escalation include substitution of other fuels for oil, marginal sources of conventional oil that become reserves when prices rise and non-conventional sources of oil that become reserves at still higher prices. Advances in exploration and production technologies are likely to bring prices down when such additional oil resources become part of the reserve base.

Capacity Issues

The projected increase in world oil demand would require an increment to world production capability of more than 42 million barrels per day, relative to the 2002 crude oil production capacity of 80 million barrels per day. Producers in the Organization of Petroleum Exporting Countries (OPEC) are expected to be the major source of production increases. In addition, non-OPEC supply is expected to remain highly competitive, with major increments to supply coming from off-shore resources, especially in the Caspian Basin, Latin America and deepwater West Africa. The estimates of incremental production are based on current proved reserves and a country-by-country assessment of ultimately recoverable petroleum.

Criticism leveled at OPEC countries for present market conditions and for not having expanded production capacity in the past few years is ironic. In order to defend the price of oil, OPEC drastically reduced its production in the early 1980s and was left with 15 million bpd of idle capacity. More recently, between 2000 and 2002, OPEC reduced its production by 2 million bpd. Most importantly, until late 2003 and even in early 2004, the general expectation was for low demand growth, greater growth in non-OPEC production and continuation of the squeeze on OPEC in the coming year.

The world oil market apparently wishes for 4-5 million bpd of spare oil production capacity as well as large crude and oil product inventories, available around the world at all times. These conditions might have been fulfilled in the past, but they can no longer be taken for granted. As noted earlier, private oil companies have been reducing inventories for the past decade. A large inventory is an unproductive asset that reduces profits, is expensive to maintain and increases operating costs.

Moreover, developing and maintaining unused spare production capacity are much more costly than holding inventory. No private oil company would undertake this. The national oil companies in OPEC are also under pressure to reduce costs and become more efficient. They are less inclined than before to invest heavily in capacity to be used only as a buffer against vagaries of the international oil market. Large spare oil production capacities can no longer be taken for granted. They require public policy decisions in the producing countries and a justification for their high cost.

Short-Term Oil Market

Tempered by high world oil prices, growth in world petroleum demand in 2005 is expected to remain strong, while retreating somewhat from its 2004 pace. Any expectation of incremental supply tightness in non-OPEC supply or downstream refinery capacity could cause crude oil prices to increase even further. As a result, the refiner acquisition cost of imported crude oil in 2005 is expected to average more than $ 47 per barrel. OPEC producers may find it more challenging to maintain high oil prices over the next few years, however, given the projected increase in non-OPEC supply.

Despite evidence that OPEC members have achieved some of their price goals in recent years by using a price-band strategy, production cutbacks have historically had only limited success. OPEC's market management strategies have often ended in failure and its successes for the most part have been the result of tight market conditions and disciplined participation by OPEC members.

Currently, spare production capacity worldwide with the exception of two or three Persian Gulf members of OPEC—is negligible, making OPEC's consensus building easier. Non-OPEC production is expected to show significant increases over the next 5 years and a number of OPEC member countries have announced plans to expand production capacity in the short term. In an oil market environment with substantial spare production capacity, it will be more difficult for OPEC to achieve agreement among its members; however, obstacles to investment in new production capacity in some areas with abundant resources may keep the growth in supply below its expected potential.

The uncertainties associated with the International Energy Outlook (IEO) 2005 projections are significant. The war in Iraq, the international war on terrorism, uncertain economic recovery in emerging Asia and Japan, the success of China's economic reforms and its political situation, the potential for social unrest in Venezuela and Nigeria, Brazil's impact on other Latin American economies and uncertain prospects for the pace of economic recovery in the FSU all increase the state of uncertainty and the associated price regime globally.

Geo-Politics and Oil

A discussion of the oil market and its future must include an examination of politics—global, regional or domestic. Politics distorts operations of the industry, the oil business and the oil market. Nevertheless, politics has played an important role in oil in the past; it is critical in the world oil scene today and it seems certain to continue playing such a role in the future.

Long-term Outlook

Any view of oil industry operations decades from now must account for the major changes to the business and world that have occurred since the days of oil concessions. In general companies and countries acknowledge their need for one another. Moreover, a third dimension of the global oil scene is evolving. Consolidation in the oil field services industry has created a new species of major company. In this category are firms offering the whole spectrum of upstream operations such as field, laboratory and office services. Their operations include work traditionally performed by oil companies, such as seismic interpretation, reservoir analyses, production planning and even operations management.

If capital is available, producing countries can enter contracts with these service companies or establish strategic alliances with them and apply advanced technology and field practice in their oil industry. An example is the impressive performance of the oil industry in Russia in the last few years; much of it is based on alliances with service companies. Growth of the service sector thus might foster alternative arrangements for the producing sector. Incorporating the recent price turbulence in to the construction of an intermediate and long term oil market outlook is difficult and raises the following questions:

- Will OPEC maintain its cutback strategy in order to keep prices within a certain price band, or will the anticipated increase in non-OPEC production exert downward pressure on prices?

- Will China and other emerging economies of Asia be able to sustain the current robust economic growth and a corresponding increase in their demand for oil in the long term?' Will technology guarantee that oil supply development will move forward even if a low world oil price environment returns?

Oil Supply Security

A key factor in future oil supplies is that all countries that produce oil beyond their own needs are and will remain keen to sell the excess in the global market. This statement is valid for members of OPEC, producers outside the organization and countries in which oil might be discovered in the future. Politics might cause temporary disruption of exports in specific countries but will not end them. Oil supplies have become geographically diversified. More importantly, major producing and exporting countries have become dependent on revenue from their oil exports. Any possible disruption would be temporary. Obviously, a disruption of exports from a major oil producer will cause a crisis in the world oil market. However, the disruption would not be sustainable. The global oil market should not be concerned about the security of long-term supplies due to political development.

Global scenario in Natural Gas

Proved world natural gas reserves are estimated at 6112 trillion cubic feet. The worldwide undiscovered natural gas is estimated at 4221 trillion cubic feet. Of the total natural gas resources, an estimated 3000 trillion cubic feet is in 'stranded' reserves, usually located too far away from pipeline infrastructure or population centres for its transportation to be economical. Consumption of natural gas worldwide is likely to increase from 95 trillion feet in 2003 to 182 trillion cubic feet in 2030.Non-OECD Europe and Eurasia and the Middle-east account for almost three-quarters of the world's natural gas reserves. Together these two regions account for 47 % of the projected increase in global natural gas production from 2003 to 2030 of it for export to OECD countries.

Availability and Utilization of Natural Gas in India

Natural gas has emerged as the most preferred fuel due to its inherent environmentally benign nature, greater efficiency and cost effectiveness. The demand of natural gas has sharply increased in the last two decades at the global level. In India too, the natural gas sector has gained importance, particularly over the last decade, and is being termed as the Fuel of the 21st Century.

Production of natural gas, which was almost negligible at the time of independence, is at present at the level of around 87 million standard cubic meters per day (MMSCMD). The main producers of natural gas are Oil and Natural Gas Corporation Ltd. (ONGC), Oil India Limited (OIL) and JVs of Tapti, Mukta and Ravva. Under the Production Sharing Contracts, private parties from some of the fields are also producing gas. Government have also offered blocks under New Exploration Licensing Policy (NELP) to private and public sector companies with the right to market gas at market determined prices. Out of the total production of around 87 MMSCMD, after internal consumption, extraction of LPG and unavoidable flaring, around 74 MMSCMD is available for sale to various consumers.

Most of the production of gas comes from the Western offshore area. The on-shore fields in Assam, Andhra Pradesh and Gujarat States are other major producers of gas. Smaller quantities of gas are also produced in Tripura, Tamil Nadu and Rajasthan States. OIL is operating in Assam and Rajasthan States, whereas ONGC is operating in the Western offshore fields and in other states. The gas produced by ONGC and a part of gas produced by the JV consortiums is marketed by the GAIL (India) Ltd. The gas produced by OIL is marketed by OIL itself except in Rajasthan where GAIL is marketing its gas. Gas produced by Cairn Energy from Lakshmi fields and Gujarat State Petroleum Corporation Ltd. (GSPCL) from Hazira fields is being sold directly by them at market determined prices. Natural gas has been utilized in Assam and Gujarat since the sixties. There was a major increase in the production and utilization of natural gas in the late seventies with the development of the Bombay High fields and again in the late eighties when the South Basin field in the Western Offshore was brought to production.

Utilization of Natural Gas

The gas produced in the western offshore fields is brought to Uran in Maharashtra and partly in Gujarat. The gas brought to Uran is utilized in and around Mumbai. The gas brought to Hazira is sour gas which has to be sweetened by removing the sulphur present in the gas. After sweetening, the gas is partly utilized at Hazira and the rest is fed into the Hazira-Bijaipur-Jagdhishpur (HBJ) pipeline which passes through Gujarat, Madhya Pradesh, Rajasthan, U.P., Delhi and Haryana. The gas produced in Gujarat, Assam, etc; is utilized within the respective states.

Natural Gas is currently the source of half of the LPG produced in the country. LPG is now being extracted from gas at Duliajan in Assam, Bijaipur in M.P., Hazira and Vaghodia in Gujarat, Uran in Maharashtra, Pata in UP and Nagapattinam in Tamil Nadu. Two new plants have also been set up at Lakwa in Assam and at Ussar in Maharastra in 1998-99. One more plant is being set up at Gandhar in Gujarat. Natural gas containing C2/C3, which is a feedstock for the Petrochemical industry, is currently being used at Uran for Maharashtra Gas Cracker Complex at Nagothane. GAIL has also set up a 3 lakh TPA of Ethylene gas based petrochemical complex at Auraiya in 1998-99.

Natural Gas Allocation and Supply Scenario

As against the total allocation of around 118 MMSCMD, the gas supplies by GAIL is of the order of 63 MMSCMD spread over about 300 major consumers. Around 32% is supplied to the fertilizer sector, 41% to power, 4% to sponge iron and the balance 23% (including shrinkage) goes to other sectors (Table 2.20).

Table 2.20: All India Region-wise and Sector-wise Gas Supply by GAIL, (2003-04) (in MMSCSD)

Region/Sector	Power	Fertilizer	S. Iron	Others	Total
HVJ & Ex-Hazira	12.61	13.63	1.24	9.81	37.29
Onshore Gujarat	1.66	1.04		2.08	4.78
Uran	3.57	3.53	1.33	1.41	9.85
K.G. Basin	4.96	1.91		0.38	7.25
Cauvery Basin	1.07			0.25	1.32
Assam	0.41	0.04		0.29	0.74
Tripura	1.37			0.01	1.38
Grand Total	25.65	20.15	2.58	14.23	62.61

OIL is also supplying around 3 MMSCMD in Assam against allocations made by the Govt. Around 8.5 MMSCMD of gas is being directly supplied by the JVs/ private companies at market prices to various consumers. This gas is outside the purview of the Government allocations.

Import of Natural Gas through Transnational Pipelines

(a) Iran-Pakistan-India (IPI) Pipeline Project

In pursuance of Government decision in February 2005, Minister (P&NG) led a delegation to Pakistan during 4-8 June 2005. During the talks, the two Ministers reviewed the Iran-Pakistan-India gas pipeline proposal. They agreed that the project, which envisaged supply of gas to Pakistan and India through a transnational pipeline, would go a long way in meeting the energy security requirements of the two countries, and thus should be seen as a significant project for the benefit of the people of these countries. The Indian and Pakistani delegations agreed to exchange information in regard to the financial structuring, technical, commercial, legal and related issues to realize a safe and secure world class project. To this end, it was agreed that the momentum pertaining to the project should be accelerated by constituting a Joint Working Group at the Secretary level at the earliest, which will meet regularly and report the progress to the Ministers to facilitate definitive decisions by them.

- An Indian delegation also visited Iran from 11-14 June 2005 and discussed the issue of import of natural gas from Iran through on-land pipeline transiting via Pakistan. Both sides noted with satisfaction that as a result of regular discussions on technical issues pertaining to the project, a Heads of Agreement between NIGEC and the Indian companies concerned had been finalized. With a view to undertaking further studies and discussions in regard to relevant issues so that the project could take off by early next year, it was agreed to establish a special JWG on the Iran-Pakistan-India gas pipeline project.
- A Pakistani delegation led by the Secretary, Ministry of Petroleum and Natural Resources, Govt. of Pakistan visited New Delhi on July 12-13, 2005

for the first meeting of India-Pakistan JWG. The second meeting of the JWG was held in Islamabad on 8-9 September, 2005. The first meeting of the Special JWG on Iran-Pakistan-India Pipeline Project was held in New Delhi on 3-4 August, 2005. The second meeting of the Special JWG on Iran-Pakistan-India Pipeline Project was held in Tehran on 24th October, 2005. The Indian side was led by Secretary (P&NG). Indian side has already appointed financial consultants i.e., M/s Ernst & Young and is in the process of finalizing appointment of legal and technical consultants for the project. During the 2nd JWG meeting, the Pakistani side informed that they will also shortly be appointing their Financial Consultants.

(b) Myanmar-Bangladesh-India Gas Pipeline Project

To pursue the matter at the Government level, for bilateral and trilateral discussions with Myanmar and Bangladesh, the Minister (P&NG) visited Yangon during 11-13th January 2005. A Memorandum of Understanding (MOU) for cooperation in the petroleum sector between the two Governments was signed. The MOU provides for furthering cooperation in the hydrocarbon sector and for establishing a cooperative institutional relationship in the field of petroleum industry on the basis of equality and mutual advantage, taking into account the possibilities for cooperation available in each country. The two Governments will designate a body of experts comprising three representatives of each party to identify and implement the projects in the hydrocarbon sector.

- A trilateral meeting between the Petroleum Ministers of India, Myanmar and Bangladesh held on 12.1.2005. After the meeting a Joint Press Statement was issued by the three Ministers. The three sides agreed to transport of natural gas from Myanmar to India by pipeline transiting through Bangladesh. The route of the pipeline will be determined by mutual agreements of the three Governments. It was also decided to establish a Techno-Commercial Working Committee (TCWC) comprising duly designated representatives of the three Governments to prepare a draft MOU prescribing the framework of cooperation among the three Governments, including the Myanmar-Bangladesh-India gas pipeline project. The MOU would be signed at Dhaka at the earliest mutually convenient date.
- In pursuance of the MoU, a Techno-Commercial Working Committee has been constituted by the three Governments. The First Meeting of the TCWC was held on 24-25 February, 2005. The TCWC has finalized draft MoU proposed to be signed by the three oil Ministers.
- However, there are certain bilateral issues which have to be sorted out with Bangladesh. Simultaneously, India is also exploring the other option of import of natural gas from Myanmar. A high level delegation led by Minister, Energy, of Myanmar recently visited India during July 5-7, 2005. All aspects of Myanmar-Bangladesh-India gas pipeline were discussed. Minister (P&NG) visited Bangladesh during 5-6 September 2005 to pursue the matter with Government of Bangladesh. The matter is being pursued

vigorously and the proposed gas imports from Myanmar would be finalized shortly notwithstanding the response of Government of Bangladesh. GAIL has been asked to do a pre-feasibility study of the onland pipeline route from Myanmar to India through North-Eastern Indian States, bypassing Bangladesh territory. The option of getting Bangladesh on board is also being simultaneously pursued. Another official level meeting was held in Yangon on 29-30 August 2005, where two sides agree to take definite steps for gas supply from Myanmar.

(c) Turkmenistan-Afghanistan-Pakistan (TAP) Pipeline

Daulatabad area of Turkmenistan has reported to have sufficient gas reserves. The Governments of Turkmenistan-Afghanistan-Pakistan (TAP) proposed the transnational gas pipeline to exploit the available gas reserves in Turkmenistan. They designated ADB as the lead development partner. ADB has carried out the study and approached India for participating in the project. Minister (P&NG) discussed this matter with Pakistani side during his visit to Pakistan 4th to 8th June 2005. This was also discussed by Secretary (P&NG) with President ADB during the latter's visit to New Delhi on 1.9.2005. Although, India is not yet formally involved in TAP project, Minister (P&NG) was invited to the next Steering Committee Meeting to be held in Ashgabat in early December, 2005.

Liquefied Natural Gas (LNG)

Natural gas at –1610C transforms into a liquid: This is done for easy storage and transportation since it reduces the volume occupied by gas by a factor of 600. LNG is transported in specially built ships with cryogenic tanks. It is received at the LNG receiving terminals and is regassified to be supplied as natural gas to the consumers. LNG projects are highly capital intensive in nature. The whole process consists of five elements:

- Dedicated gas field development and production.
- Liquefaction plant.
- Transportation in special vessels.
- Regassification Plant.
- Transportation and distribution to the Gas consumer.

LNG supply contracts are generally of long-term nature and the prices are linked to the international crude oil prices. However, the LNG importing countries in recent times had started asking for medium/short term contracts with varying linkages.

LNG Imports to India

- The LNG trade started in mid 60's and has increased rapidly. In 1992 it was around 80 Billion Cubic Metres (BCM) per annum and crossed the 100 BCM mark in 1996. World trade in LNG is currently in the range of 150 BCM. The major exporting countries of LNG are Algeria, Qatar, Indonesia, Malaysia, Australia, whereas, the major importers are Japan, South Korea, Taiwan and Western Europe.

- Geographically, India is very strategically located and is flanked by large gas reserves on both the east and west. India is relatively close to four of the world's top five countries in terms of proven gas reserves, viz. Iran, Qatar, Saudi Arabia and Abu Dhabi. The large natural gas market of India is a major attraction to the LNG exporting countries. In order to encourage gas imports, the Government of India has kept import of LNG under Open General License (OGL) category and has permitted 100% FDI.

LNG Projects

- Petronet LNG Limited (PLL), a JV promoted by GAIL, IOCL, BPCL and ONGC was formed for import of LNG to meet the growing demand of natural gas PLL has constructed a 5 MMTPA capacity LNG terminal at Dahej in Gujarat. The terminal was commissioned in February 2004 and commercial supplies commenced from March 2004. PLL is planning to expand this terminal to 10 MMTPA capacities by 2008-09 to meet the growing demand of LNG.
- Shell's 2.5 MMTPA capacity LNG terminals at Hazira have been commissioned. Dabhol LNG terminal (total 5 MMTPA capacities, with about 2.9 MMTPA available for merchant sales) may also become operational by 2006 subject to availability of LNG for the project. LNG terminals at Kochi in Kerala, Mangalore in Karnataka and Krishnapatnam/Ennore in Tamil Nadu are also under active consideration and may fructify in next 4-5 years time.
- The price of LNG for the Dahej project is linked to the JCC crude oil price. It has a fixed price for the first five years, i.e. upto December 2008 and a floating floor and ceiling price thereafter. At present the selling price of LNG in Gujarat is $4.87/MMBTU (Rs. 8777/MCM) and outside Gujarat is $4.88/MMBTU (Rs. 8800/MCM). At this price, LNG is comparatively cheaper than alternative fuels/feedstock's e.g. naphtha, Furnace Oil, LSHS, Light Diesel Oil, LPG, etc.

Gas Pricing

Prior to 1987, gas prices were fixed by ONGC/OIL. The price is being fixed by Government w.e.f. 30.1.1987. The price of APM gas of ONGC and OIL was last revised effective 1.7.2005. The salient features of the revised pricing order effective 1.7.2005 are as follows:

- ONGC and OIL produced about 55 MMSCIMD APM gas from nominated fields. The determination of producer price for this gas will be referred to the Tariff Commission. Till the Commission submits its recommendation and a decision is taken thereon, the consumer price of APM gas will be increased from Rs.2850/MCM to a fixed price of Rs. 3200/MCM on ad-hoc basis.
- It has been decided that all available APM gas would be supplied to only the power and fertilizer sector consumers against their existing allocations along with the specific end users committed under Court orders/small

scale consumers having allocations upto 0.05 MMSCMD at the revised price of Rs. 3200/MCM. This price is linked to a calorific value of 10,000 K.cal/cubic metre. However, the gas price for transport sector (CNG), Agra-Ferozabad small industries and other small scale consumers having allocations upto 0.05 MMSCMD would be progressively increased over the next 3 to 5 years to reflect the market price.

- The gas supplies through GAIL network to non-APM consumers will be at the price at which GAIL buys from JV producers at landfall point, subject to a ceiling of ex-Dahej RLNG price of US$3.86/MMBTU for the current year i.e. 2005-06. For the North-East region, Rs.3200/MCM will be considered as the market price during 2005-06.
- The price of gas for the North-Eastern region will be pegged at 60% of the revised price for general consumers. Thus, the consumer price for the North-East region will increase from the existing price of Rs.1700 to Rs.1920/MCM.
- Subject to the determination of producer price, based on the recommendations of the Tariff Commission, any additional gas as well as future production of gas from new fields to be developed in future by ONGC/ OIL will be sold at market-related price in the context of NELP provisions.

Regulatory Framework of Gas Industry

The Ministry of Petroleum and Natural Gas (MOP&NG) has been regulating the allocation and pricing of gas produced by ONGC and OIL by issuing administrative orders from time to time. The gas produced by the JVs and by NELP operators is governed by the respective production sharing contracts (PSC) between the Government and the producers. The setting up of a Petroleum and Natural Gas Regulatory Board is under the consideration of the Government and the bill is being drafted.

Under the existing policy, 100% Foreign Direct Investment (FDI) is allowed through the FIPB route for both LNG projects and natural gas pipeline projects. Import of LNG and natural gas is on OGL. If an entity requires the acquisition of Right of User (ROU) in land, it approaches MOP&NG for the acquisition under the Petroleum and Mineral Pipelines (Acquisition of Right of User in Land) Act, 1962 (P&MP Act, 1962). The draft natural gas pipeline policy covering transmission pipelines and local or city gas distribution networks is under formulation, with proposed provision in line with those under the draft regulatory board bill.

Hydrocarbon Vision-2025

India's Oil and Gas sector development road map has been laid down by the Hydrocarbon Vision: 2025 Report. Most of the planning of the Indian Oil and Gas sector is done by MoP&NG keeping this roadmap in mind and therefore the report's extract have been discussed in detail in this chapter.

Objectives for the Hydrocarbon Sector

- To assure energy security by achieving self-reliance through increased indigenous production and investment in equity oil abroad.

- To enhance quality of life by progressively improving product standards to ensure a cleaner and greener India.
- To develop the hydrocarbon sector as a globally competitive industry that could be benchmarked against the best in the world through technology upgradation and capacity building in all facets of the industry.
- To have a free market and promote healthy competition among players and improve customer service.
- To ensure oil security for the country keeping in view strategic and defence considerations.

Exploration and Production Sector

The gap between supply and availability of crude oil, petroleum products as well as gas from indigenous sources is likely to increase over the years. The growing demand and supply gap would require increasing emphasis to be given to the exploration and production sector. The objectives of the exploration policy as defined under HV2025 are as follows:

Objectives

(a) To undertake a total appraisal of Indian sedimentary basins for tapping the hydrocarbon potential, and to optimize production of crude oil and natural gas in the most efficient manner so as to have a Reserve Replacement Ratio of more than one.

(b) To keep pace with technological advancement and application and be at the technological forefront in the global E&P industry.

To achieve the above objectives, the following actions are required to be taken.

Medium-Term Objectives

(a) Continue exploration in producing basins.

(b) Aggressively pursue extensive exploration in non-producing and frontier basins for knowledge building and new discoveries, including deep-sea offshore areas.

(c) Finalize a program for appraisal of the Indian sedimentary basins to the extent of 25 per cent by 2005, 50 per cent by 2000, and 75 per cent by 2015 and loan per cent by 2025. Sufficient resources to be made available for appraising the unexplored/partly explored acreages through Oil Industry Development Board (OIDB) cess and other innovative resource mobilization approaches, including disinvestment and privatization.

(d) Provide internationally competitive fiscal terms, keeping in view the relative prospectively perception of Indian basins, in order to attract major oil and gas companies and through expeditious evaluation of bids and award of contracts on a time bound basis.

(e) Optimize recovery from discovered/future field's to improve archival practices for data management.

(f) Continue technology acquisition and absorption along with development of indigenous Research and Development (R&D)

(g) Ensure adequacy of finances for R&D required for building knowledge infrastructure
(h) Make Exploration and Production (E&P) operations compatible with the environment and reduce discharges and emissions
(i) Support R&D efforts to reduce adverse impact

Long-Term

(a) 100 per cent exploration coverage of the Indian sedimentary basins by 2025
(b) Leapfrog to technological practices to restore the original base line
(c) Put in place abandonment practices to restore the original base line
(d) Conserve resources and adopt clean technologies

Natural Gas

Natural Gas is emerging as the preferred fuel of the future in view of it being an environment friendly, economically attractive fuel and also because it is a desirable feedstock. Increased focus needs to be given to this potential sector.

Objectives

(a) To encourage use of natural gas, which is relatively a clean fuel?
(b) To ensure adequate availability by a mix of domestic gas imports through pipelines and import of LNG.
(c) To tap unconventional sources of natural gas such as coal bed methane, natural gas hydrates, underground coal gasification etc.

To achieve the above objectives the following actions are required to be taken.

Medium-Term Objective

- Timely and continuous reviewing of gas demand and supply options to facilitate policy interventions.
- Pursuing diplomatic and political initiatives for import of gas from neighboring and other countries with emphasis on transnational gas pipelines.
- Expediting the setting up of a regulatory frame work.
- Formulating a national policy on underground.
- Importing LNG to supplement the domestic gas availability and encourage domestic companies to participate in the LNG chain.
- Providing a level playing field for all the gas players and ensuring reasonable transportation tariffs.
- Rationalizing customs duty on LNG and LNG projects.
- Putting in place an effective organizational structure that would facilitate progress in the National Gas Hydrates Program.
- Personalizing the CBM Policy with a time bound program

Long-Term Strategy

- Review of LNG option in the light of economic political and energy security considerations

- Exploit the gas hydrates reserves
- Produce gas from Coal Bed Methane and through Underground Coal Gasification
- Commercialize the production and use of alternate fuels such as di-methyl ether

Tariff and Pricing

A rational tariff and pricing policy is vital to ensure the healthy growth of the hydrocarbon sector and to protect the consumers as well resources and also to eliminate adulteration.

To achieve the above objectives the following actions are required to be taken into account:

Medium-Term

(a) Phase out existing subsidies as early as possible.

(b) Set up a Group of Experts to determine appropriate levels of tariffs and duties for introduction in a phased manner as early as possible.

(c). Transfer freight subsidy on supplies to far flung areas and subsidies on products to fiscal budget Necessity for concession is to maintain the supply line to hilly and remote areas after decontrol of marketing.

(d) Increase linkage of consumer price of natural gas from the current level of 75 per cent fuel oil (FO) import parity to nearly 100 per cent.

Restructuring and Divestment

The core objective of industrial restructuring is to maintain long-term profitability and strengthen the competitive edge of the concerned companies in the context of changes in market forces and also to ensure that the consumers benefit by the restructuring and divestment policy.

Objectives

(a) To provide incentives for cleaner greener and quality fuels to promote an environment friendly hydrocarbon sector.

(b) To balance the need to boost government revenue with the need to align duties with Asia-Pacific countries and moving the prices to international levels.

(c) To promote new investments by ensuring adequate protection to domestic producers.

(d) To remove subsidies and cross-subsidies to pro mote efficient and optimal utilization of scarce resources.

The following sequence needs to be followed:

(a) Announce a policy with regards to specific public sector enterprises in alignment with the overall disinvestment policy of the Government of India.

(b) Complete the internal restructuring of oil PSUs making full use of information technology.
(c) Implement proposals of mergers and alliances of oil PSUs with the objective of enhancing shareholder value.
(d) Disinvest in a phased manner in oil PSUs down to appropriate level to realize best shareholder value.

The H-Group report succeeded by the HV-2025 report prescribes the policy framework for the hydrocarbon sector in India. As regards the policy itself the Government of India came out with bold initiatives in the upstream sector in the form of NELP and CBM policies.

New Exploration Licensing Policy (NELP): The Backdrop

In the nineties it became increasingly evident that India is heavily dependent on imports to meet the rapidly growing demand for petroleum products. Demand and supply projections indicated that the level of self-sufficiency was likely to decline to about 30 per cent over the next few years. It was realized that substantial efforts are, therefore, necessary to boost the level of exploration activity in the country so that new finds can be made and the levels of crude oil and gas production increased in the years to come. As India remained one of the least explored regions with well density per 1000 km^2 being among the lowest it emerged that vast amounts of capital investments are necessary if exploration' efforts are to be substantially augmented. Therefore, a need was felt to attract both the National Oil Companies (NOCs), as well as private sector oil companies to invest in this critical area of E&P.

Why NELP?

1. Large sedimentary areas remained unexplored/ under explored in the country
2. Ever increasing demand-supply gap
3. Requirement of vast capital investment
4. Early application of prudent and appropriate technology
5. Need for acceleration in existing leads and commercialization and development of existing discoveries
6. Only 28 PSCs could be awarded under different rounds to Pvt/JV companies in 11 years under Pre-NELP rounds
7. Level playing field between NOCs and Pvt./JV E&P companies

With this background NELP was formulated by the government in 1997-98 to provide a level playing field in which all parties could compete on equal terms for the award of exploration acreage. The salient features of the NELP are:

A. General

- Fiscal stability provision in the contract
- Finalization of contract on the basis of Model Production Sharing Contract (MPSC)

- Petroleum tax guide is in place to facilitate investors
- Possibility of seismic option in the first phase of the exploration period
- NOCs to compete for acreages

B. Fiscal and Contractual Terms

- No payment of signature discovery or production bonus
- No customs duty on imports required for petroleum operations
- No minimum expenditure commitment during the exploration period
- No mandatory state participation/carried interest by NOCs
- Freedom to sell crude oil and natural gas in domestic market at market related prices
- Biddable cost recovery limit up to 100 per cent

Sharing of profit petroleum based on pre-tax investment multiple achieved and is biddable. No cess on crude oil production. Royalty payment for crude oil on ad-valorem basis:

— 12.5 per cent for on land areas

— 10 per cent for offshore areas

  - Royalty on deep water areas (beyond 400m bathymetry)

— 5 per Cent for first seven years after commencement of commercial production

  - Option to amortize exploration and drilling expenditures over a period of 10 years from first commercial production

Salient Achievement under NELP

- The Phase I investment commitment includes $321.15 million for exploration in deep sea, $598.255 million for exploration in shallow waters and $572.75 million has been committed for onland blocks, according to a presentation on bid evaluation done by Directorate General of Hydrocarbons.
- The investment committed for Phase II and III, which are optional only upon a discovery, was not stated in the presentation.
- Of the 57 blocks offered in Nelp-VII, bids were received for 45. Besides seismic surveys, 141 exploration wells have been committed in the mandatory Phase I by the winning firms.
- The DGH has recommended to the government to award seven out of the 12 deep water blocks to the consortium of BHP Billiton and GVK Oil and Gas.
- Two blocks have been recommended for ONGC-GSPC consortia, while one block each would go to Cairn Energy, Reliance Industries-British Petroleum JV and ONGC-Oil India consortia.
- Of the shallow water blocks, the consortia of ONGC, GSPC and HPCL-Mittal Energy emerged winners for two Krishna Godavari basin blocks.
- ONGC-GSPC, Adani Welspun and Essar-Nobel were recommended winners for one shallow water offshore block each.

- ONGC and its partners were recommended for 11 onland blocks, while the consortia of OIL, HOEC and HPCL-Mittal Energy were recommended for a Rajasthan block.
- Spurt in E&P activity
- New hydrocarbon discoveries in challenging areas totally changed earlier notion about prospectivity of these areas
- Exponential growth of knowledge base in different domains of hydrocarbon exploration concepts and technology
- Wider coverage of Basins under exploration
- Upgradation of Basin category : Mahanadi, KG Basin and Deep Water East Coast

Conclusions

Based on past and recent experience of NELP (I-VII), the following conclusions can be drawn (http://www.infraline.com/UpstreamConference/Presentations/VKSibal-DGH.pdf):

- India is highly under/unexplored.
- Possibility of striking of rich oil and gas reserves in hitherto poorly explored/unexplored older sediments quite high.
- Recent discoveries in virgin areas are not a chance factor, but they are due to:
  - Envisioning of sound geological models,
  - Choosing of right exploration strategies,
  - Utilization of appropriate technology for better imaging and delineation of subsurface configuration,
  - Using right type of drilling/testing technology for reaching the targets and their evaluation.
- Need for acquiring geo-scientific data across the country.
- Integration of entire geo-scientific data for better geological understanding of regional and local prospectivity.
- A paradigm shift towards "open acreage" system.

References

Andrew McKillop (2008), Oil Shock and Energy Transition, European Commission Presentation to POGEE Conference, Karachi, May 27, 2008.

Beck, Robert J.(1999), "Low oil prices cause US and Canadian firms to curtail capital outlays in 1999", *Oil and Gas Journal*, April, 5, p. 44.

Bourdaire, Jean Marie (1998). "World energy prospects to 2020", Paper presented at the British Institute of Energy Economics, London, U.K. 2, July, pp. 5-6.

BP Statistical Review of World Energy, 2003.

British Petroleum (1998), "BP statistical review of world energy", pp. 4-5

British Petroleum (2008), *BP Statistical Review* 2008.

Campbell, Colin (1997), "The coming oil crisis", as reviewed in petroleum review, November, p. 34.

Campbell, C.J. (1995), "Proving the improvable", Petroleum Economist, May, p. 27.

Emerson, Sarah (1997), "Was 1996 a pricing anomaly", Middle East Economic Survey, 6, January.

Energy Information Administration (1999), "World energy projections system", Washington.

Euro-oil (1997), "Oil in 2001", April, pp. 37-39.

Ghanem, S. Launnas, D. Ghasemzadeh and Brennand, G., (1998), "Oil and energy outlook to 2020: Implications of the Kyoto Protocol", OPEC Review, June.

International Energy Agency (1999), Monthly oil market report, July, London, U.K.

International Energy Outlook, 2003 by EIA.

International Petroleum Statistics Report, (1998), "Future Projections", EIA, DOE/EIA-0520, Washington.

Jennings, J.S. (1996), "The millennium and beyond", Energy World, June, p. 13.

Laherrere, J.H. (1997), "Production decline and peak reveal true reserve figures", World Oil, December, p. 77.

Mabro, Robert, (1990), Oxford Energy Forum, May, p. 2.

Masters, C.D, Attanasi, E.D and Root, D.H. (1994), "World Petroleum assessment and analysis", Proceedings of the 14th World Petroleum Congress.

Odell, P.R., (1997), "Oil reserves: much more than meets the eye", Petroleum Economists, November, p. 29. Petroleum Review, (1998), April, pp. 33-34.

Oil Market Report by IEA, 2004.

Press Trust of India (2008), $1.49 billion committed in Nelp-VII, New Delhi August 21, 2008: http://www.business-standard.com/india/storypage.php?tp=on&autono=45046

Salameh, Mamdauh G. (1999), "Technology, oil reserve depletion and the myth of the reserves to production ratio", OPEC Review, June, p. 116.

Tempest, Paul ed. (1993), "The Politics of Middle East Oil", Royanmon Group, Graham and Trotman, p. 249.

Websites

www.eia.doe.gov/neic/press283gifs/fig1.gif

www.eia.doe.gov/neic/press283gifs/fig2.gif

http://www.pwc.com/extweb/pwcpublications.nsf/docid/5EBE732379E5428ECA257184005E7A2B/$file/oil_gas.pdf

https://www.oilmarketreport.org/textbase/speech/2003/va_nice.pdf

http://www.iea.org/dbtw-wpd/Textbase/speech/2004/haug/CSLF.pdf

http://www.infraline.com/UpstreamConference/Presentations/VKSibal-DGH.pdf

CHAPTER III

Oil and Natural Gas Exploration, Drilling and Production (Upstream Sector)

Introduction

At the beginning of the 21st century, the world reserves of petroleum were estimated to be roughly 1.3 trillion barrels. By 2003, worldwide consumption of petroleum totaled 29 billion barrels a year. The world's natural gas reserves were estimated to be roughly 170 trillion cubic meters (6,000 trillion cubic feet). Worldwide consumption of natural gas by 2003 totaled 2.7 trillion cubic meters (96 trillion cubic feet) a year. At the beginning of the 21st century the world coal reserves were estimated to be roughly 1 trillion metric tons, and by 2003 worldwide consumption of coal totaled 5 billion metric tons a year. Total worldwide energy consumption is expected to grow at about 2.2 percent per year until 2015. Theoretical models can be developed to estimate how many years the world fossil fuel supply will last. However, these models are complicated by technological advances in the energy production industry, unexpected discoveries of new fossil fuel deposits, and political, social, and economic factors that influence energy production and consumption (http://encarta.msn.com/encyclopedia_761586407_5/fossil_fuels.html).

Although India has significant coal and hydro-resource potential, it is relatively poor in oil and gas reserves. As a result, it has to depend on oil imports to meet its growing energy requirements for industrial, commercial and domestic operations. The geographical distribution of available primary commercial energy sources in the country is quite skewed, with 77 per cent of the hydro-potential located in the northern and north-eastern region of the country. Similarly, about 70 per cent of the total coal reserves are located in the eastern region, while most of the hydrocarbon reserves lie in the west. India has to cater to about 16 per cent of the global, and nearly one-third of Asian population. Coal, oil and gas are the most important sources of energy. Table 3.1 represents the recent reserves of these energy sources. The Reserves/Production (R/P) ratio indicates the length of time the reserves would last if production is to continue at the current level. It could be seen from the Table 3.1 that the R/P ratio for natural gas has declined over the years, but is still higher than that of crude oil, which implies that the production of natural gas would be higher than at present. For crude oil, the ratio has remained same over the last few years. The increase in production of crude oil and natural gas for meeting future energy needs would come from raising the rate of accretion.

Table 3.1: Proven Reserves of Fossil Fuels and R/P Ratio

Fuel	Reserves		R/P Ratio	
	India	World	India	World
Coal (billion tonnes)	84.00	985.0	235.0	204.0
Crude oil (billion tonnes)	0.73	142.7	19.4	40.6
Natural gas (trillion cubic metres)	0.75	155.3	27	60.7

Source: BP Statistical Review of World Energy.

The share of petroleum products and natural gas in the total energy consumption has been increasing over the years and this was at the level of about 45 per cent in 2001-02. The country is heavily dependent on imports of crude oil and this dependence will increase in the years to come. This underscores the need for increasing indigenous production. The national oil companies have made efforts to discover oil and gas to meet the ever rising demand. Recently natural gas, being environment-friendly and clean, has gained an importance as a fuel/feed stock for power plants, fertilizer industries, iron, steel plants and transport sectors. These options are being explored to maximize the share of gas in energy sector through domestic and imported sources to meet the energy demand.

In this chapter, an attempt has been made to analyze and discuss the growth and development of oil industry in India in the area of exploration and production. The major aspects that are analyzed include: exploration process, crude oil reserves, oil demand and production, problems and areas of concern, review of policy options and new exploration and licensing policy.

Regulated Industry

The oil industry in India has been highly regulated until in recent past. All business decisions used to need government sanction and improving efficiency of refineries. Marketing functions were the only avenues that companies had to improve for returns. But like many industries, the controls on oil industry have been easing and succeeded in getting completely deregulated by 1.4.2002. India's oil industry was greatly insulated from international movement in oil prices. Beginning September, 1997, several of these regulations started getting rolled back. Prices were decontrolled and administered price mechanism was dismantled. The future growth will witness the India's oil industry moving from regulated to hyper-competitive one. In this transformation, the trend shows that Tariffs will decline, government intervention will be withdrawn and the entry of private players, especially in foreign direct investment will be encouraged (IRIS study, 1999).

Exploration and Production

Exploration and Production encompasses discovery and production of oil and gas by undertaking geological and geophysical surveys like remote sensing, airborne magnetic and field gravity to identify the principal areas of adequate sediment cover. The areas thus identified are assessed for the most likely hydrocarbon potential through various methods of resource appraisal. Depending on the resource estimated, available technology and the current economic factors, each basin is ranked in terms of risk and reward and exploration priorities assigned. Basins/areas of low to medium risk and high to moderate reward are taken up first for systematic exploration which begins with detailed geological and regional seismic surveys. The results of such surveys highlight area of cost intensive exploratory inputs like seismic surveys on adequate grid and structural/ parametric/information drilling. Favourable results of these inputs lead to the next stage of exploration during which targets are decided and prospects identified. Each prospect thus demarcated is evaluated, techno-economically (Singh, 1996).

The exploratory test-well is generally located on the most viable prospects and in the event of a discovery is followed immediately by a quick assessment of prospects based on updated geological analysis and prevailing economic factors. In case the test-well fails to strike hydrocarbons, the other 'rated prospects' are evaluated immediately as a part of dynamic exploration process. Once a discovery is delineated the field is re-appraised techno-economically and its commercial viability assessed before formulation of any development plan. A technological scheme of development is adopted and executed after careful selection of optional variants related to well-spacing and maximum production based on sound reservoir management principle and economic evaluation (Mahapatra et al, 1996).

The principal activities involved in Exploration and Production activity are undertaking seismic surveys, drilling and exploratory well, economic evaluation of the project, entering into agreements with the state, formulation of field development and production plan and decommissioning of the well. The upstream oil sector is a typical case of a very high risk and high return industry. The process of oil exploration and production (O&P) can be broadly classified under the following heads and stages of activities:

Exploratory Surveys: Seismic surveys are the first stage of oil exploration wherein the companies study the area and attempt to identify locations with potential. The signals obtained are studied and the formations that exit are interpreted. On this basis further exploration is initiated. Surveys are undertaken to find out the presence of a hydrocarbon structure and then decide whether an exploratory well can be drilled. Cost of surveys would depend on the total area that is explored. It has been found that offshore seismic costs are lower than onshore costs. Onshore exploration in remote areas can be expensive compared to desert. Two dimensional (2D) surveys cost much less than the three dimensional (3D) surveys. As compared with 2-D, 3-D surveys provide more correct information, though costs are high in this case.

Against the revised 2D departmental survey target of 130370 seismic line kilometre the actual achievement was 145604 seismic line kilometre during the period of Eighth Plan, i.e., an achievement of 127.9%. For contractual survey the target was 22973 ground line kilometre and the achievement was 21286 ground line kilometre, i.e., 98% of the target. For 3D seismic surveys against the target of 4281 Seismic Square Kilometre (SSK) the achievement was 4786 (SSK); an achievement of 124.6% for onshore areas. For offshore areas against 2D survey target of 126023 SLK the actual achievement was 109682 SLK, i.e., an achievement of 93% and for 3D surveys against the target of 77093 SSK the achievement was 79846 SSK, giving an achievement of 104%.

Exploratory Drilling: An exploratory well is required to confirm the existence of oil and gas in a terrain and extract required information from the geological history and the nature and organizational aspects of reservoir. The surveys whether 2D or 3D can give us the signals of structure containing oil or not. It is the exploratory drilling which can ascertain whether the oil is there or not. The costs involved in exploratory drilling are very high and also require huge amount of capital. The costs may escalate if exploratory activities are further stepped up. In this way it would put a pressure on the resources of the Oil Company. On the contrary, if oil is actually found under the identified structure the whole costs involved in exploration could be capitalized. Otherwise, in case of dry well the entire costs would be written-off by the concerned company. As against the target of 3042 thousand metres for both the onshore and offshore regions during the Eighth Plan period the achievement was 2883 thousand metres, an achievement of 95 per cent. This was due to lower drilling activities in upper Assam basin. The main reasons for low drilling achievement were land acquisition and environmental problems.

Development Drilling: It is the phase in which oil which has been explored can be commercially extracted. Development of drilling is meant for commercial extraction of oil but it is highly capital intensive and requires a long gestation period. In most Asian countries the governments have managed to extract between 80 to 90 per cent of the total revenue in the form of various royalties, levies, duties and taxes.

In consonance with the objective of Five Years Plans, the drilling activities have expanded over the years. The Plan indicates that there has been a considerable growth in the quantum of meterage drilled as well as the productivity of the rigs expressed in terms of cycle-speed, i.e., metres per rig month. The achievement of development drilling during the Eighth-Plan was 2718 thousand metres against the target of 3809 thousand metres, i.e., an achievement of 71 per cent. The lower achievement in development drilling target was due to the fact that some of the fields which were proposed to be developed by ONGC at the time of formulation of Eighth Plan were offered for development to joint venture companies (JVCs).

Commercial Production: Commercial exploitation commences in accordance with the available infrastructure. Initially the reservoir pressure would be adequate to push oil and gas to the surface but pressure decreases with increase in production. The natural drive mechanism can be scientifically used to maintain the rate of production. However, secondary recovery methods, like injection of additional energy will be needed only if there is a fall in production with poor recovery rates. Enhanced Oil Recovery (EOR) techniques involving injection of hot water, steam or addition of solvents could also be used to increase production; though, at current oil prices, use of EOR may not be commercially viable.

Off-shore Drilling Operations

Onshore drilling operations include building access roads to the drill site, preparing the site for the drilling rig, transporting the rig to the site, and drilling the wellbore. Most drilling operations in the U.S. are done by drilling contractors. A drilling contract is an agreement between the lessee (WI owners) and a drilling contractor for the drilling of a well. The contract details the rights and obligations of the lessee and the contractor. Drilling contracts generally provide payment on a day rate (payment based on the number of days drilled), a footage rate (payment based on the number of feet drilled), or a turnkey basis (payment of a fixed sum of money based on drilling to a certain depth or stage of completion).

The first step in drilling an oil and gas well is selecting the actual drill-site. Seismic studies, particularly 3D seismic studies, are usually performed and the results of the studies are examined to determine the optimal site for the well. Once the site has been selected and a drilling contract signed, site preparations can begin. The well site is normally surveyed and staked, then access roads are built, and the site is graded and leveled. Reserve and waste pits are also prepared and a water supply is obtained. After the site is prepared, often the initial 20 to 100 feet of the well will be drilled with a small truck-mounted rig. The drilling rig and related equipment are next moved in and set up, a process called rigging up. The well is then ready to be spudded in. The spud date is the date the rotary drilling bit touches ground.

Routine drilling consists of rotating a drill bit downwards through the formations towards target depth, cutting away pieces of the formation called cuttings. During the drilling process, drilling fluid, *i.e.*, mud, is constantly circulated down the wellbore. Drilling mud serves several purposes. It raises the cuttings to the surface, lubricates the drilling bit, and keeps formation fluids from entering the wellbore.

Approximately every 30 feet as the hole is deepened, a joint of drill pipe is added, a process called making a mouse hole connection. Periodically, when the drill bit becomes worn or damaged, the entire drill pipe has to be removed from the hole in a process called tripping out. After a new drill bit is attached, the pipe is lowered back into the hole, called tripping in. Normally the drill pipe is removed and lowered three joints, *i.e.* a stand at a time depending upon the height of the derrick or mast. A derrick or mast is a four-legged, load-bearing structure that is part of the drilling rig. The height of the derrick correlates with the depth of the well since the derrick must support the weight of the drill string suspended down hole. Tripping out is also necessary when casing must be set. Casing is steel pipe that is set, *i.e.*, cemented into the wellbore. Functions of casing include preventing the caving in of the hole, protecting fresh water sands, excluding water from the producing formations, confining production to the wellbore and controlling formation pressure.

As an illustration to various drilling operations, some diagrammatic presentations are depicted on the following: Fig. 3.1: Anatomy of an oil-rig; Fig. 3.2: Mud circulation in the hole, Fig. 3.3: Drill Mud circulation system; Fig. 3.4: Schematic Diagram of a Petroleum Trap; Fig. 3.5: Slant-hole and Horizontal Wells.

Drilling for Oil

To identify a prospective site for oil production, companies use a variety of techniques, including core sampling—physically removing and testing a cross section of the rock—and seismic testing, where the return vibrations from a man-made shockwave are measured and calibrated. After these exploratory tests, companies must then drill to confirm the presence of oil or gas. A "dry hole" is an unsuccessful well, one where the drilling did not find oil or gas, or not enough to be economically worth producing. A successful well may contain either oil or gas, and often both, because the gas is dissolved in the oil. When gas is present in oil, it is extracted from the liquid at the surface in a process separate from oil production.

Historically, drilling a "wildcat" well—searching for oil in a field where it had not yet been discovered—had a low chance of success. Only one out of five wildcat wells found oil or gas. The rest were dry holes. Better information, especially from seismic technology, has improved the success rate to one out of three and, according to some, one in two. After a successful well identifies the presence of oil and/or gas, additional wells are drilled to test the production conditions and determine the boundaries of the reservoir. Finally, production, or "development," wells are put in place, along with tanks, pipelines and gas processing plants, so the oil can be produced, moved to markets and sold.

Types of Rigs

1. *Mobile Rigs*

These types of rigs are suitable to drill shallow wells. Mast, packs, draw works etc. are installed on trailers resulting in rig-building time is very less.

2. *Desert Rigs*

These types of rigs are suitable in desert areas where trailor with heavy loads cannot be moved and preparation of roads is difficult and costly. In desert rigs, rig equipments are installed on specially designed trailors whose tyres are of very big size.

3. *Heli Rigs*

These rigs are useful in logistically difficult areas where roads etc. are either very narrow or cannot be prepared to transport rig equipments. In Heli rigs, rigs equipments are manufactured in such as way that they can be dismantled in smaller modules or 4000-5000 1b so that they can be transported by Helicopters.

These rigs are similar to conventional rigs when assembled. All the rig equipments are transported by Helicopters as such operation of these rigs is very costly.

4. *TBA Rigs*

TBA Rigs are 'Transportable by any means' rigs which are similar to Heli rigs. In these rigs also rig equipments are manufactured in such a way that they can be dismantled in smaller modules of 4000-5000 lb. each and can be transported by small trucks or by helicopters.

5. *Off-Shore Rigs*

Rigs which are used for drilling in water e.g. sea, lake, pond, river etc. These can be further sub-classified as:

(i) Jack-up Rigs
   (a) Independent Log Jack up.
   (b) Mat supported Jack up.
(ii) Semi Submersible
(iii) Drill Ship

Preparing to Drill

Once the site has been selected, it must be surveyed to determine its boundaries, and environmental impact studies may be done. Lease agreements, titles and right-of way accesses for the land must be obtained and evaluated legally. For off-shore sites, legal jurisdiction must be determined.

Once the legal issues have been settled, the crew goes about preparing the land preparatory to drilling operations:

1. The land is cleared and leveled, and access roads may be built.
2. Because water is used in drilling, there must be a source of water nearby. If there is no natural source, they drill water well.
3. They dig a reserve pit, which is used to dispose of rock cuttings and drilling mud during the drilling process, and line it with plastic to protect the environment. If the site is an ecologically sensitive area, such as a marsh or wilderness, then the cuttings and mud must be disposed offsite —trucked away instead of placed in a pit.

Once the land has been prepared, several holes must be dug to make way for the rig and the main hole.

A rectangular pit, called a cellar, is dug around the location of the actual drilling hole. The cellar provides a work space around the hole, for the workers and drilling accessories. The crew then begins drilling the main hole, often with a small drill truck rather than the main rig. The first part of the hole is larger and shallower than the main portion, and is lined with a large-diameter conductor pipe. Additional holes are dug off to the side to temporarily store equipment—when these holes are finished, the rig equipment can be brought in and set up.

Setting the Rig

Depending upon the remoteness of the drill site and its access, equipment may be transported to the site by truck, helicopter or barge. Some rigs are built on ships or barges for work on inland water where there is no foundation to support a rig (as in marshes or lakes). Once the equipment is at the site, the rig is set up.

Fig. 3.1: Anatomy of Oil Rig

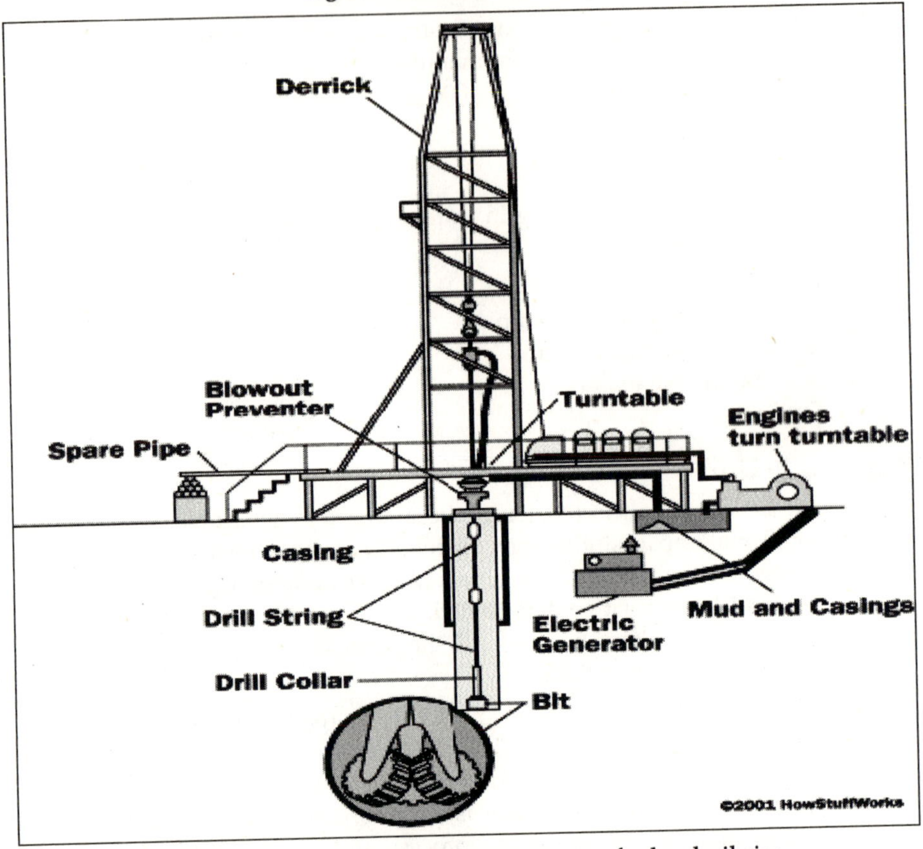

Here are brief descriptions of the major systems of a land oil rig:

- **Power system**
  - large diesel engines—burn diesel-fuel oil to provide the main source of power
  - electrical generators—powered by the diesel engines to provide electrical power
- **Mechanical system**—driven by electric motors
  - hoisting system—used for lifting heavy loads; consists of a mechanical winch (drawworks) with a large steel cable spool, a block-and-tackle pulley and a receiving storage reel for the cable
  - turntable—part of the drilling apparatus
- **Rotating equipment**—used for rotary drilling:
  - swivel—large handle that holds the weight of the drill string; allows the string to rotate and makes a pressure-tight seal on the hole
  - kelly—four- or six-sided pipe that transfers rotary motion to the turntable and drill string
  - turntable or rotary table—drives the rotating motion using power from electric motors

- drill string—consists of drill pipe (connected sections of about 30 ft/10 m) and drill collars (larger diameter, heavier pipe that fits around the drill pipe and places weight on the drill bit)
- drill bit(s)—end of the drill that actually cuts up the rock; comes in many shapes and materials (tungsten carbide steel, diamond) that are specialized for various drilling tasks and rock formations
- Casing—large-diameter concrete pipe that lines the drill hole, prevents the hole from collapsing, and allows drilling mud to circulate
- Circulation system—pumps drilling mud (mixture of water, clay, weighting material and chemicals, used to lift rock cuttings from the drill bit to the surface) under pressure through the kelly, rotary table, drill pipes and drill collars
- pump—sucks mud from the mud pits and pumps it to the drilling apparatus
- pipes and hoses—connects pump to drilling apparatus
- mud-return line—returns mud from hole
- shale shaker—shaker/sieve that separates rock cuttings from the mud
- shale slide—conveys cuttings to the reserve pit

Fig. 3.2: Mud Circulation in the Hole

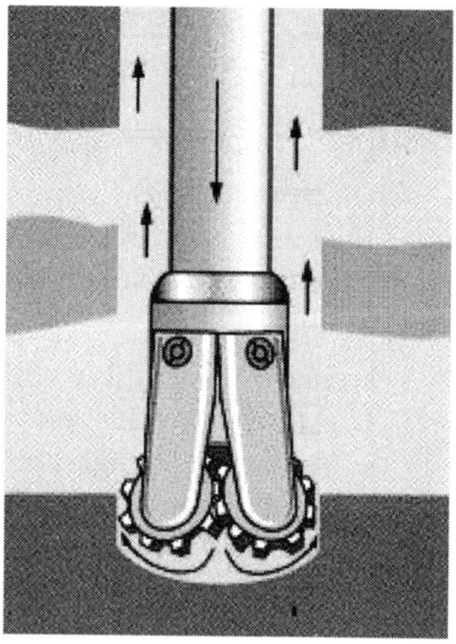

- Reserve pit—collects rock cuttings separated from the mud pits—where

Fig. 3.3: Drill Mud Circulation System

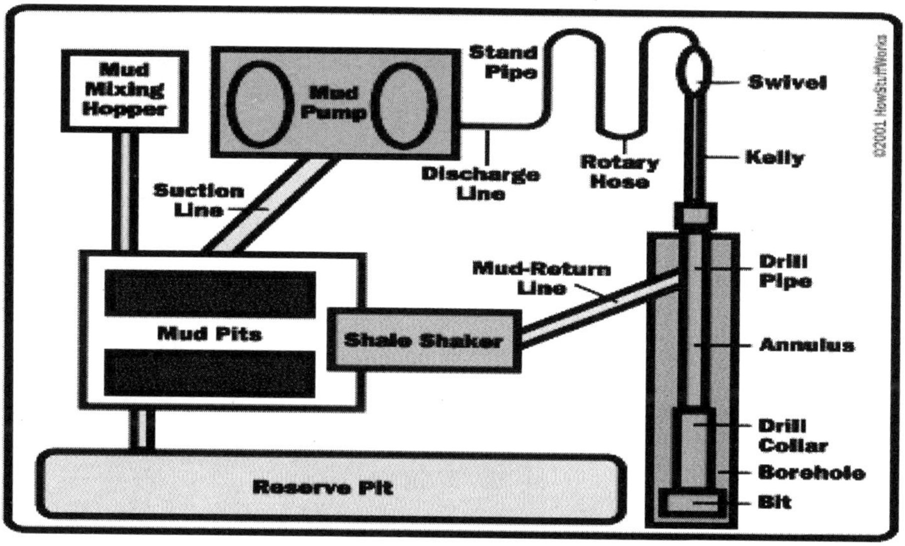

drilling mud is mixed and recycled mud-mixing hopper—where new mud is mixed and then sent to the mud pits.

- Derrick—support structure that holds the drilling apparatus; tall enough to allow new sections of drill pipe to be added to the drilling apparatus as drilling progresses
- Blowout preventer—high-pressure valves (located under the land rig or on the sea floor) that seal the high-pressure drill lines and relieve pressure when necessary to prevent a blowout (uncontrolled gush of gas or oil to the surface, often associated with fire)

Drilling Operation

The crew sets up the rig and starts the drilling operations. First, from the starter hole, they drill a surface hole down to a pre-set depth, which is somewhere above where they think the oil trap is located. There are five basic steps to drilling the surface hole:

1. Place the drill bit, collar and drill pipe in the hole.
2. Attach the Kelly and turntable and begin drilling.
3. As drilling progresses, circulate mud through the pipe and out of the bit to float the rock cuttings out of the hole.
4. Add new sections (joints) of drill pipes as the hole gets deeper.
5. Remove (trip out) the drill pipe, collar and bit when the pre-set depth (anywhere from a few hundred to a couple-thousand feet) is reached.

Once they reach the pre-set depth, they must run and cement the casing place casing-pipe sections into the hole to prevent it from collapsing in on it.

The casing pipe has spacers around the outside to keep it centered in the hole.

The casing crew puts the casing pipe in the hole. The cement crew pumps cement down the casing pipe using a bottom plug, cement slurry, a top plug and drill mud.

Fig. 3.4: Schematic Diagram of a Petroleum Trap

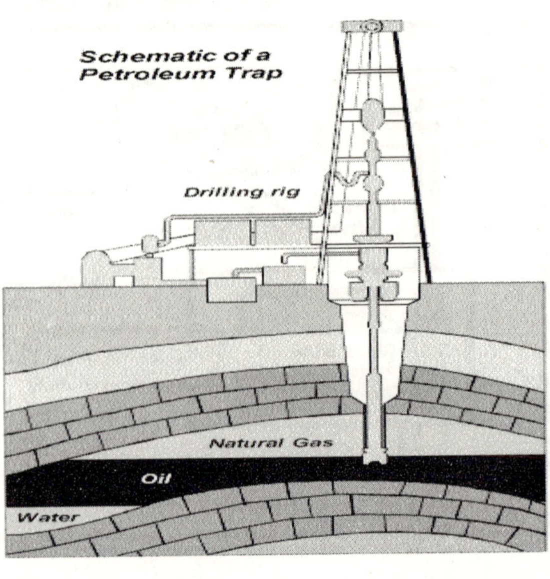

The pressure from the drill mud causes the cement slurry to move through the casing and fill the space between the outside of the casing and the hole. Finally, the cement is allowed to harden and then tested for such properties as hardness, alignment and a proper seal.

Although most well bores are drilled vertically, some wells are drilled at an angle. These wells can be either directional or horizontal wells.

Fig. 3.5: Slant-hole and Horizontal Wells

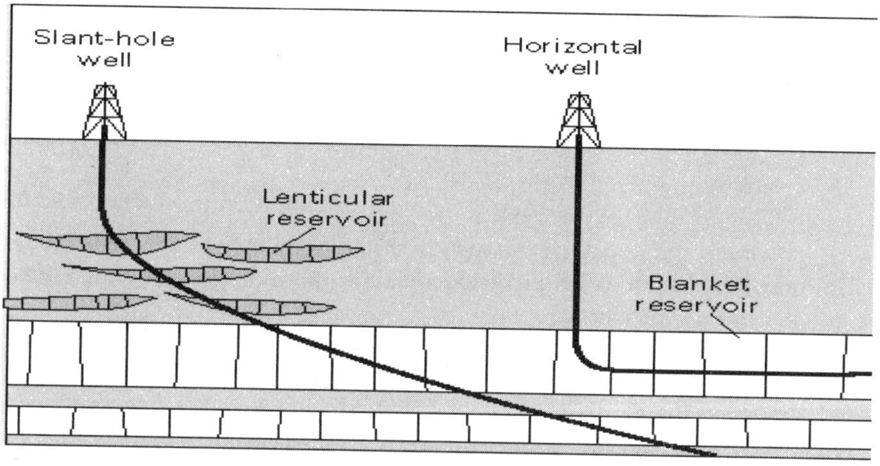

Directional wells are wells that are normally drilled straight to a predetermined depth and then curved or angled so that the bottom of the well bore is at the desired location. Horizontal wells are also initially drilled straight down but then ate gradually curved until the hole runs parallel to the earth's surface, with drilling actually achieving a horizontal direction through the formation. Figure 3.6 shows a conventional well, a directional well, and a horizontal well.

Fig. 3.6: Types of Wells

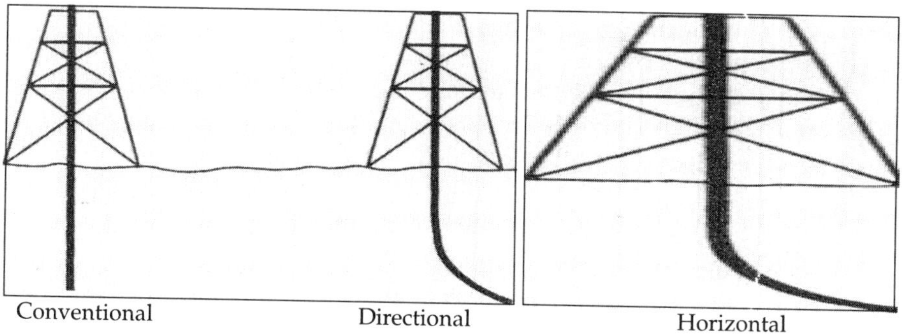

Directional drilling may be used when it is necessary to avoid drilling along a fault line, when the rig cannot be placed over the selected drillsite, when the straight hole misses the reservoir, to sidetrack around a fish (an object lodged in the borehole), or to drill multiple wells from the same offshore drilling platform. Horizontal drilling is advantageous when oil and gas are contained in several vertical, narrow pockets or reservoirs that would be missed by conventional straight drilling. Horizontal wells are also often used as lateral injection wells in enhanced recovery projects.

During drilling operations, the petroleum engineer or geologist examines cuttings and other data to decide whether there is sufficient oil or gas to justify completing the well. As the well is drilled, the cuttings are analyzed to determine fluid content and rock structure. Periodically, a larger piece of formation rock may be obtained by placing a core barrel on the end of the drill stem and cutting a cylindrical core approximately 4 inches in diameter and up to 60 feet in length from the formation. This piece of formation rock, called a core sample, is then analyzed to determine formation rock characteristics, sequence of rock layers in the earth, and fluid content of the formation.

Activities incident to completing a well and placing it on production include:

- obtaining and installing production casing (steel pipe lining the wellbore);
- installing tubing (steel pipe suspended in the well through which the oil and gas are produced);
- perforating (setting off charges to create holes in the casing and cement so formation fluids can flow from the formation into the well bore);
- installing the Christmas tree (valves and fittings controlling production at the well-head that somewhat resemble a Christmas tree);
- constructing production facilities (separators, heater treaters, tanks, etc.);
- installing flow lines.

Drilling operations are much more expensive offshore, consequently, most offshore drilling is done in the form of a joint venture or joint interest operation, *i.e.*, several companies pooling capital resources to explore, develop, and produce an offshore tract. While joint interest operations are also common onshore, they are generally the rule offshore. In some offshore areas, very little may be known about the types and depths of the sub-surface formations. In those areas, a stratigraphic test well, a well drilled for information only, may be drilled. Often, such a well will be drilled prior to the bidding process and paid for by multiple companies, who agree to share the information. Exploratory-type stratigraphic test wells are often drilled offshore to determine the existence and quantity of proved reserves and also to determine the location for the permanent development drilling and production platform. (Exploratory wells are wells drilled in area not known to contain oil or gas.). Exploratory drilling offshore is almost always done from mobile rigs. These temporary rigs can take the form of:

- drilling barges, which are towed to location;
- jack-up rigs, which are towed to location, and then four legs are jacked down to rest on sea bottom;
- submersible rigs, which sink to the ocean floor and are used only in shallow water;
- semi submersible rigs, which rest in a partially submerged position;
- drill ships, which look like ordinary ships bur contain a derrick.

Recovery Processes

Several types of production processes move the oil from the reservoir to the well. The production processes are commonly divided into three types of recovery methods: primary, secondary, and tertiary. The initial or primary recovery of oil and gas is either by natural reservoir drive or by pumping. Natural drive occurs when sufficient water or gas exists in the reservoir under high pressure. The reservoir pressure provides the natural energy needed to drive the oil to the wellbore. If insufficient natural drive exists, the oil may be pumped to the surface using a beam pumping unit. When the maximum amount of oil and gas has been recovered by primary recovery methods and the reservoir pressure has been largely depleted, secondary recovery may be instituted. Secondary recovery consists of inducing an artificial drive into the formation to replace the natural drive. The most common method is water-flooding, which involves injecting water under pressure into the formation to drive the oil to the wellbore.

Production and Sales

Fluids produced from a well normally will contain oil, gas, and water. Before the oil and gas are sold, the well fluid must be separated, treated, and measured. Flow lines take well fluid from individual wells to a central gathering point where separators divide the fluid into liquids (oil and water) and gas. Undergo Heater treaters, and then remove the water and other impurities from the oil. From this point, oil generally goes to stock tanks for storage until it is delivered to a buyer. When the oil is sold, it is measured as it is transferred from the storage tanks to either a truck transport or an oil pipeline. Gas, which is not stored on the lease, is measured as it is gathered, processed, and transferred to a gas pipeline. The amount of oil transferred from the storage tanks to a transport truck or pipeline is recorded on a document called a run ticket. The amount of payment for the oil is based upon information contained in the run ticket. The gas settlement statement is used to record similar information for the production and sale of gas.

Future Outlook

The oil and gas industry is currently facing a challenge to survive and prosper in the future. The U.S. has less the 3% of the world's reserves of oil in contrast to the Middle East, which is estimated to have 65% of world reserves. Further, the average Middle East well out-produces the average U.S. well by more than 1,500 to 1. Technology is the key if oil production is to have a future in the global economy. Many oil and natural gas reserves remain in the ground in wells that have been plugged because remaining reserves cannot be economically produced with current recovery methods. Enhanced recovery methods are currently being researched that may take it economically feasible to produce many of those reserves. For example, the method of horizontal drilling is now being used to produce from areas that were once abandoned as not economically feasible. The development of horizontal drilling in the oil industry has been compared to the invention of the transistor in the electronics industry. Further, increases in the price of oil in the future, which will happen eventually, will make even currently expensive enhanced recovery methods economically feasible.

Environmental issues will be at the forefront as a concern for the industry for many years to come. The industry has a long tradition of acting responsibly to develop environmental safeguards in order to protect the environment. Hopefully, a balance can be reached between environmentalists and the Industry, which will allow for exploration activities to continue and increase in both onshore and offshore oil and natural gas exploration operations in explored and new areas.

Finally, as the industry has realized that many of the best opportunities for exploration are in other countries, U.S. oil companies have increased operations in those areas. Companies are working with governments allover the world to explore for and develop new oil and gas reserves. The future of the industry is going to be largely dependent on the successful exploration and production operations in foreign countries.

Exploration and Development in the Ninth Plan: The Indian Scene

With evolving geological concepts and experience in other parts of the world it is seen that the less explored basins in India, e.g., Gondwana basins could be more prospective and need to be accorded top priority for exploration. Exploration efforts should spread over all the basins including unexplored/less explored having favourable geological formations. This requires a change in exploration strategy. 3D technology has been identified as a major seismic input for the development of the field as well as for monitoring EOR processes. The focus of 2D surveys in Assam and Arunachal Pradesh areas would be on the North Bank of Brahmaputra River, the belt of Schuppan and further detailing of Eocene prospects in this region. The 2D surveys would also be carried out in Ganga Valley, Rajasthan and Saurastra offshore areas. In view of the rapidly increasing demand for oil in the coming years there is an urgent need to step up the level of indigenous oil production which has remained more or less stagnant during the last 5-6 years. This will call for enlarging exploration coverage of the different sedimentary basins in the country. A new thrust needs to be given for exploration in deep waters, in the North Bank of Brahmaputra. A certain minimum level of exploration by the National Oil Companies may be necessary for upgrading the hydrocarbon resources and attracting private investments in this area. The Ninth Plan focused on strategies required for achieving the above objectives (Planning Commission, GOI, 1997 & 2002).

Tools for Measuring Exploration Efficiency: The most commonly used parameter for measuring exploration efficiency is the finding cost. The index is a good indicator of how successful a petroleum firm is in finding and developing new reserves at reasonable costs. Finding cost provides the cost per barrel of finding and developing new reserves depending upon what parameters have been used in deriving it.

International Exploration and Production companies use three different definitions of finding costs, which are:

- Exploration expenses and leasehold costs divided by the reserve addition from exploratory efforts.
- Exploration expenses and leasehold costs divided by reserve addition and revision.
- Exploration, leasehold and development costs divided by reserve additions, revision and enhanced recovery or reserve purchase.

If exploration efficiency of a company is measured, one should consider reserves accreted through exploration activities in the basin and the expenditure incurred on it. All other reserves which may be added into the company's account through reserve purchase technology upgradation or developmental activities should be excluded. It may be significant to note that reserves accreted through procurement of property signify the business efficiency of the company and not the exploration efficiency. Similarly, upgradation of technology may increase the reserves for the company but it is due to advanced and improved production technology which has helped in increasing the recoverable component of reserves accreted much earlier.

Another parameter used by the companies is their reserve replacement ratios. This is the ratio of barrels of reserves accreted to barrels of reserves produced. In other words, it depicts how many produced hydrocarbons have been replaced. Exploration Discovery Index (EDI)—another parameter gives the amount of hydrocarbon added (in tons) to the inventory by every exploratory metre drilled by the company. Another method is the reserve accretion value which indicates the net value of the reserves accreted as on date. By comparing it with the corresponding exploration investments, an idea of whether the exploration efforts are giving some returns or not, can be obtained. In case the expenditure on exploratory efforts is exceeding the reserve accretion value, it is better to call it a day. Different index characterizes each area by virtue of its unique geographic and geologic nature. It shows a need for properly balanced exploration budget. Company maintaining the highest ratio is the most successful which means that the company has found most oil for lesser investments on exploratory inputs (Loomba et al., 1999).

For a rational treatment of the theme as also to develop a deeper understanding about the principles and methodologies of exploration and production technologies of oil and natural gas it would be only apt to cover some aspects of genesis and technology options of oil exploration, as given below.

Increasing Role of Technology in Finding Oil

Technology's contribution to finding oil is huge. It cannot change geology, but by revolutionizing the information available on the features of a geologic structure, it has enhanced the likelihood of success. A primary benefit is the ability to eliminate poor prospects, thus wasted expenditure on dry holes. In addition, drilling and production technologies have made it possible to exploit reservoirs that would have formerly been too costly to put into production and, as described above, to increase the recovery from existing reservoirs.

Seismic Exploration

The biggest breakthrough in petroleum and natural gas exploration came through the use of basic seismology. Seismology refers to the study of how energy, in the form of seismic waves, moves through the Earth's crust and interacts differently with various types of underground formations. In 1855, L. Palmiere developed the first 'seismograph', an instrument used to detect and record earthquakes. This device was able to pick up and record the vibrations of the earth that occur during an earthquake. However, it wasn't until 1921 that this technology was applied to the petroleum industry and used to help locate underground oil formations.

The basic concept of seismology is quite simple. As the Earth's crust is composed of different layers, each with its own properties, energy (in the form of seismic waves) traveling underground interacts differently with each of these layers. These seismic waves, emitted from a source, will travel through the earth, but also be reflected back towards the source by the different underground layers. It is this reflection that allows for the use of seismology in discovering the properties of underground geology. Geophysicists are able to artificially create vibrations on the surface and record how these vibrations are reflected back to the surface.

In practice, using seismology for exploring onshore areas involves artificially creating seismic waves, the reflection of which are then picked up by sensitive pieces of equipment called 'geophones', imbedded in the ground. The data picked up by these geophones are then transmitted to a seismic recording truck, which records the data for further interpretation by geophysicists and petroleum reservoir engineers. The source of seismic waves (in this case an underground explosion) creates vibrations which reflect off of the different layers of the earth, to be picked up by geophones on the surface and relayed to a seismic recording truck to be interpreted and logged.

Although the seismograph was originally developed to measure earthquakes, it was discovered that much the same sort of vibrations and seismic waves could be produced artificially and used to map underground geologic formations. In the early days of seismic exploration, seismic waves were created using dynamite. These carefully planned, small explosions created the requisite seismic waves, which were then picked up by the geophones, generating data to be interpreted by geophysicists, geologists, and petroleum engineers.

In addition, drilling and production technologies have made it possible to exploit reservoirs that would have formerly been too costly to put into production and, as described above, to increase the recovery from existing reservoirs. The biggest breakthrough in petroleum and natural gas exploration came through the use of basic seismology. Seismology refers to the study of how energy, in the form of seismic waves, moves through the Earth's crust and interacts differently with various types of underground formations. In 1855, L. Palmiere developed the first 'seismograph', an instrument used to detect and record earthquakes. This device was able to pick up and record the vibrations of the earth that occur during an earthquake. However, it wasn't until 1921 that this technology was applied to the petroleum industry and used to help locate underground oil formations.

The basic concept of seismology is quite simple. As the Earth's crust is composed of different layers, each with its own properties, energy (in the form of seismic waves) traveling underground interacts differently with each of these layers. These seismic waves, emitted from a source, will travel through the earth, but also be reflected back towards the source by the different underground layers.

It is this reflection that allows for the use of seismology in discovering the properties of underground geology. Geophysicists are able to artificially create vibrations on the surface and record how these vibrations are reflected back to the surface.

Onshore Seismic Exploration

In practice, using seismology for exploring onshore areas involves artificially creating seismic waves, the reflection of which are then picked up by sensitive pieces of equipment called 'geophones', imbedded in the ground. The data picked up by these geophones are then transmitted to a seismic recording truck, which records the data for further interpretation by geophysicists and petroleum reservoir engineers. The source of seismic waves (in this case an underground explosion) creates vibrations which reflect off of the different layers of the earth, to be picked up by geophones on the surface and relayed to a seismic recording" truck to be interpreted and logged.

Although the seismograph was originally developed to measure earthquakes, it was discovered that much the same sort of vibrations and seismic waves could be produced artificially and used to map underground geologic formations. In the early days of seismic exploration, seismic waves were created using dynamite. These carefully planned, small explosions created the requisite seismic waves, which were then picked up by the geophones, generating data to be interpreted by geophysicists, geologists, and petroleum engineers". Recently, due to environmental concerns and improved technology, it is often no longer necessary to use explosive charges to generate the needed seismic waves.

Instead, most seismic crews use non-explosive seismic technology to generate the required data. This non-explosive technology usually consists of large heavy wheeled or tracked vehicle carrying special equipment designed to create a large impact or series of vibrations. These impacts or vibrations create seismic waves similar to those created by dynamite. In the seismic truck, the large piston is used to create vibrations on the surface of the earth, sending seismic waves that are used to generate useful data. Seismic exploration, broadly speaking, creates a picture of the subsurface by recording vibrations as they bounce back from geologic formations.

Offshore Seismic Exploration

The same sort of process is used in offshore seismic exploration. When exploring for natural gas that may exist thousands of feet below the seabed floor, which may itself be thousands of feet below sea level, a slightly different method of seismic exploration is used. Instead of trucks and geophones, a ship is used to pick up the seismic data. Instead of geophones, offshore exploration uses hydrophones, which are designed to pick up seismic waves underwater. These hydrophones are towed behind the ship in various configurations depending on the needs of the geophysicist. Instead of using dynamite pacts on the seabed floor, the seismic ship uses a large air gun, which releases bursts of compressed air under the water, creating seismic waves that can travel through the Earth's crust and generate the seismic reflections that are necessary. Offshore, the vibrations come from vessels towing a sonar array that "shoots" with compressed air. Onshore, the vibrations come from specially designed trucks that "thump" the ground (and formerly, from a dynamite explosion).

The difference between 2-D and 3-D seismic lies in the number of vibrations from which meaningful information can be calibrated. With 2-D, geophones along a line of vibrations provided a picture that was a cross-section—a slice—of the rock formation. With 3-D, the geophones cover a grid, not just a line. With thousands of times more data points, scientists can map a cube, creating a 3-dimensional computer image of the formation. While 3-D seismic is many times more expensive than 2-D, it allows companies to avoid unlikely prospects, and hence wasting money on unsuccessful wells.

2-D Seismic Interpretation

Two-dimensional seismic imaging refers to geophysicists using the data collected from seismic exploration activities to develop a cross-sectional picture of the underground rock formations. The geophysicist interprets the seismic data obtained from the field, taking the vibration recordings of the seismograph and using them to develop a conceptual model of the composition and thickness of the various layers of rock underground. This process is normally used to map underground formations, and to make estimates based on the geologic structures to determine where it is likely that deposits may exist.

There also exists a technique using basic seismic data known as 'direct detection'. In the mid-70's, it was discovered that white bands, called 'bright spots', often appeared on seismic recording strips. These white bands could indicate deposits of hydrocarbons. The nature or porous rock containing natural gas could often result in reflecting stronger seismic reflections than normal, water filled rock. Therefore, in these circumstances, the actual natural gas reservoir could be detected directly from the seismic data. However, this does not hold universally. Many of these 'bright spots' do not contain hydrocarbons, and many deposits of hydrocarbons are not indicated by white strips on the seismic data. Therefore, although adding a new technique of locating petroleum and natural gas reservoirs, direct detection is not a completely reliable method.

Computer Assisted Exploration

One of the greatest innovations in the history of petroleum exploration is the use of computers to compile and assemble geologic data into a coherent 'map' of the underground. Use of this computer technology is referred to as 'CAEX', which is short for 'computer assisted exploration'. With the proliferation of the microprocessor, it has become relatively easy to use computers to assemble seismic data that is collected from the field. This allows for the processing of much larger amounts of data, increasing the reliability and informational content of the seismic model. There are three main types of computer assisted exploration models: 2-dimensional, 3-D, and most recently, 4-0. These imaging techniques, while relying mainly on seismic data acquired in the field, are becoming more and more sophisticated.

Computer technology has advanced so far that it is now possible to incorporate the data obtained from different types of tests, such as logging, production Source: BP information, and gravimetric testing which can all be combined to create a 'visualization' of the underground formation. Thus geologists and geophysicists are able to combine all of their sources of data to compile one clear, complete image of subsurface geology. An example of this is shown where a geologist uses an interactive computer generated visualization of 3-D seismic data to explore the subsurface layers.

3-D Seismic Imaging

One of the biggest breakthroughs in computer-aided exploration was the development of three-dimensional (3-D) seismic imaging. 3-D imaging utilizes seismic field data to generate a three dimensional 'picture' of underground formations and geologic features. This, in essence, allows the geophysicist and geologist to see a clear picture of the composition of the Earth's crust in a particular area. Obviously, this is tremendously useful in allowing for the exploration of petroleum and natural gas, as an actual image could be used to estimate the probability of formations existing in a particular area, and the characteristics of that potential formation. This technology has been extremely successful in raising the success rate of exploration efforts. In fact, using 3-D seismic has been estimated to increase the likelihood of successful reservoir location by 50 percent.

Although this technology is very useful, it is also very costly. 3-D seismic imaging can cost anywhere up to $1 million per 50 square mile area. The generation of 3-D images requires data to be collected from several thousand locations, as opposed to 2-D imaging, which only requires several hundred data points. As such, 3-D imaging is a much more involved and prolonged process. Therefore, it is usually used in conjunction with other exploration techniques. For example, a geophysicist may use traditional 2-D modeling and examination of geologic features to determine if there is a probability of the presence of natural gas. Once these basic techniques are used, 3-D seismic imaging may be used only in those areas that have a high probability of containing reservoirs.

In addition to broadly locating petroleum reservoirs, 3-D seismic imaging allows for the more accurate placement of wells to be drilled. This increases the productivity of successful wells, allowing for more petroleum and natural gas to be extracted from the ground. In fact, 3-D seismic can increase the recovery rates of productive wells to 40-50 percent, as opposed to 25-30 percent with traditional 2-D exploration techniques.

3-D seismic imaging has become an extremely important tool in the search for oil and natural gas. By 1980, only 100 3-D seismic imaging tests had been performed. However, by the mid 90's, 200 to 300 3-D seismic surveys were being performed each year. In 1996, in the Gulf of Mexico, one of the largest offshore oil and gas producing areas in the US, nearly 80% of wells drilled in the Gulf were based on 3-D seismic data. In 1993, 75 percent of all onshore exploratory surveys conducted used 3-D seismic imaging.

Technology has also contributed a variety of tools to identify and exploit reservoirs or portions of reservoirs that are less accessible, small and/or compartmentalized, incompletely drained or porous. Modern oil geologists also examine surface rocks and terrain, with the additional help of satellite images. However, they also use a variety of other methods to find oil. They can use sensitive gravity meters to measure tiny changes in the Earth's gravitational field that could indicate flowing oil, as well as sensitive magnetometers to measure tiny changes in the Earth's magnetic field caused by flowing oil. They can detect the smell of hydrocarbons using sensitive electronic noses called sniffers. Finally, and most commonly, they use seismology, creating shock waves that pass through hidden rock layers and interpreting the waves that are reflected back to the surface.

In seismic surveys, a shock wave is created by the following:

- Compressed-air gun—shoots pulses of air into the water (for exploration over water).
- Thumper truck—slams heavy plates into the ground (for exploration over land).
- Explosives—drilled into the ground (for exploration over land) or thrown overboard (for exploration over water) and detonated.

The shock waves travel beneath the surface of the Earth and are reflected back by the various rock layers.

The reflections travel at different speeds depending upon the type or density of rock layers through which they must pass. The reflections of the shock waves are detected by sensitive microphones or vibration detectors—hydrophones over water, seismometers over land. The readings are interpreted by seismologists for signs of oil and gas traps. Although modern oil-exploration methods are better than previous ones, they still may have only a 1 a-percent success rate for finding new oil fields. Once a prospective oil strike is found, the location is marked by GPS coordinates on land or by marker buoys on water.

Exploration Techniques for Petroleum

Since the beginning of exploration for oil and gas, evolution of the art consisted of refinements of older methods and the addition of new techniques. Development of the art of looking for oil and Gas involves the realization that there is no substitute for the imaginative approach and that there is no such thing as and oil finder or "black box." Geology is a science that brings virtually every scientific discipline to bear in its application, whether it is the sorting out of geologic events and processes or the exploration for important raw materials. The proper orchestration of other sciences to the performance of geologic application requires substantial skill motivated by and analytic since of imaginative investigation—Geology uses mathematics and many other sciences, however, as adjuncts to the understanding of a large scenario of multiple components.

Surface Geology

Explorations techniques start with methods involve the obvious reason: look for oil on the surface of the ground. They continue with more esoteric procedures that produce sophisticated data suggestive of occurrences of oil and gas, which require analysis and imagination including geophysics, geochemistry, and aerial photography. The latter are substantially more indirect and circumstantially more indirect and circumstantial than the former. However, even the tactile and visual reality of oil on the surface of the ground does not insure its occurrence, in quantity, in the subsurface. Large areas of the world have no outcrops or surface features or are located offshore. Surface geology is of little use in these places, which require subsurface analysis of whatever data are available. Subsurface techniques use the same parameters as surface methods but don't have the benefit of continuity typical of surface exposures. Subsurface data quality improves as they density of data increases. However, increased amounts of data often require more specific interpretations. Interpretation of subsurface geology integrates data from a number of sources. Some sources provide direct information and others provide more indirect data.

Direct Indications

Oil and gas evident upon the ground surface may promote some degree of certainty of their being in the subsurface. Surface indications are only that, however, because there is no definition of what will be found in the subsurface.

1. Oil and gas come to the surface along porous beds, fault planes, or in springs. Mobile petroleum occurrences at the surface are called seeps. Seeps are abundant and well documented worldwide.
2. Porous rock outcrops can be impregnated with oil. They are suggestive of oil, present or past, in the subsurface, Oil-soaked rocks have provoked exploration for many years in portions of the Great Basin, Nevada, and Utah.
3. Oxidation of petroleum reduces the volatile constituents and causes it to become very viscous of immobile. The asphaltic or tarry residue at the surface seals off the un-oxidized petroleum remaining in the reservoir from the atmosphere. Asphalt/tar deposits in Asphalt Ridge west of Vernal, Utah are indicative of subsurface oil in Tertiary rocks of the rocks of the Unite Basin.
4. Some plant forms have a particular affinity for petroleum. They grow on the ground surface over subsurface petroleum accumulations Identification of the particular plant varieties is essential.

Surface Data

Exploration by surface geological activity is essential where rocks appear at the surface. In offshore areas, however, surface exploration is impossible. The surface geologist maps all visible geological features to fully utilize the data toward the exploration program. The geologist's judgment sets the entire tone and control the direction of the exploratory effort. His job is to examine the rocks, evaluate their suitability as source and reservoir beds, and map their structure. Poor source beds, inadequate reservoir rocks, and improper structure do not combine to promote a favourable exploration program.

Oil Seeps

1. Geologic mapping involves plotting geologic data on a map. The geologist measures and describes the rock sections and plots the different formations on a map, which shows their distribution. He also plots surface structure on the geologic map or construct a separate structure map. Other maps that are useful include thickness maps, which illustrate thickness variations of individual formations over the area of interest, lithologic map, which show variations over the area of interest, lithologic map, which show variations in rock types within a formation, and porosity maps, which illustrate how porosity in a particulars rock unit may vary, throughout the exploration area.
2. Without source and reservoir rocks, an area has no petroleum potential. Identification of source and reservoir rocks, their distribution, and their thicknesses are essential in an exploration program.
3. Exploration, particularly over large area, requires correlation of geologic sections. Correlations produce cross-sections that give visual information on structure, stratigraphy and thickness.
4. Photogeology is particularly useful in conducting mapping operations. Aerial photographs allow accurate geographic plotting of contacts, structures, and topography, which can later be transferred to a map. Not all areas have aerial photographic coverage. However, photogeology is an important interpretive tool where there is coverage.
5. Cross-sections can incorporate a variety of geologic information including stratigraphy, structure, porosity, lithology, and thickness of important formations or groups of formations. They are often used as adjuncts to maps and enable 3-dimensional visualization of the area covered.

Well Cuttings

Well samples are produced from drilling operations, by the drill bit penetrating the formation encountered in the subsurface. They are taken at regular intervals to establish a lithologic record of the well. Cutting are examined for lithologic characters and plotted on a strip sample log. Oil and gas shows in the samples are noted on the strip log.

Cores

Cores are cut where specific lithologic and rock parameter data are required. They are cut by a hollow core barrel, which goes down around the rock core as drilling proceeds. When the core barrel is full and the length of the core occupies the entire interior of the core barrel, it is brought to the surface, and the core is removed and laid out in stratigraphic sequence. Cores are preferable to well cuttings because they produce coherent rock. They are significantly more expensive to obtain, however. Sidewall cores are small samples of rock obtained by shooting small metal cylinders from a gun into the walls of a drill hole. The tool for obtaining sidewall cores contains a number of guns oriented around its perimeter and ranged in several tiers. Sidewall cores can be taken from several levels and at different locations using this versatile tool.

Electric Logs

Subsurface information is obtained by wire line electrical well logging techniques. This involves taking measurements of the electrical properties of rocks encountered in the well bore. Several types of measurements that produce information on formation velocity, density, radioactivity, porosity, and conductivity can be made using logging tools. The method begins with the lowering of a sonde or tool to the bottom of the well bore. Logging of the hole begins as the tool is raised and electrical impulses are sent into the formations, from which the return and are measures. Porosity is indirectly measured by the SP, or spontaneous potential or self potential, curve on an accompanying electric log. Resistively (inverse of conductivity) of the formation is measured by the resistively curve on the same log. Strong SP deflections to the left indicate increased formation porosity. Prominent resistivity deflections to the right illustrate low conductivity, which can result from a hard formation or high freshwater content or the presence of oil or natural gas.

Drill Stem Tests

Formation evaluation by obtaining samples of formation fluid and formation pressure data is made possible by drill stem testing procedures. The testing equipment is lowered into the wellbore on the drill pipe and put into place by seating a packer that seals off the formation from contamination by drilling mud. The tool is opened and fluid sampled and pressure data are obtained. Drill stem tests are run in wells in which promising hydrocarbon shows (indications) are encountered in cores and samples. Segregation of the individual formations produces results from specific intervals. Pressure data are evaluated to determine the productive potential of the formation being tested. These data and fluid information can facilitate decisions on how the well is to be completed: as a producing well or as a dry to be plugged and abandoned. Development of an individual reservoir can also be augmented by evaluation of pressure and fluid data. Data similarities suggest the same reservoir. Dissimilar data are potentially indicative of separate reservoirs, permeability barriers, or contamination.

Geophysical Surveys

Several types of common geophysical surveys are in use in petroleum exploration. They provide some direct and some indirect structural data, in most instances, no direct indications of petroleum occurrences. Differences in the density of crustal rocks are measured by the gravimeter. Low-density rocks are represented as negative anomalies and high density rocks as positive anomalies. Gravity surveys are useful in exploration of salt dome terrains. Salt domes have low density and appear as negative closed anomalies on gravity maps. Gravity surveys provide indirect structural and lithologic data. Magnetometer exploration measures variations in magnetic intensity.

Geochemical Surveys

Analysis of soil samples, river, water, formation water, and oil can be useful in some exploration programs.

1. Soil analyses can indicate the presence of hydrocarbons beneath the surface. They can indicate little about the depth of the reservoir.
2. Analysis of surface water from rivers and streams might be indicative of the locations of oil seeps along the river banks.
3. Chemical analysis of subsurface formation water is often useful in correlations within a reservoir or establishing the differentiation of reservoirs.
4. Oil composition analysis can provide age determinations of crude oil beil1g produced from a well. In many cases, crude oil age data are required to establish source rocks.

Compositional variations of crude oil are also useful indiscriminating between different reservoir horizons. Oil ages and migration histories can be determined by Oil analyses, as well.

Maps and Cross-Sections

Practically any type of geologic data can be represented on a map. Some of the most useful maps are those that present clear pictures or the distribution of geologic parameters. A geologic map is an example of this because it shows the distribution of individual rock formations over the area of the map. Contour maps can illustrate thickness, percentage, topography and structure. They show variations that are useful in interpreting the complete geology of an area or individual characteristics within the entire data structure.

Contour Maps

Data upon which numerical values can be placed can be contoured, since contour lines connect points of equal value. Contour maps are important interpretive aids and can represent anything from sequential geologic events to absolute values of individual parameters within single rock units.

1. Contour interval should adequately represent the data. Too large an interval overlooks some of the data and too small an interval clutters the map.
2. Contour lines should honor the data and be properly spaced relative to them.
3. Contour lines should be drawn smoothly and as parallel to each other.
4. Contour lines should never cross; Crossing contour lines are impossibility.
5. Contour lines should be close together where gradients are steep and farther apart where gradients are shallow.
6. Contour lines should be labeled.

Geologic Maps

Geologic maps can include as much or as little data as desired. Usually they include formation and their contacts and the most prominent faults. However, geologic maps can also include topographic and structural contours, as well as structural features. Most geologic maps are coloured. But data also can be represented by the use of symbols or different tones of gray. Geographic features are essential for purposes of location.

Cross-Sections

Structural, Stratigraphic and topographic information can be portrayed on cross-sections' that reproduce horizontally represented map information in vertical section. Maps represent information in the plan view and provide a view of distribution. Cross-sections present the same information's in the vertical view and illustrate vertical relationships such as depth, thickness, superposition, and lateral and vertical changes of geologic features. Raw data for cross-sections comes from stratigraphic sections structural data, well samples logs, cores, electric logs, and structural stratigraphic maps.

Formation Evaluation

Formation evaluation is the process of using borehole measurements to evaluate the characteristics of subsurface formation. It applies to many areas of engineering where various rock properties are needed. However, in petroleum industry; it is mainly directed towards the identification and evaluation of commercial hydrocarbon—bearing formations. These measurements are grouped into following four categories:

1. **Geo-Logging (Mud logging)**: Drilling time log, cutting analysis, mud analysis, gas logging etc.
2. **Core Analysis**: Qualitative measurements (visual lithology, presence of shows, etc.) and quantitative measurements (Porosity, permeability, information factors, saturation, etc.)
3. **Wire line Well Logs**: Electrical (SP. focused and no focused current resistivity, induction), acoustic (transit time, full wave train, borehole televiewer) radio-active gamma ray, neutron, density, spectral, LOT, GST, etc.) and specific logs (production log, temperature log, etc.)
4. **Productivity tests**: Formation Testers (RFT, FIT), DST and production tests

Enhanced oil recovery (EOR)

Enhanced Oil Recovery, or "EOR," is the use of any process or technology that enhances the displacement of oil from the reservoir, other than primary recovery methods. Enhanced Oil Recovery methods and technologies' enhancements or improvements of the primary recovery methods are also known as secondary recovery methods and may be utilized in the recovery of oil at any stage of production. Enhanced oil recovery method refers to any recovery method other than primary and the conventional secondary recovery methods through "flooding" (water or fire) or through injecting steam or gas such as nitrogen or carbon dioxide. EOR projects may involve gas re-injection, carbon dioxide (CO_2) flooding or various horizontal drilling techniques.

EOR Production by Country

On a world scale, the amount of oil produced using EOR techniques is very small (around 2Y2% of all production). Table below shows that by far the greatest proportion of EOR oil is produced using steam injection (67% of total). The next most popular process is hydrocarbon gas injection (19%) followed by miscible CO_2 injection (11%).

World EOR Production by Method

EOR Process	Amount (Mstb/d)	Percent of Total
Steam	1155.2	66.8
Miscible Hydrocarbon Gas	336.6	19.5
Miscible CO_2	188.4	10.9
Polymer/Surfactant (Chemical)	16.0	0.9
Nitrogen	14.7	0.8
In situ Combustion	10.0	0.6
Immiscible CO_2	6.4	0.4
Hot Water Injection	2.4	0.1
Immiscible Hydrocarbon Gas	0.0	0.0

A variety of augmented-recovery methods have been developed and introduced. These include:

Thermal Methods

Thermal methods, particularly steam drive and steam soak, have been commercially successful for over 30 years. Thermal methods rely on several displacement mechanisms to recover oil. The most important mechanism is the reduction of crude viscosity by increasing temperature. Thermal recovery continues to be an attractive means of maximizing the value and reserves from heavy oil assets. However, the viscosity reduction is lower for lighter crude oil. Therefore, thermal methods are not nearly as advantageous for light crude.

Solvent Flooding

Solvent flooding refers to those EOR techniques whose main oil recovering mechanism is extraction, dissolution, vaporization, solubilization, condensation, or some other phase behavior change involving the crude oil. It includes CO_2 flooding, nitrogen injection, natural gas injection, etc. These methods sometimes have additional recovery mechanisms such as viscosity reduction and oil swelling, but their primary mechanism must be extraction.

Chemical Methods

Chemical methods include polymer methods, surfactant flooding, foam flooding, alkaline flooding, etc. The mechanisms of chemical methods vary depending on the chemical material added to the reservoir; chemical methods may achieve one or more effects: interfacial tension reduction, wettability, alteration, emulsification, or mobility control. The technical limitations of chemical flooding methods are insufficient understanding of the mechanisms involved and a lack of scale-up criteria. Furthermore, the process should be cost-effective.

Future of Oil

The Hubbert peak theory, also known as peak oil, is a theory concerning the long-term rate of production of conventional oil and other fossil fuels. It assumes that oil reserves are not replenishable (i.e. that abiogenic replenishment is negligible), and predicts that future world oil production must inevitably reach a peak and then decline as these reserves are exhausted. Controversy surrounds the theory, as predictions for when the global peak will actually take place are highly dependent on the past production and discovery data used in the calculation. Proponents of peak oil theory also refer as an example of their theory, that when any given oil well produces oil in similar volumes to the amount of water used to obtain the oil, it tends to produce less oil afterwards, leading to the relatively quick exhaustion and/or commercial unavailability of the well in question. The issue can be considered from the point of view of individual regions or of the world as a whole. Originally M. King Hubbert_noticed that the discoveries in the United States had peaked in the early 1930s, and concluded that production would then peak in the early 1970s. His prediction turned out to be correct, and after the US peaked in 1971—and thus lost its excess production capacity—OPEC was finally able to manipulate oil prices, which led to the oil crisis in 1973 (http://en.wikipedia.org/wiki/Hubbert_peak_theory).

Since then, most other countries have also peaked: Britain's North Sea, for example in late 1990s. China has confirmed that two of its largest producing regions are in decline, and Mexico's national oil company, Pemex, has announced that Cantarell Field, one of the world's largest offshore fields, is expected to peak in 2006, and then decline 14% per annum. For various reasons (perhaps most importantly the lack of transparency in accounting of global oil reserves), it is difficult to predict the oil peak in any given region. Based on available production data, proponents have previously (and incorrectly) predicted the peak for the world to be in years 1989, 1995, or 1995-2000. However these predictions date from before the recession of the early 1980s, and the consequent reduction in global consumption, the effect of which was to delay the date of any peak by several years.

A new prediction by Goldman Sachs picks 2007 (Fig. 3.7) for oil and some time later for natural gas. Just as the 1971 U.S. peak in oil production was only clearly recognized after the fact, a peak in world production will be difficult to discern until production clearly drops off). More optimistic outlooks, delaying the peak of production to the 2020s or 2030s and assuming that major investments in alternatives occur before the crisis, show the price at first escalating and then retreating as other types of fuel sources are used as transport fuels and fuel substitution in general occurs (as depicted below (http://www.wealthdaily.com/articles/peak+oil-production-global/374).

More dire predictions that operate on the thesis that the peak will occur shortly or has already occurred predict a global depression and even the collapse of industrial global civilization as the various feedback mechanisms of the global market cause a disastrous chain reaction. The shortfall will cause demand destruction, which may be mitigated with planned conservation measures and using alternatives. So it's not that we're running out of oil. The bottom line is this:

Fig. 3.7: Goldman Sachs Picks—2007 (The Hubert Curve)

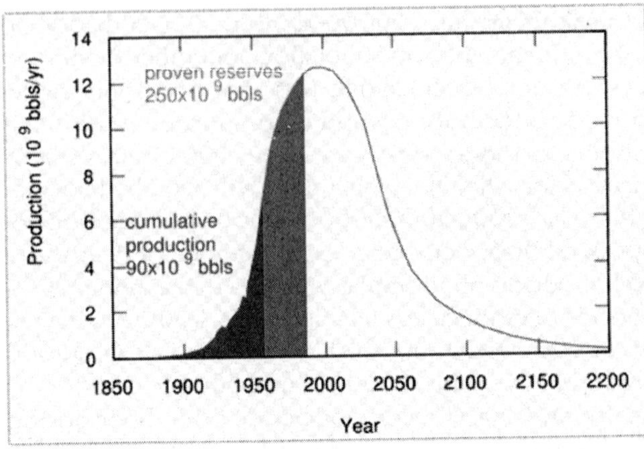

We've reached the point where we can't produce as much oil in a single day as is consumed in a single day. The other consideration is cost. There are literally billions of barrels of oil left in "alternative" structures such as oil sands or technically challenging reservoirs such as those in the North Sea. Total production from the North Sea so far is roughly 34 billion barrels. It is estimated that there are still at least 20 billion left. But the last big field to be discovered, the Buzzard, was found in June of 2001, and only started producing in June of last year i.e. 2006.

One signal is that 2005 saw a dramatic fall in announced new oil projects coming to production from 2008 onwards. Since it takes on average four to six years for a new project to start producing oil, in order to avoid the peak, these new projects would have to not only make up for the depletion of current fields, but increase total production annually to meet increasing demand. Year-2005 and 2008 also saw substantial increases in oil prices due to temporary circumstances, which then failed to be controlled by increasing production. The inability to increase production in the short term, indicating a general lack of spare capacity, and the corresponding uncontrolled price fluctuations, can be interpreted as a sign that peak oil has occurred or is presently in the process of occurring.

Historical Perspective Oil Industry in Indian Context

The history of oil exploration in India is more than 100 years old. The systematic exploration activity in India started in 1866, in the northeastern state of Assam. After the independence of India the activities of Assam Oil Company and that of Burma Oil Company operating under the aegis of Shell Oil were merged to form a semi-government and private equity partnership company known as Oil India Limited. The activities of this company were extended to the Assam plains and, as a consequence of which large accumulations, first at Naharkotiya and then at Moran, were located by systematic exploration efforts. These discoveries represent some of the best known oil and gas accumulations in the northeastern sector which continue to contribute significantly to the country's oil production till date.

With the demand for petroleum products growing, the Government of India recognized the urgency of exploring hydrocarbon resources and hence constituted

Oil and Natural Gas Commission (ONGC) in 1956. ONGC undertook systematic geoscientific surveys in most areas considered prospective on the basis of global analogies. Initially, the exploratory activities by ONGC were restricted to Himalayan foothills and adjoining Ganga plains. Later on, exploratory activities were extended to Gujarat, Upper Assam and West Bengal. The first step towards offshore exploration was taken in 1964-67, when regional seismic surveys in selected parts of western offshore were conducted. As a result, a large structure at Mumbai offshore was identified and taken up subsequently for drilling in 1974 leading to India's biggest commercial discovery. Later on, more giant discoveries like Neelam and Bassein in Western offshore and Ravva in Eastern offshore were made due to massive exploratory efforts by ONGC.

Today, we have ONGC and OIL as the two giant National Oil Companies engaged in exploration and production of crude oil and have predominant share with about 90% and 10%, respectively. These two oil companies market their products directly except natural gas which is distributed through Gas Authority of India, another public sector unit in the oil industry. The ONGC and OIL expanded their drilling activities in 1981-82 in search for oil in unexplored areas. Since then there has been massive increase in drilling activities in the offshore areas representing a rationalization of exploratory activities in line with prognostication of reserves. This is also evident from the number of wells drilled as well as the metreage drilled. However, the current reserve accretion continues to be low and this has been considered as a major area of concern (Planning Commission, 1997 and 2002). Tables 3.2, 3.3 and 3.4 provide detailed information on (i) Exploratory and Drilling performance during 1090-2003, (ii) State and Basin-wise Oil and Natural Gas Fields in India and (iii) State and Basin-wise Gross Net Production of Oil and Gas. Tables 3.5, 3.6 and 3.7 provides information on: (i) Targets in respect of major exploration, drilling and survey activities, and (ii) Targets of major downstream activities, meterage drilled, (iii) Production of Petroleum products etc.

Table 3.2: Exploratory and Development Drilling

State/Area	1990-91		1995-96		2000-01		2001-02		2002-03	
	Wells (No.)	Metreage (000)	Wells (No.)	Metreage (000)	Wells (No.)	Metreage (000)	Wells (No.)	Metreage (000)	Wells (No.)	Metreage (000)
1	2	3	4	5	6	7	8	9	10	11
(a) Exploratory										
Onshore	176	434	177	427	124	331	140	380	137	332
Offshore	73	184	27	77	30	68	15	45	20	58
Total (a)	249	618	204	504	154	399	155	425	157	390
(b) Development										
Onshore	220	455	171	384	132	316	143	300	164	378
Offshore	66	92	52	86	22	48	28	67	45	136
Total (b)	286	547	223	470	154	364	171	367	209	514
Grand Total (a+b)	535	1165	427	974	308	763	326	792	366	904

Source: Public Sector Undertakings of the National Oil Companies, Govt. of India.

Table 3.3: State and Basin-Wise Oil and Gas Fields in India as on 1.4.2005

(Number)

Company/State	Basin Fields	Oil Fields	Gas Fields	Oil & Gas Fields	Total
1	2	3	4	5	6
A. OIL & NATURAL GAS CORPN. LTD.		81	62	0	143
(a) ONSHORE					
Gujarat	Cambay	42	19	0	61
Assam	Upper Assam	16	6	0	22
Rajasthan	Jodhpur	0	1	0	1
Andhra Pradesh	K.G. Basin	6	16	0	22
Tamil Nadu	Cauvery	12	10	0	22
Tripura	AAFB	0	5	0	5
(b) Offshore					
Mumbai Offshore		5	5	0	10
B. OIL INDIA LTD.		42	8	0	50
Assam	Upper Assam	39	5	0	44
Arunachal Pradesh	Upper Assam	2	0	0	2
Rajasthan	Jaisalmer	0	3	0	3
Bikaner Nagaur		1	0	0	1
C. PRIVATE/JVCs		0	0	31	31
(a) Onshore					
Gujarat	Cambay	0	0	22	22
Arunachal Pradesh	AAFB	0	0	1	1
Assam	Assam	0	0	1	1
(b) Offshore					
East Coast	Cauvery	0	0	2	2
West Coast	KG Basin	0	0	1	1
Bombay		0	0	3	3
Cambay		0	0	1	1
Grand Total		123	70	31	224

AAFB: Assam Arakan Fold Belt.
Source: ONGC, OIL and DGH.

Table 3.4: State-wise Gross and Net Production of Natural Gas in India

(Million Cubic Metre)

State/Utilisation	1990-91	1995-96	2000-01	2001-02	2002-03	2003-04	2004-05*
1	2	3	4	5	6	7	8
A. ONSHORE							
ASSAM®							
Gross Production(GP)	2039	1926	2396	2125	2245	2416	2503
Re-injected	102	0	0	0	0	0	0
Flared	621	404	219	179	185	203	230
Net Production	1316	1522	2177	1946	2060	2213	2273
% Flared to GP	30.46	20.98	9.14	8.42	8.24	8.40	9.19
GUJARAT							
Gross Production	1696	2887	3149	3280	3531	3517	3593
Re-injected	0	0	0	0	0	0	0
Flared	402	280	436	401	323	128	49

Table Contd.

State/Utilisation	1990-91	1995-96	2000-01	2001-02	2002-03	2003-04	2004-05*
1	2	3	4	5	6	7	8
Net Production	1294	2607	2713	2879	3208	3389	3544
% Flared to GP	23.70	9.70	13.85	12.23	9.15	3.64	1.36
TAMIL NADU							
Gross Production	64	117	200	349	466	605	678
Re-injected	0	0	0	0	0	0	0
Flared	55	96	74	98	88	68	50
Net Production	9	21	126	251	378	537	628
% Flared to GP	85.94	82.05	37.00	28.08	18.88	11.24	7.37
ANDHRA PRADESH							
Gross Production	47	679	1604	1797	2038	1927	1707
Re-injected	0	0	0	0	0	0	0
Flared	5	0	23	18	18	13	10
Net Production	42	679	1581	1779	2020	1914	1697
% Flared to GP	10.64	0.00	1.43	1.00	0.88	0.67	0.59
TRIPURA							
Gross Production	70	130	376	416	446	508	496
Re-injected	0	0	0	0	0	0	0
Flared	0	0	0	0	0	0	0
Net Production	70	130	376	416	446	508	496
% Flared to GP	0.00	0.00	0.00	0.00	0.00	0.00	0.00
B. OFFSHORE							
MUMBAI HIGH							
Gross Production	14082	16581	18465	18317	18367	17805	17444
Re-injected	0	0	0	0	0	0	0
Flared	4047	613	760	878	730	570	544
Net Production	10035	15968	17705	17439'	17637	17235	16900
% Flared to GP	28.74	3.70	4.12	4.79	3.97	3.20	3.12
PRIVATE/JVCs							
Gross Production	0	322	3287	3430	4296	5184	5356
Re-injected	0	0	0	0	0	0	0
Flared	0	317	105	103	82	74	106
Net Production	0	5	3182	3327	4214	5110	5250
% Flared to GP	0.00	98.45	3.19	3.00	1.91	1.43	1.98
TOTAL (A&B)							
Gross Production	17998	22642	29477	29714	31389	31962	31777
Re-injected	102	0	0	0	0	0	0
Flared	5130	1710	1617	1617	1426	1056	989
Net Production	12766	20932	27860	28037	29963	30906	30788
% Flared to GP	28.50	7.55	5.49	5.64	4.54	3.30	3.11

*: Provisional.

@: Including Nagaland, Arunachal Pradesh and Rajasthan.

Note: Exploration activities were suspended by ONGC in Nagaland w.e.f. 5th May 1994.

Source: ONGC, OIL and DGH.

Table 3.5: Targets in Respect of Major Activities in 2003-04 (BE)

Sl. No.	Description of Activities		Targets 2003-04		
			ONGC	OIL	Total
1.	**Crude Production (MMT)**				
	i. Onshore		8.819	3.300	12.119
	ii. Offshore		17.568	-	17.568
	Total		26.387	3.300	29.687
2.	Natural Gas Production (BCM)				
	i. Onshore		6.110	1.430	7.540
	ii. Offshore		17.205	-	17.205
	Total		23.315	1.430	24.745
3.	Exploratory Drilling ('000 Metres)				
	i. Onshore		326.360	66.000	392.360
	ii. Offshore		165.500	-	165.500
	Total		491.860	66.000	557.860
4.	Development Drilling ('000 Metres)				
	i. Onshore		296.350	70.000	366.350
	ii. Offshore		135.100	-	135.100
	Total		431.450	70.000	501.450
5.	Seismic Surveys				
	i. Onshore	2D (GLK)	3.190	-	3.190
		3D (Sq. Km.)	896	-	896
	ii. Offshore	2D (GLK)	11500	-	11500
		3D (Sq. Km.)	13888	-	13888
	iii. Onshore	2D GLKm	-	500.000	500.000
	Equivalent—Sq km	-	-	-	
		3D Sq Km.	-	150.000	150.000
		2D GLKm	-	2085.000	2085.000
		3D Sq Km	-	200	200
	iv. Offshore	2D GLKm	-	-	-
		3D Sq km	-	400.000	400.00

Source: Public Sector Undertakings of the National Oil Companies, Govt. of India.

Crude Oil Reserves

The definitions of reserves are given in several reports of the international oil companies. The definitions given by Mobil Corporation are technically and practically more useful than any other ones. It provides a good framework within which industry can further evolve a set of "industry accepted practices" for the understanding of hydrocarbon assets.

Mobil's recoverable hydrocarbon volume system has three main classifications: the discovered classifications are reserves and contingent resources while the undiscovered classification is designated speculative potential. Reserves are quantities of hydrocarbons in known reservoirs that are estimated to be recoverable in future years under existing economic and operating conditions. Contingent

Number of Wells and Metreage Drilled

Area/State	Wells & Metreage Drilled									
	1990-91		1995-96		2002-03		2003-04		2004-05*	
	Wells No.	Metreage (000)	Wells No.	Metreage (000)	Wells No.	Metreage (000)	Wells No.	Metreage (000)	Wells No.	Metreage (000)
1	2	3	4	5	6	7	8	9	10	11
(a) ONSHORE										
Assam	74	252	48	172	65	246	57	201	79	260
Gujarat	253	436	232	454	178	315	156	290	139	237
Others	69	201	68	180	58	149	52	126	46	119
Total (a)	396	889	348	806	301	710	265	617	264	616
(b) OFFSHORE										
Bombay High	123	235	79	163	62	185	82	207	34	106
Others	16	41	15	3	9	7	22	35	117	
Total (b)	139	276	80	168	65	194	89	229	69	223
Grand Total (a+b)	535	1165	428	974	366	904	354	846	333	839

*: Provisional Source: Public Sector Undertakings.

Table 3.7: Production of Petroleum Products in India (in '000 MT) during 1990-2005

('000' Tonne)

Products	1990-91	1995-96	2000-01	2001-02	2002-03	2003-04	2004-05*
(a) From Crude Oil							
1. Light Distillates	10023	12433	25048	26539	28619	31971	32701
of which							
LPG	1221	1539	4088	4778	4903	5348	5569
Mogas	3552	4462	8070	9699	10361	10999	11017
Naphtha	4859	5975	9908	9180	9650	11317	14315
Others^{LD}	391	457	2982	2882	3705	4307	1800
2. Middle Distillates	26344	29941	52445	54409	55937	60018	62465
of which							
Kerosene	5471	5267	8714	9681	10028	10187	9300
ATF/RTF/JetA-1	1801	2127	2513	2595	3053	4289	5201
HSD	17185	20661	39052	39899	40207	43316	45880
LDO	1509	1351	1481	1703	2079	1659	1546
Others	378	535	685	531	570	567	538
3. Heavy Ends	12195	12707	18121	19056	19584	21474	23067
of which							
Furnace Oil	4879	5351	6479	7488	7529	8737	10519
LSHS/HHS/RFO	4550	4228	4913	4739	4638	4635	4261
Lube Oils	561	633	684	651	684	666	646
Bitumen	1603	2032	2721	2561	2941	3397	3349
Petroleum Coke	229	256	2473	2784	2659	2743	3158
Paraffin Wax	49	43	51	45	42	53	66
Others Waxes	46	63	61	37	3	Neg.	8
Others^{HE}	278	101	739	751	1088	1243	1060
Total (1+2+3)	48562	55081	95614	100004	104140	113463	118233
(b) From Natural Gas							
LPG	929	1715	2045	2205	2370	2320	2240

*: Provisional.

LD: Includes Propylene, C-3, Propane, Hexane, Special Boiling Point Spirit, Benzene, Toluene, Petroleum Hydro Carbon Solvent, Natural Heptane, Methyl Tertiary Butyl Ether, Poly Isobutine, Poly Butadine Feed Stock and Methyl Ethyl Keetone Feed Stock.

MD: Includes Mineral Turpentine Oil, JP-5, Linear Alkyl Benzene Feed Stock, Aromex, Jute Batching Oil, Solvent 1425, Low Sulphur Heavy Fuel HSD, Desulphurisation Hydrocracker Bottom and Speical Kerosene.

HE: Includes Carbon Black Feed Stock, Sulphur, Solar Oil, Light Aluminium Rolling Oil and Extracts.

Source: Public Sector Undertakings/Private Company.

resources are significant quantities of resources estimated to be recoverable but are not currently producible because of existing economic, political environmental or technical conditions. Included in this category are resources that are not producible because there are no development plans and major capital commitments are required for facilities such as offshore platforms, pipelines, or production licence.

Both reserves and contingent reserves are technically categorized as proved, probable or possible, based on the relative degree of certainty as to the presence, recovery, ability and economic viability considering all physical technical, political, economic and regulatory factors. The Mobil categories of proved, probable and possible are very similar to the recently approved joint spe/wpc definition, with a few minor exceptions. Of these, the chief difference is that currently uneconomic probable and possible volumes are categorized as contingent resources (P_5 and P_6), while they could be considered reserves (P_2 and P_3) under the SPE/WPC criteria.

Speculative potential is the quantity of hydrocarbons located in unproved traps, in undrilled provinces or deeper reservoirs underlying productive fields where geological conditions are believed to be favourable for the accumulation of hydrocarbons. Speculative potential provides estimates of the quantities which may eventually be recovered. This potential forms the basis for exploration ventures. Probability of geological success (Pg) is the probability of finding measurable hydrocarbons. It is based on the technical assessment of geologic variables, i.e., trap reservoir, source and timing of migration. A further business overlay is defined for Mobile volumes that involve future movement in addition to the current classification. These define the inventory in terms of the timing for the P_2-P_6 volumes to become proved, developed, producing hydrocarbons, i.e., to the monetized. The categories are transferable and static. The transferable volumes are sub-divided into planned and unplanned. The static volumes while they are discovered, recoverable hydrocarbons are not expected to be monetized in the next ten years.

Mobil utilizes a unique methodology for reserve and resource evaluation. The approach integrates both deterministic and probabilistic methods to evaluate and establish the full hydrocarbon potential of fields/prospects. Both methods have valid justification for utilization. When used jointly, they can provide even greater insight into the recoverable hydrocarbon volumes and the probability of recovering those volumes (Nanga, et al., 1999). In India, out of total land area of 3.2 million km, sedimentary basins account for 1.78 million km within the 200 m isobaths line, of which 1.46 million km is on onshore and the remaining is on offshore. These basins are classified into four categories:

Category I: Petroliferous basins with proven production of hydrocarbons namely, Cambay basin, Upper Assam Shelf, Mumbai Offshore basin, and the Cauvery, Krishna and Godavari basins.

Category II: Basins with known occurrences of hydrocarbons but where no commercial production on a significant scale has been started, e.g., Rajasthan, Kachch, Andamans, West Bengal, Himalyan Foothills, Ganga Valley, Tripura and Nagaland-fold belt.

Category III: Basins where significant amount of hydrocarbons have not been found. However, on general geological grounds, these basins are considered prospective, e.g., Kerala, Konkan and Mahanadi.

Category IV: Basins which are prospective on the basis of analogy with similar hydrocarbon-producing basins in the world. These include the Vindhya basin, Deccan syneclise, Narmada, Bastar and Chattisgarh.

ONGC and OIL were known as good finders. However, as they faced the challenge of exploring more difficult areas and the deep waters the technology gap has become critical. According to some experts this gap between the best globally available technology and that used by ONGC is serious and could grow larger due to the dilatory procurement methods (Das Gupta, 1997).

The accretion to recoverable hydrocarbon reserves has not been very encouraging during the Eighth Plan period. The reserves, replacement ratio (R/P) which is a measure of reserves-discovered to reserves-depleted has declined to less than unity value thereby implying that oil reserves are being depleted faster than being replenished. Against a total accretion target of about 1325 million tonnes of hydrocarbons during the Eighth Plan period, the accretion to recoverable reserves of oil and gas was 700 million tonnes. In order to intensify exploration, two major programmes have been launched in addition to the exploration programmes being implemented by National Oil Companies. Starting from September, 1991, blocks in onland and offshore areas are being offered for exploration on a continuous basis. In view of the low reserve accretion during the first two years of the Eighth Plan, an Accelerated Exploration Programmes was taken up in 1994 (Anantharaman, 1997).

The ONGC and OIL have together planned to add 865 million tonnes of oil equivalent in-place of hydrocarbon reserves during Ninth Plan. These efforts will be supplemented by addition to some reserves in the exploration blocks awarded to the private parties. An accretion of upto 200 million tonnes of oil and oil equivalent of gas (O+OEG) is envisaged in deep water areas where a breakthrough is expected in the Ninth Plan. The estimated recoverable reserves will be in the range of 245.84 to 342.72 million tonnes of oil equivalent. It may be mentioned that reserve replacement-ratio of oil and gas during the Ninth plan, was 0.813. Although a new exploration licensing policy has been announced, which offers the best terms to attract investment for exploration? The average recovery factor in India is about 28 per cent of initial oil in-place reserves. This is low by international standards. Improvement in recovery-factor would yield additional oil and gas without any corresponding additionality in the reserve-accretion. Several steps are required to be taken up for enhancing the reserve-accretion.

Strategy of 10th Plan (2002-07) for E&P Activities

During the 10th Plan, the strategy identified by the Ministry of Petroleum & Natural gas for E&P activities included:

(i) Optimization of production of crude oil and natural gas from domestic basins and existing fields especially the Mumbai High field by ONGC.
(ii) An optimal mix of intensive exploration with main thrust in producing areas and extensive exploration in other areas including frontier areas and deep waters for increasing the reserve base.
(iii) Improvement of recovery factor by the order by 3-4% in major fields.
(iv) Emphasis on quality of exploration for enhanced success.
(v) Laboratory studies and undertaking of EOR pilots in producing fields for further augmentation of recovery.
(vi) Acquisition of equity oil abroad.

(vii) Exploration of Coal Bed Methane.

The projected Petroleum Product availability during 10th plan is given in Table 3.8.

Table 3.8: Projected Petroleum Products Availability during 10th Plan

('000' Tonne)

Product	2002-03	2003-04	2004-05	2005-06	2006-07	Total
Light Distillates	34293	37057	38913	38811	38405	187479
LPG	7545	7989	8823	8749	8635	41741
MS	10478	10994	11470	11676	11580	56198
Naphtha	11878	13447	13753	13521	13333	65932
Others	4392	4627	4867	4865	4857	23608
Middle Distillates	66251	72144	78523	78976	78296	374190
ATF	3621	4367	4763	4787	4717	22255
SKO	13966	14656	15062	15110	14944	73738
HSD	47258	51921	57625	58007	57593	272404
LDO	877	701	570	570	545	3263
Others	529	499	503	502	497	2530
Heavy Ends	19567	20243	19915	19485	19265	98475
Lubes	836	900	900	882	850	4368
LSHS	4574	4206	3518	3468	3451	19217
FO	7576	7841	7128	6037	5963	34545
Bitumen	3239	3175	3112	3090	3061	15677
Others	3342	4121	5257	6008	5940	24668
Grand Total	120111	129444	137351	137272	135966	660144

Source: Draft Tenth Five Year Plan Document.

Target and Strategy for Oil Production during XIth Plan

The Ministry for Petroleum and Natural Gas, Government of India has projected a 26 per cent increase in domestic crude oil production and a 41 per cent increase in natural gas production in the XIth Plan period. Crude oil and natural gas production in the country over the last four years of the current Five Year Plan has been almost stagnant as there had been few major oil and gas discoveries by state-owned E&P companies. Some of the other reasons cited for the stagnant production include the natural decline in the ageing fields.

It is proposed to target an increase of 26 per cent in domestic production of crude oil to 211.64 million metric tonnes (MMT) over the Xth Plan achievements, which is likely to be 167.74 MMT. Similarly, the production of natural gas is projected to increase by 41 per cent in XI Plan period to 224.56 billion cubic meters (BCM) over Xth Plan estimated production of 158.79 BCM. Besides, the first Coal Bed Methane (CBM) gas production is slated to begin in 2007-08, the first year of XIth Plan. During the XIth Plan period CBM production is projected at 3.78 BCM.

The country was likely to witness gas production from another alternative source—underground Coal Specification (UCS)—towards the end of XIth the Plan. The overseas production of oil and gas during XIth Plan was projected to increase to about 45 million metric tonnes of oil equivalent (MMTOE) comprising about 35 MMT of crude oil and about 10 BCM of gas. This would be more than double of Xth Plan period production of 22.24 MMTOE (16.83 MMT of crude oil and 5.41 BCM of gas). The Ministry of Oil & Natural gas also proposes to bring 65 per cent of India's sedimentary basins under exploration by the end of XIth Plan.

Future Vision and Strategy

India's energy needs are growing with rising income levels, burgeoning population and a rapidly growing economy. Indigenous energy resources may not be sufficient in the long run to sustain a GDP growth rate of 9%. The country's energy supply system continues to be dependent on fossil fuels, which are finite. Oil and gas share in the energy consumption basket has reached a level of about 41%. Average per capita energy consumption in India is about 358 kilogram of oil equivalent (kgoe) as against 1681 kgoe world wide indicating high energy requirement in future in order to maintain the pace of economic development in the country. The total primary energy mix for India comprises Coal 51%, Crude oil 32%, Natural Gas 9%, Hydro 7% and Nuclear energy 1%. Whereas the crude oil consumption of India is about same as global average share of natural gas in primary energy mix i.e. 9% in the country is significantly lower than the world average of 24%, indicating huge potential of growth in the natural gas sector. Import dependence accounts for about 30% of our Total Primary Commercial Energy Supply (TPCES). However, oil imports constitute more than 70% of our total oil consumption.

Oil and Gas Demand Supply Scenario

Consumption of petroleum products in the financial year 2007-08 was about 129 million metric tonnes (MMT), which puts India as fifth largest consumer after USA, China, Japan and Russia. Domestic crude oil production in the country is about 34 MMT per annum. Although total imports of crude oil and petroleum products in 2007-08 were of the order of 144 MMT including 121 MMT of crude oil amounting to nearly US$ 83.2 billion (Rs.3,34,203 crore), India has also exported petroleum products amounting to 39 MMT, earning foreign exchange worth nearly US$ 26.7 billion (Rs.1,07,603 crore). After exports, our net imports amount to nearly 105 MMT of crude and petroleum products worth nearly US$ 56.473 billion (Rs.2,26,600 crore). In 2007-08, natural gas supply was of the order of 114 Million Metric Standard Cubic Metres per day (MMSCMD), out of which 88 MMSCMD was through domestic production and remaining supply of 26 MMSCMD was through import of Liquefied Natural Gas (LNG). However, gas supply position in the country is likely to improve on production of additional 40 MMSCMD of natural gas in 2008 and rising to 80 MMSCMD in 2011 (http://www.commodityonline.com/news/Augmenting-Oil—Gas-Production-11002-3-1.html).

Enhancing Oil and Gas Production

In order to increase oil and gas security for the country, Ministry of Petroleum and Natural Gas along with PSUs have adopted a multi-pronged strategy, which inter-alia, includes: increasing exploration efforts through the New Exploration

Licensing Policy (NELP). Under the Six rounds of NELP, 162 blocks have been awarded and 62 discoveries have already been made. In seventh round of NELP, 45 exploration blocks are likely to be awarded; improving the recovery factor from existing major fields by implementing Enhanced Oil Recovery (EOR)/Improved Oil Recovery (IOR) schemes. Oil and Natural Gas Corporation Limited (ONGC) has taken up 15 fields for this purpose at an estimated investment of Rs. 13,651 crore, which would also help in accelerating oil production from these fields; acquiring acreages abroad and tapping alternate sources of energy such as Coal Bed Methane.

New Exploration Licensing Policy (NELP)

The Government approved a policy called New Exploration Licensing Policy in 1999 with the objective to attract significant risk capital from Indian and Foreign companies, state of the art technologies, new geological concepts and best management practices to explore oil and gas resources in the country. 100% Foreign Direct Investment (FDI) is allowed in E&P sector under NELP regime. Companies either Indian or Foreign may bid for one or more blocks, alone or in association with other companies, through an unincorporated or incorporated venture. Licenses for exploration are being awarded only through a competitive bidding system and National Oil Companies (NOCs) are required to compete on an equal footing with Indian and foreign companies to secure Petroleum Exploration Licences (PELs). Six rounds of bids have so far been concluded under NELP, in which Production Sharing Contracts (PSC) for 162 exploration blocks have been signed. Under NELP, 62 oil and gas discoveries in 17 blocks have already been made in Cambay onland, North East Coast and Krishna-Godavari deepwater areas, for which, development plans by the operators, viz., Cairn, RIL and Niko are in progress. The NELP investment commitments are of the order of US$ 8 billions on exploration alone, out of which, about US$ 4 billons has already been made. This investment in E&P sector will increase manifolds once development of discoveries progresses. With Exploration and development efforts made under NELP, Natural Gas production in the country is likely to be doubled from the present level of gas production of about 90 million standard cubic metres per day by end of 11th Five Year Plan. Commercial production of oil and gas from two blocks from Gujarat has already commenced.

Improved Oil Recovery/Enhanced Oil Recovery Projects

Work programmes have been undertaken primarily by ONGC for IOR/EOR in its 15 largest fields, which account for 80% of ONGC's reserves and production. The challenge for ONGC is to arrest the decline of crude oil production at the rate of 7-8% per annum. To do so, ONGC has made an investment of about Rs. 13,434 crore on Improved Oil Recovery and Enhanced Oil Recovery projects. Through these efforts, incremental crude oil gain for ONGC was of the order of 40.1 MMT till 2007-08. The incremental production over the base case is expected to increase significantly from about 5 MMT in 2002-2003 to 11 MMT in 2007-2008. The total work incorporating innovative technological solutions include installations/upgradation of production facilities, laying of pipelines, drilling of about 650 new development wells, side tracking of existing wells, zone transfers, optimization of artificial lift systems etc. In addition, private sector/JV companies and Oil India Limited (OIL) are also implementing Improved Oil Recovery/ Enhanced Oil Recovery schemes in a few select reservoirs of the producing fields.

Oil and Gas from Abroad

In view of unfavourable demand—supply balance of hydrocarbons in the country, acquiring equity oil and gas assets overseas is one of the important components of enhancing energy security. The Government is encouraging national oil companies to aggressively pursue equity oil and gas opportunities overseas. Oil & gas production from overseas can be swapped, sold or brought to Indian refineries on commercial considerations. ONGC Videsh Limited (OVL) today has presence in 18 countries, viz. Russia, Sudan, Vietnam, Iran, Libya, Syria, Myanmar, Iraq, Egypt, Qatar, Cuba, Nigeria, Sao-Tome-Principe Joint Development Zone, Venezuela, Colombia, Brazil, Turkmenistan and Republic of Congo. OVL has a target to acquire 20 MMTPA of O+OEG production by 2020 but efforts are on to achieve it even earlier. OVL produced about 8.76 Million Metric Tonnes (MMT) of oil and equivalent gas during the year 2007-08 from its assets abroad in Sudan, Vietnam, Russia, Syria and Colombia. In 2007-08, OVL acquired 11 blocks and OIL-IOC acquired one block. So far, Oil PSUs altogether have presence in 22 countries.

Alternate Sources of Oil and Gas

The national endeavor to bridge the ever-increasing gap between demand and supply of petroleum products in India by intensifying exploratory efforts for oil and gas in the Indian sedimentary basins and abroad need to be supported by other alternate sources of energy like Coal Bed Methane, Gas Hydrates, Under ground Coal Gasification.

Coal-Bed Methane

Coal-Bed Methane (CBM) is a natural gas (Methane) adsorbed in coal and lignite seams and is an eco-friendly source of energy. Coal is both the source and reservoir rock for CBM. CBM production is done by simple depressurization and dewatering process. To harness this new source of energy in the country, the Government approved a comprehensive CBM policy in July, 1997 for exploration and production of CBM gas.

REFERENCES

India Hydrocarbon Vision 2025 (1999).

Tenth Five Year Plan (Energy Chapter) of Planning Commission (2000).

Annual Report (2002-2003), Ministry of Petroleum & Natural Gas, New Delhi.

International Energy Outlook 2003 by Energy Information Administration of D/o Energy US.

Indian School of Petroleum (2005), Upstream Business Process, Operational Training Manual for L&T Infotech Ltd.

Website of Director General of Hydrocarbons (DGH).

Annual Report (2002-2003) ONGC, BPC, HPC, IOC.

Research Analyst Reports on Oil & Gas Sector (2003), Govt. of India, New Delhi.

Monthly Economic Report issued by D/o Economic Affairs (January 2004).

Gazette Notification issued by Govt. of India on Dismantling of APM and granting authorization for marketing of transport fuels (2002).

Anantharaman, S.C. (1997), "Oil and natural gas sector", *Yojana*, Jan. 41(1), pp. 83-85.

Business Line (1999), Vol. 6, No. 238, August 27, New Delhi.

Business Standard (1999), August 10, New Delhi, p. 5.

Chandra, Avinash (1999), "NELP terms are comparable worldwide", *Drilling and Exploration*, Vol. 08, nos. 01 & 02, Oct.–Dec.'98 – Mar '99, p. 48.

Chhabra, Vinod, (1997), "Privatizing Petroleum", In: Infrastructure development for economic growth, edited by MVS Gowda, S. Subramanya, New Delhi, Deep & Deep, p. 204.

Das Gupta, A.B. (1997), "India's petroleum reserves, recovery and evaluation", In: Proceedings/Oil and Gas Corporation Ltd., Second International and Petroleum Conference and Exhibition, Jan. 9-12, New Delhi, p.49.

Daniel Johnston (2004), International Exploration Economics: Risk & Control Analysis. Pennwell Pub.

Editorial, (1999), "Policy needs future exploration", *The Business Line*, Vol. 6, no. 238, August 27, edit page.

GAIL (2003), Natural Gas in India, GAIL Infraline, Infraline.com.

Gidadhubli, R.G. (1999), "Sengupta proposals myopic and illogical", *Fortune India*, April 30, 17 (12), p. 70.

Investment Research and Information Services (1999), "Moving towards a free market: oil and gas", *The Economic Times—Hundred*, Vol. 1, issue 2 March, p. 100.

Loomba, A.K., Paul, Rama, Chandrashekharan, P., Thomas, J. and Sahai, S. (1999), "Measuring efficiency of hydrocarbon exploration", Papers of the Third International Petroleum Conference and Exhibition, Vol. V, pp. 354-55.

Mahapatra P. Sivarama Krishnan, T.E., Rajagopalan S., Sethi, J.R. (1996), "Producing Indian Basins and their Reserve Potential", *ONGC Bulletin*, 33(1), pp. 45-46.

Moore, David (1996), "Petroleum Industry in India: present and future trends", In: Petroleum Industry Restructuring, edited by U.K. Dikshit, Anjali Hazarika, New Delhi, NPM Programme, pp. 100-103.

Nangea, A.G. and Hunt, E.J. (1999), "An integrated deterministic/probabilistic approach to reserve estimation: and update", Papers of Third International Petroleum Conference (Petrotech, 99) Vol. 5, p.176-77.

Penn Well Publishing Co., Oklahoma, USA.

Planning Commission (1997), "Ninth five year plan: Vol. 2, Energy", Government of India, New Delhi, p. 10.

——, (1997), "Report of the working group on the petroleum sector for Ninth Five Year Plan", New Delhi, Yojana Bhawan, p. 15.

Radhakrishnan, N., Ganguli, B. (1999), "Looking for Oil", *Business India*, February 8-21, p. 57.

Robert E. Megil (2004), An Introduction to Exploration Economics (3rd. Edn.), Pennwell Books, USA.

Singh, L. (1996), "Adding reserves—an approach", *ONGC Bulletin*, 33(2), pp. 15-16.

The Times of India, (1999), August 13, New Delhi, p. 4.

Treat, John Elting (1994), Creating High Performance International Petroleum Company: Dinosaurs Can Fly.

U.S. Energy Information Agency (2007), Retrieved on 2008-04-17.

Websites

(http://encarta.msn.com/encyclopedia_761586407_5/fossil_fuels.html

http://www.oilgasarticles.com/articles/7/1/Classification-of-Oil/Page1.html

http://en.wikipedia.org/wiki/Hubbert_peak_theory

http://www.business-standard.com/india/storypage.php?tp=on&autono=45046

http://www.wealthdaily.com/articles/peak+oil-production-global/374

http://www.commodityonline.com/news/Augmenting-Oil—Gas-Production-11002-3-1.html

Chapter IV

Management and Evaluation of Upstream Assets

Scope of Asset Management

The scope of Asset Management for upstream activities covers all activities performed in acquiring, exploring, developing, producing, and disposing an asset that the internal and external stakeholders of a company is involved with. Since asset plans are developed in an area-specific manner, containing a logical collection of assets, the scope the asset management plan also need to include future prospects and opportunities such as: existing oil or gas field extensions, discoveries, exploration and analysis of third party opportunities for present and future investments.

Managing profitable upstream assets requires constant evaluation of concepts, development opportunities, reserves recovery, technology costs, and infrastructure capacities. The pillars of UAM involves extensive regional data, cost management, reservoir exploitation/optimization, and production operations/optimization give you the ability to go from the evolution of concept to effective management of upstream assets (http://energy.ihs.com/NR/rdonlyres/30281EDE-04AC-4273-A5B6-560155D07EFD/0/IHSUpstreamAssetMgmt_flyer.pdf.).

The broad areas covered under Upstream Assts Management (UAM) include (http://www.inconf.ru/projects/Management/Management_2008_eng.pdf):

- Strategic planning, setting priorities, resources management;
- Managing seismic acquisition, interpretation and other geophysical services;
- Hydrodynamic simulation and geological modeling: organizing workflows and coordination;
- Field development design: technological, economic and ecological aspects;
- Field management automation: intellectual technologies for wells and fields;

- Field data management;
- Optimizing production and surface facilities;
- Planning, design and optimization of well servicing jobs;
- Service management and supervising.

Asset Management Objectives

The objectives of managing any asset are to capture most of the intrinsic as well as perceived value of an asset without compromising Company or Host Government's policies or ignoring stake holder's and environmental concerns. Asset Management objectives can be best understood by addressing the following questions:

(a) What are Asset Management Objectives?
(b) Why are they so critically important?
(c) Why must we take into account balance-up various internal and external factors in setting asset management objectives?
(d) What are the possible consequences of not setting asset management objectives?

Following text will deal with each of these questions in turn:

(a) What are Asset Management Objectives?

Asset Management objectives are a statement of company's standards, policies, financial objectives, its vision and mission, key stake holder's expectations etc. as applicable to all activities to be carried out in conjunction with developing the asset. In other words they represent demonstration and commitment to all things that a company stands for e.g.: Asset Management objectives are a statement of company's standards, policies, financial objectives, its vision and mission, key stake holder's expectations etc. as applicable to all activities to be carried out in conjunction with developing the asset.

(b) Why are they Important?

A company's track record is by far its most important selling point for acquiring additional licenses, winning against other bidders in hotly contested exploration acreages (where all else is equal between the competing companies), or becoming a sought after partner of choice by host governments and peers in the industry. In other words a strong and consistent performance record in terms of safety, environment, financial, and asset developments is a pre-requisite for sustained growth of a company. Setting Asset Management objectives and rewarding teams for accomplishing them provides an important foundation for building a strong track record by the company.

(c) Why must we Balance Internal and External Factors in Setting Objectives?

A proper understanding of the issues surrounding this question requires discussion of the following aspects:

- Cost vs. Value trade-off.

- Balancing commercial, technical, community and regulatory needs.
- Balancing internal budgets and resources.
- Aligning rewards.

Cost vs. Value trade-offs

Having set very high standards for Safety and Environment in developing Asset Management objectives, it is recognized that in order to meet them, the asset team may need to do more engineering, spend more time on design, look at more complex technologies etc. than would be the case if the lower standards were set. The implication here is that setting higher standards increases the cost of development without a proportionate increase in revenue and hence in this instance setting higher standards will be in conflict with the objective of maximizing value of the asset, although they may lead to more business opportunities for the company in future.

Balancing Commercial, Technical, Community and Regulatory Needs

Commercial road-map for an asset consists of developing a Gantt chart (i.e. A chart showing sequence of activities against a time reference) for negotiating fiscal terms, oil and gas prices, use of local infrastructure (port, power, roads etc.), putting a transportation agreement in-place for use of oil or gas pipelines in close proximity to the asset and negotiating tariff agreements etc. Similarly, technical road-map consists of developing a Gantt chart for engineering, design, procurement, fabrication, transportation, assembling, commissioning and operating facilities and pipelines, and setting of administrative offices required to produce oil and gas from the asset.

Balancing Internal Budgets and Resources

In order to carry out all the activities just described, resources are required. Given that oil and gas companies have finite resources and finite budgets there is always a balancing act going on in the company between budgets and resources.

Scanning External and Internal Environment

Defining asset objectives requires proper assessment of internal and external factors failing which a company faces a real possibility of the objectives becoming un-realistic and un-attainable.

(d) What are the Consequences of not Setting Asset Management Objectives?

Lack of setting asset management objectives and/or defining the scope of development keeps everyone involved with development and management of the asset guessing as to the Company's true intent and desires regarding the asset. It also makes it difficult to articulate company's position and maintain any consistency when sensitive issues arise in dealings with contractors, community leaders, partners and, non-governmental organizations. Absence of clear direction and well thought out plan leads to asset managers taking positions that seem right under the circumstances of the moment, in asset manager's personal experience.

As asset managers change and situations change company's position changes along with it exposing the company and putting it in a defensive posture having to continuously defend its actions and explain its policy. In short, not setting asset management objectives upfront causes not only chaos but also significant erosion in asset value.

Asset Management Processes

Clearly, asset management takes place at various stages trough a stream of activity-based processes.

Effectively and efficiently managing an Upstream Asset therefore requires:

- A broad understanding of the asset and external and internal environment.
- Making a number of decisions.
- Interaction between many people both inside and outside an organization with expertise in a variety of disciplines and most importantly.
- Integration between the disciplines.

Publicly traded oil and gas companies have for the longest time worked with an organizational structure which focused heavily on dividing the organization in major functions such as Exploration, Production, Finance, Legal, Business Development and Administration at the top of the organizational hierarchy. The next layer would break it down into disciplines within a function e.g., Production may be divided into Engineering, Construction, Maintenance, Operations, and Drilling etc.

A survey of technical literature brings out the following characteristics as being critical for companies to consistently achieve "excellence" in maximizing value from the assets and opportunities:

- A formal well recognized Asset or Opportunity Management process which is applied consistently across the company.
- Mandatory use of the Asset Management process, hereafter called "process."
- The process is business focused and addresses the complete life-cycle of an asset.
- Assets or opportunities move through the process in a series of controlled steps. Control is assured by the need to meet defined objectives and by detailed scrutiny of recommendations and forward proposals at each step.
- Structured decision making by introducing formal decision review "checkpoints or gates" at the end of each step in the process.
- Discussing and agreeing clear performance targets with the asset/ opportunity leader.
- Benchmarking performance against peers.

Preparation of Asset Management Plans

An asset management plan, inter alia, provides:

- Details of the asset.

- Documents assumptions and uncertainties.
- ummarizes growth and development plans for the asset.
- Provides prior results in terms of exploration and appraisal.
- Provides reserves, production forecasts, budgets, cash flow, ATOI, and Capex and Opex forecasts along with a timeline of key decisions.
- An overview of opportunities.
- Benchmarking data to facilitate comparison with similar assets in the company and in the industry.

An asset management plan is a living document which is updated frequently to reflect the impact of internal decisions, changes in asset performance, and the impact of external factors. A business plan for a company is often consolidation of its asset plans. Frequently, asset plans are developed for an area in which several assets are located thus facilitating a broader strategic look and improving effectiveness of resource allocation.

Factors Affecting Asset Value

Asset Value is influenced by several factors that are broadly categorized in two parts: External Factors and Internal Factors. External factors cover host governments, partners, stake holders and macro-economic factors. Internal factors on the other hand cover such things as: company policy, external commitments, resources, roles and responsibilities, rewards and recognition program, budgeting process used inside the company, budget constraints and the decision making process used by the company. A thorough understanding of these factors leads to setting realistic expectations about the asset value, development of asset objectives, and development of work plans that are likely to be aligned with company's internal guidelines and constraints while satisfying host governments, partners, and other stake holders' expectations.

Asset Life-Cycle

A typical oil and gas company grows its business through exploration which consists of the following steps: acquiring an exploration license, identifying exploration leads, developing prospects, drilling an exploration well, appraising the hydrocarbons discovered, developing the discovery and putting it on production, operating the field until it reaches economic limit and then abandoning it. In this context, life cycle is defined as the time period between acquisition of the abandonment of the field which can range anywhere from 15 to 20 years liscence to at the low end, to 50+ years at the high end.

Key Decisions

Using the above example, the following table summarizes Phases, Objectives, and Decisions during the life-cycle of an asset (Table 4.1)

Table 4.1: Importance of Phases, Objectives and Decisions in Asset Life-cycle

Phase	Objectives	Decisions
Acquisition	Determine exploration prospectively, Acquisition cost, potential value & assess if the opportunity is aligned with business objectives	*Acquire the license?*
Exploration	Identify leads, develop prospects, select a prospect with the best potential for discovery	*Drill an Exploration Well?*
Appraisal	Evaluate the discovery, identify key uncertainties & establish need for appraisal	*Drill an Appraisal Well?*
Definition	Identify alternative concepts for developing the discovery and if it should be developed	*Sanction* a *project?*
Approval	Select a development concept & Prepare detailed cost estimates & economics to recommend approval of development	*Approve development?*
Execution	Develop the discovery, commission the facilities & put it on production	*Operate?*
Production	Produce the field, maximize revenue and reserves at minimum cost with minimal Downtime. Identify opportunities to increase value	*Pursue?*
Abandonment	Assess if there are any opportunities to add value or extend the economic limit. Prepare abandonment plans and budget	further *Abandon?*

Decision Check Points and Decision Criteria

Each of the decisions shown in the previous diagram is considered a decision gate or check point at which the following review takes place:

- A review of the work done leading up to that decision;
- Approval of the key deliverables;
- Assessment of the plans for the next phase Funding and resource approval for the next phase; and
- Each key decision is then made based on the following factors/criteria:

(a) Strategic Fit

- Does the opportunity meets the goals of the current business strategy?
- Is it the best opportunity for the funds required?
- Are the risks and uncertainties known and can they be managed?

(b) Economic Fit

- Does the opportunity meet minimum economic hurdles?
- Is it the best opportunity for the funds required?

(c) Work Quality

- Has an adequate level of work been done to support the proposed recommendation?
- Was it reviewed by the peers and subject matter experts?
- Have the issues raised in the peer review been adequately addressed?

(d) Technology

- Is the required technology available to ensure success of the project?

(e) Reality Check

- Are the costs, schedule, operability forecasts realistic as compared to similar developments in the region or for comparable analogues?

(f) Financial Considerations

- What is the NPV, IRR, PI, NCF, and capital requirements for the project?

(g) Risks

- What is the technical risks (Chance of finding commercial hydrocarbons, uncertainties related to production profiles, operating costs, capital expenditures and downtime)?
- What are the commercial risks (uncertainties in product prices, exchange rates, inflation assumptions, tariff revenues, ownership equity, and fiscal regime)?
- What are the schedule risks (time to first commitment and first production)?

Key Tools used in Asset Management

Four major tools are generally used to improve the efficiency and effectiveness of managing assets. These tools are: Front End Loading (FEL) and Value Improving Practices (VIP's) are used to enhance the value of the asset. Decision and Risk Analysis (D&RA) is used to increase decision effectiveness and Decision mapping is used for multiple purposes, such as, gaining alignment between the team members, as an aid in communications with the key stake holders and to improve the work process.

The D&RA approach encourages the evaluation of creative alternatives and assesses the impact of uncertainty so that organizations have enhanced knowledge before making important decisions. Many large organizations have used D&RA successfully. Its ongoing vitality and growth result from continual enhancements to the process and increased demand by decision-makers.

D&RA is a disciplined group process for making better decisions in conditions of uncertainty. It enables a business to:

- Understand and process issues.
- Create sound decision alternatives, including those involving real options.
- Recognize key uncertainties and determine how they relate to each other and to the expected outcome.
- Develop a financial model of the problem without having to resort to esoteric mathematical approaches.
- Use insights gained to search for better hybrid solutions.

D&RA develops a dialog between decision-makers and the line and staff specialists who evaluate those decisions. This brings out the best insights of both groups and fosters an environment of shared ownership and commitment to the result (http://www.dupont.com/consulting/consulting/dra.html).

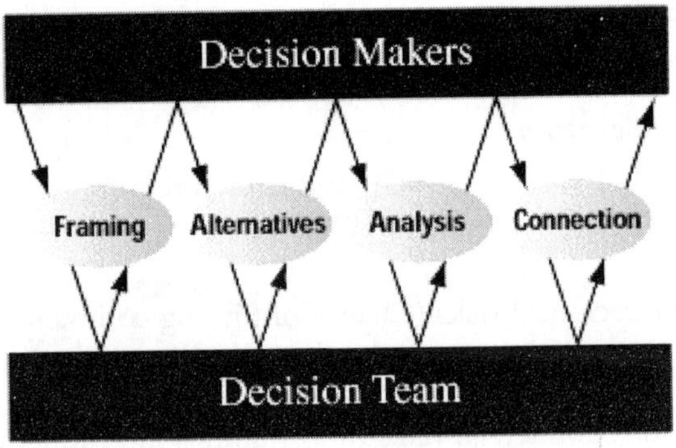

Key tools used in Asset Management start off with Front End Loading (FEL) which tries to anticipate key issues, risks and uncertainties and develops a plan to account for them before major decisions are made. FEL is further complimented with by Decision-mapping. Decision Mapping is a tool used to plan the work, develop a common understanding amongst the team members and as a communication tool with the decision makers, team, and the broader organization. Decision and Risk Analysis (D&RA) is a proven decision making and analysis approach consisting of five Steps: Problem Framing, Quantifying Risks and Uncertainties, Performing Sensitivity Analysis, Generating a Range of Outcomes, and Applying Decision Criteria. The main purpose of Value Improving Practices (VIPs) for quality asset management is to enable the identification and realization of maximum opportunity value as early as possible in the value realization process. These practices are derived from the "best-in-class" Capital Project performance companies with appropriate Benchmarking of quality performance indices.

Quality Assurance

Quality Assurance with special reference to asset management simply means how a company ensures that:

- There are no errors or omissions in the technical and commercial work, and
- All relevant aspects for building and operation of the asset were considered and included in the design and checked for performance?

Before addressing these issues, it is necessary to establish further context. This is best done by asking and addressing the following questions:

(a) How was the work accomplished between the major decisions?
(b) Who makes the decisions?
(c) Are there any conflicts between people making decisions and their authority levels?

Each company organizes things differently and therefore answers to these questions can only be provided in general terms.

Work Accomplishment between Major Decisions

Developing an asset requires use of many different skills which can be broadly classified in 6 areas, also known as functions: Exploration (includes geology and geophysics), Drilling, Engineering (includes all facets of engineering e.g. Reservoir, Infrastructure, and Production), Operations, Business Development and Administration. The extent of involvement of these functions varies as the asset moves from one phase of the life-cycle to the next. To illustrate, in the Acquisition phase major involvement is by Business Development and Exploration functions whereas in the Exploration Phase, it is Exploration, Drilling, and Engineering. Similarly, in the Development phase it is Engineering, Drilling, Exploration, Operations, and Administration and so on. In order to carry out the work an asset team is formed with core members and ad-hoc members. Core members comprise of the dominant functions required while the ad-hoc members include all the other functions whose expertise is needed on a part-time basis.

Decision-making by the Business Unit

Decisions are made by a decision board with representatives from the Business Unit, Functions and Management. The decision board provides guidance and ensures that company's value assurance guidelines have been satisfied. The decision board's role normally ends at the end of the development phase once final approval for the development has been given.

The principal objective of asset management is to achieve 'value-for-money' throughout an asset's service life. In order to provide cost-effective solutions to the various demands placed upon a facility adequate decision making tools must be available. The need for such tools is more significant when resources are limited.

The key goals for Quality Assurance during the asset life-cycle may fall under these categories (ftp://ftp.tech-env.com/pub/SERVICE_LIFE_ASSET_MANAGEMENT/QUALITY.pdf):

(i) the development of tools to assess service life and performance at any point within the service life;
(ii) the retention, via databases, of the knowledge/experience obtained;

(iii) the optimization of maintenance practices, on a life-cycle basis, in order to maximize facility service life and more effectively allocate resources; and

(iv) the on-going identification, investigation and quantification of deterioration mechanism.

With this background, Quality Assurance during the asset life-cycle is managed and monitored through formal and informal reviews. An illustration of the formal reviews and their specific purpose is detailed below in Table 4.2.

Table 4.2: Quality Assurance Criteria

Reviews	Purpose
Opportunity/Asset Initiation Review (OAIR)—Acquisition Phase	• Validate basis to pursue with the opportunity • Gain confidence in support of the milestone decision to commit resources for progressing the opportunity further
Global Prospect Ranking Review (GPRR)—Exploration Phase	"As above"
Global Appraisal Ranking Review (GPRR)—Appraisal Phase	"As Above"
Feasibility Review (FR)—Define Phase	• Confirm resolution of the uncertainties and gain confidence in support of the Field Development Plan and concept selection Gain confidence to commit resources for the next phase
Investment Decision Review (IDR)—Approve Phase	• Provide support for final Business Proposal and give confidence to stake holders that decision to proceed to project execution is sound
Pre-8tart-up Review (P8R)-Execute Phase	• To give confidence in the decision to place the Asset/facility in operation
Post Audit—Operate Phase	• Assessment of Strategic and Economic Value generated from employment of human and financial capital, document lessons learned • Document lessons learned • Make appropriate recommendation for improvements in the Asset Management Process
Health & Safety Reviews (HSR)	• To assess technical safety, operability, reliability, health and environment issues
Benchmarking Reviews	• A formal means of measuring progress and results against competitors and best-in-class companies • Leads to identification of best practices • Conducted by an outside agency
Commercial Assurance Review	• To give assurance during all phases that the opportunity/asset meets all legal and regulatory requirements and also meets commercial and business drivers
Cost Estimate Assurance	• To ensure that cost estimates are in compliance with internal guidelines and are consistently applied throughout the company

Quality Assurance Checks

The following table/format (Table 4.3) provides an overall check list of when such reviews should be done during the life-cycle phases.

Table 4.3: Quality Assurance Checks during Life-cycle

	Description	Acquire Explore	Appraise	Define	Execute Approve	Operate
1.	Project Initiation Review					
2.	Feasibility Review					
3.	Field Development Plan (Concept Selection Review)					
4.	Final Investment Decision Review					
5.	Pre Start-Up Review					
6.	Post Audit Review					
7.	Benchmarking Reviews					
8.	Health, Safety & Env. Reviews					
9.	Reserves Certification (External)					
10.	Technical Integrity Reviews					
11.	Commercial Assurance Reviews					
12.	Cost Estimate Reviews					
13.	Peer Assists/Peer Reviews					

In addition to the formal reviews there are informal Peer reviews. The Peer Review process consists of requesting the assistance of peers to review an aspect of a project and to provide documented feedback to the Asset Team as a part of the Quality Assurance process. Peer Reviews are used by all disciplines within a function to ensure discipline quality.

The success of the process depends largely on the following factors:

- Assembling peers with significant diverse experience and knowledge.
- Providing information ahead of time.
- Openness during the review.
- Commitment to follow-up on the recommendations.

Performance Measurement

Performance measures are used to track the performance of an asset, Business Units and/or regions. If designed and used properly they provide:

- Measurement against internal goals;
- Basis of comparison both internally and externally;
- A way to reveal problem areas;
- A way to track, evaluate, and develop opportunities for: cost reductions, acceleration of work schedule, and an enhancement of overall work process;
- An ability to rank options;
- A way to establish measures that can be used for compensation and rewards.

Performance measures can be broadly broken down into four major areas, activity-wise:

(a) Business Indicators (FFO, ATOI)
(b) Operating Indicators (Costs, Production Volumes, Reserves Additions)
(c) Key Performance Indictors (Funding cost/BOE, Development cost/BOE)
(d) Quality Indicators (for technical assessment).

These are four inter-dependent areas or groups of performance measurement during the life-cycle of an asset. Anyone indicator or anyone of the four groups of indicators taken in isolation can lead to bad decisions. These groups of indicators can have more or less significance when viewed from different levels i.e. Asset Management, Portfolio Management, Strategy Management, and Leadership.

Business Indicators are needed for the Company as a whole although they can also be tracked at the Business Unit or at a regional level. These may include:

- Finding Costs/BOE of proved reserves
- Reserves Replacement (as a % of production)
- Reserves Replacement costs
- Production Cost/BOE produced
- Budget Variance analysis

Performance measures for the Acquire phase may include:

- Quality Indicators (Quality of technical assessment i.e. thoroughness, risk assessment, integration with global portfolio management etc)
- Operating Indicators (Cost/sq. km. to evaluate the acquired acreage, Cost/sq. km. of bonus/commitments and value of the acreage)

Key Performance Indicators

- Acquisition Cost/BOE of proved reserves acquired (with 5 yr. rolling avg.)
- Acquisition Cost/BOE of reserves discovered
- Opportunity Value realized vs. projected

Explore Phase Measures

- Quality Indicators
- Quality of technical assessment
- Operating Indicators
  — Drilling Performance Indicators (Drilling Cost/ft.Flat time)

— Cost/sq. km of seismic program (including acquisition, processing, and interpretation)
— Safety and Environment Measures (Lost time accidents (LTAs), environmental discharges)

Key Performance Indicators

— Finding cost/BOE

Develop Phase Measures

The following Key Performance Indicators are used to develop and standardize Phase measures:

- Cost variance—actual cost vs. budgeted cost of work performed
- Schedule variance of actual work completed vs. planned
- Time variance vs. the original plan (to develop)
- Drilling Performance Indictors
- Development cost/BOE of proved/probable reserves excluding acquisition and appraisal costs
- Produce Phase Measures

Quality Indicators

- Quality of evaluations to improve production and add reserves
- Quality of evaluations and proposals for improved recovery and/or EOR projects
- Cost/Benefits of the data acquisition program
- Cost/Benefits of well workovers and stimulations

Operating Indicators

- Capital costs, operating costs, overhead costs
- Production Volumes
- Proved reserves additions
- Safety and Environmental measures

Key Performance Indicators

- Production costs/BOE produced
- Actual vs. forecasted production rate on annual basis
- Production Efficiency (Uptime analysis)

Disposal Phase Measures

- For assets produced to ultimate abandonment, all of the measures for the previous phases of the life-cycle should be updated and documented
- For major assets traded or sold, efforts should be made to use external intelligence as appropriate to determine if the asset is performing as expected
- Abandonment cost/BOE produced

- Disposal value realized vs. projected
- Comparisons of estimates of NCF, NPV, IRR, PI at the time of approval vs. at various milestones during the life-cycle
- Comparisons of original vs. current reserves estimates

In Summary, performance measures are used to modify strategy, allocate resources and otherwise mange the business and require that the following rules be observed:

- Use a balance of several measures and avoid getting focused on anyone measure.
- Set-up procedures for documenting so that the information needs for the performance measures can be simply and readily accessed as a part of post-audit process.
- Develop a rewards and recognition system that is linked to these performance measures
- Use the performance measures to continually benchmark performance against competitors.

A generic asset management process has been introduced defining various phases of the life-cycle of an asset going through Exploration and Development phases. Major decisions were defined, deliverables required for making the decisions introduced, and decision criteria and who makes these decisions in a modern exploration and Production Company was explained. The process of Quality Assurance reviews was explained in detail along with a system of maintaining technical quality through peer reviews. A system of performance measurement that begins with acquisition of the license and ends with disposal of the asset was introduced such that phase specific and full life-cycle performance of the asset can be measured, benchmarked, and used for rewarding the teams. Continuous improvement can be achieved by implementing the key learning from the post-audit process.

Portfolio Management

Portfolio Management is the process of allocating resources to a company wide portfolio of assets and opportunities in pursuit of company's objectives. It is the implementation of the selected strategy to achieve company's financial goals in the short and long term. Focusing specifically on capital allocation, there can be two objectives; (a) maximize portfolio's return, or (b) minimize portfolio risk.

In an exploration-production business, investment opportunities in different phases of the asset life-cycle have widely different risk vs. return profiles and therefore the choices made in funding opportunities have a profound influence in the expected risk and return for the total company. To illustrate, an exploration opportunity is characterized by high risk, high uncertainty but also very high return, whereas an opportunity to de-bottleneck a producing facility has very low risk and potentially high return. Similarly, a development opportunity would have low risk, medium to high uncertainty, and medium return. Invariably, companies have more opportunities than capital available and the decision they are frequently faced with is which opportunities to fund?

Portfolio optimization is often used in assisting with such decisions in which alternative portfolios are generated by combining different opportunities and calculating target risk and returns for each. Portfolio optimization is frequently used by financial institutions to manage investments. Portfolio Managers who have a goal to perform better than the market often use portfolio optimization *theory of efficient frontier* to decide a mix between different securities: CDs, common stocks, and bonds. Let us illustrate with the following example:

A company is trying to decide whether to fund drilling prospect "A" or prospect "B", or a combination of both and has following data available:

Table 4.4: Portfolio Optimization Matrix

Prospects	EMV $MM	Spread $MM	Investment $MM
A	2	+/−1	10
B	2	+/−2	10

Prospect B has a higher risk and higher reward since its expected monetary value could range from $ 4.0 MM to 0 whereas prospect A's EMV could range from $ 3.0 MM to $ 1.0 MM. Let us evaluate how the risk profile would vary if the company decided to allocate its available fund of $ 10 MM in different combinations of ownerships of prospects A and B.

Equations: EMV of portfolio = f1*VA + (1 − f1)*VB
Variance of portfolio = (f1)2 × (Sl) 2 + (1 − f1)2 × (S2)2

$$\text{Spread or Risk of the portfolio} = \frac{\text{Square root of Variance}}{\text{EMV of Portfolio}}$$

Where: S = Spread, f = Fraction of each prospect, V = EMV of the prospect

Results are shown in the following table and accompanying figure.

In this example a combination of prospect A and prospect B lowers the overall portfolio risk, for the same level of capital investment and expected monetary value.

To apply the portfolio optimization tool to the example company X will require the following steps:

(a) Rank opportunities in each of the four areas and select the best amongst them

(b) Develop alternate portfolios by combining opportunities and varying their proportions

(c) For a given level of capital expenditure evaluate portfolio risk, EMV, spread, NCF, ATOI etc. and select a portfolio or combination of portfolios that is aligned with company X's strategy and meets its short and long term financial goals.

The basic input for portfolio management and portfolio optimization comes from Asset Management Plans.

Table 4.5: Calculated Risk Profile of Portfolio with Different Proportions of Prospects A and B

Portfolio Composition (% of A in Portfolio)	Portfolio Risk
100	0.50
80	0.44
60	0.50
40	0.63
20	0.81
0	1.00

The basic input for portfolio management and portfolio optimization comes from Asset Management Plans.

Risk Profile of Portfolio

- Documents assumptions and uncertainties;
- Summarizes growth and development plans for the asset;
- Provides prior results in terms of exploration and appraisal;
- Provides reserves, production forecasts, budgets, cash flow, ATOI, and Capex and apex forecasts along with a timeline of key decisions;
- An overview of opportunities; and
- Benchmarking data to facilitate comparison with similar assets in the company and in the industry.

An asset management plan is a living document which is updated frequently to reflect the impact of internal decisions, changes in asset performance, and the impact of external factors.

Upstream Oil and Gas Companies use Portfolio Management and Portfolio Optimization methodologies to allocate finite amount of capital available each year amongst a range of assets and opportunities as a way to manage risk and increase chances of achieving their vision and business objectives.

Limitations to Portfolio Matrix and Way to Overcome

Portfolio optimization for capital investment is often too complex to allow for tractable mathematical formulations. Nonetheless, many analysts force these problems into standard forms that can utilize traditional optimization technologies such as quadratic programming. Unfortunately, such formulations omit key aspects of real world settings resulting in flawed solutions based on invalid assumptions. In this paper we focus on a flexible modeling approach that overcomes these limitations (http://www.informs-cs.org/wsc02papers/211.pdf).

Recent advances in modern finance theory and decision science are being utilized in a more systematic fashion by the upstream petroleum industry.

Corporate planning groups as well as business units in oil companies are increasingly applying techniques such as decision analysis, simulation, portfolio management, and real options analysis to improve the overall decision making and capital allocation process. An important element of improving the practice of risk management in the E&P setting is to ensure the proper integration of these analytical techniques in order to leverage their overall capabilities. The Markowitz optimization approach to portfolio analysis, for example, provides the E&P decision maker an efficient set of portfolios, based on minimizing risk subject to a particular return. However, without some guidance as to what level of risk-taking is appropriate for the E&P firm, the portfolio analysis alone does not provide managerial guidance about which of these efficient portfolios is best for the firm. There are, however, important attributes of the decision analysis paradigm that link directly to choices made by the firm regarding modern portfolio analysis. Preference analysis, an important element of a comprehensive decision analysis, provides us a mechanism for measuring and applying a corporate risk-taking policy. Knowing the firm's attitude about taking financial risk is important in terms of selecting the appropriate portfolio of activities. These linkages between decision analysis and portfolio management can improve the overall decision process, and ultimately, firm performance (http://www.sciencedirect.com/science?_ob=ArticleURL&_udi=B6VDW-4BVRTJ8-2&_user=10&_rdoc=1&_fmt=&_orig=search&_sort=d&view=c&_version=1&_urlVersion=0&_userid=10&md5=81e5ed76361d70333d3fc946326f4b8b).

Knowledge Management Perspective of Asset Management

Knowledge of the characteristics and values of oil industry assets is the key to scrutinizing an oil company balance sheet. Analysts familiar with the industry use numerous standards of comparison, known industry multiples, and rules of thumb. Outlined in the following pages are common valuation tools used in the industry for estimating value of certain related assets or business segments. The major segments of the petroleum industry are:

- oil and gas properties
- master limited partnerships (MLPs)
- refineries
- gas stations and marketing outlets
- pipelines and natural gas
- foreign operations

Role of Technology in Asset Management

Technology plays an important role in managing assets. Selecting right mix of available technological options helps in: (a) Better understanding and description of the asset, (b) Higher production rates, (c) Maximizing recovery of hydrocarbons, and (d) Minimizing Life-cycle cost. Additionally, selection of technology impacts both upfront capital investment and life—long operating cost. Since upfront capital investments have a more dramatic impact on the net present value of an asset as compared to operating costs. There is a tendency to favour technology solutions which reduce upfront capital investment regardless of the impact on life-cycle cost. This trend is changing and life cycle cost is now becoming an important consideration in selection of technology.

The key technologies used in Asset Management include: Reservoir Characterization, Reservoir Engineering, Reservoir Simulation, Accessing Surface Facilities etc. and these are used in transforming produced well fluids into marketable commodities like oil and gas. Selection of technologies in developing a hydrocarbon asset is the most important step towards controlling development cost and optimizing life-cycle cost and has a profound impact on maximizing the value of the asset. The control of life-cycle cost is best brought out in the discussion on optimizing production cost and other related services where the key message is that this consideration starts very early in the asset development life-cycle when opportunity to impact value is the highest A few other options like de-bottlenecking, commercial opportunities and operational efficiency are being introduced in the existing list of advanced technologies. The discussion on the role of technology would be incomplete without an overview of recent advances in technology and how they can assist brown field (meaning existing field) or green field (meaning new field) developments. A few critical technologies such as Time-Lapse Seismic Imaging, Horizontal Wells, Smart Well Technology, Reservoir-Surface Integration Modeling, and Knowledge Management are very important contributors to the successful development of an asset and to differentiate a company from its competitors.

Oil and Gas Properties

The most appropriate method for evaluating oil and gas properties is discounted cash flow analysis. Discounted cash-flow analysis is the workhorse of acquisition teams, bank engineers, and independent /consultants. For those who read through an annual report and try to make mental adjustments to balance sheet values, a detailed cash flow analysis is impractical. Typically, public documents do not provide sufficient information to perform detailed cash flow analysis. There are ways, however, of examining reported information to get a better understanding of oil and gas asset values.

The key factors influencing the value of producing oil and gas reserves are: product prices, capital and operating costs, production taxes, and the timing of production. Analysts have number things they look for to determine quality and value of reserves:

- book value of reserves
- SEC value of reserves
- average production rate per well
- reserves per well
- average prices
- production rates and reserve life index (RLI)

RLI is a measure commonly used to represent the longevity of reserves. It is calculated by dividing the reserves base by the current annual production rate, which the result being the number of years that the reserve base could continue to produce at its current rate. Most on average have about 8 years of reserve life left at current production rates. This means that they could sustain current production for 8 years before their reserves run out. The larger the company's (RLI) the better. If a company plans on doubling production its RLI number would be cut in half. This is why oil companies are always adding to their reserves. You can easily calculate this number yourself by finding out the company's total proven and possible reserves and than divide this number by the number of barrels produced in a year. To convert gas to boe (barrels of oil equivalent) divide gas by 7 to come up with a BOE number. In practical terms never pay more than the RLI x Cash flow. If a company had 3 years RLI left and you paid 4 times cash flow you would be considered foolish. If a company had an RLI of 8 years and were unable to add to their reserves it means that company's production and cash flow would stop in 8 years (https://www.stockhouse.com/Bullboards/MessageDetail.aspx?p=0&m=23740530&l=0&r=0&s=ODE&t=list).

Analysts will sometimes talk about *high-quality reserves.* Usually, the reference is made to fast-producing, short-life reserves with a low RLI. The value of these reserves is slightly higher on a per-barrel basis because present value discounting does not have as great an effect. The unit of value in the petroleum industry is a barrel of oil (bbl) or a thousand cubic feet of gas (MCF). When referring to acquisitions, transactions are often calibrated in terms of barrels of oil (bbls) or millions of cubic feet (MMCF) of gas purchased at some value per unit, such as $6 per barrel in the ground or $0.75 per MCF.

Target price of an oil company is equal to RLI × Cash Flow

RLI = 50,000,000 boe reserves / [oil 122,486+ gas 8147/7] = 404 years

This is what makes this company so exceptional. Most companies have only 8-15 RLI.

Cash flow (I will use the numbers from 2008 1/st quarter)

Net income ($500,461)+ depletion & amortization ($131,413) = $631,874 × 4= $2,527,496

404 years × $2,527,496 = $1,021,108,384/250,000,000 shares (full dilution)= $4.04/share.

As the production increases the RLI will begin to fall and the Cash flow will increase and eventually this 10 cent stock will be trading at several dollars per share.

Reference is often made to a *barrel* of oil *equivalent* (BOE) or *crude* oil *equivalent* (COE) used to equate gas to oil when referring to reserves in the ground. This is usually based on the heating value equivalency, in British Thermal Units (Btu) of natural gas and oil. A barrel of oil has about the same heating value as 6 MCF of gas.

Almost all $/BOE quotations are based on the Btu relationship of oil and gas. A better comparison in many situations is the relationship of price equivalency. It compares the financial value equivalent of gas to oil.

Table 4.6: Summary of U.S. Oil Well Production Statistics (OIL WELL)

		Oil WELL Average		Units
	-	-	-	-
Doily Production Rate	4	13	40	BOPD
Decline Rate	10	12	15	%
Royalty	18.75	20	25	%
Severance & Ad Valorem Taxes	4	7	10	%
Monthly Operating Costs	800	1,200	2,500	S
Well Depth		4,500		ft
Reserve-life Index	6	8	10	years
Remaining Recoverable Reserves	15	44	65	Mbbls
Total Cumulative Reserves	35	60	100	Mbbls

If oil is selling for $20.00 per barrel and gas is selling at $1.50 per MCF, the price relationship is 13:1. The reason the 6:1 thermal relationship is used so frequently is that it is a standard that does not change. In contrast, when oil and gas prices change, the price equivalency also changes.

The basic unit of production in the oil industry is a producing oil or gas well. An understanding of standards and statistics associated with oil and gas wells strengthens the analytical process. Tables 4.7 to 4.9 summarize production statistics and other information for U.S. oil and gas wells.

Table 4.7: Summary of U.S. Gas Well Production Statistics (GAS WELL)

		GAS WELL Average		Units
Daily Production Rate	100	200	400	MUD
Decline Rate	8	10	14	%
Royalty	18.75	20	25	%
Severance & Ad Valorem Taxes	3	5	8	%
Monthly Operating Costs	700	1,000	2,000	S
Well Depth		5,500		h
Reserve-life Index	B	10	12	Years
Remaining Recoverable Reserves	.3	.5	2	BU
Total Cumulative Reserves	.6	.9	5	RU

Operating Costs

Operating costs are generally broken down into three categories:

- Normal daily expenses
- Surface maintenance
- Subsurface maintenance and repair (work-over)

Nearly 95% of all oil wells in the U.S. are on some form of artificial lift to bring oil to the surface. Equipment for artificial lift requires maintenance and adds to the cost of production. The depth of a well has a large impact on operating costs because of the workover operations for downhole maintenance and repair. Wells require regular workover and maintenance. On the average, a well will require a major workover with downhole equipment and tubular (if they exist) pulled out of the hole every three years.

Table 4.8 summarizes average U.S. operating costs for oil and gas wells.

Table 4.8: (1989) Oil and Gas Well Operating Costs

Average Well Depth (*h*)	Oil Well: Primary Recovery Operations (S/Month)	Oil Well: Secondary Recovery Operations (S/Month)	Gas Well (S/Month)
2,000	900	1,810	740
4,000	1,167	2,570	1,040
8,000	1,650	3,900	1,700
12,000	2,275		2,160

Source: Energy Information, Administration costs and Indices for Domestic Oil and Gas Field Equipment and Production Operations 1987-89.

Operating costs vary substantially depending on which part of the country wells are located. Table 4.9 compares the average monthly operating costs per well for different areas around the United States.

Table 4.9: Regional Oil Well Operating Costs (1989)

Region	4,000 h Oil Well Operating Costs/ Month
California	1,465
Oklahoma	868
South Louisiana	1,410
South Texas	1,347
West Texas	890
Wyoming	1,019
Average	51,167

Source: Energy Information, Administration Costs and Indices for Domestic Oil and Gas Field Equipment and Production Operations 1987-89.

Discounted Cash-flow Analysis

Because investors prefer immediate cash returns over future cash returns, investors pay less for future cash flows—they "discount" them. The amount investors discount the future cash flows depends on the length of time until the cash is due, the amount of risk that the cash will not be tendered when due and the rate of return available from other comparably risky investments. This discounting procedure converts future income to present value usually using annual discount factors. The discount factor for each successive year declines to reflect the reduced value of revenue received in the future. The appraiser calculates the present worth of the forecast revenue stream by multiplying the projected net income (cash flow) for each year by the calculated discount factor for that year. These discount factors are derived from the discount rate (also known as the yield rate), and the process is known as discounted cash flow (DCF) analysis.

The three acceptable techniques for estimating discount rates are:

1. market surveys,
2. oil and gas sales analysis, and
3. weighted average cost of capital (WACC), also called "band of investment."

Together, these techniques provide a range of discount rates. The appraiser must estimate the risk for each oil or gas property to assign a discount rate from the discount rate range.

The DCF method is versatile and widely used to appraise income producing property. An appraiser using DCF first projects an anticipated net income for each year of the property's remaining economic life. Each annual cash flow is discounted to present value, and then all the present values are added to obtain the total market value of the real property interest being appraised.

Discount Rate Components

The discount rate used in discounted cash flow analysis has several components. These include (http://www.window.state.tx.us/taxinfo/proptax/ogman/):

The inflation rate—The annual rate of price change for a basket of consumer goods. Inflation is normally measured by the Consumer Price Index for All Urban Consumers (CPI-U), calculated by the U.S. Bureau of Labor Statistics. The inflation rate is the most basic component of a discount rate. An investor's rate of return must equal the rate of inflation just to break even in real dollar terms.

The risk-free component—A return to compensate the investor for a loss of liquidity. This component can also be defined as the risk-free rate minus the inflation rate. The risk-free rate is made up of the inflation rate plus a return to reimburse the investor for a loss of liquidity and is measured by the yield to maturity on Federal government securities with a maturity period comparable to the investment under consideration (oil or gas reserves in this case). The market perceives these securities as risk-free for all practical purposes since they are issued by the United States government.

General risk premium—A return to compensate the investor for assuming diversified company-wide risk. The weighted average cost of capital (WACC) minus the risk-free rate is the general risk premium. The WACC is measured by weighting the typical oil company debt and equity costs by the typical oil company debt and equity capital structure percentages, and then adding the weighted costs. If one were appraising companies, the WACC would be the discount rate since it reflects the market's expected yields from the stock and debt of a company. Calculation of a WACC will be explained in more detail later in this manual.

For property tax purposes, appraisers estimate the value of individual mineral reserves, not the value of oil companies. Buyers of mineral reserves usually perceive these individual reserves as riskier than the stock and debt of an entire company. Companies can spread their risk over many individual mineral reserves and often over several kinds of assets (some of which are unrelated to the oil or gas business). This asset diversification reduces the company's risk and, as a result, the WACC derived from company financial data is usually lower than an individual producing property's discount rate. However, the WACC is always higher than the risk-free rate. This increase in the rate is a general risk premium to reward investors for assuming the diversified company-wide risk.

Property-specific risk premium—A return that compensates the investor for assuming the unique risks associated with a particular mineral producing property. The discount rate minus the WACC is the property-specific risk premium. Investors demand a premium above the WACC to compensate them for this individual property risk. For certain high-risk properties, this premium can be quite high.

Evaluation of oil and gas properties in the industry is done almost exclusively with discounted cash flow (DCF) analysis. Many rules of thumb are used for quick estimates of value by those who make production acquisitions or production loans, but the bottom line is invariably determined with DCF analysis. Table 4.10 outlines the types of costs, expenses, deductions, and taxes associated with U.S. oil production. The example starts with a wellhead price of $20 per barrel.

Table 4.10: United States Production Cost and Fiscal Structure

Terminology	$/bbl	Royalties, Costs, and Taxes
Wellhead Price	$20.00	
	–3.75	18.7 5% (three-sixteenths) Royalty
Net Revenue	16.25	
	– 1.63	10% Severance, Ad Valorem and Production Taxes
	– 4.15	Operating Costs
	– 1.45	General and Administrative Costs
8efore-tax Cash-Flow	9.02*	
	– 5.15	Depreciation, Depletion and Amortization
8efore-tax Net Income	3.87	
	– .31	8% State Income Tax
	3.56	
	–1.21	34% Federal Income Tax
After-tax Net Income	$2.35	
	+ 5.15	Depreciation, Depletion and Amortization
After-tax Cash-Flow	$7.50	

'Most discounted cash flow analyses are performed at this (before-tax) stage.

The DCF method unfortunately is not practical for most people who are trying to evaluate a company's annual report or 10-K.

Adjusted Sec Value of Reserves

In accordance with provisions of the Statement of Financial Accounting Standards No. 69, oil companies report the standardized measure of discounted net cash flows for oil and gas reserves. This is often referred to as the SEC value of reserves. The information is compiled and reported in the following manner (http://www.fasb.org/st/):

- Statements of Financial Accounting Standards
- Statements of Financial Accounting Concepts
- FASB Interpretations
- FASB Staff Positions
- FASB Technical Bulletins
- EITF Abstracts

Many analysts will simply substitute the SEC value of reserves for the book value of oil and gas properties on the balance sheet to arrive at an adjusted balance sheet appraisal. This approach is a place to start, but there are a few things to consider when using SEC values. The 10-Kreport will disclose the average price received for oil or gas sold during the fiscal year. However, the SEC value of reserves found at the back of the 10-K uses year-end prices for oil and gas valuation. These year-end prices are held constant and not escalated unless actual contract terms have escalation factors built in. The SEC value of reserves is the closest many analysts will get to a discounted cash flow analysis of the oil and gas assets of an oil company. However, there are a number of things to look for:

- What were the average product prices during the year?
- What were the year-end product prices used in the SEC valuation?
- How do the year-end prices compare to projected prices?
- What value per barrel does the SEC estimate represent?
- What value per daily barrel does the SEC estimate represent?

After reviewing the SEC values, many analysts will venture an educated guess at an adjusted SEC value. This is usually done when prices used in the SEC calculation are considered to be substantially different than forecast prices.

Cash-Flow Multiple

When the information is available, a multiple of cash flow provides a rough estimate of the value of producing properties. The market for oil and gas production in the United States typically will pay from three to six times (annual) cash flow for a mature portfolio of oil or gas production. This corresponds to payouts of from four to seven years. Payout typically will be greater than the cash flow multiple for a production acquisition because production and cash flow are characterized by a decline rate.

Valuation of Undeveloped Reserves

Undeveloped reserves often represent a considerable asset, yet they can be difficult to evaluate. Fortunately, undeveloped reserves are included in the SEC value of reserves in the 10-K. The most difficult aspect for analysts is that the required capital costs to develop these reserves are unknown. Usually analysts will simply attribute to undeveloped reserves one half the values per unit given to prove developed producing reserves. For example, if a company's developed reserves based on prices, quality, and timing, is appraised at $6.50 per barrel, and then undeveloped reserves will be appraised at $3.25. This approach is very common. It is usually about all that can be done with the information available.

Acreage Valuation

Exploration acreage is an important component of a company's asset portfolio. It is a common practice for analysts to estimate value of developed and undeveloped reserves and also to attribute value to acreage even though, indirectly, some value has already been given. Ordinarily, in a mature, well-balanced portfolio of oil and gas assets, the acreage component will represent 15% of the portfolio value. It can be higher. There are always exceptions, but this is the place to start. A reasonable range would be 10-20% of the overall portfolio value. An analyst should be cautious when attributing a greater share of value to this element of the corporate asset base. Acreage values are based on:

- acreage position (size) and continuity
- location
- geological conditions
- expiration date for leases
- regional drilling success ratios
- potential size of discovery (if successful)
- costs of drilling/exploration in the area

Master Limited Partnerships

Master limited partnership (MLP) is a limited partnership that is publicly traded on a securities exchange. It combines the tax benefits of a limited partnership with the liquidity of publicly traded securities. Master Limited Partnerships are limited by US Code to only apply to enterprises that engage in certain businesses, mostly pertaining to the use of natural resources, such as petroleum and natural gas extraction and transportation. Some real estate enterprises may also qualify as MLPs. Some private equity management companies such as Blackstone Group (NYSE: BX) and Fortress Investment Group (NYSE: FIG) are structured as MLPs. In practice, MLPs pay their investors through quarterly required distributions (QRD), the amount of which is stated in the contract between the limited partners (the investors) and the general partner (the managers). Failure to pay the QRD may constitute an event of default. Because of such stringent provisions on MLPs, and the nature of the QRD, the vast majority of MLPs are pipeline businesses, which earn very stable income from the transport of oil, gasoline or natural gas (http://en.wikipedia.org/wiki/Master_limited_partnership).

The forerunner of the Master Limited Partnership (MLP) was the royalty trust. Royalty trusts provided unit holders an opportunity to own a direct working interest in oil and gas production. By doing this, one layer of income tax was avoided. This was the principal advantage of the royalty trust. The royalty trust was first used when the Tidelands Royalty Trust B was formed in 1954. This trust was established by Gulf Oil Corporation to provide for the administration and liquidation of rights to interests in 60 offshore tracts in the Gulf of Mexico. The trusts distributed royalties to unit holders who then paid income tax after adjusting for the depletion allowance credit. The royalty trust concept did not catch on immediately. It surfaced again after 14 years when the North European Oil Royalty Trust was created in 1975. This was the result of the liquidation of the North European Oil Company. This trust held overriding royalty interests in oil and gas producing properties in the Federal Republic of Germany. The measure of success of an MLP was based on its perceived ability to maintain distributions. The MLP concept provided a good example of the liquidation value of an oil and gas company. The average MLP distributed 75% of cash flow to unit holders. Some distributed virtually all cash flow, usually in quarterly dividends.

Valuation

Valuation of an MLP focuses on the reserve base and cash generating capability. The ability of the entity to maintain distributions to unit holders is the bottom line. Most MLPs are characterized by high yields, but also by the fact that they are slowly liquidating their reserve base. Reinvestment for exploration and development drilling is low by comparison to an independent oil company. The primary objective with analysis of an MLP, therefore, is to evaluate the value of the reserves. The methods for estimating reserve values are the same for an MLP as for an oil company.

Financial Analysis and Evaluation of Refineries

There are a number of ways to approach the evaluation of a refinery. The first step is to assess the book value of the refinery or the refining segment.

Book Value and Book Value Multiple

Book value of the refining segment of an oil company is often provided on the balance sheet or in supplemental information. While oil and gas assets bear little relationship to book value, this is not true of refining and storage facilities. The book value represents actual construction costs or purchase price less

DD&A

Refineries are sometimes appraised on the basis of a multiple of book value. An appraisal based on 1.25 times book value might not be unreasonable in an up-market. In a down-market, the refmery may sell for as low as 75% of book value. Regardless of book value, during the early 1980s small refineries were often worthless. Some even had negative value when mothballing or abandonment costs were considered.

Cash-Flow and Operating Profit Multiples

Typically, refining and marketing operations are part of an integrated company, and information is limited to whatever is disclosed in the segment data of the annual report or 10-K. fortunately, segment information usually provides earnings and DD&A attributable to each segment. This at least gives a general indication of cash flow for each segment. Refining and marketing segments are often appraised at from four to six times operating income, or five to seven times cash flow. While many analysts will report an appraisal based on one of these multiples, they usually are sure to check that the appraisal fits other techniques of valuation.

Comparable Sales

Comparable sales of refineries can be difficult to find because there is not an active market for them. Refineries are not bought and sold every day. Perhaps 7 to 10 refineries may change hands each year, yet during the early 1980s, many more simply closed down. Analysts and the press like to compare refinery sales on the basis of dollars paid per *B/SD* capacity. For example, if a 100,000 *B/SD* refinery sells for $400 million, the next step is to point out that it sold for $4,000 per daily barrel. This approach is convenient for a quick approximation of value. It focuses on the basic unit of production for a refinery, the distillation capacity. Analysis can go deeper with an estimate of the complexity of the processing operations. This adds an important dimension to the evaluation of a refinery. The most common index for comparing refineries and quantifying refinery complexity is the Nelson Complexity Index. Unfortunately, the complexity index of a refinery is seldom published. Many refinery employees do not even know what the complexity of their particular refinery is.

Nelson Complexity Indices

The Nelson Complexity Index (http://en.wikipedia.org/wiki/Nelson_complexity_index) for refinery construction costs is a relative measure of how many upgrading units the refinery has. The index was developed by Wilbur L. Nelson in the 1960s to quantify the relative cost of components that make up a refinery. The Nelson index compares the costs of various upgrading units, such as a catalytic cracker or a reformer, to the cost of a crude distillation unit. After the raw crude is processed in the distillation unit (or units), the components are then processed in the various upgrading and other processing units. The rated capacity of a refinery refers to the crude distillation unit capacity. Beyond that, there are numerous components that can be added. The computation of the Nelson Index is an attempt to quantify the relative cost of a refinery based on the cost of all the various upgrading units.

Nelson assigned a factor of 1 to the distillation unit. All other units are rated in terms of their cost relative to this unit. For example, assume crude distillation unit costs $200 per B/SD to construct. That is, a 50,000 B/SD unit would cost $1 million ($2001BISD X 50,000 B/SD). If another component costs $600 per B/SD to build, it would have a complexity factor of 3. Each unit has a complexity factor related to the construction cost as it compares to the cost of the distillation unit. Calculation of the complexity rating of a refinery is done by multiplying the complexity factor for a given unit by the percentage of crude oil it processes.

Duplication and Economies of Scale

Nelson was careful to point out that the cost of a 50,000 B/SD refinery with a complexity of 12 would not necessarily be the same as that of a 100,000 B/SD refinery with an index of 6. Many other factors are involved. The information normally available does not indicate the number of units used to accomplish a particular process. Small units have relatively higher per-unit construction costs. Nelson estimated that a duplication of units such as two 40,000 B/SD units, instead of one 80,000 B/SD unit, would increase the construction costs by a factor of 25%. Four units instead of one would increase costs by a factor of 60%.

The amount of duplication for larger 300,000 B/SD refineries reported by Nelson averaged 2.7 units, rather than one for each process. The industry average is 1.5 units for each process instead of one unit.

A typical refinery from each of three major refining regions is summarized in Table 4.11.

Table 4.11: Refinery Comparison

	Mid-continent	**Gulf Coast**	**West Coast**
Capacity (8/50)	45,000	200,000	120,000
Nelson			
Complexity Index	7.5 low Conversion	10.0 Medium Conversion	12.5 High Conversion

Tankers

Tankers haul crude oil or petroleum products in bulk. Their size is measured in deadweight tons (DWT). This is the total tonnage (in long tons) of cargo, fuel, water, and stores the ship can carry. Over the years, the size of tankers has grown with demand. Until the 1950s, the T-2 with 16,500 DWT capacities was standard. By the mid-1980s, Very Large Crude Carriers (VLCCs), with over 175,000 DWT, and Ultra Large Crude Carriers (ULCCs), with 300,000 tons, were used. (One long ton equals approximately 7.5 barrels). Transportation costs for crude oil from the Persian! Arabian Gulf to the United States (Houston) on a VLCC is approximately $1.25 per barrel. The average tonnage for a fleet will range from 70,000 to 150,000 DWT per ship. Exxon's fleet of 66 vessels had a combined capacity of 4.8 million DWT in 1989-72,000 DWT average. Amerada Hess has 22 vessels with a combined tonnage of 3 million DWT. The average vessel size in the Amerada fleet is 140,000 DWT.

Pipelines and Natural Gas

Gas transmission usually begins with the collection or gathering of gas at the wellhead from the original producer, but occasionally from other gas transmission companies. The transmission companies deliver the gas to someone other than the ultimate user, the utilities or local distribution companies (LDCs). The transmission operation could be equated to wholesaling rather than retailing. Gas distribution companies include the gas utilities. These companies sell gas at the retail level to residential, commercial, and industrial users. Typically, gas distribution companies are heavily regulated by local and state bodies. Gas utilities are subject to control by agencies in the states in which they operate. Like other regulated utilities, gas distribution company regulation is generally based on the price of gas or services charged to customers. Many gathering systems that transport gas from the wellhead to transmission facilities are not regulated.

Liquids pipelines are different from gas pipelines in that, since early 1981, the price of crude oil and refined products has been free of government control. Liquids pipelines can be divided into two types: crude oil lines and product lines. Mechanically, the operation of these two types of pipelines is similar. The differences between the two and the factor that limits switching from one to the other are the connections to source of supply and the market. There were approximately 230 companies involved in the interstate pipeline industry in 1990. These companies commonly have more than one type of pipeline. Gas transmission companies often have sister companies that are distribution companies. Companies involved in liquids transportation by pipeline commonly have both crude oil and refined products lines.

Rate Determination

Regulatory commissions protect consumers and utility shareholders by setting rates on tariffs or consumer prices that allow a fair rate of return for the utility. The applicable rule is usually stated as follows:

The public utility, under efficient and economic management, is to be permitted the opportunity to recover revenues sufficient: (a) to cover proper operating expenses, depreciation expense, and taxes and (b) to provide a return on investment adequate to compensate existing investors and attract new capital.

Regulations vary significantly from one state to another, but the basic elements are the same whether or not the entity is under FERC or state control. The steps in establishing utility rates are outlined as follows:

1. **Determination of revenue requirement**
    - Determine cost of service
    - Determine rate base
    - Calculate the cost of capital
2. **Determination of test year**
    - Normalization of test year
3. **Develop rate design**

Revenue Requirement

The basic equation used for regulating utilities is known as the *revenue requirement* formula:

Public Utility Revenue Requirement Formula:

$$RR = E + d + T + (V - D)\, r$$

Where:

RR = revenue requirement
E = operating expenses and cost of gas
d = depreciation expense
T = taxes
V = gross value of investments used in serving the public
D = accumulated depreciation r = allowed rate of return on net investment
$(V - D)$ = rate *base* also known as net investment
$(V - D)\,r$ = earning allowed on the rate base *(cost* of *capital)*

Cost of Service

The revenue requirement, also referred to as the *cost* of *service,* includes raw materials, operating expenses, and the cost of transmission and distribution. The cost of gas represents nearly 80% of the operating expense for most gas distribution companies. Increases in the cost of purchased gas are usually passed directly on to consumers, although regulatory bodies monitor prices paid to ensure that consumers are not paying an unfair price for gas. The other major expense that is included in the cost of service is depreciation.

Rate Base

The net investment, or the capital employed for a utility, is referred to as the rate *base.* The rate base consists of direct plant and equipment as well as working capital. Sometimes assets are excluded from the rate-base determination. Regulatory bodies may elect to omit certain investments or excess working capital from the rate base. The essential concept in the utility industry is the *used* and *useful* concept. Assets employed by a utility may not be included in the rate determination as a part of the rate base unless they are both used and useful. The rate base for a company may be less than the actual net investments, but will seldom be greater. Furthermore, utilities are often unable to obtain timely rate increases. Because of this, companies will often earn less than the authorized rate of return. Regulatory bodies will typically allow a return on equity from 12.5-15.5%. The average is close to 14%.

The capitalization structure (percentages of debt and equity) of the company is used to determine cost of capital. If regulatory bodies consider that the cost of capital is abnormally high because of too much equity financing, the regulators may use a theoretical capital structure for the company. For example, if a utility has only 20% debt, the cost of capital would likely be higher than a utility with industry average debt of around 50%. Therefore, the regulatory body may use the industry average debt percentage for determining the rate of return for the utility. This is why some pipeline industry executives talk about being penalized for being underleveraged.

Deferred Taxes and the Cost of Capital

The components that comprise the corporate capitalization structure, as it is normally explained, consist of debt and equity. The structure could be subdivided to include debt, preferred stock, equity, and deferred taxes. Deferred taxes effectively represent an interest-free loan from the government. Regulatory bodies usually require utilities to treat deferred taxes as a zero-cost source of capital in determination of cost of capital, or determination of rate of return on rate base.

Test Year

The test year is used to determine basic elements of the revenue requirement. A test year is also used for determining the number of units of sales volume over which to distribute the revenue requirement. The test period may be modified or normalized to adjust for unusual situations. For example, suppose that sales during the test year were 90 BCF of gas, but that the test period included a relatively mild winter. The forecast sales volumes for the rate period during which the rates would be applied would most likely be consistent with a normal winter. Therefore, the test year might be normalized to what might be expected for more typical weather.

Rate Design

Once the revenue requirement is determined, it is distributed among the customer classes on the basis of a particular rate design. Rate design focuses on what rate to charge each class of customer. Typical rate designs charge less for each unit as usage increases. High volume industrial users will typically pay less for each thousand cubic feet (MCF) of gas purchased. A simplified example is used here with only one class of customer. Assume that a regulatory commission and a company have agreed on a revenue requirement of $400 million per year. Assume further that, based on the normalized test year; expected sales are 95 BCF in the next rate period. A revenue requirement of $400 million divided by the 95 BCF of gas expected to be sold per year (95 million MCF) yields a rate of $4.21 per MCF.

Book Value Multiples

Gas transmission and utility companies that have been acquired give some indication of the perception of company acquisition value in the market. While the upstream oil industry may seldom make a comparison of acquisition price to book value, it is commonplace in the gas utility industry. This is because regulatory bodies will seldom allow a change in rate base due to a change in ownership. Rates are based on original cost. Any premium over book value will be ignored by regulatory agencies, and this will dilute the rate of return an investor could expect to earn. Nevertheless, utilities are of ten, appraised and acquired on the basis of a multiple of book value. A common trading range for gas pipeline stocks is 1.5-2.0 times book value and acquisitions of gas transmission companies have been taking place at around 2-2.2 times the book value.

Cash-Flow Multiples

A traditional valuation multiple for pipeline company appraisal is five times cash flow. Pipeline company acquisitions generally range from five to six times cash-flow.

Foreign Operations

Foreign operations are difficult to evaluate from the vantage point of a 10-K report. Usually, there is little information to aid in the analysis of the foreign segments of a company. Segment information will most often allow only a few clues, such as cash flow (net income + DD&A only), reserves, and SEC value of reserves. Every country has different geology, costs, laws, and fiscal regimes. Generalizations are impossible to make.

Country Risk Factor

There are many elements of risk in doing business overseas. The concept is usually termed *country risk*. The first thing that comes to mind with foreign operations is the specter of nationalization or expropriation of assets. This is a valid concern, but not quite the risk it once was. Countries pay a severe penalty for expropriating the assets of a foreign company. There are other risks associated with foreign operations that are more likely to occur. Analysis of the oil industry and the politics of a country can give some indication of stability. Some basic considerations are outlined as follows:

1. How stable is the government?
2. What type of government does the country have?
3. Are the citizens rioting?
4. What kind of neighbors does the country have?
5. Is the country at war or contemplating war?
6. How much of the country is in rebel-held territory?
7. How old is the leader?
8. Is the country a net importer of crude oil?
9. What is the oil potential of the country?
10. What does the average well produce?
11. How good are communications and transportation facilities?
12. What is the rate of inflation?
13. What is per capita income in the country?
14. What are the fiscal (tax law) conditions in the country?

Valuation of Foreign Oil and Gas Reserves

Evaluating the reserves or other assets a company has in a foreign country can be difficult. The fiscal conditions of every country and every province are different. Often each company will have an individually negotiated contract with a host government. The SEC value of reserves quoted in the 10-K is the best source of information about foreign oil and gas reserves. Foreign operations are always segregated. The 10-K SEC value of reserves on a per-unit basis in foreign operations can be compared to the SEC value of the U.S. reserves. Adjustments to the SEC values are somewhat similar. If the SEC value of reserves in the 10-K report is based on an obsolete oil price, the analyst can make some mental adjustments. If the SEC value of reserves is based, for example, on $12 per barrel oil in the 10-K and oil prices have changed since the reporting date to $18 per barrel, an upward adjustment will often be in order.

Foreign Exchange Laws

Foreign exchange laws control the amount of funds that can be expatriated or repatriated, or the amount of local currency that can be converted into an outside currency. Repatriation restrictions are usually imposed to control the level of foreign currency in the host country. For this reason, liquid assets in a foreign subsidiary may be worth less than book value. Fluctuating exchange rates also add risk to foreign operations.

Optimization of Upstream Technologies for Upgrading and Implementation

With decreasing profit margins due to more onerous fiscal terms, higher exploration and development costs, and smaller discovery sizes on average—the oil and gas industry has had to look at technology as a way to improve profitability. As the industry goes into deeper waters to search for oil and gas it is encountering yet another technological challenge—the challenge of drilling wells and developing fields in hostile deep water environments. As a result, lot of new technologies is coming to the forefront. The subject of this section is to take a look at which of these technologies can be easily applied in currently producing oil and gas fields for upgrading the underlying value of the field. After a careful review of the literature, following technologies have been selected for discussion:

- Time-lapse seismic imaging
- Horizontal wells
- Smart well technology
- Reservoir-Surface integration modeling
- Knowledge Management

Each technology will be briefly described along with its potential benefits in the following paragraphs:

1. *Time-lapse Seismic Imaging:* This technology is also sometimes referred to as 4-D technology and its main objective is to optimize reservoir management. Heretofore 3-D seismic surveys have been used in conjunction with geologic models, well data, and field production data, to form a three dimensional picture of the reservoir. Time-Lapse seismic imaging or 4-D technology is the name given to repeatedly shooting 3-D seismic surveys in the field at different time intervals after significant volume of hydrocarbons have been produced in an attempt to detect the movement of oil, gas, and water through the reservoir. Such an analysis helps to determine the connectivity of the reservoir and answer questions like: Are the hydrocarbons being produced uniformly throughout the reservoir? Or, Are there pockets of oil and gas being left behind in the reservoir? The information obtained from the survey can help in static and dynamic modeling of the reservoir and help in predicting future reservoir behavior. It helps the interpreter to determine whether the actual reservoir is behaving as expected based on the reservoir model, and how the model should be changed for future predictions. The 4-D also helps in locating

bypassed reserves and remaining oil and aids in determining optimum placement of infill or injection wells. It provides early identification of the drive mechanism as well as its effectiveness and helps to determine corrective action when fluid flow, compartmentalization or the recovery mechanism differs from the reservoir model.

4-D surveys begin to make economic sense when the cost of the survey is less than the cost of a well. There is no set schedule for repeating 3-D surveys. A minimum requirement is that the difference in the signal between the new and the original seismic survey is large enough to be distinguishable from the background noise.

In either case, 4-D seismic should be timed before major decisions are made regarding the reservoir, decisions that include placing wells, or planning a water flood project, for example. Shell conducts a business and technical feasibility study for each 4-D application. Synthetic seismic is generated for the reservoir model depicting different scenarios, in order to examine how things may have changed subsurface and how the signal might look depending on the changes. Cost savings come from not drilling wells. The large benefits come from knowing where to place wells for better reservoir recovery. In one example, Shell had already decided where to place an infill well in its North Sea Draugen Field. A 4-D survey was run across the field and showed a different picture than what the company was assuming. The result of the 4-D survey enabled Shell to decide not to drill the infill well to the west of the platform but instead to the north, where the well would not draw water out as quickly. The net result of this action was increased oil production and a value addition of $ 84 MM.

2. ***Horizontal Wells:*** Exploration wells, Appraisal wells and Development wells are generally drilled vertically through the reservoir. Where reservoirs have large pay thickness—vertical wells provide an effective conduit for draining the hydrocarbons. However, in thin reservoirs or where there is a large gas cap overlying the oil pay or a water aquifer underlying it, vertical wells represent an ineffective drainage mechanism since the production rates have to be severely curtailed to avoid "gas or water coning" in the well bore. For these situations and others horizontal well technology provides an effective mechanism to drain the hydrocarbon reserves by reducing the number of wells and increasing displacement efficiency and hence reserves recovery.

   Advances in drilling technology have now made it possible to place wells horizontally in the reservoir and open large section of the reservoir to hydrocarbon flow. The net result is much higher production rates from the well and more effective drainage of oil to the well from an advancing gas cap or an advancing water front from the underlying aquifer.

   Horizontal wells can be drilled into pockets of remaining oil in an existing field, as development wells or infill wells.

3. ***Smart Well Technology:*** In most oil and gas fields critical information about the reservoir such as reservoir pressure, temperature, completion

efficiency, fluid composition, etc. is obtained by designing well tests or by running bottom hole pressure build-up surveys at discreet time intervals. Smart well technology makes it possible to implant pressure and temperature sensors in the well which can provide real time recording of this data. Additionally, when a well is completed into multiple producing zones—smart well technology provides the flexibility to selectively close or open the producing intervals. This flexibility makes it possible to obtain dynamic reservoir information such as production rates, pressures, fluid compositions for each zone, to not only effectively manage the reservoir but also to shut-off these intervals when they start to produce large volumes of water or gas along with oil.

The intelligence of smart wells can vary dramatically, beginning with the simplest intelligence in which a well contains only a few sensors that relay down hole temperatures and pressures continuously. Down hole sensors can also measure the type and amounts of fluids being produced. The intelligence level increases with down hole valves that open or close to control flow from different zones in response to the information provided or to changing down hole conditions. The valves can be partially opened or closed to control the influx of water from a zone or they can be completely opened or closed to open or shut-off production from a particular zone. Controlling the influx of water means fewer surface facilities and a smaller environmental footprint thus minimizing both the development and the operating cost.

The next intelligence level might include oil and gas separation facilities down hole. This is currently being done in a few wells. The intelligence of the down hole control systems also varies from surface controlled manual devices to unmanned computers that can send commands to the subsurface control mechanisms. At their most intelligent and most complex level, smart wells can be automated so that the downhole devices respond directly to changing conditions without manual intervention.

4. *Reservoir-Surface Integration Modeling:* Oil and gas production systems comprise of a complex combination of wells, pipeline network, and production facilities that require intricate optimization strategies to deliver optimum returns. Accurately simulating the behavior of these components by using an integrated model, companies can make better investment and operational decisions which can be helpful in:
   - Optimizing real-time production rates
   - Construction of field development plan
   - Determining optimum size and location of various components in the production system
   - Forecasting and allocation of oil/gas production

   Heretofore, it was possible to model individual components of a complex production system by using reservoir simulators to model wells and the reservoir, pipeline simulators to model flow in pipelines, and surface simulators like HYSYS to model the surface facilities. Some companies like

Aspen Technology have now entered the market with products like the Aspen Asset Builder which provides a single integrated production system framework integrating the individual components. These are powerful tools that can be built in the engineering design phase to select the best concept, optimize a concept once it has been selected, train the operators before the facility comes on-line, and to optimize production on an ongoing basis.

Just like Smart Well technology described earlier, integrated reservoir/production system technology offers the potential to someday manage reservoirs and surface facilities on a real-time basis. Today this technology is in early stages of development and implementation.

5. ***Knowledge Management:*** In a large EandP company such as Oil and Natural Gas Commission (ONGC) of India there is a large amount of information such as: experiences with various technologies, best approach to do certain work, or experiences with certain suppliers etc. resident in the minds of certain employees, or in paper files, and of course not easily accessible when needed. ONGC is not unique in this respect. This is generally the case in most companies operating in the upstream sector today, barring a very few companies who have recognized this as a problem and taken steps to correct it. The net result is that the company learns the same lessons over and over again and by so doing significantly erodes the value of the assets. Addressing the problem requires a two prong approach: (1) Create a culture in the organization where sharing information is encouraged rather than withholding it, and (2) Provide a consistent Information Technology (IT) structure throughout the organization along with appropriate training for its use. The first part i.e. creating a culture of sharing information is more difficult because in most organizations employees have advanced in their careers by personalizing their accomplishments rather than by helping others. To do this effectively requires a wholesale change in the reward and recognition structure in the company. The second part i.e., creating a consistent IT structure requires that:

   - People are encouraged and rewarded to gather relevant information.
   - Information is gathered in a consistent format.
   - Information is accessible to all employees throughout the company regardless of their physical location.
   - Information quality is controlled.
   - Experts in key technology areas are identified and given the responsibility to scan work practices and select the best practices for dissemination throughout the company.
   - Frequent peer reviews are held to provide an unbiased feedback concerning the work.

It is difficult to quantify the value added through effective Knowledge Management (KM) in a company but suffice it to say that most successful companies list KM as not only a source of competitive advantage for them but also an important pillar in their success.

Continuous Improvement through Post-Auditing

Post-Auditing literally means auditing or carefully examining an activity after it has been completed with a view to gain the following insights:

- What went well?
- What didn't go so well?
- How can the activity be improved?

It is implied that these questions are being addressed relative to some goal or reference that was set-up prior to the start of the activity. The intent of Post-Auditing is to objectively reflect on an activity and learn from the mistakes with a view to continuously improve the results of similar actions in the future. When the focus of the audit is one task, it is usually referred to as an After Action Review (AAR), a term coined by the U.S. Army where this is routinely practiced. Beyond the scope of AAR—when the audit is focused on a group of tasks—such as those related to a discipline in the service of an asset—the review is called a Peer Review. When the review involves looking at the asset as a whole especially after a major milestone in the asset life-cycle has been completed, such as bringing a field on production, only then the review is termed a Post Audit. A Post-Audit is usually prescriptive to ensure uniformity of standards across the company.

The most important milestone in the life-cycle of an asset is when it starts generating revenue. This can take in excess of 10 years from the time a company acquires an exploratory license, and drain huge sums of money from a company's treasury in the ensuing period. Although revenue generation starts nearly coincidentally with the start of production, it reaches a peak only when the production facility is operating at its designed capacity barring large swings in the market price of oil and gas which can distort this relationship. The period between first production to peak production can be anywhere from a few months to 1-2 years depending on many factors e.g., facility design, project execution, operator training, and how completely the facilities were commissioned prior to start of production.

While start of production is a time for celebration for a company, it is also a time when reality meets expectations i.e. when a large number of assumptions used to seek management's approval of the development can be compared with actual results. This process of comparing actuals against projections (assumptions) is called Look-back or Post Auditing. Post-auditing can also be looked upon as an intermediate report card for the asset since it compares asset values before and after the development.

Summary

Evaluation of a company in the oil industry can become very complicated and exotic. The industry is certainly capital intensive, but it also has a strange blend of highly evolved technical elements and the sometimes spectacular aspects of risk and reward that make it unique. Cash-flow analysis is the key to both quick-look techniques and detailed analysis of oil companies. Analysts will usually focus on cash flow first and work from there. It is also important when evaluating oil companies to become familiar with the various assets and methods of estimating the individual asset values.

REFERENCES

India Hydrocarbon Vision 2025 (1999).

Tenth Five Year Plan (Energy Chapter) of Planning Commission (2000).

Annual Report of Ministry of Petroleum & Natural Gas for 2002-03.

International Energy Outlook 2003 by Energy Information Administration of D/o Energy US.

Indian School of Petroleum (2005), Upstream Business Process, Operational Training Manual for L&T InfoTech Ltd.

Website of Director General of Hydrocarbons (DGH).

Annual Report of ONGC, BPC, HPC, IOC for 2002-03.

Research Analyst Reports on Oil & Gas Sector (2003).

Monthly Economic Report issued by D/o Economic Affairs (January 2004).

Gazette Notification issued by Govt. of India on Dismantling of APM and granting authorization for marketing of transport fuels (2002).

Anantharaman, S.C. (1997), "Oil and natural gas sector", *Yojana*, Jan., 41(1), pp. 83-85.

Business Line, 1999, Vol. 6, no. 238, August 27, New Delhi, *Ibid*.

Business Standard (1999), August 10, New Delhi, p. 5.

Chandra, Avinash (1999), "NELP terms are comparable worldwide", *Drilling and Exploration*, Vol. 8, nos. 1 & 2, Oct.–Dec. '98—Mar '99, p. 48.

Chhabra, Vinod (1997), "Privatizing Petroleum", In: Infrastructure development for economic growth, edited by MVS Gowda, S. Subramanya, New Delhi, Deep & Deep, p. 204.

Das Gupta, A.B. (1997), "India's petroleum reserves, recovery and evaluation", In: Proceedings/Oil and Gas Corporation Ltd., Second International and Petroleum Conference and Exhibition, Jan. 9-12, New Delhi, p.49.

Daniel Johnston (2004), International Exploration Economics: Risk & Control Analysis, Pennwell Pub.

Editorial, (1999), "Policy needs future exploration", *The Business Line*, Vol. 6, no. 238, August 27, edit page.

Gidadhubli, R.G. (1999), "Sengupta proposals myopic and illogical", *Fortune India*, April 30, 17 (12), p. 70.

Investment Research and Information Services (1999), "Moving towards a free market: oil and gas", *The Economic Times—Hundred*, Vol. 1, issue 2 March, p. 100.

Loomba, A.K., Paul, Rama, Chandrashekharan, P., Thomas, J. and Sahai, S. (1999), "Measuring efficiency of hydrocarbon exploration", Papers of the Third International Petroleum Conference and Exhibition, Vol. V, pp. 354-355.

Mahapatra P. Sivarama Krishnan, TE, Rajagopalan S., Sethi, J.R. (1996), "Producing Indian basins and their reserve potential", *ONGC Bulletin*, 33(1), pp. 45-46.

Moore, David (1996), "Petroleum industry in India: present and future trends", In: Petroleum Industry Restructuring, edited by U.K. Dikshit, Anjali Hazarika, New Delhi, NPM Programme, pp. 100-103.

Nangea, A.G. and Hunt, E.J. (1999), "An integrated deterministic/probabilistic approach to reserve estimation: and update", Papers of Third International Petroleum Conference (Petrotech, 99) Vol. 5, p. 176.

Ibid, p. 177.

Planning Commission (1997), "Ninth five year plan: Vol. 2, Energy", Government of India, New Delhi, p. 10.

Ibid, (1997), "Report of the working group on the petroleum sector for Ninth Five Year Plan", New Delhi, Yojana Bhawan, p. 15.

Radhakrishnan, N., Ganguli, B. (1999), "Looking for Oil", *Business India*, February 8-21, p. 57.

Singh, L. (1996), "Adding reserves—an approach", *ONGC Bulletin*, 33(2), pp. 15-16.

The Times of India (1999), August 13, New Delhi, p. 4.

Robert E. Megil (2004), An Introduction to Exploration Economics (3rd. Edn.), Pennwell Books.

Hidustan Petroleum Ltd. (2005), Advanced Programme on Refinery Operations & Management, HPL.

Gallun, R.A.; C.J. Wright; L.M. Nichols & J.W. Stevenson (2004), Fundamentals of Oil & Gas Accounting, Pennwell Pub.

Indian School of Petroleum (2005): A Manual on Oil and Gas Accounting, Training Programme on Upstream Business Processes for L&T Infotech Ltd.

Websites

http://energy.ihs.com/NR/rdonlyres/30281EDE-04AC-4273-A5B6-560155D07EFD/0/IHSUpstreamAssetMgmt_flyer.pdf

http://www.inconf.ru/projects/Management/Management_2008_eng.pdf

http://www.fasb.org/st/

http://en.wikipedia.org/wiki/Nelson_complexity_index

http://www.sciencedirect.com/science?_ob=ArticleURL&_udi=B6VDW-4BVRTJ8-2&_user=10&_rdoc=1&_fmt=&_orig=search&_sort=d&view=c&_version=1&_urlVersion=0&_userid=10&md5=81e5ed76361d70333d3fc946326f4b8b

http://www.dupont.com/consulting/consulting/dra.html

hftp://ftp.tech-env.com/pub/SERVICE_LIFE_ASSET_MANAGEMENT/QUALITY.pdf

https://www.stockhouse.com/Bullboards/MessageDetail.aspx?p=0&m=23740530&l=0&r=0&s=ODE&t=list

CHAPTER V

Mid-Stream Sector: Pipelines

Pipeline Transportation

Pipeline transport is the transportation of goods through a pipe. Most commonly, liquid and gases are sent, but pneumatic tubes that transport solid capsules using compressed air have also been used. As for gases and liquids, any chemically stable substance can be sent through a pipeline. Therefore sewage, slurry, water, or even beer pipelines exist; but arguably the most important are those transporting oil and natural gas. The idea was first brought up by Dmitri Mendeleev in 1863. He suggested using a pipe for transporting Petroleum (http://en.wikipedia.org/wiki/Pipeline_transport).

Petroleum Industries in the Pipeline Transportation Sub-Section use transmission pipelines to transport products, such as crude oil, natural gas, refined petroleum products, and slurry. Industries are identified based on the products transported (i.e., pipeline transportation of crude oil, natural gas, refined petroleum products, and other products). The Pipeline Transportation of Natural Gas industry includes the storage of natural gas because the storage is usually done by the pipeline establishment and because a pipeline is inherently a network in which all the nodes are interdependent encompassing Sub-Sections: Pipeline Transportation of Crude Oil, Pipeline Transportation of Natural Gas, Natural Gas Transmission, Natural Gas Transmission and Distribution (Transmission), other Pipeline Transportation, All Other Pipeline Transportation (http://www.1800miti.com/links/truckin/pipeline/pipeline.html).

The transportation of oil and natural gas by pipeline basically encompasses three main domains, viz. (i) the liquid nature of oil products, volatility factor and principles of hydraulics, (ii) piping technology and (iii) the commercial prudence. The triangle created of these factors has the following features, which distinguish the pipeline mode of transportation from other conventional modes of transportation.

In case of pipeline transportation of petroleum products, the carrier does not traverse, unlike other modes and in that only the products move from source to destination: the carrier, all the same, remains static. Therefore, the energy consumption and the associated costs, including environmental pollution, in moving the carrier up and down, are nonexistent in pipeline transportation. Pipeline can navigate and traverse terrains, which are inaccessible or accessible at prohibitive costs, as opposed to other mobile and conventional modes of transportation.

Pipelines, of course, do have certain inherent limitations and implicit hazards. Firstly, pipelines are capital-intensive and largely technology-driven modes. The fixed-costs are very high and variable costs are almost negligible. Therefore, its commercial viability largely depends upon distance traveled, terrain characteristics and high degree of domestic and commercial utilization. Its minimum level of return is high, which puts the threshold production volume at a level, which is much higher than any other modes. In other words, pipeline needs higher degree of support from 'throughput' than other modes of transport available to petroleum products. The high threshold-volume warrants matching infrastructure requirement at both ends of the pipeline, involving huge investment at the time of commissioning or major expansion. Typical infrastructure that is required for pipelines are tanks, pumping unit and control and monitoring station. Operating and servicing of all these are part of pipeline operations. The hazards in pipeline transportation have two dimensions, namely, technical and social.

There are two major types of problems with regards to technical hazards, namely, corrosions of pipelines and second is generation of static electricity arising out of frictions. There are sound technological solutions available for these two. But if these two aspects are not properly taken care of, either at the time of construction or during operation, any of these can create hazards of serious nature. The hazards, which are social in nature, arise mostly from attempts of pilferage, inadequate risk awareness associated with the pipeline and the product that it carries. Leaving aside these limitations and hazards, which have sound technical and managerial solutions, the most important aspect in pipeline transportation is its economics. As the fixed cost of pipeline is huge, it has a large bearing on investment and financing decision.

Perspectives in Indian Pipeline Systems Development

India with its vast ness and peninsular size, pipeline transportation of petroleum products IS the most cost economic proposition. The network of pipelines can be further augmented with economic value in 'the supply chain of petroleum products. Need for new pipeline opens up avenues for investment, financial structuring and technological challenges. Some of the issues have been discussed below.

Cairn India Initiative in Rajasthan-Gujarat Pipeline

Cairn India, an exploration and production company, has commenced the construction of India's first heated and insulated pipeline and an associated gas pipeline from Barmer in the state of Rajasthan, to a coastal location in the Jamnagar district of the Gujarat state. The pipe-laying activity commenced at Bevta in the

Banaskantha district, about 200km from the city of Ahmedabad in Gujarat. The company noted that almost 80% of the contracts to construct the pipeline have been awarded to Indian companies. At peak production the Mangala, Bhagyam, and Aishwariya fields will aim to produce 175,000 barrels of oil per day and boost India's domestic crude production by approximately 25%. The oil field development work at Cairn India's discovery in Rajasthan is reportedly proceeding on schedule. The integrated upstream and pipe line development is on course to produce first oil from Mangala in the second half of 2009. The routing of the insulated and heated oil pipeline and gas pipeline is designed to access an extensive existing pipeline infrastructure and refinery network, with a final coastal delivery point providing access to the majority of India's refining capacity. The 600km, 24-inch diameter insulated pipeline for exporting of heated crude oil, will run from Barmer in Rajasthan to a coastal location in Gujarat. It will have an eight-inch diameter gas line running most of its length, starting from the Raageshwari gas field in the Rajasthan Block. A minimum of 32 intermediate power feeding and heating stations will be built along the length of the pipeline. These stations will help in maintaining the required temperature within the pipeline (http://www.energy-business-review.com/article_news.asp?guid=976F8032-13FE-4548-84EC-4B139F82A576).

Petronet Initiative

In view of the need for having a net work of pipelines carrying petroleum products across the country, some cross-country pipelines have already been laid in India as listed above. In order to build more of them, the following considerations were coming in the way.

Firstly, pipelines are natural monopoly. More number of pipelines under the ownership of a single company would mean strengthening of monopolistic condition. Therefore, it was considered wise to un-bundle the linkage between pipeline owner and pipeline user.

Secondly, in view of the typical nature of cost and revenue curves of pipeline projects, its financing has a non-conventional structure. Moreover, with a view to have assured stream of returns, it was felt to build in user's commitment into the project itself.

With these principal features in the mind, Petronet India Ltd (PIL) has been formed as a nongovernmental financial holding company by a directive of the Government of India for expeditious development of pipeline network in the country. Its mandate was to help build all future pipelines in India. The pipeline projects under Petronet are implemented through its Joint Venture Companies (JVC) promoted by PIL and the marketing Oil Companies, with equity holding by Refineries and other strategic investors in order to provide access to all the users of pipeline on a 'common carrier principle'. The equity share holding by the promoter Public Sector Oil Companies in Petronet India Ltd is 50%, i.e., Indian Oil Corporation Ltd. (IOC)—16%, Bharat Petroleum Corporation Ltd—16%, Hindustan Petroleum Corporation Ltd—16%, Indo Burma Petroleum Company Ltd (IBP)—2%. Financial institutions and private companies have subscribed the balance equity in PIL, i.e., SBI, ICICI Ltd, IIFS, Reliance Petroleum Ltd, each 10%.

In the JVCs formed for implementation and operation of pipelines, PIL will hold minimum 26% of the equity. Oil companies, refining companies will each hold up to 26% of the equity and the balance will be subscribed by financial institution/strategic investors so that no individual entity holds equity more than 5%. PIL and its JVCs are structured as viable, independent commercial entities with the projects financed on a stand-alone basis on the strength of their cash flows.

Other Issues of Pipeline Transportation

Pipeline Route Selection

Selection of pipeline route inevitably involves dislocation of physical and social space, which has profound implication in the implementation of the project. Following are some standard guidelines usually adopted while selecting the pipeline route:

- Shortest possible route connecting originating, intermediate and terminal locations.
- Easy approachability and accessibility during operation and maintenance stage of pipeline.
- To preserve ecological balance and to avoid/minimize environmental degradation and minimum encroachment of reserved forests and other protected areas.
- To keep the number of rail, road, river and canal crossings to the barest minimum. To avoid hilly or rocky terrain.
- To avoid pipeline route running parallel to high voltage transmission line/ D.C circuit.
- To utilize existing ROW/ROU, if any, as far as possible.

Though pipeline is always protected against external corrosion with cathodic protection system, with external coating of coal tar enamel or polyethylene, but if the ROU of pipeline passes through water logged area for the maximum period of the year, it may cause heavy external corrosion and leakage. There are quantitative route selection methodology with multi-attribute decision-making techniques, which rank alternate routes and show the life cycle cost estimate of the shortest route and optimal route.

Design Optimization

Economic design of pipeline system involves establishing an optimum relationship between pipeline size and pumping configuration in terms of number of pumps and power requirements. A smaller diameter pipeline requires a more powerful pumping systems and vice versa. Lower investment in pipeline may be offset by higher investment in pumping and consequently higher power consumption for a given throughput. Hence for a given throughput, there is an optimum size of pipeline and optimum pumping system which will give the least

Net Present Value of the investment (capital and operating) for the design life of the pipeline system.

Clearances Required

Apart from securing Right of Use (ROU) from the landowners, the following clearances are usually required for laying a cross-country pipeline.

- Environmental clearance
- Pollution Control Board clearance
- Forest clearance
- CCOE clearance
- Approval for pipe-laying
- Clearance for road, river crossing and other physical barriers

Agencies According Approval

- Ministry of Environment and Forest,
- Govt. of India Pollution Control Board of State Government
- Forest Authority of State Government
- Chief Controller of Explosives, Naqpur
- State Government
- State Govt's various Line Departments

Governance Issues

As a pipeline grows in capacity utilization, its costs increase less than linearly while throughput increases exponentially. Thus pipelines have a decreasing average and marginal costs of production. The problem with natural monopoly is that the firm can be expected to restrict its output or directly set prices higher than marginal cost without the concern for entry of a competitor. Once it is known that an industry exhibits some characteristics of a decreasing cost industry and then comes the difficult question of how to regulate the said firm.

Regulation of such firm aims to provide cost-driven prices, but it cannot achieve 'efficiency' for the fact that with marginal cost less than average cost; the natural monopoly cannot be required to set prices equal to marginal cost. Coming to regulation part of the particular industry, the regulatory mode for achieving public policy objectives in pricing has not been widely used in Europe and Asia; instead, most of these industries have been owned and operated by the governmental authorities. But now with the wave of private sector participation in virtually every industry, the role of regulation is revisited. Advances have been made in technologies to such an extent that hitherto industries, which were considered to be as natural monopoly, are increasingly seen as potential candidates for the infusion of competitive forces.

In the emerging policy regime in India, there would be a Down Stream Regulator to oversee that pipelines are used as common carrier and are accessible to all potential users at fair tariff. In a major decision towards deregulation of oil sector and to attract investment in the petroleum product pipelines, Government laid down a Petroleum Product Pipeline Policy, for laying pipelines in the country on common carrier principle in November 2002, with a supplementary guidelines in October 2004.

Processing Facilities Required at the Oil Field for Oil

Normally the following minimum processing facilities are required upstream at the oil field:

- Separation of oil, condensate and free water pumping of oil
- Metering
- Corrosion inhibitor injection

A. Well Treatment

Well treatment is conducted to optimize production and waste such as produced water and sand must be separated from the production stream. Well treatment involves the following stages of operations:

1. Corrosion inhibitors are chemicals used to counter the reaction between the acid in the gas and the iron of the tubing or other equipment. Usually it is accomplished at the wellhead, either by batch treatments or continuous injection.
2. Hydrate inhibition at the wellhead is accomplished by injection of glycol, ammonia, methanol, or brine.
   Hydrate inhibition may be accomplished by the use of indirect heaters that use bath solutions containing calcium chloride or glycol.
3. Impurities such as sand and excessive amounts of water are sometimes separated at the wellhead

B. Gathering Systems

Gathering systems are used to transport produced gas to a central treatment facility (i.e., gas plant).

1. Scraping or slug catching equipment (separators) on the pipeline removes slugs of liquid (hydrocarbons and/or water) Facilities for handling liquid hydrocarbons may be installed at these locations.
2. Hydrate inhibition is conducted at appropriate locations in the gathering system.
3. Glycol, ammonia, methanol, or brine is injected to lower the freezing point of water in the flow line.
4. Indirect heaters sometimes use bath solutions containing calcium chloride or glycol
5. The produced gas is compressed to facilitate its transport to the gas plant.

C. Gas-Plant Processing

Gas-plant processing removes impurities from the produced gas and, in some cases, includes the fractionation of the treated gas.

Oil absorption plants remove hydrocarbon products form natural gas. Oil absorption plants include:

- Stage separators (Economizers) Gas chillers
- Rich oil flash tank Presaturators
- Accumulators
- Rich oil demethanizers (RODs)

Dehydration is the removal of water from the produced natural gas and is accomplished by various methods. Recovery of natural gas liquids (NGL) is sometimes conducted at the gas plant involving the following steps:

1. Cryogenics may be used to remove NGL. Natural gas liquids (e.g., propane) are used as refrigerants and fuels. Filters are used for gas preparation (gas that is free of impurities is required for process). Electrostatic precipitators are sometimes used. Filtered substances include FeS_2, crude oil, wax, and lube oil.
2. Absorption may be used to remove NGL. Compounds from the process stream absorption oil removes the heavier Gas and product treating includes the removal of sulfur compounds (primarily H_2S) and CO_2 from gas. Sweetening processes include adsorption using various amines or a dry bed adsorbent.

Sulfur Removal

Sulfur is removed from the H_2S recovered from the produced gas. The Claus process is typically used to remove elemental sulfur from the H_2S (acid gas). Tailgas clean-up systems remove remaining sulfur from the exhaust.

Pipeline Transportation

Pipelines transport crude oil and natural gas from the wellhead to storage tanks, gas processing plants, and to market. Transportation of oil and gas includes the equipment and facilities used to move products through the pipelines.

Oil and Gas Pipelines: Comparison

Gas and oil pipelines are essentially similar, with the greatest operationa difference resulting from the varying needs of transporting gas versus liquid. Oi pipelines require pumps to propel their liquid contents, while gas lines rely o compression to force the resource through the pipe. In pump and compresso stations, corrosion of piping and vessels must be monitored constantly to preven failure. Pipelines can be cleaned and surveyed with cleaning pigs used to preven unwanted materials from contaminating the pumps or compressors. Pigs with hig technology instrumentation are used to monitor pipeline conditions and dete potential problems.

Oil Pipelines—Oil pumped from the ground travels through pipes to leas tanks, where it is treated, measured, and tested. Typically, a separator is used t separate oil, gas, and water. A fired heater is used to break water/oil emulsio to promote removal of water from the oil. Tanks store oil until it is shipped as crude oil by truck or, more commonly, by a gathering line connected to storage tanks. From these tanks, the oil is moved through large-diameter, long distance trunk lines to refineries or other storage terminals. Trunk lines rely on pumps to initiate and maintain pipeline pressure at the level required to overcome friction, changes in elevation, or other pressure-decreasing factors. Pumps are required at the beginning of the line and are spaced along the pipeline to adequately propel the oil along the line

Gas Pipelines—Gas pipelines operate at high pressures and use compressors (instead of pumps) to force the gas along the line. Unlike oil, gas does not undergo refining, and transmission lines connect directly to utility companies that distribute the gas to consumers via small, metered pipelines Gas is often treated in scrubbers or filters to ensure that it is dry prior to distribution. Gas-well flow lines connect individual gas wells to field gas-treating and processing facilities or to branches of a larger gathering system. The gas is processed at the treating facility to remove water, sulfur, acid gases, hydrogen sulfide, or carbon dioxide. Most field gas processing plants also remove hydrocarbon liquids from the produced gas stream. From field processing facilities, the dried, cleaned natural gas enters the gas transmission pipeline system (analogous to the oil trunk line system): Down stream from compressor stations, lubricating oil from the compressors is removed from the gas lines.

Pipeline Transportation Operations

Pipelines transport crude oil and natural gas from the wellhead to storage tanks, gas processing plants, and to market. This operation includes the following:

A. Routine maintenance on pipelines includes painting, repairing, pigging, and replacing.
B. Compressor stations boost the fluid in pipelines to help it travel long distances.
C. Corrosion inhibitors are used to minimize the reaction between acid in the fluid and iron in the tubing.
D. Lead acetate tape is commonly used for detection of acid gases (e.g., H_2S) in pipelines.

Configuration of Cross-Country Pipeline

A typical cross country pipeline system starting from an offshore field has the following facilities along its route:

- An offshore platform where the oil or gas is produced.
- Pipe Line End Manifold (PLEM) near the platform from where the pipeline starts (or a dispatch Terminal on land).
- An SPM (Single Point Mooring) connecting the sub sea pipeline to a tanker, if oil is transferred from a tanker instead of platform.
- Pig launcher.
- Sub-sea pipeline reaching shore at what is called landfall point.

- A receiving terminal at the landfall point. It has equipment like pig receiver, filter, storage for oil, pumping for gas, processing of gas, compression and dehydration.

From the receiving terminal, oil and gas is sent through cross country pipeline, which could be hundreds of kilometers in length to several customers along the route. For distribution to each customer, there will be a Distribution Terminal having filter, metering devices etc. Normally, there are booster stations with booster compressors for gas and booster pumps for oil after every few hundred kilometers to compensate for the pressure loss in the pipeline.

The entire facility is monitored and managed by SCADA system. SCADA is a central monitoring system, which monitors the entire pipeline parameters over several hundred kilometers by telemetry and tele-control. Table 1 gives a bird's—eye-view of the status of Petroleum pipe-lines in operation in India run by major public as well as private-sector companies. Table 5.2 provides detailed information pertaining to pipeline-specific data of major pipeline distribution network together with throughputs capacity in India.

Table 5.1: Petroleum Pipelines under Operation in India

Sr. No.	Name of the Pipeline	Capital Cost Gross Block (Rs in Crore)	Year of Commis-sioning	Length (KM)	Diameter (Inch)	Capacity (MMTPA)
1	2	3	4	5	6	7
I. Indian Oil Corporation Ltd						
A	**Product Pipelines**					
1	**GSPL** (Guwahati-Siliguri)	23.28	1964	435	8.625	0.818
2	**KAPL** (Koyali-Ahmedabad)	7.29	1966	116	8.625	1.1
3	**KNPL** (Koyali-Navagam)	16.03	2003	78	14	1.8
4	**BKPL** (Barauni-Kanpur)	202.59	1966	745	20/12.75	3.5
	Barauni-Patna-Kanpur		1966	676	12.75	3.5
	Kanpur-Lucknow Branch line		2002	69	12.75	1.7
	Barauni-Patna Replacement		2003		20.00	
5	**HBPL** (Haldia-Barauni	69.69	1967	525	12.75	1.25
6	**HMRPL** (Haldia-Mourigram-Rajbandh)		1972	277	12.75	1.35
7	**MJPL** (Mathura-Jalandhar)	76.91	1982	763	16/14/ 12.75/ 10.75	3.7
	Mathura-Delhi Section		1982	147	16	3.7
	Delhi-Ambala Section		1982	214	14	2.2

1	2	3	4	5	6	7
	Ambala-Jalandhar Section		1982	165	12.75	1.35
	Sonepat-Meerut Branch line	33.99	2001	70	10.75	0.6
	Kurukshetra-Roorkee-Najibabad Branch line	77.41	2003	167	10.75	0.9
8	**MTPL** (Mathura-Tundla)	44.52	2003	56	16	1.2
9	**KBPL** (Kandla-Bhatinda)	1967.27	1996/ 1999/ 2002	1443	22/14/ 10.75	8.8
	Kandla-Panipat Section			1113	22	8.8
	Panipat-Bhatinda Section			219	14	1.5
	KOT-Salawas Section			111	10.75	0.75
10	**PRPL** (Panipat-Rewari)	59.60	2004	155	12.75	1.5
11	**KVSSPL** (Koyali-Viramgam-Sidhpur-Sanganer)	368.53	2003/2005	249	18	4.1
	Koyali-Viramgam Section		2003	142	18	4.1
	Viramgam-Sidhpur Section		2003	103	18	4.1
	Sidhpur-Sanganer Section		2005	517	18	3.4
	Bareja-Navagram Branch Line		2003	4	10	1.1
12	**DTPL-AOD** (Digboi-Tinsukia)	NA	1956	75	8/6	0.73
	Black Oil		1956	36	8	0.2
	White Oil		1985	39	6	0.53
13	Branch Pipeline to Ajmer from SSPL	20.92	2005	21	8	0.5
B	**Crude Pipeline**					
1	**SMPL** (Salaya-Mathura)	1538.20	1978	1870	28/24/18	21
	Salaya Viramgam Section		1978	435	28	21
	Viramgam-Koyali Section		2003	148	28	12
	Viramgam-Chaksu Section		1978	716	24	13
	Chaksu Mathura Section		1978	197	24	7.5
	Chaksu-Panipat Section		1997	349	24	6
	Onshore Pipeline, Vadinar		1978	11	42	2
	SPM I Offshore line		1978	5.3	42	
	SPM II Offshore line		1997	6.3	42	
	Loop line (SPM I & SPM II) Vadinar		1997	2.1	42	
2	**HBCPL** (Haldia-Barauni)	907.29	1999/2002	943	18	7.5
	Main line—506 km		1999			
	Loop line—437 km		2002			
3	**VKCPL** (Viramgam-Koyali)	178.16	2003	148	28	12

(Contd.)

1	2	3	4	5	6	7
4	**MKCPL** (Mundra-Kandla) and conversion of Kandla-Panipat section of KBPL to Crude Oil service	305.60	2005	73	28	6
II. Hindustan Petroleum Corporation Ltd						
1	**MPPL** (Mumbai-Pune)	63	1985	162	14	3.67
2	**VVSPL** (Visakha-Vijayawada-Secunderabad)					
	(i) Visakha-Vijayawada pipeline	470	1998	349	18	5.38
	(ii) Vijayawada-Secunderabad Pipeline	326	2002	223	16/14	1.98
III. Bharat Petroleum Corporation Ltd						
1	**MMMPL** (Mumbai-Manmad-Manglia)					
	(i) Mumbai-Manmad Pipeline	474.14	1998	252	18	4.3
	(ii) Manmad-Manglia Pipeline	315.55	2003	358	14	1.4
IV. Pipelines Promoted by Petronet India Ltd						
1	**Petronet VK Pipeline** (Co-promoted by IOC) Sikka-Kandla Section	324.54	2000	100	24	7.5
2	**Petronet CCK Pipeline** (Co-promoted by BPCL & KRL)	350.21	2002	292	18/14	3.3
3	**Petronet Mangalore-Hassan-Bangalore Pipeline** (Co-promoted by HPCL)	667.00	2003	—	—	5.8
	(i) Mangalore-Neriya	—	—	89	20	
	(ii) Neriya-Hassan	—	—	76	24	
	(iii) Hassan-Bangalore	—	—	196	20	

Source: Compiled statistics of Indian Oil Cos, Petroleum Planning & Analysts Cell.

Table 5.2: Break-up of Existing Petroleum Products Pipeline in India

Oil Co.	Name of the Pipeline	Capacity (MMT) 2004-05	Length (KM) 1.4.2005	Throughput ('000' Tonne) 2001-02	2002-03	2003-04	2004-05
1		2	3	4	5	6	7
Product Pipelines							
IOC	Barauni-Patna-Kanpur	5.30	745	1697	1683	2201	4115
IOC	Guwahati-Siliguri	0.82	435	882	890	1200	1299
IOC	Haldia-Barauni	1.25	525	1176	1327	1141	925
IOC	Haldia-Mourigram-Rajbandh	1.35	277	2061	2083	1871	1909
IOC	Koyali-Ahmedabad	1.10	116	1402	1345	982	688
IOC	Mathura-Jallunder#	3.70	763	3876	3673	4575	4138
IOC	Kandla-Bhatinda	8.80	1443	5544	5091	4679	3299
IOC	Digboi-Tinsukia	1.00	75	555	486	506	550
IOC	Mathura-Tundla	1.20	56	–	–	231	277
IOC	Koyali-Navgam	1.80	78	–	–	247	269

1		2	3	4	5	6	7
IOC	Koyali-Viramgam-Sidhpur	4.10	249	–	–	424	1696
IOC	Panipat-Rewari@	0.75	155	–	–	–	254
HPCL	Mumbai-Pune	3.67	161	3152	3097	3020	3050
HPCL	Vizag-Vijayawada-Secunderabad	5.38	572	2972	3038	3110	3000
BPCL	Mumbai-Manmad-Manglia	4.30	610	2699	2376	2577	3578
Petronet	Vadinar-Kandla	11.50	100	5235	5065	4423	2097
Petronet	Kochi-Karur*	3.30	292	–	601	942	1320
Petronet	Mangalore-Hasan-Bangalore	2.30	361	–	–	305	1240
	Sub-total	61.62	7013	31251	30755	32434	33704
LPG Pipelines							
GAIL	Jamnagar-Loni	2.50	1250	1310	1520	1840	2000
GAIL	Vizag-Vijayawada-Secunderabad	1.33	600	0	0	0	140
	Sub-total	3.83	1850	1310	1520	1840	2140
Crude Pipelines							
OIL	Duliajan-Barauni	7.68	1158	N.A.	4381	4489	5920
IOC	Salaya-Mathura-Panipat	21.00	1870	19900	21052	21330	18990
IOC	Haldia-Barauni	7.50	943	3210	3095	5780	6361
	Sub-total	36.18	3971	23110	28528	31599	31271

#: Includes Sonepat-Meerut & Kurukshetra-Roorkee-Nazibabad branch pipeline.
N.A.: Not Available.
*: Operational capacity 7.5 MMT.
@: Panipat-Rewari pipeline, design capacity 1.5 MMTPA, was commissioned on 30.9.2004.
**: Commissioned in April 2004 upto Vijaywada only.
Source: Petroleum Planning & Analysis Cell.

Import Through Pipelines: pros and cons

The cross-border oil and gas trade has grown significantly in the past 50 years. How much of the oil trade is carried by pipeline is uncertain. The vast majority of oil moves in ocean-going tankers, and in addition to pipelines also is shipped by rail and trucks, with the result that precise data collection on transport methods is difficult. However, for gas there are only two serious transport options1: pipelines and liquefied natural gas (LNG).

The Future Role of Cross-Border Pipelines

In the near future, the world will need more cross-border pipelines. Two factors explain this need: the location of oil and gas reserves and the patterns of energy demand. Reserves close to traditional markets are being depleted and these markets are starting to look to newer, more remote sources of oil and gas for their needs. The successful exploitation of many of these sources will require pipeline delivery. In the case of oil, for example, some of the newer basins, notably those of the Caspian region, are landlocked. For other countries such as China, a vulnerability to naval blockade raises security-of-supply concerns against oil importation by tanker.

For gas, the case for pipelines is even more compelling. Gas reserves close to market are declining, thus requiring gas to move further. The only alternative to pipeline transportation, liquefied natural gas, is cost-competitive with pipelines only over distances in excess of 3,000 miles (4,800 km). Despite recent improvements arising from scale economies and new forms of financing, LNG projects remain extremely expensive. Changes to energy demand patterns. Regulatory, institutional, and economic barriers in the past constrained the use of gas (with the notable exception of within the former Soviet Union). The future will see a greater role for gas in the primary energy mix.

In the Organization for Economic Cooperation and Development (OECD) countries, three factors limited the use of gas. Transportation problems meant that in many countries gas was not available. In the 1970s, the so-called "premium fuel" argument posited that because gas had so many advantages it was too precious to burn. As a consequence, for example, regulation both in the United States and the European Union specifically prevented the use of gas for power generation. Outside the United States, most gas suppliers were public sector utilities with monopoly and sometimes monophony status. Gas prices thus were held artificially high and were uncompetitive.

In the developing economies, in many cases gas simply was not available. While during the 1970s some countries discovered gas reserves, their development for domestic use was painfully slow. Two reasons for this are: The realization of domestic gas consumption requires expensive infrastructure involving foreign exchange. Faced with the debt crisis of the 1980s, many developing countries could not afford the necessary infrastructure.

Despite the often attractive project economics, many foreign companies were reluctant to help develop gas resources for domestic use because of the lack of convertibility of the domestic currency. The gas export option also faced barriers:

The Size of Gas Reserves

An export project requires a minimum size of gas reserves to justify the huge upfront investments. Because of the currency convertibility problem, even those companies that had discovered some reserves lost their enthusiasm for further exploration. The reserves found often were suboptimal for export projects.

The Problems of Negotiating Export Contracts

Most export contracts are for periods of 15–20 years. In an uncertain energy market, this span of contract means that the contract must be both flexible enough to address changing circumstances but rigid enough to be worth signing. Determining price is especially problematic if the gas is being sold into a "project supply market" where no "gas price" exists. To protect the financial viability of the project for producers and consumers, an absolute floor and an absolute ceiling price must be agreed. These fixed numbers must have validity over the life of the contract, and this in a world where it is hard to determine energy prices for one year ahead, let alone 15 or 20 years ahead.

Security of Supply

Security of supply is of much greater importance for gas than it is for other fuels. For electricity or oil products the loss of supply incurs outage costs, but when supply is restored, reconnection is simple. This is not so with gas. Because there is a danger that appliances may not have been switched off or that air may have entered the pipes, supply restoration ideally requires a gas engineer at every burner tip. The inflexibility in gas supply networks means it is difficult to replace lost supply quickly, with the result that importers tend to be wary of gas.

The Problems of Long-distance Transportation

Transporting gas is far more expensive than transporting oil. Gas pipeline transit, and the alternative, LNG projects, face a range of both potential and actual problems. Those of LNG, while diminishing, can be characterized as complex, extremely expensive, and plagued by long lead times. The cost of a project, including gas field development, liquefaction plant, special LNG tankers, and the regasification plant, in the past typically would be quoted at US$ 9–12 billion. The process of liquefaction furthermore was highly energy intensive, with around 15–18 percent of the gas effectively wasted in producing the liquid. LNG also raises safety concerns since it represents highly concentrated energy. Past projects were extremely inflexible and spot trading in LNG almost unheard of. And such projects offered limited revenue benefit to the governments concerned.

Over the last 10 years, forces have been working to reduce or remove these constraints, leading to a growing role for gas in primary energy and with it a need for more cross-border gas pipelines. These forces for change include the following:

- Regulatory restrictions on gas consumption arising from the "premium fuel" argument were removed in the OECD in the early 1990s. Of the hydrocarbons, gas is relatively environmentally friendly, having high conversion efficiencies from useable to useful energy. It is also relatively clean.
- Burning natural gas emits only 75 percent of the NO_2 and 50 percent of the CO_2 released by the burning of other hydrocarbons. It emits no SO_2.

If the Kyoto Protocol emission targets are to be achieved without the use of more nuclear power, the only realistic option is considerably greater use of gas. Governments are deregulating and liberalizing electricity to encourage private sector investment, and private investors in electricity generation have a strong preference for combined-cycle gas turbine (CCGT) technology, for three primary reasons:

(a) Economies of scale are less relevant, so small plants are economic;
(b) Conversion efficiency is around 60–65 percent, compared to 30–33 percent in conventional thermal stations; and
(c) The lead time on plants is short—a plant can be completed in two years, with some generation beginning in one year.

Gas markets increasingly are being deregulated and liberalized, promoting the development of commodity supply markets and gas-to-gas competition. Prices, therefore, can be expected to fall. Developments in Cross-Border Oil and Gas Pipelines: Problems and Prospects the European gas market under pressure from the European Union exemplify this change. The gas transportation situation is improving. Work is being done on technical solutions such as gas-to-liquid and gas-by-wire transportation, and it is worthwhile also mentioning the improvements in LNG handling. A combination of technological developments, economies of scale, and new methods of project finance mean LNG project costs and lead times are falling. More projects also are coming on-stream, raising the likelihood of improved flexibility in LNG trading. In 2000, a number of companies ordered LNG tankers for independent operations, presaging a large potential increase in spot trading.

Gas consumption thus is expected to rise. The example of the United Kingdom provides an insight into how this can occur. Since the late 1980s, most of the barriers discussed earlier have been removed in the United Kingdom. As can be seen, the consequences for the share of gas have been formidable. Changes in reserve location and energy demand imbalances between oil and gas consuming and oil and gas turn implies that cross-border trade must grow. More cross-border pipelines clearly will be needed for oil and gas. Obstacles, however, exist to the implementation of these pipelines that first must be addressed.

The Problems of Cross-Border Pipelines

The number of successful cross-border oil and gas pipelines, exemplified by those in North America and Western Europe, outweigh the problem pipelines, but the problem cases nonetheless have tended to have a disproportionate affect on project planning. And cross-border pipelines have a long history, especially where transit is involved, of vulnerability to disruption and conflict. The conflicts that have affected cross-border pipelines have taken many forms. There is a widespread view that conflicts over pipelines, including those due to incompatible legal and regulatory regimes arise because of politics. Some conflicts undeniably have been political, including those that have grown out of a legacy of political divisions.

These are clear examples of political conflicts, but many conflicts are based on economic issues, ranging from failure to agree on the terms of transit and on profit and rent sharing to issues regarding the obsolescing bargain. Economic-based conflicts also can include squabbles between joint venture partners, reflecting the differences between public and private companies or between vertically integrated companies and standalone ventures. The potential for conflict that is implicit in these results can have serious implications for the producers and consumers of oil and gas at both ends of the line.

There are three primary components to the operation of a cross-border pipeline:

(a) the pipeline itself,
(b) cross-border trade, and
(c) in some cases, the use of transit

Each component has certain innate characteristics, each of which bears consequences Combinations of these consequences can give rise to one or more of the three results, outlined above, that create conflict or the potential for conflict.

CASE STUDY

A case study highlighting the application of the various aspects deliberated in the Refinery Economics and Profitability of Pipelines is presented here in order that the students will have an appreciation of all key concepts about pipeline maintenance and cost economics.

Crude Oil and Product Pipelines in India

The details of major crude oil and product pipelines under operation in India and pipeline under implementation are as under: the details of which are given in Table 5.3.

IOC's Petroleum Pipelines under Operation in the Country

Indian Oil's cross-country pipelines network is nearly 9,300 km in length and 61.72 million metric tonnes per annum (MMTPA) in capacity. Pipelines being the safest, cost-effective, environment-friendly and energy-efficient mode of transportation, have been continuously adding to the efficiency and productivity of IndianOil's refineries and marketing set-up. Transportation of crude oil to Indian Oil's inland refineries has been a very challenging task, especially so with the refineries expanding their capacities as well as capability to process a variety of crude oils. For instance, Indian Oil's Vadinar terminal in Gujarat—the country's largest offshore crude oil terminal, with two Single Point Mooring systems—set a new record during the year 2006-07 by handling 148 tankers, including 75 Very Large Crude Carriers (VLCCs). Conversion of the Kandla-Panipat section of the Kandla-Bhatinda product pipeline to crude oil service is now complete with a new 74-km section connecting it to Mundra port. The capacity of the Mundra-Panipat pipeline is being further augmented from 6 to 9 MMTPA in line with the ongoing expansion of Panipat Refinery capacity from 12 to 15 MMTPA.

In the eastern sector, Indian Oil would achieve further reduction in the transportation cost of crude oil to its Haldia and Barauni refineries once the Paradip-Haldia crude oil pipeline and a new offshore terminal at Paradip are commissioned to facilitate receipt of VLCCs. Transportation of gas by pipelines is a new growth area for Indian Oil with gas discoveries being reported from several parts of India in the recent past. LPG and natural gas pipelines are part of several new pipelines and branch lines being laid by Indian Oil. The Corporation's maiden LPG pipeline is being laid from Panipat to Jalandhar.

Indian Oil has been according high importance to energy conservation in all its operations. Among the major steps being taken in this direction are operation of the pipelines at desired flow rate with optimum combination of mainline pumping units, close monitoring of stock and ullage available at pumping and delivery stations, and avoiding frequent shutdowns. The Corporation's onshore and offshore pipelines are being monitored on a regular basis and kept in good health through state-of-the-art technology. Indian Oil's oldest pipeline, the Guwahati-Siliguri Pipeline commissioned way back in 1964, is still being operated at designed pressure and capacity. All Indian Oil pipelines are certified to ISO 14001:1996 environment management system and ISO 9001:2000 quality management system while giving paramount importance to safety too. The Pipelines Division is focused on maintaining Indian Oil's leadership in the complex business scenario and is extending full logistics support to its sister divisions of

Refineries and Marketing for enabling the Corporation to remain competitive (http://www.iocl.com/Aboutus/Pipelines.aspx).

Indian Oil Corporation operates the largest network of crude oil and petroleum product pipelines in India. Started with the construction of the 435 km long Guwahati-Siliguri pipeline in early sixties, the pipelines of Indian Oil today transport petroleum products to the various major demand centers of this geographically vast country and feed crude oil to four major inland refineries. Indian Oil is one of the leaders in, providing engineering, construction and Consultancy services to the pipeline industry. Highly qualified professionals with vast experience execute pipeline projects from concept to commissioning and provide services for construction supervision and project management.

Table 3: Investment and Technical Specifications of Major Crude-Oil and Petroleum Products Pipelines in India

Pipeline	Capital Cost (Rs. Crore)	Year of Commis-sion	Length (Km)	Diameter (inches)	Capacity (MMTPA)
1	2	3	4	5	6
Crude Oil Pipelines					
SMPL(Salaya-Mathura Pipeline)	**1555.78**	**1978/1997**	**1870**	**28/24/18**	**21.000**
Salaya-Viramgam Section			435	28	21.000
Viramgam-Koyali Section			148	28	21.000
Viramgam-Chaksu Section			716	24	12.000
Chaksu-Mathura Section			197	24	13.500
Chaksu-Patiipat Section			349	24	7.500
Onshore Pipeline, Vadinar			11	42	6.000
SPM-I Offshore Line (Vadinar)			5.3	42	
SPM-II Offshore Line (Vadinar)			6.3	42	
Loopline (SPM-I & SPM-II) Vadinar			2.1	42	
HBCPL (Haldia-Barauni Pipeline)	**910.89**	**1999/2002**	**943**	**18**	**7.500**
Mainline-506 km					
Loopline-437 km					
Crude Oil Pipelines (Total)			2813		28.50
Petroleum Product Pipelines					
GSPL (Guwahati-Siliguri Pipeline)	19.92	1964	435	8.625	0818
KAPL (Koyali-Ahmedabad Pipeline)	**6.44**	**1966**	**116**	**8.625**	**1.100**
KNPL (Koyali-Navagam Pipeline)	**19.50**	**2003**	**78**	**14**	**1.800**
BKPL (Barauni-Kanpur Pipeline)	**199.880**	**1966**	**745**	**20/12.75**	**3.500**
Barauni-Patna-Kanpur		1966	676		3.500
Kanpur-Lucknow Branchline		2002	69	12.75	3.500
(Barauni-Patna replacement)		2003		20.00	
HBPL (Haldia-Barauni Pipeline)		**1967**	**525**	**12.75**	**1.250**
HMRPL (Haldia-Mourigram-Rajbandh Pipeline)	**67.02**	**1972**	**277**	**12.75**	**1.350**
MJPL (Mathura-Jalandhar Pipeline)	**97.38**	**1982**	**596**	**16/14/12. 75/10.75**	**3.700**
Mathura-Delhi Section		1982	147	16	3.700
Delhi-Ambala Section		1982	214	14	2.200

1	2	3	4	5	6
Ambala-Jalandhar Sections		1982	165	12.75	1.350
Sonepat-Meerut Branchline		2001	70	10.75	0.600
MTPL (Mathura-Tundla Pipeline)	**45.11**	**2003**	**56**	**16**	**1.200**
KVSPL (Koyali-Viramgam-Sidhpur)	**62.50**	**2003**	**245**	**18**	**4.100**
Koyali-Viramgam tentatively Section		2003	142	18	4.100
Viramgam-Sidhpur Section		2003	103	18	4.100
DTPL-AOD (Digboil-Tinsukia		**1956**	**75**	**8/6**	**0.730**
Black oil		1956	36	8	0.200
White oil		1985	39	6	0.530
Production Pipelines (Total)			4591		28.350

Summary

IOCL Pipelines	*Capacity*	*Length*
Product Pipelines	28.35 MMTPA	4591 KM
Crude Oil Pipelines	28.50 MMTPA	2813 KM
Product + Crude Oil Pipelines	56.85 MMTPA	7404 KM

HPCL Product Pipelines

Pipeline	**Length (K.m)**	**Capacity (MMTPA)**	**Remarks**
Mumbai-Pune	161	3.67	Used for transporting MS, SKO, HSD & LDO from HPC Mumbai Refinery to terminals at Vashi and Pune
Vishakapatnam-Vijayawada	350	5.38	
Vijayawada-Secundrabad	–	1.94-3.0	

Pipeline Projects under Implementation

IOC

Name of Project	**Length (Km)**	**Diameter (Inches)**	**Quantity (MMTPA)**
Mundra-Chudwa Crude Oil Pipeline	73	28	6.0
Viramgam-Koyali Crude Oil Pipeline	146	28	12.0
Sidhpur-Sanganer Product Pipeline	506	18	3.4
Panipat-Rewari Product Pipeline	160	12	1.5
Koyali-Viramgam-Sidhpur Product Pipeline	141/98/5	18/10	4.1
Kurukshetra-Najibabad Branch Line from Panipat-Ambala Section of Existing MJPL	106	10	0.90
Mathura-Tundla Pipeline Project	60	16	1.2
Koyali-Navagam Product Pipeline	85	14	1.8
Replacement of Barauni-Patna Section of BKPL	111	20	1.8 to 3.5

Pipelines Operations

Special expertise required in pipeline operations and management includes:

- Hydrostatic testing
  Pre-commissioning
- Inspections
  Control system verification

Pipeline start up

- Commissioning, dev. of operational procedures
- Pigging and analysis of pigging data
- Selection, testing and evaluation of chemical drag reducers [) Preparation of comprehensive operation manuals

Offshore Terminals

Indian Oil owns and operates two Single Point Mooring (SPM) systems in the Gulf of Kutch on the western coast of India, for handling crude oil from Bombay High and imported crude oil (brought through tankers including VLCC), for onward transportation and feeding to three refineries through pipeline system.

Tank Farms

Pipeline division operates and maintains huge tank farms for storage of crude oil and petroleum products. Inspection and maintenance of tanks include complete de-sludge, thickness survey, repair and replacement of body and bottom plates, epoxy painting, calibration and commissioning.

Pump Stations

Pump stations of the pipelines are equipped with both engines and motors as prime movers in auto as well as manual mode. The stations have been provided with the state-of-the-art technology. Targeted capacity has been surpassed consistently, for both crude oil and product pipelines.

Pipeline Maintenance

Stations Maintenance

Preventive and predictive maintenance of pumping stations, booster stations, block valve stations and ESD valves are carried out regularly with in-house expertise. Failure analysis of rotary equipment, spare parts management, and lube oil analysis of engines are conducted to prevent any break down during the operations.

Mainline Maintenance

It includes design of impressed current cathodic protection systems and their installation, maintenance and monitoring all aspects related to cathodic protection systems and to initiate corrective measures as and when required.

Close interval potential logging (CPL) survey, current attenuation survey, direct current voltage gradient (DCVG) survey and conventional Pearson survey are carried out to maintain the smooth flow of petroleum products and crude oil.

Corrosion Monitoring

Corrosion Monitoring involves selection and injection of corrosion inhibitors and installation and maintenance of corrosion coupons and electric resistance probes for controlling internal corrosion.

Online Inspection

This involves drawing of specification for intelligent pig-survey, evaluation of various intelligent pigging techniques and undertaking intelligent pigging survey for various pipelines periodically.

Pipeline Repairs and Rehabilitation

Repair and replacement of pipeline section involves completion of the following important steps:

- Repair of leak/burst and installation of leak clamps, Installation of sleeves, Hot tapping operation, Pipeline excavation, sand padding and back-filling, Pipeline coating and re-coating,
- Hydro-testing,
- Maintenance of whole range of T&I system including Supervisory Control & Data Acquisition system (SCADA).
- Maintenance of electrical and mechanical equipment, valve maintenance.
- Maintenance of cathodic protection system etc.

Pipeline Materials Management

Procurement of equipment and materials for pipeline construction, operations and maintenance from indigenous and global manufactures in the most economical manner.

The expertise required includes:

- Vendor developments
- Cost estimation
  - Inventory management
- Materials storage and handling
  - Selection and lining up of inspection agencies
  - Insurance coverage
- All other activities related to material procurement/management areas

New Pipeline Project Implementation

- Detailed route surveys
  - Preparation of Feasibility Reports/Detailed Feasibility Reports
  - Detailed design and engineering of:
    - Mainline
    - Pumping stations/booster stations/delivery stations/block valve stations etc. "Tank farms
    - Civil Structures
    - Cathodic protection system
    - Instrumentation, Telecommunication, Tele-supervisory and SCADA system development of operational philosophy
  - Preparation and finalization of all technical specifications.
- Procurement of all materials including inspection and testing
- Acquiring rights of users
  Tendering and award of work

Preparation and issuance of approved for construction drawings
Construction supervisory of:
- Mainline
- Stations
- Tank farms
- Cathodic protection system
- Instrumentation

- Overall project management
  Testing and commissioning

Tank Wagons

The next effective mode of transportation of petroleum products after pipelines is by Rail through Tank Wagons. All the petroleum products from LPG to FO etc. are transported by tank wagons from refineries to the various demand centers in the country. White Oils are transported through 8 wheeler BTPN railway wagons of 50 MT capacities. Black Oils are however transported through 4 wheeler Broad Gauge & Meter Gauge railway wagons of 20 MT. LPG is transported through 8 wheeler Boogie Wagons as well as 4 wheeler Railway Wagons of 20 MT and 10 MT respectively.

Tank Trucks

Petroleum products are also transported through road via tank trucks also. This mode is especially effective in transporting petroleum products to far flung and hilly areas as well as smaller towns. Tank trucks in use are of 12 KL and 20 KL capacities for liquid petroleum products and 12 MT and 20 MT capacities for LPG.

Product Tankers

For coastal locations petroleum products are transported through product tankers. MR, LRI and LRII vessel are used for transporting petroleum products to and fro from coastal locations.

REFERENCES

Atmanand (2004), Growth and Deregulation of Indian Oil Industry. Excel Books.

Indian School of Petroleum (2006), Understanding Natural Gas Business. Training Manual for Gujarat Gas Company Ltd.

H.K.Abdel-AAL, B.A. Bakr & M.A.Al Sahlawi (1992), Petroleum Economics & Engineering. Marcel Deckker Inc.

Patra, D.C. (2004), Oil Industry in India. Mittal Publications, New Delhi.

Websites

http://en.wikipedia.org/wiki/Pipeline_transport

http://www.1800miti.com/links/truckin/pipeline/pipeline.html

http://www.energy-business-review.com/article_news.asp?guid=976F8032-13FE-4548-84EC-4B139F82A576

http://www.iocl.com/Aboutus/Pipelines.aspx

CHAPTER VI

Transportation of Oil and Natural Gas

Introduction

Presently, the most significant oil oriented project in India is the world biggest refining complex at Jamnagar. On the Indian West coast, the new refinery will have a 580,000 barrels/day capacity and is owned by Reliance, India's biggest privately owned conglomerate. The refinery is 90% complete and expected to come on-line in September, 2008. It will join an already operational 660,000 barrels/day refining complex at Jamnagar creating the biggest refining capacity complex in the world with expected output of 1.24 million barrels/day of refined products. The crude destined to Jamnagar is routinely transported on large vessels from the Arabian Gulf. While in principal we do not expect the source of crude to change drastically, we believe that the share of crude from more distant sources, such as West Africa and Venezuela, will increase at Jamnagar's refineries. One of the signs of more distant supply is an already signed contract for supply of 150,000 barrels/day of crude from Venezuela beginning in 2008.

This contract will result in two VLCC loads per month which will create a convenient back-haul opportunity for some VLCCs employed on the AG/USG trade. Increased volumes of crude imported by the new Indian refinery will have an effect on tanker demand. The ton miles will increase depending on the distance and volumes transported. If we assume that the share of imported crude will be equally divided between suppliers from the AG, West Africa and Venezuela, the 580,000 barrel/day of distillation capacity will absorb about 10 VLCCs or about 20 Suezmaxes annually. This number is significant in terms of tonnage supply, especially given that the two biggest tanker sectors will remain balanced in terms of supply in 2008.

Whether oil is transported from production sites to the refineries by maritime or terrestrial routes, the main issues are those of safety, security and respect for the environment. At sea, everything must be done to avoid pollution; not only accidental oil spills but also the deliberate discharging of polluting products such as the residue from tank and bilge cleaning. On land the state of oil pipelines must be continually kept under surveillance and worn equipment replaced. Enormous quantities of oil transported are not used immediately. The same is true for a part of the output from refineries, what are called the finished products. Storage facilities ensuring total safety and security must therefore be planned for petroleum products (planete-energies.com).

Annual quantities of oil transported by sea are enormous. Almost 38000 oil tankers navigate the seas and oceans, transporting this fabulous liquid energy source from the points of extraction to the points of consumption. The enormous majority of hydrocarbons transported reach their destination. For example, in the period 2000/2004, according to the accident statistics of ITOPF (International Tanker Owners Pollution Federation) almost 99.99998% of oil transported arrived at its destination without problem. The organization of maritime transport of oil is complex and many companies and skills are involved in a voyage (building and maintaining the boat, inspecting it regularly, choosing the crew, deciding the route to be taken into account). Countries have responsibility for organizing safety and security regulations worldwide and above all for ensuring their respect by all involved. These regulations, which can appear complicated, formalise many decisions taken jointly at an international level for the well-being and safety of everyone (http://www.planete-energies.com/content/oil-gas/distribution/supply-transportation-oil/tankers.html).

The petroleum industry has chosen to favour maritime transport for its products, for reasons of greater flexibility. Overland transport by pipelines nevertheless remains important, in particular in vast countries such as Russia. It is also necessary to bring oil, destined for transport by ship, to a port. Finally, in the industrialized countries, there are major pipeline networks transporting crude to refineries situated inland and also handling the finished products coming out of the refineries and destined for major centres of consumption. Oil pipelines are large diameter tubes that can transport enormous quantities of oil, up to several tens of millions of tons per year. The oil circulates by means of pressure maintained by pumping stations located every 60 to 100 km. The oil travels in the pipelines at speeds of around 2m/sec (http://www.planete-energies.com/content/oil-gas/distribution/supply-transportation-oil/pipelines.html).

Overall, the problems of transport and of storage of gas are the same as for oil. Producer and consumer countries are far apart and gas has to be taken from one to the other. But in detail, things are quite different. Overland or underwater transport by gas pipeline is preferred. Unlike oil, the gas is in a gaseous state at normal pressures and temperatures. This means that, for the same quantity of energy, it occupies a volume 600 times greater than that of oil. Therefore, there is no question of chartering vessels to transport gas in its gaseous state. The most usual method of transportation is therefore by gas pipelines. There are underwater gas pipelines, such as those which link Norwegian gas fields to European terminals or those linking North Africa to Sicily. And of course, overland gas pipelines like those that bring Russian gas to the European Union. These gas pipelines are not visible: for reasons of safety and security they are buried underground. The compressed gas circulates at high speed in a gas pipeline, with the aid of compression plants positioned at regular intervals along the network. But in certain cases the construction of gas pipelines is technically impossible or too expensive, for example to bring Nigerian gas to Europe, or to take gas from Qatar to Japan. To resolve this problem, a method of maritime transport based on the liquefaction of the gas (LNG, liquefied natural gas) introduced (http://www.planete-energies.com/content/oil-gas/distribution/supply-transportation-gas.html). Be crude oil, as natural non-renewable natural resource, is available only in limited quantities, as also in limited oil fields in the country. Crude oil is refined and blended for value-additions, to make various streams of refined products to meet various types of end-uses. Refining of petroleum products is a capital-intensive and high technology-oriented process, whose threshold scales of production aught to be very high for economies of scale. In India, there are in all only 12 refineries with the combined production capacity of 114 million tonnes, which put together, serve to meet the demand of petroleum products in the country. Therefore, logistics of movement of petroleum products from the production centre to the consumption centers in a vast country, with diverse topography/terrains, such as India, is a complex management process. Moreover, as part of petroleum products is imported and exported; to that extent the refined petroleum products move in and out of a number of well-developed sea-ports of the country to be globally competitive. In designing a sound transport system for oil and natural gas these aspects need to be considered very carefully.

Logistics and transportation of Petroleum products involves massive investment, mainly for creation of its basic infrastructure, which every consumer in this country has to share either directly or indirectly. It is important that the whole gamut of activities is surveyed and put together at a macro-conceptual level for better appreciation of transport operations modes and attendant complexities thereof by the researchers, policy-makers and practitioners in the field. It is therefore imperative that optimization in logistics and transportation of Petroleum products be made to create value in the whole end-to-end supply-chain management. This chapter attempts to bring in convergence to various interrelated issues, so that areas of optimization can be identified and models can be developed for integrated planning to capture value of the products in the chain of transportation-related activities.

A. Supply Plan Management in Oil Industry

Oil Industry Supply Chain Management

When a customer region has a demand for a quantity of an oil product, it is in general possible to meet the demand using a number of equivalent products. Many factors influence the proportions of component products that are combined to make an optimal supply chain decision. The factors include the season of the year, the locations of available equivalent products, and the availability of suitable and timely transportation.

A competitive supply chain plan depends on knowledge of the above factors, on business policy knowledge, and on inventory facts in SQL databases. Both the knowledge and the facts can change rapidly. This makes it difficult to write conventional application programs and SQL queries that can produce supply chain plans to meet demand profitably (http://www.reengineeringllc.com/Oil_Industry_Supply_Chain_by_Kowalski_and_Walker.pdf).

The code of practices in maintaining a supply-chain for oil and natural gas may involve the following critical steps/ stages (www.pilottaskforce.co.uk/files/workgroup/2015.ppt):

- Commercial Stage—Forecast/Planning all activity up to the point of tender.
- Commercial Stage—Tendering all activity up to the point of contract negotiations, including elimination of bidders.
- Commercial Stage—Negotiation agreement of contract terms.
- Commercial Stage—Implementation and review through the life of the contract and at the end of the contract.
- Commercial Stage—Monitoring and Evaluation of Code.
- Implementation and Adoption of the Code.

Supply Plan Management

Supply Plan Management in Oil Industry, involving handling of diverse nature and volume of commodities, entails two major facets:

- Crude Oil Procurement for refineries Inland Distribution of Petroleum Products.
- Crude Oil logistics has a large bearing on refinery operation and refinery margin, whereas in-land distribution management has equally significant bearing on marketing logistics and marketing margin.

The commodity balance scenario of India petroleum industry—a prerequisite for understanding Transport-related logistics requirement, is highlighted below in Table 6.1:

The complexity of supply chain management in Oil Industry in India can be gauged from the fact that 144 million tones of petroleum products and 129 million tones of crude moved across the country, from well to wheel, in 2004-05, registering a growth of 6% and 5%, respectively. Consumption of petroleum products is consistently growing at 3 to 4% per annum during last 5 years.

Supply Plan in Indian Oil Industry has been traditionally managed on a centralized basis for the whole country till March 2002 under the auspices of Oil Coordination Committee (OCC), a Standing Committee of Ministry of Petroleum & Natural Gas. Till then, the primary emphasis was to make product available at all places of the country at all time, as per availability to meet demand. Today, under the overall mandate of making product available at all places, each oil company is also aiming at cost optimization and maximization of return, subject to the constraint of governmental control on some select product prices, primarily auto-fuel and cooking fuels. At the enterprise level, this optimization is being done through various software packages and development of transportation models.

Table 6.1: The Commodity Balance Scenario of India Petroleum Industry

Commodity Balance of India	Petroleum Products in Years			Million Tonnes Per Annum		
	1999-2000	2000-01	2001-02	2002-03	2003-04	2004-05
Petroleum Products						
1 Consumption	97.09	100.07	100.43	104.13	107.75	111.56
2 Indigenous Production	79.41	95.61	100	104.14	113.46	118.23
3 Refining self-sufficiency (%)	82	96	100	100	105	106
4 Growth in Consumption (%)		3	0	4	3	4
5 Imports	16.61	9.27	7.01	6.74	7.9	8.87
6 Exports	0.75	8.37	10.07	10.29	14.62	17.52
Crude Oil						
7 Indigenous Production	31.95	32.43	32.03	33.04	33.37	33.98
8 Imports	57.80	74.10	78.71	81.99	90.43	95.86
9 Growth in Crude import (%)		8	6	4	10	6
10 Load on Supply Chain of Petroleum products (2+5+5)	96.77	113.25	117.08	121.17	135.98	144.62
11 Increase in load (%)		17	3	3	12	6
12 Load on Supply Chain of Crude (7+8)	89.75	106.53	110.74	115.03	123.8	129.84
13 Increase in load (%)	—	19	4	4	8	5

B. Transportation of Petroleum Products

Transportation of petroleum products is a specialized economic activity, distinct from that of other commodities. The features, which make it distinct and complex, are:

1. Petroleum products are hazardous and inflammable. Therefore, safety of the vehicle and its operating environment is a very significant feature of transporting petroleum products.
2. Petroleum products are transported in bulk liquid and gas form. Therefore, it needs specialized containers, built exclusively for handling those products.
3. Petroleum products are quality sensitive. Therefore, it becomes the responsibility of the transport operators to maintain quality of the products at all stages of handling, loading, unloading and transporting. Products like Aviation Fuel, food grade Hexane are very sensitive from the quality point of view. Many a time, this requires dedicated transport earners.
4. Petroleum products are volatile and liquid. Therefore, products suffer loss, real or apparent, during transit. The loss has financial and environmental impact. A transport operator can playa crucial role in saving this loss.
5. Efficient handling of loading, unloading and transportation of Petroleum products need exclusive infrastructure, many of which are built and operated by agencies other than Oil Companies. Pipelines need pumping

and storage stations, Oil tankers need oil jetties, which are built and operated by port sectors, rail sidings are built and maintained by Railways. These require huge investment, planning and co-ordination.

Integrated Transport operation

Logistics and transportation of oil and gas is closely integrated with the operation of Oil and Gas Companies. The Oil Companies primarily plans the logistics and transportation is undertaken to carry out their plan. The end users of Oil and Gas also playa role in this, as they are the ultimate customers, whose needs dictate the chain of activities.

The Oil companies themselves have built and are operating a segment of the transportation infrastructure, either by themselves or through their joint ventures. Similarly, many end users also have developed their own transport facilities for their dedicated use. The transport operators are service providers to both. The transportation activity is carried out in close link with the users, so that optimization takes place at all the links of the total chain.

Therefore transportation has links with production, import, storage of inventory, end use pattern in the domestic market and export. At every stage, value is created, optimized and is passed on to the next stage.

Players in Petroleum Transportation

Transportation of Petroleum products is carried out by multiple operators/ agencies, who over the years have developed commercial acumen and strength in their respective field as illustrated in Table 6.2.

Table 6.2: Transportation of Petroleum Products by Multiple Operators/Agencies

Mode	Operators	Companies (not exhaustive)	Comments
Pipeline	Oil Companies	ONGC, IOC, BPC, HPC, GAIL, Petronet	Public sector and JVs, shared pattern of use
Shipping	Large Shipping Companies Barge operators	SCI Great Eastern Shipping Essar Shipping Barge operators	Both public and private players are competing with each other, some sectors still reserved for public sector
Rail	Indian Railways	Indian Railways	Monopoly operation, Oil Companies have created some assets for own use purpose
Road	Oil Companies, Fleet operators and end users	Large number of transport operators	Free market, multiple players, localized operation

Transportation in Oil Industry : A Multi-Modal Operation

No other tradable commodity travels so much as petroleum products do. From well till wheel, it is a long chain of transportation, storage, handling and value addition. Depending upon distance between source and intermediate destination and the size of the parcel, the modes of transportation varies. In the current state of technology and commercial viability, following are the four modes of transportation, which are being adopted in India:

1. Ocean transportation, by tankers of various sizes ranging from 5 thousand tonne capacity till 50 thousand capacities, mostly used along both stretches of Indian coast.
2. Pipeline of various length and diameters.
3. Rail wagons of various types and types, ranging from 20 tons till 55 tons carrying capacity.
4. Tank Lorries of various capacities, ranging from 10 kiloliters to 25 kiloliter.

Modes of Transportation

Transportation by Railways

Out of its total petroleum products, 36 per cent is transported by rail wagon, which constitute 7.6 per cent of Indian Railways' total revenue earning freight traffic (2000-01). During 2000-01, 4891 wagons of conventional type, including LSHS and LPG, were loaded, which was 4716 in the previous year. Indian Railways is the lifeline of the nation sustaining the Indian economy by transporting more than 600 MMT of various commodities over the entire length and breadth of the country. Petroleum traffic constitutes 5% of Railway's revenue earning freight as may be seen from Table 6.3.

Table 6.3: Petroleum Tariff as percentage of Railway Revenues

Fig. in MMT	1999-00	2000-01	2001-02	2002-03	2003-04	2004-05
Railways Revenue Earning Traffic	456	473	492	519	557	602
POL Traffic	35.1	37.0	36.4	35.0	32.43	32.4
% share of POL traffic to total traffic	8	8	7	7	6	5

Sources: Ministry of Railways, Govt. of India.

Where ever the destination is not connected by pipeline or coastal shipping and the distance to be covered is significant, Railways are the next best choice to move petroleum products. The share of Railways in the transportation of petroleum products is steadily declining over the last few years, due to the following reasons:

- Increased pressure on the existing track capacity.
- Non-availability of locomotives and tank wagons.
- Higher operating costs as compared to pipelines, resulting in higher costs to the consumers.
- Inflated freight rates due to cross subsidization of passenger traffic by freight traffic.

Railways have attributed the shortfall to the decline in the consumption of HSD in the country, which accounts for 44% of total POL freight of the Railways. They also attribute to the loss in business due to new pipelines; namely, Mangalore-Bangalore; Kochi-Karur-Coimbatore; Vadinar-Kandla; Mathura-Tundla; Koyali-Navgam; Koyali-Sidhpur and the extension of Mumbai-Manmad to Indore.

Transportation by Roads

Petroleum products are carried from the depots or terminals to retail outlets in its proximity through tank Lorries. Roads offer the most viable option for transporting petroleum products over short distances or to destinations where rail, coastal tankers or pipelines cannot penetrate. One of the problems faced by Oil Companies in transporting petroleum products by road is that widespread pilferage and adulteration *en route*. Oil Companies are now resorting to innovative methods to check this menace in order to maintain the quality and quantity standards.

Road transportation is usually the last leg of the long journey of petroleum products and it is mostly associated with the retail segment of the petroleum industry. As an economic activity, its significance is very wide as it touches a wide segment of small employers of capital and manpower. Not withstanding its economic value, road transportation has a number of negative features. It is a high-energy consuming

Mode; its contribution to environmental pollution is high; it is hazardous to itself and to the surrounding. However, considering the retailing nature of road transportation, its service can hardly be dispensed with.

Ocean Transportation

Petroleum products are transported through the ocean transport mode by way of the following five ways:

Crude Oil

1. Import of Crude (from international markets to Indian Refineries for processing), and
2. Coastal movement of Crude (Indigenous Crude supplied to Indian Refineries through tankers)

Petroleum Products

3. Import of products (from international market to Indian market for domestic consumption).
4. Export of products (from Indian market to international market).
5. Coastal movement of products produced in the Indian Refineries (from Indian Refineries to other coastal Terminals in India).

Crude oil received in Refineries is processed and refined products are transported along the Indian coast by way of first level (primary) distribution. Twelve major ports in India handled 117 million tones (MMT) of petroleum cargo of all the above fives categories during 1999-2000, which is 43 per cent of total cargo handled in the ports. Rising from a level of 34 MMT in 1980-81, 55 MMT in 1985-86, and 66 MMT in 1990-91, the petroleum cargo handling in Indian ports has been growing at an annual average of 5 per cent during 1990s. However, there is a declining trend visible in the year 2000-01 by –8.5 per cent, which is reduced to –3.4 per cent in 2001-02 (during April-November). This is because of exclusion of data pertaining to cargo handled in private and captive port facilities (Mundra, Pipapav and Jamnagar), which were operational in last two years and also because of diversion of cargo from ports to pipeline (from Kandla port to Vadinar-Kandla pipeline). However, looking at the newly developed trend of export of petroleum products and increased import of Crude, this is likely to take an upward turn by 2002-03.

Handling at Ports

12 major ports in the country handle about 151 tonnes of Petroleum products as per table 6.4 given below, which is 36% of the total traffic handled. The share of POL Traffic in Total Traffic handled at Major Ports is given in table 6.5.

Table 6.4: POL Cargo Handled in Majors Ports in 2003-04

	Ports	POL cargo in MMT
1	Kolkata / Haldia	20.12
2	Mumbai	18.55
3	Chennai	9.48
4	Kochi	9.96
5	Kandla	23.63
6	Vishakhapatnam	17.43
7	Mormugao	1.32
8	JNPT	1.93
9	Paradip	1.364
10	Tuticorin	2.30
11	New Mangalore	17.95
12	Ennore	0
	Total	151.05

Table 6.5: Share of POL Traffic in Total Traffic handled at Major Ports

Fig in MMT	1999-00	2000-01	2001-02	2002-03	2003-04
Total Traffic	271.92	281 .1 0	287.58	313.45	344.55
POL Traffic	116.71	108.35	103.18	109.58	122.30
% of POL to Total	44	38	36	35	35

Crude Oil and Gas Shipping

A. Terminal Management

A Terminal receives, stores, and distributes crude oil, feedstocks, lubricants, petrochemicals, and bunker oils (used for fueling ships and other marine vessels). A modern terminal now also provides inventory management, storage, and distribution services for refiners and other large end-users of crude oil (Figs. 6.1-6.5).

A terminal has three basic facilities:

- Storage facilities
- Crude oil receiving facility including tanker berthing facility to along with pipeline arrangement: To give a dimension of the facilities available in a terminal, we quote that the Nederland Terminal in USA can receive crude oil at each of its five ship docks and three barge berths, which can accommodate any vessel capable of navigating the 40-foot freshwater draft of the Sabine-Neches Ship Channel. The five ship docks are capable of receiving over 1.0 million barrels per day of crude oil. The terminal can also receive crude oil through a number of pipelines.
- Delivery system: The Nederland Terminal can deliver crude oil and other petroleum products via pipeline, barge, ship, rail, or truck. Nederland Terminal is capable of delivering over 1.0 million barrels per day of crude oil to 12 connecting pipelines.

Fig. 6.1: An Overall view of Terminal Facilities

Courtesy: Indian School of Petroleum.

Fig. 6.2: A View of Storage Facility in a Terminal

Courtesy: Indian School of Petroleum.

Fig. 6.3: A View of a Tanker Loading Operation in a Terminal

Courtesy: Indian School of Petroleum.

The shipping industry has experienced a tremendous increase in regulation, which to a very large extent has concentrated on matters relating to the ship and the terminal and navigation facilities, which are equally important. Once a ship approaches a port or terminal facility, the prevention of accidents and the protection of the environment becomes a shared responsibility. Tanker owners face potential unlimited liability for oil pollution damages in the event of an oil spill and tanker operations have been subject to vigorous regulation in recent years. Shipping is a truly international business. It can only function efficiently and safely if there is maximum use of international, as opposed to local, standards. Recent navigation history, provides examples where failure to adhere to this principle causes significant problems.

Terminal Automation

There are some international companies who provide total automation solutions world-wide to terminals performing primary and secondary distribution. They are designed for managing bulk plants (e.g. crude oil terminals) or oil, gas and chemical product distribution terminals by automating them with integrated applications for inventory management, fluid movement optimization, operations planning and other sophisticated technologies that improve the efficiency of transfer operations.

Benefits of Automation for Terminals

- Better insight into ongoing terminal operations and terminal performance, even for several Terminals at once.
- Improved terminal efficiency (reduced inventory, more flexible operations, improved usage of facilities, improved throughput, minimized downtime).
- Improved terminal safety, for reliable operation in the most hazardous environments.

- Reduced system/terminal maintenance.
- Simple integration with existing automation solutions.
- More cost effective engineering, implementation and testing.

The terminal management system integrates and controls loading racks and associated equipment, pumps, valves, motors, weigh scales, flow meters, card readers, data entry terminals, remote connections, smart additive equipment and blenders, safety and shutdown systems. In addition to the core functionality, the system also provides features designed to automate truck, railcar, ship, barge and pipeline receipt and shipment. These solutions are specifically designed for managing bulk plants (crude oil terminals) or oil, gas and chemical product distribution terminals in the most efficient way and keeping the terminal operating costs to a minimum.

B. Shipping

Shipping is an integral part of Oil Industry. One of the factors behind Oil Industry's global reach is ship's ability to carry large quantity of oil all across the world. For a country like India, shipping has additional significance. Firstly, India has a long coastline of a peninsular size. That makes a great deal of prospect for coastal shipping. Secondly, Indian subcontinent is astride the critical sea lanes of communications of the Persian Gulf and the Malacca strait on ether side. Almost 70% of the world's oil supply passes this area.

Shipping activity in Indian Oil & Gas Industry has the following three facets:

- Coastal shipping for products movement across the coast.
- International shipping for Crude Oil import.
- LNG & LPG Shipping.

The State owned Shipping Corporation of India dominates the Indian Shipping Industry, owning more than 40% of gross registered tonnage (Table 6.6). Major Private Sector players include Great Eastern Shipping, Essar Shipping, Varun Shipping, Shahi Shipping and Tolani Shipping.

Table 6.6: Indian Tonnage as on March 31, 2003

	Gross Registered Tonnage (GRT)	Dead Weight Tonnage (DWT)
Coastal Trade		
Oil Tankers (Product Carriers)	40,776	61,027
Oil Tankers (Crude Oil Carriers)	50,080	82,246
Overseas Trade		
Oil Tankers (Product Carriers)	1,955,129	3,592,087
Oil Tankers (Crude Oil Carriers)	893,676	1,493,043
LPG Carriers	134,447	162,592

Size of Vessels

Ship size has direct relevance to the cargo carrying capacity and port related facilities required for the ship to berth. The following terminology speaks about the dimension of ships:

- **LOA (Length over-All):** LOA is the overall length of a ship from foremost to the aftermost part. VLCC 300m, Suezmax 275m, Aframax 240m.
- **Beam:** The width of a vessel at its widest part.
- **Draft:** The depth of the vessel below the waterline, which varies depending on the amount of cargo on board and the density of the water the vessel, is lying in.
- **Hull:** The Hull is the Shell including the superstructure.
- **Double Hull:** A design of tanker which has double sides and a double bottom. The space in between are used for ballast.
- **Ballast:** Ballast is required in an empty ship to give her sufficient draft to ensure stability and sea handling.
- **Dead weight (dwt):** The cargo carrying capacity of a vessel plus the weight of bunkers, stores, fresh water etc (in MT).
- **Gross Tonnage (GRT):** A measurement of volumes including most of the confined spaces on board.

Types of Ship

I. With Reference to suitability for Cargoes and Trades:
   A. DRY Trades
   B. WET Trades

II. With Reference to Tonnage

Dry Trade

- *Liner Trades*: Ships are designed to carry a variety of cargo between specific ports on fixed schedules.

  Example: Containership, Barge carriers.
- *Tramp Trades*: Ships are designed to carry no specific types of cargo and travel anywhere in the world.

  Example: Conventional Bulk Vessels (Handy max, Panamax, Capesize), ore carriers and combination carriers.

Wet Trade

- Crude Carriers
- Product Carriers
- Chemical Carriers
- Gas Carriers
- Specialist Vessels

Tonnage

- **ULCC** = A tanker of 320,000 + dwt
- **VLCC** = A tanker of 160–319,999 dwt

- **Suezmax** = Tanker between 120–159,999 dwt.
- **Aframax** = Tanker of 80–119,999 dwt
- **Panamax** = Tanker between 50–80,000 dwt
- **MR Tankers** = Tanker between 40–49,999 dwt
- **Parcel Tankers** = Tanker between 10–39,999 dwt

Fig. 6.4: A view of Tanker Chartering

Courtesy: Indian School of Petroleum.

Tanker Chartering

A vessel can be chartered in any of the following ways:

(i) Voyage Charter
(ii) Time Charter
(iii) Bareboat Charter
(iv) Trip-Time Charter
(v) Contract of Affreightment (COA)

• *Voyage Charter*

Ship is engaged for either a single voyage or for consecutive/round voyage for shipments of an agreed quantity of cargo. The ship owner undertakes to provide the vessel to the charterers for carriage of agreed cargo within the certain range of rates and conditions mutually agreed in advance.

• *Time Charter*

Ship is hired for a fixed period of time for operation within the defined territories or between safe ports. The responsibility of scheduling the ship employment and meeting port expenses, canal dues, fuel cost, cargo expenses etc remains with the charterers. Running expenses have to be met by ship owners

• *Bareboat Charter*

Ship owner let out the bare ship for a period of time to the charterer. The ship in the bare form lies at the disposal of the charterer who has the full responsibility of operating and manning the ship. Thus charterer in this case becomes the despondent owners.

- *Trip-Time Charter*

Ship is chartered on single or round voyage basis, where charterers bear greater responsibilities in ensuring timely performance of the voyage.

- *Contract of Affreightment (COA)*

Owner & Charterer agree to carry a certain quantity of specified cargo from one port to another during a fixed period at an agreed freight rate. The ship owner may engage the number of ships to complete the assignment or contract within the agreed period.

Freight Market

Freight is what a tanker charter pays to the tanker owner. Depending upon the type of chartering used, it would essentially cover all the variable costs of running a vessel and a part of the fixed cost. The type of chartering as described above, would essentially apportion the cost either to the charter or to the owner, as the case may be.

Freight market is highly sensitive to time. For a particular cargo type and cargo size, specific vessels are required. For example, crude vessel of a 100,000 tonnes, would require an 'afra max' vessel or a 'Suez max' vessel with dead freight. Similarly, LNG and LPG vessels are specialized carriers. White oil and black oil vessels cannot be interchanged from voyage to voyage. It would mean grade changeover, for which there are stipulated keys (tables prescribing washing the tanks). There are vessel with registration restriction, like coastal voyage and international voyage. Various terminals have age restriction for vessels, like certain terminal would not accept a vessel more than 20 years. Most of the modern terminals have their own ship vetting system. All the restrictions coupled with the lay days requirement (period during which a vessel is required to report at the terminal), make the vessel selection quite a limited option. Within limited option available to a charterer, he has to enter the market through a broker and come out of it very carefully, so that he can get the best deal. Al the same time, from the tanker owner's perspective, a tanker should get good business. Idling time of a tanker is a costly proposition for the tanker owner.

Besides these cargo specific points, the charter party contract has got inbuilt provisions as per international maritime law, specifying liabilities and responsibilities of the charterer and the ship owner.

INCHOE TERMS

The liabilities and responsibility of the seller and buyer of the cargo is spelt out in a document, called INCHOE TERMS. That would essentially mean, whether the cargo is to be uplifted on FOB or CFR or CIF basis. That would essentially mean, who pays the freight. Irrespective of FOB or CFR, the title and ownership of cargo gets transferred to buyer at the flange of the manifold connecting the ship and the hose.

Bill of Lading

Bill of Lading is an essential shipping document that bears the ownership of cargo, quantity assessment, load and discharge port and the date of completion of loading.

World Scale

- The new World wide Tanker Nominal Freight Scale is a catalogue of theoretical freight rates expressed as US dollars per tonne for most of the conceivable spot voyages in the tanker trade.
- World scale is used because it gives the flexibility required for the oil trade. If a tanker fixture takes place, this would involve the ship owner to calculate separate individual freights for a wide variety of discharge points.
- World scale provides a solution to this problem in that it offers a set of nominal rates designed to provide roughly the same daily income irrespective of discharge point.

- Standard Vessel : 75,000 tonnes
- Average service speed : 14.5 knots
- Bunker Consumption : 55 tonnes/day
- Grade of fuel oil : 380 cst
- Port time : 4 days basis 1 load/1 discharge
- Fixed hire element : USD 12,000 /day
- Bunker price : USD 167.75 per tonne
- Port Costs : Current
- Canal Transit Time : 30 hrs for Suez Canal, 24 hrs for Panama canal

Shipping of Liquefied Natural Gas

Liquefied natural gas or LNG is natural gas that has been processed to remove impurities and heavy hydrocarbons and then condensed into a liquid at atmospheric pressure by cooling it to approximately –160 degrees Celsius. LNG is transported by specially designed vessels and stored in specially designed tanks. LNG is about 1/640th the volume of natural gas at standard temperature and pressure (STP), making it much more cost-efficient to transport over long distances where pipelines do not exist. Where moving natural gas by pipelines is not possible or economical, it can be transported by LNG vessels, where the most common tank types are membrane or moss (Fig. 6.5).

Trade in LNG

LNG is shipped around the world in specially constructed seagoing vessels. The trade of LNG is completed by signing a Sale and Purchase Agreement (SPA) between a supplier and receiving terminal, and by signing a Gas Sale Agreement (GSA) between a receiving terminal and end-users. Most of the contract terms used to be DEX or Ex Ship, which meant the seller, was responsible for the

Fig. 6.5: A Cross-sectional view of LNG Ship's Hull and Containment System

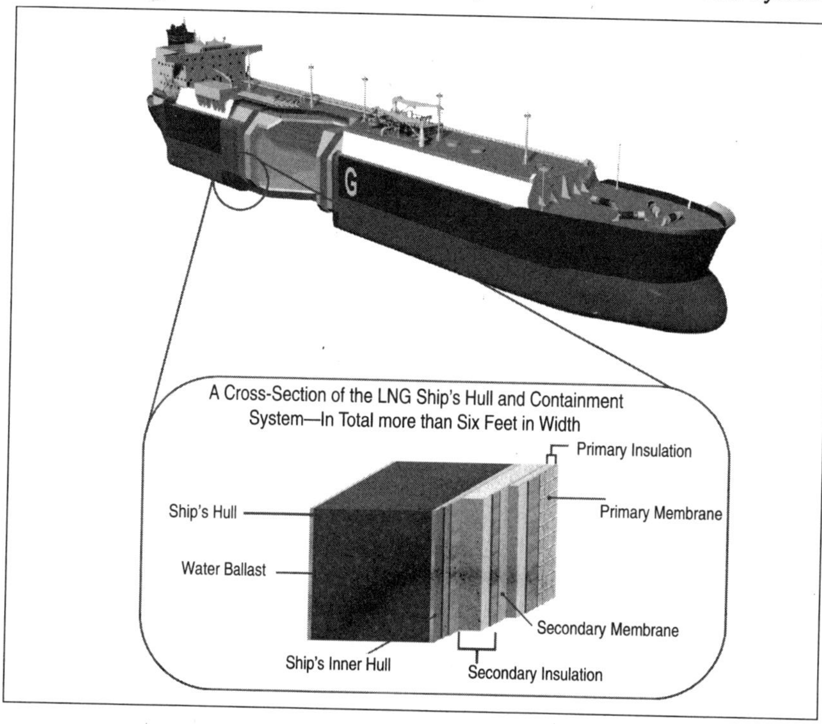

transportation. But with low shipbuilding costs, and the buyer preferring to ensure reliable and stable supply, there are more and more contract terms of FOB, under which the buyer is responsible for the transportation, which is realized by the buyer owning the vessel or signing a long term charter agreement with independent carriers. The pricing structure that has been widely used in Asian LNG SPAs is as follows: PLNG = A+B×Pcrude oil, where A refers to a term that represents various non-oil factors, but usually a constant determined by negotiation at a level that can prevent LNG prices from falling below a certain level. It thus varies regardless of oil price fluctuation. Typical figures of ex-ship contracts range from USD 0.7 to 0.9. B is a degree of indexation to oil prices; typical figures are 0.1485 or 0.1558, and Pcrude oil usually denominated in JCC. PLNG and Pcrude oil stand for price of oil in USD per million British Thermal Unit (MMBTU (in the fuel industry, M stands for 1000 and MM for 1,000,000)). With the demand of LNG moving up and down, the price of LNG moves in an "S" curve. With new demand from China, India and US increasing dramatically, and crude oil price skyrocketing, the LNG price is on the rise too. In the mid 1990s LNG was a buyer's market. At the request of buyers, the SPAs began to adopt some flexibility on volume and price. The buyers had more upward and downward flexibilities in TOP, and short term SPAs less than 15 years came into effect. At the same time, alternative destinations for cargo and arbitrage were also allowed. By the turn of the 21st century, the market was again in favor of sellers.

Sellers now propose rigid SPAs and would like an association similar to OPEC to be established to protect their interests. It is certain that the competition between sellers and buyers will go on. The United States Department of Energy's Energy Information Administration (EIA) provides the estimates of LNG Trade in 2002 as follows (Table 6.7):

Table 6.7: Profile of LNG Trade in 2002 in Major Destination Countries

Country	Export volume		Country	Import volume	
	(10^9 ft^3)	(10^6 t)		(10^9 ft^3)	(10^6 t)
Indonesia	1,100	23.0	Japan	9,200	188.3
Algeria	935	19.6	South Korea	2,000	40.7
Malaysia	741	15.6	France	511	10.7
Qatar	726	14.9	Taiwan	363	7.5
Nigeria	394	8.2	United States	229	4.8
Australia	367	7.7	Turkey	224	4.6
Oman	356	7.3	United Kingdom	356	7.3
Brunei Darussalam	351	7.2	Portugal	146	3.3
United Arab Emirates	278	5.7	Spain	131	2.7
Russia	234	4.8	Italy	130	2.6
Trinidad and Tobago	189	4.0	Belgium	124	2.7
United States	68	1.4	India	122	2.5

Source: USDE.

Natural Gas Pipelines in India

In India, natural Gas did not find much use and almost all the associated gas was being flared. The 1960s saw some developments in the natural gas market with QIL supplying gas to local producers and state electricity boards in Assam. ONGC started supplying associated gas from its Ankleshwar fields, discovered in 1960, to Alembic Glass and Sarabhai Industries at Baroda through a gas pipeline that was laid by the then Gujarat Pipelines project of ONGC.

Supply of free-gas from Cambay to Dhuvran thermal power station started in 1964. The 24 kilometer Nahorkatiya-Namrup pipeline was commissioned in 1965 to supply feedstock to FCI and fuel to the Assam State Electricity Board. In December 1970, another gas pipeline was laid to market gas from Navagam in Gujarat to Calico Mills. The 150 km long Ankleshwar Koyali gas pipeline was commissioned in September 1971 at a cost of Rs 36 million. 1974 saw the discovery of the giant Bombay High oil and gas field by ONGC. Commercial production started in 1976 and it was only by 1978 that gas pipelines were laid to the shores of Mumbai for supplying gas to power generation and fertilizer manufacturing units. Transportation and marketing of natural gas was entrusted to GAIL (India) Ltd.

GAIL started its Hazira-Bijaipur-Jagdishpur (HBJ) trunk pipeline in 1986. In 1987-88, country's first cross country 1,700 km long, 18.2 MMSCMD capacity HBJ pipeline was commissioned. In March 1996, GAIL expanded the capacity of HBJ system to 33.4 MMSCMD by laying an additional 505 km pipeline.

Other players in the gas transportation business are:

- Gujarat State Petronet Limited (GSPL), a SPV floated by Gujarat State Petroleum Corporation Ltd (GSPCL) to set up a Rs 32 billion, 2,500 km pipeline network for transportation of gas within the state of Gujarat.
- Assam Gas Company has a 600 km pipeline network in Assam, including the 250 km pipeline from Sibsagar to Marsharita in Assam.
- Gujarat Gas Company Ltd, a private player, has a pipeline network spanning more than 1,800 km in Gujarat. Its pipeline network caters to Surat, Bharuch and Ankleswar. GGCL has also extended its network to Jhagadia.

India has recently started importing LNG at the Petronet LNG (PLL)'s 5 MMTPA terminal at Dahej, Gujarat and at Hazira-developed by Shell. Major company-wise performance of Pipelines for Natural gas transportation is given in Table 6.8.

Table 6.8: Performance of Existing Natural Gas Pipelines (length & capacity) in India

	Owner	Length in km	Dia. in inches	Capacity MMSCMD	Year of Commission
Hazira-Bijaipur-	GAIL	2,800	18/36	33.4	1 987/1 997
Chainsa-Maruti	GAIL	60	16	2.25	12003
Kalol-Ramol	GAIL	44	12	0.8	2003
Aqra-Ferozabad loop	GAIL	35	10	1.2	2003
Dahei-Bijaipur	GAIL	610	42	23.9	2004
Bomaby Hih-Uran	ONGC	203	26	12.5	1978
Heera-Uran	ONGC	81	26	16	1989
Bassein-Hazira	ONGC	231	36	23	1985
Bassein-Hazira	ONGC	244	42	37	1995

Pipeline Transportation

There are 12 product pipelines in India, running into total length of 5018 km, which are used to transport 32 per cent of total products consumed in India (2000-01), which was only 23 per cent during 1990-91.

Table 6.9 presents the list of pipelines and their use pattern for three years (1998-2001).

Table 6.9: Pipelines and their Use Pattern in India

Major Pipelines in India	Capacity (mm) as oil 1.4.2001	Length (km.)	1998-99 tmt	1999-00 tml	2000-01 tmt	Capacity Capacity utilization per cent
1	2	3	4	5	6	7
Barauni-Kanpur	1.80	669	1591	1903	1671	93
Mumbai-Pune	3.67	161	3630	3456	3388	92
Guwal1ati-Siliguri	0.818	435	1010	1048	995	122
Haldia-Barauni	1.25	525	1541	1528	1364	109
Haldia-Mourigram-Rajbandh	1.35	277	1723	2024	2249	166

(Contd.)

1	2	3	4	5	6	7
Koyali-Ahmedabad	1.10	116	1577	1605	1549	141
Mathura-Jullandhar	3.70	596	4363	3506	3550	96
Kandla-Bhatinda	7.50	1443	5532	6421	5933	79
Digboi-Tinsukia	0.73	75	466	506	584	80
Mumbai-Manmad	4.33	252	1178	3261	3195	74
Vizag-Vijaywada	4.10	356	1304	2523	2980	73
Vadinar-Kandla (May, 2000)	11.50	113			4054	35
Total	41.85	5018	23915	27781	31510	75

LPG Transportation by Road and Rail

The demand for LPG in the country in *2003-04* was 9.31 MMT against the domestic production of 7.65 MMT. The balance requirements were met through imports. The imported LPG is shipped at the ports from where they are further transported by road, rail or pipeline. The domestic production of LPG is derived either from the refineries or from the gas fractionators. LPG within the country is transported by road (bulk or packed), rail or pipeline. Tank trucks of different capacities are used to service the needs of different consumers. Hence there are tank trucks of 7 meter to 20 meter; Tank wagon 4 wheelers and 8 wheelers and ships from 22,000 cubic meters to 54,000 cubic meters. These tank wagons are operational on broad gauge of Indian Railways. There are approximately 2,600 tank wagons operational. The state of LPG import infrastructure as well as shipping fleet available for LPG transportation in India is given in Tables 6.10 and 6.11 respectively.

Table 6.10: LPG Import Infrastructure

Sl. No.	Disport	Achievable Capacity (MMTPA)
1	Kandla	1,000
2	Mangalore	1,000
3	Haldia	*800*
4	Ratnairi	*300*
5	Vizaq	4,00
	Total	3,500

Table 6.11: Shipping Fleet for LPG in India

Sl. No.	Vessel	Built	DWT
1	M. Viswamitra	1974	38,705
2	M. Vashist	1976	17,650
3	Nana Parbat	1991	17,601
4	Annapurna	1991	17,601
5	M. Vyas	1975	18,165
6	Nayantara	1991	2,628
7	Ishita	1991	2,628
8	Vikram	1991	1,060

Transportation of LPG by Pipeline: Jamnaar-Loni Pipeline

GAIL completed the world's longest and India's first cross-country LPG pipeline in 2001. The Jamnagar Loni pipeline covering 1,246 km passes through Gujarat, Rajasthan, Haryana, and Delhi and UP. The pipeline had a capacity of 1.7 MMTPA in Phase I and was upgraded to 2.5 MMTPA in Phase II, which was completed with the commissioning of the 68.5 km long Kandla to Samakhiali LPG pipeline with maximum throughput capacity of 0.8 MMTPA. The LPG is sourced from RIL's Jamnagar refinery and subsequently from the import terminal of IOC at Kandla and evacuated at Ajmer and Jaipur in Rajasthan, Piyala in Haryana, Madanpur Khadar in Delhi and Loni in Uttar Pradesh. The overall position of LPG pipeline throughput in India is shown in Table 6.12.

Table 6.12: LPG Pipeline throughput

Year	Fig. in MT
1999-2000	0
2000-01	100
2001-02	1,310
2002-03	1,520
2003-04	1,840

CNG Marketing

GAIL, in joint venture with some other companies, is engaged in city gas supply activities. Basically, it means, making CNG available for auto, domestic and commercial uses through pipelines. In Mumbai, the JV is Mahanagar Gas and in Delhi it is Indraprastha Gas. The potential in this sector is huge. The issues involved in this are: pricing and scarcity of gas.

Sectoral Use of Petroleum Products

Petroleum products are used primarily in three sectors, *viz.*, household, transport and industrial. As large segment of our population still uses bio-fuels and agricultural wastes in the household sector for domestic energy requirement, petroleum products are not used in a significant way in the domestic sector. However, use of bio fuels in household sector is sensitive from environmental point of view and the dependence of household sector on mineral fuels is increasing very fast. Out of the total production of LPG, 80 per cent is used in domestic sector and its use is increasing by 9 per cent per annum during 1990s. During the last decade, transport sector has consumed 35 per cent of total petroleum products and the industry has used 17 per cent and the share of power generation comes to 4 per cent. With the increasing trend of industrialization and urbanization, use of fossil fuel is going to increase in all sectors and, to that extent, the transportation activities are going to multiply in volume and complexity.

Market Segments and Transportation Legs

From the logistics point of view, petroleum products traverse three intermediate points, taking resort to multi modal transportation system as depicted below (Table 6.13):

Table 6.13: Transportation Legs in Petroleum Transportation System

Sl. No.	Origin	Destination	Mode
1.	Primary supply point, i.e., Refineries (both coastal and inland), and Port locations	Secondary supply points, i.e., Major Terminals and Tap off points	Cross country Pipelines, Coastal Ships, Rail and Road
2.	Secondary supply points	Distribution storage points (Depots) and major customers	Rail, Road and Pipelines
3.	Depots	Retail outlets and customers	Road

Marketing of Transportation Fuels in India

The process of liberalization of the downstream sector in India began in February 1993, with the decanalising of imports of Superior Kerosene Oil (SKO), Liquefied Petroleum Gas (LPG) and Furnace Oil (FO) and allowing private marketers to import and sell these products at market determined prices.

In November 1997, the Government of India passed a resolution to allow marketing rights for transportation fuels—motor spirit (MS), high speed diesel (HSD), and aviation turbine fuel (ATF) conditional on owning and operating refineries with an investment of at least Rs. 2000 crore or oil exploration and production companies producing at least three million tones of crude oil annually.

With the dismantling of the APM, the GOI has amended the provisions of the resolution of 1997, in line with announcement of the India Hydrocarbon Vision, 2025, under which marketing rights are also available to a company investing or proposing to invest Rs. 2000 crore (about US$ 415 million), in exploration and production (E&P), refining, pipelines, or terminals. The Government to its satisfaction will do the valuation of the investments. In case of future investments, the time frame for making such investments in the eligible activities would be counted as ten years from the date of grant of authorization for marketing of transportation fuels. A bank guarantee of Rs. 500 crore would have to be provided to the GOI, which would be discharged on completion of the investment of Rs. 2000 crore.

Every eligible company would get only one authorization for marketing transportation fuels, and the authorization for marketing transportation fuels, and the authorization will not be transferable without permission of the GOI. The Company seeking authorization to market transportation fuels will be required to make an application in a specified form. There shall be no limit to the quantum and size of the scheme and the number and location of retail outlets.

The marketing scheme shall contain details of:

- The source of supply of products to be marketed.
- Tankage and other infrastructure proposed to be established along with their capacity;
- Means of transportation of products to depots and to RO's;
- The number of locations of RO's proposed to be established and details of their storage and dispensing capacity;
- The total quantum and type of products to be covered under the marketing scheme.

Company will have to follow GOI/Regulatory board guidelines on retail service obligations (to make available MS and HSD to retail consumers through out the specified working hours) and marketing service obligations (to set up retail outlets in remote areas and low service areas) that are set up from time to time in public interest.

Structural Shifts Envisaged in Transportation of Petroleum Products

Transportation of Petroleum products will undergo a structural transformation in the short-term future. This will be more pronounced in the road sector. Today, the fleet owners are having only limited principal users, with whom they have a long-term contract. Many of the tank Lorries used for transportation of petrol and diesel have an evergreen contract with any of the four oil-marketing companies. Secondly, as the entire principal user companies are PSUs, there is security and loyalty from both sides. At times, the fleet operators have used their collective bargaining power and attempted to extract a rent from the PSU users.

From April 2002 onwards, nine private companies have been permitted to market transportation fuels, namely, petrol, diesel and aviation fuel. These companies are Oil & Natural Gas Corporation (ONGC), Reliance Petroleum Ltd (RPL), Gas Authority of India Ltd (GAIL), Oil India Ltd (OIL), Mangalore Refineries and Petrochemical Ltd (MRPL), Essar Oil Ltd, Cairns Energy of UK, Petronet LNG Ltd and Nagarjuna Group. With the entry of these firms, there will be stiff competition among the users of fleet and a new tariff level will be drawn.

Second development goes in favour of fleet owners, which is that Oil Companies are coming up with new customer serving measures or loyalty programmes which provide multiple service packages for the fleet owners and transport operators. Those measures are known as 'smart fleet cards', 'one truck stop shop' etc.

Import through Pipelines: pros and cons

The cross-border oil and gas trade has grown significantly in the past 50 years. How much of the oil trade is carried by pipeline is uncertain. The vast majority of oil moves in ocean-going tankers, and in addition to pipelines also is shipped by rail and trucks, with the result that precise data collection on transport methods is difficult. However, for gas there are only two serious transport options1: pipelines and liquefied natural gas (LNG).

REFERENCES

Atmanand (2004), Growth and Deregulation of Indian Oil Industry. Excel Books.

GAIL (2004), Natural Gas in India. GAIL-Infraline. I.Infraline.com

Indian School of Petroleum (2005), A Manual on Oil and Gas Accounting. Training Programme, on Upstream Business Processes for L&T Infotech Ltd.

H.K. Abdel-AAL, B.A. Bakr and M.A.Al Sahlawi (1992), Petroleum Economics & Engineering, Marcel Deckker Inc.

Patra, D.C. (2004), Oil Industry in India, Mittal Publications, New Delhi.

Websites

Planete-energies.com

http://www.planete-energies.com/content/oil-gas/distribution/supply-transportation-oil/tankers.html

http://www.planete-energies.com/content/oil-gas/distribution/supply-transportation-oil/pipelines.html

http://www.planete-energies.com/content/oil-gas/distribution/supply-transportation-gas.html

http://www.reengineeringllc.com/Oil_Industry_Supply_Chain_by_Kowalski_and_Walker.pdf

www.pilottaskforce.co.uk/files/workgroup/2015.ppt

CHAPTER VII

Economics of Crude Oil

Introduction

This chapter is designed as a basic study material on the subject, drawn from applied knowledge in the field of crude oil management, with focus on cost implications and cost advantage. The chapter provides an insight into the basic understanding of crude oil economics with adequate knowledge to take up a professional assignment in the following fields of operations:

Basic Petroleum Supply Chain Economics

Petroleum economics has a value chain. Value is created at each of the following links of the chain:

(a) Raw material cost (cost of the crude oil),
(b) Primary transportation cost,
(c) Manufacturing cost (cost of refining),
(d) Primary storage and throughput cost,
(e) Wholesale downstream markets,
(f) Secondary transportation,
(g) Secondary storage and final distribution, and
(h) End user's total cost.

The scope of this lesson is confined to only the first link: that is the economics of crude oil. However, it will highlight the interface with the second and the third link, *viz.*, primary transportation and refining, for holistic comprehension of the theme.

Crude Oil is a Composite Product

Crude oil is seldom used in its natural form. It is refined through a process of distillation and blended to form mixtures of various refined streams. Each mixture would be having a range of close distillations, which makes the properties of the mixture homogeneous, suitable to a particular application. In this process, a barrel of crude oil outputs a range of refined products. Therefore, crude oil, in its natural form is a composite product. The value of crude oil is, therefore, a function of the use value of the constituent units, which are the refined products.

The basic process of refining is distillation, where a liquid is heated in order to vaporize it. The vapors then cool and condense into a liquid. Crude oil contains several hydrocarbon compounds with different boiling points. The lighter compounds boil first and then the heavier compounds boil as the heat increases.

Crude Oil is Quality-Specific

Crude oil has geo-chemical properties, depending upon its natural composition. It is usually specific to a location where it is available and extracted from. Therefore, all grades of crude oil are not equal with regard to their quality and value. Crude oil available world over is not a homogeneous product, but what is available in a particular field has a large degree of homogeneity and consistency in it. As a natural commodity, which is predominantly used as raw material, the quality specifications of any crude oil are very broad and, therefore, may not conform to precise laboratory specifications. Crude oil available in the world market is so diverse that there are as many grades of crude oil as there are oil fields.

From the user point of view, crude oil in the world oil market has been classified into three broad categories. This classification helps to identify the nature and use value of crude. Given below is a brief exposition on these classifications, with their dominant features and distinguishing a grade from other grades. Crude oil is categorized and evaluated according to three characteristics. The first is sulfur content, which is important because sulfur is a major harmful pollutant. Low sulfur crude oil or ' sweet' crude contains less than 0.5 per cent sulfur by weight. Intermediate crude oil has between 0.5 and 1.0 per cent and high content crude has more than 1.0 per cent sulfur by weight.

The second characteristic is density. Low density or 'light' crude oil is desirable because it yields higher value light products, such as gasoline (petrol), jet fuel and light distillate fuel oil. Density is measured in terms of gravity, which is determined by the American Petroleum Institute (API) and is quoted in terms of degrees. Light crude oils have gravity greater than 35 degrees and heavy crude oils have gravity less than 24 degrees.

The third characteristic of crude oil is field of origin, which is important because it summarizes many other characteristics, such as viscosity, colour and metal content.

Besides the above mentioned broad classification, crude oils are also known to be classified as (a) bituminous and non-bituminous, (b) lube bearing and non-lube bearing, (c) high pour and low pour, etc.

How Crude Oil is converted in the Refinery Process?

An oil refinery is an industrial process plant where crude oil is processed and refined into more useful petroleum products, such as gasoline, diesel fuel, asphalt base, heating oil, kerosene, and liquefied petroleum gas. (Gary and Handwerk,

1984 & Leffler, 1985) Oil refineries are typically large sprawling industrial complexes with extensive piping running throughout, carrying streams of fluids between large chemical processing units.

Raw or unprocessed ("crude") oil is not useful in the form it comes in out of the ground. Although "light, sweet" (low viscosity, low sulfur) oil has been used directly as a burner fuel for steam vessel propulsion, the lighter elements form explosive vapors in the fuel tanks and so it is quite dangerous, especially so in warships. For this and many other uses, the oil needs to be separated into parts and refined before use in fuels and lubricants, and before some of the byproducts could be used in petrochemical processes to form materials such as plastics, detergents, solvents, elastomers, and fibers such as nylon and polyesters. Petroleum fossil fuels are used in ship, automobile and aircraft engines. These different hydrocarbons have different boiling points, which means that they can be separated by distillation. Since the lighter liquid elements are in great demand for use in internal combustion engines, a modern refinery will convert heavy hydrocarbons and lighter gaseous elements into these higher value products (http://en.wikipedia.org/wiki/Oil_refinery).

Refining process takes place inside a maze of hardware that one observer has likened to "a metal spaghetti factory"; Employees regulate refinery operations from within highly automated control rooms. Because so much activity happens out of sight, refineries are surprisingly quiet places. The only sound most visitors hear is the constant, low hum of heavy equipment.

The complexity of this equipment varies from one refinery to the next. In general, the more sophisticated a refinery, the better its ability to upgrade crude oil into high value products. Whether simple or complex, however, all refineries perform three basic steps: separation, conversion and treatment.

Separation: Heavy on the Bottom, Light on the Top

The liquids and vapours are discharged into distillation towers, the tall, narrow columns that give refineries their distinctive skylines. Inside the towers, the liquids and vapours separate into components or fractions according to weight and boiling point. The lightest tractions, including gasoline and Liquid petroleum gas (LPG), vaporize and rise to the top of the tower, where they condense back to liquids. Medium weight liquids, including kerosene and diesel oil distillates, stay in the middle. Heavier liquids, called gas oils, separate lower down, while the heaviest fractions with the highest boiling points settle at the bottom. These tars like fractions, called residuum, are literally the "bottom of the barrel." The fractions now are ready for piping to the next station or plant within the refinery. Some components require relatively little additional processing to become asphalt base or jet fuel. However, most molecules that are destined to become high-value products require much more processing that follows in the continuous stream of value-chain.

Conversion: Cracking and Rearranging Molecules to Add Value

This is where refining is fanciest footwork takes place, where fractions from the distillation towers are transformed into streams (intermediate components) that eventually become finished products. This also is where a refinery makes money because only through conversion cans most low-value fractions become gasoline. The most widely used conversion method is called cracking because it uses heat and pressure to "crack" heavy hydrocarbon molecules into lighter ones. A cracking unit consists of one or more tall, thick-walled, bullet-shaped reactors and a network of furnaces, heat t exchangers and other vessels. Fluid catalytic cracking, or "cat cracking," is the basic gasoline-making process. Using intense heat (about 1,000 degrees Fahrenheit), low pressure and a powdered catalyst (a substance that accelerates chemical reactions), the cat cracker can convert most relatively heavy fractions into smaller gasoline molecules.

Hydro-cracking applies the same principles but uses a different catalyst, slightly lower temperatures, much greater pressure and hydrogen to obtain chemical reactions. Cracking and coking are not the only forms of conversion. Other refinery processes, instead of splitting molecules, rearrange them to add value. Alkylation, for example, makes gasoline components by combining some of the gaseous byproducts of cracking. The process, which essentially is cracking in reverse, takes place in a series of large, horizontal vessels and tall, skinny towers that loom above other refinery structures.

In India, secondary processing facilities are available in seven refineries, of which IOC's Koyali only uses both the hydro-cracking and the catalytic cracking method. All other refineries use the carbon rejection process. Today, a major portion of refining involves blending, purifying, fine-tuning and otherwise improving products to meet these requirements. Among the variables that determine the blend are octane level, vapor pressure ratings and special considerations, such as whether the gasoline will be used at high altitudes.

Sources and Availability

The Middle-East remains the largest crude oil producing, region. It holds about two-thirds of the one trillion barrels of global proven oil reserves. So the region's critical role in world crude oil supply will continue and will grow. The core developments given in following paras have shaped the pattern of regional oil production:

The higher crude oil prices of the 1970s and early 1980s afforded a strong economic incentive to explore and produce oil and the production rose in many areas. At the same time, oil demand declined in response to high prices. Saudi Arabia became the 'swing supplier', reducing its production as necessary to balance supply and demand. Rejecting of that role in mid 1985 (when its output had fallen to about 25 per cent of its 1980 peak), brought the full force of supply-demand imbalance on to the markets and resulted in price collapse of 1986 : Prices did not return to the pre-1986 level until the Persian Gulf conflict of 1990-91, and even then only briefly. Again, in 1998, when Asian demand faltered with the region's economies and Northern Hemisphere demand faltered with the warm winter, the high production levels resulted in another price collapse. The market reaction in 1998, however, was not the same as in 1986, as demand did not recover as quickly and supply did not fall as quickly. Hence, the low price period lasted longer and showed lower prices in 1998 than in 1986. In early 2000, crude oil prices exceeded the levels of the Persian Gulf conflict in nominal terms. Although price increases were sharp in early 2000, yet, crude oil prices remained less than half of the early 1980s peak in terms of real buying power.

Saudi Arabia, the market-balancer in the early 1980s, has been the world's largest producer during 1990s. Not only did Saudi Arabia increase its production to fill the gap caused by the loss of Iraqi and Kuwaiti supplies after Iraq invaded Kuwait in 1990, but production declined in the other two large production regions, i.e., the United States and the Former Soviet union. Middle East's production would have been higher throughout the 1990s if Iraq's production had not been constrained by the United Nations sanctions imposed after Iraq invaded Kuwait in 1990. The so-called 'Humanitarian oil Sales' has provided Iraq only limited and closely controlled re-entry into 'world crude oil market. Middle-East's production also would have been higher at various times if it had not been for the market balancing role played with varying degrees of success by the Organization of Petroleum Exporting Countries (OPEC).

North America is the second largest producing area after the Middle East. The United States, the second largest producing country in the world, accounts for almost 60 per cent of the North American region's total. Canada, the United States and Mexico all have long production histories and production from mature fields has been declining. However, a new surge in technology has benefited both new field development and more complete production from the existing fields.North Sea production, off the United Kingdom and Norway, began in the late 1970s. In contrast to prediction from the early 1980s of the imminent decline in the region's production, the North Sea has yet to see its peak. The regions success with new exploration and production technology, and hence its continuing volume growth, has been a central factor in world crude oil market for a decade.

Production in the Soviet Union peaked at about 12 million barrels a day in early 1980s, when it was the top world crude oil producer. The region's demand collapse, in combination with its aggressive production targets set to maintain foreign exchange, marked its rapid production decline in the late 19805 as the Soviet Union broke up. The former Soviet Union has recently been the third ranked producer, after Saudi Arabia and the United States. One of the most visible new production prospects has been the Caspian Sea in Central Asia, in spite of the enormous logistic and political hurdles involved in making available the crude oil produced in this area to world markets.

Gasoline is made from crude oil. Refineries take crude oil and break down its hydrocarbons into different products, called "refined products," including gasoline, diesel fuel, heating oil, jet fuel, liquefied petroleum gases, and residual fuel oil. The characteristics of the gasoline depend on the type of crude oil that is used and the setup of the refinery at which it is produced. Gasoline characteristics are also impacted by other ingredients that may be blended into it, such as ethanol. The performance of the gasoline must meet industry standards and environmental regulations that may depend on location (http://www.eia.doe.gov/neic/experts/contactexperts.htm).

Crude oil is classified by the location of its origin (e.g. West Texas Intermediate, WT, Brent, Dubai or Minas) and often by its relative weight or viscosity (light, intermediate or heavy); refiners may also refer to it as 'sweet', which means it contains relatively little sulphur, or as 'sour', which means it contains substantial amounts of sulphur and requires more refining in order to meet current product specifications. The number of carbon atoms determines the oil's relative 'weight' or density. Gases generally have one to four carbon atoms, while heavy oils and waxes may have 50, and asphalts, hundreds. Crude oil from an area in which the crude oil's molecular characteristics have been determined and the oil has been classified are used as pricing references throughout the world. These references are known as Crude oil benchmarks. After considering availability of indigenous crude oil, balance crude oil is required to be imported. Indian Oil sources its crude oil requirement from Far East, Gulf region, Mediterranean, West Africa and Latin American sources (http://www.iocl.com/Products/CrudeOil.aspx).

Crude Oil Pricing and Evaluation

Pricing

Crude Oil price formation does take place in two markets, namely, Physical market and Paper market. Both the markets have their own dynamics and both interact with each other in a complicated way. In economic sense, price is what a buyer pays for the utility of the goods that he buys. In that sense, the price of Crude Oil is the market price in the physical market. Paper market is actually a derivative market, where physical Crude is not available. Paper market is a backward extension of physical market, where right on physical Crude is traded and thereby its future price is formed.

At present, the attention of most observers of the international oil industry is firmly on the current price of oil and the prospects for an immediate price shock. There is much discussion as to the causes of the relatively high prices. These are clearly complex and controversial. There tend to be two schools of thought. One argues high prices are cyclical and arise from a coincidence of potentially reversible factors pushing in the same direction. Thus physical shortages as a result of booming demand and problems in Iraq and other producers combine with a bull run in the paper market. The other school argues that we are witnessing a fundamental structural change in the oil market reflecting insufficient investment over the last 10 years or so. The difference between the two schools is crucial. If current prices are cyclical in origin they will eventually go down, if structural they will stay high (Paul Stevens, 2004).

Physical Market

Physical market is the market, where physical oil is sold and bought and the actual seller and actual buyer meet and enter into a contract to deliver and accept the cargo at a price. A refiner is the final buyer in the physical market, who buys Crude for processing and pays the price, which he can not pass on to any other buyer of Crude. Besides the final buyer, there are many buyers in this market, who buy Crude and sell them at appropriate time, may be at same place or at different places. They are: (a) traders and (b) refiners. Sellers in this market are: (a) the original producers of Crude Oil, (b) traders, (c) refiners.

For a refinery in India, purely from geographical proximity (therefore freight economics) point of view, the physical Crude Oil market presents itself in three regions: (a) Middle East, (b) West Africa, and (c) Far East. The countries in Middle East, mainly producing sour Crude Oils, are: Saudi Arabia, Kuwait, Abu Dhabi, Yemen and Egypt. Countries in West Africa, mainly producing sweet Crude Oils are: Nigeria, Angola and Libya. Country in Far East, mainly producing sweet Crude Oils, is Malaysia. Besides these three regions, there are two more regions, which present alternate economic sources, are Egypt, Venezuela and Australia.

Players in the Physical Market

Original producers of Crude Oil are of two types: a) the National Oil Company (NOC) of the country of Crude Oil origin, like Saudi Aramco, Abu Dhabi National Oil Company (ADNOC), Kuwait Petroleum Corporation (KPC), Petronas in Malaysia and many others. Each oil-producing country has one such company, who holds the ownership of the oil in their geographical territory.

All such NOCs do not necessarily play the same role for their respective countries. Some NOCs are actively into Crude Oil selling business, refining business and are in control of the sale and destination of their cargo. They in fact allocate the quota among their buyers. They also declare their price, what is called official selling price (OSP). They are the price makers in the market. Example of such NOC is Saudi Aramco. Their OSP level determines the revenue for their country on the one hand and sets the price level in the market on the other. While fixing the OSP, these companies do a balancing act on multiple fronts. Some of these fronts are: (a) demand and supply of Crude in the physical market, (b) revenue for the producing country and margin for the refineries (the buyers), (c) current production level and investment for future oil fields, and (d) some other geo-strategic fronts as having political and military dimensions.

There are some NOCs whose main role is to set the price for their Crude (OSP) and ensure the revenue for their respective country. They have given the act of marketing their Crude wholly or partly to some multinational Oil Company. Examples of such NOCs are Egyptian General Petroleum Corporation (EGPC), Yemen Oil & Gas Company (YOG). EGPC has given the marketing right of their Crude Gulf of Suez Mix to British Petroleum, while retaining with them the right to fix the price (OSP) for their Crude. YOG holds ownership of certain portion of the Crude Oil, Masila produced in Yemen and the ownership (equity) of the remaining part rests with multinational Oil Company, Nexen. There is one more type of NOC, like Petronas (of Malaysia), who are quite diversified in their activities. First, they are the sole equity holder of Malaysian Crude, viz, Labuan, Miri, Tapis. Secondly, they declare OSP. Thirdly, they market their Crude. Fourthly, they have E&P activities in other countries like Sudan. Fifth, they trade Crude Oils of other country's origin. Sixth, they run refineries and do domestic marketing of products. Seven, they sell refined products to other countries.

The second category of players in the physical Crude Oil market is the trading companies. They buy Crude Oil from the market and sell to others. They invariably have some equity holdings in some Crude Oils some where in the world. Alternatively they have purchase contract from the original Crude Oil producers. They buy and sell, depending upon their relative position and price at the moment of selling and buying. They swap their Crude Oil with others. Some time, they also hold physical stocks at some parts in the world. They take advantage of price movement in all markets across the globe. Usually they are having operation all over the world. They keep tab on the requirement of the refineries. They closely monitor the developments in the world Crude Oil market affecting the price. They own or operate fleet of vessel, so that they can quickly seize arbitrage opportunities arising between two markets. Thus they play an intermediary role between buyer and seller across the world and make margin for themselves taking advantage of price movement.

The last twenty years have seen the emergence of a new type of trader: the Wall-Street refiners. They were given this name when the US investment banks set up oil trading arms to deal in oil derivatives in much the same way as they deal in other financial instruments. They are assuming the risk for a number of companies involved in the oil market and laying these risks off in the physical or futures market in the same way as an insurance company does in other sectors. Several of them also take substantial outright position in their own right.

The third category of players are integrated multinational oil companies (MNCs) having integrated operations in the Oil market, namely, E&P, refining, marketing and trading. They are very powerful operators in the Crude Oil market by virtue of their scale of operation, volume of transaction and financial strength. They are very few in numbers and the number of has been further narrowed down in the wake of mergers that took place in recent past. They are: British Petroleum, ExxonMobil, Shell, TotalElfFina, and ChevronTexaco. They play multiple roles in the Crude Oil market, such as: (a) they are suppliers of Crude Oil, as they bring equity Crude Oil to the market; (b) they buy Crude Oil for their own refinery system; c) their trading wing buy and sell Crude Oil and make margin.

The fourth and final category of players in the Crude Oil market is the refiners. They are the users of Crude Oil and are the ultimate buyers. They are the ones who pay the price, whatever may the level. At times they can also be the sellers of Crude Oil, which they have bought. They do resell the Crude Oil due to various reasons like: (a) to take opportunity in price movement; (b) the swap the Crude Oil, inter grade or inter month; (c) unscheduled change in demand pattern.

Refiners have interest not only in the price they pay for the Crude Oil, they also have interest in the value of Crude which they realize from the refined products that are produced from the same Crude Oil. Therefore, a particular type of Crude Oil has an economic value for a particular refinery, which is other wise called as 'Gross Product Worth' (GPW). Given the GPW of a type of Crude Oil for a particular refinery, the CFR (Cost and freight) price of Crude determines the margin that a refinery gets by processing a type of Crude Oil.

Paper Market

Paper markets are basically markets where right to Crude Oil is traded. It is a mixture of Crude Oil market and financial market. Here the players are not necessarily having any interest whatsoever with Oil. This market has multiple uses, the principal among which is price risk management. Since Oil price is volatile, which creates risk for the buyer and seller of Crude Oil, this market provides avenues where this risk can be transferred. This is an integral part of Oil Market. This market consists of institutions like Oil Exchanges, Financial Institutions and Brokers, in which instruments like Futures and swaps are bought and sold. The futures and swap in the paper market helps to form the price in the physical market. However this is beyond the scope of this material.

Fundaments of Physical Market

The factors bringing about equilibrium price in Crude Oil market are many. One would presume that it is the cost of production. Alternatively, it would be presumed that the demand and supply or some such economic law would be able to explain the price behavior. Economists have attempted to explain the Crude Oil prices in order to forecast them in both short and long terms. However no theory has thus far been able to use economic variables in a model that can accurately predict future oil prices. Still there are consultants, who take in to account the fundamentals of the market and factor anticipated political developments and project the future price both in short and long term under various probable scenarios. We need to be aware of the fundamental factors that work in the market and influence the price.

The region by region demand patterns interact to establish the price level. The interaction is constant and usually invisible to any one not directly involved in the Oil Industry. As a general rule, the thousand of transactions that take place simultaneously are complete without fanfare. The price fluctuations are small and of interest to the buyers and sellers within the Industry.

The steady state stability gets disrupted by a number of factors, suddenly bringing Crude Oil prices to the headlines. Demands surge, refinery outages and supply cutbacks can all cause prices to run up. Some developments, like refinery outages, logistics snags or demand surges in a cold snap etc cause a price spike. Prices shoot up initially and then recede again when the supply and demand balance has been reestablished. Long term factors like OPEC cut or a recession have long-term impacts. Like the Crude Oil price declines experienced during 1998 or the Crude oil price increase experienced during 2000 and record high in 2005, take longer time to return to the underlying price trend.

The marginal cost of a barrel of Crude Oil differs not only from one country to another, but also from one well to another. Both the varying reservoir characteristics and the physical characteristics of the Crude oil are important components of the cost of producing Crude Oil. The costs can range from as little as 4 dollar per barrel in the Middle East to more than 15 dollar per barrel in some fields in the United States, including capital recovery. It is interesting to note that technological advances in finding and producing Crude Oil have made it possible to bring once expensive deep water Gulf of Mexico oil into production for less than 10 dollar per barrel.

More than the production cost, the supply and demand conditions in the global market over all, and more particularly, in the main refining centers: Singapore, Northwest Europe and the US Gulf Coast influence the price. Crude Oil market is essentially a global auction; the highest bidder wins the supply. Like any auction, the bidder does not want to pay too much. When markets are 'strong' (when demand is high and/or supply is low), the bidder must be willing to pay a higher premium to capture the supply. When markets are 'weak' (demand low and/or supply high), a bidder may choose not to outbid competitors, waiting instead for later, possibly lower priced supplies.

Prices in spot markets, cargo by cargo and transaction by transaction, send a clear signal about the supply / demand balance. Rising prices indicate that more supply is needed and falling prices indicate that there is too much supply for the prevailing demand level. While most Crude Oil flows under term contract, its price (OSP) varies with spot market. Futures market in Oil Exchanges also provides information about the physical supply/demand balance as well as the market's expectations.

Seasonal swings are also an important underlying influence in the supply/demand balance and hence in price fluctuations. Other things being equal, Crude Oil markets would tend to be stronger in the fourth quarter on a global basis, when demand is boosted both by cold weather and by stock building. It is supposed to be weaker in the late winter as global demand falls with warmer weather. The overall supply picture is of course influenced by the level of inventories. Stocks keep the global supply system operating. Stocks indicate whether any regional market has too little, too much or just the right quantity of Oil. When stocks in a given market are high, they represent incremental supply immediately available, so prices tend to be weak. The opposite is true in low stock situation. Price change patterns can vary between regions, depending on the prevailing supply/demand conditions in the regional market, especially in the short term. That price response and the differences in regional price movements are critical to the way the Crude Oil market redistributes to rebalance after an upheaval.

Tradable and non-tradable crude

For a refiner in India, the time frames for buying Crude Oil are two: (a) annual term contract, and (b) spot-purchase. There are some types of Crude Oil in Middle East, which can only be bought by annual contract and these Crude Oils are destination specific. These are therefore called non-tradable Crude. These Crude types, like Arab Heavy, Arab Light, Arab Medium and Kuwaiti Crudes, are sold by the respective NOC under annual contract and are bought by the refiners directly.

The Crude Oil types other than these non-tradable types, which change hands of multiple sellers, are available in spot market. Physical Crude Oil market is such that it is to be booked at least two-month prior to the month of loading the cargo. For example, generally if a cargo is to be loaded any time in the month of March, the loading terminal will plan the month's loading in the first week of February and the allocation of the cargo by the original seller will be finalized by the first half of January.

Formula Price

When a refiner book a cargo, say in January for loading in March, what is agreed between the buyer and seller in January is the quantity and a price. The price has two elements. One is the basic price (say B) and another is the premium and discount (say P). This type of price is called floating price or formula price.

Invoice Price = B + P

At the time of booking, what is agreed between buyers is the 'P', which remains fixed. As far as 'B' is concerned, it is usually linked to the price of a Benchmark Crude or Official Selling Price (OSP) of an NOC. The price of the Benchmark Crude is assessed by independent price assessing agencies like Platts or Petroleum Argus on daily basis.

Usually payment is made 30 days after the date of loading. Therefore the payable amount looks like the following:

Invoice Price (payable in April) = B (of March) + P (as agreed in January)

The basic price ('B' in the equation) is the floating element and is linked to a Benchmark Crude Price, which is assessed by a price assessing agency like Platts on daily basis. What is considered for the purpose of determining a payable price is an average of a Benchmark Crude price for a specific period, called the pricing period. Typically it is average of the calendar month in which the cargo is loaded. A variant of the pricing period could be five or six day average after the date of loading.

A typical pricing clause in a contract would read like this:

"Mean of Platts Dubai average for the calendar month of loading plus 1.18 dollar per barrel" (hypothetical value)

This formula has the following characteristics:

- The price has been agreed in advance.
- The major part of the price, that is the basic price, remains relevant to the time when cargo is loaded (i.e., the pricing period around the loading period; could be a month or five or six days).
- The basic price is market determined, as assessed by an independent expert body in the Industry, which is acceptable to the buyer and seller.
- At the time of signing the contract, neither buyer nor the seller has knowledge of the basic price. Their respective fundamental position and knowledge of the market guide them to agree the fixed part of the formula, that is premium or discount ('P' in the equation).
- 'P' also captures the quality difference of the cargo booked with respect to the benchmark crude.

- As it is a monthly average of the daily assessment, the price gets moderated by the law of average.
- Neither buyer nor the seller gets affected by the specific loading window, as long as the loading window falls in the calendar month (i.e., the pricing period).

This formula at times gets modified by taking average of, say, two benchmark Crudes for 'B', like Oman Dubai average. The practice in the Industry is to make the formula as objective as possible, so that the value of the Crude under deal is accurately captured, without discriminating the either party. Industry has developed many variants of this formula to suit the risk management objective of the buyer and/or seller, but the spirit of the formula remains the same.

Benchmark Crude

Because there are so many different varieties and grades of Crude Oil, buyers and sellers in Oil Industry have found it easier to refer to a limited number of references or benchmark Crude Oils. Other varieties are then priced at a discount or premium, according to their quality. The main criteria for a marker Crude is for it to be sold in sufficient volumes to provide liquidity (many buyers and sellers) in the physical market as well as having similar physical qualities of alternative Crudes.

Brent is generally accepted to be the world benchmark. Brent is used to price two thirds of the world's internationally traded Crude Oil supplies. In the Middle-east, Dubai Crude is used as a benchmark to price sales of other regional Crudes into Asia. Dubai is one of the few Gulf Crudes available on the spot sales, as opposed to long-term supply contracts. In the United States, the benchmark is West Texas Intermediate (WTI). Tapis is generally used as benchmark for Far-East Crude.

OSP of NOCs

NOCs with original hold on their country's Crude usually announce the FOB price of their Crude Oils for their term buyers. This rate is applicable for all the cargoes loaded during a specified period and uniform for all the buyers in the region, irrespective of the volume. Some companies like Saudi Aramco and KPC announce a premium or discount to the average of a Benchmark Crude (Oman and Dubai). They announce in the first week of the month for the next month. As distinguished from above, company like ADNOC announces an absolute number in the first week of the month, applicable for all the cargo loaded in the previous month. Some other companies like the NOC of Yemen and Nigeria announce a premium or discount to a Benchmark Crude (Brent). The applicable price is average of 5 or 6 days after the Bill of Lading days.

The underlying principles in the OSP system are the following:

- It is a declared price (or posted price) by the seller, uniformly applicable to all the buyers in the region. There is no room for negotiation. Buyers have little choice with regard to price.
- While setting the price, the sellers usually make the price level in line with the spot price in the respective destination market.

- The sellers also see that the buyer gets the value for the price they pay. In other words, they see that the refiner gets his net back at the price fixed by them.

In this process, a producer NOC realizes different FOB price (net back) for the same type of Crude Oil, loaded for different destinations.

Crude Oil Evaluation

Crude oil evaluation is an important activity for a buyer, that is, a refinery. At the time of deciding to book a cargo, a buyer has to choose from multiple offers that he would be having. The choice to buy a specific grade of crude for a particular time goes through a techno-economic evaluation process. Along with the type of crude also goes the decision as to who would be the supplier and what would be the terms and conditions. Crude Oil evaluation has some features, which makes the methodology of evaluation distinct from other product evaluation. The distinctive features are relating to, (a) the value of Crude, and (b) price of Crude, which are explained below.

Value of Crude

Crude is a natural product available from underground at various regions in the world. The Crude, when available in the market for sale, is not a homogeneous product. There are types of Crude with specific qualitative parameters. It is not possible to compare the Crude types on the basis of their quality. Though some representative specifications like API and sulfur would indicate the broad features of a particular type of Crude, but these features do not indicate their full value. There is no composite index, which could perhaps bring out the value of Crude and can put the various types of Crude on a scale and compare their relative worth. Therefore, Crude is evaluated based on the value that it would provide to a refinery. A Refinery derives value from particular Crude in terms of the output that it can make out of the Crude. The output from a unit of crude, say a barrel is a range of refined products, produced through various stages of refining process. Therefore, the output that gets generated from Crude is Refinery specific. When that output (refined products) is sold at a price, the Refinery gets the value of the Crude.

To summarize the above discussion, the value of Crude to a Refinery is a function of the following variables:

- The yield pattern of a Crude for a particular Refinery (Refinery specific)
- The price of products in the market (market specific and time specific)

Price of Crude

Each Crude price is a formula linked to a marker Crude and each marker Crude is priced differently on a floating (changing with the prevailing market condition) basis. Therefore, when we receive a price offer for a particular type of Crude, it would typically quote a premium or discount to a marker Crude, whose price would be known when it loads, say the average price of the month of loading.

Therefore, at the stage of evaluation, the price of Crude is not known; it is to be estimated on certain basis.

Price of Products

Prices of petroleum products are market specific and time specific. At the stage of evaluating Crude, it is not known when and at what price the products produced from a parcel of Crude will be sold. Therefore, like Crude price, the product prices are also to be estimated at the time of evaluation.

Gross Refinery Margin (GRM)

A Refinery retains the difference between what price it pays for buying Crude and what it recovers by selling its products. A Refinery aims to maximize the difference between the two sets of prices, which is of Crude and Product. Crude offers are to be evaluated based on their relative GRM.

Drivers of High Refining Margin

- Advantageous crude supply
- Strong purchasing power
- Flexible crude slate
- Refineries designed for sour crude
- Favorable transport costs
- A strong position in import infrastructure
- Pipeline links and reduced storage needs for key customers
- High exporting ability

Evaluation Methodology

Summarily, the evaluation will be based on the relative outcome of GRM from each Crude:

GRM = GPW—(Estimated landed cost of Crude + cost built up on account of difference in terms of payment and credit)

GPW

GPW for Crude will be weighted average of product prices, where the yield pattern of the Crude will be used as weights. Product prices will be calculated on import parity basis (landed cost), based on the Platts price for the previous month (M-1). (M month is the one in which the evaluation is being done). Refinery will use the yield pattern for each Crude along with API, based on Refinery process experience.

Landed Cost of Crude

Landed cost of Crude would be estimated by taking into account FOB price of Crude of previous month (M-1), freight and other cost of operation and financial transaction. Freight from the port of loading till disport including freight of daughter vessel in case of transshipment will be provided by Shipping Group.

Pecking Order

Pecking order is drawn based on the ranking of GRM for a particular refinery for a specific time period. The type of crude with highest GRM is the one to be selected.

Platts and Argus

Platts is a leading energy news service agency. It was set up by Mr. Warren Platt in 1923. In course of time, the agency has widened its operation to a wide gamut of services in the energy sector worldwide. Platts is known for its expertise in price assessment in energy sector. It has earned a unique place for itself by meeting the need for impartial information, market price transparency and real time news. In the Crude Oil market, Platts plays a crucial role in the daily assessment of Crude Oil prices, including those of benchmark crudes. It does assess the price of Crude Oil for each market. It has established methods, networks and institutional arrangements to keep track of market developments and price movement. With all these arrangements and after having extensive interactions with market players, Platts, at the end of the day, assess and reports a high, mean and low price, at which a particular Crude Oil was traded in a particular market. The Platts assessed price is considered to be the price for that day for the particular type of Crude. The price of benchmark Crude as assessed by Platts is used to workout the formula price of Crude Oil as per contracts.

Trade and Transportation

Oil Trade—The Balancing Flow

The main oil producing areas are not the same as the main consuming areas. Hence, oil must be moved from regions where supply is greater than demand (exporting regions) to regions where demand is greater than supply (importing regions). These flows dictated by economics, logistics and temporary imbalances in supply and demand are central to the efficient operation of the crude oil market. The world's three largest consuming regions, North America, Europe and Asia Pacific, are all importers. All the other regions are exporters. The Middle East still exports vastly more oil than any other region, despite strong growth in production in other areas in recent years. There is less variation among the importing regions. In the decade preceding the 1997-98 financial crises, Asia Pacific's economic boom propelled it into the number one spot; with import growth more than double that of any other regions. Even though the United States is the largest individual importer, both net and gross, North America as a region ranks third; because Canada and Mexico are two of the United States three top suppliers.

There is more trade internationally in oil than in anything else. This is true whether one measures trade by how much of a good is moved (volume), by its value or by the carrying capacity needed to move it. All the three measures have economic significance. Volume provides insight about whether markets are over- or undersupplied and whether the infrastructure is adequate to accommodate the required flow. Value allows governments and economists to assess patterns of international trade and balance of payments. Carrying capacity allows the shipping industry to assess how many tankers are required and on what routes.

Generally, crude oil flow to the markets that provide the highest value to the supplier. Every thing else being equal, oil moves to the nearest market first, because that has the lowest transportation cost and, therefore, provides the supplier with the highest net revenue or the highest net back. If this market cannot absorb all the oil, the balance moves to the next closest one and the next and so on, incurring progressively higher transportation costs, until all the oil is placed. In practice, however, trade flows do not always follow the simple 'nearest first' pattern. Factors like refinery configuration, product-demand mix, product quality specifications, and politics can change all the rankings. Different markets frequently place different values on particular grades of crude oil. Thus, African crudes, low in Sulfur, are worth relatively more in Asia, where these grades may allow a refiner to meet tighter sulfur limits in the region without investing in refinery upgradation. In addition, both buyer and seller may impose restrictions. For instance, the United States prohibits the importation of Iranian and Libyan crude and the United Nations allows only limited sales of Iraqi oil. On the seller's side, Mexico formerly limited sales to the United States to 50 per cent of its exports, reflecting concerns about dependence on the United States specifically and about dependence on one geographic market in general. Saudi Arabia's national security concerns, on the other hand, dictate that it maintain a very high profile as a supplier to the United States market, even at the cost of lower net-backs.

Tanker—The Most Economic Transport Mode

Transportation and storage play critical role in the flow of trade in crude oil. They are not just the physical link between the importers and the exporters and, therefore, between producers and refiners, refiners and marketers and marketers and consumers; their associated costs are a primary factor in determining the economics and pattern of world trade.

There are two modes of transportation for inter-regional trade: tankers and pipelines. Tankers have made global transport of crude oil possible. They are low cost-efficient and extremely flexible. Pipelines, on the other hand, are the mode of choice for transcontinental oil.

Not all tanker trade routes use the same size ship. Each route usually has one size that is the clear economic winner, based on voyage length, port and canal constraints and volume.

Pipelines are critical for landlocked crudes and also complement tankers at certain key locations by relieving bottlenecks or providing shortcuts. The only inter-regional trade that currently relies solely on pipelines is crude from Russia to Europe. Production from Caspian Sea region also depends upon pipeline for evacuation.

Taxation

For a refiner in India, the landed cost of imported crude includes customs duty and applicable Octroi duty. Currently customs duty is advalorem @20 per cent calculated on CIF value plus one per cent landing charge. Octroi duty is four per cent at Mumbai. As per the latest ruling of Supreme Court of India, duty is to be paid on the quantity received in the shore tank not on Bill of Lading quantity, as used to be the practice earlier. The difference in customs duty applicable for crude and on refined products is of great economic significance in the pricing structure of oil. If customs duty on crude oil is say 10 per cent and that on refined products is say 20 per cent, then the refineries in the country get duty protection of 10 per cent, in a regime when product pricing is on import parity basis.

OPEC's Role in Price Structuring

OPEC vis-à-vis World Oil Market

Organization of Petroleum Exporting Countries (OPEC) was founded in September 1960 and its member countries include Algeria, Indonesia, Iran, Iraq, Kuwait, Libya, Nigeria, Qatar, Saudi Arabia, the DAE and Venezuela. Original OPEC members include Iran, Iraq, Kuwait, Saudi Arabia, and Venezuela. During 1960 and 1975, the organization expanded to include Qatar, Indonesia, Libya, the DAE and Algeria. Ecuador and Gabon were members of OPEC, but Ecuador withdrew in 1992 and Gabon followed suit in 1995.

OPEC members share common interests and as a group have a significant influence on world oil market, despite their lack of monopoly over world oil production. EIA (Energy Information Administration) estimates the current eleven members account for roughly 40 per cent of world oil production and about 80 per cent of the proven oil reserves. Following are some significant characteristics of OPEC member countries:

1. Member countries of OPEC are important world oil exporters. Excluding Indonesia, members' net exports averaged 85 per cent of total oil production in 2001.
2. OPEC countries' oil industries are mostly nationalized, allowing OPEC members' political establishments to increase or decrease oil production. Through managing world oil supply, OPEC can control world oil prices to help meet the group's economic and/or political goals. Member governments tend to rely heavily on oil revenues.
3. The lion's share of the world's spare oil production capacity lies in OPEC countries. Non-OPEC countries hold approximately a combined 500 thousand barrels per day (bb/d) of spare production capacity, while OPEC spare production capacity estimates for 2002 are as high as eight million bb/d.
4. As per January 2002 estimates, 80 per cent of proven world crude oil reserves are located in OPEC member countries.
5. Production costs are far lower in OPEC countries. Prolonged periods of low oil prices make the world more reliant on cheap-to-produce OPEC oil. In contrast to OPEC countries; non-OPEC countries share the following characteristics:

   (a) Most non-OPEC countries are net oil importers. The seven largest non-

OPEC producers' 2001 net exports averaged 15 per cent of total oil production.

(b) Because major non-OPEC countries have private oil sectors (Mexico is one notable exception), the political establishment generally has very little control over production levels. Companies react to international price expectations, exploring and drilling more and in higher cost areas when prices are high and focusing on lower cost production when prices are low.

(c) Private companies keep very little spare production capacity. Hence, in case of a significant world oil production disruption, OPEC would be the primary immediate source of additional oil to displace the loss.

(d) Non-OPEC lifting costs tend to be higher than OPEC lifting costs, which makes non-OPEC production more vulnerable to price collapses. Prolonged periods of low prices can drive higher cost producers out of business and make major oil companies focus less on higher cost areas.

There is one important early document of relevance to OPEC's role—the "Solemn Declaration" adopted by a conference of OPEC sovereigns and heads of state in Algiers in 1975. This declaration carried a proposal for a "New International Economic Order" aimed at promoting a more equitable global economic system, with particular emphasis on alleviating poverty and other injustices affecting developing countries by encouraging greater interdependence among nations from the north and south. The proposal for a new international economic order led to the establishment of the OPEC Fund for International Development, which is a multilateral development finance institution seeking to promote cooperation between OPEC members and other developing countries. Over the years, the OPEC Fund has distributed loans and grants to 104 countries located in Africa, Asia, Latin America, the Caribbean and Europe. Including grants and contributions to other institutions, the Fund's total approved commitments, as of the end of September 1999, stood at $5.4 billion (U.S.), with disbursements reaching $3.7 billion (http://www.eppo.go.th/inter/opec/RoleOfOPEC.html).

World Oil Production and Exportable Surplus

The world's oil supply comes from a wide variety of sources. While the Middle East (home to the largest OPEC producers) was the largest producing region in 2001 with 29 per cent of total world production, North America accounted for 20 per cent, with the remaining 51 per cent dispersed fairly evenly throughout the globe.

OPEC member countries together accounted for almost 40 per cent of world production in 2001. As the table below would show, of the 14 countries that produced more than two million barrels per day in 2001, seven were OPEC members.

Among the world's top net exporters, OPEC countries are better represented. Nine of the 12 countries exporting more than one million barrels per day in 2001 were OPEC members, as in the Table 7.1.

Table 7.1: Top World Oil Producers and Exporters, 2001

(OPEC members in italics)

(Million barrels per day)

Sl. No.	Country	Total oil/ Total of Production	S. No.	Country	Net oil exports
1	United States	9.02	1	*Saudi Arabia*	7.38
2	Saudi Arabia	8.73	2	Russia	4.76
3	Russia	7.29	3	Norway	3.22
4	Iran	3.82	4	*Iran*	2.74
5	Mexico	3.59	5	*Venezuela*	2.60
6	Norway	3.41	6	*UAE*	2.09
7	China	3.30	7	*Nigeria*	2.00
8	Venezuela	3.07	8	*Iraq*	2.00
9	Canada	2.80	9	*Kuwait*	1.80
10	United Kingdom	259	10	Mexico	1.65
11	Iraq	2.45	11	*Libya*	1.24
12	UAE	2.42	12	*Algeria*	1.24
13	*Nigeria*	2.26			
14	*Kuwait*	2.15			

*The Table (IEA, 2001) includes all countries whose total oil production exceeded two million barrels per day and those countries whose net exports exceeded one million barrels per day in 2001.

In the emerging world oil scene, non-OPEC production is expected to rise, with the greatest increase in the FSU (Former Soviet Union) countries, including Russia and the countries bordering the Caspian sea and in North America (Mexico, Canada and USA).

OPEC Reserves

Of the world's 1.03 trillion barrels of proven reserves, 819 billion barrels (80 per cent) are held by OPEC Because non-OPEC countries' smaller reserves are being depleted more rapidly than OPEC reserves, their overall reserves-to production ratio—an indicator of how long proven reserves would last at current production rates—is much lower (about 15 years for non-OPEC and 80 years for OPEC). This implies increased OPEC production as a proportion of world production over the long term.

OPEC's Oil Policy

The single most important objective of OPEC is to maximize the revenue of its member countries. This objective can be achieved only if oil prices remain at a level that can sustain demand and supply and remain stable over a secular period. OPEC cannot determine the price level of oil by its dictates. OPEC is a cartel and not a monopoly producer. The dynamics of oil market is such that oil prices are volatile and are subject to multiple forces. One of those factors is oil production at a particular time, which determines supply of oil in short term. Second factor is oil reserves, which determines supply of oil in the long run. OPEC, by virtue of its having, large exportable surplus and proven reserves does attempt to control price through output variation.

The revenue maximization objective of OPEC is dictated by a number of compulsions, a few of which are mentioned below:

- Meeting budgetary requirements of its member states: Oil revenue form around 90 per cent of the total budgets in most OPEC countries. OPEC countries need a stable income primarily for two purposes: (a) to develop their economies and afford a fair standard of living for their people; (b) to expand their oil production capacity to cover the expected future increase in oil demand.
- Transfer of technology: OPEC countries need new exploration and production technologies and expertise, which require massive investment. This is a challenge for OPEC countries, which has to be faced in line with their political philosophy of not accepting production-sharin agreement with Oil Majors.
- In the revenue earning game played by both the oil producing countries and oil consuming countries, OPEC does not want to be a losing party. OPEC has been observing that oil consuming industrial countries are levying high taxes of various types to gain revenue on the one hand and also to reduce consumption of oil. OPEC secretariat has studies that taxes levied by the government of industrialized countries constitute 65 per cent of the price of petroleum products. For example, taxes in UK on gasoline are 70 per cent of its price.
- Another compelling purpose for which OPEC countries barter their output and price control is to earn measures of political stability and military security.

In a paper authored by Ali Hussain (2004) the implication of OPEC's short-term and long-term policy impacting oil price and the global economy has been described as follows:

"OPEC's short-term policies have led to continuous fluctuations, sometimes drastic, in OPEC's oil prices and consequently its oil revenues, which in turn had negative effects on the economic development of OPEC countries. What happened in 1986 is a good example in this respect.

OPEC must adopt a long-term pricing policy taking into consideration not only the above-mentioned factors but also the following ones:

1. OPEC has vast reserves of oil and gas, which can be produced at relatively low cost and must maximize the utilization of such resources. For example, at the end of 2003 OPEC's oil reserves represented 77% of total world oil reserves.
2. OPEC countries are still developing countries that need revenues from oil exports (received in foreign currencies) to import much required goods and services for their economic developments. Keeping oil prices at relatively low rates will generate economic, social and even political instability.

3. OPEC's oil revenues' purchasing power—in other words, the real price of the organization's oil in the international market, taking into consideration imported inflation into OPEC countries and the devaluation of the US dollar, which is used to price OPEC oil, vis-à-vis other major currencies.
4. OPEC investments in the oil industry.

Other international factors must also be considered:

1. The effect of oil price increases on the world economy.
2. Required future investments in the international oil industry with adequate return.
3. The cost of finding new oil to replace depleted stocks.
4. The effect of using oil on the environment.
5. Oil conservation and the optimum use of oil.
6. Availability and cost of alternative sources of energy. In many cases oil is still more competitive and in certain cases oil cannot be replaced by other sources of energy.
7. Taxation on oil products in major economies.

OPEC's long-term pricing policy, to be successful and realistic, must be based on scientific studies undertaken by the organization, which must take the above factors into consideration, but with full consultation with oil consuming countries and major international oil companies. Such a policy may help OPEC to adopt oil prices that will protect the interests of OPEC countries, secure oil to oil consuming countries, provide adequate and reasonable return to international oil companies and simultaneously ensure that oil will be available for sometime to come for our future generations." (http://www.mees.com/postedarticles/oped/a47n50d01.htm)

OPEC's Production Cut and Compliance

In the prevailing condition of depressed demand world over, OPEC's curb in production has maintained a kind of balance, which can be seen from the two tables given below. While table 1 gives a snap shot of world demand and supply split in terms of OPEC and non-OPEC, table 7.2 presents the degree of compliance of quota by OPEC member countries. It can be seen that the major producing countries in OPEC block are adhering to their ceiling production. Saudi Arabia is the only country with the capability to further increase its capacity significantly in short period, say 30 days.

The vast majority of development projects in OPEC countries, accounting for incremental capacity is being operated and funded by MNCs. Governments of OPEC member countries are increasingly finding it hard to comply with the quota restriction beyond a point, to the extent the surplus capacity is being funded by MNCs.

Table 7.2: World Demand Supply Balance: Summary

Particulars	Million barrels per day	
	2001	2002
Demand	76.1	76.2
Y-O-Y change	–0.1	+0.1
OPEC Crude Supplies	27.2	26.0
Other supplies	49.5	50.5
Less US SPR additions	0	0.1
Total Oil Supply	76.7	76.4
Y-O-Y change	–0.1	–0.3
Global Stock change	+0.6	+0.2

Source: IEA, 2001.

The Impacts of OPEC Policy

OPEC Crude oil production vs. quota restriction scenario is given in Table3 for OPEC countries.

Summarily, OPEC operates its policy through the following four instruments: viz., (a) output variation, (b) destination control, (c) declaration of official selling price, and (d) policy announcement.

Table 7.3: OPEC Crude Oil Production vs. Quota
(Excludes condensate and natural gas liquids)

(Thousand barrels per day)

Countries	1Q 2002 Production	2Q 2002 Production	January 2002 Quota	1Q 2002 Production Capacity	2Q 2002 Surplus Capacity
Algeria	779	803	693	1100	297
Indonesia	1,140	1,120	1,125	1,200	80
Iran	3,344	3,367	3,186	3,850	483
Kuwait	1,835	1,870	1,741	2,400	530
Libya	1,277	1,290	1,162	1,500	210
Nigeria	1,974	2,003	1,787	2,350	347
Qatar	593	593	562	850	257
Saudi Arabia	7,275	7,430	7,053	10,000	2,570
UAE	1,955	1,997	1,894	2,600	603
Venezuela	2,567	2,567	2,497	3,100	533
OPEC (10)	22,740	23,041	21,700	28,950	5,909
Crude Total	45479	46081	43400	57900	11819
Iraq	2,450	1,642	exempt	3,050	1,408
OPEC Crude	25,191	24,683	21,700	32,000	7,317
Oil Total	27641	26325	21,700	35050	8725

Source: IEA, 2003.

These instruments directly impact the availability of physical crude in certain segments of market with different time lags. For example, if OPEC cuts reduce availability of physical cargo in the region of South Asia and Asia Pacific in the same month, it affects USA after a lag of 45 days.

Reduction in physical loading of crude by OPEC-member countries, impacts on the crude inventory with refineries. Through the invisible hand of market, reduction in supply brings about disequilibrium in the price, which triggers ripples in the price level. By fine tuning the output, OPEC attempts to keep the price of OPEC basket crude in a certain band, which currently is 22-28 US dollar per barrel.

The output and price linkage is not a linear linkage. Like any other market phenomena, it has its own complexities. *Firstly,* there are powerful non-OPEC producers, who may have domestic compulsions not allowing them to toe the line of OPEC dicta. *Secondly,* there are substitute fuels, like gas, coal, nuclear, which compete with oil for their commercial use. *Thirdly,* the transportation and handling of physical crude also impacts the price formation of crude, as ships, pipeline, and storage may pose bottlenecks, hindering availability of crude at the point of consumption. *Fourth,* the paper market and financial market also plays a significant role in price formation of crude oil. OPEC members do not participate in these markets and the forces operating in these markets have dynamics, which are different from those of physical oil market.

India's OPEC Policy

India has large stakes in OPEC countries. A country with refining capacity of 2.2 million barrels per day, with barely 0.6 million barrels per day indigenous crude production, has a large import intensive structure of feedstock. The geographical proximity of Middle East is really an opportunity for India by way of security of supply and economic freight. *Second,* some of the Indian refineries are configured to process the types of crude produced in Middle East. During 2000-02, 87 per cent of India's import was procured from OPEC countries. Countries providing large volumes are Nigeria (for low sulfur type of crude), Saudi Arabia and Kuwait (for high sulfur). Together these three countries have supplied 70 per cent total OPEC crude. This shows a large and concentrated dependence on OPEC countries for India's crude requirement (Table 7.4).

Table 7.4: Sources of India's Imported Crude

(Figures in Thousand Metric Tonnes)

Countries	2000-01	2001-02
OPEC Countries		
Saudi Arabia	7,204	6,352
Iraq	1,788	905
Qatar	62	85
UAE	5,815	6,809
Iran	2,607	2,249
Kuwait	6,828	9,216
Nigeria	12,556	11,409
Libya	138	1081
Venezuela	Nil	279
OPEC Total	36,998	38,385

(Contd.)

Countries	2000-01	2001-02
Non-OPEC Countries		
Malaysia	1,681	,853
Egypt	1,192	1,594
Yemen	313	2,164
Oman	Nil	259
UK	1,629	Nil
Brunei	Nil	84
Angola	260	395
Non-OPEC Total	5,075	6,349
Grand Total	42,073	44,734

Source: Ministry of Petroleum, GOI, New Delhi.

Objective of India's OPEC policy can be classified under two headings: *viz.*, (a) to have a security of supply at all times and especially at the time of exigencies like war or natural calamities; and (b) to get crude at the best price.

Till recently, Indian refineries were operating in protected environment and under administrative pricing regime. The features of crude import which were then operating under the previous regime were:

1. Canalized procurement by Indian Oil Corporation, under the operating guidance of Oil Corporation Committee.
2. Crude types were limited, which formed a common basket for all the PSU refineries.
3. Sources of import were also limited, dominated by protocol and convention of Indian Government with National Oil Companies of Middle East.
4. Operational practices were constrained by existing infrastructure, which were highly inadequate, and therefore, built in costs were incurred for crude import.
5. The total operating costs were shared amongst all the PSU companies in proportion to their throughput. Therefore, there were invisible costs.
6. Import procedures were strongly tied by Government guidelines. All activities were subject to retrospective scrutiny of audit, vigilance and parliament.

There have been substantial improvements during past four years. The changes have been brought in under a phased liberalization programme being pursued since 1991 and culminating in the following three landmarks:

I. Effective April 1998, all PSU refineries were taken out of administered pricing mechanism. Ex-refinery gate prices were fixed on import parity basis.

II. Effective April 1998, refineries in private sector (viz. Reliance refinery at Jamnagar) and joint sector (MRPL at Mangalore) were allowed to import crude directly.

III. Effective April 2002, crude import for PSU refineries was de-canalized.

Policy Direction for India

In the short and medium term time frames, that is, within two to five years, Indian refiners and policy-makers need to take few policy initiatives, keeping in view the objectives of security and economy with respect to crude oil import.

Indian government and business associations (like FICCI & ASSOCHAM) need to step up commercial diplomacy in the OPEC member countries. Commercial, economic and diplomatic relationship with OPEC member countries and oil producing companies would go a long way in taking care of India's crude oil import.

It is important to realize that a vibrant and growing economy, with competitive export and adequate foreign exchange reserve are a few pre-requisites for the success of any policy drive in the external sector. Middle East countries need collaboration in technology and expertise in drilling, exploration and information technology. Indian companies having comparative advantage in these fields need to be marketed in these countries. India's premier companies like ONGC Videsh Limited (OVL), the consultancy JV of ONGC, IOC and GAIL (ONGIO) and Petroleum India International (PII) can play constructive role in this venture.

Indian companies have to secure equity in overseas oil fields. OVL has done well by doing this in Sakhalin, Iraq, Vietnam and Sudan. This is an area where Multinational Oil Companies like British Petroleum (BP), TotalElfFina, Caltex-Chevron-Texaco and Shell have considerable expertise world over. Indian companies have to penetrate into this area, which require huge capital, risk taking ability, institutional arrangement and above all managerial vision.

Areas of Action for Indian Refineries

Indian refineries have to learn and practice and art and science of buying high value crude at competitive price. Certain areas requiring attention are:

1. Diversification of crude basket, which means continuous search for non-conventional crude; trial processing of crude from new fields and up-gradation of refinery configuration to process new varieties of crude and to extract maximum yield.
2. Diversify the supply sources. New Crude sources are to be tapped. For example, countries like Venezuela, Angola, Egypt, and Libya have not been properly examined. There are of course constraints like shipping, which are to be addressed.
3. Have port related facilities to handle VLCC. It requires a focused attention to overcome of the infrastructural bottlenecks to bring in large parcel size from a remote source.
4. Vigorously enter into risk management areas. It is commonly known that crude price? are highly volatile and considering the volume, stakes are very high. Therefore, we need to resort to techniques of passing on the price risks to others, which have specialized in risk taking business. A well-designed policy framework is to be built by the Indian oil companies for this. Institutional set ups and support systems in this filed are already available. This is an area where Indian oil companies are lagging behind their counterparts operating in international oil market.

Crude Oil of Indian Origin

India has a proven reserve of 674 million tonnes of Oil. During 2000-01; India produced 32.4 million tones of crude oil. The field wise production of crude oil is given below in Table 7.5:

Table 7.5: Major Oilfield-wise Indian Crude oil Production

Sl. No.	Oil Field	Production in 2000-01 (TMT)
1	Assam Fields	5200
2	Arunanchal Pradesh Fields	31
3	Tamil Nadu Fields	698
4	Gujarat Fields	5785
	Sub-Total	11 714
	On Shore	11714
5	Mumbai High	16629
6	Private / JVC	4083
	Total All Fields	32426

The entire indigenous crude oil gets processed in Indian refineries. Besides processing 32.4 million indigenous crude, Indian refineries imported 74 million tones in 2000-01 and processed 103 million tones of crude. Currently the crude produced by India's E&P companies is being allocated to the closest refineries. Therefore, crude oils of Indian origin are not traded in the sense that it does not change hands multiple times at market price. However, the price at which it is sold to Indian refiners was determined on a 'fixed benchmark' principle to qualitatively similar crude in international market.

After abolition of Administered Pricing System from April 2002, a new pricing method is being evolved. This principle being talked about is import parity, on freight sharing basis between buyer and seller. Here, the FOB price of Nigerian sweet crude is taken as benchmark and it is adjusted for the yield differential. Half of VLCC freight from the Nigerian load port to a designated port in Indian West Coast is \ considered for working out import parity. Similarly, saving on account of customs duty and sales tax is also shared between the buyer and seller.

Based on the prevailing international price, the indigenous crude oil was provisionally priced at Rs. 8325 per tonne (approximately 22 dollar per barrel), of which the producing company gets Rs 5310, excluding Cess of Rs 1800, royalty of Rs. 850 and Sales tax of Rs. 380. Indian market is poised to undergo a massive transformation in the coming years. The emerging scene will see multiple buyers and sellers, new discoveries and more production spurred by updated technology, novel commercial practices and so on. The macro-economic policy of the country driving towards globalization is an added stimulus to the Indian oil.

Summary

Crude oil is a heterogeneous and composite raw material and serves as mother liquor of major Petrochemical and allied industries. Its value is realized from the price, which its yields fetch in the product market. Crude oil's price is determined by plethora of forces and geo-political factors operating in both physical and financial market. Crude oil is transformed into value-added refined products, which have got a wide-ranging utility-value to its consumers. Crude oil is made available to a refinery by transportation using different modes, which adds to its cost. Tax from petroleum products is a major revenue item for governments of all countries. Therefore, tax structure of a country has a direct and indirect bearing on its cost. As various regions of the world are asymmetrically endowed with crude oil, it moves from surplus region to deficit consumption regions for operating the supply-chain with economies of scale in order to penetrate the global market at competitive price. Crude oil being a highly traded commodity a refiner, who is the ultimate buyer of crude oil, pays for all these costs and realizes its profit margin by selling refined products, which are processed out of crude oil. Hence, cost economics of crude oil is critical to sustainable growth of petro-industries world-over.

REFERENCES

Alberto Clo (2004), Oil Economics & Policy, Springler.

Gary, J.H. and Handwerk, G.E. (1984), *Petroleum Refining Technology and Economics*, 2nd Edition, Marcel Dekker, Inc, ISBN 0-8247-7150-8.

Hussain, Ali (2004), OPEC's Policies: A Critical View, Middle East Economic Survey, Vol. XLVII, No. 50, 13-December-2004.

Ian Lerche & Shiela Noeth (2004), Economics of Petroleum Production: A Compendium (Vols. I & II), Multi-Science Publishing Company Ltd., U.K.

Leffler, W.L. (1985), *Petroleum Refining for the non-technical person*, 2nd Edition, PennWell Books, ISBN 0-87814-280-0.

Patra, D.C. (2000), Oil Industry in India, Mittal Publications, New Delhi.

Stevens, Paul (2004), The Future Price of Crude Oil, Middle East Economic Survey, Vol. XLVII, No. 37, 13-September-2004.

Websites

http://en.wikipedia.org/wiki/Oil_refinery

http://www.mees.com/postedarticles/oped/a47n37d01.htm

http://www.mees.com/postedarticles/oped/a47n50d01.htm

http://www.eppo.go.th/inter/opec/RoleOfOPEC.html

CHAPTER VIII

Refinery Economics

Introduction

Crude oil differs from one another in a large number of chemical and physical properties, many of which play an important part in their refining and subsequent sale as refined products. It has been known that heavy crude contains many impurities. Many of the impurities are in concentrated form. Sulfur has been recognized as one of the major impurity, which affects the quality of the final refined product and processing cost. Moreover there are certain impurities, which affect properties of crude oil and create many operational and quality issues. Apart from affecting the cost of recovery and refining, amount of waste produced is high. Due to high concentration of these impurities, these crudes are labeled as poor quality crudes and have a lower price in the market. The conventional methods used in overcoming poor quality crudes are very cumbersome and not cost effective. World refineries have spent more than $190 billion producing cleaner petroleum and diesel fuels. Indian refineries, which process more than 2.3 million bpd of crude oil, need to invest $ 8.2 billion (estimate based on available technologies) by 2010 to meet strict emission rules to reduce pollution. In many parts of the world automotive fuels have 0.25% sulfur content, which is being reduced to 0.05% and further below. Profit margins are very low; hence any technology that takes cost out of refining and production is an asset. Typically crude is valued based on its yield of Intermediate and finished products (increased quantities) and on its sulfur content (Doctor & Mustafa, 2005).

Oil is crucial for the growth of industry and infrastructure. In the face of the growing supply-demand gap in petroleum products, oil security in India has, of late, been a matter of prime concern. Oil security implies a regulated balance between supply and demand and affordable prices within stable macro-economic prices. The deregulation and restructuring of oil and gas industry in India is a sequel to the macro-economic reforms initiated in the areas of industry, finance, banking operations and trade as was initiated in 1991-92. It aims at a smooth and graded transformation of the oil sector into a vibrant, efficient and market-friendly system which meets the domestic as well as global demands.

The strategy for attaining oil security will require an investment of around Rs 1000 billion over the next ten years. Such massive funds cannot be arranged by the public sector alone. In the past, the global oil economy and domestic oil security have been the victims of volatile product price and supply disruptions. Political and military events too have had a share in deranging the settled state of affairs. There can be no insurance against such events. The answer lies in intensifying exploration within the country and looking for equity oil in prospecting ventures abroad. ONGC Videsh Limited, a subsidiary of ONGC, is exclusively engaged in acquiring equity oil abroad. Other upstream companies are also gearing up to take up this challenging task. The country has attained self-sufficiency in the refining capacity with the joint efforts of the public and private sectors drawing upon overseas financial and technological support.

In addition to oil, it is also important to prospect for and establish alternative sources of energy. There is a huge internal demand for natural gas. To bridge the demand supply gap in gas, Government is keen to import natural gas through transnational gas pipelines. The import of LNG has already started at Dahej terminal and is being planned at other locations.

The restructuring process of the public sector oil companies had begun even before the announcement of the policy reforms in November, 1997. As a first step towards financial restructuring of these companies, disinvestment of a certain portion of government holdings in the equity to the oil companies has been carried out since 1991-92. The goal of organizational restructuring is to instill a proactive approach in effective decision-making. The public sector oil companies have already initiated comprehensive analysis of the existing corporate structures, of the threats and opportunities for business in the new environment and of the strategies to develop and strengthen their competitive advantage.

The challenges faced by the companies today are varied and complex. With new competitions relentlessly trying to take away a slice of the market, the focus of the management has now shifted to the customers it serves and the community it lives in. The strategies to remain ahead of others would require continuous adoptions of innovative techniques to nurture customer's needs and expectations. Asia is expected to be the hub of business in oil and gas in future. Within Asia, India and China are well positioned as choice destinations.

Successful refiners are maximizing the productivity of current refineries by adapting advanced refining technology to achieve optimal refinery configuration. It is therefore crucial for refiners to develop effective financial projection techniques to reduce cost and maximize profit. It is also essential to take immediate advantage of favourable economic conditions, technological advances and best in class operating processes in the whole processes of refinery. Only then can there be continued success in refinery operations and petro-chemical industrial businesses. Before we embark on the Refining technology as well as reining economics in some depth, it would be apt to cite some historical backdrop of refining globally.

Historic Backdrop of Refining: Global Scene

- 3000 BC Sumerians use asphalt as an adhesive
- Egyptians use pitch to grease chariot wheels
- Mesopotamians use bitumen to seal boats
- 600 BC Confucius writes about drilling a 100′gas well and using bamboo for pipes
- 1500 AD Chinese dig oil wells >2000′ deep
- 1847 First "rock oil" refinery in England
- 1849 Canada distills kerosene from crude oil
- 1856 World's first refinery in Romania
- 1857 Flat-wick kerosene lamp invented
- 1859 Pennsylvania oil boom begins with 69′ oil well producing 35 bpd
- 1860-61 Refineries built in Pennsylvania and Arkansas
- 1870 US Largest oil exporter; oil was US 2nd biggest export
- 1878 Thomas Edison invents light bulb
- 1901 Spindletop, Texas producing 100,000 bpd kicks off modern era of oil refining
- 1908 Model T's sell for $950/T
- 1913 Gulf Oil opens first drive-in filling station
- 1942 First Fluidized Catalytic Cracker (FCC) commercialized
- 1970 First Earth Day; EPA passes Clean Air Act
- 2005 US Refining capacity is 17,042,000 bpd, 23% of World's 73MM

Refining Techniques and Processes

The petroleum refining industry provides products that are critical to the functioning of the economy. Virtually all transportation; land, sea, and air, is fueled by products that are refined from crude oil. Industrial, residential, and commercial activities, as well as electricity generation, use petroleum based products. Along with volatile changes in crude oil prices, the industry has faced evolving health, safety, and environmental requirements which have changed and multiplied product specifications and required capital investment in refineries (Pirog, 2005).

Once produced, crude oil has to be refined to manufacture the various oil products and it is refining that provides the key to the oil industry. Although the basic principles of refining remain virtually the same, refinery technology has improved dramatically in the last forty years. There are likely to be more alterations yet as the industry seeks to come to terms with the changes in demand that are forecast to continue.

When considering the economic performance of a petroleum refiner, several characteristics should be noted. First, the production process is capital intensive and technological improvements are embodied through investments in the basic refinery. As a result, any circumstance which affects the availability, or allocation, of capital investment can have significant structural effects on the firm and the industry. Second, the major variable cost in the production process is crude oil, the price of which is determined in the world petroleum market. Third, while labor and other variable costs are relatively small fractions of total costs, a great deal of attention is given to minimizing them in the interests of enhancing profit margins. Finally, regulatory costs, both capital and operational, required to meet congressionally mandated environmental standards on both refined products and refinery sites increase as new requirements are phased in. Evaluating the economic performance of the petroleum refining industry is complicated by the fact that many refineries can use crude oil of different quality as an input, while others cannot. Crude oil can be of lighter or heavier density, as well as having higher or lower sulfur content. The density of the crude oil is important because, in general, a lighter crude oil input yields a lighter product mix. A lighter product mix is important because lighter products are generally in higher demand, and yield higher prices for the refiner (CRS, 2005).

The Product Lines

Crude oil

Crude oil is a complex mixture of hydrocarbons, contaminated with sulfur, metals, salts and other compounds. The principle of refining is the application of heat to crude oil in order to separate the different constituents.

Gases

As heat is applied to the crude oil, different constituents boil at different temperatures and can be collected at various points in the distillation column. The temperature decreases as the oil moves up the column, so the compounds with the lowest boiling points, the gases, are collected at the top. The gases are primarily butane and propane, with some methane, ethane and other gases. They have a variety of uses, ranging from chemical feed stocks to gasoline additives and bottled gas for domestic cooking and heating. Gases are a small percentage (usually 3 to 6 percent) of the total yield from the heated crude oil.

Light Gasoline

Collected at the next stage down from the gases are the light gasolines, which are used for the blending of motor gasoline. These account for only 5-10 percent of the total yield. Gasoline is a mixture of chemical compounds and is blended to meet local requirements. High octane gasoline requires a higher proportion of naphthenes (also called cyclo-alkanes), which are made up of six and five-member carbon rings, than paraffins or straight-chain carbon compounds. However, octane numbers can also be boosted by the addition of a variety of other compounds: lead used to be the main booster but has now been largely replaced by toluene and other aromatics and specially developed products such as methyl tertiary butyl ether.

Naphtha

Naphtha is the next product to be collected in the distillation column. This joins the light gasolines in the production of motor spirit. Both fractions are fed to a catalytic reformer, with butane and any other additives, for blending. Naphtha is also a major feedstock for the petrochemical industry in Europe, though not in the United States, where the LPGs (liquefied petroleum gases such as the alkanes) are preferred. There are differences, however, between the naphtha used for blending and those used for petrochemical production. The chemical industry prefers naphtha with a high paraffinic content, while the gasoline blenders like a high naphthenic and aromatic content (The type produced in any particular refinery is determined by the crude used, not the type of plant). Naphtha accounts for a slightly higher proportion of the whole yield than gases and gasolines: usually 5-15 percent. Gases, light gasolines and naphtha are known as the light end of the barrel, because they consist of lighter hydrocarbons and are lighter in weight per unit volume than the other compounds.

Middle Distillates

At the next stage of collection come the middle distillates, made up primarily of kerosene and gas oil/heating oil. Kerosene are mainly used as aviation fuel, though they also have applications as domestic burning and cooking fuel, particularly in the developing world and for upgrading heavier products. In general, kerosenes are a fairly small fraction: usually 5-10 percent of the barrel. Gas oil, the heavier of the middle distillates, accounts for 25-30 percent of the total. It has two major applications—space heating and diesel fuel. It can also be used by some European companies as a chemical feedstock in place of naphtha. Naphtha is preferred but, when the price differentials widens, gas oil can become attractive. Not all European naphtha crackers have this capability to use gas oil, although those that do can have an effect on gas oil prices from time to time. Some smaller industries also use gas oil as a fuel source, but these are few. Almost all middle distillates consumption demands low sulphur content and this will be determined largely by the crude oil used. Middle Eastern and South American crudes, for example, tend to have a high sulphur content, while North African and North Sea crudes are 'sweet' or low in sulphur.

Residual Fuel Oils

Finally, when all the other products have been boiled off, some fuel oils are left. These are used for electricity generation and as industrial fuel and fuel for ship's bunkers (although some ships use marine diesel, a kind of gas oil). Increasingly, however, these residual fuel oils are being used to feed upgrading facilities and to produce more light and middle distillate products. The sulphur concentration in residual fuel oil is higher than that of the crude from which it is produced because very little of it is removed during the distillation process.

Changing Patterns of Demand and Consumption

The refining of residual fuel oils in order to upgrade them was needed because of the changes in the demand for different products over the last quarter century. Gasoline demand as a percentage of all oil product demand has risen from 12 percent in 1970 to 29 percent in the mid 1990s. There has been a significant change in demand for different grades of gasoline within that overall total, most notable being the shift from regular grades to premium and the increasing strength of low lead and unleaded gasoline.

Gas oil demand rose from 29 percent in 1970 to around 37 percent over the same period. Diesel cars and increased commercial road transport during the economic boom in the industrialized countries in the mid 1980s contributed to the good demand for gas oil. This continued into the 1990s as one in four new cars in some countries are diesel fuelled.

Fuel oil has lost market share over many years, dropping from 40 percent of all products in 1970 to 17 percent in the mid 1990s. The tendency is most pronounced in high sulphur fuel oil, which has very limited applications following the introduction of tighter environmental controls in many countries. Fuel oil is the only oil product that can be easily substituted (apart from gas oil's space heating demand) and many fuel oil consumers are now flexible in their feedstock requirements, capable of taking gas and, in some cases, coal as an alternative, making price the determining factor in demand. Natural gas usage in particular has grown rapidly in recent years, accounting for almost 24 percent of total energy consumption in 1996, up from 22 percent in 1990 and less than 20 percent in 1980. The rate of growth is likely to accelerate over the next decade.

In different geographical areas, oil demand patterns vary considerably. The United States has traditionally been a high consumer of gasoline, which accounts for 42 percent of total demand. This proportion has been more or less steady for the last few years. The fast growing Asian market has seen gasoline's share increase to around 20 percent. In Europe, the gasoline share has fallen as the popularity of diesel cars has increased, largely due to a more favorable tax regime.

Refinery economics has been under pressure for much of the last two decades. In 1996, consumption was around 90 percent of total worldwide refinery capacity, one of the highest levels seen for some time. It took the refining industry a long time to recover from the demand falls of the late 1970s and early 1980s. The lead times in building a refinery are long and decisions on closure also have to reflect long term views.

There have been a number of years when refineries have lost money: variable costs, such as crude oil purchases, are almost always covered, but fixed costs may not be. Refineries tend to keep operating despite making losses because of the heavy depreciation costs suffered whether refinery is operational or not. There are also strategic reasons, particularly for state owned refineries, to keep operating. In 1978, oil accounted for 53.3 per cent of total primary energy consumption in the OECD countries, but by 2005 this had fallen to below 40 percent. The main beneficiaries have been natural gas, nuclear energy and coal, illustrating one of the main problems with alternative fuel. All of these fuels substitute for fuel oil in power generation and space heating but not for the other major use of oil that is transportation. As yet there have been no real alternatives developed for transportation that are both efficient and practical.

Some scheme, such as the Brazilian gasohol project where alcohol produced from sugar is added to gasoline, can be effective in a small area and when the circumstances are right. But in this case, a plentiful supply of cheap sugar is essential and as the price of sugar increases it becomes a less attractive option. A similar project was looked at in the US Mid-West using corn as the alcohol feedstock, but this was rejected as economically unfeasible. Because of their use of agricultural products as feedstock, small scale (in world terms) projects are likely to be initiated from time to time as politically expedient, but there seems little likelihood at the moment that gasohol will really take hold.

Global demand for energy is projected to rise 54 percent by 2015 from 1995 levels, according to the Energy Information Administration (EIA). In its annual International Energy Outlook 1997, EIA agency of the US department of energy, forecasts that almost half of the increase will be the result of rising demand in the newly emerging Asian economies. If energy consumption reaches the levels predicted by the report, released May 6, 2008, carbon emissions will rise to 9,700 million metric tons by 2015-61 percent higher than in 2000 (http://www.allbusiness.com/energy-utilities/energy-utility-sector-performance-oil/8006793-1.html).

The dynamics of the current oil market rely on four major interdependent areas of uncertainty: geo-strategic risks, macroeconomic fluctuations, nature of resources risks, and the uncertainty in current and future oil production capacity. At this point, about all that is certain is that the global energy market is unpredictable and that recent oil prices have been high and volatile. In four years, the price per barrel of oil has increased by roughly 108%. The price of crude oil averaged $25.9/barrel in 2001 and for the first eight months of 2005, the average price crude oil increased to approximately $54.1/barrel. By August-September, 2008, the price of crude sky-rocketed to circa $ 140/ barrel. Rigorous, transparent, and credible analysis, however, can improve our understanding of the forces at play and provide policy makers and analysts the tools necessary to forge sound energy policy based on real-world realities and risks (CSIS, 2006: www.igloo.org/igloo/community.igloo?r0=community-download&r0_script=/scripts/document/download.script).

Refinery Process and Technology

Refining process comprises of four types of process:

- Primary Separation
- Conversion Processes
  - Product up gradation
  - Conversion of heavy residue to light product
- Lube Oils Processing
- Treatment Processes

A generic Process of Refining is illustrated in Fig. 8.1.

Primary Separation

Primary separation is done by Atmospheric Distillation and Vacuum Distillation. Distillation is defined as a process in which a liquid or vapour mixture of two or more substances is separated into its component fractions of desired

Fig. 8.1: Generic Process of Oil Refining-Schematic

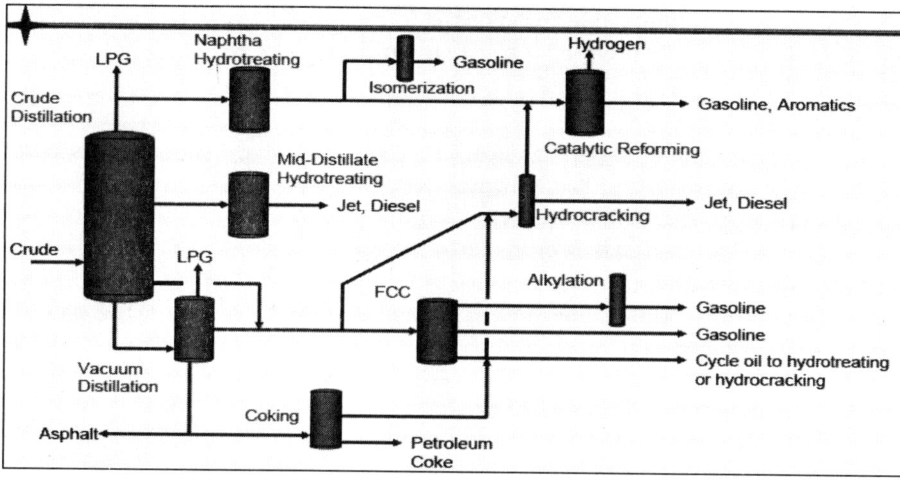

Source: API Energy.

purity, by the application and removal of heat. Distillation separates components of a liquid mixture based on their different boiling points. Distillation is based on the fact that the vapour of a boiling mixture will be richer in the components that have lower boiling points. Therefore, when this vapour is cooled and condensed, the condensate will contain more volatile components. At the same time, the original mixture will contain more of the less volatile material. Distillation columns are designed to achieve this separation efficiently. The strengths of distillation are that it has a simple flow sheet, low capital investment, and is generally low risk. Its weaknesses are that it is not energy-efficient, cannot separate components having overlapping boiling points of an azeotropic mixture, such as ethanol and water, and can degrade thermally sensitive materials.

Distillation is the leading separation process and by far the most popular technique for many applications. New developments in distillation technology promise further improvements in performance. Spurred in part by the increasing costs of feedstocks and energy, distillation has seen new developments in high efficiency trays and packing, enhanced process configurations and hybrid systems. Newer cross-flow trays are finding important applications, particularly when it is desirable to increase capacity in distillation columns operating at pressures of about 100 psig and higher. Meanwhile, the latest random packings boast thinner walls and occupy less of the volume of the column than traditional packings—freeing up more space for fluid traffic. They have been found to be especially attractive for high-pressure applications. At low pressures, structured packing has become prominent as a device that gives high efficiency at high capacity.

Atmospheric Distillation

A distillation unit operating at a little over the atmospheric pressure and processing crude is called an Atmospheric Crude Distillation Unit (CDU). It is also the backbone of refinery operations as it forms the first of a chain of various processes employed in producing distillate products from the crude.

CDU Process Objective:

- To distill and separate valuable distillates (naphtha, kerosene, diesel) and atmospheric gas oil (AGO) from the crude feedstock.
- Primary Process Technique:
  - Complex distillation
- Process steps:
  - Preheat the crude feed utilizing recovered heat from the product streams.
  - Desalt and dehydrate the crude using electrostatic enhanced liquid/ liquid separation (Desalter).
  - Heat the crude to the desired temperature using fired heaters.
  - Flash the crude in the atmospheric distillation column.
  - Utilize pump around cooling loops to create internal liquid reflux.
  - Product draws are on the top, sides, and bottom.

A crude distillation unit normally consists of a pre topping column, a main fractionating column, side stream strippers and stabilizers, all equipped with internal trays/ packings, as describe above. A reboiler or stripping steam is used to strip out light ends from column bottom product. Overhead condensers are provided to condense top vapors, while various pump-arounds exchange heat with incoming crude. Preheat exchanger trains are provided for waste heat recovery from rundown products and pump-arounds, a desalter for removing salt and water from crude, and process heater to heat the crude. (Fig. 8.2)

Crude distillation is an energy-intensive process. It consumes fuel at the equivalent of 2% of the crude processed. Crude is mixed with water and heated in a heat exchanger network before entering a desalter, where most of the water containing the salt is removed. The desalted crude enters another heat exchanger network and receives heat from hot streams. Both heat exchanger networks make use of the vapours of the main column condenser, the pump around circuit streams, and the products that need to be cooled. The preheated crude then enters the furnace, where it is heated to about 340-370°C. The partially vapourised crude is fed into the flash zone of the atmospheric column, where the vapour and liquid separate. The vapour includes all of the components that comprise the products, while the liquid is the residue with a small amount of relatively light components in the range of gas oil. These components are removed from the residue by steam stripping at the bottom of the column. In addition to the overhead condenser, there are several pump-around circuits along the column, where liquid streams are withdrawn, cooled, and sent back to upper trays. Products are withdrawn in the liquid state from different trays and then stripped by steam in side stripper to remove light components. Residue which is left behind at the bottom of the distillation column after atmospheric distillation is called long residue (LR).

Fig. 8.2: Crude Distillation Unit—Process Schematic

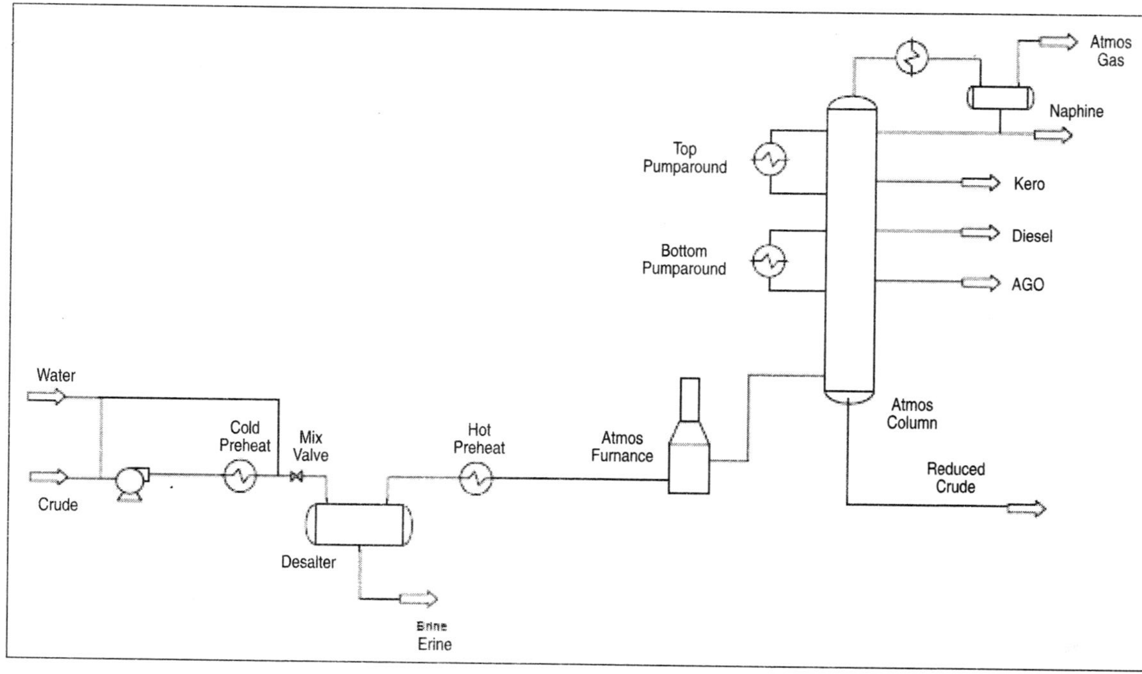

Source: API Energy.

Vacuum Distillation

The limitation of distilling at high temperature is that above 350 to 370°C temperature, crude oil starts cracking, that is, the heavier molecules start breaking into smaller molecules. Uncontrolled cracking process results in coke formation and production of unstable olefinic (double bonded) hydrocarbon products.

In vacuum distillation, the residue from atmospheric distillation is heated to around 350 to 370°C, and the heated and the partly vaporized reduced crude enters the flash zone of the vacuum column. In this column the feed is fractionated to recover the following products:

- Diesel fraction as the top side stream
- LVGO fraction as the second side stream
- HVGO fraction as the third side stream
- Slop cut as the fourth side stream
- Vacuum Residue as the bottoms product

The salient feature of the simplest form of Vacuum Distillation Unit (VDU) is as give below with schematic diagram (Fig. 8.3)

Primary Objective:

- To recover valuable gas oils from reduced crude via vacuum distillation.

Process technique:

- Reduce the hydrocarbon partial pressure via vacuum and stripping steam.

Fig. 8.3: Vacuum Distillation Unit—Process Schematic

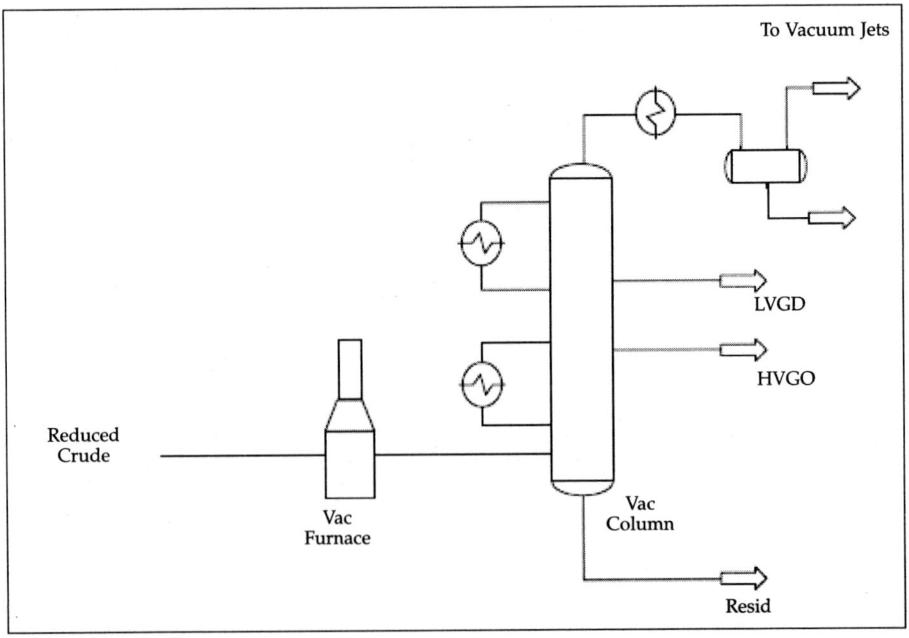

Source: API Energy.

Process steps:

- Heat the reduced crude to the desired temperature using fired heaters
- Flash the reduced crude in the vacuum distillation column
- Utilize pump around cooling loops to create internal liquid reflux
- Product draws are top, sides, and bottom

Immediately above the flash zone, a wash section is provided.

The HVGO section packing is essentially a heat transfer packing and its height is governed by the HVGO circulating reflux duty. Similarly the LVGO section packing is governed by heat transfer requirements for the LVGO circulating reflux. A packing equal to two theoretical stages is generally provided between the LVGO and diesel section. The diesel section packing is again governed by heat transfer requirements. The packing is designed to take care of the increased heat transfer requirements in this section during winter operation when diesel production will be much higher than in a summer.

Vacuum in the column (about 65-70mm Hg at the top) is maintained by a system consisting of precondenser ejectors, inter and after condensers. A two stage ejector system is provided. The precondenser consists of four shells having a total capacity equal to 110% of the design capacity. The ejectors are provided with three elements of 4/7, 2/7, 1/7 capacity and the total capacity of the elements is equal to 150% of the design capacity. The inter and after condensers too are sized for 150% capacity. The condensate from the condensers is routed to the hot well from where it is pumped to the sour water stripper in SRU. The uncondensed cracked gases are released to the atmosphere at safe location. Following heat exchange with reduced crude in the preheat train, the products from the vacuum column are further cooled and sent to storage/other destinations as described below.

Diesel stream (product and pump around reflux) is first cooled in air cooled exchanger to 60°C. The pump around is then returned to the vacuum column while the product is cooled in a trim cooler and sent to the diesel or LDO pool. The LVGO stream is mixed with HVGO which is cooled by steam generation. The combined VGO stream is cooled by tempered water in exchanger. Hot VGO can be supplied to downstream units before cooler. The VGO is used as feedstock for cracking in the Fluid Catalytic Cracking Unit (FCCU) and/or Hydro-cracker Unit (HCU) for cracking to lighter products. VGO can also form the base oil for processing into lubricating oils.

Slop distillate after heat exchange with RCO, is cooled by heat exchange with boiler feed water and finally with tempered water. The slop distillate can be routed independently to the IFO feed tanks or to the LSHS pool. Vacuum residue is routed to various destinations. The vacuum residue is cooled in tempered water cooled exchanger and sent to the FO pool/LSHS pool and Visbreaker Unit feed tanks.

Vacuum distillation unit yields VGO, which are used as feedstock for cracking to lighter products. VGO also can form the base oil for processing into lubricating oils. Various cuts obtained during the above Distillation processes, together with their routings are indicated in the table below (Table 8.1).

Table 8.1: Primary Separation: Atmospheric and Vacuum Distillation Cuts

Crude Oil	Atmospheric Distillation	< 35 deg. C	Butane and lighter	LPG Recovery
		35–80 deg. C	Light Gasoline	Motor Gasoline Blending
		80-140 deg. C	Naphtha	Cat Reforming
		140-250 deg. C	Kerosene	Hydro-treating
		250-350 deg. C	Gas Oil	Diesel Oil Stock
	Vacuum Distillation	350-400 deg. C	Light Vac. Gas Oil	Lube Base Stock
		400-500 deg. C	Heavy Vac. Gas Oil	Lube Base Stock or Cracking
		> 500 deg. C	Straight Run Residue	For Bitumen Processing

Conversion Process

Primary separation processes are essentially physical separation of the raw products by distillation. Conversion process means change of the molecules of the raw products obtained from distillation by reaction process under heat, pressure, along with or without a catalyst, from one type of molecule to another.

There are two types of conversion process:

- Conversion for up-gradation of product quality.
- Conversion to change heavy residual products into light and high value products like gasoline and diesel.

Conversion for Upgradation of Product Quality

There are several processes, which come under this category:

- Catalytic Reforming
- Isomerization
- Alkylation

These processes are essentially restructuring of molecules to improve the specifications.

Catalytic Reforming

Catalytic Reforming is a major conversion process having applications in Petroleum Refining and Petro-chemical Industries. It transforms low Octane Naphtha to:

(a) High Octane Motor-Gasoline Blending Stock.

(b) Produces Aromatic Concentrates rich in Benzene, Toluene and Xylene (BTX).

Hydrogen and LPG are produced as by-products during the Catalytic Reforming Process. The costly Hydrogen thus produced is used for Hydro-de-sulphurisation, Hydro-treating and Hydro-cracking processes, thus making the process economically viable process.

Feed Naphtha Quality and Pre-treatment

Naphtha (IBP-140 deg C) produced from Atmospheric Distillation Unit is split into various cut ranges depending on the end objectives:

C5-70 Cut: Used for blending in MS or Naphtha.
70-90 Cut: Used as feedstock for production of Benzene/Toluene
90-140 Cut: Used as feedstock for production of Reformate used as MS Blend.

As Reformer contains costly Platinum catalyst, Pretreatment of Naphtha feed to Reformer is carried out in presence of hydrogen in a Naphtha Pretreating Unit to meet the Sulphur limit of less than 0.5 ppm. Pre-treater acts as a shield for more expensive reformer catalyst against the presence of metallic impurity. Catalyst used for Naphtha Preheating is either Co–Mo or Ni–Mo or a combination of both. These catalysts are sulphited to form sulphur metal complex which activate the catalyst.

Chemistry of Naphtha Hydro Treatment

The Naphtha Hydro treating Process is a catalytic refining process employing a select catalyst and hydrogen-rich gas stream to decompose organic sulfur, oxygen and nitrogen compounds contained in hydrocarbon fractions. In addition, hydro treating removes organo-metallic compounds and saturates olefinic compounds. Main reactions in Naphtha Hydro-treatment are:

1. Conversion of organic sulfur compounds to hydrogen sulfide.
2. Conversion of organic sulfur compounds to ammonia.
3. Conversion of organic sulfur compounds to water.
4. Saturation of olefins.
5. Conversion of organic halides to hydrogen halides.
6. Removal of organo-metallic compounds.

Organo-metallic compounds, notably arsenic and lead compounds, are known to the permanent poisons to platinum containing catalyst. The complete removal of these materials by hydrotreating will give longer ultimate catalyst life in the Platforming unit. Sulfur is a temporary poison to Platforming catalysts. If alternate Platforming catalyst activity causes an unfavorable change in the product distribution and increases coke laydown. Organic nitrogen is also a temporary poison to Platforming catalyst. It is an extremely potent one; however, a relatively small concentration of nitrogen in the Platformer feed will cause a large activity offset as well as the deposit ammonium chloride salts in the Platforming unit cold sections. Oxygen compounds are detrimental to the operation of a Platformer. Any oxygen compounds which are not removed in the hydrotreater will be converted to water in the Platforming unit, thus affecting the water/chloride balance of the Platforming catalyst. Large amounts of olefins contribute to increase coking of the Platforming catalyst. Also, olefins can polymerize at platforming operating conditions which can result in exchanger and reactor fouling.

The Naphtha Hydrotreating Process makes a major contribution to the ease of operation and economy of Platforming. Much greater flexibility is afforded in choice of allowable charge stocks to the Platforming unit. Because this unit protects the Platforming catalyst, it is important to maintain consistently good operation in the Hydrotreating unit.

Pre-Process Disposition of the Pre-treatment Process

Naphtha feed from the charge pump combines with a hydrogen-rich gas stream, and this combined feed enters the combined feed/reactor effluent exchangers, where the feed is heated and the reactor effluent from the second reactor is cooled. The combined feed leaving the exchanger is all vapors, and flows to the charge heater where it is heated to the required reaction temperature. Most reactors are designed for down—flow operation, and contain sufficient catalyst to remove contaminants to the level required. In a two reactor configuration, the effluent from the first reactor is cooled through the second Combined Feed Exchanger (CFE) and then enters the second reactor. A three-way valve which controls a slip stream around the CFE is used as the temperature control. In the two reactor system, the purpose of the first reactor is to remove the sulfur and to saturate the olefins while the second reactor hydrogenates any recombinant sulfur formed with the higher temperatures seen in the first reactor. In some units, rather than having a recycle gas compressor, a comparable amount of a hydrogen-rich gas stream is brought into the unit on flow control, and flows on a once-through basis through the reactor section to the product separator where it is vented on pressure control.

The liquid hydrocarbon in the separator is pressured on level control through the stripper feed/bottoms exchanger, and thus heated enters near the top of the stripper. A reboiler is provided to supply the required heat input for generating vapor. This vapor strips hydrogen sulfide, water, light hydrocarbons and dissolved hydrogen from the feed to the stripper, which then passes overhead to the overhead condenser and to the overhead receiver. The reflux is pumped into the stripper on receiver level control. To increase the amount of reflux, the reboiler heat input must be increased to provide more overhead material. The net overhead gas leaves the receiver on pressure control, usually to amine scrubbing and then to fuel gas. The stripper overhead system is equipped with inhibitor addition facilities to prevent corrosion of the process lines and equipment by hydrogen sulfide in the overhead vapor. The stripper bottoms material is pumped through the feed/bottoms exchanger and is usually charged directly to the Platforming Unit.

Platforming Process

Platforming is the UOP name given to a group of reactions by which low octane, low-aromatic content Naphtha is catalytically converted to a high Octane Naphtha containing a high concentration of Aromatics. The reactions which take place are catalyzed by Platinum and Halogen impregnated on an Alumina base. Platforming catalysts are dual function catalysts, which promote reactions which are catalyzed by both the Platinum and Halogen (normally Chloride).

Reactions in Catalytic Reforming

The Chemical reactions involved in reforming processes are of two types:

Desirable Reactions: reactions which lead to an increased Octane Number and to high purity hydrogen production. These are:

- With Hydrogen production: Naphthenes Dehydrogenation, Paraffin Dehydro cyclisation
- Without Hydrogen Production: Linear Paraffin and Naphthenes Isomerization.

Adverse Reactions: reactions which lead to a decreased Octane Number, a decrease in hydrogen purity and a loss in products yield. These are the reactions to minimize. These are:

- Cracking, Demethylation, Ring Opening, Production of polycyclic and Coke, and cracking of non-Hydrocarbon compounds.

Types of Process Configurations

Commercial Catalytic Reforming Processes are furnished below:

Process Name	Licensor	Process Type
Catalytic Reforming	IFP, IFP-IIP in India	SR, CCR, Hybrid
Magnaforming	Engelhard	SR
Platforming	UOP	SR, CCR, Hybrid
Powerforming	Exxon	SR, Cyclic
Rheniforming	Chevron	SR
Ultraforming	Standard Oil Co., AMOCO R&D	SR, Cyclic

Isomerization

Light naphtha Isomerization can significantly boost octane in light gasoline fractions. Isomerization is the process used to up-grade the octane of light naphtha and similar refinery streams by molecular rearrangement. Branched isomers of light paraffinic hydrocarbons have higher octane blending numbers than the equivalent straight chain paraffins.

Isomerization Process Objective

- To convert low-octane n-paraffins to high-octane iso-paraffins.

- Primary Process Technique:
  - Isomerization occurs in a chloride promoted fixed bed reactor where n-paraffins are converted to iso-paraffins. The catalyst is sensitive to incoming contaminants (sulfur and water).
- Process steps:
  - Desulfurized feed and hydrogen are dried in fixed beds of solid dessicant prior to mixing together
  - The mixed feed is heated and passes through a hydrogenation reactor to saturate olefins to paraffins and saturate benzene
  - The hydrogenation effluent is cooled and passes through a isomerization reactor

Fig. 8.4: Schematic Diagram of Isomerization Process

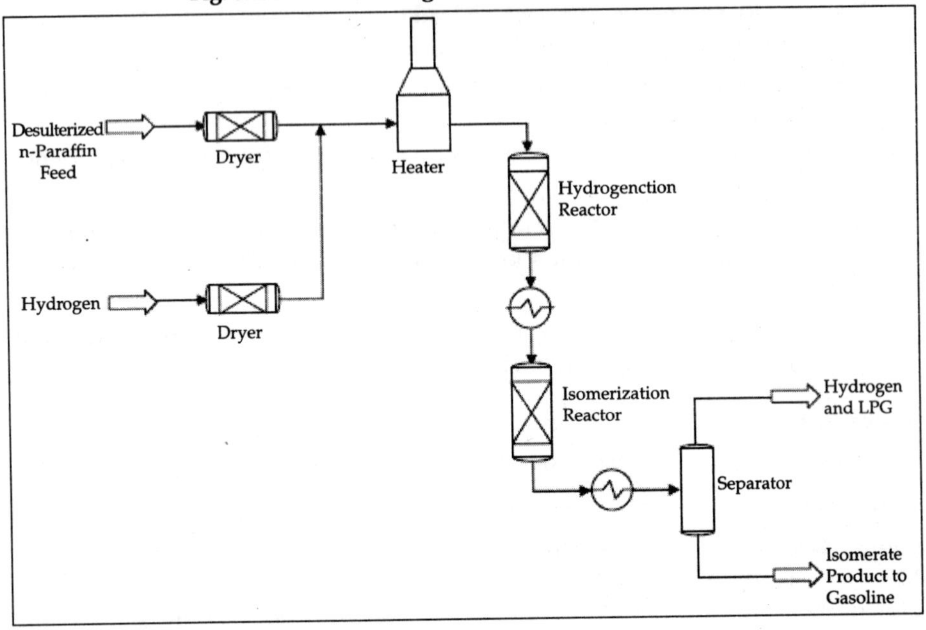

Source: API Energy.

- The final effluent is cooled and separated as hydrogen and LPGs which typically go to fuel gas, and isomerate product for gasoline blending

A Schematic Diagram of Isomerization Process is given in Fig 8.4.

Main Reactions

The main paraffin reactions that take place are the formation of iso-pentane from normal pentane and the formation of di-methyl butanes and methyl-pentanes from normal hexane. These reactions are equilibrium limited. Iso-pentane (iC_5) has a significantly higher octane value than n-pentane and the branched C_6 paraffins have a much higher octane than n-hexane. The highly brached C_6 iso-paraffins, 22-dimethyl butane (22-DMB) and 23-dimethyl butane (23-DMB) have the highest octane numbers and maximization of the formation of these components is therefore highly desirable. In addition to these reactions a number of cyclic reactions take place. Benzene in the feed will undergo complete saturation to cyclohexane. Some cyclohexane will be isomerized to methylcyclopentane. The C_6 naphthenes, cyclohexane (CH) and methylcyclopentane (MCP) exist in equilibrium. Subsequent ring opening of some of the cyclohexane and methylcyclopentane to form normal hexane will occur. These reactions although not providing a net octane boost do provide the refiner with the advantage of reducing benzene. These reactions are exothermic and so higher equilibrium conversions are favored by lower reaction temperatures.

Advanced Recycle Technologies

Molecular sieve separation: For full conversion of all normal paraffins, recycling normal paraffins to extinction is required to convert them entirely to branched isomers. This involves separating and recovering the normal paraffins from their isomers. An efficient separation path uses molecular sieve adsorption Technology. Using molecular sieves to separate normal paraffins from their isomers either in the vapor or liquid phase, is a proven industrial technique and has been applied to Isomerization processes. This separation method relies on the pore size of the molecular sieve to adsorb normal paraffins selectively, taking advantage of their smaller molecular diameter. The adsorption step is followed by a desorption step for a net recovery of the normal paraffins. These steps are carried out cyclically or pseudo-continuously and often rely on third fluids for the desorption and delivery steps. Hydrogen can be used in processes that are integrated with the isomerization reaction. The more volatile butanes are used in liquid phase non-integrated processes. In the latter, the use of butanes for desorption calls for two debutanizers to recover the desorbing fluid from both the isomerate and the normal paraffin extract streams. When using recycles hydrogen to desorb the normal paraffins, the non-chlorinated less active zeolite isomerization catalyst is required to avoid molecular sieve degradation. As such, it cannot attain the same RON performance—as does the chlorinated alumina catalyst. For the highest octane isomerate, it is best to use a chlorinated alumina catalyst with a segregated molecular sieve normal paraffin separation section. Two patented separation processes are offered, Ipsorb and Hexorb enabling attainment of 89 to 92 RON.

Ipsorb

With the Ipsorb process a cyclic vapor-phase adsorption system follows the isomerate stabilizer to remove unconverted normal paraffins from the raw isomerate. Desorption of adsorbed normal paraffins takes place using an isopentane rich vapor stream to recycle the normal paraffins to the upstream deisopentanizer column. Separating isopentane from the fresh feed reduces flow to the reaction section thereby affording increased per-pass conversion of normal pentane to isopentane. The increased per-pass conversion in turn reduces the recycle of normal pentane for conversion to extinction. The net reaction section feed rate is a maximum of 10% above the fresh feed rate for a chlorinated alumina catalyst system.

Deisopentanizer

A low pressure, conventional deisopentanizer column is required in the separation scheme as an integral part of the Ipsorb process. One feature is that it is not necessary to attain a very sharp separation in the column because the isopentane-rich distillate is used as a desorption stream for the molecular sieve section where any n-pentane present is removed. The distillate is combined with the molecular sieve effluent to make the final product which can tolerate a reasonable concentration of n-pentane (isomerate contains less than 1% n-pentane). In 1994, the first Ipsorb isomerization unit was commissioned in Italy.

Hexorb

Ultimately, to go beyond the 90 Ron thresholds, substantial conversion of the methyl pentanes is required. This can be achieved with full conversion of normal paraffins by integrating the Hexorb separation process with the reaction section. This patented process provides Isomerate having over 90 RON (typically 91-91.5RON) with a 40:60 C5/C6 feed. The Hexorb isomerization process combines a cyclic molecular sieve adsorption system with a downstream deisohexanizer that splits raw isomerate from the molecular sieve section into an isomerate overhead stream rich in isopentane and dimethyl butanes and poor in the lower octane methyl pentanes (MPs) from two streams containing higher boiling components. The first is a bottoms section side-stream from the deisohexanizer, containing essentially all the MPs, is recycled to the isomerization reaction system. It is also used as a desorption fluid through the molecular sieve system. This desorption fluid acts in the same manner as the isopentane rich vapor stream in the Ipsorb process. The second stream, a bottoms purge, is removed and combined with the isomerate product since it is high in C_6 naphthenes and C_7+hydrocarbons. This avoids catalyst inhibition by naphthenes and hydrocracking of C_7's to extinction in the Isomerization reactor.

REACTOR-REGENERATOR SECTION

Fluidic Catalytic Cracking Process (FCC)

Process Objective:
- To convert low value gas oils to valuable products (naphtha and diesel) and slurry oil.

- Primary Process Technique:
  - Catalytic cracking increases H/C ratio by carbon rejection in a continuous process.
- Process steps:
  - Gas oil feed is dispersed into the bottom of the riser using steam.
  - Thermal cracking occurs on the surface of the catalyst.
  - Disengaging drum separates spent catalyst from product vapors.
  - Steam strips residue hydrocarbons from spent catalyst.
  - Air burns away the carbon film from the catalyst in either a "partial-burn" or "full-burn" mode of operation.
  - Regenerated catalyst enters bottom of riser-reactor.

A Schematic diagram of the Fluidic Catalytic Cracking Process (FCC) is given in Fig. 8.5.

Reactor-Riser

The reactor riser is a vertical pipe in which all the cracking reactions take place. Hot regenerated catalyst ex the Regenerator enters the "wye" section at the bottom

Fig. 8.5: Schematic diagram of Fluidic Catalytic Cracking Process (FCC)

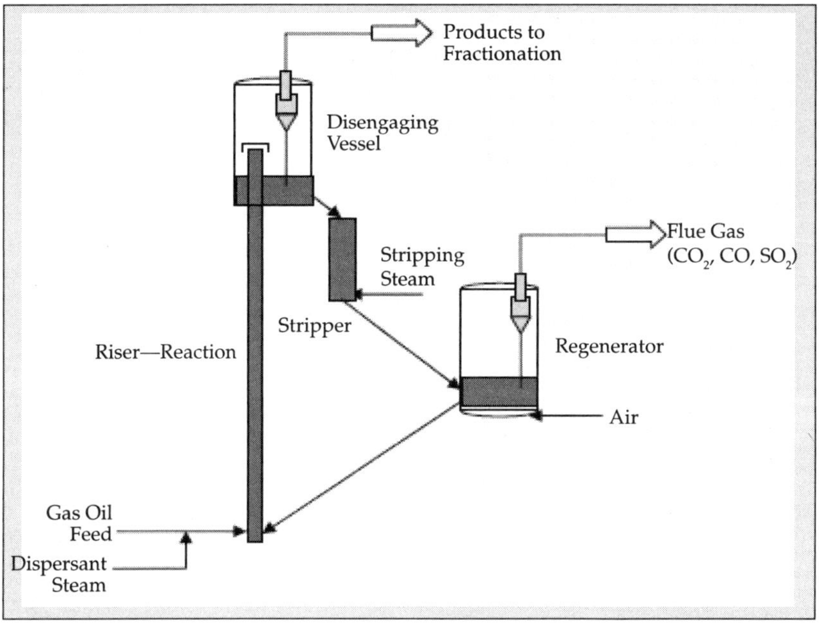

Source: API Energy.

of the riser, and meets the raw oil and riser steam. The flow of catalyst is controlled in the Regenerator Standpipe to maintain the desired reactor temperature. The raw oil and riser steams are premixed in a feed distributor to form an emulsion. The raw oil/riser steam emulsion vaporizes upon contacting the hot regenerated catalyst, accelerating the catalyst and hydrocarbon vapors up the riser. Cracking reactions are carried essentially to completion in the riser with a minimum of over cracking and coke formation. Catalyst and oil contact time using this system is approximately 3 seconds.

Catalyst and hydrocarbon vapors exit the riser into the reactor. Various new devises are available to disengage the catalyst. The basic objective is to provide a quick method of separating the catalyst and hydrocarbon vapors. Catalyst falling from the disengaging devise combines with catalyst recovered from the reactor cyclones to enter the reactor stripping section (Fig. 8.6).

Reactor

The upper section of the reactor contains the cyclones and the disengaging device. The disengaging arm provides the primary separation of catalyst and hydrocarbon vapors. A singles stage of cyclones, located at the top of the reactor, recovers the remainder of the catalyst. The hydrocarbon vapors exit the top of the cyclones through the plenum chamber to the main column. Recovered catalyst flows from the cyclone dip-legs to enter the reactor stripping section. The dip pipes

Fig. 8.6: Fluid Catalytic Cracking Unit

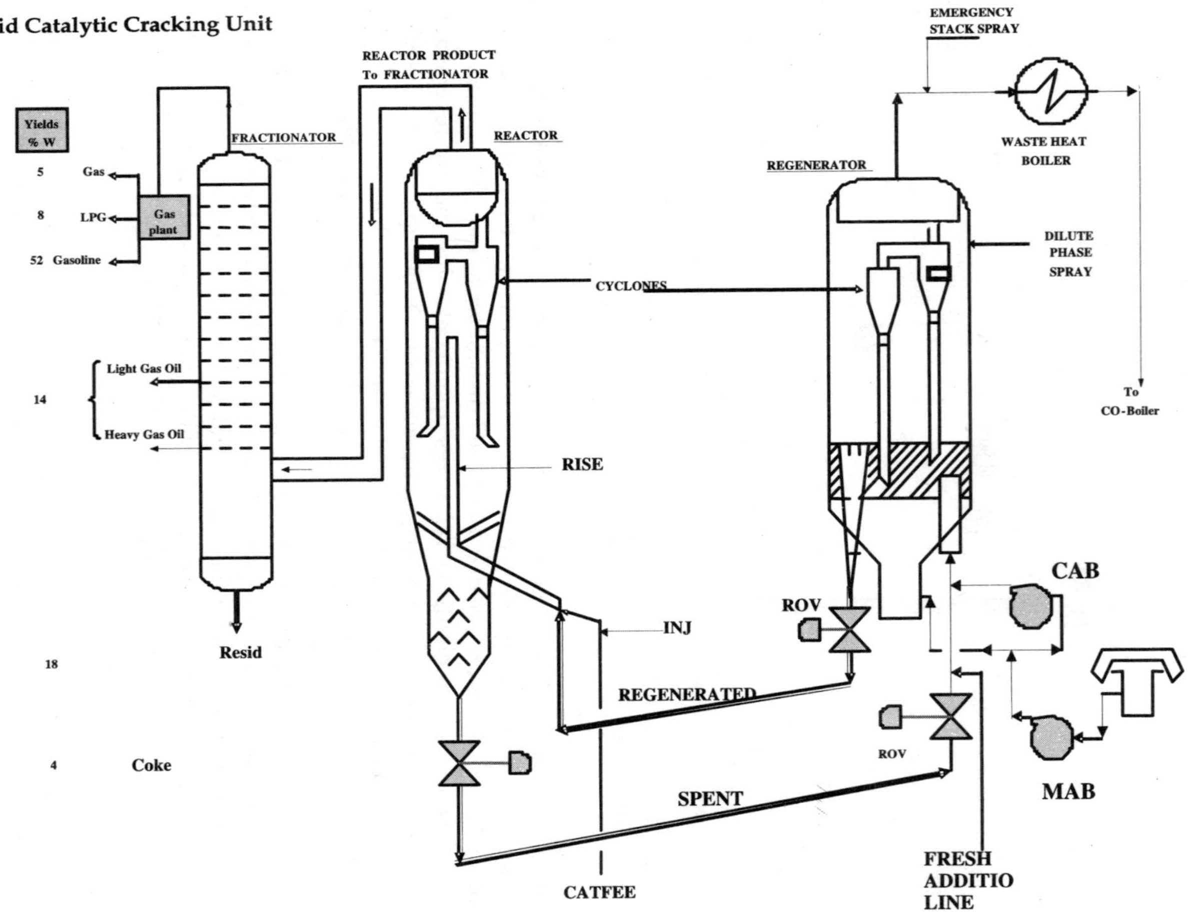

are equipped with counter weighted flapper valves to maintain a catalyst seal in the cyclone dip-legs. Reactor catalyst level is maintained above the top grid in the reactor stripping section. Stripping steam from the catalyst stripper flows through the reactor to enter the cyclones. This steam carries hydrocarbon from the catalyst to mix with the hydrocarbon product from the reactor riser.

Regenerator

The regenerator is lined with an insulating refractory concrete united on a reinforcing support. This lining is necessary to protect the metal wall of the vessel from the high temperatures at which the regenerator operates and should keep the out shell of the regenerator below its design temperature at all times. The coke deposited on the catalyst in the reactor is burned off by air distributed by perforated pipe grid mounted at the bottom of the regenerator. The combustion of coke is an exothermic reaction yielding a great quantity of heat. The FCC catalyst absorbs approximately seventy (70) percent of the heat generated and most of that remaining leaves with the hot flue gas. Spent catalyst enters the regenerator on level control from the reactor. Air, which is injected through the pipe air grid distributor, provides catalyst fluidization as well as the necessary combustion oxygen. There are basically two modes of operation for Regenerators, one is the full combustion mode and the other is the partial combustion mode. In a full combustion Regenerator, the coke on the regenerated catalyst is almost negligible, but in the partial mode the coke would about 0.2 wt%.

FRACTIONATION SECTION

The effluent vapors from the reactor must be condensed and fractionated into the desired products. The main column performs both of these operations, yielding net gas and un-stabilized gasoline as the net overhead products, light cycle oil as net side-cut product, and a main column bottoms net product. Heavy cycle oil is also drawn as a side-cut and circulated for heat exchange, but no net HCO product is produced. The column is designed to handle the superheated reactor effluent vapors, and the large quantity of vapor which rises through the column.

Reactor vapors at approximately 500°C enter the bottom of the main column below the disc and donut trays. Disc and donut trays are used because of the large vapor load in the bottom section of the column. The superheated vapors must be cooled below 365°C before fractionation can commence. The vapors are de-superheated, partially condensed, and washed of entrained catalyst by contact with a cooled, circulating bottoms stream returning below the top disc and donut tray. Coke can from in the column bottoms if the bottoms material has too great a residence time at a high bottoms temperature. A quench stream of cooled bottoms material returning below the disc and donut trays is used to keep the bottoms temperature below the 365°C cracking temperature to prevent coking. A hot bottoms circulating stream returning below the top disc and donut tray is used to maintain a high wash rate over the trays when the unit is operated at reduced throughputs.

De-superheated vapors rise from the main column bottom into the cooled heavy cycle oil section. This section contains two valve type trays, and an accumulator tray. The cooled HCO circulating stream, returning through a distributor, condenses the HCO fraction from the rising vapors. The liquid is collected on the HCO accumulator tray from which it is withdrawn for the pumped, flow controlled, circulating heat exchange streams. Uncondensed vapors from the heavy cycle oil section rise to the light cycle oil section. The cooled light cycle oil circulating stream returns through a distributor and condenses the light cycle oil material from the hot rising vapors. The refluxing liquid collects on the accumulator LCO tray from where it is withdrawn for the pumped, flow controlled circulating stream. Liquid from the accumulator also flows to the top tray of the light cycle oil stripper. Stripped vapors return to the main column above the LCO accumulator tray and rise with the lighter vapors to the naphtha section.

The remaining uncondensed gasoline range vapors, light hydrocarbon gases, and water vapor pass through top trays into the overhead system where the gasoline and water are condensed by the main column overhead condenser, and collected in the main column overhead receiver. Condensed gasoline is pumped from the overhead receiver on temperature control (cascaded to flow control) to the top of the main column above top tray. This maintains the desired endpoint of the final stabilized gasoline product. The gasoline and separated water are individually pumped on level control. From the overhead receiver, uncondensed light gases flow to the gas concentration unit on pressure control. The condensed gasoline is pumped on level control to the gas concentration unit as net overhead liquid. Water from the Softened Water Vat in the Gas Concentration Unit is injected upstream of the main column overhead condenser to prevent salt buildup in the exchangers. Water is pumped from the overhead receiver water boot on level control to the sour water stripping unit.

Hydrocracking

Chemically, the most efficient cracking process is Hydro-cracking. Hydrogen is reacted with residual Fuel Oil, in presence of a catalyst, to increase the proportion of Hydrogen atoms to Carbon atoms and to produce more light constantans. This process is more flexible than the other two—its major disadvantage is cost.

Process Principles

Process Objective

- To remove feed contaminants (nitrogen, sulfur, metals) and to convert low value gas oils to valuable products (naphtha, middle distillates, and ultra-clean lube base stocks).

- Primary Process Technique:
  - Hydrogenation occurs in fixed hydrotreating catalyst beds to improve H/C ratios and to remove sulfur, nitrogen, and metals. This is followed byone or more reactors with fixed hydrocracking catalyst beds to dealkylatearomatic rings, open napthtenerings, and hydrocrack paraffin chains.

- Process steps:
  - Preheated feed is mixed with hot hydrogen and passes through a multi-bed reactor with interstage hydrogen quenches for hydrotreating
  - Hydrotreated feed is mixed with additional hot hydrogen and passes through amulti-bed reactor with quenches for first pass hydrocracking
  - Reactor effluents are combined and pass through high and low pressure separators and are fed to the fractionator where valuable products are drawn from the top, sides, and bottom
  - Fractionator bottoms may be recycled to a second pass hydrocracker for additional conversion all the way up to full conversion

Hydro-cracking process is a catalytic process for treating hydro-carbonaceous feed under conditions of high hydrogen partial pressure and high temperatures in the presence of a catalyst containing a hydrogenation component selected from the groups VI and VIII of the periodic table and with an overall net chemical consumption of hydrogen to produce a range of products lighter than the feed.

Hydro-cracking is probably the most versatile petroleum process which can handle feed stocks ranging from naphtha to de-metalized oils/de-asphalted oils to produce almost any desired products lighter than feed as indicated below :

	Feed	Products
(i)	Naphtha	Propane, Butane, LPG
(ii)	Natural Gas Condensate, Kerosene, Light Cycle Oil, Coker Distillate.	Naphtha
(iii)	Atm. Gas Oil, DMO, DAO	Naphtha
(vi)	Vac. Gas Oil, DMO, DAO	Naphtha, Jet Fuel, Lube oils, Gas oils
(v)	Residues	Distillates, Low Sulphur fuel oils

In a Distillate Hydro-cracker, the application of which is more relevant in the Indian context, feed-stocks such as Vacuum Gas Oils, Heavy Gas Oils, FCC Cycle Oil, de-asphalted oil/de-metallized oil are subjected to cracking over catalyst beds in presence of hydrogen at pressure above 150 atmospheres and temperatures ranging between 370-450 deg C. The process removes almost all the sulphur from the feed to produce H_2S and the entire nitrogen to produce NH_3. The products obtained are therefore almost free of sulphur and nitrogen compounds, are fully saturated and hence stable and on the whole are much more superior as compared to products from other secondary processes. Generally, no post treatment is necessary for any of the products. The products can be blended with other inferior quality straight run products and upgrade them to a great extent.

Process Configurations

Depending upon the feed quality, the product mix desired and also the size of the unit, one of the following process flow configurations can be adopted:

(a) Single stage Scheme: For 100% conversion
(b) Two stage Scheme: Feed into products.

(c) Once through operation: For partial conversion of feed (50-80%).
(d) Hydro-cracking for Lube production.

In the Single stage scheme the unconverted material from the fractionator bottom is recycled to the first reactor along-with fresh feed. In the Two-stage scheme the unconverted material is routed separately to another reactor. In both these schemes cracking takes place to extinction and on the other hand in the once through operation there is no recycle and fractionator bottom is also taken out as a product. A schematic presentation of a typical Hydrocracking Unit is give below (Fig. 8.7)

Reaction Chemistry

Following main reactions are stated to be taking place in the hydrocracking process:

(a) Hydro-de-sulphurisation
(b) Hydro-de-nitrogenation
(c) Hydro-Isomerization
(d) Hydro-cracking
(e) Hydrogenation

The cracking reactions namely, hydro-cracking, hydro-de-alkylation, hydro-isomerisation and hydro-de-cyclisation, are carried out on the acidic support of the catalyst (Silica/Alumina, Zeolite). The Hydrogenation reactions such as hydrogenolisis, polyaromatics hydrogenation, olefins hydrogenation, hydrogenation of monoaromatics, etc., take place with the help of the metal sulphides present in the Catalyst. Ni/Co/Fe, Mo/W/V is the metals normally used.

Catalysts

Hydro-cracking reactions which combine both cracking and hydrogenation reactions demand a dual function catalyst. Cracking reactions are permitted by acid sites and hydrogenation by metal sites. The acid function is normally supplied by the catalyst bases and these are primarily amorphous silica, Alumina or Zeolite. The hydrogenation function is supplied by metals selected from group VI and group VIII of the periodic table. Favored metals are Molybdenum and Tungsten (Group VI) Cobalt, Nickel, Platinum, Paladium (Group VIII) respectively. The selected metals are dispersed on the catalyst base.

The preferred catalyst base depends on the type of product required. Silica/ Alumina is normally used where waxy distillates (350-550 degree C boiling range) are hydrocracked to maximize the yield of Middle Distillates, whilst zeolite catalysts which have a higher intrinsic acid activity are more favoured where the main product requirements are gasoline and naphtha. Of late, zeolite bases are also being developed for use in middle distillates production. The highly acid catalysts are sensitive to nitrogen compounds in the feed stocks. The nitrogen in the feed gets converted to ammonia through reactions and the ammonia so formed partially neutralizes the acidic sites thus reducing the catalytic activity. Zeolite

Fig. 8.7: Schematic Presentation of a Hydro-Cracking Unit

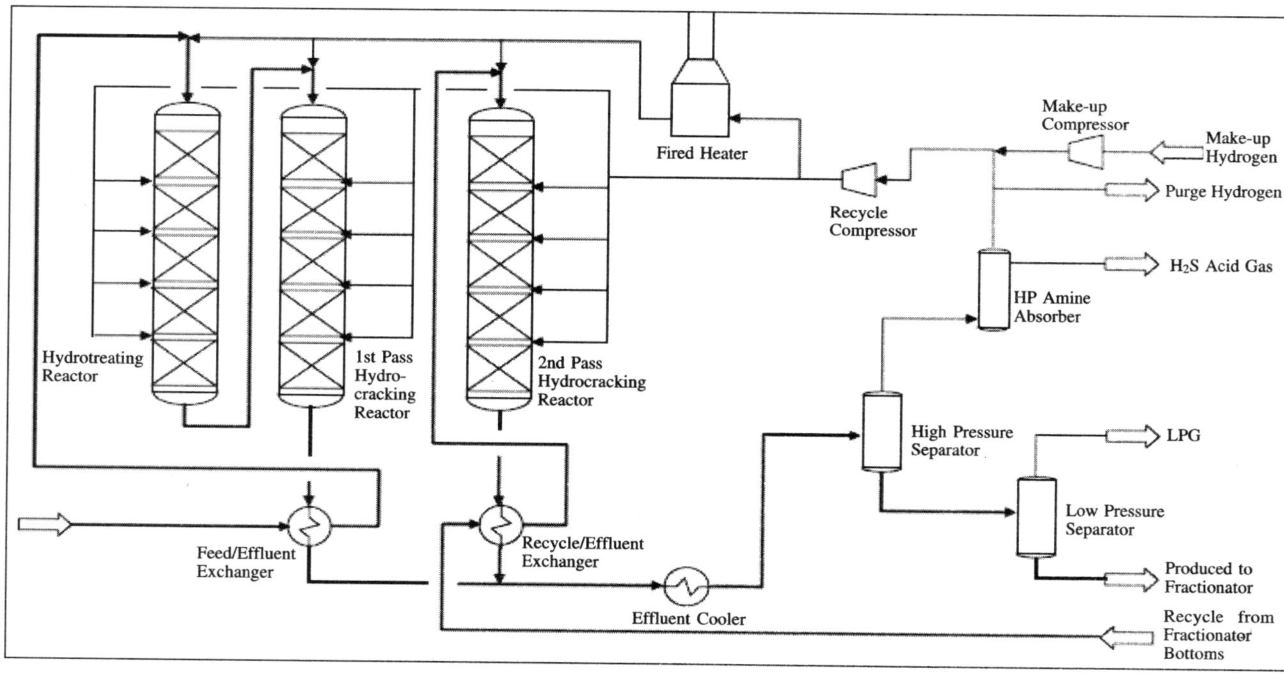

Source: API Energy.

catalyst on the other hand is poisoned by organic nitrogen compounds which adsorb strongly on the catalyst. It is therefore, necessary to have a feed pretreatment for ue-nitrogenation which is carried out using a cobalt/molybdenum or Molybdenum on Alumina or Silica-Alumina Catalyst.

Catalytic Reforming Process

Process Objective

To convert low-octane naphtha into a high-octane reformate for gasoline blending and/or to provide aromatics (benzene, toluene, and xylene) for petrochemical plants. Reforming also produces high purity hydrogen for hydro-treating processes.

Primary Process Technique

Reforming reactions occur in chloride promoted fixed catalyst beds; or continuous catalyst regeneration (CCR) beds where the catalyst is transferred from one stage to another, through a catalyst regenerator and back again. Desired reactions include: dehydrogenation of naphthenes to form aromatics; isomerization of naphthenes; dehydrocyclization of paraffins to form aromatics; and isomerization of paraffins. Hydrocracking of paraffins is undesirable due to increased light-ends make.

Process Steps:

- Naphtha feed and recycle hydrogen are mixed, heated and sent through successive reactor beds.
- Each pass requires heat input to drive the reactions.
- Final pass effluent is separated with the hydrogen being recycled or purged for hydro treating.
- Reformate product can be further processed to separate aromatic components or be used for gasoline blending.

A Schematic Presentation of the Catalytic Reforming Process is given in Fig. 8.8.

Lube Oil Manufacture

Functions of lubricating oil is to reduce friction and wear, prevent scuffing and seizure of moving parts, remove heat from the contact surface, prevent rust, corrosion, excessive deposit and sludge formation, dispersion of contaminants, maintenance of water reparability and remissibility, maintenance of sealing in critical parts, maintenance of resistance to degradation in presence of oxygen and catalytic materials. Any lubricating oil available in the market is a blend of Lube Oil Base Stocks (90%) and additives (10%). The additives used for Lubricants include Surface Protective Additives like Anti-wear Agents, Corrosion Inhibitors, Detergents, Dispersants, Friction Modifiers, and Rust Inhibitors etc. Performance Additives like Pour Point Depressants, Viscosity Index Improvers, Emulsifiers and

Fig. 8.8: Schematic Presentation of the Catalytic Reforming Process

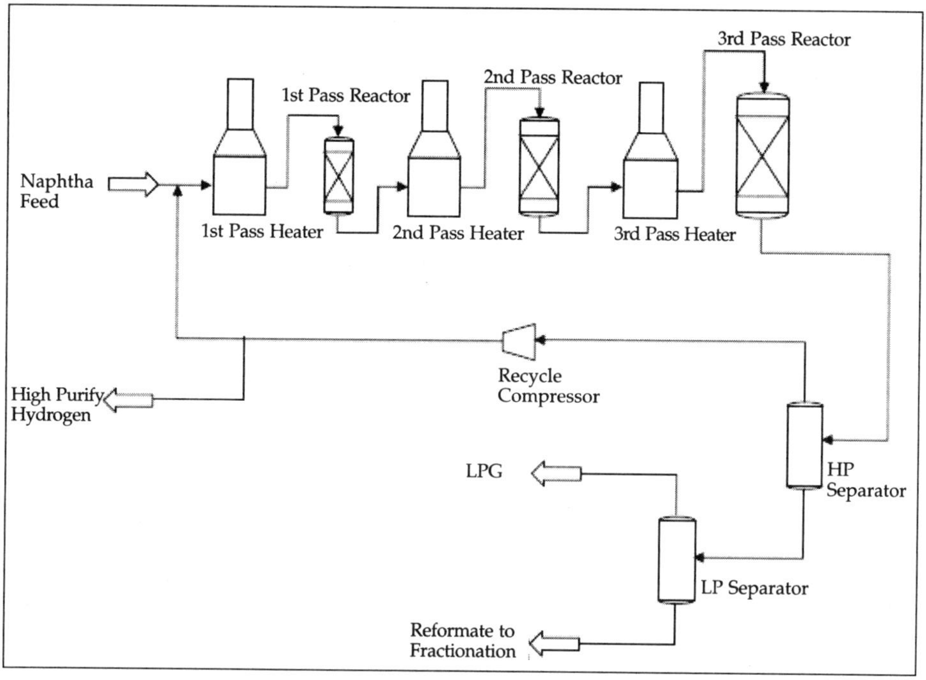

Source: API Energy.

Demulsifiers etc. and Lubricant Protective Additives like Antioxidants, Antifoamants, Metal Deactivators, Biocides and Fungicides.

Sulphur Recovery Unit

The modified Claus process basically converts hydrogen sulphide from an amine unit into sulphur and water vapor. Besides Hydrogen sulphide, the acid gas typically contains Carbon dioxide, water vapor and eventually some amounts of hydrocarbons.

The feed to the Sulphur Recovery Plant is H_2S rich Acid and Sour Gas generated in the ARU and Sour Water Stripper units respectively. The acid gas feed is the principal feed stock for the unit. Sour gas is fed in comparatively lower quantities to supplement acid gas feed. Acid gas and sour gas compositions are dependent on the upstream amine regeneration and sour water stripping units.

Reaction Chemistry

In the sulphur plant, elemental sulphur is recovered from this feedstock using the Claus Reaction. The two principal reactions used in SRU are:

(i) H_2S COMBUSTION:

$$H_2S + 3/2\ O_2 \Leftrightarrow SO_2 + H_2O + \text{HEAT}$$

(ii) CLAUS REACTION:

$$2H_2S + SO_2 = 3/n\ S_n + 2H_2O \text{ (- HEAT AT HIGH T + HEAT AT LOW T)}$$

The Claus reaction is endothermic at high temperatures, i.e. in the Main combustion chamber (MCC) and exothermic at low temperatures, i.e. in the reaction section. As is apparent from the Claus reaction and coefficient of sulphur, i.e., 3/n, it is clear that the sulphur produced in the MCC is of the S_2 type while the sulphur produced in the reaction section is of the S_6/S_8 type.

Sour Water Stripping

Sour water strippers do not enjoy the same constant feed rate and composition that most refinery hydrocarbon processes thrive on. Sour water systems have been described as garbage disposals or toilets of refineries. Any water soluble waste, whether produced continuously, intermittently or in a slug will be dumped into this system. Because sour water is produced from most refinery processes, a refinery processing sour crudes will supply sour water from such the units such as:

(a) Atmospheric crude columns
(b) Vacuum columns
(c) Hydrodesulphurization units
(d) Steam crackers
(e) FCC units and
(f) Catalytic hydrocracking units

Product Specifications

Since most of the operations in the refinery are to meet certain specifications of products, it is necessary to know of certain important specifications and their significance.

No.	Refinery Products	Specifications
1	LPG	Vapor Pressure at 65 deg. C, Propane content
2	Gasoline	Octane No., Boiling Range, Sulfur, Aromatics,Olefins, Benzene content
3	Naphtha	Boiling Range
4	Kerosene	Smoke Point, Flash Point, Sulfur
5	Jet Fuel	Freezing Point, Flash Point, Boiling Range
6	Diesel Oil	Cetane No., Carbon Residue, Pour Point, Flash Point, Sulfur, PAH content,
7	Lubricating Oil	Viscosity, Viscosity Index, Carbon Residue

Vapour Pressure: It is a property of LPG for safety and handling, particularly as LPG is used as cooking fuel in households. It restricts maximum pressure a cylinder can develop and helps to set the design pressure for the cylinder. Propane, being more volatile than butane, it can develop more pressure and hence its content in LPG is limited by specification.

Flash Point: It is the minimum temperature at which the product generates enough vapour to form an explosive mixture with air. Flash point is significant to the safety during storage and handling.

Octane Number: Octane number is defined as the percent volume of iso-octane in a mixture of iso-octane and normal heptane that gives the same knocking as that of the fuel when tested under defined conditions. Iso-octane is assigned a value of 100 and normal heptane is given the value of zero. Other octane numbers emerge as relative ignition quality or anti-knock quality of the component. This signifies ignition quality of the gasoline in automobile engines. The engine has cylinders with pistons where the fuel and air mixture is injected. The cylinders of automobile pass through a cycle of expansion, compression and ignition for movement of the pistons, which drive the wheels through a crankshaft. For optimum delivery of power to the engine, the fuel air mixture injected to the engine should ignite at the right time. The different hydrocarbon content in gasoline is straight chain paraffin, iso-paraffins, naphthenes and aromatics. Normally for the same carbon number and size of the molecule straight chain paraffins have the lowest octane number. Branched chain paraffins (isomers), naphthenes have the higher octane number. Olefins also have high octane number, but they are undesirable in gasoline because they tend to polymerize to form resins or gum in the tank.

Aromatics: Although it has high ON, its content in gasoline is being limited by specification due to its carcinogenic nature.

Pour Point: When heavy petroleum products like fuel oil or diesel containing wax are cooled to certain temperatures, the wax separates out from them making the oil immobile. It becomes difficult to move or pump the oil. The temperature at which the oil becomes immobile is termed as pour point. It happens because separated wax forms honeycomb like structures.

Boiling Range: The volatility of oil is indicated by its boiling range and distillation characteristics. The oil should have suitable boiling range (volatility) so that it can be used in a particular application.

Smoke Point: It is the length of flame in a standard laboratory test, which produces smoke. It is an important property of kerosene. Smoke point depends on the type of hydrocarbon constituents of the fuel. Paraffins have high smoke points followed by naphthenes and then by aromatics. Higher smoke point means less smoky.

Cetane Number: While the octane number indicates ignition quality of engines using spark ignition (gasoline fuelled cars), this test is applicable to diesel fuels which use ignition by compression. Cetane number is defined as the percent by volume of n-cetane in a mixture of n-cetane and alpha methyl naphthalene that would give the same ignition quality and engine performance as that of the fuel under test.

Sulfur: Sulfur is corrosive to the fuel systems and also is a pollutant to the environment. The specifications on sulfur content in petroleum products are becoming more and more stringent worldwide.

Viscosity: Viscosity is the resistance to flow. Viscosity is an important property of lube oils because higher viscosity is required to prevent wear and tear in the moving parts of a machine. For fuel oils, it gives flow properties which are needed for pump selection for transporting.

Viscosity Index: This specification signifies change of viscosity with temperature. This is an important specification for lubricating oils. In machinery, friction generates heat. For any petroleum product, viscosity is lower as the temperature increases. The lube oil viscosity not expected to go down too much with heating, as it would lose its lubricating property. Higher the Viscosity Index less is the effect of temperature on viscosity.

Carbon Residue: Fuel as it burns, forms a carbon deposit. This carbon deposits on burner tips or cylinders reduces efficiency. Carbon residue test gives an indication of the amount of carbon that would form when the oil is cracked and burned.

Process Control Basics

Process Definition

A process is phenomenon that chemically or physically changes matter or converts energy.

Examples of processes are:

- Heating
- Separating
- Refining
- Mixing
- Filling

Process Parameters

A process parameter is a characteristic of the process—something that you can monitor and measure, which will give you information about the process. If the process is Air conditioning of the Office, a parameter is room air temperature. If the process is mixing, a parameter is the consistency of what is being mixed.

Few Processes and their parameters are listed below:

Processes	Parameters
Conveying boxes along a conveyor belt	Speed of the conveyor belt
Filling a tank	Level of the liquid in the tank
Mixing ingredients for a chemical	Consistency of the ingredients
Cooling air	Temperature of the air

Control Functions

The control function has three stages:

(1) Gathering information about the process parameter—*Measurement*
(2) Making a decision about the process parameter—*Control*
(3) Taking action based on the decision—*Correction*

In the process control in industry, you must repeat the three stages continually in order to keep your process running efficiently. Instruments can perform all three stages. Instruments monitor process parameters to gather information, make decisions and cause action. There is often a separate instrument system for each parameter of the process that is monitored, although computers and distributed control systems combines functions.

Process Control

Process control means regulating the parts of the process to achieve a desired result. It is the continuous performance of the three stages of control: measurement, control, and correction. For example: Filling a tank is the process. What are the parameters of this process that you want to control? Level of liquid in tank is one. Other may be temperature in the tank, pressure in the tank. For maintaining the level in the tank inlet and outlet flow rates are important.

Control of Parameters

Parameter	Control
Temperature	Measure the temperature of the liquid by thermometer and adjust the steam supplied to the steam heater until the liquid is at the right temperature.
Level	Measure the level of liquid in the tank and adjust the inlet or outlet flow rates.

Process control is a phrase, which often brings to mind black boxes and high technology. Process control can be very complex using complicated hardware and automated techniques. However, process control is found in simple, everyday applications and basic principles on which process control is based are not difficult to understand.

Growth of Refinery Industries

In the last over 50 years the country witnessed a remarkable growth in refining facilities, from one to eighteen in number, throughput increasing from 0.25 MTPA to 110 MTPA. The refining capacity as on 1.4.2003 was 116.97 Million Metric Tonnes Per Annum (MMTPA). Availability of petroleum products during 2002-03 from domestic refineries was adequate to meet the domestic demand except for Liquefied Petroleum Gas (LPG). The availability of petrol and diesel is in excess of domestic requirement and the surplus quantity was exported during the year.

At present, there are 18 refineries operating in the country, (16 in Public Sector, one in joint sector, and one in private sector). Out of the 16 Public Sector refineries, 7 are owned by Indian Oil Corporation Limited (IOCL), two by Chennai Petroleum Corporation Limited (subsidiary of IOCL), two by Hindustan Petroleum Corporation Limited (HPCL) and one each by Bharat Petroleum Corporation Limited (BPCL), Kochi Refineries Limited (KRL) (subsidiary of BPCL), Bongaigaon Refinery & Petrochemicals Limited (BRPL) (subsidiary of IOCL), Numaligarh Refineries Limited (NRL) (subsidiary of BPCL) and Oil and Natural Gas Corporation Limited (ONGC). There is one refinery in joint sector viz. Mangalore Refinery & Petrochemicals Limited (MRPL) and one refinery in private sector viz. Reliance Industries Limited (RPL)–now subsidiary of ONGC.

The first decade of independence (1947-57) was the establishment of three coastal refineries by multinational oil companies operating in India at that time, viz. Burmah Shell, Stanvac and Caltex; the first two at Mumbai and the last at Visakhapatnam. These were set up primarily to refine imported crude and raise the indigenous throughput capacity to about 4.8 MTPA.

The second decade, (1957-67) witnessed the commissioning of three fully owned public sector oil refineries. The development of a close co-operation between Romania and Soviet Union with India Ltd, inter alia, to the selling up of three refineries at Guwahati (Assam), Barauni (Bihar) and Koyali (Gujarat) in the public sector. These three inland refineries were set up essentially to process the indigenous crude; Guwahati and Barauni for Assam crude and Koyali for Gujarat crude. The refinery throughput capacity reached about 12.7 MTPA by the end of the decade.

The next ten-year period, (1967-77) witnessed establishment of two refineries, one with equity participation from the American and Iranian companies at Chennai, and another in the public sector at Haldia set up by IOC with assistance from Romania and France. The refining throughput capacity by the end of third decade had reached about 22.9 MTPA.

The period 1987-97 saw the commissioning of two more refineries in the public sector. The refinery at Bongaigaon was the first experiment in having an integrated petroleum refinery-cum-petrochemical unit. The other refinery, at Mathura, was set up in 1982 utilizing Soviet assistance but, to a considerable extent, utilising indigenously developed know-how and equipment. With the commissioning of this refinery, the throughput capacity reached about 35 MTPA. Major expansion of the coastal refineries at Mumbai, Cochin, Madras and Visakhapatnam were also completed during this period taking the refining capacity to about 47 million tonnes per annum.

The refining capacity at the beginning of the Eighth Plan was 51.85 million tonnes. The Eighth Plan envisaged augmentation of the domestic refining capacity to 65 million tonnes by 1996-97. The actual refining capacity at the end of Eighth Plan was 61.55 million tonnes. The shortfall in the refining capacity was mainly due to delay in the commissioning of Gujarat Refinery Expansion by 3 million tonnes per annum. The highest priority has been accorded to low cost expansion of the refining capacities. The new grassroot refining capacities already commissioned during the Plan period are at Mangalore (3 million tonnes).

The period 1997-2002 saw commissioning of two more refineries in public sector and one in private sector taking the total to 114.67 million tonnes by the end of Ninth Plan. With the expansion of existing refineries and new refineries, the country achieved self sufficiency in refining capacity. As of July, 2005 there are a total of 18 refineries in the country comprising 17 in the Public Sector, one in the private sector. The company-wise locations and capacity of the refineries as on 1.7.2005 are given in Table 8.2.

Table 8.2: Company-wise Locations and Capacity of the Refineries as on 1.7.2005

S.No.	Name of the company	Location of the Refinery	Capacity (MMTPA)
1.	Indian Oil Corporation Limited (IOCL)	Guwahati	1.00
2.	IOCL	Barauni	6.00
3.	IOCL	Koyali	13.70
4.	IOCL	Haldia	6.00
5.	IOCL	Mathura	8.00
6.	IOCL	Digboi	0.65
7.	IOCL	Panipat	6.00
8.	Hindustan Petroleum Corporation Limited (HPCL)	Mumbai	5.50
9.	HPCL	Visakhapatnam	7.50
10.	Bharat Petroleum Corporation Limited (BPCL)	Mumbai	6.90
11.	Chennai Petroleum Corporation Limited (CPCL)	Manali	9.50
12.	CPCL	Nagapattnam	1.00
13.	Kochi Refineries Ltd. (KRL)	Kochi	7.50
14.	Bongaigaon Refinery & Petrochemicals Ltd. (BRPL)	Bongaigaon	2.35
15.	Numaligarh Refinery Ltd. (NRL)	Numaligarh	3.00
16.	Mangalore Refinery & Petrochemicals Ltd. (MRPL)	Mangalore	9.69
17.	Tatipaka refinery (ONGC)	Andhra Pradesh	0.078
18.	Reliance Petroleum Ltd. (RPL) Pvt. Sector	Jamnagar	33.00
	Total		127.37

Performance of Refineries in India

The details of Refineries capacity are shown in Table 8.3. Performance of individual Refinery units is described below:

Guwahati Refinery, IOCL (Assam)

Guwahati Refinery, the first in public sector, was set up in collaboration with Rumania at a cost of Rs.17.29 crore and commissioned on 1st January, 1962 with a design capacity of 0.75 MMTPA. The present capacity of this Refinery is 1.00 MMTPA. Hydrotreater Unit for improving the Quality of diesel has been installed and was commissioned in 2002. The refinery has also installed in 2003 Indmax Unit, a novel technology developed by its R&D Centre for upgrading heavy ends LPG, motor spirit and diesel oil.

Barauni Refinery, IOCL (Bihar)

Barauni Refinery in Eastern India was built in collaboration with the Soviet Union at a cost of Rs.49.4 crores and went on stream in July, 1964. By November, 1967, the initial capacity of 2 MMTPA was expanded to 3 MMTPA by 1969. The present capacity of this refinery is 6.00 MMTPA. A Catalytic Reformer Unit (CRU) was also added to the refinery in 1997 for production of unleaded motor spirit. Projects are also planned for meeting future fuel quality requirements.

Koyali Refinery-IOCL (Gujarat)

The Gujarat Refinery was built with Soviet assistance at a cost of Rs.26.00 crores and went on stream in October, 1965. The Refinery had an initial installed capacity

Table 8.3: Installed Capacity and Refinery Crude Throughputs

('000' Tonne)

Refinery	Installed Capacity as on 1.4.2004 & 1.4.2005	Refinery Crude Throughput						
		1990-91	1995-96	2000-01	2001-02	2002-03	2003-04	2004-05*
(a) PUBLIC SECTOR	94368	51772	58741	77411	77620	82015	89495	92808
IOC, Guwahati, Assam	1000	783	839	707	656	458	891	1002
IOC, Barauni, Bihar	6000	2416	2322	3122	2876	2994	4304	5082
IOC, Koyali, Gujarat	13700	9334	10167	12006	11697	12434	12758	11698
IOC, Haldia, West Bengal	6000	2835	3416	3873	4026	4513	4518	5418
IOC, Mathura, Uttar Pradesh	8000	7808	8332	7133	8031	8207	8248	6387
IOC, Digboi, Assam	650	566	559	678	653	581	602	651
IOC, Panlpat, Haryana	6000	0	0	5707	5822	6101	6338	6387
Total IOC	41350	23742	25635	33226	33761	35288	37659	36625
BPCL, Mumbai, Maharashtra	6900	6957	7460	8683	8744	8711	8757	9138
HPCL, Mumbai, Maharashtra	5500	5766	5965	5575	5641	6078	6108	6118
HPCL, Visakh, Andhra Pradesh	7500	3464	5037	6405	6706	6851	7591	7825
Total HPCL	13000	9230	11002	11980	12347	12929	13699	13943
KRL, Kochi, Kerala	7500	5006	7421	7520	6797	7580	7854	7924
CPCL, Manali, Tamil Nadu	9500	5698	5599	6046	6123	6176	6387	8181
CPCL, Narimanam, Tamil Nadu	1000	0	370	579	566	643	653	742
Total CPCL	10500	5698	5969	6625	6689	6819	7040	8923
BRPL, Bongaigaon, Assam	2350	1139	1215	1488	1475 1	463	2126	2311
NRL, Numaligarh, Assam	3000	0	0	1451	2307	1879	2200	2042
ONGC, Tatipaka, Tamil Nadu	78	0	0	0	13	93	91	93
MRPL, Mangalore, Karnataka	9690	0	39	6438	5487	7253	10069	11809
(b) PRIVATE SECTOR	33000	0	0	26033	29654	30544	32345	34309
RPL, Jamnagar, Gujarat	33000	0	0	26033	29654	30544	32345	34309
Total (a+b)	127368	51772	58741	103444	107274	112559	121840	127117

*: Provisional.

Notes: (1) CPCL and BRPL are subsidiaries of IOC. (2) KRL and NRL are subsidiaries of BPCL. (3) MRPL is subsidiary of ONGC.

Source: Public Sector Undertakings/Private Company.

of 2 MMTPA and was designed to process crude from Ankleshwar, Kalol and Nawagam oilfields of Oil & Natural Gas Commission in Gujarat. In September, 1967, the capacity of the Refinery was expanded to 3 MMTPA. The capacity of the Refinery was further increased to 4.3 MMTPA through de-bottlenecking measures and to 7.3 MMTPA in October, 1978 by implementing an expansion project of Rs. 56.07 crores. With the implementation of additional processing facilities the Refinery could achieve capacity of 9.5 MMTPA in 1989. The refining capacity was further expanded to 12.5 MMTPA with commissioning of 3.0 MMTPA CDU in September, 1999. The present refining capacity of this refinery is 13.70 MMTPA. In order to meet future fuel quality requirement, MS quality improvement facilities are planned to be installed by 2006.

Haldia Refinery—IOCL (West Bengal)

The Haldia Refinery, with the objective of processing of 2.5 MMTPA of Middle-east crude was commissioned in January, 1975 with two sectors—one for producing fuel products and the other for Lube base stocks. The fuel sector was built with French collaboration and the Lube sector with Romanian collaboration. The refining capacity of the Refinery was increased to 2.75 MMTPA in 1989 through debottlenecking measures. The refining capacity was further expanded to 3.75 MMTPA with the commissioning of new crude distillation unit of 1.0 MMTPA in March, 1997. The present refining capacity of this Refinery is 6.00 MMTPA.

Mathura Refinery—IOCL (Uttar Pradesh)

The Mathura Refinery with a capacity of 6.00 MMTPA was set up at a cost of Rs. 253.92 crores. The Refinery was commissioned in January, 1982 excluding FCCU and Sulphur Recovery Units which were commissioned in Jan, 1983. The refining capacity of this refinery was expanded to 7.5 MMTPA in 1989 by debottlenecking and revamping. A DHDS Unit was commissioned in 1989 for production of HSD with low sulphur content of 0.25% wt. (max.). The present refining capacity of this Refinery is 8.00 MMTPA.

Digboi Refinery (Assam)

The Refinery was set up at Digboi in 1901 by Assam Oil Company Limited. The Indian Oil Corporation Ltd. took over the Refinery and marketing management of Assam Oil Company Ltd. with effect from 14.10.1981 and created a separate division. This division has both Refinery and marketing operations. The Refinery at Digboi had an installed capacity 0.50 MMTPA. The refining capacity of the Refinery was increased to 0.65 MMTPA by modernization of Refinery in July, 1996. A new delayed Coking Unit of 1,70,000 TPA capacities were commissioned in 1999. A new Solvent Dewaxing Unit for maximizing production of micro-crystalline wax was installed and commissioned in 2003. The refinery has also installed Hydrotreater to improve the quality of diesel.

Panipat Refinery—IOCL (Haryana)

The refinery was set up in 1998 at Baholi Village in Distt. Panipat, Haryana at a cost of Rs.3868 crores. The refining capacity of this refinery is 6.00 MMTPA. The expansion of refining capacity from 6 MMTPA to 12 MMTPA is in under implementation and is expected to complete by end 2005.

Mumbai Refinery (HPCL) (Maharashtra)

The Refinery at Mumbai came into stream in 1954 under the ownership of ESSO. In March, 1974, Govt. of India acquired it. Hindustan Petroleum Corporation Ltd. was formed on 15.7.1974 after the merger of these companies. The capacity of the Mumbai Refinery of HPCL was 3.5 MMTPA which was increased to 5.5 MMTPA during 1986 after implementation of expansion programme.

Visakh Refinery (HPCL) (Andhra Pradesh)

In 1957, Visakh Refinery went on stream under the ownership of M/s Caltex India Ltd. In May, 1978, M/s Caltex Oil Refinery (India) was amalgamated with Hindustan Petroleum Corporation Ltd. The installed capacity of 1.5 MMTPA was increased to 4.5 MMTPA in 1985 and 7.5 MMTPA in 1999, through an expansion programme.

Bharat Petroleum Corporation Ltd. (BPCL) (Maharashtra)

The Refinery at Mumbai came into stream in January, 1955 under the ownership of Burmah-Shell Refineries Ltd. Following the Government's acquisition of the Burmah-Shell, name of the Refinery was changed to Bharat Refineries Limited on 11.2.1976. In August, 1977, the Company was given its permanent name, viz. Bharat Petroleum Corporation Ltd. The installed capacity of 5.25 MMTPA was increased to 6 MMTPA in 1985. The present refining capacity of the refinery is 6.9 MMTPA.

Manali Refinery—Chennai Petroleum Corporation Ltd. (CPCL), Tamil Nadu

Chennai Petroleum Corporation Limited (CPCL), formerly known as Madras Refineries Limited (MRL) was formed as a joint venture in 1965 between the Government of India (GOI), AMOCO and National Iranian Oil Company (NIOC) having a share holding in the ratio 74% : 13% : 13% respectively. From the grassroots stage CPCL Refinery was set up with an installed capacity of 2.5 Million Tonnes Per Annum (MMTPA) in a record time of 27 months at a cost of Rs. 43 crore without any time or cost over run.

In 1985, AMOCO disinvested in favour of GOI and the shareholding percentage of GOI and NIOC stood revised at 84.62% and 15.38% respectively. Later GOI disinvested 16.92% of the paid up capital in favor of Unit Trust of India, Mutual Funds, Insurance Companies and Banks on 19th May 1992, thereby reducing its holding to 67.7 %. The public issue of CPCL shares at a premium of Rs. 70 (Rs. 90 to FIIs) in 1994 was over subscribed to an extent of 27 times and added a large shareholder base of over 90000.As a part of the restructuring steps taken up by the Government of India, Indian Oil Corporation Limited (IOCL) acquired equity from GOI in 2000-01 Currently IOC holds 51.88% while NIOC continued its holding at 15.40%. In view of the CPCL become subsidiary of IOCL in 2001. The Manali Refinery has a capacity of 9.5 MMTPA and is one of the most complex refineries in India with Fuel, Lube, Wax and Petrochemical feedstocks production facilities.

Cauvery Basin Refinery-CPCL (Nagapattinam-Tamil Nadu)

CPCL's second refinery is located at Cauvery Basin at Nagapattinam. The initial unit was set up in Nagapattinam with a capacity of 0.5 MMTPA in 1993 and later on its capacity was enhanced to 1.0 MMTPA.

Kochi Refineries Limited (KRL) (Kerala)

The Kochi Refineries Ltd. is a public sector undertaking set up in pursuance of a formation agreement dated 27th April, 1963 between Govt. of India, Phillips Petroleum Co. of USA and Duncan Brothers of Calcutta with an authorized capital of Rs.15 crore. Subsequently, the authorized capital was increased to Rs.75 crore and the paid up capital in March, 1989 stood at Rs.68.47 crore after issue of shares on rights basis. During the year, the Phillips Petroleum Company also completed withdrawal of their equity by disinvesting of shares. With this, in March 1989, Government was holding 61.58 percentages of equity shares of the Company. At present authorized capita of KRL is Rs 1150 crore and paid up capital Rs. 138.47 crore. M/s Bharat Petroleum Corporation Limited (BPCL) holds 54.81% of the total shares, the balance of the shares being held by Government of Kerala, Financial Institutions and the Public. The installed capacity of 2.5 MMTPA was increased to 3.3 in September, 1973 and to 4.5 MMTPA in November, 1994. The capacity of the Refinery was further increased to 7.5 MMTPA in December, 95.

Bongaigaon Refinery & Petrochemicals Ltd. (BRPL) (Assam)

On 20th January, 1974, M/s BRPL was incorporated in Assam under the Companies Act, 1956 with an authorised capital of Rs.50 crores. With the objective of installation of the Refinery having a crude processing capacity of 1 MMTPA and a Petrochemicals Complex consisting of Xylene, Di-Methyl Terephthalate (DMT) and Polyester Staple Fibre (PSF) Units. The complex was built and commissioned in phases. The capacity of Crude Distillation Unit was increased to 1.35 MMTPA from April, 1987 by debottlenecking. Now the authorized capital (equity) of the company is Rs.200 crores. The paid-up capital as on date is Rs.199.82 crore. As a part of the restructuring steps taken up by Govt. of India, Indian Oil Corporation Limited acquired Govt's equity in 2000-01. In view of this BRPL became subsidiary of IOCL in 2001. The capacity of the Refinery has been increased to 2.35 MMTPA in June, 1995 by installing additional unit.

Numaligarh Refinery Limited (Assam)

Numaligarh Refinery, Popularly known as "Assam Accord Refinery" has been set up a grass-root refinery at Numaligarh in the district of Golaghat (assam) in fulfilment of the commitment made by Government of India in the historic "Assam Accord", signed on 15-8-1985 at an approved cost of Rs, 2,724 crore.

Numaligarh Refinery Limited (NRL) was incorporated on 22-4-1993. Presently Bharat Petroleum Corporation Limited holds 51% of the company's equity. The other equity holder is Government of Assam, Oil Industry Development Board and Oil India Limited with equity participation of 10% each. The balance 19% equity is earmarked for a Public Issue. The refining capacity of this refinery is 3.0 MMTPA.

Mangalore Refinery and Petrochemicals Ltd. (MRPL) (Karnataka)

Government approved on 11.4.1991 the setting up a 3.0 MMTPA Oil Refinery at Mangalore at an estimated cost of Rs.1160 crore, including foreign exchange component of Rs.300 crore. The project has been implemented by a Joint Venture Company with Hindustan Petroleum Corporation Limited, Mumbai and Indian Rayon and Industrial Limited, Gujarat as Co-promoters. The Refinery was commissioned in March, 1996. MRPL which was a Joint Sector Company become a PSU subsequent on acquisition of its majority shares by ONGC. The capacity of the refinery was assessed at 3.69 MMTPA and has been further expanded to 9.69 MMTPA in September, 1999.

Tatipaka Refinery-ONGC (Andhra Pradesh)

A mini refinery of ONGC with capacity of about 0.1 MMTPA with an approved cost of Rs.29.9 crore was commissioned in September, 2001 at Tatipaka in East Godavari District of Andhra Pradesh.

Reliance Petroleum Limited (RPL) Private Sector Jamnagar (Gujarat)

The Private Sector Refinery (RPL) was commissioned on 14th July, 1999 with an installed capacity of 27 MMTPA at Jamnagar. The present capacity of this refinery is 33.00 MMTPA.

Refining Capacity and Capacity Utilisation

To meet the growing demand of petroleum products, the refining capacity in the country has been gradually increased over the years by setting up of new refineries in the country as well as by expanding the refining capacity of the existing refineries. The total refining capacity in the country as on 1.7.2005 stands at 127.37 MMTPA.

The refining capacity, actual crude throughput and capacity utilization during the last five years are indicated in Table 8.4.

Table 8.4: Refining Capacity, Actual Crude Throughput and Capacity Utilization during 2000-05

	2000-01	2001-02	2002-03	2003-04	2004-05
1. Refining Capacity(As on 1st April)	114.59	114.66	116.96	127.37	127.37
2. Actual Crude throughput (MMTPA)	103.1	106.5	10.6	118.7	124.3
3. Capacity Utilization (%)	91.00	93.00	95.00	99.00	—

Expansion of Existing Refineries

Expansion plans of refining capacities of existing refineries are as under:

(i) Expansion of Panipat Refinery of IOCL from 6 MMTPA to 12 MMTPA is under implementation at an estimated cost of Rs. 4165 crore and is expected to be completed by end of 2005.

(ii) Expansion of Mumbai Refinery of BPCL from 6.9 MMTPA to 12 MMTPA is also under implementation at an estimated cost of Rs. 1831 crore. The project is expected to be completed by July, 2005.

(iii) HPCL is expending the refining capacity of Mumbai Refinery from 5,5 MMTPA to 7.9 MMTPA with an estimated cost of Rs. 1152 crore. The project is expected to be completed by December, 2006.

(iv) Expansion of Visakh refinery of HPCL from 7.5 MMTPA to 8.33 MMTPA is under implementation at an estimated cost of Rs. 1635 crore. The project is expected to be completed by December, 2006.

Following three new refineries has been planned for commissioning:

Name of Refineries	Capacity	Expenditure (Rs. in Crore)	Anticipated Completion Date
IOC, Paradip	9 MMTPA	8312	March-2010
BPC, Bina	6 MMT	6354	Sept.-2009
HPC, Bhatinda	9 MMT	9806	Decm.-2006

Guidelines for Laying Petroleum Product Pipelines

In a major decision towards deregulation of oil sector and to attract investment in the petroleum product pipelines, in November 2002, Government had laid down a new Petroleum Product Pipeline Policy for laying pipelines in the country on common carrier principle. Guidelines for laying petroleum product pipelines were notified on 20.11.2002. Supplementary guidelines in this regard have also been notified on 26-10-2004.

Auto Fuel Policy

Schedule for Introducing Improved Quality Fuels as per Auto Fuel Policy

(i) Euro-III Petrol and Diesel has been introduced from 1-4-2005 in all 11 identifies cities (Delhi/National Capital Region, Mumbai, Kolkata, Chennai, Bangalore, Hyderabad, Ahmedabad, Pune, Surat, Kanpur and Agra) in line with Auto Fuel Policy.

(ii) BS-II Petrol throughout the country has been introduced w.e.f. 1-4-2005 in line with Auto Fuel Policy.

(iii) BS-II Diesel in all states except Rajasthan, West U.P., Uttaranchal, M.P., Punjab H.P. and Jammu & Kashmir has been introduced from 1-4-2005 as per Auto Fuel Policy.

(iv) As per the revised programme BS-II diesel has been introduced in Rajasthan from 1-6-2005 and in West U.P. and Uttaranchal from 1-7-2005.

(v) Introduction of BSII Diesel is proposed in a phased manner as per the revised programme as under:

(a) M.P. from 1-9-2005

(b) Punjab, H.P. and J&K from 1-10-2005

Refining Capacity Additions during Tenth Plan

Refinery sector is de-licensed and, as such, it is not possible to correctly assess the plans of refining capacity additions in future. The actual capacity additions would depend upon several factors including domestic demand, duty structure which would impact import and export possibilities, refining margin, and export potential for the products.

The approved capacity expansion of PSU refineries alone works out to about 22.0 MMTPA. As many of these revamps are also linked to fuel quality upgradation programmes it is likely that these companies would go ahead with the expansion plans. The work of RPL expansion by 6 MMTPA is also almost complete. Considering all expansion programmes alone, the refining capacity at the end of Tenth plan period would be about 143.1 MMTPA.

PSU companies are actively pursuing three new grass-root projects, i.e., Bhatinda refinery of HPCL and Paradeep refinery of IOC in the public sector, Bina refinery of BPCL in the joint sector—with an aggregate new capacity of 24 MMTPA. Also, work on two private sector refineries, i.e., Essar and Nagarjuna, are in progress with a planned capacity of 16.5 MMTPA. Thus, there is likelihood of at least some of these projects getting commissioned in Tenth Plan period. However, in view of the likely surplus scenario, many of the projected capacity additions may be reviewed by the concerned companies and deferred if the project economics are not found favourable. The spread and growth of refineries in India is shown below (Fig. 8.9).

Refining Capacity Addition during the Eleventh/Twelfth Plan (2007-12/2012-17)

During the Eleventh Plan period, capacity addition of 40.05 MMTPA (comprising of 34.05 MMTP A in the public sector and 6.0 MMTPA in the private sector) is expected to be added. With this capacity addition, the total refilling capacity in the country is expected to go up to 260.80 MMTPA. In view of estimated surplus scenario many of the projected capacity additions may be reviewed by the concerned companies and likely to be deferred to Twelfth Plan period if the economics are not favourable.

Considering the projects under implementation and the project under various stages of approval, the companies have plans to increase the refining capacity by 106.08 MMTPA in future, which includes PSUs, Joint Venture Companies (JVCs) and the private sector companies subject to favourable economics. The petroleum products demand is expected to go up to 120 MMT by the end of the Tenth Plan (2006-07) and to 147 million tonnes by the end of the Eleventh Plan (2011-12). Additions to refining capacity are not likely to be more than 28.43 MTPA by the end of Tenth Plan.

In other words, by the end of the Tenth Plan, while the demand would be 120 MT, the capacity would be around 143 MT giving a finished product of around 130 MT. There would thus be a surplus of 13 MT in refined products. There is, of course, talk about a lot of other new refineries as well as expansion plans, prominent among them being BPCL/Shell in Uttar Pradesh, HPCL's Punjab

Fig. 8.9: Refineries in India (Capacities in MMT)

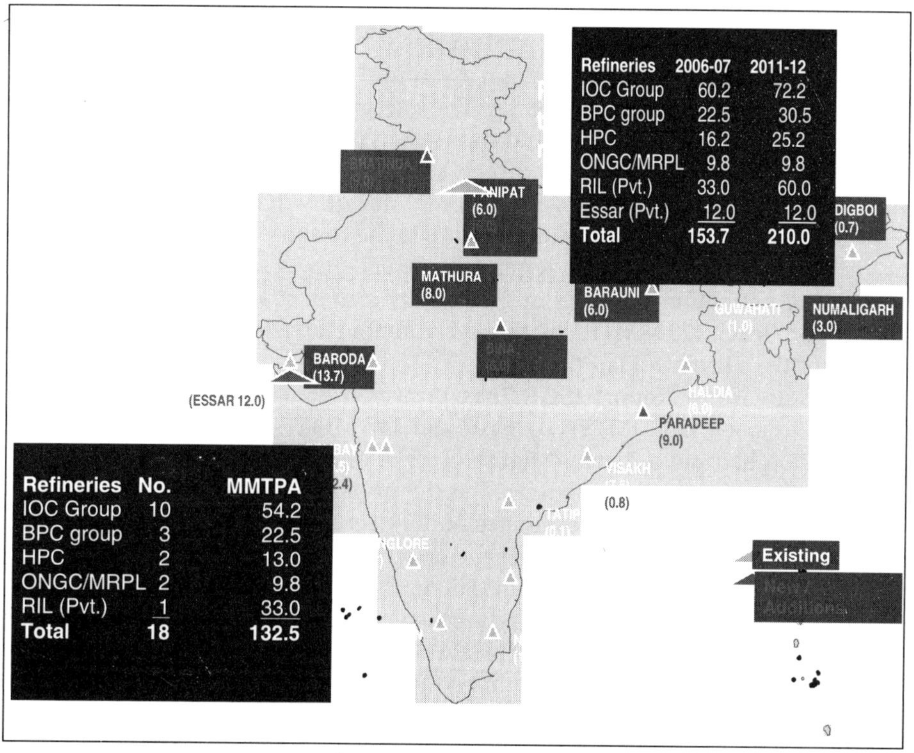

Refinery, IOC's Orissa refinery. Various other private sector refineries are having second thoughts on taking up the huge investments required (Planning Commission, 1997 and 2002).

Market share and Infrastructure

	Market Share (As % of Total Volume Sales) Retail outlets)	Retail Sales (Sales % of total Co. sales through	Retail outlets (as % of total outlets in India)
IOC	49	29	51
HPCL	19	49	25
BPCL	18	54	24

The oil industry has drawn up plans to add another about 26 MMPTA in the next few years. These include low-cost expansions and de-bottlenecking at existing refineries, capacity addition. With these additions, the country will have a refining capacity of about 143 million tonnes per annum by the terminal year of the Tenth plan, which is 2006-07.

Oil and natural gas now contribute about 32% and 8%, respectively to the primary energy needs of the country. These figures, however, are still lower compared to the world average of 40% oil and 23% natural gas. As per the latest statistics available, the per capita consumption of primary energy in India is around 228 Kg of oil equivalent against the world average of 1,435 Kg. Out of this, the per capital oil consumption is around 71 kg for India as against the corresponding world average 588 kg. The energy requirement of the country is gradually increasing with the rapid industrial growth. The GDP is growing at a rate of about 6 to 7%. The hydrocarbon sector, therefore, is expected to play an important role commensurate with the economic growth of the country.

The consumption of petroleum products in the country has not been increasing at a rate of past trend. Last year it grew an annual growth rate of 3.2%. The current demand of petroleum products in the country stands at about 104 MMTPA. It is projected to reach 120 MMTPA by the end of Tenth Plan (2006-07) and 147 MMTPA by end of the Eleventh Plan (2011-12).

The Sub-Group Report (SGR) has projected consumption for petroleum products to reach 123 MMTPA by FY07 and 147 MMTPA by FY12. The Planning Commission had put a demand figure of 120.4 MMTPA for 2006-07.

A number of refineries announced in the private sector may not see the light of the day and thus, supply estimates of SGR could be on the higher side. With the removal of APM for the refining sector, a lot of new capacities, especially the EOUs, would probably fail to materialize. Even the JV refineries of PSUs are expected to see considerable time and cost overrun. HPCL is planning JV refineries at Bhatinda (Punjab). Indian Oil's, 9 MTPA Paradeep refineries, BPCL's refineries—at Bina (MP) are under plans. Reliance Petroleum's 27 MMTPA refineries at Jamnagar seem to be the only refineries which have been implemented in the private sector.

Demand supply gap has already reversed significantly with the commissioning of Reliance Petroleum. Surplus situation in some products has already been projected.

The demand for petroleum products in the Asia-Pacific region is also growing rapidly. Though the economic crisis experienced recently by some of the countries in this region adversely affects the demand growth rate, long-term future projections indicate a deficit scenario. India with its vast coastline, proximity to growing demand centres and being enrooted from the main source of crude oil, the Middle East, offers ample opportunities for settling up export oriented refineries. Apart from refining capacities planned for the domestic market, the India Government had issued Letters of Intent for EOU refineries with an aggregate capacity of 29 MMTPA. They are being given several concessions, including duty free import of capital goods and other inputs. However, in view of the economic crisis in the Asia-Pacific region, the projected growth may not materialize and hence finding a market for products of these refiners could become a challenge (Pathan, 1998). The overall position on India's dependence on Crude in so far as Refining is concerned, is shown in Fig. 8.10.

Liberalization in Indian Oil Industries

With the initiation of economic reforms in India in 1991, the Oil Sector witnessed massive transformation. There was reformation across the segments, upstream and downstream. In the upstream sector, change was brought about by offering identified blocks for exploration and development to private sector including foreign oil companies. Some ONGC's discovered medium size fields were also offered for development to private sector in addition to small fields, which were offered to private sectors for development in joint venture with PSUs. In the downstream, refineries were permitted in the private sector either as JV with PSU or a wholly owned subsidiary with a 100% export obligation. Import by private parties and parallel marketing of selected petroleum products, viz., Kerosene, LPG and LSHS were permitted. Further, steps were also taken to provide greater degree of autonomy to PSUs. The Ninth plan period marked a watershed in the chronology of policy for the hydrocarbon sector in terms of two profound policy packages announced by the government: The notification in November 1997 heralding major Oil Sector reforms such as gradual dismantling of Administered Pricing Mechanism (APM) and long term policy frame work in the shape of India Hydrocarbon Vision 2025 in April 2000.

In line with the 1997 notification and in order to give boost to investments and promote efficiency in refining sector, the APM regime was dismantled for refining sector w.e.f. 01.04.1998 and the refining industry were de-licensed in June 1998. As per the policy, any company can set up refinery without specific permission from the Government subject to fulfilling the statutory requirements. The cost plus

Fig. 8.10: India's Dependence on Crude in the Refining Industry

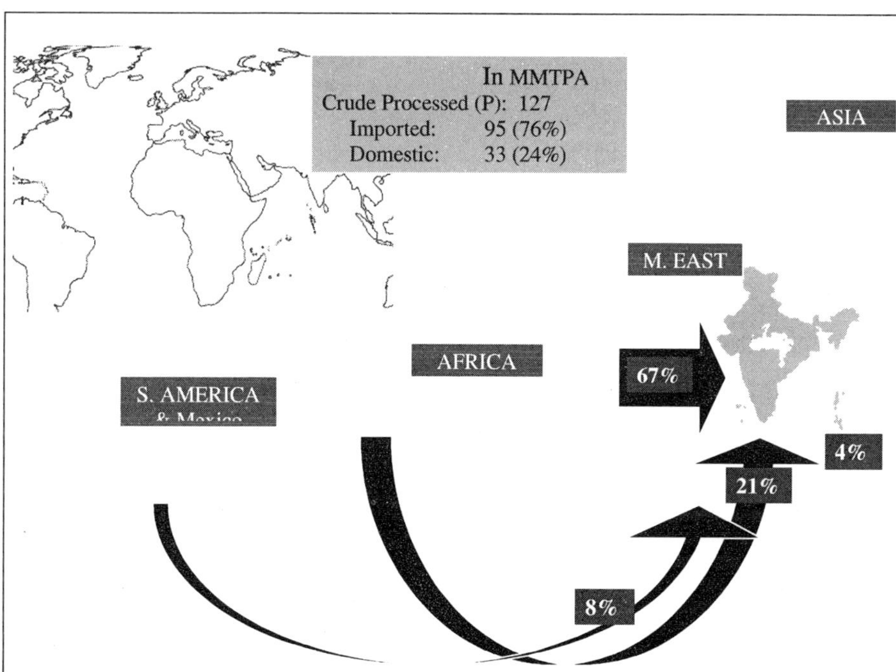

pricing of domestic crude oil and refinery products was replaced by import parity pricing from 1 st April 1998. It was also envisaged that after March 2002, market forces would determine prices and the domestic markets would be brought under a regulatory framework. As a result of the de-licensing, MRPL came up in 1996-97 in Joint Sector and Reliance Jamnanagar refinery came up in 1999-2000, both adding 30 MMT capacities to Indian then existing refining capacity of 58 to 68 MMT. Further as per the policy notification of November 1997, downstream marketing including dismantling of APM was affected from 1.4.2002.

To understand what needs to be done beyond the dismantling of the APM, one need to go back in time to see how the APM actually came into existence in a market, which was then relatively free and generally competitive. With the quadrupling of oil prices in 1973/74, India had the difficult task of regulating oil product prices consistent with the increase that had taken place in the global oil market while protecting the economy from sudden shock, and the APM was introduced to help the government decide on oil product prices. Had system been done away with in the late 1980s when oil prices reached much lower levels, the industry would have had a much higher level of competition than is currently seen. The APM imposed certain constraints and resulted in several distortions in the pattern of consumption of oil products.

In the deregulated scenario, refineries have to improve their efficiency to meet the challenges of the competitive forces. Another challenge is to meet the increased demand of light and middle distillates with stringent quality specification that requires refinery complexity to increase. The refinery output has to match the changing profile in market demand. The fastest growth in demand for light and middle distillates is expected to occur in Asia. Asian refineries have low complexity and will need large investments in conversion capacity to keep up with the falling share of heavy fuel demand. Further, variation in the fuel quality standards between countries and in some cases, within countries could hamper inter-regional trade over the next few years.

The refining capacity is projected to reach a level of 140 million tones by the year 200607 from the current level of 122.97 million tones. The 'India Hydrocarbon Vision 2025' projected a refining capacity of 364 million tones by the year 2025. This will of course depend on the demand materialization. The demand of petroleum products has been projected as 120 million tones for the year 2006-07. Thus, in all probability the refining capacity will be surplus.

Paradigm Shift in Business Process

With deregulation in the Oil Sector, a paradigm change is envisaged in the approach to doing business. New players have entered into the market. On the one hand, multinational Oil Companies are vying with each other to take the share of the growing market in India. On the other hand, Indian private sector also wants to playa big role in the Oil Sector. Thirdly, the Public Sector Oil Companies (PSUs) themselves have become competitive and expansive by undertaking various measures including joining hands with private and multinational companies. Each PSU Oil Company has started to protect their market share by taking competitive position with others. In the emerging scenario, the customer focus will be a key *to* success with quality, quantity, prompt service and speed of response. The way of doing business will be different with emphasis on customer relations. E-business and innovative style will replace the traditional way of doing business. In the circumstances whosoever is competitive would be able to survive in tile competitive market.

In view of the above it has become necessary to optimize the operations and be competitive. In this context the refining economics, which is the vital component of the value chain, assumes importance and need to be given proper consideration.

Crude Oil Pipelines in India

Bombay High (BH) Imported Crude Oil is supplied to IOC Koyali, Mathura and Panipat inland refineries through crude pipeline from Salaya at Gujarat coast.

Salaya-Viramgham-Koyali crude pipeline supplies imported/BH crude to Koyali.

Viramgham-Chaksu-Mathura crude pipeline supplies—imported/BH crude to IOC's Mathura refinery.

Chaksu-Rewari-Panipat branching of the above pipeline supplies imported/ BH crude to IOC's Panipat refinery.

Indigenous Crude Oil from South and North Gujarat oil fields is supplied through pipeline from Crude Oil fields to IOC Koyali. Crude Oil from Assam oil fields is supplied to Guwahati, Bongaigaon and Numaligarh refineries through the Naharkatia-Barauni pipeline of Oil India Limited.

Imported/Indigenous crude is also supplied through Haldia-Barauni crude pipeline to IOC Barauni and through reserve pumping through pipeline from Nahakatia-Barauni from Assam oil fields, to Bongaigaon refinery.

Products

Refinery products after crude oil refining are transported to consumption centers through the following modes:

(a) Product Pipeline.
(b) Tank Wagons.
(c) Tank Trucks.
(d) Tankers for Coastal Product movements.

Product Pipelines

Product pipelines are safest and economical mode of transportation of petroleum products from the refineries to demand centers. In addition to safety and economy, this mode also is extremely effective where the chances of adulteration are the least.

Some of the important product pipelines in India are as under (also given in Fig. 8.5):

- Kandla, Kota, Panipat, Bhatinda Pipeline
- Mathura, Delhi, Panipat, Jalandhar Pipeline
- Haldia, Rajbandh,Barauni Pipeline

- Haldia Maurigram Rajbandh Pipeline
- Barauni, Allahabad Pipeline
- Guwahati, Siliguri Pipeline
- Mumbai Manmad, Manglia (Indore) Pipeline
- Mumbai, Pune Pipeline
- Vizag, Vijawada, Secundarabad Pipeline
- Mangalore, Bangalore Pipeline
- Cochin, Karur Pipeline

Like crude oil pipelines product pipelines also have a number of pressures boosting pumping stations enrouted to make the products available at the demand centers (Fig. 8.11). Petroleum products are transported by the above mentioned various modes from refineries to marketing terminals and installations from where they are further distributed to bulk and retail customers.

Refinery Cost Elements

Besides the capital cost involved in the refining operation, various operating costs involved in refining of crude into products can be categorized under the following heads (also shown diagrammatically in Figs. 8.12 and 8.13:

Elements of Crude Costs

(a) Crude Cost Elements, (b) Refining Cost Elements.

Fig. 8.11: Pipeline Network in India

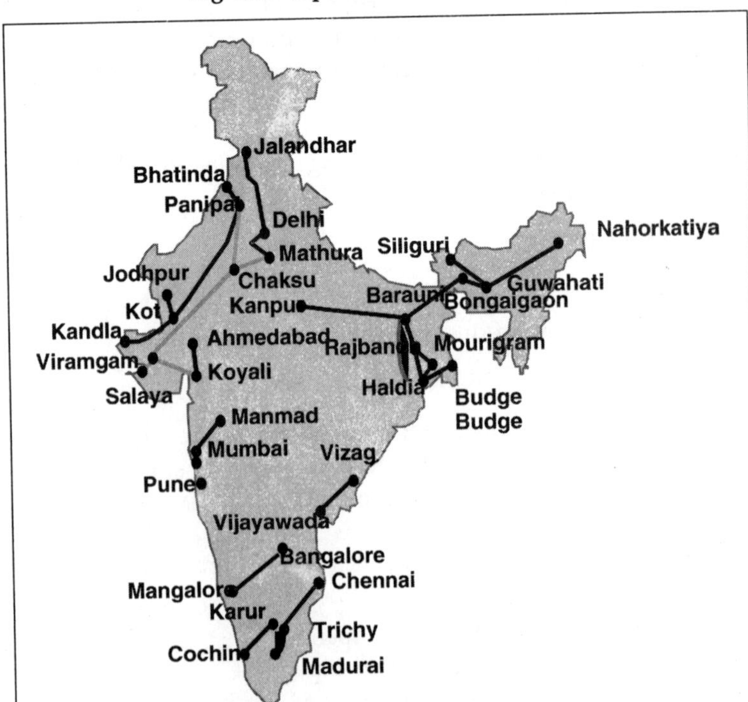

Fig. 8.12: Cost Implications and Break-up of Refinery Cost Elements

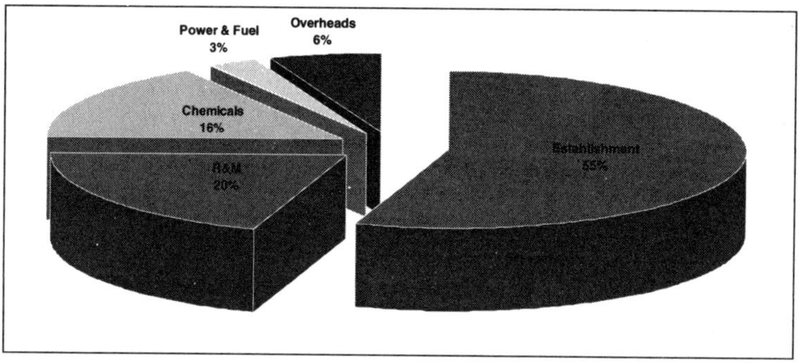

Fig. 8.13: Break-up of Crude Oil and Operating Costs

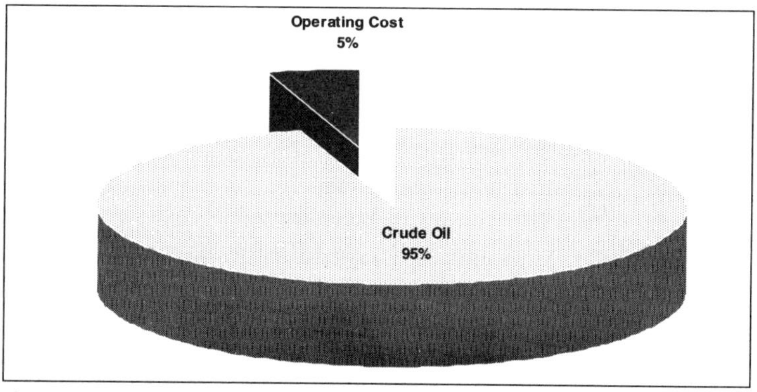

Crude Cost Elements:

- Crude Sourcing—FOB Crude Cost
- Primary Transportation Cost—Crude Freight Cost
- Ocean losses
- Insurance
- Wharf age(port related charges)
- Custom duties
- Secondary Transportation Cost—Crude Oil Pipeline Costs for land locked Refineries

The various elements of refining crude oil into useful products for meeting the energy needs are:

- Chemicals and Catalysts
- Fuel and Utilities
- Consumables
- Salaries and Wages
- Repairs and Maintenance
- Overheads
- Depreciation

Operating Cost Elements

- Controllable
  - Chemicals, Stores and Spares
  - Overtime
  - Traveling Expanses
  - Staff Car Expanses
  - Communication Expanses
  - Printing
- Non-Controllable
  - Power & Fuel
  - Establishment (Salary, PF, Gratuity, Bonus, Medical etc.)
  - General Administration (Rent, Electricity, Water, Security etc.
  - Other overheads (advertisements, Insurance, etc.)
  - Depreciation

Crude Freight Cost

World Scale (WS), Revised every year.
Average Freight Rate Assessment (AFRA), Published Monthly
Percentage of WS, Varies with size of vessel
Suppose freight from Ras Tanura to Mumbai for vessel
LRII is \$5/MT for voyage and AFRA for LRII for the month = 110

$$\text{Freight} = \frac{5 \times 110}{100} = 5.5/\text{MT}$$

Ocean loss comprises of the loading loss at the load port, transit loss during voyage and unloading loss at the disport. Ocean loss is normally taken as 0.3% to 0.5% of the quantity.

The various elements of crude cost are:

(a) FOB crude cost
(b) Freight cost
(c) Ocean loss
(d) Insurance
(e) Wharfage
(f) Custom duties etc.
(g) Crude Oil pipeline operating expenses for pumping crude oil from port location to inland refinery.

FOB crude cost refers to the free on board cost at the load port as per the prevailing Crude Oil price in the international market.

International crude oil prices vary from time to time based on a large number of factors such as world political developments, intensity of winter in Europe and US etc. The major factor is the role of Organization of Petroleum Exporting Countries (OPEC), which by and large controls the crude oil price in the market place by altering the production of crude oil whereby the price varies based on the Supply Demand syndrome. The Middle East OPEC countries include Iran, Iraq,

Kuwait, Qatar, and Saudi Arabia and UAE. Among these countries Saudi Arabia is the largest crude oil producer. The non-Middle East OPEC member countries are Algeria, Indonesia, Libya, Nigeria and Venezuela.

OPEC reviews the prevailing prices of crude oils in the market place on regular intervals and directs its member countries to vary their production quotas to increase/decrease the crude availability with consequent impact on the price based on supply demand balance. The non-OPEC crude producing nations have maximum crude oil production from countries like Norway, UK, Former Soviet Union Canada, Mexico and US. Although developments in countries like US, Canada, Mexico and Former Soviet Union do have some impact on world Crude Oil prices through diplomatic and political pressure, yet OPEC still to a larger extent controls the international Crude Oil prices. India imports oil from Gulf (High Sulfur) and West African (Low Sulfur) countries. Our import dependence has grown over a period of year as follows (Table 8.5).

Table 8.5: Self-sufficiency in Petroleum Products

(Quantity in MMT)

		1975-76	1980-81	1985-86	1990-91	1995-96	2000-01	2002-03
1.	Total Consumption/ Demand	22.447	30.896	40.872	55.035	74.671	100.075	104.126
2.	Crude Imports	13.624	16.248	15.144	20.699	27.226	74.097	81.989
3.	Production from imported crude	12.735	15.171	14.075	19.416	25.521	68.709	77.265
4.	Product imports	2.218	7.269	3.865	8.660	21.85	9.267	6.264
5.	Product exports	0.170	0.036	1.963	2.648	2.971	8.365	10.289
6.	Net imports	14.783	22.404	15.977	25.428	44.400	69.611	73.240
7.	Import dependence % [6/1]	66	73	39	46	59	70	70
8.	Self sufficiency [1–{6/1}] ×100	34	27	61	54	41	30	30

During 2025, the import dependence could go up to 80-90%, depending upon accretion of new reserves. In absolute terms import of nearly 200-230 million tonne of Oil would require huge dependence on Middle-East. Existing level of imports from various sources are given in Table 8.6.

Proximately, 66% of the imported Crude is being met from Middle-East. During 2025 the share of this region may go up as the share of OPEC countries in the overall availability increases to 43% from 29% as of now.

Freight cost refers to the cost of transportation of Crude Oil from the load port to discharge port. Per unit freight cost depends on the size of the vessel utilized for transporting Crude Oil. The shipping industry publishes the tanker rates for various DWT vessels as per the World Scale (WS). During the year AFRA, (Average Freight Rate Assessment) on a monthly basis publishes the prevailing percentage of world scale for different sizes of Crude vessels.

Table 8.6: Crude Oil Imports from Middle-East and Other Countries

(In MMT)

		2001-02	2002-03
Middle-East Region			
1	Iran	8.446	7.424
2	Iraq	3.800	4.166
3	Kuwait	11.956	9.212
4	Neutral zone	2.372	2.626
5	Oman	0.902	0.420
6	Qatar	0.527	0.209
7	Saudi Arabia	13.321	18.816
8	UAE	7.634	9.002
9	Yemen	4.471	3.165
	Sub-total	53.429	55.040
Other Region			
10	Angola	0.395	
11	Brazil	0.412	2.802
12	Brunei	0.259	
13	Cameroon		0.107
14	China	0.065	
15	Congo		0.246
16	Egypt	4.002	3.066
17	Equatorial Guiena		0.139
18	Gabon		0.450
19	Indonesia	0.620	
20	Kazakisthan		0.262
21	Libya	1.081	1.074
22	Malaysia	1.791	2.714
23	Mexico	1.376	2.275
24	Nigeria	11.679	11.579
25	Russia		0.285
26	Venezuela	3.516	1.739
27	Vietnam	0.081	0.075
28	West Asia		0.136
	Sub-total	25.277	26.949
	Total	78.706	81.989

The percentage WS for various sizes of vessels is broadly taken as global standard. It is however never fixed. It reflects the prevailing freight rate in the shipping market.

ULCC	40-50
VLCC	50-70
LRII	70-100
LRI	100-120
MR	120-150

(1) World Scale (WS)—Revised every year.

(2) Average Freight Rate Assessment (AFRA) published monthly

Percentage of WS—Varies with the shipping market condition

Suppose WS from Ras Tanura to Mumbai = \$5/MT per voyage AFRA for LR-II for a month = 110

$$\text{Applicable freight} = \frac{5 \times 110}{100} = \$5.5/\text{MT}$$

Ocean loss comprises of the loading loss at the load port, transit loss during voyage and unloading loss at the disport. Ocean loss is normally taken as 0.2% to 0.3% of the Bill of Lading (BL) quantity for arriving at the landed cost. Insurance is the charge incurred for covering the voyage risk. It is normally taken as 0.060.1 % on FOB Crude cost but could be higher in case of a war or other eventualities prevailing at a particular time in the international arena. Wharfage refers to port related charges such as piloting, water tax, port usage charges etc. Custom duties refer to the prevailing duty on Crude Oil. Currently the custom duty is on Crude Oil is 10%.

For transporting Crude Oil to inland refineries from the port through pipeline, the operating expenses for the Crude Oil pipeline is also a crude cost element for inland refineries. For coastal refineries, which are at locations other than where VLCC or ULCC cannot discharge, additional cost in terms of supply through smaller crude carriers is also an input for total cost.

Elements of Refining Cost

The various elements of refining cost for refining Crude Oil into refined products for meeting the energy needs are as under:

(a) Chemicals and Catalysts;
(b) Fuel and Utilities;
(c) Consumables;
(d) Salaries and Wages;
(e) Repairs and Maintenance;
(f) Overheads; and
(g) Depreciation.

Refinery Profitability/Margins

Before April, 2002, petroleum products were regulated under Administrative Pricing Mechanism (APM) and were thus characterized by oligopolies and cartel like industry structure, which operated on the basis of Guaranteed Profitability (retention margin concept, otherwise known as cost plus pricing formula).

The deregulated form of the oil sector currently prevailing however is under Market Determined Pricing Mechanism (MDPM) where in, there is not only a sizeable reduction in government control in the affairs of the industry, but also the profitability is based on Market Forces such as Crude & Product Prices, Tanker Freights prevalent in the international market as well as other factors such as Refining & Marketing/Distribution Performance Efficiency, Product Quality, Benefits of Lower Cost Due to Scale Economics, etc.

In view of the transition of APM to MDPM in the recent past it would be worthwhile to understand the profitability of refining under the erstwhile APM as well as the current Free Market Scenarios.

Refining Profitability under APM

The administrative petroleum pricing in its latest form was based on Retention Price System (RPS).

Under the retention concept the individual oil refineries were reimbursed their Factual Operating Cost Subject to Certain Pre-Set Norms and 12% Post Tax Return on Net Worth and Actual Weighted Average Interest Rate on Borrowings, through the pricing of various petroleum products.

Retention price per MT of crude was being computed from the base delivered cost of Crude and adding refining cost of individual refineries and return on capital. The retention price per MT of crude for each refinery was translated into petroleum product prices by the method of apportionment on the basis of set of indices for different products produced as per Standard Product Patterns fixed for each refinery.

The indices for various petroleum products were based on various factors such as supply demand position and socio economic considerations; need to encourage domestic production of deficit products and to discourage production of surplus products. The Standard Product Pattern for each refinery was fixed based on the available capacities of primary & secondary units at the refineries, pre-set norms for unit wise yield patterns, blending techniques and fuel and utilities consumption etc., in consultation with Oil Coordination Committee (OCC), then a standing committee of MOP&NG. The weighted average of the retention prices of the products was escalated by the addition of Rs. 25 per KUMT to arrive at Ex-Refinery Price. The Selling Prices of the petroleum products were determined by addition of excise duty, marketing margin, and return on capital for marketing companies & pool surcharges to ex-refinery prices. These prices were termed as basic ceiling selling prices.

Need and Importance of Refining Margin

- Benchmark for Profitability of Refining Operations.
- Guide for incentive to refine more Crude.
- Determining optimum level of Capacity utilization:
  - For optimum selection of Crude for Refineries vis-à-vis Refinery Hardware;
  - Trigger for future investment decisions for Yield Optimization, Bottoms Up-gradation, Energy Optimization, Product Quality Improvements etc. for enhancing bottom line;
  - Used as performance indicator for comparing relative performance for various refineries.

Pooling Mechanism

The price build up of petroleum products recovered from the consumers by

Oil Companies represents the industry-weighted average of the individual retention cost elements. The pricing system allowed reimbursement of retention costs to the Oil Companies while the Oil Companies recovered industry weighted average costs from consumers. The difference between such weighted average cost elements and the individual oil company retention cost elements were allowed to be adjusted in centrally administered funding stream known as 'Industry Pooling Mechanism'. For this purpose various pool accounts were maintained and are administered by acc. Each pool account was funded by levy of surcharge included in consumer price build up. The Oil Companies were to recover these surcharges from consumers and fund the pool account through account.

Special Products

For major consumption products, the prices had been fixed individually on the basis of recommendation of various pricing committees from time to time and these products were called formula products. Certain other products, not brought within the bounds of the price control, were called non-formula products.

The latest pricing committee i.e., Oil Cost Review Committee (OCRC) recognized the continuance of the concept of formula and non-formula products for pricing but in additional category called free trade products. The free trades products were totally out of the pricing control and ail Companies were free to fix the price of these products purely on the basis of prevailing market forces.

Fixation of Retention Price per Ton of Crude 'Throughput' for each Refinery

Retention price concept was introduced in the country w.e.f. 14.07.1975. Under that regime, refineries were compensated on the basis of retention prices. The elements that go into the build up of the retention price for the refineries are given below by way of illustration for two refineries, viz., Haldia (coastal) and Mathura (inland). The retention price fixed per tonne of crude, as in 1988 is given in Table 8.7.

Refinery Profitability I Margins under Free Market Scenario

Under the presently prevailing free market regime, the profitability of refineries is determined based on Net Back Margin ($ per barrel) on the principles of import parity.

Definition of Key Terms

GPW—Gross Product Worth

Value of yield of products from particular crude based on the prevailing product prices.

Refinery Gate Value

Gross Product Worth less variable Refining Cost such as Energy costs.

Net Back Margin

Net Back Value less Crude Price.

Table 8.7: Fixation of Retention Price per ton of Crude 'throughput'

(Rs./MT as in 1988)

Sl. No.	Cost Elements	Haldia	Mathura
1	Fooled FOB Cost	1700.00	1700.00
2	Ocean/Inland Freight	95.64	133.78
3	Marine/Inland Insurance	2.55	2.28
4	Ocean Loss	10.61	7.02
5	Wharfaqe/Other Landing Charges	34.60	12.90
6	Customs Duty	502.68	251.34
7	Delivered Cost of Crude Oil (1 to 6)	2346.08	2107.32
8	Chemicals & Catalyst		
9	Utilities		
10	Consumables		
11	Salaries and Wages		
12	Repairs and Maintenance		
13	Overheads		
14	Depreciation		
15	Refining Cost (8 to 14)	74.64	89.17
16	Return on Capital Employed	70.17	115.87
17	Retention Price per MT of Crude Throughput (7+15+16)	2490.89	2312.36

Net Back Value

Refinery Gate Value less freight costs or worth of products "Netted Back" to crude loading terminal.

Factors Dermining Net Back Margin

- Type and Quality of Crude
- Refineries Type, Hardware and Complexity
- Efficiency of utilization of the given hardware
- Energy efficiency of Refining Operation
- Prevailing Crude and Product prices
- Crude Freight Cost

Methodology of Evaluation of Net Back Margin

The key factor for evaluation of Net Back Margin of a Refinery is the determination of the Gross Product Worth from the Refinery. Gross Product Worth from a Refinery is evaluated by multiplying the product pattern achieved on processing a mixture of crudes through the available refinery processing units by the prevailing product prices at a given point in time. The first step to evaluate the Gross Product Worth is to evaluate the product pattern available from a Refinery from processing a basket of available Crudes. Product Pattern from a Refinery is dependent on the type of Crudes processed and the Refinery configuration of primary and secondary processing units. Refineries process a wide variety of Crudes, which can broadly be categorized as light, and Sweet Crudes (Low Sulfur) and heavy and Sour Crudes (High Sulfur).

Typical Product Pattern of a Modern Refinery

In order to illustrate the evaluation procedure for determining the Product Pattern of a modern Refinery, a refinery configuration of Crude Processing Unit (CDU), Once through Hydro-cracker (HCU), Fluidized Catalytic Cracking Unit (FCC) and Bitumen Blowing Unit (BBU) is assumed.

Typical and illustrative yield patterns for HCU, FCC, and BBU are taken and Dubai Crude Oil is assumed to be processed in CDU under the above configuration.

Crude Distilation Unit (CDU)

Feed **Products**	**Dubai Crude Oil [100 MT]**	
	%	MT
LPG	1.5	1.5
NAPHTHA	12.4	12.4
SKO	14.4	14.4
HSD	22.8	22.8
RCO	49.2	49.2
Total	100	100

Vaccum Distilation Unit (VDU)

Feed Reduced Crude Oil (RCO) [49.2 MT]

Products	%	MT
Light Vaccum Gas Oil (L VGO)	6	3.0
Vaccum Gas Oil (VGO)	44	21.7
Short Residue (SR)	50	24.5
Total	100	49.2

Once Through Hydro-Cracker (OTHC)

Feed Vacuum Gas Oil
(VGO ex VDU) [21.7 MT]

Products	%	MT
Gas	1.6	0.4
LPG	2.5	0.6
Naphtha	7.2	1.5
SKO	23.0	5.0
Gas Oil	23.2	5.0
Residue	42.5	9.2
Total	100	21.7

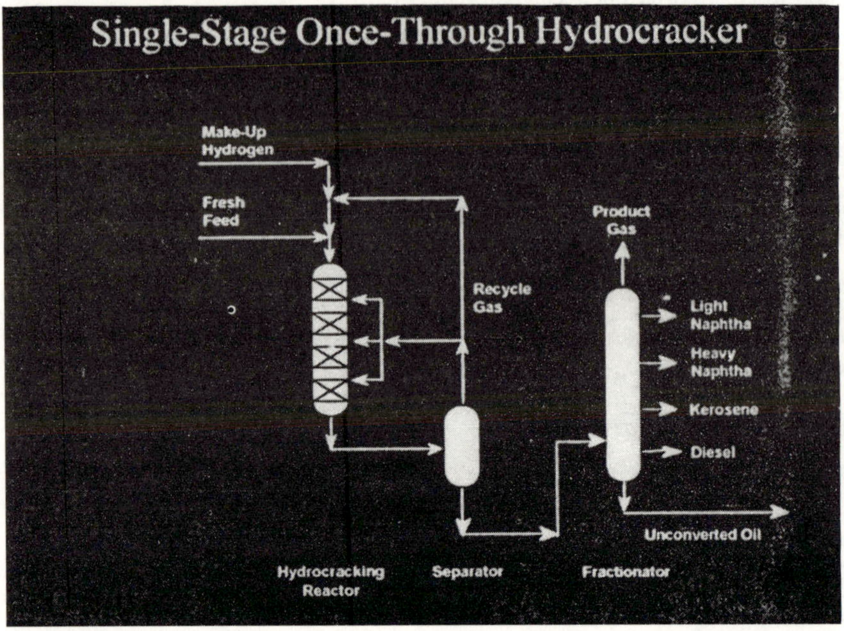

Fludized Catalytic Cracking Unit (FCC)

Feed HCU Residue [9.2 MT] + Short Residue Ex. VDU [1.4 MT] = [10.6 MT]

Products	%	MT
LPG	14.0	1.5
FCC Gasoline:28.0		
Total Cylce Oil :40.1		
(TCO)		1.0
Clarified Oil (CLO)	9.8	
Gas + Coke	8.1	0.8
Total	100	10.6

Product Pattern after Blending Streams from Various Processing Units

Crude		100
LPG	[1.5+0.6+1.5] [12.1+1.5]	3.6
Naphtha	[12.1+1.5]	13.6
FCC Gasoline		
(MS component)	(3)	3.0
SKO	[14.4+5]	19.4
HSD	[22.8+3+5+4.3]	35.1
BIT	[10]	10
FO	[24.5-(10+1.4)+1]	14.1
Gas & Coke	[0.4+0.4+0.4]	1.2
Total		100

Final Product Pattern

The final product pattern after taking MS production as 10 MT as per demand after processing part Naphtha through Reformer, considering Gas & Coke (1.2 MT) as equivalent to FO and correction of Fa viscosity to meet the prevailing IS specification by blending about 6% SKO (1 MT) in Fa pool is as under.

Dubai Crude Processed		100
Products		
LPG	3.6	4
NAPHTHA	6.6	7
MS	10	10
SKO	18.4	18
HSD	35.1	35
FO	16.3	16
BITUMEN	10	10

Prevailing Crude and Product Prices

Table 8.8: Prevailing Crude and Product Prices in International Market

AVQ FOB Price ($BB)	AVQ	Freight ($ per T)
Dubai Crude	28.2	207
Products		
LPG		300
Naphtha	32.71	294
MS	38.03	324
SK/ATF	34.05	269
HSD	34.03	254
FO	24.98.	160
BITUMEN		155

- For products except LPG a flat freight of $6/MT and insurance/ocean loss at 0.6% is considered extra.
- For LPG a freight of $20/MT and 1.0% insurance is considered extra.
- The above is based on simplified, but reasonable assumptions.

Production Pattern

Dubai Crude Products	MT	100 MT Prices($/MT)	Realization($)
LPG	4	323	1292
Naphtha	7	302	2114
MS	10	331	3310
SK/ATF	18	277	4986
HSD	35	261	9135
FO	16	167	2672
BITUMEN	10	162	1620
Total Product Value:			25129

Evaluation of Net Back-Margin

A	Gross Product worth (Value of Products)	$ 25129
B	Energy Cost at 8% Fuel Consumption [8 x FO Price]	$ 1336
C	Refinery Gate Value [A-B]	$23793
D	Crude Freight Cost @ 0.5$/BBL Or Rs. 3.7 *I* Tonne for 100 Tonnes	$ 370
E	(C-D)	$23423
F	Crude Cost @ $28.2 IBBL or $207 *IMT* for 100 Tonnes	$20700
G	Net Back Margin (E-F)	$ 2723
	$/MT	$ 27.23
	$/BBL	$ 3.71
	Say: $ 3.7/BBL	

Need and Importance of Net Back Margin

- Benchmark for Profitability of Refining Operations.
- Guide for incentive to refine more Crude into Products, thereby determining optimum level of Capacity utilization.
- Used for optimum selection of Crude for Refineries vis-à-vis Refinery Hardware.
- Trigger for future investment decisions for Capex, Yield Optimization, Bottoms Upgradation, Energy Optimization, Product Quality Improvements etc. for enhancing bottom line.
- Used as performance indicator for comparing relative performance for various refineries.

Measures for Improving Refinery Profitability

As already indicated that in the free market scenario the Refinery Profitability is very much dependent on external market forces such as crude and Product prices, shipping rates, acts of competition etc on which refiners have very little control. In spite of the above constraints refineries still have a host of factors under their control to improve Refinery Profitability.

These factors can be classified under the following broad categories:

(a) Optimizing Existing Operations, including proper selection of Crude mix, scheduling and blending planning in line with product slate.
(b) Technological Up gradations.
(c) Planning for Economics of Scale.
(d) Optimization of Refinery Configuration.
(e) Forward and Backward Integration.
(f) Human Resource Gradation and Manpower Empowerment.

(A) Optimising Existing Operations

Reduction in inputs costs for refining Crude into refined Petroleum Products directly adds to refinery profitability. Some of the key actions under this category are:

(i) Optimizing Crude FOB Cost
(ii) Reduction in Shipping Costs
(iii) Reduction in Refinery Energy and Losses
(iv) Reduction in Refinery Operating Costs

Optimizing Crude FOB Cost

This process begins with proper selection of Crude Oil basket for a given refinery. Once Crude basket is identified, and then sourcing Crude is an important economic activity. This is a very dynamic and market sensitive activity in the whole value chain of refining. Day by day Crude

Oil market is evolving itself to a highly knowledge based area of operation. One such emerging area is Risk Management, which requires both individual skill and organizational policy to operate in the sensitive field of international Oil Exchanges.

Reduction in Shipping Costs

Proper planning for transportation of Crude Oil in large parcel sizes in ULCC's saves crude transportation costs. For Indian refineries, this is a very live issue, which is largely infrastructure related. Many Indian refineries suffer from the constraint of inadequate tankage, which prevents them from taking large size parcel. Indian ports are ill equipped to handle large size tankers. Massive investment planning at national level and at Industry level is called on this aspect. However, given the constraint, proper chartering of vessels is a very significant economic activity. International shipping market is a sensitive and well-knit market. As far as Crude Oil chartering is concerned, there are national level policy issues, which are mostly addressed by Director General of Shipping and Ministry of Surface Transport. Given the policy framework, substantial optimization can be done, with proper scheduling and planning with the Supplier of Crude on the one hand and the Shipping Company on the other. This activity calls for high degree of coordination, timely decision and knowledge in the area of maritime conventions and legal aspects of ship chartering and operation.

Reduction in Refinery Energy and Losses

Modern refineries are highly energy intensive with energy and losses constituting 7 to 8% on crude intake. Constant efforts such as regular monitoring of energy efficiencies of refinery furnaces and boilers, heat integration, implementation of various energy conservation schemes as well as efforts to reduce refinery losses has direct impact in improving refinery margins.

Reduction in Refinery Operation Costs

Refinery operating cost other than energy and losses is in the range of $1 per barrel and accordingly optimizing the operational costs results in significant improvement in refinery profitability. Benchmarking, target setting and rigorous monitoring of chemicals and catalyst consumption, predictive and preventive maintenance of refinery process equipments resulting in higher on stream factor and higher run lengths between successive planned shutdowns, avoidance of losses due to unscheduled outages with consequent lower repairs and maintenance cost significantly reduce operating cost resulting in improving the refinery margins.

(B) Technological Upgradations

Technologies need to be constantly scanned to evaluate appropriate cost effective options for reducing the bottom of the barrel and increasing production of useful high value products thereby enhancing refinery margins.

(C) Planning for Economics of Scale

Refinery crude and secondary processing capacities as well as other related facilities have to be planned or upgraded to economic sizes to bring down the operating cost with resultant improvement in refinery bottom line, keeping in view the comfort level of disposal of products in view of surplus refining capacity.

(D) Optimization of Refinery Configuration

Continuous efforts need to be made for evaluating the existing refinery configuration using simulation/modeling techniques to identify investment needs for upgrading the configuration to the most optimum level for enhancing the yield from the barrel of crude processed. An optimum configuration thus results in improving the refinery profitability. The ultimate aim is to maximize distillate yield and reduce heavy ends.

(E) Backward and Forward Integration

Backward integration by investment in upstream exploration and production activities either directly or through equity participation with reputed Crude Oil producers, besides providing crude supply security also results in lowering crude cost inputs thereby improving margins. Forward integration by diversification to petrochemicals and power generation from low value refinery residue results in value addition with consequent enhancement in refinery margins. This is a long-term capital-intensive strategy, which results in transforming a refinery to a fully integrated oil and utility company with immense value addition to the operating margins.

(F) Human Resource Development

In the present day environment of constantly changing technologies, shrinking margins forcing organizations to adopt effective cost cutting measures and cut throat competition, human resources are the cutting edge in helping organizations to improve their profitability. Manpower has to be exposed to latest technologies on an ongoing basis, best industry practices, latest simulation/modeling and cost optimization techniques etc and appropriately motivated and empowered to take effective and quick decisions related to day-to-day operational management issues. Such a proactive approach shall in the long run help the refineries achieve its objective of most optimum refining with least possible cost and thereby improving refinery margins.

Optimizing Crude Cost: Summing-up

- Study current mix of LS and HS crudes
- Identify other crude for trail
- Examine the impact with partial quantity for processing blended crude
- Calculate gain in GRM
- Widen Crude Basket
- Optimise Crude Mix
- Mix of Spot and LT contract

Reduction in Shipping Cost

- Study mode of transport whether through VLCCs
- Identify crudes which could be transported through VLCCs
- Time chartering of vessels
- Study and Identify alternate port

Benchmarking

- Evaluate the performance of refineries
- Know the gaps with pacesetters in global scenario
- Comparative rankings in various performance areas

Performance Indicators

- Refinery Utilization, %
  - Capacity Utilization of Process Units
- Volumetric Expansion Index (VEI)
  - Conversion of Hy. Ends to Light Ends
- Energy Intensity Index (EII)
  - Comparison of Energy consumption
- Hydrocarbon Loss, % on Crude
- Inventory (Bbl/Utilized EDC)
  - Comparison of Hydrocarbon Inventory
- Manpower (Eq. Personnel/100 thousand EDC)
  - Manpower deployment
- Maintenance Index (US$/EDC)
  - Comparison of Maintenance Cost

Equivalent Distillation Capacity (EDC)

- Plant Availability, %
  - Mechanical, Operational
- Cash Operating Expenses (US Cents /Utilized EDC)
  - Comparison of Operating Cost
- Value Added Index (VAI)
  - Comparison of Gross Margin
- Net Margin (US$/Bbl Input)
  - Gross Profit

Operating Cost

- Catalyst/Chemical management
- Inventory reduction
- Fuel & loss control
- Overhead/Establishment cost
- Maintenance cost reduction
- Demurrage

Energy and Hydrocarbon Loss

Reduction in Energy Loss

- Study trend
- Compare with the best in the company
- Compare with the best in the industry
- Compare with the best in the World
- Study unit wise energy consumption and loss
- Optimize operations
- Implement advance process controls

Refining Strategy and Operations

The starting point for any refining strategy must be the existing physical configuration of the company's refinery or refineries. Refineries range from small and simple topping units that boil crude oil into a very simple slate of basic products to extremely large plants that produce a wide variety of end products. However, there are three basic types of refiners-complex, cracking, and hydro skimming-found in most developed country markets today. They differ dramatically in their ability to produce lighter products (e.g., gasoline, diesel) at the expense of heavier products (e.g., residual fuel oil). For each refinery, the desired set of products is one starting point, while' the crude selection process is the other. In reality, these two are inextricably linked and should be considered jointly. The goal for any refiner should be to maximize uplift across the refinery. Determination of the appropriate refining strategy is an iterative process, balancing the changing product yields with the changing crude slate to optimize the dollars per barrel uplift.

All refiners must decide whether they can make money being a low complexity/low-cost refinery or a high-capital/complex refinery with a large gross margin sufficient to support the additional debt load. Some refineries do not have a choice: they maybe simple refineries without access to capital and therefore have to be as innovative as possible with a fairly constraining set of assets. Other complex refineries already have committed the capital and must continually look at a variety of crude and other feedstock and new ways to best use a more flexible set of assets.

The following examples are designed to illustrate the complexity of refining strategy choices.

- Strategies must contend not only with the structural differences between refineries, but also with the effect those strategies will have on the markets being served.

- For a given refining region, it is in fact possible to construct an aggregate refining margin curve. Of course, this curve is an oversimplification, since it only examines the average margin for all products. A more sophisticated approach would measure the marginal supply curve for each product.
- Only with a thorough understanding of a refinery's position in such a regional market can a manager make strategic and tactical decisions.
- If an oil company fundamentally disadvantaged, it is quite unlikely to earn a consistent profit unless demand growth and margins are robust over a prolonged period of time. One should therefore consider if major improvements in the assets build-up or in operational performance are possible or whether it would be better to leave the market.
- A key activity for senior refinery management is continuously looking out into the future and assessing the impact of known and possible future events. For example: What impact will new Coker capacity have? What will the introduction of reformulated gasoline do? Will a new pipeline suddenly allow additional refineries to market products in our region?

How to Run an Individual Refinery

There are eight critical success factors that generally apply to the management of an individual refinery (some also apply across refineries). If one applies these best practices consistently, this will transform into a high performance refining organization (Treat, 1996).

1. ***Listen to the market:*** Price volatility can swamp refinery economics. If you are losing money, you can't make it up on volume. In both crude buying and product sales, you must stay carefully tuned to the market signals.

2. ***Optimization continuously:***
   - Refineries must have a good LP representative of the operation and run soon after crude or product price changes.
   - Once the crude throughput and mix has been determined, individual unit models should continuously optimize each unit.

3. ***Organize around asset or area teams:*** Functional silos in refineries are legendary fiefdoms. Maintenance, operations, and engineering are often sovereign kingdoms with inefficient and ineffective interfaces. Organizing the refinery around cross-functional work teams will break down these barriers, thereby reducing costs and improving reliability.

4. ***Trust the operators:*** They know the equipment best, and they want to do a good job. The problem is they often lack the tools to make the right decisions. If you give them the right information and training, they can work wonders.

5. ***Stay flexible:*** There will always be peaks and valleys of work. Your organization should have the flexibility to share resources in order to conquer the peaks and to take advantages of the valleys. This is particularly true in the maintenance and engineering functions.

6. ***All maintenance is not equal:*** Refineries require a lot of maintenance, but

determining how much by whom to what units and when can make a big difference to the bottom line.

7. *Energy is not free:* Surprisingly, many refineries do a poor job of tracking energy costs-particularly steam-by unit.

8. *Build project discipline:* Refinery turnarounds are major events and cost big bucks. The downtime is often the most expensive component of cost. Refinery managers should insist on careful advance planning that minimizes downtime and leverages the organization's skills in procurement, logistics, and doing the work. Operators should play important roles in turnarounds along with contractors.

In addition to these general principles, there are a number of function-specific issues which require special attention. These include:

- ***Procurement:*** We have already mentioned procurement in the discussion of project discipline above. However, this is often a major area for operational improvement as well. Consolidation and standardization combined with implementation of full life cycle cost analysis can yield major benefits.
- ***Health, Safety, and Environment:*** Refineries are under intensive scrutiny by both company and government HSE personnel. The key to success in this sensitive area is to understand the appropriate distribution of roles and responsibilities between the corporate center and the refinery. In general, it pays to place accountability with the asset team, with clearly defined performance measures monitored by a small corporate HSE group.
- ***Process Controls and Information Technology:*** Refineries are often burdened by islands of technology which do not communicate with each other. The greatest disconnect is usually between the operational/ process control systems and the financial/management systems. Moreover, many refineries have developed in-house LP models and other systems that can be better performed today by third party software like the Bechtel RIMS model.

However, in-house systems shops often view such "off the shelf" products as threatening their own empires and convince management that only a proprietary (i.e. in-house system) will do the job. Yet in-house solutions typically cost more and become outdated more rapidly than third-party products that are forced to innovate to remain competitive. Advanced process controls offer a means to automate operations, reducing cost, improving reliability and optimizing performance. The lack of capital has often prevented refiners from making investments in this area which offers very high and short-term paybacks. Dynamic matrix control and even simple feed-forward control loops are impossible to implement on old pneumatic/local instrumentation.

REFERENCES

Bhattacharya, S.C., 1996, 'Deregulation of petroleum product prices: the case of India', *Natural Resources Forum*, 20(4), p. 281.

Business Line, 1998, November 29, New Delhi, p. 15.

Chittal, Nitin, Joshi, Pankaj, 1997, 'Refineries: justice delayed', *Express Investment Week*, Feb. 10-16; 7(7), p.16.

Doctor, H.V. and H. D. Mustafa (2005), Innovative Refining Technology—Crude oil Quality Improvement (COQIR): http://www.ese.iitb.ac.in/aer2006_files/papers/199.pdf

The Economic Times, 1999, 'Investor's guide', August 9, New Delhi, p. 5.

The Economic Times, 1998, 'Investor's guide', March 30, New Delhi, p. 5.

The Economic Times, 1999, 28 June, New Delhi, p. 1.

Ministry of Petroleum and Natural Gas, 1998, Annual Report, New Delhi, p. 13.

Ministry of Petroleum and Natural Gas, 1999, Annual Report 1998-99, Govt. of India, New Delhi, p. 44.

Patha, M.A., 1998, 'Oil and Gas: meeting the challenges in the downstream sector; *Oil Asia*, Oct.-Dec., Vol. 19, No. 4, p.45.

Pirog, Robert, L (2005), Petroleum Refining: Economic Performance and Challenges for the Future, CRS Report for Congress, Order Code RL32248, May, 9, 2005.

Planning Commission, 1997, 'Ninth five year plan, Vol. 2, Energy; Govt. of India, New Delhi, p. 10.

Prasana, K., 1999, 'Investor's guide', The Economic Times, New Delhi, p. 5.

Rao JSN, Pushpalatha, 1992, 'Restructuring of petroleum pricing', Urja Oil and Gas International, 1 (5B6), p. 17.

Wahi, S.P., 1999, 'Strategy for oil security', Discussion Paper, presented at ASSOCHAM, New Delhi.

India Hydrocarbon Vision 2025-(1999), Ministry of Petroleum and Natural Gas, GOI, New Delhi

Tenth Five Year Plan (Energy Chapter) of Planning Commission (2000), New Delhi.

Annual Report of Ministry of Petroleum & Natural Gas for 2002-03.

International Energy Outlook, 2003, by Energy Information Administration of D/o Energy US.

Website of Director General of Hydrocarbons (DGH).

Annual Report of ONGC, BPC, HPC, IOC for 2002-03.

Research Analyst Reports on Oil & Gas Sector by Citigroup, ABN Amro, HSBC etc. (2003).

Monthly Economic Report issued by D/o Economic Affairs (January 2004).

Leffer, William L. (2000), Petroleum Refining: In Non-Technical Language (3rd. Edn.) Pennwell Publication, USA.

Hidustan Petroleum Ltd (2005). Advanced Programme on Refinery Operations & Management, HPL

Treat, John Elting (1994). Creating High Performance International Petroleum Company: Dinosaurs Can Fly, Penn Well Publishing Co., Oklahoma, USA

CSIS, 2006: www.igloo.org/igloo/community.igloo?r0=community-download&r0_script=/scripts/document/download.script

CHAPTER IX

Strategy for Petroleum and Natural Gas Trading

Fossil-fuel products such as crude oil, natural gas, refined products, and petrochemicals are all sold into commodity markets globally for serving customers and in exchange earn reasonable profits. These commodities are bulk-produced initially as unspecialized products, with high fusibility, having characteristics so similar that they are mutually interchangeable. For example, light sweet crude oil is fungible because a barrel produced in Venezuela and one produced in Saudi Arabia would produce similar mixes of products if processed in the same refinery. But when produced in different refineries, both composition and price of selling of products could vary within given parameters.

Taking a broad view of petroleum marketing it generally involves the following mix of operations:

- Transporting the Product to a point where custody transfer is feasible
- Providing storage facilities wherever necessary
- Balancing Product and demand
- Obtaining the best possible price

Crude Oil Marketing

Refineries are normally located near population centre, often in processing clusters that include petrochernica1 plants. The overall pattern is for crude to be shipped to these clusters from around the world in smaller tankers.

Since crude is so easily transported by marine tanker in remote areas of the world the development of a new field generally includes building a pipeline connecting the field to a marine loading terminal. This gives complete access to the world market. An oil company may use its own tankers to ship to its refinery in Europe or the U. S. but more often it will sell at the terminal to the highly organized and efficient third-party market. Crude oil traders responsible fo procuring feedstock for the world's refineries are in constant contact with the producers, negotiating prices and arranging transportation.

When a new field is discovered in the U.S., the operator normally connects it to the nearest crude oil pipeline and receives the per barrel "posted price" published by the pipeline company. Producers also have the option to rent space in the pipeline to transport their crude. Because of the well established market between producers and refiners in the U.S. and abroad, and because it is a fungible product, no particular attempt is made by companies to run their own crude in their own refineries.

OPEC's Role In International Oil Trading

OPEC was formed way back in 1960 to give the producing countries a unified voice in dealing with the western oil company's crude pricing. Its major impact, however, has been experienced since 1973, when it began functioning as a cartel to control crude prices to such an extent that it created first-ever 'Oil-shock' in the global market. In 1999, the OPEC member states consisted of: Saudi Arabia, Iraq, Iran, Venezuela, Nigeria, Kuwait, Libya, United Arab Emirates, Indonesia, Algeria, Gabon, and Qatar.

From its beginning, the international crude market was highly volatile and under geo-political pressure. Since major crude oil and natural gas reserve-related discoveries were random events that defied planning or scheduling, the supply of crude was usually too long or too short, generating a wide-ranging swings in price. This environment was discouraging to investment of the huge sums the emerging industry needed. Some stabilization was clearly in everyone's interest.

The first effort to bring order to the market was made by the Texas Railroad Commission (TRC) in the 1930s, and it was quite successful. At that time the United States-principally Texas-was the world's biggest crude producer and exporter. The TRC was therefore able to cut-back or increase Texas production as needed to bring world supply and demand into rough balance. Working closely with the major oil companies who controlled the foreign-produced crude, the TRC was able to maintain relative price stability well into the 1960s.By the early 1970s, the United States had lost its position of leading producer in the world, and in fact had become a net importer. This eliminated the TRC as a player, leaving the multinationals to manage the international crude markets alone. It also gave OPEC new life as it members realized that they now dominated world crude supplies. In 1973, a wave of nationalizations by the producing countries started. OPEC quickly took control of the crude market and in October of 1973 more than tripled prices. Since then, OPEC has tried to stabilize prices by adjusting member's production rates to meet market demand. Their efforts have been successful at times, but at other times major price fluctuations have occurred. This is not surprising considering the diversity of interests that exist between individual member states. For example, OPEC member Iraq invaded fellow member Kuwait in the Gulf war. Another factor weakening OPEC is the substantial non-OPEC production that has recently been developed around the world. As of the late 1990s OPEC production has been reduced to only 40% of world production. It is significant, however, that OPEC, particularly Saudi Arabia, still has virtually all the world's surplus producing capacity. This assures them continued influence on crude prices.

Trading Petroleum Products

Trading Petroleum products involves the customers from Commercial, Industrial and Construction Industries. These customers normally require Diesel, Fuel Oil and other Petroleum Products to cater their own consumption in their related fields (viz. Petroleum Products, Petroleum, Petroleum Coke, Petroleum Equipment, Petroleum Gas, Petroleum Jelly, Petroleum Oil, Petroleum Production, Petroleum Resin, Petroleum Wax, Calcined Petroleum Coke, Liquefied Petroleum Gas, Liquid Petroleum Gas, White Petroleum Jelly, IT Products, 3M Products, ABS Products, Acoustic Products, Acrylic Products, Adult Products).

Trading process includes:

- Marketing
- Providing Customer Services
- Ordering Process
- Product Delivery Process
- Billing/Invoicing Process
- Account/Payment Collection
- After Sales Services

Other Process Involved:

- Assisting in License Application (Stock License—LHDN—HEP)
- Supplying Skid Tanks and Other relevant process (Pump & Meters) upon request.

Indian Oil and Gas—Industry Report (2007)

India is the sixth largest consumer of oil. There is a huge demand-supply gap in oil and gas in India. The country imports more than 70% of its crude oil requirement. In 2005, oil and gas accounted for 38% of primary energy consumption in India, followed by coal at 55%. Oil and gas industry is broadly classified into Upstream and Downstream segments and comprises 18 refineries, with total refining capacity of 132.47 mmtpa as of April 1; 2006. Consumption of crude oil was estimated at 130.11mmt, whereas consumption for natural gas was estimated to be 31.02bcm in the same year. The production and consumption of petroleum products was estimated at 119.75mmtpa and 111.92mmt respectively. Recently, India has emerged as net exporter of petroleum products.

In the Indian petroleum industry, refining of crude oil is a profit making business, but marketing of those refined products is loss making due to a cap on selling prices. The state-owned oil marketing companies, HPCL, BPCL, IOC, have to sell petroleum products—petrol, diesel, kerosene and cooking gas—at a controlled price and typically have to bear losses which at best is mitigated through oil bonds. The fiscal saw unabated rise in crude prices. The average Indian Basket of crude oil prices increased to US$79.55/bbl for the 12 months ending Mar'FY08 as against US$62.4/bbl in FY07 (http://www.capitalmarket.com/BrokerResearch/

PDFs/21-229496-030408.pdf). However, the increase in product price was higher than the increase in crude price, thereby leading to improved refiners' margins across the world. The position of Indian Refineries, in terms of number in Public and Private sector, capacities and relative market share is given below.

Refineries in India	No. of refineries	Capacity (MMTPA)	Market Share
Public Sector	17	105.5	71%
Private Sector	2	43.5	29%
Total	19	149.0	100%

Indian Oil Marketing Companies are using latest/modern technology including hydro cracker to process complex and sour crude oil in some of their refineries. This type of crude oil is $4/bbl-$5/bbl cheaper than Brent crude oil. Also, the Indian basket of crude comprised of Oman-Dubai sour (high sulphur) grade crude oil and Brent dated sweet (low sulphur) crude oil in the ratio of 61.4:38.6 ratio which is having a large proportion of sour crude oil. Asian refiners are adding capacity to feed demand in developed nations where there has been little expansion in recent years and India, Asia's third-largest oil consumer, plans to add 2.14mn bpd to its existing 2.98mn bpd nameplate capacity by 2012 as it seeks to become a global refining hub.

Current installed capacity of 149 MMTPA, is the 10th largest refining capacity in the world. Also, capacity utilization of PSU refineries is more than 100% as compared to world's refineries, which are having capacity utilization of around 88%. Whereas the Existing installed refining capacity 149.0MMTPA, the expected addition by 2012 [11th 5 yr plan (2007-12)] will be in the region of 112.0MMTPA. Indian Oil companies are coming out with new refineries in the 11th 5-year plan (2007-12) having new technology to refine complex crude oil.

Internationally, apart from crude which is in short supply, the refining capacity is even in greater short supply. Even a country like Iran, which is the second largest producer of crude oil, doesn't have enough refining capacity and has to import the finished product. The Singapore Benchmark refining margin is at $7.7/bbl for the nine months ending December '07 and it may rise further in the range of $8-10/bbl. We expect for Indian OMCs, average GRM for the full fiscal year 2008 will be approximately $1/bbl lower than the Singapore benchmark refining margin around $6.5/bbl-$7/bbl (http://www.capitalmarket.com/BrokerResearch/PDFs/21-229496-030408.pdf).

The oil sector is the country's largest foreign exchange earner. Starting from virtually no exports in 1999-2000, the oil sector now rings in 17% of the country's foreign exchange. Gross exports of petro-products from India during 2006-07 stood at $18.6bn (with volumes at 32.4 MMT). On $48.3bn of crude imports in 2006-07, 17% amounts to $8.2bn. For the nine month ended December'07, Indian Oil and Bharat Petroleum got Rs. 10.43bn and Rs. 2.98 bn respectively towards gain on foreign exchange variation which is accounted in other income as compared to gain of Rs 679mn and loss of Rs 779mn. (Loss was accounted as other expenditure).

On the effects of the rise in the value of the rupee (10% appreciation), the under-recoveries have reduced to that extent in the last nine months during 2007, while crude prices appreciated 30% during the period.

In India, prices for kerosene & LPG are determined on the basis of import parity prices and for petrol and diesel, it is determined on the basis of trade parity pricing model.

In a situation where there is no domestic manufacture of a product, the cost of supplying it in the domestic market would be the landed cost, which would be the *import parity price,* the international price plus the insurance and freight cost plus the customs duty. In a situation (as in India) where there is domestic manufacture, the import parity price can be taken as the international competitive price that sets the ceiling for the domestic price. Notional charges are taken as $2/ bbl which includes the free on board price, ocean freight, insurance, exchange rates, customs duties, losses during transit and port charges. The import parity principle, in effect, enables Indian refining companies to import at inflated prices, which bear no relation to the actual cost of production in the country. The notional method of pricing petroleum products overstates the losses of OMCs. It is important to differentiate between oil companies' "losses" and "under-recoveries." The latter is purely related to the notional price that the companies would charge if they were free to do so.

The *trade-parity* pricing model for diesel and petrol is the weighted average of the import parity and export parity prices in the ratio of 80:20. Trade parity pricing takes into account the emergence of India as an exporter of products like petrol and diesel. Oil companies buy petroleum products from their own refineries on a trade-parity basis, which to a large extent reflects global prices.

However, the government regulates the sale of petroleum products in India and the PSU oil marketers are compelled to sell their products below cost. However, under the current subsidy mechanism, the government compensates for almost 76% of the losses by way of oil bonds and discounts from the upstream oil firms namely, ONGC, GAIL and OIL leaving 24% to be borne by the oil firms. The government has been issuing special oil bonds at various intervals to the oil marketing Companies (OMCs) in lieu of the under-realization on sale of sensitive petroleum products. Under recoveries by the Oil Marketing Companies (OMCs) have been rising with the spiraling crude prices.

Oil Marketing Companies (OMCs) are likely to get bonds worth Rs 92.87bn as part compensation for selling fuel below cost during the quarter ended December 31, 2007. IOC will be getting Rs 51.00bn worth of bonds, HPCL Rs 19.67bn and BPCL Rs 22.20bn. Also, these companies got Rs 70.83bn from upstream firms and the remaining of the Rs 212.64bn under-realizations on sale of petrol, diesel, LPG and kerosene was borne by IOC, BPCL and HPCL.

The government had previously issued bonds worth Rs 112.57bn to three PSU oil marketing companies to compensate them for under recoveries on selling petrol, diesel, domestic LPG and PDS kerosene in April-September 2007 period. IOC got Rs 63.62bn worth of oil bonds, BPCL Rs 25.39bn and HPCL Rs 23.56bn worth of bonds carrying coupon rate of 7.95 per cent and maturing in 2025. Also, Rs 87.88bn assistance was received from upstream companies like ONGC and OIL. The total under-realization on sale of the four fuels during April-December has been pegged at Rs 476.28 bn, of which the government compensated Rs 205.54 bn through bonds and Rs 158.71 bn from upstream companies. Issuance of oil bonds and discounts by upstream companies, to OMCs are in line with the government's policy to compensate the public sector oil marketing companies for their under-recoveries on domestic sale of sensitive petro products. Oil bonds have been calculated at the rate of 42.7 per cent of the total under-realization on sale of the four fuels. One-third of the losses get compensated by way of discounts on crude oil from upstream companies such as ONGC and the remaining of under-realization are borne by the fuel retailers.

Crude oil accounts for some 90 per cent of the cost of production of refined petroleum products, it is to be expected that crude and retail product prices move in tandem. However, the Indian retail prices are not fully reflective of the changes in crude prices. Despite the Government announcement to dismantle the Administered Price Mechanism (APM) effective from April 2002, Government is still controlling the prices of petrol, diesel, PDS kerosene and domestic LPG.

Despite increase in international oil prices, the Government has not increased prices of kerosene sold under the public distribution system and cooking gas. The Government has only brought a marginal increase in petrol and diesel prices.

The three oil marketing companies—Indian Oil Corporation, Bharat Petroleum and Hindustan Petroleum—are losing around Rs 4.4bn per day by selling petroleum products at subsidized prices. Indian Oil Corporation is losing Rs 2.2bn per day on sale of auto and cooking fuels, below the cost price and rest shared by remaining two marketing companies.

The average price of the Indian basket for this month is $100.37/bbl, compared with $92.37/bbl in Feb and $89.52/bbl in Jan. The steep increase in international crude prices saw the Indian crude oil basket hover around $103.8/bbl. The oil companies' net realization from petrol and diesel sales is one of the lowest in the world. Since government-owned oil marketing companies, which also operate refineries, sell most of their petrol and diesel domestically, it results in losses for them.

The government is considering increasing the proportion of oil bonds to 57%, against the existing 42.7% of the under-recoveries, along with granting SLR status to the bonds, to reduce the burden borne directly by OMCs.

The under-recoveries by the oil companies are estimated at Rs 718.08bn for 2007-08. Based on the existing burden-sharing formula, the government is likely to issue bonds worth Rs 306.62bn. The formula specifies the government would issue oil bonds worth 42.7% of the losses while 33.3% would be borne by upstream companies, and the remaining 24% by the OMCs.

As Government-owned oil companies are forced to sell petroleum products at subsidized prices, each increase in crude oil prices means additional burden of so-called under recoveries on the companies.

Therefore, the oil companies are cutting costs by:

- Reducing fuel inventories to cut daily working capital
- Processing sour crude oil in large amount, which is cheaper than sweet crude oil

- Increasing refinery capacity utilization
- Liquidating oil bonds
- Borrowing more funds

The present market share of the oil PSUs are 98.85% for diesel and 96.8% for petrol which makes it clear that the competition from the private sector has been virtually eliminated due to avoidance of private companies from the subsidy package. Also, the under-recoveries for the oil marketing companies are partly getting compensated by high refining margins and to some extent by the issue of oil bonds by the Government and discounts from upstream companies like ONGC and GAIL.

Refining margins may continue to be high because of a shortage of petrol and diesel globally and higher capacity utilization of refineries. Refining margins are continuing to increase almost in tandem with crude oil. With the dwindling inventories the world over, petrol and diesel prices have gone up to over $120/bbl over the last two months, leading to healthy margins for oil refiners (Net Worth, Stock Broking Ltd, 2007).

Natural Gas Marketing

Because natural gas must be compressed/condensed under pressure (or else it will dissipate), commercializing (marketing) of remote gas inevitably involves heavy investment in creating right kind of downstream facilities. One obvious option is liquefied natural gas (LNG), where the gas is converted in situ to a more easily transportable liquid with reduction of bulk. Another approach is to bring demand to the gas field by building, for example, a fertilizer plant in the remote location. The high-value fertilizer can then be economically transported to the consuming area.

Unlike crude oil, it is not feasible to build surface storage facilities for gas. Gas is, in effect, stored in the reservoir and not produced until it can be consumed. Underground gas storage usually using depleted gas fields near the market, is a variant of this. In the U.S., the bulk of gas production is in the southwest of the country while the population and consumption is concentrated in the northeast. Demand is highest in the winter, so the pipeline operates at maximum rates during cold weather. In the summer, when demand slows down, production is normally reduced and the pipeline operates at reduced levels. With the underground storage facility, the pipeline throughput is kept high. When the gas reaches the northeast, instead of being consumed, it is injected into the subsurface storage reservoir. During the next winter the gas is produced out of storage to augment the gas coming-up in the pipeline.

With remote gas developments the gas reserves are totally committed to the project, which may last 20 years or longer. This pattern prevails throughout most of the world. In recent years however the gas industry in the U.S. has become a great deal more flexible. Deregulation of the industry has freed up pricing, so short-term markets for gas, even "spot" markets, and have now developed. The contract chain has been altered so that the producer no longer must sell its gas to the pipeline company, who then sells it to the consumer. Instead, the producer and consumer can make the deal direct *or* through intermediary trading companies, and hire the pipeline to transport it. This flexibility and efficiency is benefiting all parties. 'Gas futures' are now being traded in financial derivative markets, much the same way as are crude futures. Companies have become quite sophisticated in hedging to cushion themselves from possible financial losses arising out of short-term gas price fluctuations in the international oil market.

LPG Marketing by Public Sector Oil Marketing Companies (OMCs)

Four Public Sector Oil Marketing Companies (OMCs) viz., Indian Oil Corporation Limited, Bharat Petroleum Corporation Limited, Hindustan Petroleum Corporation Limited and IBP Co. Limited are engaged in marketing of LPG in the country. With increased availability of LPG, the number of LPG customers enrolled by them has also been increasing. The number of LPG customers served by them, as on 1.4.2005, was about 845 lakh through their network of 9,001 LPG distributors. Consequent upon liquidation of LPG waiting list in urban areas and availability of new LPG connections across the counter, in existing markets throughout the country, OMCs had set the target for release of about 63 lakh new LPG connections during financial year 2004-05 with a thrust on smaller towns/rural areas which were hitherto virgin markets. OMCs have already commissioned 535 distributorships. During the year 2004-05, OMCs had released about 73 lakh new LPG connections and commissioned 675 LPG distributorships.

Marketing of Mini-LPG Cylinders by OMCs

PSU Oil Companies had launched 5 Kg cylinders on 16th August 2002 at Shimla, Himachal Pradesh. Since then, scheme has been expanded to all other States as per demand of product. Basic purpose for launching 5 Kg cylinder was that the small size LPG cylinder in the domestic sector will help in fulfilling the demand of low income groups in urban, semi-urban and rural pockets and also extend reach to hilly terrain and interior areas on account of convenience in transportation. The LPG connection with 5 Kg domestic cylinder in terms of deposit of Rs. 350 per cylinder and low cost of refills costing approximately Rs. 110 is affordable for the low income groups. This will also help in meeting the requirement of economically weaker sections of the society for LPG refills and help in restricting deforestation, ensuring pollution-free, happy and healthy environment. During the year 2004-05, OMCs had released about 1 lakh number of 5 Kg connections in 27 States and 2 UTs. Total customers of 5 kg cylinders are about 2.42 lakh with OMCs as on 1.4.2005.

Promoting LPG as Auto-Fuel

Government has permitted the use of LPG, being a clean and eco-friendly fuel, as an auto fuel. For this purpose, MOP&NG along with other concerned Ministries/departments has formulated necessary Legislative and Regulatory framework for safe usage of LPG as an automotive fuel. The Supreme Court has mandated conversion of old vehicles to LPG/CNG in cities which are equally or more polluted than Delhi like Ahmedabad, Agra, Bangalore, Chennai, Hyderabad, Kanpur, Kolkata, Lucknow, Mumbai, Pune, Surat and Sholapur.

Public Sector Oil Companies had initially identified 228 Locations for setting up of Auto LPG Dispensing Stations in various Metros and some other major cities. However, in view of directive of the Supreme Court to oil marketing companies are at present primarily concentrating on increasing their infrastructure in above mentioned cities. As on 1st January, 2005, OMCs have commissioned 99 ALDS in 16 cities and have planned another 60 ALDS to be commissioned in a phased manner. Auto LPG pricing is market determined and there is no subsidy on Auto LPG. At present about 13 manufacturers of Conversion kits for 4 Wheeler vehicles and about 11 manufacturers of Conversion kits for 3 Wheeler vehicles have been approved by various Testing Agencies like ARAI, Pune, VRDE Ahmednagar and IIP, Dehradun.

Parallel Marketing of LPG

In order to increase the availability of LPG and to foster competition, the private sector was allowed to participate in the scheme of parallel marketing of LPG in April 1993 by decimalizing imports of LPG. Under the scheme, a private party can undertake import of LPG after obtaining a rating certificate from one of the approved rating agencies given in the LPG (Regulation of Supply and Distribution) Order, 2000. Under PMS LPG is to be sold at market-determined prices by the private parties. LPG imports during 2004-05 have been about 265.3 TMT against about 216.3 TMT during the last year. Recently Government have authorized ONGC, GAIL and RIL to market their seasonally surplus LPG through parallel marketing system or directly. Likewise, Government has authorized RIL and MRPL to sell SKO directly at market price, after meeting PDS requirement projected by OMCs.

Marketing of Transporation Fuels

As a consequence of dismantling the APM and allowing competition, Government have granted the authorization to market transportation fuels in favour of new entrants namely; Oil and Natural Gas Corporation Limited (ONGC), Mangalore Refinery and Petrochemicals Limited (MRPL) and Numaligarh Refinery Limited (NRL) (All Public Sector Oil Companies) and M/s. Reliance Petroleum Limited (RIL), M/s. Essar Oil Limited (EOL) and M/s. Shell India Pvt. Ltd (SIMPL).

The details of the Retail Outlets being set up by new entrants are as under:

Name of Company	Number of Retail Outlets	Commissioned as on date (17.2.2004)
ONGC	1,100	Nil
NRL	510	04
RIL	5,849	243
EOL	1,700	153
MRPL	500	Nil
SIMPL	2,000	Nil
Total	**11,659**	**400**

Petro-Retail Outlets in sufficient numbers would be set up by these companies as per their commercial considerations subject to the condition that they would set up at least 5.6% of the retail outlets in remote areas and at least 5.3% of their retails outlets in low service areas. Further they would abide by other marketing service obligations and retail service obligations as notified by the Government from time to time.

Refined and Petro-chemical Product Marketing

Plant operators not only have to organize and procure their slate of feed-stocks, they also have to keep the products they produce moving smoothly out to retail markets. Although temporary storage of excess liquid products, is more feasible than storage of natural gas, the available storage capacity is I miniscule compared to the enormous volume of petroleum products moving through the system. This smoothly running enterprise again depends on well-developed markets for traders to easily dispose of their surpluses and. pick up their shortfalls. As with crude oil, there is no particular attempt made by refiners to move the gasoline they produce through their *own* service stations only. Instead, a Gulf Coast refiner would typically deliver its surplus gasoline to other marketers in the immediate area in trade for similar volumes received from other refiners on the east coast, west coast, and elsewhere. This saves the cost of physically moving the products around the country, so everyone benefits.

Products are transported from plants by truck, barge, ocean-going ship, and pipeline. A pipeline can handle a variety of different products introduced as sequential batches. Some mixing occurs at the batch interfaces and this material is reprocessed. LPG is produced not only as a refinery byproduct, but also direct from gas wells. As a byproduct, its production volumes are not determined by its own demand, but rather by the demand for gasoline and natural gas. As a result, the LPG market is notoriously cyclic, swinging rapidly from surplus to deficit and back again. It is therefore necessary to have more LPG storage capacity than for other products. On the U.S. Gulf Coast and elsewhere around the world, this has been accomplished by washing out caverns in sub-surface salt formations.

Trading of Oil and Natural Gas

Deregulation of the natural gas industry and pricing set by supply and demand, has opened the industry to traders. As in any commodity market, traders try to buy low and sell high to turn a profit; gas is bought and sold as a commodity. Pipelines providing basic transportation of gas from one location to another connect regions of supply to market areas. Some pipelines bridge the gap between other pipelines or storage areas. Finally, the gas reaches end users. It is here, at the burner-tip or burning point, that the now of gas stops and it is consumed.

There are several types of end users-some of which arc regulated, depending on what type of business they are in. For example, local distribution companies (LDC) provide a pipeline or distribution system and gas supply for consumers in towns and cities. Since LDCs are considered public utilities, they arc subjected to rate approval and regulation by their slate Public Utility Commission (PUC) Other end users include nnn-regulated industrial consumers that burn gas to generate heat, powering machines that manufacture their products, Cogeneration plants use natural gas to produce heat, creating steam that in turn generates electricity. The Commercial end-users burn gas to provide space, heat, hot-water as well as power for air-conditioning units. These consumers include offices, schools, hotels, and restaurants.

Electric utilities are the single largest end users of natural gas in terms of the volume of natural gas consumed per user. They burn large quantities of natural gas to generate electricity, which they then sell to electricity buyers. Because they are utilities, the price they can charge for electricity is regulated by their state PUC.

This is in the process of changing as the electricity industry undergoes deregulation, and the price of electricity will also be set by supply and demand. Electricity is already traded as a commodity on a limited basis, and some states are well on the way to deregulating their industry. This means if natural gas prices rise to the point that it is no longer economical to make the energy conversion to electricity-based on the price received for the electricity-the utility will switch to alternate fuels or generate more power from facilities that burn other fuels such as coal or nuclear energy.

Although they are neither producers nor end users, marketing companies play a big role in the business activity on a pipeline. Also called resellers or third parries, they are in the business of capturing profits from opportunities presented. Their best-known function here is as trading companies buying and reselling natural gas for a profit. These companies are not paid a fee by any one, but earn the difference between the price they pay for gas and the price at which they sell it. As a result of deregulation, my company is free to buy and sell natural gas to anyone. In addition, it is entitled to contract for pipeline capacity on almost any pipeline system. The ability to enter the market with opportunities like these has led to the explosive growth in the number of natural gas trading companies.

Each day trading companies look for areas of excess supply or high demand. If they find the region that is temporarily oversupplied, e.g., they can inexpensively buy and take title to the supply when they sell and transfer title to another party, they capture a profitable spread in between. Transactions like this can occur either at the same place or where the gas is consumed. The goal is the spread.

Service, marketing, and trading companies are important to the natural gas Industry for several reasons. As service providers, they perform necessary administrative business procedures, at a low cost, for companies that don't have established departments or the know-how to perform them. As traders, they keep supply and demand in balance by searching for profitable arbitrage opportunities where there are discrepancies.

Import and Export of Petroleum

India's Gross import bill of petroleum products, valued at Rs.131756 crore during 2004-05 was almost four times as much as the export bill valued at Rs. 28386 crore, as may be seen in Table 9.1. The quantum of sale of Petroleum products during 2002-05 by the public sector companies/government undertakings was 5 times higher than the private sector enterprises, as cited in Table 9.2.

Table 9.1: Imports / Exports of Crude Oil and Petroleum Products

(Qty: '000' Tonne, Value: Rs. Crore)

Item	2001-02		2002-03		2003-04		2004-05*	
	Qty.	Value	Qty.	Value	Qty.	Value	Qty.	Value
GROSS IMPORTS								
A. Crude Oil	78706	60397	81989	76195	90434	83528	95857	116806
B. Petroleum Products								
I. Light Distillates	3967	4287	3857	5418	4529	6034	5419	10015
1. LPG	659	810	1073	1867	1708	2558	2362	4455
2. MS	0	0	0	0	0	0	233	501
3. Naphtha	3308	3477	2784	3551	2371	2884	2214	4029
4. Propane/MTBE	0	0	0	0	450	592	610	1030
II. Middle Distillates	424	425	806	934	906	1015	1079	2123
1. ATF	2	92	72	9	3	14		
2. SKO	391	388	698	808	804	890	210	429
3. HSD	31	28	106	119	100	116	866	1680
III. Heavy Ends	2618	2537	2565	2495	2566	2674	2374	2812
1. FO/LSHS	1425	1030	1256	1084	953	810	761	709
2. Lubes/Others[HEI]	1193	1507	1309	1411	1613	1864	1613	2103
Total (B)	7009	7249	7228	8847	8001	9723	8872	14950
Grand Total (A+B)	85715	67646	89217	85042	98435	93251	104729	131756
EXPORTS								
Petroleum Products								
I. Light Distillates	5008	4927	4493	5475	5448	7100	6162	11188
1. LPG	0	0	0	0	0	0	69	110
2. MS	2406	2570	2336	3011	2979	4021	2836	5475
3. Naphtha	2515	2234	2067	2325	2176	2653	2926	5030
4. TAME	87	123	90	139	83	117	0	0
5. Reformate	0	0	0	0	210	309	331	573
II. Middle Distillates	3084	2747	3875	4337	7841	8713	9440	15507
1. SKO	0	0	0	0	0	0	11	22
2. HSD/LDO	2890	2571	3178	3547	6181	6763	7001	11165
3. ATF	194	176	697	790	1660	1950	2428	4320
III. Heavy Ends	1973	545	1921	1056	1331	968	1922	1691
1. FO/LSHS	482	255	1120	902	1310	928	1781	1504
2. VGO/Lubes	272	211	101	109	17	36	99	125
3. Coke/Bitumen/ White Oil/Paraffin	1219	79	700	45	4	4	42	62
Total	10065	8219	10289	10868	14620	16781	17524	28386
NET IMPORTS								
A. Crude Oil	78706	60397	81989	76195	90434	83528	95857	116806
B. Pol. Products	-3056	-970	-3061	-2021	-6619	-7058	-8652	-13436
Grand Total	75650	59427	78928	74174	83815	76470	87205	103370

TAME: Tertiary Amyl Methyl Ether; *: Provisional.

HEI: Includes Bitumen. Lube Oil Base Stock, Low Sulphur Waxy Residue. Carbon Black Feed Stock, Rubber Processing Oil and Paraffin Wax.

Source: Petroleum Planning & Analysis Cell, New Delhi.

Table 9.2: Sales Performance of Petroleum Products in Public and Private Sectors

(000' Tonne)

	Products	1996-97	1997-98	1998-99	1999-00	2000-01	2001-02	2002-03	2003-04	2004-05
					A. PUBLIC SECTOR					
1	**Light Distillates**	14384	15742	17958	20473	21770	22916	23567	25002	25317
	LPG	4184	4581	5041	6029	6613	7310	8143	9089	9967
	Mogas	4955	5182	5507	5909	6613	7011	7570	7895	8162
	Naphtha	4015	4716	6652	7970	8059	8128	7284	7329	6550
	NGL	682	768	330	91	6	27	32	0	0
	Others	548	495	428	474	479	440	538	689	638
2	**Middle Distillates**	48544	49716	51686	54259	52854	50661	50555	50548	51923
	SKO	9646	9878	10599	10731	10714	10114	9707	9426	9393
	ATF	2154	2108	2112	2197	2249	2256	2269	2484	2811
	HSDO	35019	36071	37217	39287	37938	36515	36534	36875	38091
	LDO	1223	1235	1278	1512	1399	1202	1413	1181	1086
	Others	502	424	480	532	554	574	632	582	542
3	**Heavy Ends**	14296	14380	15122	15919	15362	15515	16002	16580	17360
	FO/LSHS	10847	10974	11304	11579	11360	11616	11652	11840	12461
	Lubes/Greases	705	835	885	915	797	819	938	816	779
	Bitumen	2273	2178	2412	2879	2618	2428	2847	3367	3318
	Petroleum Coke	276	227	315	328	414	367	335	308	445
	Paraffin Wax	58	28	36	53	43	45	41	41	60
	Other Waxes	57	45	76	89	62	51	13	20	20
	Others	80	93	94	76	68	189	176	188	277
	Total (A) (Excl. RBF)	77224	79838	84766	90651	89986	89092	90124	92130	94600
					B. PRIVATE SECTOR					
1	**Light Distillates**	160	2124	2573	4058	7544	6702	8188	9333	10087
	LPG	83	222	311	392	403	418	208	216	236
	MS	0	0	0	0	0	0	2		89
	Naphtha/NGL	15	1874	2239	2831	3614	3600	4645	4539	7443
	Benzene	0	0	23	33	8	0	0	0	0
	Others	62	28	0	802	3519	2684	3335	4576	2319
2	**Middle Distillates**	507	1187	1644	1175	613	778	1510	1475	1987
	SKO	507	1187	1644	1167	593	318	698	804	0
	HSDO	0	0	0	8	20	31	110	199	1564
	LDO	0	0	0	0	0	390	650	438	391
	Others	0	0	0	0	0	39	52	34	32
3	**Heavy Ends**	1277	1141	1579	1202	1931	3860	4304	4813	4887
	Furnace Oil/LSHS	660	517	1206	874	1293	1366	1086	1105	1099
	Lubes/Greases	308	246	212	328	246	318	312	611	538
	Bitumen	0	0	0	0	96	156	139	6	21
	Raw Petroleum Coke	0	0	78	0	34	1431	2228	2569	2684
	CBFS	0	0	83	0	230	75	74	230	243
	Others	309	378	0	0	32	514	465	292	302
	Total (B)	1944	4452	5796	6435	10088	11340	14002	15621	16961
	Total (A+B)	79168	84290	90562	97086	100074	100432	104126	107751	111561

Source: Petroleum Planning & Analysis Cell, Government of India, New Delhi.

Supply Strategy

North America, for instance, has an abundant supply of this particular natural resource. Much of our natural gas comes from a few regions and must be transported for use. Some is less expensive to produce because it is found in shallower depths, and some is more expensive because it is more difficult to drill.

But the biggest factor affecting supply in North America is price. The higher natural gas prices are the more incentive producers have to look for more supplies. As prices fall, wells that are only marginally profitable will be closed to ensure that maintenance and production costs do not exceed sales revenue. Also the risk of loss in new drilling projects increases relative to the potential reward when evaluating prospective wells. Natural disasters can temporarily affect supply. Due to the vast amount of production in offshore wells in the Gulf of Mexico, hurricanes pose a threat to the stability of this supply region. Whenever a hurricane threatens, producers evacuate workers and stop production. This causes a temporary shortage. If a storm actually damages these rigs, as Hurricane Andrew did in 1992, shortages become more serious. During Andrew, several rigs were damaged and made inoperable, and supply couldn't be restored for about six months Natural gas prices soared as buyers scrambled to replace lost supply. During the outage, supply from throughout the U.S. and Canada was re-routed to make up for the lost supply from the Gulf of Mexico area. Prices around the country continued to rise as demand outweighed supply. However, when production from the damaged rigs resumed, supply caught up with demand and natural gas prices gradually fell back to pre-disaster levels. On a smaller scale, wellheads can freeze during prolonged periods of intense cold weather. When this happens, the wells in a specific production area become inoperable and the supply from that region is temporarily unavailable to the market. As temperatures return to normal, production is restored, and the gas is again available to the market. The relative Industry-wise position of off-take of Natural Gas in India is given in Table 9.3. The Power generation and Natural gas as industrial fuel occupy prominent positions. In non-energy sector, Fertilizer industry and Petro-chemical industry are the two major consumers of Natural gas.

In India industry-wise off-take of natural gas can be seen from Table 9.3; where it could be seen that whereas the consumption in the energy sector was 21328 MCM, in the non-energy-sector the consumption of natural gas was much lower at 9446 MCM during 2004-05, which in effect maintained a 70; 30% ratio. In a period of 15 years (1990-2005) the LPG market in India has expanded by almost 5 folds in terms of volume and value of total sales (Table 9.4 refers). The status of growth of LPG industries in India is shown in Table 9.5. It is observed that there has been almost five fold increase both in production and consumption of LPGs during the period 1990-2005.

Demand Profile

The demand side of the natural gas market is more dynamic than one might expect. Natural gas has more uses than just heating and air conditioning although natural gas is primarily used as a fuel to generate heat; there are also more obscure uses. Crude oil producers in California will sometimes use natural gas to extract more crude oil from old, low-pressure wells. This is accomplished by injecting highly pressurized natural gas into the ground beneath the oil reserves to increase

Table 9.3: Industry-wise Off-take of Natural Gas in India

(Million Cubic Metre)

Industry	1990-91	1995-96@	2000-01	2001-02	2002-03	2003-04	2004-05
(a) Energy Purposes							
1. Power Generation	3634	6836	8801	9214	10510	11478	12099
2. Industrial Fuel	827	2301	2870	2979	2939	3099	3569
3. Tea Plantation	89	111	151	147	119	142	142
4. Domestic Fuel	50	178	335	485	654	93	343
5. Captive use/LPG Shrinkage	1775	589	5004	5339	5409	4865	4944
6. Others	0	0	38	70	136	1263	231
Total (a)	6375	10015	17199	18234	19767	20940	21328
(b) Non-Energy Purposes							
1. Fertilizer Industry	5612	7602	8480	7957	7955	7889	8173
2. Petro-Chemicals	409	474	779	909	1027	1128	1236
3. CNG	0	0	0	0	0	1	0
4. Others	370	0	1402	937	1215	948	37
Total (b)	6391	8076	10661	9803	10197	9966	9446
Grand Total (a+b)	12766	18091	27860	28037	29964	30906	30774
%age to Grand Total Energy Purposes	49.9	55.4	61.7	65.0	66.0	67.8	69.3
Non-Energy Purposes	501	44.6	38.3	35.0	34.0	32.2	30.7

@: Excludes offtakes of natural gas by ONGC.
Source: ONGC, OIL, DGH and GAIL.

Table 9.4: Marketing of Petroleum Products by Oil Companies

Item	Unit	1990-91	1999-00	2000-01	2001-02	2002-03	2003-04	2004-05*
1. Total Sales (excl. RBF)	Mn. Tonne	55.04	97.09	100.07	100.43	104.13	107.75	111.56
2. Percentage Share								
IOC/AOD	%	57.1	50.9	47.8	46.9	44.5	43.4	43.0
BPCL	%	18.9	19.5	19.4	19.0	19.1	18.8	18.5
HPCL	%	19.2	18.0	17.9	17.4	17.5	17.2	17.1
Others (PSUs)	%	4.8	5.0	4.8	5.4	5.5	6.1	6.2
Private Parties	%	Nil	6.6	10.1	11.3	13.4	14.5	15.2
Total	%	100.0	100.0	100.0	100.0	100.0	100.0	100.0

*: Provisional.
RBF: Refinery Boiler Fuel.
Source: Petroleum Planning and Analysis Cell.

the crude oil reserve pressure. This type of use accounts for only a tiny fraction of overall demand, however Industrial companies represent the largest portion of natural gas demand, powering machines and heavy equipment. Residential consumption also accounts for a large portion of total natural gas demand.

Table 9.5: Growth in LPG Marketing in India

Item	Unit	1990-91	1995-96	2000-01	2001-02	2002-03	2003-04	2004-05*
Consumption (PSU/Pvt.)	(TMT)	2415	3849	7016	7728	8351	9305	10182
LPG Customers (PSUs)@	(Lac)	169.8	257	579	635	700	772	845
LPG Distributors (PSUs)@	(No.)	3930	5165	6477	7486	7910	8325	9001
LPG Markets (PSUs)@	(No.)	1669	2018	2604	3209	3438	3669	4105
Enrolment	(Lac)	6.30	20.54	107.17	60.75	67.1	78.1	73.0
Indigenous Production (PSU/Pvt)	(TMT)	2150	3254	6133	6983	7273	7668	7809
of which								
(a) Refineries	(TMT)	1221	1539	4088	4778	4903	5348	5569
(b) Fractionators	(TMT)	929	1715	2045	2205	2370	2320	2240
Imports (PSU/Pvt.)	(TMT)	329	678	853	659	1073	1708	2362
Bottling Capacity@	(TMTPA)	2503	3182	5595	6263	6840	7402	7702

*. Provisional.
@: Year end position.
Source: Public Sector Undertakings.

Residential consumption is very straightforward-home heating, or as a fuel for stoves, fireplaces, and hot water heating tanks. Power generation is the third largest market for natural gas. Electric utilities and independent power produces use natural gas to power gas-fired turbines to generate electricity.

The level of demand for natural gas rises and falls as a result of changes in price for several other reasons as well. By far the most important force altering the level of demand is weather. The economy also effects demand. A strong economy that generates demand for steel products, for example, will cause steel manufacturers to run their equipment at maximum capacity to manufacture additional products. Their demand for natural gas increases as they use it to heat ovens over additional work shifts. Demand for gas, in terms of consumption, is less sensitive to changes in price than the supply is. This is true as prices increase, but even more apparent when prices decrease. That is due to the nature of this uses for natural gas, more consumers do not eagerly rush into the market to buy if prices fall. However, if prices fall to a certain level, it is not uncommon for producers to shut-in wells in a matter of a few hours.

Transportation Mechanism of Pipeline Nominations

A pipeline nomination is a notification given by a third party shipper to a pipeline. It requests the pipeline recognize, account for, and physically implement a transportation transaction for that shipper. If the shipper is planning to transport gas on a particular pipeline from point A to point B, it must notify that pipeline of its intentions through a nomination. A nomination must include all details needed to ensure that the pipeline can perform the requested service properly Nominations generally include:

1. Shipper's transportation contract number
2. Delivering party's transportation contract number

3. Start date
4. Stop date
5. Shipper's receipt location
6. Shipper's receipt amount
7. Shipper's Delivered amount
8. Shipper's delivered amount
9. Receiving party's transportation contract number.

Because natural gas transactions are done on a daily basis, natural gas pipelines monitor their systems on a day-to-day basis as well. With little variation, physical operators of wellheads, gathering systems, and the pipelines themselves begin measuring and accounting for volumes flowing through their respective systems at 7 A.M. central time and end at 7 A.M. the following day. The typical nomination deadline is 10 A.M. central time for gas to flow the following day As a result of these deadlines, trading activity is busiest in the early morning hours as traders conduct their business for the following day.

Once it receives a nomination from a shipper, the pipeline follows a confirmation procedure, matching all the details of the shipping party to those of the delivering party, and the details of the delivering party to the details of the receiving party If any of the relevant information does not match, the nomination will not be confirmed and must be resubmitted.

Once a nomination is confirmed, the pipeline schedules the gas to flow. It notifies its operations personnel to expect the amount of the gas in the shippers nomination to flow through the shippers designated receipt meter and the shipper's designated delivery meter on the start date and every day thereafter until further notice There is typically more gas flowing through meters other than the amount in one shipper's nomination, so pipeline operators designate the amount specified in the shipper's nomination at a particular meter as "gas supply intended for the shipper's account".

In the day-to-day market for physical natural gas, buyers and sellers conduct the majority of their transactions with each other over the telephone. Electronic bulletin boards are available for physical trades to be cleared at a few major trading points by third-parry operators. Natural gas traders maintain lists of contacts at other companies whom they know to be traders of gas on a particular pipeline, at a specific point, or in a designated region of the country. It is through these contacts that most transactions are done and market information is disseminated.

Although the daily market for natural gas is active, the majority of gas trading occurs during the last week of each month. This period of time is known in the industry as bid-week It is the time when market participants buy and sell the majority of their gas requirements and available volumes of gas for the following month. Gas transactions are prepared in terms of volume per day, but the standard industry practice is to deal for a month at a time. During bid-week, trading volume is heaviest as producers try to sell their core supply, end users try to buy for their core needs, and marketing companies try to get in between the two.

Electricity is also traded as a commodity on a limited basis, but the volume of trading is increasing. As deregulation progresses, it should one day mirror natural gas trading. Commodity status is one of the many similarities between the natural gas and the electric industries, and these similarities are pulling the industries together. Similar knowledge and skills are helpful in trading both electricity and natural gas. In fact, most .of the pioneers in the electric trading market was the gas traders.

Pipeline Economics

Economics of scale are the major element in pipeline economies. From a theoretical point of view, doubling the pipeline diameter will tend to increase the amount delivered by more than fourfold in a given period of time-other factors remaining constant. This implies that total cost might double while the cost per unit delivered would decline.

At the construction and operation stages, pipeline economics involve two cost elements: initial capital cost and operating cost. Pipeline construction in costs constituted about 40% of total investment. These costs vary among diameter classifications and are affected by geographic location, terrain and pipe length. It has been noted that the cost per mile for a given diameter is lower where the pipeline is longer.

The major cost components of pipeline construction are material, labor and right-of-way damages. In most cases, material and labor account for more than 75% of construction cost. As to the pipeline operating costs, they seem to vary among different sizes, uses and locations. For example, total operating costs for the U.S. interstate natural gas pipelines were estimated by natural gas companies to be $3.41 billion in 1985. A major part of operating costs is the cost of pipeline power consumption. This figure has grown manifold in next two decades due to partial replacement of industrial use of oil by natural gas in the industrial and transport sectors in the USA.

LNG Transportation Policy of GOI (FOB)

Background

According to the Hydrocarbon Vision 2025 envisaged by the Government of India, by the year 2012, the demand for LNG in the country would be to the tune of 300 MMSCMD which would increase to 400 MMSCMD by 2025. As against this, currently the availability of domestic gas is 75-100 MMSCMD which is expected to remain static in future. The extrapolation of demand and supply of LNG for future suggests that in the year 2012, the country would require to import 200 MMSCMD of gas while in 2025 the import would be even higher at 300 MMSCMD. To make these imports realize, by 2012, we would need 22 LNG vessels while by 2025, 34 LNG vessels would be required. With the kind of need we have, the industry has started talking of FOB policy as in due course of time, it is likely to become a strategic necessity.

Description	2012	2025
Demand	300 MMSCMD	400 MMSCMD
Availability	75-100 MMSCMD	75-100 MMSCMD
Import Needed	200 MMSCMD	300 MMSCMD
LNG Vessels needed	22	34

Source: Hydrocarbon Vision: 2005.

LNG Transportation Policy

LNG is the fuel of the future. It is a strategic commodity. Today, it has become the lifeline of India's power and agriculture (fertilizer) sector. In such a situation, it becomes imperative that India must exercise control over LNG shipping in times of war and scarcity. Such a control over LNG shipping would work in favour of meeting national energy security requirements. It would also deter monopoly of suppliers and international shipping companies.

Rationale for FOB

The Free-on-Board basis results in lower delivered cost to buyer for long-term supply contracts. It is simply because the risk and profit element associated with the LNG transportation is removed from the supplier's list of responsibilities. The FOB imports also ensure flexibility of gas sourcing which results in competitive pricing of gas. FOB basis by controlling shipping enables LNG buyer (importer) to better address the huge 'Take or Pay' obligations for LNG Sale and Purchase Agreement (SPA). Control over long-term shipping moderates the freight level for the country.

LNG Carriage Cost—Indian Flag vs. Foreign Flag

Indian shipping has recently been granted a globally competitive Income Tax regime that is Tonnage Tax. However, ship owning firms in India are still subject to other forms of direct and indirect taxation such as Dividend distribution tax, Withholding tax, Service tax, Fringe benefit tax etc. A foreign flagged vessel may be exempt from all such taxes if owned in a tax-free jurisdiction. If we take the current Indian Tax Regime into account, the cost impact per day per mBtu would be as under:

Dividend tax	$ 931.50
Withholding tax	$ 3109.59
Tonnage tax	$ 45.67
Service tax	$ 139.73
Total Additional Tax	**$ 4226.49**
Total annual outgo per ship	$1.543 million
Additional cost per ton	$ 0.617
Additional cost per MMBTU	$0.0134 or 1.34 cents

Incremental cost of shipping on account of Indian taxes would be approximately 1.34 cents per mBtu. Assuming an FOB cost of $2.53 per mBtu and the cost of shipping at 27 cents per mBtu the landed cost would be $2.80. The incremental cost of 1.34 cents, on account of Indian taxation would hence be 5 per cent of the shipping cost and a mere 0.5 per cent of landed cost. The government may exempt Indian shipping companies from the above taxes so that costs differential between Indian and foreign flag vessels are eliminated. It may be pertinent to mention here that Indian shipping companies were in the past exempted from Withholding Tax vide Section 10(15)(4)(C) of Income Tax Act until June 2001.

Indian Flag—Value Addition to the Nation

The Rakesh Mohan Committee Report in its report has well amplified the significance of national tonnage.

TERI Report

- Gross Register Tonnage (GRT) = Gross Value Added (GVA) to the economy of Rs 2211
- 1 per cent change in GRT = 0.0068 per cent change in GDP

Under the Indian Tonnage Tax regime, it is mandatory to invest 20 per cent of book profit into additional tonnage acquisition. If LNG is permitted to be imported on foreign flag vessels, then this opportunity of national fleet expansion and value additions thereof are totally lost.

It has been calculated that for every 8 years, 1 VLCC can be added to the Indian fleet for every 1 LNG carrier owned under Indian flag, which is a huge value addition of Rs 33.32 crore (assuming 150,000 GT for 1 VLCC × Rs 2211). In other words, the country will lose 1 VLCC or Rs 33.32 crore every 8 years for every single foreign flagged LNG vessel employed.

According to Hydrocarbon Vision 2025, about 56 million tonne per annum and 84 MTPA respectively of NG will be required by 2012 and 2025. This will be about 22 and 34 LNG ships respectively. Thus from year 2025, 33 VLCCs (22×1.5 VLCCs) value addition to the Indian economy will be to the tune of Rs 1095.6 crore per year.

LNG shipping closely controlled either by importing countries (Japan, South Korea, Spain) or exporting countries (Algeria, UAE, Malaysia, Brunei, Qatar). Control of shipping offers opportunity not only to conserve freight outgo but also to effectively control the FOB cost of LNG imports, through diversification of supply sources.

Japan, Korea strongly encourage not only LNG ship owning, but also shipbuilding.

Major importing countries and their tonnage as of end-2003:

Country	LNG imports in 2002 (in '000 tonne)	Number of ships required	Ships under national ownership	Ships under co-ownership/JV
Japan	54,000	47	25	14 (Co-ownership) 30 (Joint venture)
South Korea	18,000	16	17	

Control over LNG shipping will provide long-term fiscal and energy security benefits. Incremental cost of Indian flag tonnage is virtually non-existent (0.5% of landed cost) and exists only due to taxation and government levies. Value addition through the growth of Indian fleet is substantial and outweighs any marginal cost on account of Indian flag. In the wake of all these issues, it is not a matter of surprise that the Indian shipping industry has been demanding an LNG policy based on Indian flag tonnage on FOB basis.

Asian Gas Market Overview

The final market overview segment is the emergence of an increasingly important natural gas market in Asia. This growing importance of natural gas in Asia's energy mix is being driven by a variety of factors, including the abundance of gas within the region, environmental considerations, the drive to use domestic energy resources wherever possible, and efforts to diversify sources of energy supply away from dependence on Middle East oil.

Importance of Natural Gas in Asia's Energy Supply Chain

The coincidence of five factors is driving rapid growth in the consumption of natural gas in Asia:

Resources: The proven reserves of natural gas in Asia have increased by 43 per cent over the last decade and now amount to 10.2 trillion cubic meters (TCM)-over 35 years supply at the current region-wide demand rate of 294 BCM per year and over 41 years supply at current regional production levels.

Technology: Ongoing developments in the technology for combined cycle gas turbine systems combined with their lower capital costs and shorter development cycles compared to coal fired plants have opened vast new applications for gas in power generation.

Environment: Major Asian countries are getting serious about local environmental quality, and natural gas provides a cost-effective means of improving air quality.

Nuclear concerns: Growing public concern over the safety of nuclear power in Japan, Korea, and Taiwan will slow nuclear power development in all three countries, opening yet further markets for natural gas.

LNG costs: The cost of new LNG facilities is declining, making LNG a more competitive fuel.

Asia's Natural Gas Supply and Demand

The results of these driving forces is that natural gas demand in Asia is projected to grow from the current level of about 225 billion cubic meters per year to over 600 billion cubic meters by 2020. This represents growth rates at an average annual rate of 6 per cent through 2010 and 4.5 to 5 per cent for the following decade. The extensive use of combined cycle gas turbine systems in the power sector will account for about two-thirds of that total growth in gas demand. On a

Fig. 9.1: Total Asia Gas Demand Profile

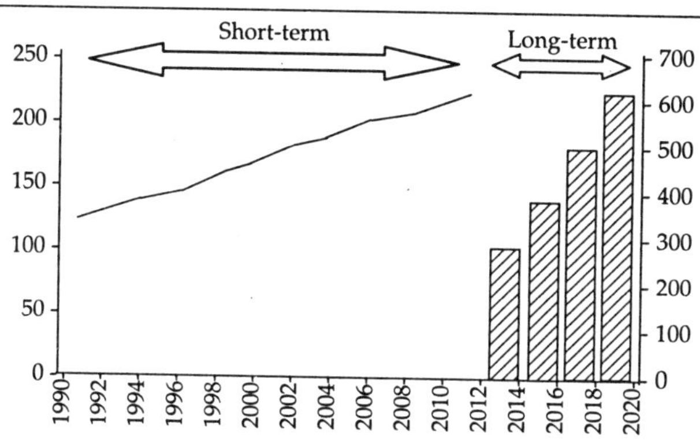

Annual Growth Rates

	Gas Demand	GDP
1990-1995	6.4	3.8
1996-2000	5.1	2.6
2001-2010	6.2	4.1
2011-2020	4.9	4.5

Source: Cambridge Energy Research Associates

regional basis, the development of new gas productive capacity in the region will mirror demand developments over at least the next decade, creating increased competition in the market as supplies from the Middle East and eventually from Russia increasingly compete for the regional market. Key gas resources that will be developed in the region include Bangladesh (Bay of Bengal), Indonesia (expansions in Bontang, Sumatra, and Irian Jaya), Australia (Gorgon, Northwest Shelf, and Bayou Undan), Russia (Sakhalin Island), Malaysia (Tiga), China (Ordos, Sichuan, and Tarim Basins), Vietnam (Nam Con Son), Papua New Guinea, and others.

Global and Regional LNG Supplies Continue to Expand

Of critical importance to India's LNG import plans is the outlook for regional and global liquefaction capacity. In CERA's view, global liquefaction capacity could increase to as much as 235 million tons per year (MTPA) by 2010 from the 1999 level of 102 MTPA. However, this growth assumes that regulatory frameworks and pricing dynamics develop in supportive directions. Planned liquefaction capacity additions in Asia and the Middle East are more than sufficient to meet CERA's projections of demand potential beyond 2010. (Refer Fig. 9.2). Key expansions will be:

Indonesia: Expansion of Bontang, Greenfield project at Irian Jaya (Tanguh), with decline at Arun.

Malaysia: Tiga project already under development.

Brunei: Minor expansion.

Australia: Expansion of Northwest Shelf, Gorgon development, Bayou Undan.

Russia: Sakhalin II Greenfield project.

Fig 9.2: Middle East: Expansions at Qatar, Abu Dhabi, and Oman Greenfield project in Yemen

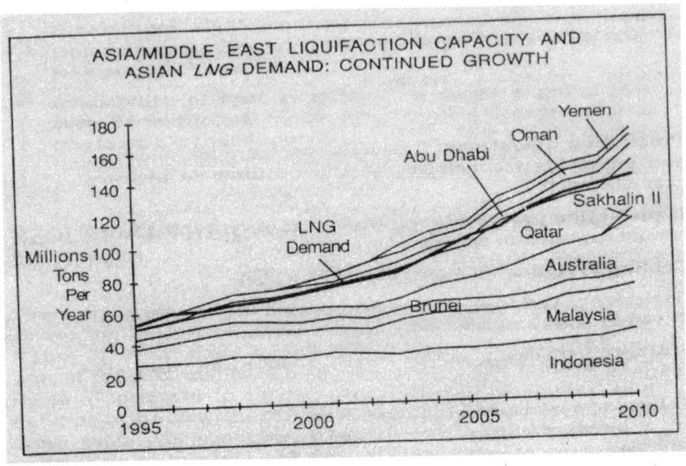

Source: Cambridge Energy Research Associates

Downward Pressure on LNG Prices: A Feature of the Next Decade?

Historically, the development of the LNG business has been based on tightly integrated projects involving all aspects of the LNG value chain from liquefaction to transportation to regassification. This structure has been necessitated by the need to project-finance huge infrastructure projects. In turn this meant long-term take-or-pay contracts, and hence all parties involved in the project required the security of these long-term relationships. CERA expects in the long-run this structure of the LNG industry to change into fundamental directions with lower prices and greater contract flexibility. These changes are driven by new circumstances in both the supply and demand side of LNG trade.

Plentiful supplies: The next 10 years in the LNG business are expected to be a buyer's market, with abundant supplies and aggressive development of a number of large remote gas resources. This will meet aggressive competition among suppliers for new LNG business opportunities.

Reduced costs: LNG development costs are declining as a result of better technology and the increasing competitiveness of LNG markets.

Buyer price pressures: LNG buyers are becoming more cost conscious as they are in turn being pressured by their customers and by their host governments to reduce the cost of energy throughout the value chain. Sellers to Japan's LNG market are already seeing this pressure. Japanese buyers have traditionally been able to directly pass on the cost of LNG to their customers. This, however, is becoming increasingly difficult, particularly for majority of Japan's LNG, which goes into electric power. Japan's power companies are being pressured by their customers and by the Ministry of International Trade and Industry (MITI) to lower the cost 'of power to Japan's industries in order to make those industries more competitive in international markets. The intense pressure to lower tariffs is being reflected directly in the utilities and LNG price negotiations.

Fragmented negotiations: CERA expects that in the near future, the buying practices of Japanese LNG importers will change. The current practice of negotiating *en masse* with sellers will give way to individual negotiation for each LNG importer. This will add to downward pressure on prices.

Buyers seeking greater flexibility: There are increasing buyer demands for increased flexibility to lift schedules in order to avoid future take-or-pay obligations. These demands have arisen from two factors. First, several buyers face take-or-pay obligations as a result of the economic downturn of 1997. They seek to avoid any future repeat of the experience. Second, electric utilities, particularly those in Japan, face uncertainty in future load growth because of the evolution of independent power generators. Under these circumstances, they are more reluctant to make long-term take-or-pay obligations.

Availability of spot supplies: The excess supplies that seem certain to materialize over the next decade will give rise to an expanded spot trade in LNG. This will encourage buyers to demand greater contract flexibility.

OTC Energy and Oil Derivative Markets

Nearly all the key terms of an OTC derivatives deal are negotiable, which means that the pricing reference, the payment terms and the volume can all be adjusted to suit the counterparts to the deal. This is a benefit if an organization has a very specialized or unique price risk which requires a one-off hedging tool. Basically, anything is possible in the OTC energy markets, although, of course, the price of the derivative instrument quoted to suit a customer's precise and perhaps esoteric needs, may not always be attractive. Fortunately, for risk management purposes, the core energy markets, like the larger oil, gas and electricity (power) markets have some active and fairly standardized OTC contracts. They are standard both in their floating price reference, and in the sort of minimum contract volume that would normally be traded. Indeed, the increasing standardization in the plain vanilla OTC markets has led to the development of a number of electronic trading platforms. People often ask why regulated futures exchanges seem to be unable to launch new petroleum futures contracts. The answer is that the needs of the market are already being met by the now well-established and liquid OTC derivatives market. Another supporting factor of this observation is that futures exchanges have been successful in launching futures contracts in both the natural gas and power markets. The reason for this is that the regulated futures markets were launched soon after deregulation prior to or at the same time as an OTC market was establishing itself.

The effectiveness of the OTC market can also be seen in Asia, which overtook Europe as the second largest oil consuming region in the world several years ago. Today, Asia includes the world's second, third, seventh, eighth and ninth largest importers of oil: Japan, Korea, India, China and Taiwan. However, Asia still does not have a liquid and internationally recognized futures exchange for energy market. This is because its needs for energy-related derivatives contracts seem to be well served by the established OTC market, for which Singapore is the key trading hub. There is only one bastion of support for the energy futures industry in Asia, which is the Tokyo Commodity Exchange or TOCOM. It is making great progress with its Middle East crude futures contract and product futures, but the range of market participants and liquidity is still a long way away from that seen on the IPE and the NYMEX. Singapore Exchange launched the TOCOM Middle East crude contract in Singapore but in US dollars and barrels instead of yen and kilolitres in Q4 2002, and it is still not clear whether this will be successful. Rather than trying to create a brand new contract, an interesting approach by SGX has been to create a forex hybrid of the TOCOM Middle East crude contract. Since traders should be able to offset margin calls between the SGX contract (in US$ per barrel) and the TOCOM contract (yen/kilolitres) either at the exchange/ clearing house level or at their clearing broker level, there are interesting opportunities to trade the forex arbitrage between the two contracts, and also to trade the arbitrage between TOCOM and SGX contract with the OTC Dubai/ Oman, WTI Crude Futures on NYMEX and/or Brent Futures on the IPE. Apparently, there is already some speculative trading between the TOCOM Middle East crude contract and the Dubai/Oman OTC swaps arbitrage and also against the WTINYMEX Futures.

The OTC Oil Derivatives Market

The vast majority of physical transactions and OTC swaps are priced using an industry-recognized publication—Platts, which is a division of McGraw-Hill. Platts publishes a daily assessment of the price of any given crude oil or oil product in any given location, according to Platts' own specifications, and also publishes an assessment of the forward curve. These daily value assessments are based on the aggregated bids and offers from many brokers and dealers around the world during a specified time window for each geographic region (usually towards the end of each business day in each major time zone: Asia (Singapore), Europe (London), USA (New York, and then the West Coast). Swaps are usually priced off the monthly average of these Platts assessments and lead to a monthly financial payment equivalent to the difference between the traded fixed price and the calculated average floating price multiplied by the contractual monthly quantity. The main Hubs of OTC Oil derivative markets can be clustered as follows:

- **Asia:** Singapore is the main pricing hub.
- **Europe:** Mediterranean prices, Arab Gulf Prices, North West Europe (NWE) and Amsterdam–Rotterdam–Antwerp (ARA) as the main pricing hubs.
- **USA:** New York Harbor, US Gulf Coast, US West Coast (L.A. Pipeline)

These are some international reference points for oil markets.

Futures and Options Contracts and Markets

Commodity futures contracts are legally binding and negotiable contracts that call for the delivery of agricultural, industrial, or financial commodities in the future, hence the term "futures contract". Options are also legally binding and negotiable contracts that give the holder the right, but not the obligation, to purchase or sell the underlying futures contract at a specified price and time for a one-time premium payment. Futures and options contracts are traded on futures and options markets, which are composed of exchanges and brokers that facilitate the buying and selling of contracts. Commodity futures and options markets are central marketplaces, located primarily in Chicago and New York, although recently markets have developed in such diversified locales as London, Tokyo, Beijing, Frankfurt, Paris, and Sao Paolo. Today there are more than sixty marketplaces worldwide where trading in futures or options contracts occurs (Errera & Brown, 2002).

Futures markets are primarily financial markets that trade commodity futures and options contracts. Even though futures contracts may involve actual delivery of physical commodities, such delivery is a relatively rare occurrence in mature futures markets.

Commodity futures markets in the United States, Canada, Europe, and Asia serve an important economic function. The markets facilitate the transfer of risk among various market participants and in the process reduce risk for producers and processors and improve the flow of commerce.

Commodity futures contracts are traded for a variety of commodities. Agricultural commodities such as wheat and corn have been traded in Chicago since about 1860. During the last fifty years futures contracts have been developed for industrial commodities such as platinum and copper. There are also well-developed futures markets for foreign currencies such as the British pound and the Japanese yen. Contracts on financial instruments such as treasury bonds and Eurodollars are dramatically changing the financial system, while futures contracts on stock indexes and options on commodity futures are dramatically increasing risk-reduction alternatives for commerce.

Yet, the most exciting development in recent years was the introduction of contracts in energy products such as heating oil, crude oil, gasoline, natural gas, and electricity Energy futures contracts are enhancing the operation of the petroleum distribution system and changing the way petroleum is priced worldwide. A complete list of actively traded energy futures contracts is presented in Table 9.5 and a list of actively traded energy options contracts is presented in Table 9.6 (Errera & Brown, 2002).

Participants in futures markets may be classified under two broad categories: commercials and noncommercial (also known as speculators). Commercials are those market participants who own or will own actual commodities and are motivated to use futures markets to reduce the risk of price variation in those commodities. This is called hedging. Noncommercial, or speculators, seek price

Table 9.5: Energy Futures Contracts Trading More Than 100,000 Contracts/Year

Contract	Market	Delivery Point
Crude Oil	New York	Cushing, Oklahoma
Natural Gas	New York	Henry Hub Louisiana
Brent Crude Oil	London	EFP/Cash Settlement
No. 2 Heating Oil	New York	New York Harbor
Unleaded Regular Gasoline	New York	New York Harbor
Gas Oil	London	A. RA. Area
Natural Gas	London	UK NPB

variation risk and in the process attempt to profit from it. This is called speculation. Futures markets are arenas where risk is transferred among market participants.

Table 9.6: Energy Options Contracts Trading More Than 50,000 Options/Year

Option	Market
Crude Oil	New York
Natural Gas	New York
No. 2 Heating Oil	New York
Unleaded Regular Gasoline	New York
Brent Crude Oil	London
Gas Oil	London

Hedging refers to any action taken to reduce risk. Hedging in commodity futures markets is undertaken to reduce the risk of price fluctuations. An example of this kind of price risk is the risk the refiner faces because he does not know when he purchases crude oil what the market price will be for gasoline, heating oil, and residual oil 30 or 60 days later. Another example is the risk the heating oil distributor faces when he contracts with his customers to deliver fuel oil at a fixed price but doesn't know ahead of time at what price he will be able to purchase the heating oil. Changes in the cash or spot market prices of various agricultural and industrial commodities and financial instruments can be hedged in futures markets.

Risk reduction is accomplished by assuming a futures position opposite to the position the hedger has in the underlying commodity. The position in the actual physical commodity is known as a "cash" or "spot" market position. The terms are used interchangeably The combination of the cash and futures positions causes price changes to cancel, and the resultant net position is one in which price changes are reduced or eliminated. This is the essence of hedging.

The opportunity to hedge price risk is valuable to the firm because it allows the firm those hedges to focus on business concerns rather than expending time and energy attempting to forecast prices. Because risk is reduced, the: hedger can typically afford to operate on narrower but mote certain margins. In some instances, profitability is actually increased. In general, by reducing price uncertainty, hedging improves the flow of commerce and ultimately results in lower and more stable prices to the consumer.

Speculators are motivated by profits to participate in futures markets. In the process they perform the economic functions of assuming risk and providing liquidity to the market. The speculator hopes to profit from price changes of various agricultural and other commodities. Speculators use various types of analysis to forecast prices and price changes. They buy when they think prices are too low and sell when they think prices are too high. This contributes to the efficient pricing of commodities in the future and provides liquidity to the futures market. One of the most important functions of futures markets is to provide the public with information about the prices of commodities. Petroleum products are traded worldwide, and there are many different prices of product depending on grade and location. Futures markets provide a central marketplace and a centrally determined reference price, which can be used to price product worldwide. This is called "price discovery" and is one of the major benefits of futures markets.

The business world has become increasingly aware of futures markets and especially of energy futures markets. The introduction of contracts on financial instruments, energy, and stock indexes has dramatically increased the range of potential users of futures markets. In addition, changes in the business climate, OPEC (Organization of Petroleum Exporting Countries), deregulation of the energy industry, fluctuating interest rates, and governmental monetary and fiscal policies have greatly increased the risks of doing business. Participation in futures markets has been growing dramatically and is expected to accelerate in the future. The introduction, in the mid 1980s, of commodity options contracts has also contributed to the rapid growth of futures markets. As business people become more familiar with the workings of futures markets, hedging should become a more common business practice. Familiarity with futures markets and hedging techniques will become a necessity for all businesses that are subject to price risk.

Commodity Futures and Options

Contracts and Markets

Hedging and speculating in commodity futures markets is accomplished by trading commodity futures contracts. A commodity futures contract is a contract to make or take delivery of a standardized amount of a specific quality of a commodity at a specified time in the future. Energy futures and options contracts are traded for all 12 delivery months. The prices of futures and options contracts are determined by a highly competitive auction process on commodity futures exchanges. The majority of energy contracts are traded on the New York Mercantile Exchange (NYMEX) and the International Petroleum Exchange (IPE) in London. Agricultural and financial futures contracts and options are traded primarily in Chicago on the Chicago Board of Trade (CBOT) and the Chicago Mercantile Exchange (CME). There are other exchanges that trade contracts on various commodities in New York and in other parts of the country. There are also almost 50 exchanges outside the United States that trade in futures or options contracts, although most of their trading volume consists of financial contracts.

The prices of futures contracts for any particular delivery month often change sharply from day to day and week to week depending on numerous developments that influence market prices. Prices often change when there is news of factors that will influence the supply and demand for the underlying commodity in the future. For energy-related commodities, factors such as weather conditions, OPEC pricing policies, forecast gasoline consumption, and a myriad of technical and other factors will cause the prices of futures contracts to change. The prices of commodity futures contracts are determined in a highly efficient central marketplace and at any point in time prices reflect the market's best estimate of the correct price of the commodity given all of the factors that are known to have an impact on the current and future level of energy prices.

Futures contracts involve a contractual obligation by both parties to either make or take delivery of the underlying commodity. Physical delivery of the underlying commodity is always possible with futures contracts. However, futures contracts recently have been introduced which call for cash settlement rather than physical delivery. An example of this is the stock index futures contract where delivery of the several hundred different stocks that comprise the stock index would be impossible.

Actual delivery is quite rare. Less than 2% of all futures contracts traded result in actual physical delivery. It is more common that the contractual obligation to make or take delivery is satisfied by selling a similar contract in the futures market. This is called an "offset". An offset occurs when the holder of a commodity futures position assumes another position opposite to the original position. Because there is now an obligation to buy and sell, the exchange allows the two positions to offset each other and thus the obligation to make or take delivery is satisfied. Of course, the trader assumes financial responsibility for the difference in price between the two positions. Thus, because there is a ready and liquid market to buy or sell futures contracts, commodity futures markets are able to act principally as financial markets. The exchanges are public in the sense that anyone who makes the necessary arrangements with member brokerage firms can trade. The ability to satisfy the obligation on a futures contract by offsetting means, for example, that speculators don't have to be in the heating oil business to trade heating oil futures contracts or in the propane business to trade propane futures. Like the financial market for stocks and bonds, futures markets are international in scope and regulated to insure the smooth and honest fulfillment of trades. Perhaps because of the regulated nature of these markets, the record for legal and ethical operation is excellent. It is the ability to offset futures positions in futures markets that allows hedgers in all areas of the world to hedge. The refiner in Illinois, the heating oil distributor in Maine, or the electric consumer in California can use the futures market to hedge even though there is no intent to make or take delivery on the contract. Indeed, in most cases transportation costs are prohibitive. Financial transactions take place via telephone and there is no necessity to ship commodities to and from remote delivery points. Typically, hedgers will offset their futures positions at the same time that they eliminate cash market positions in local cash markets.

Comparison of Forward and Futures Contracts

Forward and futures contracts are similar in that they both involve an element of futurity. Forward contracts, also known as cash forward contracts, are cash or spot market transactions in which the parties agree to the purchase and sale of the commodity at some future time under agreed-upon conditions. Each forward contract is a unique legal instrument that is tailor-made to suit each particular situation. Thus, forward contracts are not standardized and are usually not transferable except with the consent of the other party, often for some consideration. Delivery is typical in forward contracting and the market is geographically dispersed. It is primarily a telephone market made by major dealers, and the time periods involved are relatively short.

In contrast, futures contracts are completely standardized. The terms of each contract (natural gas, crude oil, gasoline, wheat, gold, etc.) on a particular exchange are the same in all respects except price. Futures contracts are readily transferable with only a small transaction cost. The commodity exchange provides a mechanism whereby contracts may be purchased or sold.

With forward contracting there is typically an element of concern regarding the ability of the parties to perform on the contract. This is called "default risk" In futures contracts there is no such concern because the futures exchange places itself between the buyer and seller of each futures contract. Once the agents for the buyer and seller meet on the floor of the exchange and negotiate the price, all connection between the buyer and seller is severed. The exchange becomes the buyer's seller and the seller's buyer so that the solvency of a particular transaction as far as the parties are concerned is dependent only upon the solvency of the exchange involved. Default is very rare in organized futures markets.

It is not unusual for forward and futures markets to exist for the same commodity. A good example of this coexistence is the market for foreign currencies, also known as foreign exchange. Large multinational banks operate foreign exchange departments for the convenience of their customers. They trade currencies for both immediate delivery and for delivery in the future (forward contracts). In the forward market, delivery will typically take place, although it is usually possible to assign the rights of a forward contract to third parties. As previously mentioned, there are also completely standardized futures contracts for foreign exchange traded in futures markets.

Commodity Futures Exchanges

Until recently, all commodity futures exchanges in the United States have been not-for-profit membership associations. Each association limits the number of individuals that may become members. Every membership, called a "seat" on the exchange, is owned by an individual. In certain instances, companies, partnerships' and cooperatives may be registered for certain membership privileges. The New York Mercantile Exchange (NYMEX) and the Chicago Mercantile Exchange (CME) have recently become for-profit corporations of which the members are stockholders. The International Petroleum Exchange (IPE) in Europe has also converted to a for-profit corporation.

Exchange members may be placed in three broad categories. Some members represent commercial interests that are primarily engaged in the producing, marketing, or processing of commodities and use the market to hedge against price risk. Others may speculate for their own accounts. A third group, called brokers, executes orders for individuals, partnerships, and corporations that are not members of the exchange. Some members may engage in all three activities at one time or another. Nonmembers trade through brokerage firms, which hold memberships through partners or officers. The exchanges are supported by dues and assessments on members as well as exchange fees on each transaction on the exchange.

Each exchange member must meet certain standards of financial responsibility, credit standing, and character. The exchanges are self-regulating. Members elect a board in which is vested the power to promulgate rules, create committees, hire staff, discipline members, and so on.

The world's oldest and largest commodity futures exchange, the Chicago Board of Trade, was founded in 1848. The New York Mercantile Exchange, also known as the energy exchange, is the third oldest exchange and was founded in 1872. It has 816 memberships and a board of directors and several standing committees charged with various responsibilities.

Exchange members buy and sell contracts on the floor of the exchange. Trading is conducted in trading areas called "pits" which are generally octagonal in shape and are made up of a series of steps on which the brokers and traders stand, all facing one another. There is a different pit for each type of contract being traded, but the method of trading is the same in all pits. Every offer to buy or sell a contract must be called or cried out publicly, resulting in a process that appears to an outsider to be total bedlam amid chaos. Open outcry is supplemented by hand signals.

Exchange members may trade for their own accounts, in which case they may be hedgers or speculators, or they may execute orders for hedgers and speculators located off the floor of the exchange. In these cases members are acting as brokers and receive commissions for their efforts. Strict exchange rules require that members acting as brokers place the interests of customers before their own interests.

Associated with each exchange is a clearing corporation or clearinghouse. It performs all clerical and financial tasks involved with keeping track of the thousands of trades that occur on the floor of the exchange each day. Each trade must be cleared through the clearinghouse. For each futures contract there is a chain of financial responsibility from the buyer or seller to the brokerage firm to the clearing corporation.

The New York Mercantile Exchange owns and operates its own clearinghouse where all the trading positions are fully margined and marked to market at the end of each day. The International Petroleum Exchange in London clears its trades through the London Clearing House (LCH). The LCH is able to guarantee contract performance by the collection of a margin payable on any outstanding position at the end of each day, calculated according to the value of that position.

Although not all members of the exchange are members of the clearinghouse, each exchange member must clear his trades through a clearing member. Each clearing member has funds on deposit with the clearing houses. These funds serve as a guarantee that the member has the financial means to support his trading activities. In addition to individual members, brokerage firms are members of the clearinghouse of each exchange. The brokerage firms in turn require that their customers who trade futures contracts also maintain margins against their futures contracts.

Electronic Trading

During the I980s, the combination of the technological revolution and the increasingly competitive nature of world business encouraged futures exchanges to reach out beyond their normal borders and time zones in the form of electronic trading. Some exchanges used electronic trading as their only trading medium, while others used it to expand their traditional floor trading day. In 1993, the New York Mercantile Exchange introduced after-hours trading with its NYMEX ACCESSS system which effectively extended the trading day to almost a full 24 hours. At present, the International Petroleum Exchange has electronic trading from 8:00 A.M. to 9:00 A.M., but expanded to a fully electronic trading system in 2002.

Regulations

In the United States, the major regulatory provisions regarding commodity futures contracts are contained in the Commodity Exchange Act (CEA) which is enforced and administered by an independent governmental regulatory commission called the Commodity Futures Trading Commission (CFTC). Futures trading may be conducted only on exchanges officially designated by the CFTC The markets so designated must comply with certain stipulations of the CEA and the rules and regulations issued and administered by the CFTC The CEA also forbids cheating, defrauding, dissemination of false information, and manipulation. The National Futures Association (NFA), authorized by an act of Congress, is the futures industry's first industry-wide self-regulatory organization. The NFA is responsible for the registration of futures professionals, arbitration, auditing, and other duties as they develop.

With an increase in the demand and supply for petroleum and natural gas products, and with multiple new players entering the market, the Indian government has enacted the Petroleum and Natural Gas Regulatory Board Act, 2006 (http://www.touchoilandgas.com/recent-indian-petroleum-petroleum-a7063-1.html).

Its aim is to:

- promote competition among entities;

- avoid infructuous investment;
- maintain or increase supplies;
- secure equitable distribution; and
- Ensure adequate availability of petroleum, petroleum products and natural gas nationwide.

The act is to provide for the establishment of the Petroleum and Natural Gas Regulatory Board (the 'board') in order to regulate the refining, processing, storage, transportation, distribution, marketing and sale of petroleum, petroleum products and natural gas, excluding production of crude oil and natural gas. This is to protect the interests of consumers and entities engaged in specified activities relating to petroleum, petroleum products and natural gas, and to ensure uninterrupted and adequate supply of petroleum, petroleum products and natural gas in all parts of the country whilst promoting competitive markets.

Foreign Direct Investment

The Ministry of Finance, Government of India, now permits up to 100% foreign direct investment (FDI) into the petroleum and natural gas sector, under the automatic approval route of the Reserve Bank of India. The caps on FDI are as follows:

- FDI up to 100% is permitted on the automatic route on petroleum product marketing. FDI for this sector would be permissible subject to the existing sectoral policy and regulatory framework in the oil marketing sector.
- FDI up to 100% is allowed on the automatic route in oil exploration in both small and medium-sized fields, subject to and under the policy of the government on private participation in: (1) exploration of oil, and (2) the discovered fields of national oil companies.
- FDI up to 100% is permitted on the automatic route for petroleum product pipelines subject to and under the government policy and regulations thereof.
- FDI up to 100% is permitted for natural gas/liquefied natural gas (LNG) pipelines with prior government approval.
- FDI up to 100% is permitted in, other than refining and including market study and formulation; investment/financing, setting up infrastructure for marketing in petroleum and natural gas sector subject to sectoral regulations, issued by the Ministry of Petroleum & Natural Gas, and in the case of actual trading and marketing of petroleum products, divestment of 26% equity in favour of Indian partner/public within five years.
- FDI up to 26% are permitted in the refining sector in case of public sector undertakings (PSUs), with prior approval of the Foreign Investment Promotion Board (FIPB) and up to 100% in case of private companies under the automatic route.

Policies and Procedures

A number of policy initiatives have been taken by the Government of India for facilitating the inflow of foreign capital and for encouraging entrepreneurs to invest in India, such as:

- equity participation in commercial and industrial ventures, which has been freed from all restrictions, FDI is now permitted up to 100% in different activities in the petroleum sector;
- rupee convertibility on the current account;
- deregulation and delicensing of various petroleum products in the country;
- gradual decontrol of pricing and distribution;
- freedom to form joint venture companies (JVCs) for the development of infrastructure and for marketing and refining activities; and
- Procedure for obtaining industrial licences has been simplified by making an application to the Secretariat for Industrial Approvals (SIA), Department of Industrial Policy and Promotion, Ministry of Industry. Approvals will normally be available within six to eight weeks under a fast time-bound schedule.

Natural Gas Futures Market: A Case Study

"The SMC Report—Natural Gas Futures Advisory Report"

SMC's goal is to produce a thoughtful, understandable report that takes a systematic and seasoned approach to the natural gas futures market. While the reports are intended as a tool for entities looking to hedge purchases or sales, they are also considered very useful to others interested in market direction such as marketers, hedge funds, mutual funds, pipelines, and LDC's and government entities. The idea is to make sense of the futures market and attempt to identify high probability situations for best hedging opportunities. The reports focus on the seasonal nature of the market and consider fundamental and technical aspects as well as history. There is also a good dose of market experience. Serious entities are encouraged to subscribe to the full package of reports which include monthly and weekly reports and occasional midweek updates.

The SMC Report is used by top industry executives in North America as a primary tool in identifying anticipated significant highs and lows in the natural gas futures market. Both fundamental and technical considerations are integral in SMC's disciplined approach, and both timing and price targets are presented in each report. Reports are geared for hedging, but they are also of great value to anyone seriously interested in movement in the natural gas futures market.

The majority of readers are large industrial users and producers in North America, but the reports are also perfect for the smaller company and individuals that need the information at a minimum cost. You can get one of the best seasoned perspectives in the natural gas industry at a bargain price.

SMC Reports: Natural Gas Price Forecasting and Advisory Services

The control of energy pricing is becoming an essential component of economic survival in today's world. With the increasing volatility in the natural gas futures market, the SMC reports are designed to provide an ongoing perspective of the market and assist participants in identifying higher probability timeframes and price levels that are best suited for satisfying a company's risk management goals. By using the reports, industrials and natural gas producers should be better able to systematically implement hedges or market positions at logical points and avoid emotional or panic decisions. Also, Mutual Fund and Futures Fund managers may use the reports to better time investments in energy related securities and futures instruments.

Navigating the Natural Gas Futures Market

The natural gas futures market provides an opportunity for market participants to come together to contract for future purchases or sales of natural gas. Because of the differing reasons and motivations of the participants, movement in natural gas futures is often viewed as random or even counter logical. Having been involved with natural gas futures since 1991, SMC has found strong, overriding seasonal tendencies that can affect market movement despite situations existing in fundamental factors. As such, SMC uses a seasonal approach to the market and looks to fundamentals to initiate and determine the magnitude of trends within seasonal periods.

REFERENCES

Atmanand (2004), Growth and Deregulation of Indian Oil Industry, Excel Books.

Errera, S. & S.L. Brown (2002), Fundamentals of Trading Energy Futures & Options, Penn Well.

GAIL (2004), Natural Gas in India, A Reference Book in India, Gail-Infraline, I.Infraline.com

H.K. Abdel-AAL, B.A. Bakr and M.A.Al Sahlawi (1992), Petroleum Economics & Engineering. Marcel Deckker Inc.

Patra, D.C. (2004), Oil Industry in India, Mittal Publications, New Delhi.

Net Worth, Stock Broking Ltd. (2007), Sectoral Update of Indian Oil Marketing Companies: http://www.capitalmarket.com/BrokerResearch/PDFs/21-229496-030408.pdf

SMC Report on Natural Gas Futures Market: www.ogjresearch.com

Website

http://www.touchoilandgas.com/recent-indian-petroleum-petroleum-a7063-1.html

CHAPTER X

Petro-Retailing

Understanding Petroleum Retail Business

The modern world could not exist without the low-cost and free movement of people, services and commodities. Oil-powered transport dominates the economic infrastructure that links and sustains present day communities, agricultural systems and the global economy. Billions of people now depend on food production that requires substantial inputs of petroleum fuels to power farm machinery, for fertilizers, herbicides and transport. Industrial agriculture, for some, is a way of converting petroleum into food. Oil supplies 40% and natural gas 22% of the world's commercial energy. Road, rail, water and air transport consume 60% of this oil. Other fuels have a negligible transport role. The remaining petroleum products are used for power generation, heating, in agriculture and mining, and for the manufacture of plastics, fibres, petrochemicals, paint, fertilizers and pesticides. Oil has overtaken coal as the main fuel since 1945. In 1859, Pennsylvania's Colonel Drake drilled one of the first oil wells. Another 40 years of invention led to the invention of internal combustion engine, the beginning of oil powered transport and the many other uses of oil. Oil triumphed over coal fired steam for shipping after World War-I and for rail after World War-II.

Road and air transport have triumphed since 1950. There was a rapid expansion of electric power grids from 1920 and the take-off of oil-powered industrial agriculture began in the 1930's. US fears of oil shortages during World War-II, along with the invention of welded steel pipelines, saw the first marketing of natural gas, previously flared at oil fields. Natural gas has been widely recognized to be the world's growth fuel since 1970.

Conventional oil rapidly displaced the direct use of coal as an industrial and transport fuel because of its ease of storage and transport, the fine control possible in its various uses and its high power-weight ratio. Oil is the most economically effective of all the fuels, especially for transport and domestic use. Contemporary industries and services using coal, gas and electricity require petroleum powered transport to be economically effective and viable. The availability of cheap oil is the most critical factor for the future of our contemporary industrial world. To maintain smooth working of all these sectors, it is very important to supply oil in time in sufficient quantity. A major requirement of oil is met through the retail sector as the entire requirement of transport sector, barring exception of state-run road transport, is met through oil. A major portion of requirement in power generation (both factories as well as domestic), agricultural demand of petroleum fuels, etc. is also met through the retail sector.

Retailing Concept

Evolution of retailing to its present form traces its origin to the 'barter' system prevalent in the pre-currency days. People exchanged their surplus products with each other on a 'perceived value'. This 'perceived value' was actually based on the need of both the giver and the receiver. (We probably cannot call them the seller and buyer!). The receiving power (purchasing power!) was determined by the surplus product available with him at prices mutually agreed to be exchanged to benefit both. With the emergence of 'standard' for bartering, initially salt and later in the form of currency, the concept of selling emerged. Selling is seen as a comprehensive process of exchange between the product and its price-transfer of ownership of product from the seller to buyer and flow of money from the buyer to seller in lieu of the products. Such selling over the years, as the concept expanded, included all types of products.

In earlier days, since the supply outstripped demand, there was no effort on branding and development of merchandise. Whatever was produced, it was sold out. With the advent of industrial revolution and subsequent competitive selling, the concept of retailing, direct marketing, etc. emerged.

Retailing is defined as a business that sells products and/or services to consumers for their personal or family use. This definition includes the interface of retailers with both vendors and consumers, as well as other processes like supply chain management that impact retailers.

Retailers, therefore, have to do many tasks, namely such as these:

1. They analyze their customers.
2. They develop strategies.
3. They choose markets and channel in which to compete.
4. They make location decisions.
5. They find, design, purchase, price and promote merchandise and services.
6. They organize their operations and manage their employee and stores.
7. They create an atmosphere that is inviting to customer and conductive for buying.

Strength of Retailing

- Retailing is the last link in the supply chain—the journey from well to wheel
- Retail is the face of the Oil Company
- Retail assumes the feature of service while dispensing product

Retailing is Selling

- Retailing is selling—a point at which the ownership of product gets transferred to the buyer
- Selling involves meeting customer's need in exchange of price

Retail function Involves

- Identify the customer and his need
- Develop selling strategy
- Locate market and channel
- Position the product and show room/dispensing station
- Design the product, price and promotion
- Manage operation, employees and store
- Create ambience for customer's visit and transaction
- Basics of Petroleum Retail Business
- Financial Aspects
- Performance Assessment

The Effect of Retailing

- The changing face of shopping
- Who feels the effect?
  - The city centre
  - The corner shop
- The long-term effect
- Some implemented schemes encompass:
  - 'Town centre management'

Social Consequences

- Benefits
  - Increased Choice
  - Late night shopping
  - Clean functional buildings
  - Single Storey Buildings
  - Fun-Shopping
- Costs
  - Excludes those without a car
  - Traditional service is lacking

Economic Consequences

- Benefits
  - Employment
  - Investment
  - Encourages spending

- Costs
  - Threatens other forms of retailing
  - Supermarkets import goods

Encourages car use at the cost of public transport

Establishing a New Retail Outlet

For opening a New Retail outlet the following important features need to be considered carefully:

- The process required for setting up a new Retail Outlet, though appears to be simple but in fact requires a great deal of knowledge combined with a lot of hard work both in the field as well as on the desk.
- A thorough survey, field study of the area in general is carried out and especially of the Trading Area where the Retail Outlets (RO) is proposed to be set up.
- A Trading Area is selected and a map study is done.
- Extensive field surveys are carried out and vital inputs taken.
- All ROs including those of the competitors are marked on the map.
- A stretch and side of the road is selected and the proposed location of the site indicated on the map.
- Having done so, a shorter stretch on the road is selected.
- Class of Market to be identified.
  - Traffic Census
  - Once done so, the search should be started for the plot of land for the proposed RO.
  - The EO must also accompany the SO for site selection.

Site Selection Criteria

- The land should be free of encroachments.
- There should not be any proposal of a fly-over or road widening.
- That there should not be any dwellings at the site or in the immediate vicinity.
- That there should not be any such industry in the immediate vicinity having open flames.
- Should not be at the immediate bank or catchments area of a river or canal.
- The land should not be earmarked by town planning for some other purpose.
- The site should be away from crossings as per requirements.
- The land is not mortgaged.
- Water table to be checked and soil taken for testing.
- There are no court cases on this land.
- The site meets all the requirements of Explosives, IRC, PWD, NHAI, local Govt. etc.
- The site should not be on a curve.

Market Intelligence (MI)

- MI is a very important part of data requirement necessary for planning and setting up a new RO.

Information for MI should contain:

- Population counts
- Age profile
- Spending habits
- Business counts by type
- New development profiles
- Average spending profiles (by product)
- Affluence levels, Social class
- Nearby facilities (viz. ATMs, Petrol Stations, C-stores, etc.)
  - Transport sector details
  - Agriculture details

Franchising Models in the Petroleum Industry

Franchising not new to the Oil industry – has been used for over a hundred years in this country. Oil industry has the largest franchisee network spread across the country. Started with franchising packed Kerosene tins in 1890s with the following Mission:

- A vast network spanning the length and breadth of the country was set up quickly.
- With the advent of Petrol vehicles a franchisee network for marketing Petrol and subsequently Diesel was set up.
- In the 1950s domestic LPG was introduced and a separate network was established.
- Since then we have a very vast network of franchisees for special products and lubricants as well.

The following Table 10.1 illustrates the growth of Franchisee-based Petro-Retail Market in India set up by major oil companies in India:

Table 10.1: Growth of Franchisee-based Petro-Retail Market in India

Name of Oil Company	No. of Dealers/Distributors		
	Retail	SKO/LDO	LPG
IOCL	7931	3443	4029
BPCL	4748	994	1802
HPCL	4781	1639	1865
IBP	1663	379	54
Total	19123	6455	7750

Franchisees are of different types with varying franchising models for different products as shown below:

- Individuals
- Partnerships
- Industrial houses
- Cooperatives
- Govt. Bodies
- COCOs

Modus operandi of Franchisee-based Petro-Retail business can be evolved on these lines:

- The decision on how to franchise was strongly driven by the product category, investments required and the need for control of operations
- Accordingly Petrol/Diesel network was predominantly company controlled while other products had a more loosely structured dealer controlled network
- Lubricants and special products are also franchised to a non exclusive network
- However over a period of time some of the models have been diluted with changing priorities
- The decision on how to franchise was strongly driven by the product category, investments required and the need for control of operations

Historically, franchisees treated as partners by oil companies in manners, as given below:

- Dealer selection was a extremely critical activity with a very clear idea of what sort of person was the right candidate
- The compensation or dealer profitability was very attractive
- Comprehensive training
- Strict control of all activities at the outlet
- Limited product category
- Competitive pricing
- Close interaction and relationships with network

Dramatic changes in market dynamics in Petro-Retailing in India are taking place in this direction:

- Evolving consumer needs
- Market becoming highly competitive
- Large formats with state-of-the-art facilities
- Non-fuel offerings like convenience stores, ATMs, Fast food outlets, medical shops, grocery, Dhabas etc.
- Branded fuels
- Quick oil change centers
- Loyalty programs
- Use of Technology
- From just selling fuel to managing all these activities is a completely new game for the organization and the network.

Franchisee mindset, capabilities and requirements:

- Newer business areas require Dealer to acquire new skills

- Effort to reward ratio is initially much less than that for fuel trade
- Focus on category management
- Most franchisees do not want to expose large fraction of personal wealth at risk
- Enhanced customer interaction—multiple touch points
- An understanding of customer acquisition costs as an investment for the long term rather than cost.
- Maintenance of standards and consistency of operations.
- Stricter financial control—MIS and data management

However, many franchisees are highly averse to any new concepts/plans. Therefore, several key priorities for both franchisors and franchisees need to be demarcated, considering the following:

- Creating a positive Brand image and clear brand positioning
- Creating high brand awareness and recall
- Developing a sustained business model
- Developing a strong national marketing policy
- Choosing the right location
- Selection of Franchisees—akin to selecting partners in business
- Understanding from day one that the real customer is the buyer of the product or service that is sold, it is not the Franchisee
- Developing systems, structures, suppliers for achieving consistency
- Developing a flexible and low cost structure

There is a clear need to significantly strengthen partnership with mutual obligations between the franchisor and franchisees in terms of following:

- Written contract
- Partnership requiring delivery by both parties
- Leverage of existing business system/brand equity
- Finite period of operation-potential for renewal
- Sharing of financial gain
- Specific operational procedures to be adhered to
- True partnership with mutual obligations and focus on several aspects in addition to financial returns

Franchising increases attractiveness for entry of independent entrepreneurs by:

- Offering comparatively lower risk option as compared to independent retailers in other sectors
- Management training and support
- Brand name appeal
- Standardized quality of goods and services
- National advertising program
- Financial assistance
- Proven products and business formats
- Centralized buying power

The Wheel of Retailing

This theory suggests that new retailing institutions enter the marketplace as low-status, low-margin, low-price operations and then move toward higher status, margin, and price positions. With respect to the wheel of retailing theory, a low spot on the wheel, once occupied by a low-margin retailer that has traded up, is left open for an innovative retailer that can operate at a margin lower than those earned by existing retailers. Some observers suggest that modern marketing methods, including research and positioning, will stop or slow the wheel of retaining as retail marketers (Fig. 10.1) resist abandoning market positions they have carefully selected.

The ongoing cycle of retail passes through three phases:

The Entry Phase: When new retailers enter the market

The Trading-up Phase: When retailers begin improving upon their trade volumes and move from the initial low status, low price, to higher status and better margins.

The Vulnerability Phase: When the competition increases, margins get squeezed, and return on investment begin declining.

Each phase attracts its own set of retailers who retail their merchandise to get maximum advantage. The merchandise is designed to meet the demands of the market. Innovative retailers mark their entry with merchandise which is typically low priced, low status, etc.

Commodity v/s Brand Retailing

There was time in not so recent past when salt was retailed as simple, plain salt till brands like Tata salt, Dandi, etc. marked their entry. The petroleum sector

Fig. 10.1: Explains the Various Stages of the Wheel of Retailing

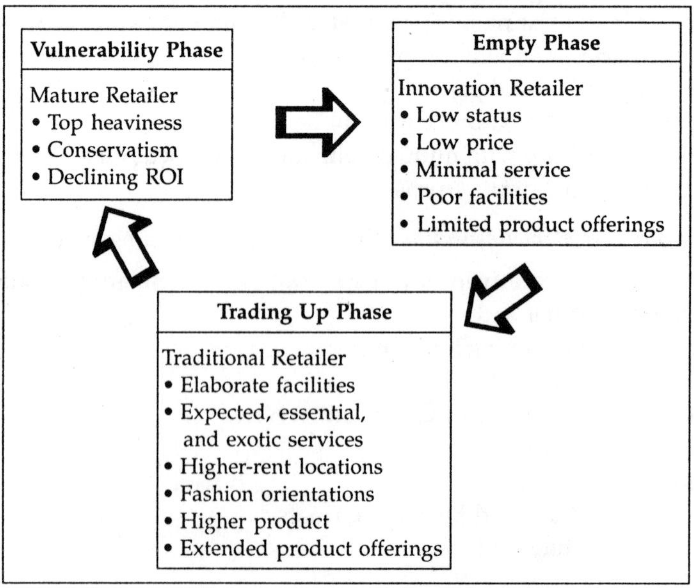

was typically selling motor spirit, high speed diesel, etc. till recently. However, last couples of years have seen entry of specialty, branded fuels like Speed, Hi-Speed, Josh, Premium, etc.

Why did that happen? In a stagnant market where the overall demand is not growing at a satisfactory rate, one way to expand margins is by expanding the market share. That means wresting some of sales volumes from the competitors. Alternatively, company can decide to charge a higher price than the competition. Typically, customers are not willing to pay a higher price till the merchandise is 'perceived' different from other. The perceived value of the product differs in customers' minds with respect to product's additional features. In times of increase competition, companies often adopt strategies aimed either at increasing cost competitiveness or at growing revenues. A strong brand helps in shifting the demand curve as depicted in Fig. 10.2.

Brand Personality is what distinguishes one brand from another. It is the sum of intangible assets of the brand. It is the symbolic aspect of brand. Southgate defines brand personality as the human characteristics of the brand. For example Harley Davidson motorcycle is seen as a macho, freedom-seeking person.

David Aaker has identified five different personality factors found among the brand personality. These are:

- Sincerity (Kodak)
- Excitement (Bacardi)
- Competence (Wipro, Pentium)
- Ruggedness (Levi, Marlboro)

Brand Image is the totality of impressions about the brand. David Aaker says, "Brand image as an association and image both represent perceptions which mayor may not reflect objective reality... as image of competence may be based upon the appearance of a doctor's office and the manners of his staff rather than on the

Fig. 10.2: Importance of Brand Personality and Brand Image

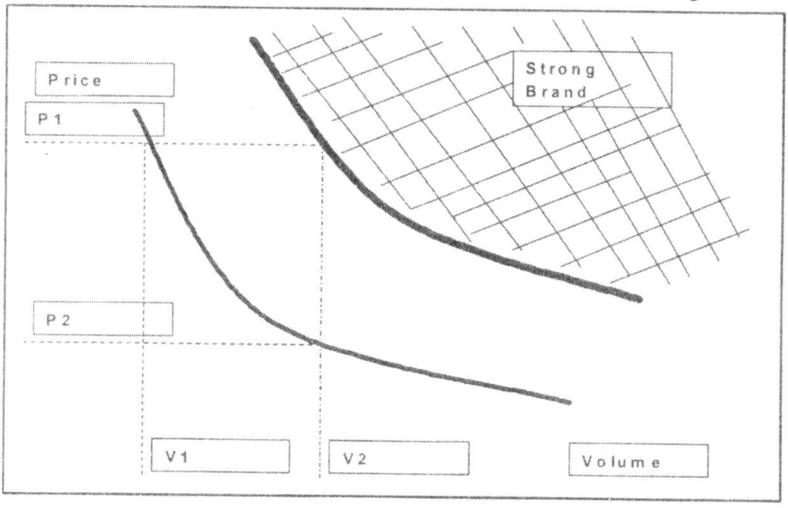

objective measure of the health of former patients." Brand personality is the sum total of all the significant tangible and intangible assets that a brand possesses. Whereas, brand image is how the brand is perceived by the consumer. It can be said the brand personality is the cause while brand image is the effect.

Table 2: Differences amongst Brand Name, Brand Personality and Brand Image

Brand Name	Brand Personality	Brand Image
Lifebuoy	Price Carbolic	Value for money Hardworking
Kinetic Honda	Gearless Ignition start	Comfort Comfort
Little Hearts	Puffed biscuits Distinct packing Heart shaped	Novelty Attractive Romantic

Brand Equity, as the price at which one brand is preferred over other, can be referred to as the final outcome of a brand identity (personality and image). This is the payback of investment into a brand. Brand equity is what makes the demand curve shift upwards (Fig. 10.3).

Therefore, to drive revenue growth, petroleum retailers have to either attract new consumers or increase their share of the existing consumer's wallet. Key to this lies in creating a strong brand adds perceived value which can command a price and or volume premium by differentiating from commodity products.

Basic Difference Between Brand and Product

- A product is something that is made in a factory
- A brand is something that is bought by a customer

Fig. 10.3: Building the Brand Equity

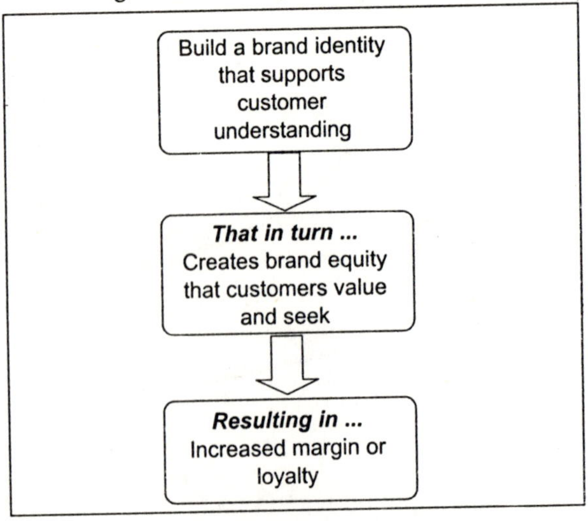

- A product can be copied by a competitor
- A brand is unique
- A product can be quickly outdated
- A successful brand is timeless

Special Nature of Petro-retail

When we go and buy a packet of Amul butter, we can see the packet, feel it, examine its condition unlike most the petroleum products which can not be seen, feel it, examine its condition unlike most the petroleum products which can not be seen, felt, or examined unless special efforts we made. Have you ever seen LPG? While fueling your vehicle at a petrol pump what you see is the nozzle going inside the tank and a metering assembly registers the volume of product dispensed-you never get a chance to see what is going inside the tank. In a way petro-retailing works on trust-consumers believe that they are getting what they are buying. It's like gold—you can't check the purity yourself so you trust the goldsmith. It is this special nature of petro-retailing which introduced a new element of product attribute the correct quality and quantity delivered by the petrol pump, or by the gas distributor. When compared with developed markets like USA, the Indian market, therefore has its own interpretations of some of the key constitutes of products mix.

Indian Market	US Market
Quality interpreted as no adulteration	Quality interpreted as impact on fuel efficiency and engine performance.
Quality interpreted as getting the right amount of fuel	Quality is not a parameter for consideration
Price is not a differentiating factor always	Price is a very important factor

However, as the Indian market evolves parameter such as quality and quantity may become hygiene factors.

Another major difference between other retailing (like apparels, white goods, foods stuff, etc.) and petroleum products retailing is that the former retailing is often treated by customers as a form of 'Leisure' where as petro-retailing is a specific need drive on purchase situation. This divides the Indian petroleum shopper into four distinct segments.

- **Routine Chore Doer**
  - Looks for minimization of hassle at the petrol pump. Petroleum purchasing is seen as drudgery, a menial job.
  - Seeks addition vehicle repairs and maintenance services.
  - Likely to be a persons indulging in monotonous routine jobs.

- **Time Poor (The Rabbit)**
  - Strong need for location convenience and other non-fuel related services.
  - Characterized by his need for quick service and convenience.

  - Likely to be a professional, 24 × 7 worker.
- **Trust seeker**
  - Unique to emerging market, is driven by a strong desire for integrity and by strong relationships with the retailer.
  - A typical late adopter.
  - The 'quality-guarantee' is the underlying driver for purchase decisions.
- **Prestige seeker**
  - Higher level emotional needs for reinforcements of self esteem.
  - Relatively more brand conscious.
  - May often be stereotyped as the 'self-made man'.
  - Potential target for international or premium brands.

A.T. Kearney Report on Petro-retailing:

Research Findings

To understand the buying behavioural pattern and drivers for petroleum and non-fuel products and services, A.T. Kearney conducted a quantitative research with 500 consumers in New Delhi. The findings clearly indicated that the location is a key factor-most consumer prefers to purchase their fuel from petrol stations near their residence or office. Why do consumers exhibit this behavior? Probing into the reasons for selection of their regular petroleum station of their regular petroleum stations threw up some expected responses—over 90% cite assurance of quantity and quality of petrol to be the key drivers of choice. However, a number of less expected responses were also received. For example, 70% of the respondents say that having air filling facilities is important in their decision making process.

Key Finding of Research

- Trust in "Fuel quality and quantity" and location conveniences are the primary drivers for choice of petrol pumps amongst consumer in New Delhi.
- 85% of consumers also attach significant importance to the "experience" in terms of quick service, attendant disposition and station ambience.
- Consumers have very low brand locality—over 50% are indifferent to the brand of petro-retailer.
- 70-80% of consumer would prefer their station to stock fuel-based products and offer air refill facilities, small facilities, small repairs etc.
- Only 45% of car and 35% of two-wheelers have ever purchased at a conveniences stores-snacks and beverages being the most common items.
- More than 90% of the consumers do not usually fill their tanks.

The latter may have two implications—petrol marketers building a brand proposition around speed of service may need to incentivize consumers to buy larger quantities of fuel in each visit to reduce the frequency of visits. However, companies building a non-fuel retailing model could focus on offering cross-sell products and services.

Linked Retailing

Under this concept your main product is the anchor while some other products one retailed as add on. Typical example is a Multiplex Mall where the main product is entertainment at multiplex, but a shopping mall or food plaza adds to the customer's convenience. Most of the car dealers sell customized car accessories as linked retailing. The origin of this form of retailing can be traced to the cinema halls or colleges of earlier days where a canteen was set as for sale of food stuff to customers who actually came for a movie or studies respectively.

Petroleum retailing companies have been successfully trying it for a long time. The major categories under this "allied retailing" are convenience stores (urban or rural), food services, and ancillary services. There is always a positive rub off from one products category to another. For example a petrol pump may have an ATM as an ancillary service. A customer who actually comes to the site for a transaction at the ATM may buy fuel to avoid another trip to petrol pump.

Convenience Stores

These are small stores selling categories such as impulse items, gifts, daily need items, snacks, arid other packaged foods. There are branded stores. In rural areas, there are stores which cater to farmers such convinces stores sell various brands fertilizers, pesticides, and other farming inputs to farmers. Such stores are set-up in typical rural markets. DCM Shriram Consolidated Limited has very successfully implemented this concept at their Hariyali Kisan Bazaar.

Food Services

At the petrol pumps depending upon the availability of space, retailing companies are adding food services. Bharat Petroleum has opened McDonald's outlets. Domino's is present at some of the India Oil petrol pumps. There are Cafe Coffee Day outlets at Bharat Petroleum and Hindustan Petroleum petrol pumps. To cater to the highway trucker segment, oil companies have set up low-end dhabas which offer quality food at affordable prices.

Factors to be considered in deciding the food services model:

1. Space available (including parking).
2. Labour implications.
3. Skills/resources requirements.
4. Consumer demographics/psychographics.
5. Competitive environment.

Ancillary Services

These include products like ATMs, Courier Services, Dormitory, Insurance Counters, Automated car wash, Laundry, etc. Some oil companies have put up pool tables at their petrol pumps. Even swimming pools have been commissioned at large stations. Rub-off from other products has been proven through some surveys conducted by oil industry. One of the surveys conducted to link ATM with fuel has established that about 60% of ATM customers buy their fuel from the same RO. (Fig. 10.4)

Fig. 10.4: Ancillary Services by Retail Outlets

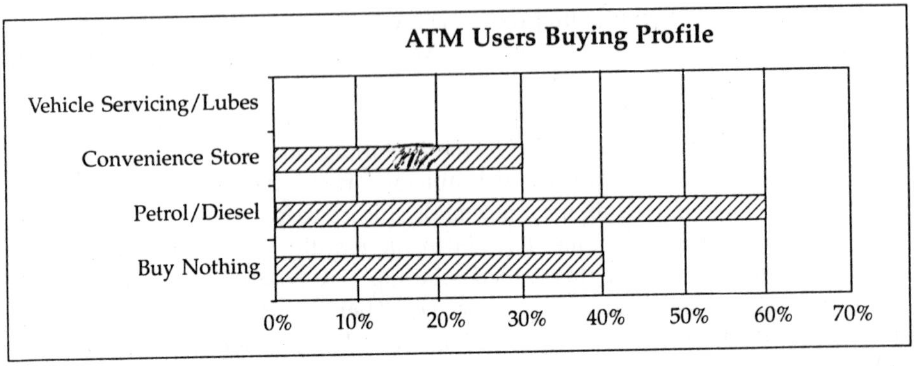

Another survey has clearly shown retention of sales at ROs with allied facilities in an otherwise declining market. A survey of dealers conducted in Delhi had 87% dealers saying, "A shop adds to the overall ambience of our RO making the customer believe that our RO is better than others. That's how it increases our sales." In response to a question that how much of fuel sales will be lost if the non-fuel retail shop were to be closed, they clearly indicated an expected loss of 15%-25% in MS sales and about 5%-10% in HSD sales. At two ROs of a national oil company where McDonalds outlet was commissioned the company registers 225-350% of sales growth on weekends (when compared to weekly average) when families visit the McDonald outlet. That clearly indicates purchase of fuel while foot-fall at the outlet is due to some non-fuel offering.

Indian Experience in Petro-Retailing

Indian consumers have very low brand loyalty towards petroleum products, which in place brings in the need for strong brand-building exercise by the petro-retailers. The following section explains lessons learned for Indian petro-retailers from successful strategies of major international players. Segmenting shoppers, understanding their behaviour patterns and drivers, fuel based differentiation, and providing value added products and services are some of the interesting areas coved under Petro-Retailing, especially from Indian perspectives.

With growing competition and deregulation, the rules of the game in the petroleum retailing industry in India will undergo some major changes in the next few years. The revolution in the Indian telecom sector is a recent example of the impact of free market dynamics on the structure of the industry and on the strategies of various players. Deregulation of the petroleum retailing sector in India will undoubtedly lead to a similar battle for market share, with new players attempting to gain share from current incumbents. This will exert a downward pressure on profit margins and force industry players to adapt their organizations and strategy.

To succeed in this environment, the two key questions are: How can the industry prepare for the change? What will be the most effective strategies for petroleum retailers in India in the medium term?

To explore the strategic option for petroleum retailers in India, A.T. Kearney has conducted a study of successful strategies adopted by petroleum marketing companies worldwide and drawn lessons relevant to the Indian environment. The findings clearly demonstrate the value to be gained from adopting a consumer centric approach and in building strong brand equity.

From analysis of the Indian market, it would appear that there is an opportunity for petroleum retailers in India to develop differentiated value propositions that will boost their revenues and improve competitiveness and profitability in the new market economy. In this study, we have identified key imperatives for successful petroleum retailing in the Indian subcontinent and suggested some strategic alternatives.

Petro Retailing: A chronology of the Evolution of Concept

- 1882: Petro-Retailing started in India with the supply of kerosene by Standard Oil Co.
- Oil was first struck in India in 1890 at Digboi in north-eastern India.
- India's first refinery was built at Digboi in 1901.
- 1950-55 : Refineries were set up by Burma Shell, Esso and Caltex
- 1964: IOC was formed by the merger of Indian Refineries Ltd. and Indian Oil Company.
- 1981: Assam Oil Co. was taken over by IOC as AOD.

In the early 70's there were six Oil-Marketing Companies

1. Indian Oil
2. Burma Shell
3. Esso
4. Caltex
5. Indo-Burma Petroleum (Balmer Lawrie & Co. Ltd.)
6. Assam Oil Company

Importance of the 70's

Petro-retiling assumed historical significance in the 70's, 80's and 90's as given below:

In 70's

1970: World Oil crisis
1971: Indo-Pak war
1975: Esso and Caltex merged and nationalised as HPCL
1976: Burma Shell nationalised into Bharat Refineries and then changed to BPCL
1977: Indo-Burma Petroleum became IBP Co. Ltd.
1977: (Dec. 16th): APM came into existence

During: 1980-2002

IOC: Refining and Marketing
BPC: Refining and Marketing

HPC: Refining and Marketing
IBP : Purely Marketing
AOD: Purely Marketing
1991: Demand management was implemented
1992: Post-liberalisation: LPG, naphtha, Aviation fuel
1997-98: Dismantling of Administrative Pricing Mechanism announced
1999: RPL started with Direct Sales
2001: IBP taken over by IOC
2002: Post APM (effective 1st April '02)

Entry of private players in the field of Petro-Retailing

Oil Industrial Structure in India

The overall position of Oil Industrial Structure in India, as in October 2005 is illustrated below. The Industrial Structure includes participation of major Oil Corporations, involved in mainly in 3 categories of activities, viz. Upstream (Exploration & Production), Downstream (Refining & Marketing), Oil and Natural Gas Transportation. The Major Oil Companies involved include: ONGC, OIL, IOCL, HPCL, MRPL, RIL, Essar, GAIL (Fig. 10.5)

A Deregulation Overview of Petro-retail Business

- Refineries deregulated w.e.f. 1 April '98:
  - All products except five-Gasoline, Gasoil, ATF, LPG and Kerosene decontrolled
  - ATF decontrolled w.e.f. April 2001

Fig. 10.5: Oil Industry Structure
(As on Oct. 2005)

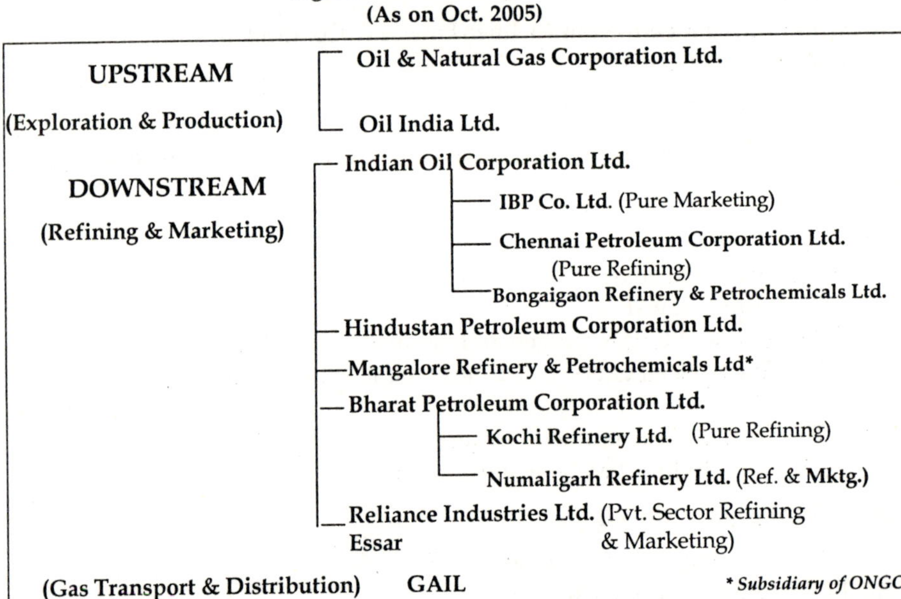

- Marketing and Pipelines sector deregulated w.e.f. 1 April '02
  - Market determined pricing of all products-Prices of MS/HSD reviewed fortnightly
  - Oil Pool dismantled:
    * Petroleum Regulatory Board to be set up;
    * Subsidies on LPG and Kerosene borne thru' fiscal budget and to be phased out in the next 3-5 years;
    * Upstream companies share under recovery on subsidy;
    * Freight subsidy for far flung areas continues;
    * Marketing rights for transportation fuel awarded to new entities;
    * Marketing service obligation for rural and far flung area for all players;
    * Guideline for laying new pipelines announced.

Deregulation has brought forth balance between reasonable earnings for the industry and protection of consumer interest.

Strong Brands Drive Revenue Growth

Findings of A.T. Kearney Report

In times of increased competition, firms often adopt strategies aimed either at increasing cost competitiveness or at growing revenues. A.T. Kearney's work across industries globally, has shown that in growth markets, the major imperative should be revenue enhancement through profitable share and market growth (Figs. 10.6 and 10.7).

To drive revenue growth, petroleum retailers will have to either attract new consumers or increase their share of the existing consumers' wallet. Creating strong brand equity will be the key to achieve these objectives, consistently and profitably. Empirical evidence shows that strong brands add perceived value which can command a price and/or volume premium by differentiating from commodity products.

Among consumers in India today, brand recognition and differentiation of existing petroleum retailers is currently low. This presents a potential opportunity to new players as well as existing companies, to adopt a differentiated consumer-focused strategy centered on building a strong petroleum retail brand.

Know your Consumer

To develop a strong brand and product proposition, a key imperative is to understand the target consumers' psyche, behavior and needs. Segmentation is a powerful tool to help marketers identify the most profitable consumer segments and to develop an offer which fulfills their needs better than competition. Psychographics segmentation is more often used today than traditional demographic measures, as it captures better the key behaviors and underlying attitudinal drivers. Many successful global petroleum brands have used detailed psychographic segmentation as the foundation of building strong brands. For example, Mobil split the US petroleum consumer population into five psychographic segments—Price shoppers, Homebodies, Road Warriors, True Blues

Fig. 10.6: Demand-Driven Revenue Curve

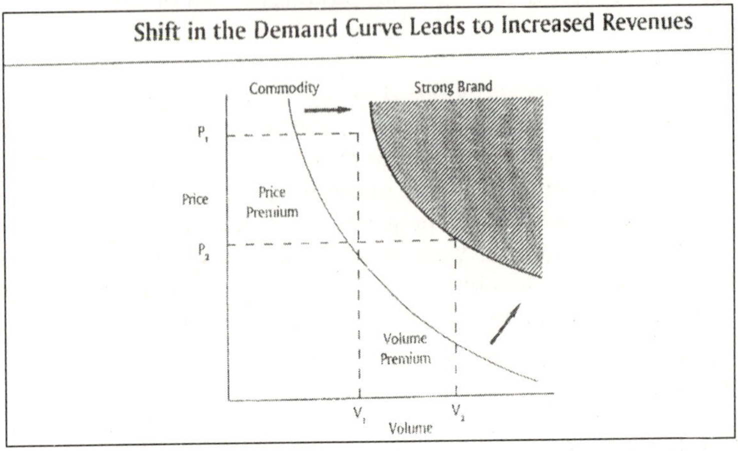

Source: A.T. Kearney.

Fig. 10.7: The Brand Building Processes

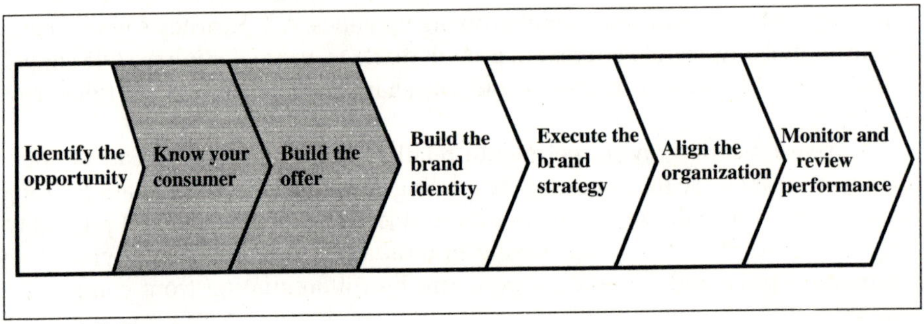

Source: A.T. Kearney.

and Generation F3. Research showed that the latter three segments had high purchase frequency and low price sensitivity and were therefore identified as the most profitable target segments. Mobil's marketing strategy was then built around these consumer segments. Similarly, a detailed psychographic segmentation was developed by A.T. Kearney for a leading Oil and Gas company in Canada, as the basis for their national marketing strategy. Their value proposition was built on satisfying the common emotional and rational needs of the consumer segments, which were identified as the most attractive (Fig. 10.8).

The relative attractiveness of each consumer segment is usually evaluated against criteria such as:

- Segment size in terms of numbers and purchase value.
- Competitive intensity in each consumer segment.
- Key Success Factors (KSFs) required serving each segment.
- Firm's existing competencies and ability to develop/access the required skills.

Fig. 10.8: Consumer Segmentation Pattern of US Petroleum Buyers

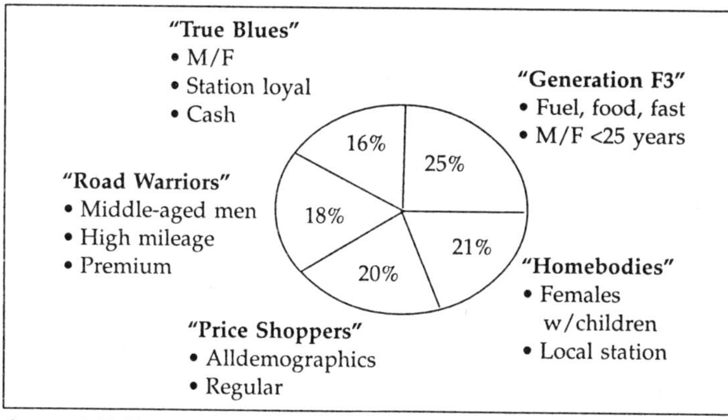

Source: A.T. Kearney.

- Objectives of the firm, both financial and non-financial.

The Petroleum Shopper in India

Often, in less developed or regulated markets, such psycho graphics segmentation is not always so revealing. To test this hypothesis, A.T.Kearney recently initiated qualitative market research amongst petroleum consumers in New Delhi to check if distinct consumer segments exist. Interestingly, our research identified four psychographic consumer segments, and we believe these offers a strong basis to develop differentiated value propositions.

Routine Chore Doer

- Main driver is to minimize the hassle at the petroleum station; petroleum purchasing is seen as 'drudgery'.
- Seeks additional vehicle repair and maintenance services.
- Likely to be a person indulging in monotonous routine jobs.

Time Poor

- Strong need for location convenience and other non-fuel related services.
- Characterized by his need for quick service and convenience.
- Likely to be a professional, 24×7 worker.

Trust Seeker

- Probably unique to emerging markets such as India.
- Driven by a strong desire for integrity and by strong relationships with the retailer.
- A typical late adopter, akin to the Indian middle class.
- The 'quality-guarantee' is the underlying driver for purchase decisions.

Prestige Seeker

- Higher level emotional needs for reinforcement of self-esteem.
- Relatively more brand conscious.
- May often be stereotyped as the 'self-made man'.
- Potential target for international or premium brands.

As the consumer in India has not been exposed to differential pricing in petroleum, the price sensitive consumer is not as well-defined as in other markets. However, our experience of consumers in India in other product categories, as well as international learning, indicates that there will be a sizeable segment of consumers in India who are extremely value conscious and whose primary evaluation of value will be price-based. To understand better the buying behavioral patterns and drivers for petroleum and non-fuel products and services, A.T. Karney conducted a quantitative research with 500 consumers in New Delhi. The findings clearly indicate that location is a key factor—most consumers prefer to purchase their fuel from petrol stations near their residence or office.

Key findings emanated from this research were:

- Trust in "fuel quality and quantity" and locational conveniences are the primary drivers for choice of petrol pumps amongst consumers in New Delhi.
- 85 percent of consumers also attach significance to the "experience" in terms of quick service, attendant disposition and station ambience.
- Consumers have very low brand loyalty—over 50 percent are indifferent to the brand of petro-retailer.
- 70-80 percent of consumers would prefer their station to stock fuel-based products and offer air refill facilities, small repairs etc.
- Only 45 percent of car owners and 35 percent of two-wheeler owners have ever-purchased at a convenience store snacks and beverages being the most common items.
- More than 90 percent of the consumers do not usually fill their tanks.

The latter may have two implications—petrol marketers building a brand proposition around speed of service may need to incentives consumers to buy larger quantities of fuel in each visit to reduce the frequency of visits. However, companies building a non-fuel retailing model could focus on offering cross-sell products and services. Comparing the drivers of petrol station choice with more developed markets such as the United States, there are some stark differences which may give some pointers as to how consumers may evolve in India. In the US, while location (71 percent) is the primary parameter, price (56 percent) is also a very important factor. Product performance or quality (24 percent) is the third most important factor. However, there is a big difference in the consumer's interpretation of quality. In India quality is interpreted as 'no adulteration', but in the US it means impact on fuel efficiency and engine performance. Quantity (interpreted in India as getting the right amount of fuel, i.e. integrity) is not a parameter for consideration in a market such as the US. As the Indian market evolves, parameters such as integrity of fuel quantity and purity are likely to become hygiene factors, and not bases for differentiation. However, a brand proposition built on a broader platform such as quality can be an enduring differentiator. For example, marketers would be able to evolve their brand offering in line with the development of consumer needs—from purity to higher order needs such as performance, fuel efficiency, or even the quality of the buying experience.

Build the Offer

The choice of the target consumer segment drives the development of the brand offer and impacts many aspects of the organizational strategy such as location, pricing and human resource policies. The target consumer should determine the value proposition; for example, a company which is targeting the "Prestige Seeker" would design its offerings very differently from a competitor targeting the "Time Poor" consumer type.

Company A: The Prestige Seeker

- Brand positioning—"a superior product for the discerning consumer".
- Product-service offerings could include differentiated fuel products-premium grade petrol, additives and services such as an automated car wash.
- The look of the petrol stations would be "international" with technology enabled services.

Company B: Time Poor

- Brand positioning—build entirely on a "Time is money" value proposition.
- Focus on offering rapid transaction times, swipe-at-the-pump facilities, smart cards, medicine shops, etc. to ensure that the "time-poor" consumer gets the quickest service possible.

Petroleum retailing is both a product and a service, and differentiation is possible around either or both of these axes. From our analysis of successful international strategies, we have identified four main platforms for differentiation: 1. Fuel-based, 2. Value added products/services, 3. Price based, and 4. Consumer experience. We shall consider the manner in which of these parameters can be exploited by petroleum marketers to develop a differentiated brand strategy.

1. *Fuel-based Differentiation*

The Key Success Factors in Fuel-based Differentiation Strategies are:

- Product Development Competencies—Offer Superior Products
- Brand Image Creation—Perception of Product Superiority

In markets such as the US, petroleum retailers sell multiple grades of fuel-based on their octane ratings, additives added and/or process differences. Multiple grades cater: to an evolved consumer segment who seek enhanced fuel performance and can support the premium price/margin business model. For example, in USA a leading petroleum brand has built a strong equity around' good performance', enabling it to capture a greater share of the 'performance' motivated consumer segment. The impact of this has been the relatively high contribution of premium grades to the brand's product mix, translating into correspondingly higher revenues and profitability (Fig. 10.9). Premium grade petroleum consumers in the US have been found to be less price-sensitive and more brand-loyal. In India, the growth in the number of cars in the large car segment, adoption of multi-point fuel injection engines and the introduction of stringent pollution emission norms suggests that there maybe an opportunity for fuel-based differentiation targeting the 'Prestige Seeker' and 'Trust Seeker' consumers.

2. *Value-added Products and Services-based Differentiation*

Apart from being used as a basis for differentiation, non-fuel products and services can contribute significantly to revenue and profit enhancement. Non-fuel revenues of petroleum retailers contribute as much as 38.6 percent in the US and 28 percent in France, and their significantly higher profitability makes them particularly attractive; average profit contribution of non-fuel products and services is 65.8 percent in the US and 40 percent in France.

There arc a number of products and services which petroleum retail stations can offer, but they can all be broadly grouped into three categories—convenience stores, food service outlets and ancillary service.

Convenience Stores (C-store). The concept of convenience stores has not as yet taken off in India and we believe that in the near term this may not be a profitable opportunity for petroleum retailers. The Report analysis of the Indian consumer

Fig. 10.9: Brand Image to Promote the Sales of Premium-Grade Petro-Products in USA

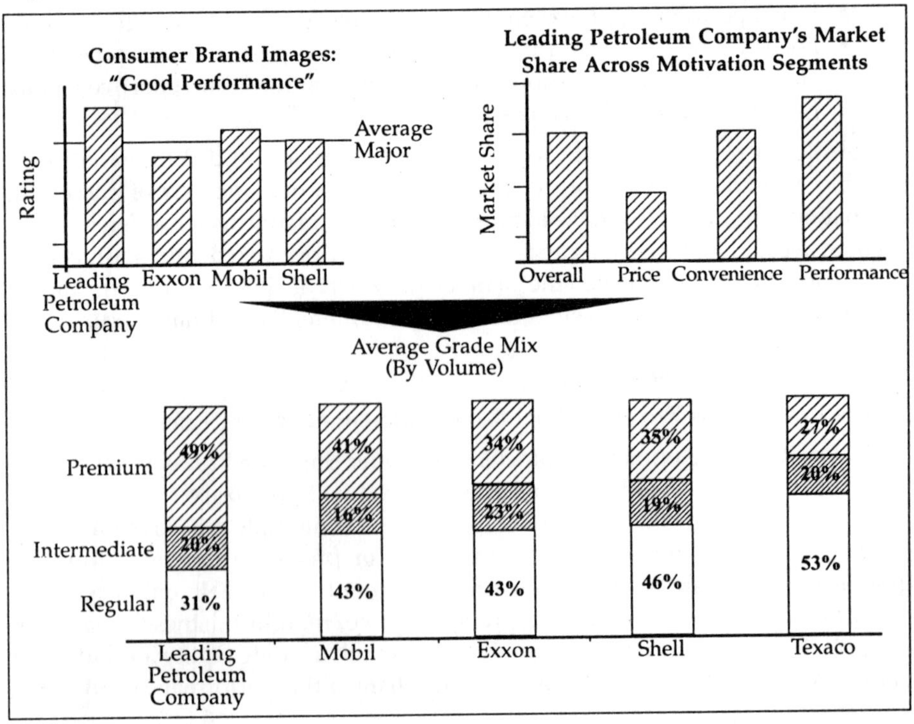

showed that their need for convenience is currently reasonably well-satisfied at competitive prices by the unorganized retail sector such as the neighborhood 'kirana' store, the 'thelawallah' with his fresh vegetables and the friendly 'paanwallah'. Most consumers in India today are unwilling to pay the price premiums required to support the organized convenience store business model; the 'MRP' regime also restricts the c-store operators' ability to charge a premium for the higher service levels that it may provide. Coupled with this are the difficulties in operating a profitable convenience store business model in India, where the supply chain for most products remains highly fragmented and inefficient. To overcome these shortcomings BPCL have pioneered to venture into Petro-retail business by adopting the following BPCL's Additional Value Propositions as outlined below:

BPCL'S Additional Value Propositions
Bharat Petroleum has launched an 'Enhanced Fuel Proposition' (EFP) program—A nation-wide effort at dispensing pure quality and correct quantity of fuel, and at the same time delivering courteous, fast and efficient service. The retail outlets covered under this program display the 'Pure for Sure' sign —an out-turned palm forming a circle with the thumb and the first finger— also imprinted on the dispensing units and on the back of the blue uniform sported by DSMs, and TUV's certificate displayed at the outlet At such retail outlets, Bharat Petroleum guarantees that the correct quality and quantity are dispensed. Market research has revealed important lacunae in terms of time, convenience, and ambience in the shopping experience of households in 'A' class cities. The In and Out concept aims to address these need gaps by inviting you to "save time by shopping at a conveniently located, single point for a number of typical household needs" and by offering an up-market ambience.

Operating a c-store requires an entirely different set of capabilities from petroleum retailing. Sourcing and supply chain management is critical skills for a c-store operator and may need to be outsourced by Indian petroleum marketers as they build other consumer facing kills. A reduced risk model could be an alliance with an established retail chain e.g. Food-World or *'Subhiksha'* which would provide the required skill synergies and also ensure immediate consumer credibility and—trials. This model has worked well in more mature markets where consumers require greater choice and assortment mix. Fig 10.10 shows how to create diffentiation in product-line/brands in the C-store businesses.

It is also important that the petroleum c-store operator develops a strategy that differentiates its convenience store from other similar stores as well as the traditional retailer. There are multiple opportunities for differentiation in the convenience store market; the key is to make a consumer-based choice. For an international brand entering the market in India, targeting the 'Prestige Seeker' consumer segment, the 'smart shop'—clean, well-lit, wide aisles may offer a differentiated value proposition. A convenience store operator can select from eight

Fig. 10.10: How to Create Product/brand Differentiation in c-Store Businesses

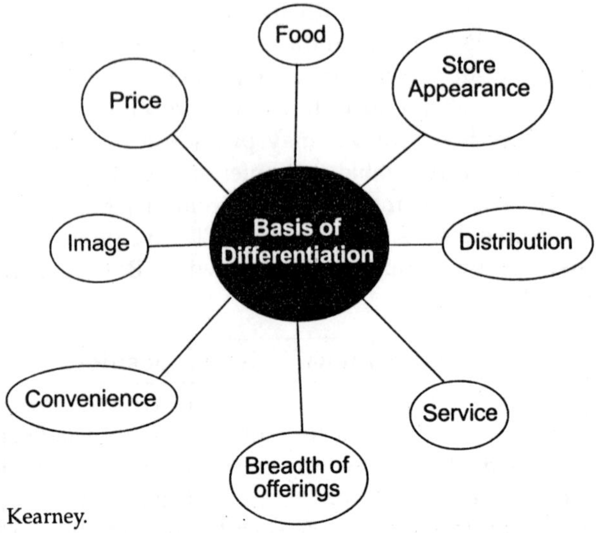

Source: A.T. Kearney.

levers which provide a basis for differentiation depending on the needs of the target consumer segments.

Food Service Outlets—This is an emerging sector in the non-petroleum range of products from sandwiches to full branded fast food operations; and our research in New Delhi indicates that 40 percent of car owners seek food service facilities at petrol stations. The critical issues are: what services should be offered, and how should they be provided? In the US, food prepared on-site for take-away is a significant category of food service sales and caters to the habit of grazing the eating 'on-the-move'. In India, eating-out is more of a social event, and thus the platform of 'Food-on-the-go' may be less relevant. Our observation is that convenience stores are likely to be 'destinations' and not' traffic interceptors' in India. Therefore, full-fledged fast food operations could offer greater appeal at petroleum stations. The exact nature of food service provided is a function of the target consumer; a Barista coffee pub appeals to a very different consumer type from a 'Chinese van' consumer, but a 'Haldirams' and a McDonald's may be complementary. An interesting option could be to capitalize on the growth of organized Indian fast food retailing, using relatively well-located and spacious real estate (petrol stations) to establish 'chat' corners jointly with brands such as 'Haldirams', particularly in the smaller towns. Petroleum marketers can adopt a number of operating models for food service. From an alliance with an established brand such as McDonald's to the retailer's own brand/label.

Factors to be considered in deciding which food service model to adopt:

1. Space available (including parking);
2. Labour implications;

3. Skills/resource requirements;
4. Consumer demographics/psychographics; and
5. Competitive environment.

Branded food service offers the benefit of immediate brand recognition by consumers. It also provides assurance of quality, freshness and consistency. In India, where the concept of food service *at* petroleum stations itself is new, *an* alliance or joint venture is likely to be the most suitable operating model.

Ancillary Services—Ancillary services complement regular convenience stores and food service by providing additional reasons for consumers to visit the non-fuel area of the stations while increasing the retailers' share of the consumers' wallet on each visit. The range of ancillary service that can be sold through petroleum stations is large, and includes ATMs, insurance sales agents, courier services, pre-paid card sales, laundry services, car wash, newspaper and magazine stand, and even lotteries.

Key Success Factors in Value-added Product/Services-based differentiation Strategies

1. Manage barriers to trial and usage, such as consumer' perceptions of differentials in price, selection and service
2. Customize the assortment and offering to local market conditions
3. Maintain low operating *costs* and tight inventory control

3. Price-based Differentiation

This is an obvious differentiator for any product or service, and in markets such as the USA where as many as 56 percent of petroleum buyers cite price as a reason for selecting their brand; it is a powerful platform for differentiation. In India, where there are a large number of 'bargain hunters', a price-based strategy could be potentially very powerful. The challenge of such a strategy however, is to maintain uniqueness and sustainability. When a number of petroleum retailers adopt a low price positioning, other factors such as the associated offerings to ensure customer retention become critical. Internationally, there are 2 broad categories of petro-retailers which differentiate themselves based on price—the grocery retailers selling petroleum and the high volume, low margin convenience store retailer.

Grocery Retailers—Hypermarket retailers are rapidly gaining share of the fuel market in the West. In the USA, hypermarkets have 3.3 percent of the market value and in Europe, 5.2 percent of the number of petroleum retailing locations. In India, hypermarket operations are nascent and unlikely to be a near term threat to petroleum marketers. However, the likely success of the hypermarket retail model in India will pose a longer term threat to petro-retailers here.

Key Success Factors for Price-based Differentiation Strategies

1. Ability to sell more profitable products/services to subsidize lower margin 'loss leader' petroleum sales.
2. High degree of consumer price elasticity which ensures that lower margins are compensated through greater volumes.
3. Supply chain optimization and sourcing efficiencies to deliver lower-priced fuel consistently.

The High Volume, Low Margin Operating Model—Exemplified by companies such as QuikTrip and RaceTrac in the US, these retailers have developed operating models building on the high price elasticity in petroleum retailing. Selling petroleum at prices that are typically 5 percent less than the average market price, companies such as Quick-Trip are able to achieve as much as 75 percent higher sales throughputs through their stations. Although their margins are as much as 40 percent lower than the majors, their overall profitability is high. As in the hypermarket model, they use the higher traffic through their stations to drive sales in their convenience stores, which also typically sell at discounts to the market. The challenge to such a strategy in the Indian context is that non-fuel sales are currently so low that the discount retailers would be unable to boost overall profitability of their petrol stations sufficiently through this route. Like Quick-Trip, discount petroleum marketers in India would also need to develop other consumer hooks such as 'consumer experience' to build consumer loyalty.

4. *Consumer Experience-based Differentiation*

Petroleum marketing has a strong service element which can be used as a powerful lever for differentiation, especially in a commodity market environment. The consumer experience, or 'Moment of Truth', as it is also called, has been very successfully used by petroleum brands internationally to protect market share and to garner loyalty. A leading Oil and Gas company in Canada has clearly differentiated its consumer experience by ensuring warm and caring attitude towards its consumers. It builds "environmental consciousness" and "community orientation" in its overall image through sponsorships and theme creation. The company also continuously improves and up-dates the retail ambience through systematic renovation at their premises.

Indian Oil's Initiatives

BSNL will have the opportunity to set up and offer communication business centres at attractive rates to customers at Indian Oil petrol stations. Indian Oil's Indane distributorship network will be engaged by BSNL for selling products like Recharge Coupons, Sanchamet cards, .as well as BSNL's bill collection.

With an eye for enhancing customer convenience, Indian Oil has already introduced cashless transactions through co-branded credit cards at its petrol stations. The Corporation has also tied-up with reputed agencies like Akbarallys' for Coiwenio stores, with Dominos and Kamats for food courts, with ICICI Bank, Centurion Bank, etc., for ATMs etc. to provide an exhilarating retail experience to its customers.

In USA, Quik-Trip also uses consumer experience to reinforce its price-based strategy. Surveys of Quik-Trip consumers show extremely high value attached to their overall experience at the pump premises. While Quik-Trip ensures a warm and congenial experience for its consumers by recruiting and grooming highly motivated individuals, it also strikes the right chord with its consumers by storing their favorite drinks and snacks. QuikTrip's management believes in reflecting an image of "we do everything right" in all its direct and indirect consumer interaction.

Technology can also be used to greatly enhance the consumer experience. Many petroleum majors have adopted latest technology to ensure that consumers have a fast and hassle-free service. These are mainly in terms of the "swipe at pump" facilities, "at pump ordering" of non-fuel items through wireless microphones, customized electronic reports for corporate fleet programs etc. Mobil Speed pass is a good example of successful differentiation through technology-enabled service. Automatic miniature radio transponders attached to key chain or affixed to vehicles' rear window. Transponder automatically transmits unique secure ten digits that are recognized by an electronic system located at the pump. These electronic devices enable automatic charging of fuel purchases to a designate credit or check card. All these are at no direct or indirect cost to consumers.

In India, where many shoppers are highly relationship-oriented, personalization of the consumer experience could offer potential for differentiation and maintaining loyalty. Our research in New Delhi showed 85 percent of consumers attach significant importance to the "experience" within the premises in terms of quick service, attendant disposition and overall ambience in choosing their petrol pumps. Most have a stronger loyalty to the specific station than the petroleum brand. Developing a brand offering for the 'trust seeker' with a promise of "We make you feel special" could be a powerful strategy as long as the retailer is able to ensure consistency of delivery across locations and over time.

An experience-based differentiation strategy could be particularly relevant to existing petroleum retailers in India who would benefit from strengthening of their bond with the existing consumer franchise, thereby increasing the barriers to entry for new players.

Conclusions

Key Success Factors in Service-based Differentiation Strategies

1. Ensure quality of the human interface through people selection, training and development.
2. Ensure consistency of service delivery across location and over time.
3. Systemize the consumer experience delivery process.
4. Establish service recovery procedures.
5. Use technology to enable better consumer experience.
6. Personalize the experience.

Petroleum retailers in India will have to become more consumer-focused as competitive pressures increase and new players enter the market. Retailers can no longer treat all consumers alike and offer an undifferentiated set of products and services. We believe that there is an opportunity for petroleum retailers in India today to build revenues and enhance profitability by building strong and differentiated brand propositions based on in-depth consumer understanding.

AT Kearney research amongst petroleum consumers in New Delhi indicates that there are already distinct consumer psychographic segments emerging

(Routine Chore Doer, Time Poverty, Trust Seeker and the Prestige Seeker) which may offer potential to develop a differentiated offering in this 'commodity-like' market currently characterized by weak brand recognition and low levels of loyalty. A petroleum retailer can differentiate its offer on the basis of a number of different platforms: fuel-based differentiation, value-added products/service, and price and consumer experience.

Petroleum marketers need to develop a consumer centric strategy which addresses some key questions:

- What consumer segments should target?
- What differentiation strategy should adopt?
  - Is there an opportunity to build a petroleum retail brand around the concept of speed of service'?
  - How can the potentially large 'Price Shopper' consumer segment be tapped-profitably?
  - Is the convenience store concept as a revenue driver or brand differentiator premature in the Indian context?
- Is my basis for differentiation unique and sustainable?
- What operating model would deliver my brand promise most profitably?

CASE STUDY I: PETRO-CANADA

Gas Station Canopy

Conversion to LED-based canopy border tubing from neon results in energy savings of 85%

Like most high-traffic retailers, gas stations and convenience stores rely on a carefully designed brand image and visually attractive store-fronts to appeal to drive-by customers. Traditionally, the bright lights and attention-getting benefits of neon have been a critical design element for most of these outlets. Today, however, the exceptional energy savings, low maintenance costs and rich, bright colors associated with LED-based neon-replacement border tubing and lettering are proving an attractive alternative for retailers and store owners. Petro-Canada is a case in point.

Petro-Canada is one of Canada's largest petroleum retailers, with a network of more than 1,600 retail and wholesale outlets selling gasoline and other products across the country. In addition, as a responsible petroleum company interested in protecting the environment, Petro-Canada is keenly aware of the issue of global warming. The chance to reduce greenhouse gas emissions while taking advantage of the energy savings potential and brightness of LED-based products was attractive to the company.

"The engineers and staff in Petro-Canada's asset management team are focused on constantly looking for ways to increase visual appeal while reducing the costs of managing their stations," said Ken Piaggio, Vice-President, Service Delivery and Corporate Quality for TIR Systems, a leading global manufacturer of LED-based signage systems.

"In an industry such as gasoline retailing in which competition is fierce, cost containment is a key to profitability. Therefore, adopting a border tubing solution that reduces energy consumption by approximately 85 percent from existing solutions has been a valuable contribution to managing costs on site. Ultimately, however, the increased visual impact was a very important factor."

Better known as solid state lighting (SSL) in the lighting community for its foundation using solid-state technology from the semiconductor industry, it is important to understand that LED-based border tubing is a significant advance beyond neon. One reason is that SSL signage does not have filaments and glass that can be broken or ignite. Another is that semiconductor technology is a much more energy-efficient user of electricity; the energy savings alone can range up to 85 percent in applications such as border tubing and there are operational savings too.

Project Overview

Energy savings measured at 85 percent

Petro-Canada, which had been looking at LEDs for as long as ten years, already knew quite a bit about TIR's energy efficient SSL technology and the benefits of LEDs prior to initiating discussions with the company. The particular application Petro-Canada had in mind is usually called "border tubing" or "contour lighting." This border tubing delineates the canopy that shields the customers from bad weather at the gas pump, and provides a long-distance visual marker. Looking from a distance, the effect is that of a single unbroken band of light around the canopy. TIR's LightMark™system offers a continuous bright appearance that surpasses neon. This helps passersby to see and recognize the canopy from a distance, and therefore is a key element in the station's lighting architecture. For petroleum retailers, the border tubing around the canopy is possibly the second most important aspect of its canopy branding and visual look, after its logo.

This project started during the summer of 2003, when Petro-Canada contacted TIR to order its first test site of LightMark™border tubing. The test application was installed at a new facility in the Mont Tremblant region of Quebec and would enable Petro-Canada to trial TIR's product under the tough Quebec cold-weather conditions as the year went on. (As an interesting aside, SSL signage is brightest at around –20 degrees and is most effective in ambient temperatures ranging between –20 and 40 degrees Celsius). Another key feature of LightMarkTM border tubing is that it is very rugged. This is critical for customers such as Petro-Canada that have locations exposed to extreme winter weather conditions. The extruded plastic casing for the LEDs is sealed against the elements and, unlike neon, is very difficult to vandalize or break.

After successfully completing the first test phase, Petro-Canada wanted to check the energy savings of SSL lighting and review the visual look of LightMarkTM more closely. The company decided to set up a head-to-head trial to truly compare neon with SSL. It installed LightMark™on another site in Mississauga, Ontario in early 2004, close to a near identical site nearby lit with neon, where factors were the same or similar. This became the main test site and Petro-Canada began to monitor and compare performance. The company measured the electrical consumption on the canopy delineation for both stations over the period of several months and determined that SSL lighting used just 15% of the electricity required to light neon. In addition to this significant saving on energy consumption, LightMark™ also offered reduced operational costs due to lower maintenance requirements, and showed a decrease in greenhouse gas emissions.

The importance of greenhouse gas reductions cannot be overstated. Global warming continues to rise and this issue is gathering momentum for the world economy and the implementation of the Kyoto Protocol. Lighting and the use of energy-efficient SSL technologies is one area where significant efficiencies can be gained relatively quickly. Twenty five percent of all electricity generated around the world is used for lighting, and today the majority of that energy is wasted as heat, a byproduct. SSL technologies are using LEDs, an inherently more efficient light source, with the potential of converting up to 85 percent and more of the energy needed into usable light.

This means that the amount of power required for lighting would decline significantly, and so, consequently, would the quantities of harmful emissions from power stations. In addition, conventional light sources contain mercury and other potentially hazardous materials that enter the environment upon disposal. With life spans of up to ten years or more, LEDs won't need replacing as often, greatly reducing this waste. The potential of SSL technologies to assist in the battle against global warming and environmental pollution is enormous.

"While there are other benefits such as reduced maintenance costs and increased safety, customers find that LED-based solid state lighting solutions deliver significant energy savings over neon. That not only contributes to the bottom line, it helps reduce greenhouse gas emissions," notes Piaggio. "In the case of Petro-Canada, the company measured the energy-use reduction and found it to be 85%. It was an important validation of the magnitude of the savings that switching to LightMark™can bring".

Visual impact and curb appeal – day and night – critical for Petro-Canada

Yet despite these significant operational savings, the most important factor for Petro-Canada and most other retailers is almost always the final appearance of the gas station canopy. Bright border tubing is vital for visual impact and curb appeal. So how did the SSL border tubing look once in place? According to Piaggio, "SSL lighting has that visual punch that sign makers and their corporate clients are looking for with LEDs able to emit light of a single saturated color giving them a rich, bright appearance. For Petro-Canada the benefits of having excellent energy savings were matched by the look projected by the new SSL technology."

An additional visual benefit exhibited in the Petro-Canada project was that using the red SSL border tubing not only delivered vibrant color at night, it also presented rich color during the day. The resulting look was clean and even (by contrast, during the day neon is unable to provide any of the impact one sees at night and can look messy and detract from the overall appearance of a facility). It also didn't hurt that modifications to the existing canopy or design were not required—the installation was a clean, straight replacement.

After testing, the new system was approved by Petro-Canada which has made LightMark™ the design standard for all new-build stations across the country. "We were impressed with the proven field performance of TIR's LightMark™ product," said Lance Ubell, Manager, and Engineering and Construction for Petro-Canada's Asset Management team. "It allowed us to meet our key objectives of reducing our operating costs and our energy requirements while doing our part to protect the environment. Plus, we really liked the look of it compared to the neon we were using."

Summing up, Petro-Canada put TIR's SSL LightMark™border tubing to the test, using rigorous testing and head-to-head comparisons to see if the technology had flaws and how it stacked up against traditional neon. End result: TIR's SSL signage provided bright lights and exceptional savings. In short, it passed the test with flying colors.

Petro-Canada new station canopy border tubing

- Strong visual impact—a clean continuous illumination effect also provides an enhanced day-time visual effect
- No modifications to existing canopy required—LightMark™ fits the canopy well and provides a clean straight replacement
- LightMarkTM uses just 15% of the electrical energy required for neon
- Operational savings provide a solid business case – strong Total Cost of Ownership and ROI will only improve as electrical costs continue to rise in the future
- Red LightMark™ is an excellent match with the existing corporate image and therefore the color of the canopy
- LightMark™ is ruggedly constructed for harsh outdoor climates – it fares much better in cold Canadian winters than its neon counterpart
- Reduced maintenance requirements
- LEDs have up to ten years or more of useful life
- Significant reduction in GHG emissions (due to reduced electrical requirements)
- Increased safety—low voltage; inherently safer design; material will not ignite
- Approximately 350 feet of border tubing per station canopy

CASE STUDY II: DESIGN INNOVATIONS BY NRL

As part of its efforts to create a distinct identity in petro-retailing, NRL has developed a new look Energy Station. Design Innovations in the Petro-retail Centre is highlighted in this case study.

Retailers are constantly striving to come out with revolutionary design concepts to lure customers and get that extra edge over their competitors. Not just lifestyle and food but petroleum retailers, too, are considering this option to sport a 'different look'. Be it a Multi-Purpose Dispensing unit to fuel the vehicle, a sleek unit (in front) having TV monitor and LED display of the quantity, price and amount or a TV monitor exhibiting entertainments and advertisements which automatically switch on to unveil the fuelling activities of the dispensing boy behind the car. Seems too good to be true? But this is what the new-look petro retail outlets have in store for its customers. The first such energy station was launched at Kaziranga highway in Assam in January 2006 by Numaligarh Refinery Ltd (NRL) and 500 more are planned to be set up all over the country in phases. BPCL, which owns 63 per cent stake in NRL, has developed this new concept to create a 'retail visual identity' for the NRL brand. Recognizing the innovative and creative effort of the designers in effective retail display in making the consumers purchase decision memorable and enticing at NRL Energy Stations, BPCL was awarded a 'Silver Medal' at the prestigious POPAI, India OMA contest (Point-of-Purchase Advertising International, Outstanding Merchandising Award) in the Permanent automobile category. Let's take a look at the unique design concepts adopted by BPCL that helped NRL to bring out some of the innovative concepts in their venture to petro retailing business.

Inception

With the privatization of petrol pumps and new entrants in the industry, the Government of India granted license to NRL to operate 510 retail outlets for marketing transportation fuels. The Indian oil industry has undergone a metamorphosis and the rules of the game have changed with each company being a lot more professional. With this, providing service to the customer has gained importance. "NRL's composite marketing strategy was developed as more customer centric and is projected as dynamic and sensitive to the prospective customers.

CHAPTER XI

Financial and Accounting Systems for Oil and Natural Gas

(Petro-Accounting)

An understanding of basic accounting concepts and principles is a must for oil-industries personnel to go a long way in conducting in-depth financial analysis of an oil company. The basic issues that govern the treatment of financial statement entries are fairly straightforward and usually based on common sense. Knowing the rationale behind accounting convention can leverage into aiding systematic financial statement analysis. The practice of accounting dates back hundreds of years. In 1494, Luca Pacioli was the first to publish the 'double-entry system' of accounting in Venice. Fortunately, there is no need to mention debits or credits to explain the basic principles of accounting as it relates to petroleum and allied industries.

Generally Accepted Accounting Principles

The organizations that govern the accounting industry and monitor financial reporting practices in the United States are: the American Institute of Certified Public Accountants (AICPA), superseded in 1973 by the Financial Accounting Standards Board (FASB), the Securities and Exchange Commission (SEC), and the American Accounting Association (AAA).

The Financial Accounting Standards Board (FASB) is an independent self-regulating organization. It establishes the standards for the industry known as the generally accepted accounting principles (GAAP). The FASB outlines procedures and rules that define accepted accounting practices for financial reporting. The FASB publishes broad guidelines and detailed procedures for financial accounting practices. These principles govern the auditor's report or opinion letter that is published with corporate financial statements.

It is well understood that financial statements based on GAAP do not provide the petrified truth as far as value is concerned, but they do necessarily provide a place to start. Accounting theory is founded in economic and financial theory, yet different opinions exist as to what constitutes GAAP in different situations. There are some strict rules that provide some consistency, but accountants must exercise their professional judgment on many issues to arrive at consensus.

Accounting Concepts: The Basic Elements

Eleven basic accounting concepts put-together provide the foundation of accounting theory. These principles are fundamental to the understanding of financial statements. They may not be perfect. In nearly every case where there is a weakness in a particular principle or accounting practice, it is easy to point out the inherent short-comings, but in a way difficult to find a better solution.

The following represents some of the basic elements of Accounting Concept:

1. Money Measurement Concept
2. Entity Concept
3. Going Concern Concept
4. Dual-aspect Concept
5. Accounting Period Concept
6. Materiality Concept
7. Conservatism Concept
8. Consistency Concept
9. Realization Concept
10. Matching Concept
11. Cost Concept

A brief outline of 11 basic concepts of Accounting is given below:

The Money Measurement Concept: Financial information is expressed in monetary terms. It would not be practical to record on the balance sheet the number of barrels of oil or acres a company owns. Money is the common denominator. Fortunately, the number of barrels and acres can be found elsewhere.

The Entity Concept: Accounts are kept for business entities. The answer to any accounting issue must address the question: "How does it affect the business?" According to the entity concept, accountants are not concerned with persons who own or operate the business, but with the business itself.

The Going Concern Concept: Accounting assumes that a business will continue forever. If there is evidence to the contrary that the entity is going to liquidate, the accounting function might need to assess what the entity is worth to a potential buyer. Under the going concern assumption, current resale value or economic value of balance sheet items is usually irrelevant.

The Dual-aspect Concept: The resources owned by a business or entity are called assets. The claims against these assets are called equities. The two types of equities are: (1) Liabilities that represent the claims of creditors and (2) the owners' equity. The total claims on the assets are equal to the assets.

Assets = Equities
Assets = Liabilities + Stockholders' Equity

This is why both sides of the balance sheet balance. The essential concept is that for every resource available to a company, somebody has a claim on it.

The Accounting Period Concept: Accounting practices are based on the need to report periodically the status of a business entity. The basic time period is the fiscal year (12 months). Many companies use interim (usually quarterly and/or monthly) reports.

Materiality Concept: Insignificant items do not require attention. To a small company, a $5 million asset may be a very important item, but to the US based US company-Exxon, it may not be sufficiently material to deserve a separate balance sheet entry or even a footnote. The Exxon 1989 balance sheet listed $1,941 million worth of odds and ends under "other assets, including intangibles."

The Conservatism Concept: This principle dictates that given a choice, an asset will be recorded at the lowest or most conservative value. As far as the income statement is concerned, this principle provides that potential losses be accounted for, and yet potential gains or profits are not registered until they are realized. The result theoretically is that financial statements will provide a conservative view of the business.

Consistency Concept: The consistency concept stipulates that once an entity embarks on an accounting methodology, it must be consistent in its treatment of accounting issues unless it has good reason to do otherwise. At times, companies decide to make changes in accounting policies. These changes are explained in the footnotes.

The Realization Concept: The realization principle dictates that revenue should be recognized only at the time a transaction is completed with a third party, or when the value is reasonably certain. One common concern centers on the applicability of the realization principle to the petroleum industry. Some feel this principle should not be applicable because the major asset of an oil and gas company is its reserves, and the value of a company's reserves is not directly reflected on the balance sheet.

Neither the balance sheet nor the income statement allow appropriate recognition for important oil and gas discoveries in the accounting period in which a discovery is made. When a company makes a major discovery, there is no mechanism for reporting the results from an accounting point of view. The impact on the income statement comes when the discovery begins to produce, yet economic value was realized the moment the discovery was made. But just how much could be the economic value? This is the first natural question posed by the accountant. It is a fair question, too, because at the point of discovery, the uncertainty as to the quantity and value of reserves is greatest. Fortunately, the analysis of a company does not end with the financial statements.

Accrual vs. Cash

Another aspect of the realization concept is the accrual method of accounting for revenue and expenses. Under this method, revenue is recorded as it is earned, or is said to have accrued, and does not necessarily correspond to the actual receipt of cash. This concept is important for the understanding of the Statement of Cash-Flows and the concept of cash flow. For example, assume that a company sold 1,000 barrels of oil for $20 per barrel, but had only received $17,000 by the end of the accounting period. From an accrual accounting point of view, revenues are recorded as $20,000.

Revenues	$20,000	
Beginning Receivables	1000	
Cash Flow Potential	21,000	
Ending Receivables	(–) 4000	
Realized Cash Flow	$17,000	= Sales less increase in receivables

The income statement would reflect $20,000 because the accrual method of accounting realized the income at the point of sale, not at the point of actual cash exchange. The balance sheet would show the $17,000 increase in cash as well as an increase in accounts receivable for the $3,000 not yet received. However, the actual cash received is $17,000. This is why the statement of cash flows treats increases in the working capital account as a reduction in cash flows. As a business grows, the required amount of working capital also increases, and therefore, most detailed cash flow analyses include a negative adjustment for increases in working capital.

The Matching Concept: The matching principle provides that revenues should be matched with the corresponding costs of producing such revenues. A serious accounting issue in the oil and gas industry deals with the matching principle because it is so difficult to match the costs of finding oil and gas with the revenues from production. Under GAAP, assets reported on the balance sheet consist of capitalized historical costs. Earnings are recognized as reserves are produced, rather than when they are discovered or revised. Two separate systems of accounting in the industry are based primarily on this issue as it pertains to the treatment of exploration costs. The two systems are called Full-Cost and Successful Efforts accounting. While revenues are typically recognized when oil or gas are sold, the fundamental difference between the FC and SE accounting systems lies in how the corresponding costs of finding those reserves match those revenues.

The Cost Concept: In accounting, an asset is recorded at its original cost. This cost is the basis for all subsequent accounting for the asset. The primary rationale behind the cost principle is that the value of an item may change with the passage of time, and determination of value is subjective. There is no subjectivity associated with the actual cost of an item. Because of the cost principle, the accounting entry on the balance sheet for oil and gas assets usually has little to do with the actual value of the assets. For instance, if a company were to obtain a lease and then discover a million barrels of oil, the accounting entry would not change because of the discovery. It would never reflect anything other than the associated costs less depreciation. Only the net tangible costs would represent all that oil. In this example, there is substantial appreciation in value that is ignored by GAAP. However, accountants do not ignore economic value completely. The cost principle provides that assets should be reflected on the balance sheet at cost, unless there has been a decline in their utility or economic value. Accountants do not mind an asset on the books at less than its true market value, but they are careful to keep accounting entries from exceeding economic value.

Reserve Recognition Accounting

Many methods have been considered in an effort to find a way to adequately represent the actual value of oil and gas assets. In 1978, in response to a request from the SEC of the USA, the FASB announced a programme of financial reporting, FASB Statement No. 19, termed Reserve Recognition Accounting (RRA of USA). Here the value of a company's reserves was recognized as an asset. Also, additions to proven reserves could be recognized as assets, and the additions could be included in earnings (http://books.google.co.in/books?id=sYIqxibXy1kC&pg=PA244&lpg=PA244&dq=FASB+Statement+No.+19,+termed+Reserve+Recognition+Accounting+(RRA+of+USA)&source=web&ots=k_6D7NtTFl&sig=2nl-PSXB1Q31EGAcGWYLRQf741M&hl=en&sa=X&oi=book_result&resnum=1&ct=result#PPA212,M1).

The SEC originally intended RRA to replace FC and SE accounting methods. But RRA was only required as supplemental information during a trial period from January 1979 to November 1982. The FASB issued Statement No. 25 in February 1979, suspending all but the disclosure requirements of FASB Statement No. 19. It was determined that RRA could not replace FC and SE accounting due the inaccuracies of reserve reporting. In response to a request from the SEC, the FASB then developed disclosure requirements that were issued in November 1982 in Statement No. 69, Disclosures about Oil and Gas Producing Activities.

These disclosure requirements provide a substantial amount of information. The basic information pertaining to reserve recognition is summarized as follows:

1. Quantification of proved oil and gas reserves. Reserves are further categorized as developed or underdeveloped.
2. Annual production information and results of exploratory drilling, production, acquisitions, and revisions to previous reserve estimates.
3. Capitalized costs associated with producing properties and costs incurred for lease acquisition exploration and development activities.
4. Standard Measure (SEC Value of Reserves) based on standardized discounted cash flow analysis of proved reserves.

   The SEC requirements that provide the basis of standardization are as follows:

   - prices received at fiscal year end for products (oil, gas, coal, sulfur) sold
   - prices are held constant, no escalation
   - costs are not escalated
   - a 10% discount rate is used

5. Changes in Standard Measure and reasons for change are reported.
6. Accounting method used must be disclosed as well as the manner of disposing of capitalized costs.

Costs associated with oil and gas exploration and production fall into four fundamental categories:

Lease Acquisition Costs: Costs associated with obtaining a lease or concession and rights to explore for and produce oil and gas.

Exploration Costs: Costs incurred in the exploration for oil and gas such as geological and geophysical costs (G&G), exploratory drilling, etc.

Development Costs: Costs associated with development of oil and gas reserves: Drilling costs, storage and treatment facilities, etc.

Operating Costs: Costs required for lifting oil and gas to the surface, processing, transporting, etc.

Treatment of these costs is fairly straightforward. The one exception is the way that exploration costs are treated. This provides the basis for the two different accounting practices that are used in the industry.

Full-Cost and Successful Efforts Accounting

These two accounting methods, Full-Cost (FC) and Successful Efforts (SE) can give very different results on earnings, return on equity, and book value. Both systems follow as best they can the accounting principles of matching, realization, and cost, yet there is debate about which system is most appropriate. Primarily, the two systems differ on how capital costs associated with exploration drilling are treated. The main difference is that drilling costs of unsuccessful exploration wells are capitalized under FC accounting and expensed under the SE accounting system (Gallun et al, 2004).

Successful Efforts Accounting

Prior to the 1950s, virtually all oil companies used some form of Successful Efforts (SE) accounting. The rationale behind SE is that expenditures providing no future economic benefit should be expensed at the time incurred. The SE approach will expense or write off exploratory dry-hole costs in the accounting period in which they are incurred. This is similar to many other businesses that will write off business failures. Proponents of SE agree that only expenditures directly associated with the discovery of hydrocarbons should be capitalized. SE companies treat exploration expenditures like other companies would treat research and development. If a research project results in a viable product, then capital expenditures are capitalized, otherwise, the costs are expensed.

In 1969, the American Institute of Certified Public Accountants published *Accounting Research Study* No. 11 on "Financial Reporting in the Extractive Industry." The basic thesis of the report was to promote the use of the SE method. In understanding the broad concepts of Accounting for oil and natural gas industries the salient findings of the research study contained in the report will hereafter be referred to (http://books.google.co.in/books?id=t_wYPe8arT0C&pg=PA56&lpg=PA56&dq=Certified+Public+Accountants+published+Accounting+Research+Study+No.+11+on+%22Financial+Reporting+in+the+Extractive+Industry.%22&source=web&ots=n30xTsd_s&sig=ZGYEVAlkeYZNEKFnM5K4t2BR_rk&hl=en&sa=X&oi=book_result&resnum =1&ct=result).

Ceiling Test

Full-cost accounting requires a write-down on the book value of oil and gas assets if it exceeds the SEC value of reserves. For this reason, FC companies use large cost centers. This is the *ceiling test* required by the SEC for the cost of oil and gas properties on the balance sheet. The recorded capitalized costs for producing oil and gas properties are limited to the net present value of the reserves discounted at 10%. This is the SEC value of reserves or standard measure. If the SEC value of reserves falls below the capitalized costs on the balance sheet, a ceiling write-down occurs. For example, if a company had a book value for proved oil and gas properties of $100 million, and the SEC value of these reserves was $130 million, there would be no write-down. The company would have a cost ceiling cushion of $30 million. In 1986, when oil prices dropped so dramatically, cushions disappeared, and many FC companies experienced substantial write-downs. The most important problem that this caused was that many companies suddenly found themselves in violation of covenants in their loan agreements. Impairments and write-downs occur under SE accounting, too. It is usually not considered as great an issue because such a large part of exploration costs are expensed and not capitalized. But, consistent with the conservatism principle, the carrying value of BE oil and gas properties are subject to write-downs if the economic value of a property is less than the recorded value. Periodic assessments are made to ensure that the value of leases has not been impaired due to negative results of drilling or approaching expiration dates.

Comparison

With each system, lease bonus payments, related legal costs, and development drilling costs are capitalized. Capitalized costs within a cost center are usually amortized on the unit-of-production method. Basic elements of the two systems are compared in Table 11.1.

Book Value, Sec Value and Market Value of Reserves

The book-value of oil and gas reserves that appears on the balance sheet bears no direct relationship to reserve values under either FC or BE accounting methods. Because the BE company will expense. G&G costs and exploratory dry holes, the book value of reserves will be lower than under FC accounting. Primarily, the two systems differ on how capital costs associated with exploration drilling are treated. The main difference is that drilling costs of unsuccessful exploration wells are capitalized under FC accounting and expensed under the SE accounting system.

Table 11.1: Comparison of Accounting Systems

	Successful Efforts Methods	Full Cos) method
G&G Costs	Exp	Cap
Exploratory Dry Hole	Exp	Cop
Lease Acquisition Costs	Cap	Cap
Successful Exploratory Well	Cop	Cap
Development Dry Hole	Cap	Cap
Successful Development Well	Cap	Cap
Operating Costs	Exp	Exp
Which Companies Typically Use Each Method	Major Oil Companies	Smaller Independent Companies
Size of Cost Center Used	Small	Large
	Single Well, Lease or Field	Company, Country, or Hemisphere
Comment	Favored by FASB Approved by SEC	Approved by SEC

G&G = Geological and Geophysical.
Exp = Expensed (Written off in accounting period).
Cop = Capitalized (Written off over a number of accounting periods).

Full-cost Accounting

Full-Cost Accounting (FCA) was developed in the 1950s. The First Corporation to use FC accounting was Belco Petroleum in 1957, which at that time was just going public. FC allowed smaller companies and especially startup companies to access the capital markets more easily. These companies believe that the system is fairer and reported earnings are less volatile. The philosophy behind FC accounting is that costs of acquisition, exploration, and development are necessary for the production of oil and gas. This rationale acknowledges that dry holes are an inevitable part of the exploration effort. With FC, the entire company can be a cost center, and all costs of exploring for oil and gas are capitalized. Companies with international operations typically treat each country as a separate cost center.

Full-Cost Accounting (FCA) generally refers to the process of collecting and presenting information (costs as well as advantages) for each proposed alternative when a decision is necessary. A synonym, true cost accounting (TCA) is also often used. Experts consider both terms problematic as definitions of "true" and "full" are inherently subjective. Full cost accounting embodies several key concepts that distinguish it from standard accounting techniques. The following list highlights the basic tenets of FCA (http://en.wikipedia.org/wiki/Full_cost_accounting).

1. Accounting for costs rather than outlays
2. Accounting for hidden costs and externalities
3. Accounting for overhead and indirect costs
4. Accounting for past and future outlays
5. Accounting for costs according to lifecycle of the product

In 1977, the FASB *Statement* No. 19 struck down FC with seven of the Big Eight accounting firms ruling against FC. While the FASB did not consider FC accounting an acceptable accounting method under GAAP, the SEC in 1978 declared the FC method acceptable. The SEC ruled that FC could coexist with SE and that companies could choose whichever method they desired. The FASB refused to develop the rules for FC accounting, so the SEC developed the FC guidelines. In 1979, the FASB rescinded their requirement that all companies use BE accounting. By 1986, 60% of the publicly traded oil companies had adopted FC accounting.

Comparison of Accounting Impact for a Start-up Company

Table 11.2 shows an example of a company with $10 million startup capital. In its first year, the company drills 15 wells and has two discoveries. The following table outlines the general features of how the two accounting methods would report the financial results of the first year of operations. Under the SE method, all exploratory dry holes are expensed. For the startup company, reporting a $5.5 million loss in the first year can be devastating. This is one of the reasons why so many small startup companies prefer FC accounting. The company managed to find 1.6 million barrels of oil. The company might believe the reserves would be unfairly represented by a book value of only $2.5 million under BE. Events affecting net income will also be represented differently under the two accounting systems. This is particularly true of a startup company. With moderate reinvestment of cash flow, the earnings of an established company would be nearly the same under either accounting system.

Table 11.2: Company Start-up Results under FC&SE Accounting

Exploration Wells Drilled	Drilling Costs ($000)	Results
6	3,000	Plugged and Abandoned
1	1,500	700,000 Barrel Discovery
7	2,500	Plugged and Abandoned
1	1,000	900,000 Barret Discovery
15	$8,000	1,600,000 Barrels

Generalized Financial Reporting

	SE Accounting (S000)	FC Accounting ($000)
Revenue	0	0
Expense	– 5,500	0
Income*	(5,500)	0
Assets		
Cash	2,000	2,000
Property	2,500	8,000
Equity	4,500	10,000

No Income Taxes or G&A Costs considered

Events affecting net income will also be represented differently under the two accounting systems. This is particularly true of a startup company. With moderate reinvestment of cash flow, the earnings of an established company would be nearly the same under either accounting system. Statement in above table depicts how the income statement under the two accounting systems would reflect changes in drilling activity. It is assumed that drilling efforts result in the same degree of success as in the past. With increased exploratory drilling, net income drops under SE accounting compared to FC accounting methods. This is because SE will expense exploration dry-hole costs. Decreased exploratory drilling under both methods will increase net income initially, but the change will be greater under SE.

Depreciation, Depletion and Amortization

Depreciation is a means of accounting for the recovery of the costs of a fixed asset by allocating the costs over the estimated useful life of the asset. When this concept is applied to mineral resources such as oil and gas reserves, it is called *depletion*. The concept is called amortization when the allocation of costs is applied to intangible assets. The terms depreciation, depletion, and amortization (DD&A) are sometimes used interchangeably, or more often collectively as DD&A. The importance of DD&A is that these expenses are deducted from income for federal and state income tax purposes. The depreciable life of an asset is usually determined by legislation to emulate the useful life of that asset. Table 11.3 gives some examples of basic oil industry assets.

Table 11.3: Typical Asset Lives for Depreciation and Amortization

Asset	Life
Intangible Drilling Costs that must be Amortized (30% of IDCs)	5 Years
Vehicles and Drilling Equipment	5 Years
Production Equipment and most Field Equipment	
Office Equipment	
Processing Plants	7 Years
Refining Equipment	10 Years
Transmission Pipelines	15 Years
Buildings	30 Years

Cost Depletion and Percentage Depletion

Depletion for tax purposes is based on the concept of the removal and sale of a wasting or depleting asset in this case, oil and gas. Depletion is analogous to ordinary depreciation. The Internal Revenue Code authorizes a deduction from income for depletion of oil and gas properties. It is a relatively simple concept, but it is complicated by many limitations and exemptions. Two types of calculating depletion must be considered when estimating taxable income. The two methods are cost depletion and percentage depletion. The taxpayer is entitled to the higher of either the cost or percentage depletion. Cost depletion of producing oil and gas properties is allowed under the unit-of-production method on a property-by-property basis. This method requires a reasonably accurate estimate of the remaining recoverable reserves. The basic formula is outlined as follows:

Formula for Unit of Production Method

$$\text{Annual Depreciation} = (C - AD - S)\,\frac{P}{R}$$

where:

C = capital costs of equipment
AD = accumulated depreciation
S = salvage value
P = barrels of oil produced during the year
R = recoverable reserves remaining at the beginning of the tax year

The tax advantages of percentage depletion were eliminated for all integrated oil companies in 1975. Cost depletion is available to both independent producers and integrated oil companies.

Oil and Natural Gas Accounting: Broad Principles

Oil and gas accounting relates to accounting for the four basic costs incurred by companies with oil and gas exploration and producing activities. These four basic types of costs are explained in a nut-shell as follows (Gallun et al, 2004):

- **Acquisition costs**—costs incurred in acquiring property, *i.e.*, costs incurred in acquiring the rights to explore, drill, and produce oil and natural gas. Domestically, these rights are normally acquired by obtaining an oil, gas, and mineral lease.
- **Exploration costs**—costs incurred in exploring property. Exploration involves identifying areas that may warrant examination and examining specific areas, including drilling exploratory wells.
- **Development costs**-costs incurred in preparing proved reserves for production, i.e., costs incurred to obtain access to proved reserves and to provide facilities for extracting, treating, gathering, and storing oil and gas.
- **Production costs**—costs incurred in lifting the oil and gas to the surface and in gathering, treating, and storing the oil and gas.

To account for these costs, knowledge of the industry terms and procedures discussed is imperative. Additional and important terms are defined in the following Glossary as they are used in accounting.

Historical Cost Accounting Methods

The four basic types of costs incurred by oil and gas companies in exploration and production activities must be accounted for using one of two generally accepted historical cost methods: successful-efforts accounting (SE) or full-cost accounting (FC). In connection with the four basic costs, the fundamental accounting issue is whether to capitalize or expense the incurred costs. If capitalized the costs may be expensed as expiration takes place either through abandonment (SE only), impairment (SE only), or depletion as reserves are produced. If expensed as incurred, the costs are treated as period expenses and charged against revenue in the current period. The primary difference between SE and FC is in whether a cost is capitalized or expensed when incurred. In other words, the primary difference between the two methods is in the timing of the expense or loss charge against revenue. The other basic difference between the two accounting methods is the size of the cost center over which costs are accumulated and amortized. For SE, the cost center is a lease, field, or reservoir. In contrast, the cost center under FC is a country. The cost center size has implications in computing depreciation, depletion, and amortization (DD&A) and also in computing ceiling write downs

In the presently accepted financial accounting framework, an asset is an economic resource that is expected to provide future benefits, and non-monetary assets in general are accounted for at the cost to acquire or construct them. Costs that do not relate directly to specific assets having identifiable future benefits normally are not capitalized-no matter how vital those costs may be to the ongoing operations of the enterprise. If costs do not give rise to an asset with identifiable future benefits, they are charged to expense or recognized as a loss. Under SE, a direct relationship is thus required between costs incurred and reserves discovered. Consequently, under SE only successful exploration costs that directly result in the discovery of proved reserves are considered to be part of the cost of finding oil or gas and are capitalized. Unsuccessful exploration costs do not result in an asset with future economic benefit and are therefore expensed. In contrast, because there is no known way to avoid unsuccessful costs in searching for oil or gas, FC considers both successful and unsuccessful costs incurred in the search for reserves as a necessary part of the cost of finding oil or gas. A direct relationship between costs incurred and reserves discovered is not required under Fe. Hence, both successful and unsuccessful costs are capitalized, even though the unsuccessful costs have no future economic benefit. Specifically, SE treats exploration costs that do not directly find oil or gas as period expenses and successful exploration costs as capital expenditures. Under FC, all exploration costs are capitalized. Under both methods, acquisition and development costs are capitalized and production costs are expensed. Although development costs could include an unsuccessful development well, all development costs are capitalized under SE because the purpose of development activities is considered to be building a producing system of wells and related equipment and facilities, rather than searching for oil and gas. Table 11.4 shows the accounting treatment of these costs under SE compared to FC.

SE vs. FC

The divergent accounting treatment of unsuccessful exploratory drilling costs

Table 11.4: The Accounting Treatment of these Costs under SE Compared to FC

Item	SE	FC
Acquisition costs	C	C
G&G costs	E	C
Exploratory dry hole	E	C
Exploratory well, successful	C	C
Development dry hole	C	C
Development well, successful	C	C
Production costs	E	E
Amortization	Cost center	Property, field, Country or reservoir

under SE versus FC can have a substantial impact on the income statements of exploration and production companies. A company with a large exploratory drilling program and a normal unsuccessful drilling rate would, under SE, have a significant amount of dry-hole expense. Those dry-hole costs would adversely affect the net income of a successful-efforts company. On the other hand, a full-cost company would capitalize exploratory dry-hole costs, and therefore, these costs would typically have no immediate effect on net income. They would, however, reduce net income through future amortization. The adverse effect on net income of expensing exploratory dry-hole costs under SE may be especially significant for smaller companies.

The following example illustrates the impact of the FC and SE accounting methods on the financial statements of Lucky Company.

EXAM PLE

Financial Statements

Star oil Company began operations on March 3, 1995, with the acquisition of a lease in Texas. During the first year, the following costs were incurred, DD&A (depreciation, depletion, and amortization) taken, and the following revenue was earned.

G&G costs	$ 30,000	
Acquisition costs	50,000	
Exploratory dry holes	1,200,000	
Exploratory wells, successful	400,000	
Development costs	200,000	
Production costs	25,000	
DD&A expense	40,000	(SE) 90,000 (FC)
Revenue	100,000	

Income Statements

	SE	FC
Revenue	$ 100,000	$100,000
Expenses:		
G&G	30,000	0
Exploratory dry holes	1,200,000	0
Production costs	25,000	25,000
DD&A	40,000	90,000
Total Expenses	**1,295,000**	**115,000**
Net Income	$(1,195,000)	$(15,000)

Partial Balance Statements ·

	SE	FC
G&G costs		$ 30,000
Acquisition costs	$ 50,000	50,000
Exploratory dry holes		1,200,000
Exploratory wells, successful	400,000	400,000
Development costs	200,000	200,000
Total assets	650,000	1,880,000
Less accumulated DD&A	(40,000)	(90,000)
Net assets	$ 610,000	$ 1790,000

Historical Development of Accounting Methods

Accounting history has emerged as an academic discipline over the last 40 years within English speaking countries. There is now a critical mass of researchers, dedicated journals and conferences, and a significant body of literature that is increasing in scope and depth. This article examines the strategies that, ex-post can be seen as important in developing accounting history as a discipline. Three strategies are identified: (1) making accounting history relevant (to education, standard-setting, and organizational memory/identity), (2) making accounting history controversial (by identifying positive and negative exemplars, providing historical critiques of mainstream research, and encouraging methodological/ theoretical pluralism within accounting history), and (3) institutionalizing accounting history (by developing academic associations, journals and conferences, and embedding accounting history within a network of supporting organizations including universities, professional associations, libraries, research centers and publishers). The article concludes by identifying the weak points in the disciplinary project (Richardson, 2008)

Accounting for oil and gas producing activities poses many technical and theoretical problems involving basic characteristics of the industry such as:

- high risk
- high cost of investment
- lack of correlation between the size of expenditure and the value of any resulting reserves
- long time span from when costs are first incurred until benefits are received are four important reasons for the controversy surrounding the

accounting procedures used by oil and gas exploration and production companies.

In addition, taxation and regulation have placed demands on companies' accounting and reporting systems. The federal taxation statutes contain many specialized rules applying only to oil and gas operations (e.g., intangible drilling costs and depletion rules). Further, federal and state governments have a long history of regulating the production and pricing of oil and natural gas. Finally, companies typically undertake oil and gas exploration and produce any resulting reserves as joint venture operations. In addition to placing extensive accounting responsibilities on the operator, joint venture accounting requires each of the parties to account for its proportionate share of costs and revenues and to separately report their income to the state and federal taxing authorities. For all the above reasons, accounting for oil and gas operations has complex and specialized accounting rules and procedures.

In 1969, the American Institute of Certified Public Accountants (AICPA) issued *Accounting Research Study No.* 11, "Financial Reporting in the Extractive Industries." This study supported the successful-efforts method of accounting. Despite this study, the Accounting Principles Board chose not to issue an Opinion thus requiring its successor, the Financial Accounting Standards Board (FASB), to deal with the complex and politically sensitive issues surrounding an appropriate method of accounting for oil and gas exploration, development, and production costs. In 1975, in response to OPEC's embargo and the consequent oil and gas shortage in the United States, the Federal Energy and Conservation Act was passed. This act required that the SEC must either prescribe oil and gas accounting rules or approve oil and gas accounting rules developed by the FASB.

The Historical Development of Accounting Standards on Deferred Tax

To fully understand the historical developments of accounting for deferred tax in the UK it is first necessary to gain an appreciation of how a tax liability can be 'deferred', and how such a liability may be measured. A tax can appear to be deferred because of differences between the profit before tax reported in the profit and loss account following UK accounting legislation and accounting standards, and the profit that is considered to be taxable by the Inland Revenue. It is, therefore, possible to effectively incur a tax liability in one accounting period but, because of the differences between the way activities are included in accounting profit and taxable income, pay the tax in a much later period (Steve Lawrence, 2000).

Methods of Computation

1. The Deferral Method

This method is based on the concept that, in the year in which a timing difference originates, a benefit arises which is deferred until a later period when the timing difference reverses. The deferred tax balance is viewed as deferred income and, therefore, subsequent changes in the rate of tax give no cause for adjustment. The reversal amount will be matched exactly with the original difference. It is necessary to keep detailed records of timing differences arising under varying tax rates to ensure that there is a correct match. Emphasis is placed on the profit and loss account charge.

2. The Liability Method

The tax effects are regarded as amounts of tax ultimately due by the entity. Thus, deferred tax provisions are maintained in the balance sheet at the future tax rates that will apply when the relevant originating timing difference reverses. (For practical purposes it is often necessary to assume that the current rate is the best estimate of future rates). Emphasis is placed on the balance sheet provision.

Bases of Calculation

1. *Full provision*
   The full tax effects of all timing differences are provided for irrespective of the future investment plans of the company.
2. *Partial provision*
   Deferred tax should be provided for in respect of the net amounts by which it is probable that any payment of tax will be temporarily deferred by the operation of timing differences which will reverse in the foreseeable future without being replaced.

Introduction to Full-Cost Accounting

Figure 11.1 presents a flowchart overview of the treatment of the four basic costs under FC (Gallun et al, 2004). The example used to illustrate SE accounting is also used to illustrate FC accounting. As shown in the flow chart and in the example, acquisition, exploration, and development costs are capitalized under the full cost method, regardless of whether the costs result in a discovery of reserves. As in SE accounting, gross acquisition costs are placed in an unproved property account and are moved to a proved property account if proved reserves are found. If the property is abandoned or impaired, the costs continue to be capitalized but are transferred to an abandoned or impaired cost account.

Drilling Costs

Over the past several decades, various methods have been proposed to evaluate drilling cost and complexity, but because of the large number of factors and events that impact drilling performance, predictive models are difficult to construct. Quantifying well costs and complexity is challenging, due either to restrictions on data collection and availability, constraints associated with modeling, or combinations of these factors. Drill rates are often constrained by factors that the driller does not control and in ways that cannot be documented. The Joint Association Survey and Mechanical Risk Index the most popular methods used to evaluate drilling cost and complexity in the Gulf of Mexico, and specialized indices have been introduced to characterize are the complexity of drilling directional and extended reach wells. Recently, the concept of Mechanical Specific Energy has been used to obtain a more objective (Kaiser, 2007). This section discusses two types of exploration drilling costs and both drilling and no drilling

Fig. 11.1: Full-Cost Overview

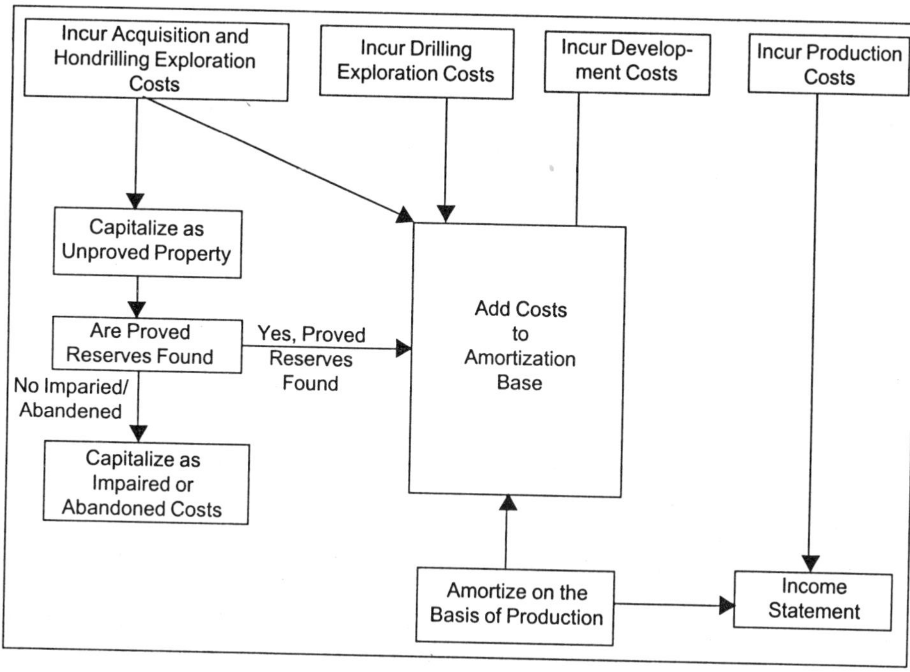

development costs. Under SE accounting, a direct relationship is required between costs incurred and specific reserves discovered before costs are ultimately identified as assets. In contrast to exploration costs, the purpose of development activities is considered to be building a producing system of wells and related equipment and facilities rather than searching for oil and gas. Thus, both successful and unsuccessful development costs are capitalized as part of the cost of the oil or gas (Gallun et al, 2004).

Exploratory Drilling Costs

Figure given below diagrams the accounting treatment of all five types of exploration costs. The last two types are: (1) the costs of drilling and equipping exploratory wells, and (2) the costs of drilling exploratory type stratigraphic test wells. These drilling exploration costs are defined as follows:

Exploratory well: A well drilled to find and produce oil or gas in an unproved area, to find a new reservoir in a field previously found to be productive of oil or gas in another reservoir, or to extend a known reservoir. Generally, an exploratory well is any well that is not a development well, a service well, or stratigraphic tests well as those items are defined.

Stratigraphic test well: A drilling effort, geologically directed, to obtain information pertaining to a specific geologic condition. Such wells customarily are drilled without the intention of being completed for hydrocarbon production. This classification also includes tests identified as core tests and all types of expendable holes related to hydrocarbon exploration. Stratigraphic test wells are classified as

(i) "exploratory-type," if not drilled in a proved area or (ii) "development-type, "if drilled in a proved area.

The cost of drilling exploratory wells and the costs of drilling exploratory-type stratigraphic test wells shall be capitalized as part of the enterprises uncompleted wells, equipment, and facilities, pending determination of whether the well has found proved reserves. If the well has found proved reserves the capitalized costs of drilling the well shall become part of the enterprises wells and related equipment and facilities (even though the well may not be completed as a producing well); if, however, the well has not found proved reserves, the capitalized costs of drilling the well, net of any salvage value, shall be charged to expense. The following example (Fig. 11.4) illustrates typical drilling and completion costs and their accounting treatment under SE. As shown in the example, drilling costs are temporarily classified as (1) wells in progress-IDC or (2) wells in progress-lease and well equipment. (The term wells in progress is used in place of the FASB terminology uncompleted wells, equipment, and facilities). When drilling reaches the targeted depth, a decision must be made as to whether the well has found proved reserves. If proved reserves have been found, both wells in progress account balances will be transferred to wells and related equipment and facilities accounts. In addition, if the well is the first successful exploratory well drilled on the property, the unproved property account will be reclassified or transferred into a proved property account because proved reserves have been found and are now attributed to that property.

Development Drilling Costs

Development wells are defined by the SEC as follows:

Development well: A well drilled within the proved area of an oil or gas reservoir to the depth of a stratigraphic horizon known to be productive. Although a reservoir is discovered by exploratory wells, drilling additional development wells is typically necessary to produce the reservoir at a satisfactory rate. Development wells may not significantly increase the total amount of oil and gas that is ultimately recoverable from a formation; however, the additional wells do increase the ultimate rate of recovery.

Development costs are accounted for as follows:

Development costs shall be capitalized as part of the cost of an enterprises wells and related equipment and facilities. Thus, all costs incurred to drill and equip development wells, development-type stratigraphic test wells, and service wells are development costs and shall be capitalized, whether the well is successful or unsuccessful. Costs of drilling those wells and costs of constructing equipment and facilities shall be included in the enterprises uncompleted wells, equipment, and facilities until drilling or construction is completed. For entries n and o the well was assumed to be a dry hole. Entries n and o transferred to dry hole expense the cost of drilling, evaluating, and plugging and abandoning the well. If the well had been a development well, these costs would have been capitalized, regardless of the well's outcome, as wells and related equipment and facilities.

Fig. 11.2: Typical Drilling and Completion Costs and their Accounting Treatment under SE

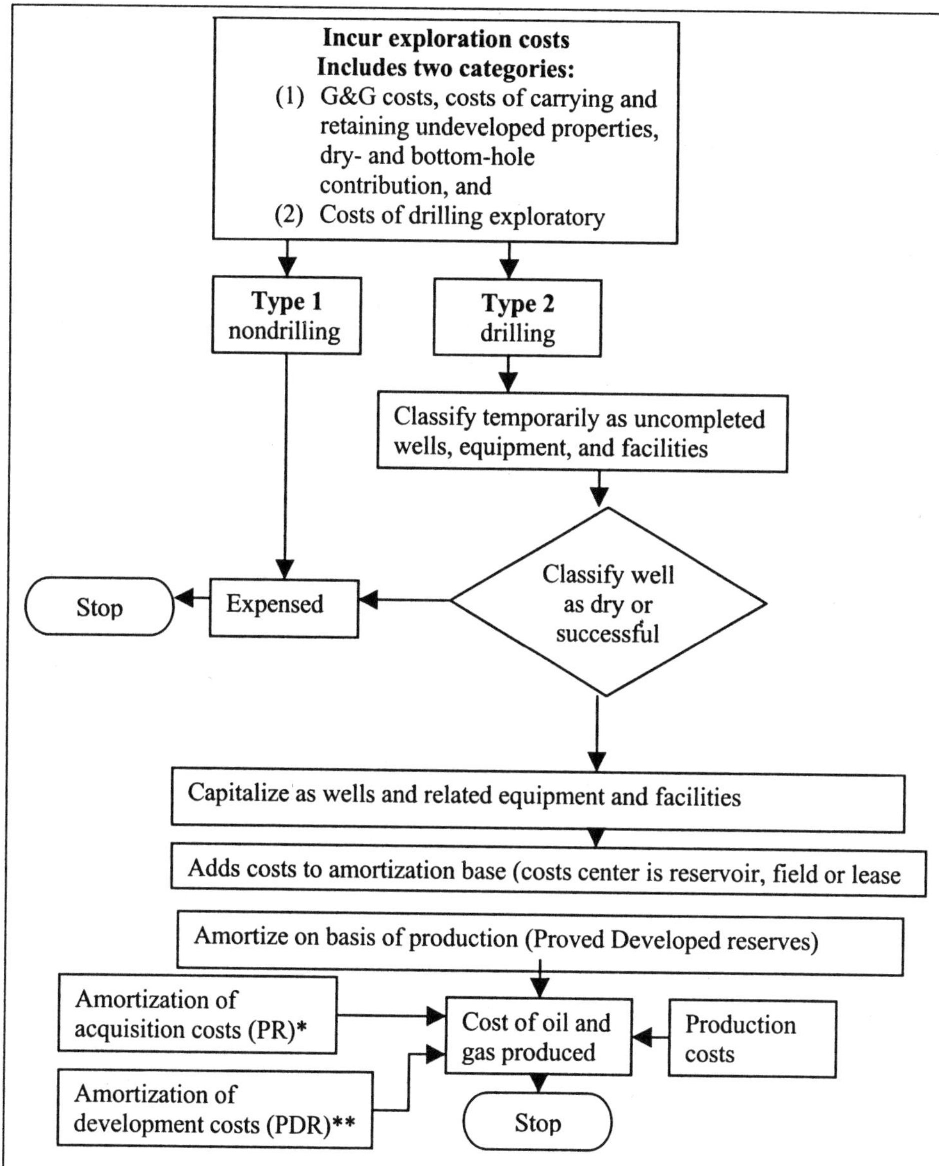

Stratigraphic 'Test Wells'

The rules for capitalizing or expensing costs of exploratory-type and development-type stratigraphic test wells are the same as the rules for capitalizing or expensing the costs of exploratory and development wells. As a result, dry exploratory-type stratigraphic test wells are expensed; successful exploratory-type stratigraphic test wells are capitalized. All development-type stratigraphic test wells, whether dry or successful, are capitalized. Thus, capitalization is not dependent upon whether the well will be completed as a producer, but upon whether the well has either found proved reserves or is a development well.

Full-Cost Accounting

Under Full-cost (FC) accounting, both successful and unsuccessful costs incurred in the search for oil and gas is considered necessary to finding oil or gas. In other words, it is necessary to drill a certain number of dry holes as well as successful wells-and incur other nonproductive exploration costs-in order to find oil and gas reserves. According to this reasoning, both successful and unsuccessful expenditures should be capitalized and amortized over production as part of the cost of the oil and gas. Thus, directly relating costs incurred to specific reserves discovered is not relevant under full-cost accounting. In contrast, under successful-efforts accounting, only those exploration costs that can be directly related to specific reserves are capitalized. Some would argue that FC is a departure from traditional historical cost accounting since nonproductive exploration costs, having no future economic benefit, are capitalized. Others contend that FC actually produces more meaningful financial statements. Unlike other industries, the primary assets of oil and gas companies are not the property, plant, and equipment, bur the oil and gas in the ground. FC financial statements are based on the fact that unsuccessful expenditures are a necessary and unavoidable part of discovering those assets.

Specifically, under full cost, all costs associated with property acquisition, exploration, and development activities are capitalized. Consequently, G&G studies, delay rentals, and exploratory dry holes are capitalized. Even when property is impaired or abandoned, the costs of impairment or abandonment continue as part of the capitalized costs of the cost center. Any portion of general and administrative costs directly related to acquisition, exploration, and development activities, such as the internal costs of the land department, may also be capitalized. Costs related to production, general corporate overhead, and similar activities are expensed. General corporate overhead cost normally includes all costs incurred in maintaining the various administrative offices throughout the company unless those office costs can be identified with acquisition, exploration, and development activities. Examples of general corporate overhead include executive compensation and offices, salaries of accounting personnel and the costs of their offices, and other administrative costs not related to acquisition, exploration, and development activities.

Figure 11.3 shows the accounting treatment of the four basic types of costs incurred in exploration and production activities under full cost in a summarized form. These four costs-acquisition, exploration, development, and production-are defined for full cost as they are for successful efforts. The following is an example of accounting for costs using the full-cost method. In studying the example, compare the accounting treatment under full cost to that under successful efforts-which costs are capitalized versus expensed, as well as account tides used. Because

Fig. 11.3: Accounting Treatment of the Four Basic Types of Costs

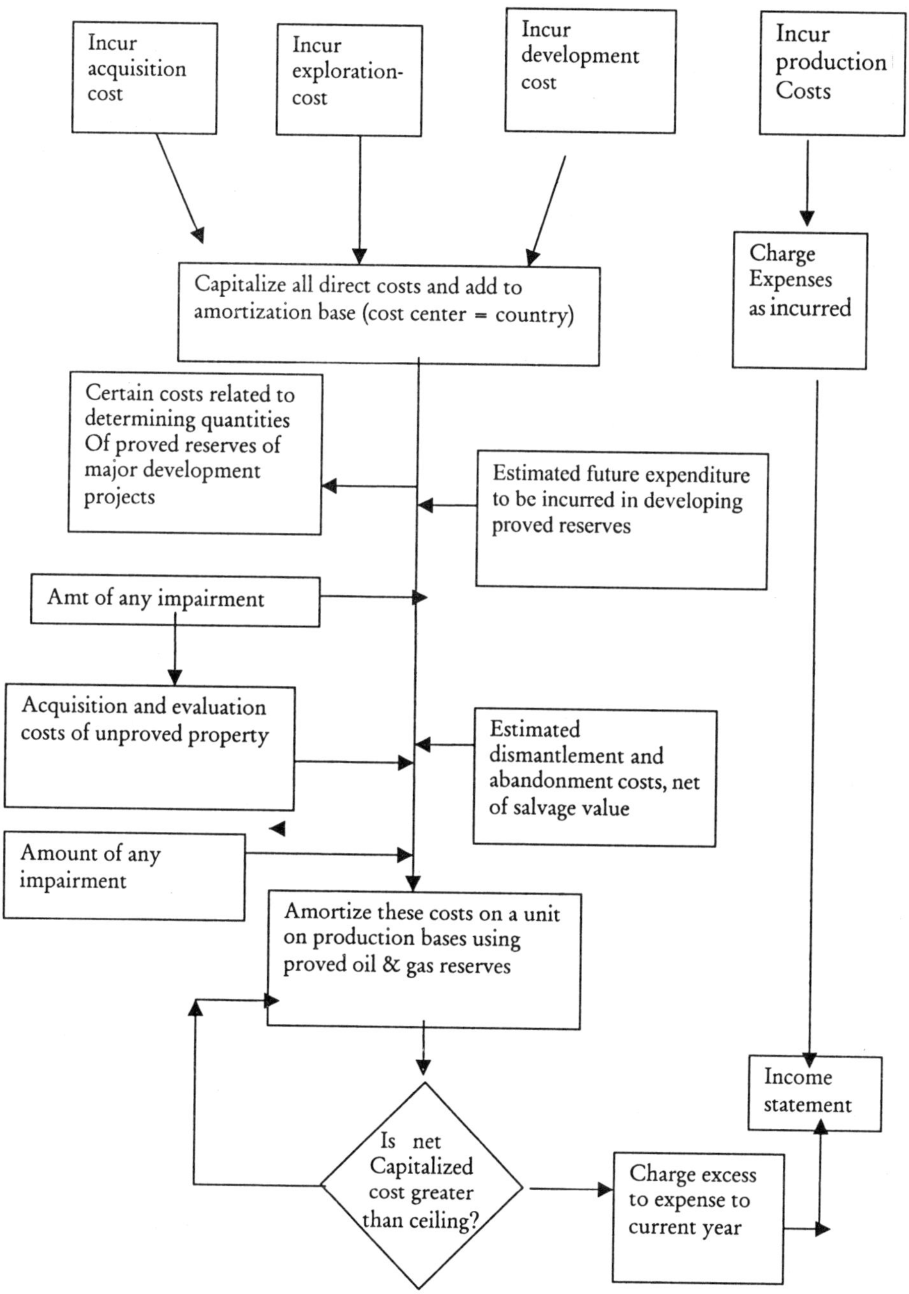

(he full-cost rules allow exclusion of certain costs from the amortization base, all non-drilling costs that can be associated, when incurred, with specific unproved properties are debited to an unproved property control account. Drilling costs are initially charged to wells in progress (W/P) and, if proved reserves are found, transferred to wells and related E&F. If proved reserves are not found, exploratory wells in progress are transferred to exploratory dry holes. Although different accounts are used for successful exploratory wells versus exploratory dry holes, both accounts are asset accounts under FC accounting and are written off to expense through DD&A. Development wells in progress that do not find proved reserves are transferred to wells and related E&F in the same manner as under successful efforts.

Measurement and Sale of Oil and Gas

Oil and gas must be measured either when produced or when sold. Understanding the measurement process is important to the accountant because the amount of revenue recorded is based on information obtained during this process. The following sections discuss the measurement and sale of oil and gas.

Oil Measurement and Sale

Fluids produced from an oil well normally contain oil, gas, and water. Before the oil can be sold, well fluids must be separated, treated, and measured. Flow lines transfer the well fluids from individual wells to a centralized separating, treating, and/or storage facility. At the centralized facility, the fluid enters separators that remove the gas from the liquid (oil and water). The liquid is then treated in heater-treater units to remove the water and other impurities from the oil. The water and other impurities, called BS&W or basic sediment and water, must be below an established limit in oil sold. The limit is usually 1%.

The BS&W, API gravity, temperature, the number of barrels of oil removed from a tank, and the calculations converting the barrels to standard conditions, net of BS&W are recorded on a run ticket at the time of delivery of the oil. The run ticket is the source document for recording the amount of oil sold. When the oil is sold, the pipeline gauger, observed by the lease pumper-gauger, measures the oil removed and determines its characteristics. When the amount of oil removed from the tank and its characteristics have been recorded on the run ticket, both the pipeline gauger and the lease pumper-gauger sign the ticket. Another method of measuring oil delivered is used when the oil is delivered or transferred automatically into a pipeline. In this case, measurement of the oil is performed by a lease automatic custody transfer (LACT) unit. A LACT unit is an unattended unit that automatically transfers oil from the lease to the pipeline, takes samples, and collects and records production/accounting data. i.e., volume measurement, temperature and BS&W content while the use of LACT units appears to be much more efficient than manual measurement.

Gas Measurement and Sale

Gas, unlike oil, is not stored on the lease after production but is instead transferred immediately to a pipeline. Gas measurement is more complicated than oil measurement because of different State and federal measurement standards and because of the physical characteristics of natural gas. Gas volume varies significantly with changes in pressure and temperature. Therefore, it is especially important that measured volumes of gas be converted to volumes are a standard set of conditions. Generally, standard conditions are a temperature of 60°F and a pressure at 14.05 psia. Federal standard conditions are a temperature of 60°F and a pressure at 14.73 psia for onshore leases and 15.025 psia for offshore leases.

Gas volume is measured in thousand cubic feet, i.e., Mcf adjusted to standard conditions. Several instruments are used for measuring natural gas. One of the most important and widely used instruments is the orifice meter. An orifice meter records the flow of gas through pressure differentials. The data are recorded and are then converted to standard cubic feet by using conversion factors based upon the size of the line, the size of the orifice, the flowing temperature, the flowing pressure, the specific gravity of the gas, and the differential pressure.

Recording Oil Revenue

Gross revenue from oil sales is determined by multiplying the net amount of oil delivered by the price for that particular grade of oil. The net amount of oil delivered is recorded on a run ticket, which serves as the source document for determining the quantity of oil sold. The price of oil is dependent in part on the quality of the oil, measured in terms of gravity. Gravity, as used here, refers to degrees of gravity on the American Petroleum Institute (API) scale. On this scale the greater the density of the petroleum, the lower the API degree. Generally, higher the API gravity, the greater is the value of the oil.

In the past, the price of the oil has generally either been given as a posted field price or negotiated as a spot price. A posted field price is the price purchasers are willing to pay for oil in the area. This price, which is published in a crude oil price bulletin, is based on factors such as the API gravity, location of the oil, grade, and market center prices, actual negotiated transactions in the field, the NYMEX oil futures market and other available information. A spot price refers to a short-term price negotiated between the buyer and the seller in the spot market, without a long-term contract. Once the sales price has been determined and the oil sold, the accounting entries are made.

ISI-Developed Integrated Oil and Gas Accounting Software

ISI Software has over 30 years experience of programming Oil and Gas accounting systems for exploration and operating companies. ISI expertise focuses on providing customization for individual companies at a low cost and incorporating the changes into the total system. ISI specialize in converting data from IBM system 3x mini-computers to the PC environment. Training, support and program updates are accomplished via modem allowing us to service a client anywhere very effectively.

The Integrated Oil and Gas Accounting System is made up of several application modules (http://www.isisoftware.net/):

A. Master Files
B. Accounts Payable
C. Accounts Receivable
D. General Ledger
E. Joint Interest Billing
F. Revenue
G. Production
H. Lease Records
I. Payroll

Crude Oil Exchanges

Producing companies often exchange crude oil in order to operate more efficiently. For example, crude oil production in one area may be exchanged for crude in another location closer co the purchaser so that the oil does not have to be physically transported. Alternately, future production could be exchanged for an immediate delivery of crude oil in order to meet refinery demands. Crude oil exchanges are often tracked and accounted for using volumetric information. Under the inventory method, the number of barrels received in an exchange is debited co a volume-based physical inventory account with a corresponding credit to exchange inventory. The reverse entry would be made when the oil received is paid back with a future delivery. A common alternate method of recording exchanges is based on the monetary value of the oil exchanged. The gross purchase and sales method treats each exchange receipt as a purchase and each exchange delivery as a sale, with corresponding entries made to accounts payable and accounts receivable, respectively. Regardless of which basic method is used, differentials will usually exist because the monetary values of the barrels exchanged will normally not be equal due to differences in quality, crude type, or gravity. These differentials are settled in cash and are recorded as revenue by the company receiving the payment and as an expense by the company making the payment.

Crude oil is the world's most actively traded commodity, and the NYMEX Division light, sweet crude oil futures contract is the world's most liquid forum for crude oil trading, as well as the world's largest-volume futures contract trading on a physical commodity. Because of its excellent liquidity and price transparency, the contract is used as a principal international pricing benchmark. Additional risk management and trading opportunities are offered through options on the futures contract; calendar spread options; crack spread options on the pricing differential of heating oil futures and crude oil futures and gasoline futures and crude oil futures; and average price options. The contract trades in units of 1,000 barrels, and the delivery point is Cushing, Oklahoma, which is also accessible to the international spot markets via pipelines. The contract provides for delivery of several grades of domestic and internationally traded foreign crudes, and serves the diverse needs of the physical market (http://www.nymex.com/lsco_pre_agree.aspx).

Crude Oil Pricing

In general, crude oil is sold through a variety of contract arrangements and in spot transactions. Oil is also traded on futures markets but not generally to supply physical volumes of oil, more as a mechanism to distribute risk. These mechanisms play an important role in providing pricing information to markets. In fact, the pricing of crude oils has become increasingly transparent from the 1990s onwards through the use of marker crudes such as (http://www.aip.com.au/pricing/crude.htm):

- West Texas Intermediate (WTI—USA)
- Brent (Europe and Africa)
- Dubai and Oman (Middle East)
- Tapis and Dubai (in Asia)

The main criteria for a marker crude is for it to be sold in sufficient volumes to provide liquidity (many buyers and sellers) in the physical market as well as having similar physical qualities of alternative crudes. In addition, the marker crude should provide pricing information. WTI does this through its use on the New York Metals Exchange (NYMEX) as the basis of a futures contract where trade is equivalent to many hundreds of millions of barrels per day, even though physical WTI production is less than 1 million barrels per day. A futures contract for crude oil is a promise to deliver a given quantity of crude oil but this rarely occurs as participants are more interested in taking a position on the price of the crude oil. Futures markets are a financial instrument to distribute risk among participants with the side effect of providing transparency on the pricing of crude oil.

Brent offers pricing information based more on the physical trading of oil through spot trading, and forward trading but also offers futures trading but not to the same extent as WTI. In Asia there is no futures exchange where crude oil is traded and which would provide pricing information to the same extent as WTI and Brent. In Asia the pricing mechanism for say Tapis, a marker for light sweet crudes in the region, is based on an independent panel approach where producers, refiners and traders are asked for information on Tapis crude trades. Tapis is used as the appropriate Australian crude marker because of the strong trade relationship Australia has with the region as a source for crude oil and also petroleum product imports.

Prices of crude oil markers and petroleum product markers are affected by a myriad of factors including:

- overall supply/demand for crude
- supply/demand for petroleum products
- freight rates
- competition in the crude markets
- Competition in the regional and domestic markets for petroleum products.

They all have a role in determining the final price charged to consumers and the role that each of these elements plays can change over time. It is this very complexity in markets which makes it very difficult to determine a theoretical price as part of regulation in markets because there may be a perception that because the theoretical price is different from the market price that the market price is 'not fair' for some reason (http://www.aip.com.au/pricing/crude.htm).

Pricing of Physical Crude Oil Trades

Generally this is based on a formula approach where marker crude is used as the base and then a quality differential (premium/discount) as well as a demand/supply (premium/discount) is added depending on the crude being purchased. Thus in times of tight supply this premium will rise and gradually drag up the Marker crude price, whilst in times of surplus supply, a reduced premium or even a discount will drag down the Marker crude price. Of course big changes, announcement or events that can significantly influence crude supply levels will sometimes result a large step change in the prices of crude oil (e.g. OPEC announcements, civil unrest or wars, hurricane activity, major refinery shutdowns or outages etc). That is, crude oils being purchased do not always slavishly follow marker crudes. Marker crudes are indicators of what is happening in regional markets.

Crude Oil as an Input Cost to Refiners

It is true to say that the cost of crude oil is the major input cost for refiners. However, the relationship between such a cost and the final price for a petroleum product produced from that crude, such as petrol or diesel, is not as direct as one would think. There are, for instance, additional petroleum product markers which give a guide to prices. That is, prices are not just a function of cost-push, but are also strongly influenced by demand-pull. For example, USA environmental requirements for gasoline (petrol) have at times pushed up the prices in the USA by significantly more than the movements in crude prices. This is the market working as refiners who see these prices work hard to increase production to capture some of these high prices before they dissipate under competitive pressure – both from within the USA and from the resulting massive influx of product cargoes from other producing centers in the world. There are also a number of other variables which affect the price of products such as petrol. In addition the perception of the purchasers and sellers in the market as to the price risk over time can also add or subtract premiums to the product marker price.

Oil and Gas Revenue: A Case of ATP Oil and Gas Corporation

ATP Oil & Gas Corporation Announces Record Revenue and First Quarter 2005 Results HOUSTON, May 6/PRNewswire/—ATP Oil & Gas Corporation (Nasdaq: ATPG) today announced first quarter 2005 results which include:

- Oil and gas revenues of US$37.0 million, an increase of 54% over the comparable period in 2004 and the largest single quarterly revenue in the Company's history;
- Production of 5.8 Bcfe, an increase of 24% over the comparable period in 2004;
- Net income of US$1.0 million compared with a US$2.4 million net loss in the first quarter 2004;

- A US$21.0 million improvement in cash flows from operating activities from the first quarter 2004, and
- continued development operations in the Gulf of Mexico and the North Sea, including initial production from the West Cameron: 432 No. 1 well and the Eugene Island 71 A-1 well.

(Logo: http://www.newscom.com/cgi-bin/prnh/20030428/ATPGLOGO)

Results of Operations

Oil and natural gas revenues totaled US$37.0 million for the first quarter 2005 compared to US$24.0 million for the first quarter 2004. First quarter 2005 oil and gas revenues exceeded all previous quarters in the Company's history and represented a 54% improvement over the same period in 2004. Driving the revenue increase was both improved production and increased price realizations. Natural gas and oil production increased 24% in the first quarter 2005 to 5.8 Bcfe from 4.6 Bcfe during the first quarter 2004. With 10 additional wells producing in the Gulf of Mexico during the first quarter 2005, the Gulf of Mexico accounts for 91% of ATP's year-to-date production compared to 82% during the same quarter in 2004. The Company also increased its average realized price in 2005 as a result of higher oil and natural gas prices in general and higher prices for those quantities the Company hedged compared to the same period in 2004. For the first quarter 2005, ATP realized an average price including the effect of cash flow hedges for natural gas of US$6.32 per Mcf, an increase of 24% over the same period in 2004, and US$40.15 per barrel of oil, an increase of 29% over the first quarter 2004. A significant factor in the natural gas price increase was the realized price of US$7.97 per Mcf received in the North Sea, an increase of 113% over the first quarter 2004.

ATP's lease operating expenses (LOE) per Mcfe decreased 18% to US$0.79 in the first quarter 2005 compared to the same period in 2004, primarily due to the increase in production while a portion of the expenses remained fixed. DD&A per Mcfe for the first quarter 2005 was US$3.55 compared to US$2.49 in the same period in 2004. The increase was primarily due to production from wells for which the company incurred higher development costs in 2004 compared to wells completed in previous years. ATP's general and administrative expenses increased US$0.1 million to US$4.2 million for first quarter of 2005. Included in the 2005 amounts are increased overall compensation costs and fees related to Sarbanes-Oxley 404 compliance. These costs were offset by a reduction of expenses related to professional and legal fees incurred in the first quarter 2005 compared to those incurred in the first quarter 2004. The Company reported net income of US$1.0 million or US$0.03 per basic and diluted share for the first quarter 2005 compared to a net loss of US$2.4 million or US$0.10 per share in the comparable quarter in 2004.

The Company's selected operating statistics and financial information, included within this press release, contain additional information on ATP's activities for the three months ended March 31, 2004 and 2005.

All figures in US Dollars.

	Three Months Ended March 31,	
	2005	**2004**
Selected Operating Statistics (Unaudited)		
Production		
Natural gas (MMcf)	4,594	3,617
Oil and condensate (MBbls)	198	172
Natural gas equivalents (MMcfe)	5,779	4,646
Gulf of Mexico (MMcfe)	5,238	3,791
North Sea (MMcfe)	541	855
Percentage natural gas	79%	78%
Average Prices (includes effect of Cash-flow hedges)		
Natural gas (per Mcf)	$6.32	$5.11
Natural gas (per Mcf) — GOM	6.10	5.54
Natural gas (per Mcf) — North Sea	7.97	3.74
Oil and condensate (per Bbl) — GOM	40.15	31.13
Natural gas, oil and condensate (per Mcfe)	6.40	5.13
Lease operating expenses (per Mcfe)	0.79	0.96
Other Expenses, per Mcfe		
Depreciation, depletion and Amortization	$3.55	$2.49
Selected Financial Data (In Thousands, Except Per Share Data)		
Oil and gas revenues, including Settled derivatives (1)	$36,980	$23,829
Net income (loss)	1,000	(2,393)
Per share, basic and diluted	$0.03	$(0.10)
Average number of common shares Outstanding		
Basic	28,924	24,523
Diluted	29,782	24,523

Capital Resources and Liquidity

On April 14, 2005, ATP announced that it had amended and improved the terms of its Senior Secured Credit Facility by expanding the credit facility to US$350.0 million and reducing the interest rate. Significant terms of the amendment included:

- adding US$121.0 million in additional liquidity;
- paying off and eliminating the second lien tranche of the credit facility which carried an interest rate of LIBOR plus 10%;
- decreasing the overall interest rate of the credit facility from LIBOR plus 6.847% to LIBOR plus 5.500%;
- amending covenants within the credit facility to provide more flexibility to ATP, and
- extending the maturity by one year to April 2010.

Net cash provided by operating activities increased US$20.9 million. Cash provided by operating activities for the first quarter 2005 was US$10.7 million compared to cash used in operating activities of US$10.2 million for the first quarter 2004. Cash used in investing activities for oil and gas properties increased to US$42.3 million in the first quarter 2005 compared to US$22.6 million for the same period in 2004. In the first quarter 2004, ATP received US$10.5 million for the sale of an undivided interest in seven properties. Net cash used in investing activities, after accounting for the proceeds of the sale of the seven properties and other additions in the first quarter of 2004, was US$12.2 million. In the first quarter 2005, net cash provided by financing activities was only US$0.2 million compared to US$53.1 million in the first quarter 2004 when the original Senior Secured Credit Facility was initiated (http://www.prnewswire.co.uk/cgi/news/release?id=145506).

Recording Gas Revenue

Prior to 1985, most sales of natural gas were made on long-term contracts, often for terms of 10 or more years. In contrast, most gas sales today are made on the spot market on a short term basis. Spot sales of gas involve the sale of gas at current market prices by the producer co pipelines or their affiliates. Spot sales of gas also include direct sales that are made by the producer to the end-user or local distribution company. In direct sales, the gas is transported by a third-party pipeline company, which charges a transportation fee. Spot sales also include sales to marketers or middlemen who buy and resell gas. Brokers may also be used. Brokers, instead of taking tide co the gas find a buyer for the gas and charge a brokerage fee for their services. This change to selling gas in the spot market has led to significant seasonal price volatility, which is expected co continue in the foreseeable future.

In the domestic market and many foreign markets, the volume of gas sold is measured in Mcf (1,000 cubic feet). The selling price of gas, however, is usually based on the heating value of the gas, as measured in MMBtu's (1,000,000 British Thermal Units: A Btu is the quantity of energy necessary to raise one pound of water by Fahrenheit). Because of this difference in measurement units, it is important to know how to convert gas measurements to MMBtu's and to Mcf's. (Gas volumes are determined by metering the gas. The heating value, on the other hand, is determined through sampling and analyzing the gas in the pipeline. Gas, like oil, is also often used for lease operation. The gas may be used as fuel for operating lease equipment such as pumping units, heater-treaters, and compressors or as fuel for the lessor's residence or other activities. Such gas is measured by metering if the quantities involved are substantial; otherwise, the volume used is normally estimated based on engineering estimates of fuel used by the various pieces of equipment.

Natural Gas Processing

Often gas is not of marketable quality when produced because of impurities and liquids. Since gas may not usually be disposed of by flaring, the gas must be processed to make it marketable. Such processing involves removing impurities and saleable liquids and compressing the gas to meet pipeline pressure specifications. Typically the gas is either sold to a processing plant or is processed by a plant for a fee. In either case, accounting entries to record the sale are similar to the accounting discussed above.

The demand for gas is highly seasonal. As a result, if wells are to produce at capacity during the low demand summer months, the excess gas must be placed in underground storage facilities for use in the higher demand winter months. Royalties usually must be paid to royalty interest owners when the gas is severed from the lease, even if the gas is being stored by the producer for sale at a later time.

Timing of Revenue Recognition

Theoretically, revenue from oil and gas sales should be recognized when the sale is made rather than when the oil or gas is produced. Legally, tide normally passes when physical control of the oil or gas is transferred from one parry to another. Therefore, theoretically, revenue should be recognized at the point of delivery.

Revenue from Oil

In practice, revenue from oil sales is typically recognized either when the oil is produced or when the oil is sold. When oil revenue is recognized at the time of sale, the revenue is recognized based on pipeline runs or run tickets.

Allocation of Oil and Gas

Production from different wells or leases is often commingled and measured at the point of delivery, Total production sold may need to be allocated back or reconciled to the individual well or lease production in order to comply with tax requirements and management needs or because of different ownership of the properties involved. The method for determining production quantities from individual wells depends upon whether the well is metered individually. Each gas well/completion is usually metered individually, as is generally required by state law. Oil wells are not required to be metered individually and, as a result, usually are not metered individually bur instead are put on test periodically to determine or estimate the total amount of oil, gas, and water produced from the well.

A well put on test means that the stream of fluid from the well is diverted from the production separator to a test separator. The test separator measures the amount of oil, gas, and water produced nom the well for 24 hours. The test results are used to estimate the production from that well for a period of time-usually a month. When all wells have been tested, the test result is used to allocate total production to the various wells or properties. This allocation method is similar to the relative sales value method used for many other accounting purposes. The exact method of allocation depends upon the points at which the production is measured or metered. The allocation procedure may be complicated when the quality of the oil varies. The value of a barrel of oil is partially dependent on the quality of the oil, specifically the API gravity of the oil, which can vary from lease to lease. Consequently, when significant differences in gravity between the various leases exist, the allocation procedure illustrated above must be modified to determine sales revenue due each lease from the quantities of oil produced and sold from each lease. While conceptually the allocation of gas is the same as allocation of oil, the actual allocation process is much more complicated.

Gross Refining Margin

Gross Refining Margin (GRM) is the differential between the product realization and the cost of crude processed to obtain these products. GRM of a particular refinery will depend upon various internal and external factors. Some of these factors are discussed below:

Internal Factors

- The crude mix (low sulphur and high sulphur) processed by the refinery
- The secondary processing facilities available with the refinery which affect the product yield of the refinery
- The fuel used and losses incurred in the production processes.

External Factors

- The international prices of various crudes and products
- The demand and supply balance of various products refined by the refinery
- The duty structure prevailing in the country relating to crude and products

Operating Cost of the Refinery

The operating cost of the refinery includes various elements, some of which are as under:

- **Power and fuel:** Fuel is used either directly in the refining process or to generate power and utilities to be used in the refining process. Fuel may be purchased from outside suppliers (like natural gas), power from electricity board or internal refined products (like LSHS, FO or HSD) may be used as fuel.
- **Chemicals and catalysts:** During the refining process of petroleum products, various chemicals and catalysts are used. The purpose of chemicals is mainly to improve the quality of products so as to meet the desired specifications. Catalysts are used in various reformers and other secondary processing facilities.
- **Establishment cost:** This is related to the manpower deployed and includes the salary and wages paid to staff, overtime, bonus etc.
- **Repair and maintenance cost:** It is incurred in various mechanical,

electrical and civil jobs carried out for the maintenance of plant and machinery.

- **General administrative cost:** This cost includes expenses such as traveling. Printing, insurance and other related overhead expenditure.
- **Depreciation:** Operating cost includes depreciation on plant and machinery, furniture, equipment and other fixed assets used in the refining process towards general wear and tear.

Net Margin

The net margin is the difference between gross margin and operating cost. This is virtually the net profit to the refinery.

Net Margin = Gross margin – Operating cost.

For higher profitability, gross margin should be increased and operating cost reduced by increased efficiency in refining operations. Attachment 1 shows a sample calculation for gross and net margin for a refinery.

Components of Gross Refining Margin

The following table illustrates the various components considered for computing Gross Refining Margin as a typical case for a Refinery (http://www.eia.doe.gov/emeu/perfpro/ref_pi2/tab1.html):

Table 11.5: Components of the Gross Refining Margin and Average Refined Product Revenues for FRS Companies, 1988, 1995, and 2001

	1988	1995	2001	Percent Change 1995-2001
Average Refined Product Revenues	29.36	27.04	33.88	25.3
Raw material Acquisition Costs and Refined Product Purchases	20.05	20.87	26.04	24.8
Gross Margin	9.31	6.17	7.85	27.2
Energy Costs	1.45	0.92	1.37	49.3
Marketing Costs	2.14	1.95	1.59	–18.6
Environmental Operating Costs	0.36	0.49	0.34	–29.8
Other Refining Costs	2.94	2.26	1.82	–19.4
Net Refining Margin	2.43	0.55	2.72	397.0
Average Refined Product Revenues				
Motor Gasoline	33.59	30.26	36.96	22.1
Distillate	27.59	24.70	32.96	33.4
Other Products	23.20	23.17	26.30	13.5
All Refined Products	29.36	27.04	33.88	25.3

Source: Energy Information Administration, Form EIA-28 (Financial Reporting System).

CASE FOR INDIAN OIL COMPANIES: 3 ATTACHMENTS

Attachment 1: Gross Margin

	(Rs. Crore)
Realization of transfer of products	4050
Cost of crude (inclusive of freight, wharfage, customs duty)	3720
Gross margin	330
Thorough put-MMT	3.98
GROSS margin Rs/MT	829
Margin—Rs/BBL	112
Margin US $/BBL	US $ 2.30
Less: Operating cost Rs/MT	500
Net margin Rs/MT	329

Net-back Estimation

In the net back system the estimated realization is calculated on the basis of expected yield from the particular refinery for specific crude. For the purpose of procurement of crude for a particular refinery, net back estimation is used to evaluate the suitable crude for the refinery. The crude which is having higher net back to the refinery is normally procured for it.

Attachment 2 gives a sample netback calculation to select the best crude out any of seven crudes, considered. All these 7 crudes are sweet (low sulphur) crudes. F.ODS gives the highest netback of INR 1054/MT vs. TAPIS with lowest netback of INR 41/MT.

Attachment 2: Sample Working of Netback Calculations

	PROD PRICE	BRENT BL	F.ODS	BON. LT.	LABUAN	ESCRA-VOS	TAPIS	MIRI
CRUDE PRICE	RS/MT	11987	11361	11714	11994	11987	12859	11994
LPG	14599	7	5	5	4	2	5	4
NAP	12260	8	0	5	2	5	10	3
MS	14832	12	12	12	12	13	12	12
SKO	13617	11	11	11	11	11	11	11
HSD	14361	48	58	54	58	51	53	59
OF	10100	0		0	0		0	0
LSHS	10100	1	0	0	0	6	0	0
RPC	5535	2	1	1	2	6	I	1
SUIPHUR	258	1	1	1	I		0	1
SL WAX	13851	0	0	0	0	0	0	0
F&L	0	10	12	11	10	6	8	9
TOTAL		100	100	100	100	100	100	100
DIST%		860	86.0	87.0	87.0	82.0	91.0	890
CRUDE ALUE,RS/MT		11987	11361	11714	11994	11987	12859	11994
PROD VALUE, RSIMT		12408	12415	12454	12570	12593	12900	12780
LESS IPN COST, RS/MT					100			100
NET BACK, RS/MT		421	1054	740	476	606	41	686

Accounting for International Operations

A company electing to engage in operations outside the U.S. will likely encounters many issues and difficulties not encountered in domestic operations. For example, a company must consider that the costs of operating in a foreign country are likely to be higher than undertaking similar operations domestically. In some locations there may be risks associated with factors such as the stability of the government, stability of the currency, adequacy of the supply of materials and equipment, and availability of a qualified labor pool. In addition, local laws and customs may affect the way business is conducted in the country. For example, an oil and gas exploration and production company will encounter different laws and customs regarding the ownership of the minerals in the earth. The local government rather than an individual or company will, with limited exception, own the minerals. Consequently, an oil and gas company must enter into a contract with the local government for the right to explore for and produce oil and gas reserves. These contracts are complex and vary widely from country to country. All of these issues impact on oil and gas companies engaging in exploration and production activities outside the U.S. This chapter provides an overview of some of the issues and difficulties encountered in international oil and gas operations. Of special interest are contracts between oil and gas companies and governments that dictate how costs, revenues, and reserves are to be shared.

Petroleum Fiscal Systems

One of the first things geologists, engineers, landsmen, lawyers, and economists encounter in the international sector of the petroleum industry is the diversity of fiscal systems. Countries are vastly unique in the way they structure their taxes, and natural resource taxation can be complicated (http://www.danieljohnston.com/pdf/fiscal_systems_course_outline.pdf). Evaluating upstream investment opportunities is a very demanding task. Exploration projects are intrinsically risky as quantity and quality of the hydrocarbons are uncertain. Project risks increase due to volatility of prices and costs, and geopolitical developments. Fiscal regimes should ideally balance geologic as well as other risks (http://www.beg.utexas.edu/energyecon/documents/UT-CEE%20Seminar%20on%20Petroleum%20Contracts.pdf).

Since mineral rights are typically owned by the government of the foreign country or "host" country, the government and the oil and gas company must come to an agreement as to what collective payments are to be received by the government in return for allowing the company to operate there. Collectively these payments are referred to as the fiscal system of the country. Examples of such payments include:

- Up-front bonuses paid to the host country
- Royalties paid to the host country
- Federal and provincial income taxes
- Various other taxes collected by the host country including duties and special petroleum taxes

- Production sharing wherein oil or gas is allocated between the parties for the purpose of recovery of capital and/or operating costs
- Infrastructure development for the host country

The exact nature of payments that the government receives is determined by the legal system in the country. In the United States and in limited situations in Canada and Trinidad it is possible for individuals to own mineral rights. Outside the U.S., Canada, and Trinidad mineral rights are owned exclusively by the host government. Some countries allow non-government ownership of oil and gas after it is produced while others do not. Countries that allow non-government ownership of oil and gas are referred to as having concessionary systems. With the limited exceptions noted above, in all other concessionary systems the government owns the rights to all minerals but will transfer ownership of the minerals to oil and gas companies when the minerals are produced or sold. In these countries, the contract between the government that own the minerals and the oil and gas company wishing to explore, develop, and produce the minerals is referred to as a concessionary contract or agreement.

The two most common contracts in a contractual system are production sharing contracts (PSCs) and service contracts. The fundamental difference between these two types of contracts relates to whether the oil and gas company is paid in the form of oil and/or gas or in the form of money. Conceptually, in a PSC the oil and gas company, referred to as the contractor, is allowed to recover certain costs and receives a share of the profits. The company typically receives payment in-kind (in the form of oil or gas). In a true service contract, the contractor receives money representing a fee for conducting exploration, development, and production activities. In practice, most contracts have terms and conditions that make it difficult to classify them as being either PSCs or service contracts. Most are simply referred to as PSCs. Each of these types of arrangements is discussed in detail below. It should be noted that the term contractor is used collectively to refer to one company or several companies who are acting together in a joint operation.

Almost every contract has its own unique terms and characteristics. Often it is not only difficult to classify the contracts as being PSCs or service contracts but also as being concessionary or contractual in nature. Each country negotiates the terms it believes are most beneficial to the citizens of the country. Consequently, contracts and agreements generated by any given country may be contractual in nature but have some aspects that resemble a concessionary contract and vice versa. It is important to remember that any discussion of these contracts reflects the most usual case given. Contracts can be very different since they are the product of intense negotiation and can include whatever clauses and conditions the negotiators agree to.

Contractual Systems

In some countries the legal system as it pertains to mineral ownership is based on the principle that natural resources are owned by all citizens of the country, and the government should act in such a manner as to maximize the value of the resources flowing back to the people for a result, the government owns and retains title to all minerals. The contractor is entitled to minerals or money from the sale of minerals as a "fee" for the services it performs (i.e., exploration. drilling, development, and production). In some countries the contractor may be entitled to an ownership interest in the minerals at the point of sale. In other instances the contractor may not ever receive title to the minerals but instead is entitled to a share of the revenue from the sale of the minerals. Some agreements require that all or part of any oil or gas produced within the country be sold to the host government.

Government Involvement in Operations

In a contractual system the government plays an active role in exploration, development, and production typically by acting through a government-owned oil company. The contractor (or one of the contracting companies) usually acts as the operator. Contracts frequently call for the formation of a joint management group to oversee operations and vote on all major operating decisions. Such a joint management group is typically made up of representatives from the contractor (or each of the companies that compose the contractor), the government-owned oil company, and the government (i.e., representatives from the Ministry of Petroleum or some other government agency). The contractor is typically required to submit an annual work program and budget to the joint management group for review and approval. In addition to the annual budget, the joint management group generally makes all major decisions regarding the management of the project including approval of all major expenditures, evaluation of the results of exploration, planning and drilling of wells, and determination of the commerciality of drilling results.

The contractor is typically required to provide all technology and financing. In most contractual systems, any equipment or facilities brought into the country by the contractor become the property of the local government. In some cases tide to the equipment and facilities passes to the government at the time the goods are brought into the country or upon installation. In other cases, tide passes to the government when the costs of the equipment and facilities have been recovered by the contractor.

As mentioned earlier, the two types of agreements prevalent in contractual systems are production sharing and risk service contracts, with the production sharing contracts being, by far, the most common. These contracts arc discussed below.

Production Sharing Contracts

Production sharing contract is an agreement between the parties to a well and a host country regarding the percentage of production each party will receive after the participating parties have recovered a specified amount of costs and expenses (http://www.glossary.oilfield.slb.com/Display.cfm?Term=production%20sharing%20contract). Production sharing contracts first emerged in the 1960s when governments began to evaluate alternative strategies to maximize the value of their resources. Under a concessionary agreement (where the government is not a working interest owner), the government has little or no involvement in the management and decision-making related to day-to-day drilling and operations. Governments generally were looking for ways to increase their total share of petroleum-related revenues and profits. Governments were also frustrated due to their inability to be involved in the management of petroleum operations. In addition to the legal constraints related to the ownership of minerals, these factors largely led to the trend toward production sharing contracts and away from concessionary agreements.

Signature and Production Bonuses

A common feature of both concessionary agreements and PSCs is that the contractor agrees to pay the government an up-front bonus for signing the agreement. This bonus is often referred to as a signing or signature bonus. Typically, signature bonuses are payable in a lump sum of money but sometimes may involve payment in the form of equipment. In some instances a lump sum of money is paid at the signing of the contract and subsequent payments are made to the government when production reaches an agreed upon level. These later payments are referred to as production bonuses. For example, a contractor may agree to pay the government, in U.S. dollars, a $3 million bonus at signing, $2 million when production reaches 2,000 barrels of oil per day, and $1 million when production exceeds 4,000 barrels of oil per day. In other words, rather than paying $6 million at signing, the bonuses are phased in as certain levels of production are achieved. This arrangement theoretically allows the contractor to use its capital in exploration and drilling with production bonuses being paid as money is coming in from the production and sale of oil or gas. On the other hand, the government is taking on some degree of risk since it receives a lower signing bonus and may not receive any additional bonuses if production does not occur or if it does not reach the specified level. However, that risk is balanced with the expectation or hope that exploration and development will increase and will result in higher royalties, etc.

Payment of Royalties

An interesting feature of production sharing contracts is the inclusion of a royalty provision. Payment of a royalty is a logical concept in a concessionary system where tide to oil and gas passes to the contractor at some point. In a contractual system tide to the oil and gas in place never passes to the contractor; nonetheless, many PSCs contain royalty provisions. In practice, royalty provisions range from as low as zero to 15% or higher. Since a royalty represents a payment to the government off the top of gross receipts, many argue that royalties can actually discourage capital investment in new drilling and development and, in marginal situations, actually work against further development and production. For example, if the royalty is 10%, only 90% of gross revenue is available to cover capital costs and operating costs. This may discourage an oil and gas company from developing a marginal field or may result in the abandonment of a marginal field earlier than would otherwise be the case. To help offset this effect to some extent, some contracts contain sliding scale royalties. A sliding scale royalty provides for a lower royalty amount when production is lower and increases as production increases. Thus, in marginal situations where production is lower, the lower royalty may allow production that would otherwise not have been profitable. The following example illustrates a sliding scale royalty:

EXAMPLE

Sliding Scale Royalty

Average Daily Production	Royalty
Up to 7,000 barrels per day	5%
7,001 to 14,000 barrels per day	10%
Above 14,000 barrels per day	15%

In this example, when production is low the royalty payment is low and when production increases the royalty increases. By using a sliding scale, when production is low there is more cash available to the parties for additional exploration and development.

Government Participation

As in concessionary systems, some PSCs allow the government to participate in oil and gas projects through a government-owned oil company. In most cases, the contractor must pay all costs and bear all risks during the exploration phase of a project. The government does not reimburse the contractor for its share of the exploration costs. Instead, the contractor must look to production and cost recovery to recoup those costs. If there is no production, the contractor bears all of the costs without any provision for reimbursement. If oil and gas is discovered, the government-through the government-owned oil company—can elect to participate at whatever level of working interest it chooses up to a maximum of 51 %. If the government backs into the project, their role is similar to any other working interest owner. In other words, the government is responsible for its proportionate share of development and operating costs.

Cost Recovery

Cost recovery is a feature common to most PSCs. The contract should specify which costs are recoverable, the order of recoverability, any limits on recoverability, and whether costs not recovered in one period can be carried forward into the next period. Since title to the oil or gas in-place never passes to the contractor, cost recoverability is the mechanism whereby the contractor is able to recoup the costs that it has expended on a project. The oil (or gas) that goes to the parties to allow them to recover their costs is referred to as cost oil. In some PSCs the contractor must pay 100% of the cost incurred in the exploratory phase.

Government ownership of all equipment and facilities raises interesting questions regarding who is responsible for future abandonment and reclamation costs. Some PSCs require the companies to put money into a sinking fund to be used in the future to pay for abandonment and reclamation. If these sinking fund payments are considered to be recoverable costs, as with other exploration or development costs, the government is actually paying for dismantlement and reclamation. Most contracts indicate the order in which costs recovery is to occur. The order of cost recovery is important since it determines how quickly the contractor is able to recover certain costs. For example, assume a contractor paid 100% of exploration expenditures and shared development expenditures with the government-owned company. Obviously the contractor would prefer to be able to recover all exploration expenditures before development expenditures are recoverable. Typically, cost recovery occurs in an order similar to the following:

- Current year operating costs
- Unrecovered exploration expenditures
- Unrecovered development expenditures
- Capitalized interest (if allowed)
- Any investment credit or capital uplift (defined later)
- Future abandonment cost fund

In many contracts exploration and development expenditures are referred to as capital costs and are amortized. This means the costs are recoverable over a fixed number of years. In most cases, if the amortized capital costs are not recovered in any given year, the unrecovered portion can be carried forward and recovered in subsequent years. In some cases, however, carry forward of unrecovered amortized capital costs is not allowed and recoverability is permanently lost.

Profit Oil

The gross revenue from production typically goes first to pay royalties, next certain production-related taxes are taken out (e.g., production taxes and VAT) and, finally, to cost recovery. The gross revenue remaining after deducting royalties, taxes, and cost recovery is referred to as profit oil. The profit oil is shared between the parties based on the terms and conditions set forth in the contract.

Service Contracts

The second type of agreement prevalent in a contractual system is a service agreement. Service agreements can be classified as being either risk service contracts or no risk service contracts. In non risk service agreements, the contractor provides services in the form of such activities as exploration, development, and production and is paid a fee by the government that covers all costs. In practice non-risk service agreements are rare. Risk service contracts are much more common. In a risk service contract, the contractor bears all of the costs and risks related to exploration, development, and production activities. In return, if production is achieved, the contractor is allowed to recover its costs as production is sold. In addition, the government pays the contractor a fee for its "services." The fee is typically based on production. As with production sharing contracts, a significant task facing the accountant is the proper determination of recoverable operating and capital costs.

Joint Operating Agreements

As with domestic operations, when two or more international parties are involved in a joint operation they must execute some type of joint operating agreement. In international operations the function of the joint operating agreement depends on the parties and the detail included in the underlying concession agreement, PSC, or risk service contract. Model Form International Joint Operating Agreements are published by the association of International Petroleum Negotiators (AIPN). All operating agreement, of whatever type, has certain elements in common. First, if different companies own interests in different, segregated tracts, the agreement will need to *pool* the rights of the parties. Second, the agreement must set out a *method* for the conduct of the joint operations: who has the authority to make what decisions, and under which circumstances. Third, the agreement must contain a *formula for participation* in costs, production or revenues, and ownership of property and materials. Finally, the agreement for operational practicality should designated an "Operator" who, at a minimum, will control day-to-day activities, and should specify that Operator's powers, duties, compensation and replacement.

The *international* joint operating agreement must take into account the special circumstances involved in international operations. First, since the operating agreement is intended to implement the Government Contract, it should track its requirements and conform to its provisions: *the international joint operating agreement is **always** subordinate to the Government Contract, not vice versa*. The other attributes that are unique to operations in a foreign country in general, and to operations in *this* foreign country in particular, should also be taken into account. Finally, if the terms of the Government Contract require participation in the operations by a *Government Oil Company*, the operating agreement must take this into account (http://www.mosburgoil-gas.com/html/body_mosburg_primer_ijoa1_11_96_2a.html).

Recoverable *vs.* Non-recoverable Costs

In joint interest accounting, one of the key tasks is co determine the proper amount of costs and revenues co be shared by each of the parries. In accounting for a PSC or risk service contract, evaluation of costs and allocation of revenues are likewise issues that involve considerable accounting attention. As a general rule of thumb, costs that are defined as direct costs in domestic joint operating agreements are also recoverable under the PSC or risk service contract. In a domestic joint operating agreement, recoupment of indirect costs by the operator is specified via application of Overhead rates. Overhead rates (typically sliding scale rates) are also frequently used in PSCs and risk service contracts co determines the amounts of recoverable indirect costs.

Many of these costs would likewise appear in international accounting procedures as either direct costs or recoverable costs. There are a number of potentially sizeable costs encountered in international operations. A few of these are listed below:

- Transportation costs, in general, are likely to be much larger in international operations.
- Rig mobilization and demobilization costs are likely to be significant since rigs may have co be moved long distances.
- Companies typically have a home office in their home country. In addition they may have large, administrative offices within the Country of operations. The costs associated with the in-country offices are generally direct and recoverable. If there is more than one project and/or different projects with different owners then the cost of the in-country office will have to be allocated co the projects on some reasonable basis.
- Costs associated with expatriate employees (i.e., employees working in a foreign country) who are relocated into the country include, travel, moving, living quarters, education for dependent children, etc.
- Relocation costs associated with expatriate employees who move from one foreign assignment co another are frequently an issue that must be spelled our in the contract. For example, if an employee is relocated from an assignment in Poland co an assignment in China, and from there co an assignment in Thailand, how much of the total relocation costs would be chargeable co the operations in China?
- In most domestic joint operating agreements, charges relating to technical employees are chargeable co the joint operation only if the employee is physically on location at the joint property a minimum amount of time, typically eight hours. In international operations, technical employees working in offices located outside of the host country may nonetheless still be chargeable co the joint operation so long as their work is directly benefiting the joint property.

Financial Accounting Issues

Financial Accounting vs. Contract Accounting

Over the years, accountants have recognized that, while the contract terms and conditions are quite different for PSCs and risk service contracts, the financial accounting should be fundamentally the same. Consequently, financial accounting for PSCs and risk service con reacts is no different from financial accounting for concessionary contracts. Even though in a PSC or risk service contract the government owns the oil and gas reserves, the exploration, development, and production activities should be accounted for as oil and gas producing activities and not as contractor services. The production revenue that accrues to the contractor is to be accounted for as revenue and not as cost recovery.

International Accounting Standards

Regardless of the country in which the parent company is located, most foreign governments require companies operating within their country to file financial statements prepared in accordance with local GAAP. For example, a French company operating in Australia might be required to account for its Australian operations using Australian GAAP and, for purposes of parent company reporting, to also account for the Australian operations using French GAAP. Many foreign countries have adopted accounting standards issued by the International Accounting Standards Committee (IASC). This may be particularly helpful for companies that operate in several foreign countries, since using IASC standards allows them to apply one set of accounting standards rather than standards relating to each of the countries in which they operate. In 1999, the IASC steering committee, which was appointed to draft a standard for the extractive industries (including oil and gas and mining), began working on a draft standard. The standard will address such issues as whether to allow full-cost and successful-efforts methods, specific provisions related to many issues including capitalization of exploration, drilling, development and production cost calculation of DD&A, accounting for conveyances, and reserve disclosures. It is anticipated that this standard will be finalized by 2002.

Comparing Financial Statements

Financial statements of oil and gas companies are evaluated for several different purposes. Oil and gas companies compete in capital markets for new investment dollars. Investors and lenders must determine in which companies to invest and to which companies to lend money. In determining which companies to invest in, investors and lenders use various criteria, including the analysis of certain key ratios or performance measures. Investors and lenders then compare the ratios to identify the firms that have the greatest potential for successful performance in the future. In addition, companies are continuously seeking to improve their own performance. One technique a company can use to evaluate its performance is to compare itself to other similar companies. This comparison is commonly referred to as benchmarking. The process involves identifying a pool of companies who are "peer" companies, i.e., companies that are similar to the company in size, operations, and various other factors. Performance measures or key ratios are computed for all of those companies, and then analyzed to determine how the company compares to its peer companies. In this way, comparative strengths and weaknesses can be identified. A plan can then be established and implemented to build on the strengths and correct the weaknesses. Benchmarking is a critical step in improving the quality of business processes.

Whether the financial statement analysis is performed by outside investors or for internal benchmarking, it is important to keep in mind that an analysis which involves trends over several years is typically much more informative than the calculation of ratios for a single year. The ratios commonly used in the oil and gas industry for financial statement analysis and benchmarking are discussed in the remainder of this chapter. The ratios discussed are reserve ratios, reserve cost ratios, reserve value ratios and financial ratios. The source of the data necessary to compute most of the ratios unique to oil and gas companies is typically the SFAS No. 69 disclosures. Disclosures must be presented in the annual reports of both successful-efforts and full-cost companies. Specifically, the following disclosures are required:

Historical

1. Proved reserve quantity information.
2. Capitalized costs relating to oil and gas producing activities.
3. Costs incurred for property acquisition, exploration, and development activities.
4. Results of operations for oil and gas producing activities.

Future

5. A standardized measure of discounted future net cash flows relating to proved oil and gas reserve quantities.
6. Changes in standardized measure of discounted future net cash flows relating to proved oil and gas reserve quantities.

Reserve Ratios

Reserve Replacement Ratio

One key performance measure is the reserve replacement ratio. The reserve replacement ratio measures a company's ability to continue to operate in the future, by measuring the extent to which a company is replacing the reserves it is producing. A firm that is not replacing the reserves it produces will ultimately deplete its pool of available reserves and be forced to either purchase reserves in-place or simply cease to do business. Since purchasing reserves in-place is typically more expensive than acquisition of reserves through exploration and drilling. It is desirable for a company to consistently a1d to its reserves at a rate equal to or higher than its rate of production. Accordingly, a company replacing the reserves it produces should have a reserve replacement ratio of at least one. One problem with the reserve replacement ratio is determining which categories of reserves to include in the calculation. Specifically, reserve additions resulting from revisions in previous estimates and purchases of reserves in-place are often treated in different ways. Consequently, there are three different ways to calculate the reserve replacement ratio. Each method is discussed below. The most basic formula is:

$$\text{Reserve Replacement Ratio} = \frac{\text{Extensions and discoveries + improved recovery}}{\text{Production}}$$

Computed in this manner, the reserve replacement ratio considers only reserve additions resulting from current discoveries, extensions, and improved recovery. An alternative reserve replacement ratio that includes any current year revisions in reserve estimates in the numerator of the formula is as follows:

$$\text{Reserve Replacement Ratio} = \frac{\text{Extensions and discoveries + improved recovery + Revisions in previous estimates}}{\text{Production}}$$

If reserves acquired by purchase are included in the numerator of the reserve replacement ratio, then any reserves sold in-place (as opposed to through production) should be added to the denominator as follows:

$$\text{Reserve replacement ratio} = \frac{\text{Extensions and discoveries + Improved Recovery + Revisions in previous estimates + Purchases of reserves in-place}}{\text{Production + Sales of reserves in-place}}$$

Presumably, a firm could not consistently replace its reserves by purchasing reserves in place; therefore, the above formula might only be useful during those periods when in-place purchases are material.

Reserve Cost Ratios

The reserve cost ratios are based on costs and on reserves. When a company has oil and gas reserves, the reserve cost ratios are computed by converting the reserves to a common unit of measure based on energy content (BOE).

Finding Costs Ratios

Finding costs per BOE is one of the most common, but difficult to define, performance measures used in evaluating oil and gas operations. Finding costs per BOE is the most frequently cited ratio Utilized in evaluating the efficiency of a company in adding new reserves. The basic ratio consists of the finding costs of adding new reserves divided by the new reserves added. The difficulty with calculating and using the finding Costs per BOE ratio results from several factors.

First, there is no consensus regarding which costs should be included as finding costs. Second, companies use different methods of accounting for oil and gas exploration and development operations, i.e., full-cost and successful-efforts. Consequently, even if there were a specific definition of finding costs, the amounts would likely still differ since the various accounting methods treat the costs differently in terms of expense and capitalization. Third, there is typically a timing difference between the period(s) when the finding costs were actually expended and when the new reserves are actually reported in the financial statements. This timing difference poses a difficulty in interpreting the finding costs per BOE ratio. Finally, there is some debate as to which reserve estimates should actually be used in the calculation.

In computing finding Costs per BOE, there should be correspondence or matching between the costs in the numerator and the reserves in the denominator. The difficulty is determining which reserves should be used to correspond to the costs in the numerator. Reserves categories include reserves added through discoveries and extensions, purchases of reserves in-place, revisions in reserve estimates, or enhanced recovery. If reserves added through extensions and discoveries are to be used then finding costs per BOE should be calculated as:

Formula 1 without revisions:

$$\text{Finding costs per BOE} = \frac{\text{G\&G exploration costs + All exploratory drilling costs}}{\text{Reserve extensions and discoveries (excluding revisions)}}$$

or

Formula 2 without revisions:

$$\text{Finding costs per BOE} = \frac{\text{G\&G exploration costs + Exploratory' drilling costs + Proved properties}}{\text{Reserve extensions and discoveries + Purchases of reserves in-place}}$$

Formula 2 with revisions:

$$\text{Finding costs per BOE} = \frac{\text{G\&G exploration Costs + Exploratory drilling costs + Proved properties}}{\text{Reserve extensions and discoveries + Purchases of reserves in-place (including revisions)}}$$

Finally, sometimes finding com per BOE is computed by attempting to include all com, necessary to replace reserves. This ratio includes all of the Costs in the above ratio plus the cost, of unproved properties and develops men, drilling expenditures:

Formula 3 with revisions:

$$\text{Finding costs per BOE} = \frac{\text{G exploration Costs + All exploratory and development drilling costs + Proved and unproved property acquisition costs}}{\text{All reserve additions (including revisions)}}$$

The purpose of a development well is not to find reserves but to produce previously discovered proved reserves. Consequently, when development drilling costs are included in the ratio, this ratio is sometimes referred to as a finding and development costs, ratio or a reserve replacement cost, ratio.

These different formulae can result, in significantly different finding costs per BOE. Gaddis, Brock, and Boynton used the financial statements of several oil and gas producers to demonstrate the vastly different results in finding costs per BOE.

Method A: G&G costs and exploratory drilling costs only divided by reserve additions excluding revisions.

Method B: G&G costs and exploratory drilling costs only divided by reserve additions including revisions.

Method C: G&G costs, exploratory drilling costs and development drilling costs divided by all reserve additions, including revisions.

Reserve Value Ratios

When a company has oil and gas reserves, the reserve value ratios are computed by converting the reserves to a common unit of measure based on energy content (BOE). While the disclosures mandated by Statement no. 69 are controversial, the use of certain value-related amounts found in the disclosures in ratio analyses has become a popular means of incorporating reserve value. One such ratio is the value of proved reserve additions per BO£. This ratio is computed using certain elements of the changes in the standardized measure disclosure and the reserve quantity information disclosure.

Financial Ratios

There are many other ratios that are frequently used in financial statement analysis. These ratios are used to evaluate companies in all industries, including oil and gas companies. These ratios include:

Liquidity Ratios

$$\text{Current ratio} = \frac{\text{Current Assets}}{\text{Current Liabilities}}$$

$$\text{Quick ratio} = \frac{\text{Liquid current assets}}{\text{Current liabilities}}$$

$$\text{Working capital} = \text{Current assets} - \text{Current liabilities}$$

Financial Strength

$$\text{Debt to stockholder's equity} = \frac{\text{Total long \& short term debt}}{\text{Total stock holder's equity}}$$

$$\text{Debt to assets} = \frac{\text{Total long \& short term debt}}{\text{Total Assets}}$$

$$\text{Times interest earned} = \frac{\text{Net Income}}{\text{Total interest expense}}$$

Profitability Ratios

$$\text{Net income to sales} = \frac{\text{Net Income}}{\text{Sales}}$$

$$\text{Return on stockholder's equity} = \frac{\text{Net Income}}{\text{Total stockholder's equity}}$$

$$\text{Return on assets} = \frac{\text{Net Income}}{\text{Total Assets}}$$

$$\text{Cash flow from operations to sales} = \frac{\text{Cash flow generated in the current year}}{\text{Current year sales}}$$

$$\text{Price/Earnings ratio} = \frac{\text{Market value of common per share}}{\text{Adjusted earning per share}}$$

$$\text{Price/Cash flow ratio} = \frac{\text{Market value of common per share}}{\text{Cash flow per share}}$$

Some analysts incorporate Statement No. 69 reserve values into some of these formulae. For example, in computing ratios that include total assets or stockholder's equity (i.e., return on assets or return on stockholder's equity), the standardized measure of discounted future net cash flows may be substituted for proved properties as reported in the balance sheet. Additionally, a comparison between the book value of oil and gas assets and the standardized measure of discounted future net cash flows is sometimes used as a measure of the financial strength of underlying oil and gas assets.

Gas Pipeline Accounting

In today's market, pipeline companies primarily provide a transportation service. Natural gas belonging to a pipeline's customer is put into the pipeline (receipt point) and is delivered to a physical point designated by the customer (delivery point). The delivery point may be the customer's facilities, a natural gas storage field, or an inter-connect with another pipeline. Because the actual measured flow of the gas received and the gas delivered will not be the same as the expected gas flow, imbalances between pipelines and their customers will be created. Pipeline companies and their customers also store gas in storage facilities in low usage months to meet demand in peak usage months. This chapter discusses the regulations and accounting treatment related to these issues.

General Regulations

Companies involved in the transportation of natural gas are regulated by governmental authorities. For companies that transport natural gas between states, *i.e.*, interstate transportation, the Federal Energy Regulatory Commission (FERC) is the governing body. (FERC is a division of the U.S. Department of Energy.) Companies that transport natural gas within states, *i.e.*, intrastate transportation, are typically governed by state commissions.

FERC or other specific governing authorities:

- approve construction of new or expanded pipeline facilities
- approve the Tariff rates that are charged to customers
- administer various accounting and reporting requirements

FERC initially approves all interstate pipeline projects by reviewing proposed Costs associated with construction and operation, market evidence that exhibits the need for additional pipeline capacity, and the environmental and operating plans of the projects. The rates that pipelines charge customers are recorded as revenues and are based on construction and operating costs and a return on equity that have been approved by the regulator. These rates are specified in a document called a Tariff. Tariff rates may vary for different areas of transportation, for instance market area zones and supply area zones, and are established for each type of transportation service provided.

The FERC's accounting and reporting requirements are published in the Code of Federal Regulations. The code is revised at least once each calendar year and includes a chart of accounts and an accounting methodology that must be used by all gas pipelines subject to the jurisdiction of FERC. This standardization provides FERC with financial data that is comparable among the pipelines, making it easier for FERC to ensure compliance and accuracy. A summary of the account numbers used in the FERC's chart of accounts is as follows:

Type of Account	Number
Balance Sheet (except Plant detail)	100-299
Assets	100-199
Liabilities	200-299
Plant Detail	300-399
Income	400-432,434-435
Retained Ermine's	433,436-439
Operating Revenues	480-499
O&M Expenses	700-949

While interstate pipeline companies are required to report to the FERC, public pipeline companies must report to the SEC as well. Reports to the SEC and other financial statement reports 'provided to bankers or other external parties must comply with GAAP; reports to the FERC must use the chart of accounts summarized above. The Federal Energy Regulatory Commission (Commission) proposed to amend parts 352, 357, and 385 of its regulations. The Commission proposes to revise Form 6 schedules and instructions to better meet current and future regulatory requirements and industry needs, update Uniform Systems of Accounts (USofA) requirements to be more consistent with current Generally Accepted Accounting Principles (GAAP), and amend its regulations to provide for the electronic filing of Form 6 commencing with reporting year 2000, due on or before March 31, 2001. The Commission is also testing the software and related elements of the electronic filing mechanism prior to its formal implementation (http://www.epa.gov/fedrgstr/EPA-IMPACT/2000/August/Day-17/i19742.htm).

Transportation Services

In the past, pipeline companies purchased gas from a producer and transported this company-owned gas to the end user. In recent years, the number of industry players has increased, with gas producers selling directly to end users (the parries who actually use the natural gas). Additionally, marketers and brokers are acquiring gas for sales to each oilier, local distribution companies (LDC), industrial facilities, and to oilier end users. As a result, pipeline companies typically serve only as the transporter of me gas versus *both* the purchaser and me transporter of the gas. The customers are now responsible for me direct purchase of natural gas from producers or marketer/brokers to ensure that their gas supply needs are met. Pipelines provide transportation services to their customers under contracts that are in accordance with the pipeline's FERC Tariff. These contracts have historically been long-term in nature-typically more than 10 years. As these long-term contracts expire, replacement contracts are being negotiated for shorter average periods, but the contracts can range any Where from 30 days to 10 years. The transportation contract specifies me type of service to be provided, me points of receipt and delivery, me transportation fees, and oilier contractual terms such as maximum daily quantities, quality of gas, etc.

There are four types of agreements associated with transportation:

1. Transportation for Others—TFO
2. Operational Balancing Agreements—OBA
3. Transportation by Others—TBO
4. Exchange Agreements

Revenue Accounting

All charges billed to pipeline customers for transportation services are recorded to the following FERC revenue accounts:

- Account 489.1 Transportation revenue—gathering Account
- 489.2 Transportation revenue-transmission Account
- 489.3 Transportation revenue—distribution

The selection of the appropriate account depends on the nature of the facilities that transport the gas—gathering, transmission, or distribution. The majority of revenues earned by interstate pipelines is attributable to their transmission facilities, and is therefore recorded in FERC Account 489.2 Transportation revenue-transmission. Because the demand for gas is highly seasonal, gas is stored in natural gas storage fields by the customer or the pipeline company during lower-usage periods in order to have enough gas available for peak demand periods. If this storage capacity were not available, pipeline companies would need to increase their pipeline capacity significantly to meet peak demand. For storage of the gas, pipelines usually own or lease space in depleted gas fields that are used for storage. Storage service charges billed to customers for storing their gas are recorded in FERC Account 489.4 *Storage revenue.* Charges and credits for balancing transactions are usually recorded in FERC Account 495 *Other Gas Revenues,* although there are also numerous special instructions for recording balancing transactions.

Kelkar Committee on Price Structure and Pricing Policy

In March 1989, Government of India appointed another Committee under the Chairmanship of Dr. Vijay Kelkar, the then Chairman, BICP. The Committee was to review the existing pricing policy, including structure and levels of prices and recommend changes, if any, required either in the principles for determining these prices or in the actual levels of the prices or in both.

The Committee inter-alia observed the following:

(i) As distinct from crude oil and oil products, natural gas cannot be easily stored or transported as much larger capital investment are required for storing and transporting natural gas than for crude oil and petroleum products.

(ii) Due to high transport cost, one of the major characteristics of the natural gas is that it is not easily tradable internationally.

(iii) While gas by itself is not tradable, it can substitute a number of tradable liquid and solid fuels, which are used as feedstock in process industry or as a fuel for domestic and industrial uses for power generation. Natural gas price would, therefore, need to bear some relationship to the prices of these fuels as is the trend emerging the world over.

(iv) On the demand side, there are competing demands for gas from different sectors. It is, however, difficult to precisely establish the effective demand for natural gas since the bulk of is it is used by fertilizer and power sectors where the demand will be largely generated by investment decisions taken by the Government.

(v) An important issue analyzed was the impact of prices on the consumers in the context of the alternative that would be available to the sectors in the absence of natural gas for this purpose. The report brought out in this context, the replacement value of gas especially in the context of power, fertilizer and sponge iron industries. vi. For the purpose of determining replacement value of gas, both the capital cost and the prices of alternate fuels other than gas were considered. This means, if gas is to replace an alternate fuel, the incremental investments due to shifting to the gas and incremental cost savings by using gas vis-à-vis the replaced alternate fuel are considered.

The recommendations of the Committee followed the following objectives:

(i) The consumer price should encourage optimal inter-fuel substitution and ensure optimum use of natural gas.

(ii) The producer price should be such as to encourage efficient production and transportation of natural gas so as to enlarge production at the maximal rate.

(iii) The prices should be fixed in such a way that the markets are cleared on the basis of prices and not on the basis of physically fixed quotas.

The pricing of gas recommended by the Committee followed the basic principle of long run average cost of production of gas of ONGC and OIL to work out the consumer price of gas.

After considering the recommendations of the Committee, the Government of India, vide letter dated 31st December 1991, fixed gas prices from 1st January 1992 till 31st December 1995. The Producer Price of natural gas was fixed at Rs. 1500/MCM for gas with calorific value in the range of 9000-9500 kcal/M^3. The Consumer Price of gas for the calendar year 1992 was fixed at Rs.1550/MCM increasing every year by Rs. 100/MCM to reach Rs. 1850/MCM during the year 1995. For gas supplies in the North East, the gas price was retained as Rs. 1000/MCM while the maximum discount was brought down to Rs. 400/MCM on case-to-case basis.

For gas supplies with calorific values beyond the above range (9000-9500 kcal/M^3) there was a discount/premium based on the mid-point of the range i.e. 9250 kcal/M^3 as in the case of 1987 pricing order.

Sankar Committee on Gas Pricing

In January 1995, the Government constituted another Committee under the Chairmanship of Shri T.L. Sankar, Principal, ASCI to review the existing gas pricing policy, including structure and levels of the prices and recommend changes required either in the principles for determining these prices or in the actual levels of prices. The Committee was also to take into account the requirements of the existing consumer industries as well as the need and the feasibility of encouraging new markets of utilizing natural gas.

The Committee brought out that both in 1987 and 1992; while fixing the prices the implicit assumption was that only indigenously produced gas would be available for use in India. However, the Committee noted major developments in the gas sectors as follows:

1. Gas is proposed to be imported in significantly large quantities and several industrial and power generation proposals have been identified.
2. Gas would be produced by few private sector companies under PSC and some more fields may be granted in the near future. While awarding the gas fields to private sector companies, Government has agreed at a price, which is indexed to the price of basket of fuel oils in the international markets with floor and ceiling price.
3. In the proposal for import of natural gas through major pipelines, the price of natural gas has been fixed with reference to basket of crude oils, fuel oils etc.

In view of the changed circumstances and availability of imported gas in the country, Sankar Committee deliberated on the gas pricing options based on:

(a) Cost of production;
(b) Market determined prices; and
(c) Import parity prices.

The Committee recommended adopting the gas pricing system for the producer price, which compensates the producer, the cost of production including the rate of return on investment, which is large enough to act as an incentive. The recommended consumer price is to gradually increase every year and approach the import parity prices.

Taking all the factors, Sankar Committee recommended that the Consumer Price to be gradually de-linked from cost of production and should move towards import parity price. The difference between the Consumer Price and the Producer Price is a rent, which should be deposited in a fund for the development of gas industry. Therefore, the Committee recommended that in addition to the Producer

Price, the consumers must pay a contribution, which could be called the contribution to the "Gas Pool Account."

Domestic Price Structure of Natural Gas

The Ministry of Petroleum and Natural gas currently controls the price of majority of domestic natural gas in India sold by Gas Authority of India Limited (GAIL). It does not control price of gas sold by entities like Gujarat Gas Limited. GAIL buys gas from national oil and gas companies ONGC and OIL and also from Joint Venture producers who have been awarded gas fields pursuant to New Exploration and Licensing Policy (NELP). The consumer price of gas i.e., the price paid by the final consumer is combination of land fall price of gas, royalty charges (which in turn depends on the producer price i.e., the price of gas paid by GAIL to ONGC/OIL), transmission charges of GAIL and applicable taxes and duties.

GAIL pays producer price to ONGC and OIL and negotiated price to JV producers based on the contract entered into by GAIL with them. The producer price of gas is set by MoP&NG on quarterly basis after making suitable adjustments in the land fall price. The price setting mechanism is explained in detail in subsequent sections.

Producer Price of Gas

The Producer Price is the price for gas paid to upstream producers like ONGC. ONGC is paid for gas supplied on a netback basis after deduction of the Gas Pool Account charges and compensation to GAIL for the higher cost of gas purchases from the Joint Venture Companies (JVCs) from the *Consumer Price* of gas payable by off takers.

Producer Price = Total Consumer price payable—GAIL's
Compensation for JVC Purchases- Gas Pool Charge

However, the actual Producer Price varies according to a number of variables, including calorific value at the point of purchase from ONGC and the price of the international basket of fuel oils. The producer price is set by MoP&NG in consultation with ONGC every quarter. The producer price is set such that a contribution of INR 2.5 billion can be made by GAIL to the Gas Pool Account annually.

Components of Producer Price

Consumer Price

Consumer Price is the gas price charged by GAIL from its consumers based on 75% linkage to the price of a basket of fuel oils.

Gas Purchase from JVCs

There are currently three Joint Venture Companies (JVCs) from which natural gas is purchased by GAIL. The gas price from JVCs to GAIL has been negotiated. The gas purchase prices from the JVCs are denominated in US dollars per MMBTU and are linked to calorific value of gas. Gas from Tapti and Panna-Mukta has a floor price of US$2.11/mmbtu (million British thermal units) and a ceiling of US$3.111 mmbtu, while that from Ravva has a floor ofUS$1.75/mmbtu and a ceiling of US$3/mmbtu. The price paid by GAIL to JVCs in excess of the price paid by GAIL to the ONGC/OIL for purchase of gas is deducted from the total amount payable by GAIL to ONGCI OIL. This ensures that the cost of gas purchased by GAIL is same irrespective of the seller being ONGC or the JVCs.

Gas Pool Account

The Gas Pool Account is funded by a flat charge of INR.2.5 billion deducted from the total gas revenues payable to ONGC and transferred to the Gas Pool Account annually. The pool money is used for:

- Inflation adjustments to GAIL's transmission charges to compensate GAIL at the rate of 1% for every 10% increase in the consumer price index (CPI)
- Compensation to Oil India Limited (OIL) for gas sold at concession rates in the Northeast. OIL is also compensated for the effect of inflation on its margins.

R&D: The Gas Pool provides for exploration activities and the exploitation of small fields.

Any sum in the pool account remaining after deducting the above is credited to the central exchequer.

Price Build-up for Gas Transporter

GAIL currently buys gas from either the state owned gas companies ONGC/ OIL or from private sector JVCs. GAIL pays JVCs based on the negotiated prices. GAIL pays the Producer Price to ONGC as explained in the previous section. GAIL is allowed to build up only the transportation cost into the gas price and does not get any margin on marketing and sale of gas.

Price Build-up for End Consumers

Till January 1996, the pricing of gas was controlled and the upstream producers of natural gas like ONGC were paid Rs.1500 per thousand cubic meters (tcm) ($0.79 per mmbtu @ 48 Rs/US$) for natural gas. This pricing scheme allowed a 25% pre tax return to the upstream companies. With effect from October 1, 1997, pricing for marketed natural gas has been linked to a basket of international fuel oils. The new policy is largely based on the recommendations of the T.L. Sankar Committee. The details of the current policy for natural gas pricing are as follows:

Total Gas Price = Consumer Price based on Calorific Value of gas
+ Transmission Charge + Royalty + Sales Tax

Consumer Price

The Consumer Price is linked to a "reference price" based on a predetermined basket of international fuel oil prices. The fuel oil basket chosen by the government is an equally weighted mix of two low-sulfur and two high-sulfur oils as follows:

(a) Cargoes Mediterranean Basis, Italy (1% Sulfur), f.o.b.
(b) Cargoes NWE Basis ARA (1% Sulfur), c.i.f.;
(c) Singapore HSFO 180 cst (3.5% Sulfur), f.o.b.;
(d) Arab Gulf, HSFO 180 cst (3.5% Sulfur), f.o.b.

- Consumer Prices for natural gas were 55% of the price of the basket of fuel oils in 1997-98, 65% in 1998-99 and are currently at 75%.
- Currently natural gas prices are reviewed quarterly and fluctuate with the international price of the basket of fuel oils. There is a floor price of Rs 2,150 per tcm ($1.121 mmbtu) and ceiling price of Rs 2850 per tern ($1.491 mmbtu) for the Consumer Price of natural gas.
- These prices are fixed for natural gas having a calorific value of 10000 kcal per SCM and are adjusted for the actual calorific value of delivered gas.

Royalty: The present rate of royalty applicable to natural gas is 10% of the Producer Price.

Transmission Charges

GAIL has entered into gas supply with each of its consumers. The transmission tariff for each of the consumers is defined by the contracts. The transmission tariff is fixed for the term of the contract. The transmission charges have nominal escalation element of around 3%. The average transmission charges of GAIL for its consumers in Maharashtra and Gujarat (non-HBJ) is around Rs 200 per thousand standard cubic meters.

For HBJ Pipeline, the Government has fixed the transportation charge at Rs. 1150 per TCM. This is a postalised transportation charge i.e. the same transportation charge is applicable to all the consumers on the HBJ pipeline. This transportation charge increases at the rate of 1% for every 10% increase in the consumer price index. The increase in tariff is however not passed on to the consumers and is recovered from the Gas pool Account.

Sales Tax: The sales tax varies from state to state. The sales tax on natural gas sales in Gujarat is currently 22% and in Maharashtra it is 16%.

Sample build of gas price (for consumer on HBJ Pipeline) is given below in Table 11.6.

Table 11.6: Current Price Build-up of Domestic Gas

Item	Amount (Rs. per thousand SCM)
Land Fall Price	2850 (current prices)
Producer Price	2116 (June 2002)
Royalty (10% of Producer Price)	211
Transmission Charges	1150
Total (without Sales Tax)	4347
Sales Tax (22% for Gujarat)	956
Total Price	5303
Total price in $/ mmbtu	$2.842 per mmbtu

1 Based on a calorific value of 8500 kcal per scm.
2 At Rs 49.5 per US$ and Calorific value of 9500 kcal per standard cubic meters (scm).

Currently, the Land fall price of domestic gas is linked to 75% of a basket of fuel oil prices with a ceiling of Rs 2850 per thousand scm and a floor of Rs. 2150 per thousand scm. Based on the fuel oil prices, the domestic landfall gas prices have been restricted to the ceiling of Rs 2850 per thousand scm since October 1999. The relative gas prices in $ per mmbtu terms has been however falling on account of depreciation of Indian rupee. Price applicable for gas produced under medium sized discovered fields awarded by the Government to consortium of private sector companies and ONGC under PSG arrangement as follows.

Panna-Mukta and Tapti

Natural Gas Price: Base Price × (Linkage fuel price for 12 months preceding the quarter) 1 (Linkage fuel price for April 1993 to March 1994 which is US$ 1.9486/ mmbtu)

Base Price: US$ 2.32/mmbtu

Linkage fuel: 99% of the price of a Low Sulphur Fuel Oils basket consisting of the following in equal parts:

1% sulphur Fuel Oil, Cargoes, FOB Med, basis Italy

1 % sulphur Fuel Oil, Cargoes, CIF NWE, basis ARA

- 3.5% sulphur Fuel Oil, Singapore HSFO, 180 cst Arab Gulf, FOB HSFO 180 cst.
- In view of the above formula, 119.06% of Fuel Oil parity price is admissible for Panna-Mukta and Tapti fields subject to the floor and ceiling, which are US $ 2.11/mmbtu and US $ 3.11/mmbtu respectively.

Ravva

Linkage fuel: Basket of High Sulphur and Low Sulphur Fuel Oils consisting of the following in equal parts:

3.5% Sulphur Fuel Oil, Singapore HSFO, 180 cst

1% Sulphur Fuel Oil, NEW, Barges, FOB Rotterdam

1% Sulphur Fuel Oil, Cargoes, FOB Med, basis Italy

Prices to be fixed on quarterly basis based on previous 12 months prices of above fuel oils with the floor of US $ 1.751 mmbtu and ceiling of US $ 3.00/mmbtu.

Price Applicable for Gas Produced under pre-NELP Exploratory Fields

The pre-NELP exploratory blocks PSG provide full marketing rights to the contractors along with right to fix prices based on market forces. In one of the blocks (CB-OS-2) where the gas production is to start shortly, gas sale agreements have been finalized with Gujarat Gas Company and Gujarat Powergen Energy Corporation Limited. While in the former case, the gas price has been linked to Dated Brent crude oil and Naphtha prices with floor of US $ 2.74/mmbtu and ceiling of US $ 4.00/mmbtu, gas price in the later case works out to about US$ 3.67/mmbtu.

Price Applicable for Gas Produced under NELP Blocks

No gas sale agreement understood to have been concluded in respect of any NELP block. While the gas price in such cases would depend upon the local demand and supply conditions, the gas price may be near to the ones concluded in pre-NELP exploratory blocks, as above, where the regulatory environment is similar to the NELP. No gas sale agreement concluded so far; the gas price may be near to the agreements concluded in pre-NELP exploratory blocks where the regulatory environment is similar to the NELP. Currently, natural gas is one of the most economical fuels domestically, largely on account of controls on prices. Once gas prices are decontrolled, the differential advantage vis-à-vis other liquid fuel should decrease. However, even then, natural gas is expected to be the preferred fuel as it is cleaner compared with other fuels like coal and petroleum. Because of environmental reasons, the GoI also encourages its use.

Further, the capital costs and operating costs for plants using natural gas as feedstock are lower vis-à-vis liquid fuels. The transportation problems associated with natural gas are more since it requires a large infrastructure. The economics of alternative fuels keeps changing with time, as oil and gas prices are very volatile. However, the above economics largely hold true as the prices of these alternative fuels are linked to each other in the long term. Fuel oil is the most economic liquid fuel in terms of heat value. This is because naphtha can be used for the production of more value-added petrochemicals/polymer products. At current prices, natural gas is most economical in India, but as the natural reserves of the fuel are not significant in the country, its availability remains a problem.

Increase in Gas Costs

In India, where there is an acute scarcity of NG, its prices have been administered and kept low. Currently, the domestic NG prices are at a discount of over 40% to the price of internationally traded fuel oils. Globally, because of the absence of trading in NG, the prices of fuel oil act as the benchmark for NG prices. In countries where there is shortage of NG, the prices of NG are close to fuel oil prices (as in Japan). However, in countries where there is no major demand for NG and it is produced as associated gas (with crude oil), NG prices are incredibly low (as in the Middle East and Venezuela), given that its storage cost is very high and the gas produced has to be flared. Thus, Natural Gas prices are different in various markets, reflecting the demand supply position in these countries. Following table highlights recent gas prices in various countries. In a country like India, where the demand for NG is far in excess of the supply, gas prices for industrial use are expected to increase to the level of fuel oil (the highly traded lowest priced liquid hydrocarbons) prices if allowed to be determined by market forces. Although the current linkage of gas prices with fuel oil is 75%, a low ceiling price restricts the gas price to Just 55% of fuel oil price.

LNG Pricing

LNG is traded generally on the basis of its energy contents and the prices are usually expressed in the US Dollar per million BTU. The energy contents are

Table 11.7: International Gas Prices of Representative Countries

	International Gas Prices (US $ as per mm btu)
Western Europe	3.0
Russia	0.6
Venezuela	0.5
Argentina	1.5
Trinidad	1.25
North Africa	0.4
Middle East	0.5
Indonesia	1.2
US	3.15

Source: Completed by ICRA Information Services.

measured on the basis of Gross Heating Value. The pricing formula for LNG typically has a base price with some form of indexation and can be calculated on an FOB (Free on Board) or C.LF (Ex ship) basis. Today most new contracts are on FOB basis, since this gives buyers more control over the landed and perhaps a boost to the importing country shipping industry.

LNG prices are benchmarked to the competing fuels in the market place. There are distinct and relatively independent LNG markets in the world i.e. North America (US), Western Europe and Asia Pacific. The benchmarking in these markets has been as follows:

Table 11.8: Benchmarking of LNG Price with Competing Fuels

Region	Linkages
North America	Domestic Gas
Western Europe	Competing Fuels (Heating oil, Gas oil, Pipeline gas etc.)
Asia Pacific	Imported Crude

Japan (Asia Pacific) which is the largest LNG importing country has following formula for importing LNG from Malaysia/Brunei.

$$P = A \times JCC + B$$

Where

P = Ex ship price LNG.

A = Constant (negotiated).

B = Agreed Constant

JCC = Japan Custom Cleared (Published every month) crude oil, in US$/Bbl

Such formulas in the past were not suitable to buyers (when price of benchmark fuel were very high) and Seller (when price of benchmark fuel were very low). Over the years some changes have been made to protect buyers and sellers against extreme fluctuations in oil prices by introducing other variables.

The two techniques used generally are:

Floor & Ceiling: LNG price would remain static below specified (floor price) and above specified (Ceiling) price of benchmark fuel.

S curve: The formula 'Flattens' out the pricing curve on both the high and low ends (so that in the case of extreme fluctuations in oil prices, both seller and buyer share the risk).

Planning and Measuring Financial Performance

This section deals with the basic concepts on IRR/return on investment which is used for planning of new retail outlets, Tracking of sales; leading indicators *vs.* lagging indicators of sales performance, and the comparative advantages/ disadvantages of the concepts of Sales maximization *vs.* profit maximization.

Internal Rate of Return/Return on Investment

- Any Investment (Rs. 100) is meant to generate a series of cash flows.
- Rs. 100 today will generate Rs. 10 as return in one year.
- Rs. 100 given after one year is equivalent to Rs. 91 as of today.
- Similarly; Rs. 100 given after 10 years is equivalent to Rs. 39 as of today.
- All future cash flows converted to equivalent amount of today should equal or more than today's Investment amount to justify investment.
- Conceptually, present value of future cash inflows should be equal to present value of Cash outflow i.e., Net Present Value (NPV) = 0.
- % rate by which future cash inflows are discounted to present equivalent amount to equate with proposed investment is Internal Rate of Return (IRR).

The internal rate of return (IRR) takes into consideration the time value of a stream of revenues generated over a period of time. A retail outlet, typically, has a long gestation period. It is expected to generate a stream of revenue for many years. To calculate the discounted value of returns spread over next couple of years from the date of investment the concept of IRR is applied. If IRR of a retail outlet project is more than the 'cost of capital' the project is considered favourably.

Return on Investment is simply the ratio of operating income and total investment. It is a one time figure as against IRR which consider a long period of 5-10 years (Table 11.9).

Table 11.9: Return on Investment Computation for a Retail Outlet

(Rs in lakh)

Investment	**150**											**PV**	**NPV**
Year	**0**	**1**	**2**	**3**	**4**	**5**	**6**	**7**	**8**	**9**	**10**		
Returns	–150	20	30	40	22	26	28	30	32	35	40		
Discounted	10%	1800	2410	2916	14 43	1535	1488	1435	1377	1356	1395	17116	21.76
Returns(a)	11%	17.80	23176	28.20	13.80	1452	1392	13.27	1260	1226	1247	16260	12.66
	13%	17.60	21.23	2720	2736	1319	1372	1226	11 51	1108	1114	153 99	3.96
	13%	1740	2271	26.34	1260	12.6	1214	11.32	1050	999	994	14590	-4.10
IRR	12.486%	1750	22.98	2681	12.90	13.35	1258	11 79	1101	1054	105	15000	0.00

In this example IRR is 8.97 %o which can be compared with cost of capital.

Tracking of Sales

Sales tracking is an important performance evaluation tool for any retailing. For the purpose of retailing two important performance evaluators are:

Revenue per sq feet = Gross Revenue (in Rs.) generated per month is divided by the area in sq. ft to arrive at this ratio. This ratio is an indicator of the utilization of land/buildings. It can be improved by changing the product mix in a manner so as to improve the gross revenue. In the case of fuel retailing this can be achieved by increasing the share-out of branded fuels (high priced product) at the retail outlet. In the case of non-fuel category mix can be altered to improve the revenues.

Revenue to Stock ratio = Gross Revenue (in Rs.) generated per month is divided by the value of average inventory for the month to arrive at this ratio. This is an indicator of inventory management. A healthy ratio indicated a better inventory management indicating lesser money tied-up by way of working capital in stocks. Most retailing companied follow the pattern of monthly, weekly, or fortnightly sales reviews. Among oil retailing companies in India, sales figures are collected, and analyzed at the end of the month. An 'Industry Performance Review' coordinated by IOCL takes place by 10th of the following month where 'Regional Sales Reviews' (RSR) brought by regional RSR Coordinators from North (Delhi), South (Chennai), East (Kolkatta), and West (Mumbai) are discussed and analyzed to arrive at the overall performance.

This is a typical example of what are referred to as lagging indicators of performance. Lagging Indicators are those indicators which are collated after the review period. Performance is measured against some pre-set target and analysis typically conveys whether sales are lagging behind the target or not. Lagging indicators are like a post-mortem. In contrast leading indicators are those data or events which indicate the correctness or otherwise of a direction. So, weekly sales data collected against a monthly target can convey whether our sales are progressing in the right direction, if not a corrective action can be taken during the period of review it. While driving a car from Delhi to Baroda, the landmarks as seen in the rear view mirror are lagging indicators of performance whereas the milestones that we see on the road in front are leading indicators.

Gap Analysis

Data on monthly sales of petrol pumps for the period April 2000 to March 2001, and April 2001 to September 2001 collected from the respective sales officers for 54 Trading areas from the Sales Officers is shown in tables below. All these Trading areas have at least one outlet of each oil company. Data is collected for a total of 241 outlets. Based on the average monthly sales calculated from the sales data of 241 retail outlets, it is observed that an IOC outlet is market leader in 18 Trading areas (TA), a BPC outlet is market leader in 18 Trading areas, HPC in 15, and IBP in 3 Trading areas.

The Table 11.10 summarizes the data obtained from the companies.

Table 11.10

Company Name	Leader in TAs	No. of Outlets in 54 TAs
IOC	18	64
BPC	18	62
HPC	15	61
IBP	03	54
Total	54	241

There are trading areas where a company has more than one outlet, and thus competing with it. But even in those cases individual outlet average sales are considered for this analysis. Those Trading areas where a BPC outlet is at number 2 to number 4, and the gap from the industry leader was more than 1, 00,000 litres per month are considered *to* be strategic Trading areas and the outlet concerned is identified as low performing strategic outlets. The overall average, sales per outlet is 3, 00,000 litres per month. So an outlet doing less than 33% of the average is considered poor performing, as there are four players in the market. It is recommended not to consider 25% of the average because in a competitive market a leader should lead with a wide margin for others to catch up. Accordingly the following data has emerged (Table 11.11)

Table 10.11: Planning and Measuring Financial Performance

Trading Area No.	Mar leader	Average Monthly Sales (Litres)		Gap (Litres)
		Market leader	BPC Pump	
3	IOCl	670000	434000	236000
7	IOC	440000	310000	130000
8	HPC	220000	120000	100000
11	IBP	340000	230000	110000
19	HPC	303000	200000	103000
20	IOC	275000	175000	100000
21	IOC	503000	398000	105000
33	HPC	440000	325000	115000
41	IOC	531000	298000	233000
42	IOC	531000	277000	254000
44	IOC	404000	299000	105000
45	IOC	603000	302000	301000
46	IOC	402000	300000	102000
47	IOO	367000	250000	117000
51	IOC	311000	211000	100000

The sales gaps will then analyzed in terms of their impact on company's business and the efforts involved in improving the marketing mix in that particular Trading area. For example, the Trading area no 3 is more attractive than the Trading area no 51 in terms of its impact on the company's business. All the Trading areas identified in the above mentioned table should be plotted in the following 2x2 matrix ranging from high impact to low impact on the one axis and high effort to low effort on the other. The effort is in terms of man-hours required, money to be spent, and the expected gestation period for the improvement of marketing mix.

Effort/Impact Matrix

High Effort	Least Attractive	*Moderately Attractive*
Low Effort	*Moderately Attractive*	*Most Attractive*
	Low Impact	High Impact

The Trading areas, which fall under "most attractive" box, are further analyzed for the gap study. For this purpose the marketing mix of each company is studied in detail and compared with each other for their ease of replication—what is it that the competitor could easily copy. Now it is easily identifiable that hardware impacts business because better facilities, attractive outlets, and well-lit pumps attract more customers. But in the overall systemic approach this would call for higher investments. High cost of capital coupled with the long time required to actually spruce-up the outlets make this particular element a high effort one, The fact the any oil company can invest same amount of money to bring their facilities at a comparable level renders this initiative less effective. And overall it would find a place in the 'least attractive' box of the 2×2 Effort v/s Impact matrix. On the other hand improved services, being low cost and highly individualistic would find their place in the 'most attractive' box.

It can be easily deduced from the above tabulated data that for BPC the best competitive advantage could come through the assurance to customer on correct Product Quality and Quantity, improved software in terms of better and efficient customer service, and through innovative add-ons being provided to the customer, This marketing mix through a suitably chalked out promotional campaign and loyalty programmes could be the final deliverable of this strategy.

The specific strategic initiatives for this purpose are called 'Pure for Sure' for the correct quality and quantity with better traffic flow and improved customer service, 'In & Out' for the allied retail business, and 'PetroCard' & 'Fleet Card' for the loyalty programmes. The results obtained at 22 outlets in Delhi where the company has implemented these strategies show a growth of 11% during the months of September and October 2001 as against the industry average of 8%. The author was shared data for Calcutta where the growth has been 34% against the industry growth of just about 6%. In Bombay these figures are 9% v/s 5%. And in Chennai the growth figures for this period are 6% v/s 3%.

This data suggests that the strategy devised through 'Gap Analysis' has bore fruits. Therefore, as a technique it can be relied upon. Also it provides an opportunity to explore each market as a strategic component of the 'whole' marketing mechanism. For example a promotional scheme in one market can be agriculture oriented (and hence diesel fuel based) whereas in the other it could have an urban outlook (thus petrol based). Therefore, the strategic importance of driving the target market, devising action plans for each one of them, and finally collating these plans to achieve synergies is the systemic approach that can prove to be vital. A final measure of the overall health of a retail network in petro-retailing is market effectivity. Market effectivity can be defines as the ratio of your company's sales market share and your company's network market share.

Market Share = Your Sales Market Share/Your Network Market Share

Consider the hypothetical data in the table given below (Table 11.12).

Table 11.12

Sample Calculation of Market Effectivity in an area

Company	MS Sales in KL	Sales Market Share = Sales / Total Sales	No. of ROs	Network Mkt. Share = No. of ROs / Total ROs	Market Effectivity = Col 3/ Col 5
IOCL	234560	41.08%	31	4627%	0.888
PCL	144000	25.22%	13	19.40%	1.300
HPCL	121563	21,29%	13	19.40%	1.097
mp	69312	12.14%	7	10.45%	1.162
Reliance	1108	0.19%	2	2.99%	0.065
.Essar	432	0.08%	1	1.49%	0.051
Total	570975	100.000%	67	100.00%	1.000

A market effectivity of 1 or more for a company signifies that the company is able to generate more sales than the competition. This could be due to better placed ROs, better services, better product, etc. A good retailing company must try to maximize its market effectivity. Ideal figure is above 1 and around 1.25. In the above example BPCL has an effectivity of 1.3. A very high market effectivity for a company means that its RQs are likely to be attacked by new or improved ROs from the competitors. Therefore, very high market effectivity is also no reason for companies to become complacent. All the elements of marketing mix which can be replicated easily will be copied and even improved upon by the competition. Low market effectivity for a company indicates that each of its retail outlets needs to be examined in greater detail to improve the performance. For deeper analysis company can use the earlier discussed techniques of gap analysis, or quadrant analysis.

Sales Maximization vs. Profit Maximization

Very often sales maximization is taken as the single largest target of retailing. Often the battle is fought on market share of sales. However, it is equally important to understand the overall financial implication of high sales—sales at what cost?

Consider the following example (Table 11.13). Here sales volume is increased through greater promotional effort. The increased sales promotion has some additional cost to it which has nullified the effect of improved realization on account of more number of units sold.

An Increase in revenue realization does not mean an increase in Profit:

Table 11.13

	Existing	Revised
Sales Volume	1000 units	1125 units
Profit per unit	Rs 10	Rs10
Promotion cost per unit	Rs 1	Rs 2
Profit	Rs 9000	Rs 9000

No change in profit in spite of increase in sales volumes and revenue realization. Sometimes, higher sales are achieved through reduction in price, rather than through promotion. Even in that case the overall profitability may not improve as can be seen from the following example. Actually, depending upon the price elasticity of demand a product sales may not go up with decrease in price. Even within the price band when sales have an inversely proportional relationship to price the marginal increase in sales may be far less than the marginal decrease in price resulting into less overall profit. The following Table 11.14 will clarify this point:

Table 11.14

	Price	Variable Cost	Fixed Costs	Total Revenue	Total Profit
100	1100	800	200	1100	100
150	10,50	8,00	200	1575	175
200	10,00	800	200	2000	200
280	9,50	800	200	2660	220
350	900	7,85	200	3150	203
430	8,75	7,85	200	3400	190
435	8,70	785	200	3200	170

For this data, graph should be plotted for both sales volumes and profit which can be placed with respect to price. The maximum profit volume point on this graph can be easily spotted; this will indicate that sales volumes higher than this level do not add to the bottom line of the company.

Petroleum Accounting Management System (PAMS)

The Petroleum Accounting Management System (PAMS) is a totally integrated software solution for the Petroleum and Convenience Store Industry, encompassing the retail, wholesale, fuel oil, propane, cardlock, mobile fueling, and financial accounting necessities of the industry.

PAMS has a modular, flexible design that enables the system to be tailored for a client's particular industry focus. Each customer installs only the PAMS modules and optional subsystems that apply to his or her business. Additional modules can be easily activated and integrated into the existing database as your business diversifies. Clients can also use PAMS to maintain separate databases for a business that is divided into financially distinct companies, yet retain the ability to produce consolidated reports and cross company look-ups. The large range of processing and reporting options provided by PAMS allows the system to be set up in different ways in order to produce the desired end results (http://www.addsys.com/products/pams.htm).

PAMS Module

Financial Modules

A complete package of sophisticated financial accounting software allows you to link the home office with retail c-store, wholesale operations and home heating/

propane in the field, providing a total solution of unsurpassed power and flexibility. The modular design of the system means that all financial modules share and use the same data.

Accounts Payable

- Detailed vendor records.
- Optimizes payment strategies.
- Electronic import of vendor prices, invoices and manifests from C-Store vendors/petroleum suppliers.

Accounts Receivable

- Manages receivable amounts and simplifies collection activities.
- Maintains extensive customer records.
- Allows user-defined aging categories, finance charges, memos and live transaction processing posted to the general ledger.

Retail Modules

PAMS gives control of Petro-retail operations. This advanced soft-ware package will improve data collection and reporting, reduce daily reporting errors, eliminate redundant paperwork, reduce dependence upon individual managers and supervisors, provide timely fuel dispatching data, and improve customer satisfaction

Wholesale Modules

The PAMS package integrates bulk terminal, wholesale marketing, data transmission interface, fuel supplier/tax reporting, card lock management, equipment maintenance, purchase orders, order entry, and inventory management programs into a comprehensive system linking home office and field functions into a single operation.

Bulk Terminal Management

- Tracks and controls activities at bulk fuel terminals
- Electronically poll transaction data from auto-mated terminal equipment
- Interfaces with the Petroleum Product Exchange (PETROEX)
- Handles the many account types, such as pre-buy, exchange, and custody
- Automatically generates the proper types of invoices, manifests, bills of lading, etc.

C-Store Purchases/Price Book

- Manages bulk liquid fuel purchases
- Purchasing fuel from a supplier and shipping it to a customer, company gas station, or bulk storage location
- Accounts for the freight costs
- Track and report the fuel taxes owed to local, state, and federal authorities

Order Entry/Inventory Control

- Processes customer orders
- Tracks warehouse inventory, both bulk liquid products and packaged items
- Supports multiple order types, direct ship, direct bill, cash and credit memos
- Variety of customer invoice and delivery ticket formats

Purchase Orders

- Manages the purchase of all stock/non-stock items, lubricants, equipment/parts
- Keep track of minimum inventory quantities, vendor discounts, restocking lead times, and other purchasing data
- Generates automatic purchase orders
- Integrates Order Entry and Accounts Payable modules to facilitate inventory control and cost tracking

Wholesale Marketing

- Maximize profit margins and other benefits on fuel sales to wholesale customers
- Maintains customer information, including quote history, account status, and miscellaneous notes
- Integrates that data with up-to-date supplier cost information

Auto-Fuel

- Electronically polls and processes transaction data from card lock sites
- Interfaces with numerous types of automated fueling equipment
- Information on customer accounts, vehicles, and drivers
- Tracks taxes by transaction, monitors inventory by site
- Provides flexible customer discount options
- Generates customer statements in a variety of formats

Thus, it would be seen that RAMS software based Module, among other things, will provide complete package of sophisticated financial accounting software allowing linking the home office with retail c-store, wholesale operations and home heating/propane in the field, providing a total solution of unsurpassed power and flexibility. Thus the RAMS' IMS will also effectively link the wholesale Module with Petro-retail Module to extend the supply chain in a micromarketing mode for service optimization and effective revenue generation with low cost solutions.

References

Peter M Senge (1999), The Fifth Discipline, London, Random House Business Books.
Ralph D Stacey (1991), The Chaos Frontier, Oxford, Butterworth Heinemann
Thomas, J.G. (1988), Strategic Management, New York, Harper & Row

Ramaswamy, S & S. Namakumari (2001), Strategic Planning, New Delhi Macmillan Business Books.

Burrow, Jackie, "Treatment of Dry Holes Under the Successful-Efforts Method of Accounting—A Definitional Problem *Journal of Extractive Industries Accounting*, spring, 1982, pp. 58-59.

Gallun, R.A.; C.J. Wright; L.M. Nichols & J.W. Stevenson. (2004), Fundamentals of Oil & Gas Accounting, Pennwell Pub

Indian School of Petroleum (2005), A Manual on Oil and Gas Accounting. Training Programme on Upstream Business Processes for L&T Infotech Ltd.

Certified Public Accountants published Accounting Research Study No. 11 on "Financial Reporting in the Extractive Industry": http://books.google.co.in/books?id=t_wYPe8arT0C&pg=PA56&lpg=PA56&dq=Certified+Public+Accountants+published+Accounting+Research+Study+No.+11+on+%22Financial+Reporting+in+the+Extractive+Industry.%22&source=web&ots=n30xTsd_s-&sig=ZGYEVAlkeYZNEKFnM5K4t2BR_rk&hl=en&sa=X&oi=book_result&resnum=1&ct=result

FASB Statement No. 19, termed Reserve Recognition Accounting (RRA of USA): http://books.google.co.in/books?id=sYIqxibXy1kC&pg=PA244&lpg=PA244&dq=FASB+Statement+No.+19,+termed+Reserve+Recognition+Accounting+(RRA+of+USA)&source=web&ots=k_6D7NtTFl&sig=2nl-PSXB1Q31EGAcGWYLRQf741M&hl=en&sa=X&oi=book_result&resnum=1&ct=result#PPA212,M1

Charlotte J. Wright, Rebecca A. Gallun (2007), International Petroleum Accounting: http://books.google.co.in/books?hl=en&id=93xtSaC6EGIC&dq=Petroleum+Accounting&printsec=frontcover&source=web&ots=jmySAa0IMp&sig=RIqHt17lYfVGAP_ZGf6sTpXsejw&sa=X&oi=book_result&resnum=1&ct=result#PPR7,M1

PricewaterhouseCoopers (2007), Petroleum Accounting: Principles, Procedures and Issues, PricewaterhouseCoopers and Professional Development Institute (PDI) of the University of North Texas.

Rebecca A. Gallun, Linda M. Nichols, Charlotte (2001), Fundamentals of Oil & Gas Accounting, PricewaterhouseCoopers, 2001

Charlotte Wright and Rebecca A. Gallun (2004) International Petroleum Accounting, Pennwell.

Steve Lawrence, (2000), Historical Development of Accounting Standards-Part II: http://www.accaglobal.com/archive/2888864/31025

Richardson, Allan, J (2008), Strategies in the development of accounting history as an academic discipline, Accounting History, Vol. 13, No. 3, 247-280 (2008) DOI: 10.1177/1032373208091528

Kaiser, Mark, (2007), A survey of drilling cost and complexity estimation models, International Journal of Petroleum Science and Technology, June, +19,+termed+Reserve+Recognition+Accounting+(RRA+of+USA)&source=web&ots=k_6D7NtTFl&sig=2nlPSXB1Q31EGAcGWYLRQf741M&hl=en&sa=X&oi=book_result&resnum=1&ct=result#PPA212,M1

http://books.google.co.inbooks?id=t_wYPe8arT0C&pg=PA56&lpg=PA56&dq=Certified+Public+Accountants+published+Accounting+Research+Study+No.+11+on+%22Financial+Reporting+in+the+Extractive+Industry.%22&source=web&ots=n30xTsd_s-&sig=ZGYEVAlkeYZNEKFnM5K4t2BR_rk&hl=en&sa=X&oi=book_result&resnum=1&ct=result

http://en.wikipedia.org/wiki/Full_cost_accounting

http://www.isisoftware.net/

Websites

http://www.nymex.com/lsco_pre_agree.aspx
http://www.aip.com.au/pricing/crude.htm
http://www.newscom.com/cgi-bin/prnh/20030428/ATPGLOGO
http://www.prnewswire.co.uk/cgi/news/release?id=145506
http://www.eia.doe.gov/emeu/perfpro/ref_pi2/tab1.html
http://www.beg.utexas.edu/energyecon/documents/UT-CEE%20Seminar%20on%20Petroleum%20Contracts.pdf
http://www.glossary.oilfield.slb.com/Display.cfm?Term=production%20sharing%20contract
http://www.mosburgoil-gas.com/html/body_mosburg_primer_ijoa1_11_96_2a.html
http://www.epa.gov/fedrgstr/EPA-IMPACT/2000/August/Day-17/i19742.htm
http://www.addsys.com/products/pams.htm

- INFOSEEK (guide.infoseek.com)
  ...NETSCAPE SEARCH ENGINE
- ALTA VISTA (altavista.digital.com)
- LYCOS (www.lycos.com)
- OPEN TEXT (www.opentext.com)
- EXCITE (www.excite.com)
- WEBCRAWLER (webcrawler.com)
- WEBCOMPASS (www.quarterdeck.com)
- INFOMARKET (www.infomkt.ibm.com)

NET DIRECTORIES:

- EXCITE (www.excite.com)
  ...NETSCAPE DIRECTORY
- YAHOO (www.yahoo.com)
- MAGELLAN (www.mckinley.com)

U.S. DEPARTMENT OF ENERGY HOME PAGE: (http://apollo.osti.gov/home.html)

SAMPLES OF PETROLEUM COMPANY ADVERTISEMENTS

- TEXACO OIL COMPANY (http://www.texaco.com/default.htm)
- SHELL OIL COMPANY (http://www.shelloil.com/)
- ARCO (http://www.arco.com/)

BIG YELLOW: COMMERCE ON THE WEB: (http://s15.bigyellow.com/web_business_guide/wbg_intro2.html)

WWW VIRTUAL LIBRARY: ENERGY: (http://solstice.crest.org/online/virtual-library/VLib-energy.htm)

UTILITY DATA INSTITUTE: (http://www.udidata.Inter.net/)

IRS HOME PAGE: (http://www.irs.ustreas.gov/)

CHAPTER XII

International Hydrocarbon Economic Environment

The global oil industry has moved into the 21st century on a high profit-making market condition, especially under deregulated global business environment. Oil and Natural gas exploration, production, processing, transportation and marketing technology etc. are constantly undergoing innovations, creating the ability to find, position and market oil and gas even in increasingly remote and inaccessible areas of the world. Oil and gas companies are developing new strategies aligned to the unique customer demands in the most competitive and cost-effective manner. With added pressure from the governments as well as customers, cleaner and cheaper fuels are being introduced and offered to the customers on a continual basis at an affordable price with value-added service quality. Growing global customers/ consumers-both in the industrial and domestic sectors are demanding more petroleum products that are being catered to by substantial scaling-up of global refinery capacity and their system-managed business operations. This chapter is dedicated to review and scan through the global business environment in the context of booming Oil & gas sector to meet their growing global demands.

Global Oil Production

The following Table 12.1 sums-up information on global oil production during by major oil producing countries during 1991-2001.Regionally speaking, Middle-east were the maximum producing countries, followed by North America and Russia in that order.

Over the past two decades, the growth in non-OPEC oil supply has resulted in an OPEC market share of 41 per cent substantially under its historic high of 52 per cent in 1973. New exploration and production technologies, aggressive cost reduction programmes by industry and attractive fiscal terms to producers by governments, all contribute to the outlook for continued growth in non-OPEC oil production which is going to make a strategic balance between production, supply and pricing of oil and natural gas products in years to come.

Table 12.1: Scenario of Global oil production by the Major oil-producing countries

(Millions barrels per day)

Regions	1991	1 992	1993	1 994	1995	1996	1997	1998	1999	2000	2001
North America	1.18	1.05	13.90	13.81	13.79	14.05	14.27	14.18	13.68	13.90	14.0
South and Central America	4.75	4.84	5.04	5.35	5.78	6.15	6.49	6.94	6.83	6:89	7.00
Europe	472	5.06	5.34	6.26	6.51	6.83 '	6.86	6.79	6.90	6.93	6.81
Former Soviet Union	10.7	9.15	8.20	7.39	7.30	7.17	7.38	7.39	7.55	8.01	8.65
Middle East	17.28	18.75	19.60	19.90	20.04	20.45	21.38	22.60	21.68	22.97	22.23
Africa	6.81	6.93	6.92	*7.00*	7.11	7.43	7.75	7.64	7.57	7.79	7.81
Asia Pacific	*6.93*	6.92	7.00	7.18	7.32	7.57	7.12	7.74	7.61	7.98	7.9
Total World	63.14	63.70	65.99	f,6.90	67.85	69.67	71.85	73.28	71.83	7.48	7.49

Global Oil Consumption

Table 12.2 depicts country profile of major consumers of oil in the world during the same period, i.e. 1991-2001. North America, Asia and Europe were found to be the predominant oil consumers in the world during the period.

Table 12.2: Country Profile in Global Oil Consumption pattern

(Million barrels per day)

Region	1991	1992	1993	1994	1995	1996	1997	1998	1999	2000	2001
North America	19.91	20.28	20.50	21.H	21.06	21.7	22.19	22.59	2.1.21	2.1A7	23.39
South & Central America	3.60	3.72	3.80	3.97	.16	4.33	.57	.71	4.7	.73	.69
Europe	14.98	15.04	15.02	15.02	15.29	15.63	15.84	16.09	16.00	10.97	16.09
Former Soviet Union	7.98	6.97	5.54	4.74	4.36	3.78	3.75	3.63	3.01	3.41	3.41
Middle East	3.50	3.57	3.70	3.89	.03	4.11	4.16	4.16	4.28	4.31	4.31
Africa	1.99	2.04	2.07	2.13	2.20	2.20	2.31	2.38	2.44	2.48	2.49
Asia Pacific	14.38	15.35	16.04	17.15	18.09	18.87	19.68	19.25	20.20	20.94	20.92
Total World	66.33	66.97	66.67	68.06	69.20	70.69	72.50	72.81	7.50	75.29	75.29

Oil consumption in 2001 remained at the same level of previous year at 75.2 million barrels per day. During 1999, oil consumption rose by slightly more than 1.5 million barrels per day with industrialized nations accounting for about one-half of the increase. Before the 1998 recession, oil demand in developing Asia (including China) had governed at a robust annual rate of about eight per cent between 1991 and 1997. As the Asian economies began recovering in 1999, oil demand grew in China by 5.1 per cent and in the rest of Asia by 2 per cent. With economic problems in Brazil and political uncertainty in Colombia, Ecuador and Venezuela, oil demand in Latin America exhibited negative growth. Persistent economic problems in Russia caused declines in oil demand from 1998 onwards for the former Soviet Union countries. During 2001, some countries like Kazakhstan (10%) and Lithuania (15%) experienced positive growth and some other countries like Azerbaijan (-25%) had negative growth in consumption, leaving the whole group of countries witl1 negative growth in consumption *or* 0.4 per cent. In Asian Far-East countries like Hong Kong (–2.1%), Thailand (–2.8%), Japan (–3.2%)/Malaysia (–8.8%) and Taiwan (–5.2%) had experienced negative growth in 2001. Overall Asia Pacific had negative growth in consumption is by 0.5 per cent in 2001.

Oil provides a larger share of world energy consumption than any other energy source, at 39 per cent of the total in 1997. Petroleum world over is used heavily in the transportation sector and is also used to provide heat and power. World oil consumption is projected to increase to 112.8 million barrels per day in 2020 from the level of 75.3 million barrels per day in 2001. The industrialized countries, currently the largest consumers of petroleum, are expected to remain the largest users through 2020. Oil demand is driven by economic growth, along with rising population. The industrialized countries consume oil at much higher levels per capita than the developing countries, such as China and Brazil.

The Future of Oil

"Oil is dead. Gas is king. Long live the king." This must be the mandate to all oil company exploration companies. The ground reality is not far from this. Global Oil scenario apart, all of the tampering for position with regard to the mega mergers in no small part been driven by the desire of oil industries to find gas or strengthen their gas portfolio: the mega economies like China, India, North America, and of late, Brazil and Russia continue to have a massive projected demand for gas—both now and more importantly, in the future. Newer power generation projects will undoubtedly be fuelled by cheaper and cleaner natural gas with the two emerging economies of China and India plus the global thrust for the cleaner burning-image of gas is predicted to increase production to the detriment of both oil and coal. On top of that, transport and to a large extent, domestic sector will gradually move towards gas and duel-fuel run vehicles on the road.

E-Commerce—The Impact on Both Upstream and Down Stream Industries

The E-commerce and micromarketing boom has made a large impact upon the upstream and downstream industries. Oil companies are already predicting large cost reductions on account of logistics and administrative savings from the use of e-enabled services with much wider customer-base. The current high oil price has severely reduced margins from petrochemicals and fuels, therefore, any method to increase margins are being increasingly vied as potential future opportunities.

The oil companies are now aiming to streamline their supply chain via business-to-business networks over the internet.

The Upstream Industry

The following paragraphs analyze the future outlook in the growth prospects of upstream activities on oil and natural gas.

1. Future of the North Sea

The future of the North Sea is a two-sided coin. On one side, new investment has slumped due to the continued hangover from the low oil price in 1998. On the other side, opportunities are enormous for smaller, independent E&P companies, who are looking to re-establish mature or even capped fields with the assistance of new drilling technology. The UK Government have provided tax breaks for such E&P companies, as a further sweetener to the opportunities on offer in the UK sector of the North Sea. During 2001, production of UK at the level of 2.5 million barrels per day declined by 6.6 per cent from its previous year level. The Norwegian Government has not followed the UK's lead, but is under growing pressure to do so in an attempt to attract investment into this very mature oil province. Norway produced 3.4 million barrels per day in 2001, which is one per cent higher than the previous year. The E&P activity in this region (UK, Norway and Denmark) has declined as represented by the decline in production figure by 1.8 per cent in 2001 to the level of 6.2 million barrels per day. Another factor that has added to the low level of development work has been the mergers of a large number of companies with the investments in the North Sea.

2. Western Investment in Middle-East

European and other western oil majors are looking to expand their presence in Saudi Arabia, following the kingdom's latest investment proposals to foreign oil companies, including Royal Dutch Shell, Exxon Mobil, Phillips, and Chevron Texaco. Saudi Arabia alone accounts for over a quarter of all global oil reserves. Hence, the large oil companies are queuing up for a share of this long-term supply.

3. US Independents Prefer to Explore Overseas

More independents are going overseas to search for oil and gas because North American basins are mature, production is declining and competition is fierce for E&P deals. Foreign basins have become much more attractive with regard to their contract terms and their potential reserve size. There is limited potential in the United States, unless companies grow by acquisitions or trades. But this has been labeled a 'zero sum game' where one side wins and the other loses. Larger independents will be expected to start spending more overseas, with the exception of the deepwater Gulf of Mexico.

4. Republic of China

China is becoming more and more dependent on imported oil as it looks towards the next decade. In fact, the amount of imported oil could be as high as 40 per cent of its total consumption. The inherent problem that China is faced with is that there have been no new significant discoveries for a. number of years. China's E&P future is not as bleak as it may sound. Some geologists have claimed that there are some significant untapped resources in the Sangliao Basin in the northeast and in the Bohai Sea in the west and northwest.

5. Asia-Pacific Region

Oil producers in the Pacific Rim are expected to increase production significantly with the use of enhanced exploration and production technologies. Deepwater fields offshore from the Philippines have improved the reserve picture there and production is expected to reach almost 250 thousand barrels per day by 2005. Vietnam's long term production potential also is still viewed with considerable optimism, although exploration activity has been slower than originally anticipated. Output levels from Vietnamese fields are expected to exceed 500 thousand barrels per day by 2020. Australia has significantly added to its proven reserves recently and it is likely that Australia will become a million barrels per day producer by 2005. Papua New Guinea also continues to add to its reserve posture and is expected to achieve production volumes approaching 200 thousand barrels per day by 2005. India too is expected to show some modest production increase early in the decade. Malaysia shows little potential for any significant new finds and its output is expected to peak at around 825 thousand barrels per day in the early 2000s. Exploration and test well activity have pointed to some production potential for Bangladesh and Magnolia, but significant output is not expected before 2005.

6. Libya

Libya has been heralded with the title of "The No. 1 Exploration Hotspot" in Robertson Research International's survey in 1998.

Top ten exploration hotspots in the world as per the latest survey are as follows:

1. Libya,
2. Iran,
3. UK,
4. Australia,
5. Algeria,
6. Iraq,
7. Indonesia,
8. Angola,
9. Brazil, and
10. Egypt.

7. Africa

Several West African producers (Angola, Cameroon, Chad, Congo, Gabon, and Ivory Coast) are expected to reap the benefits of substantial exploration activity, especially considering the recent rebound in oil prices. Angola is expected to become a million barrels per day producer within five years. Given the excellent exploration results, Angola has the potential to produce volumes up to 1.8 million barrels per day in the next 10-20 years.

Electronic Trading

Both the International Petroleum Exchange (IPE) and the American Petroleum Exchange (APE) are testing the water With regard to 'electronic trading'. The days of the trading floor pit and 'open outcry' may be numbered. The APE has recently set up an internet based trading exchange for wholesale gasoline and diesel. The IPE have developed a new system that will allow trading to be carried out via the internet on a real time basis.

Downstream Industry—Refining and Marketing

The global capacity for refining crude oil has grown by 0.7 per cent during 2001 to a level of 82.2 million barrels per day.

Environmental Issues

MTBE has been banned in California and a US wide ban is but a short step away. The reason is tenuous, the impact could be far-reaching. MTBE is an additive brought in to produce a cleaner burning fuel. However, MTBE is now thought by some to have carcinogenic properties disputed by others and has now found its way into the Californian water system probably from site contamination or inland lakes with motor vessels experiencing fuel leakage. The Environmental lobby in California is very strong and has pushed through the total ban before conclusive testing has been done. The cost of development of the replacement additive will be high with the end-user the ultimate financier. Much has been made of the 'greenhouse gas effect', the Kyoto Protocol and emission trading. A rather sobering thought which should prod lice a reduction in the hysteria surrounding the subject is a recent report, which suggested that just one large volcano eruption produces more environmentally unfriendly gases than the entire world production of 'greenhouse gases' for the whole year.

Exploring Alternative Fuels

Alternative Fuelled Vehicle (AFV) is any vehicle capable of operating on an alternative fuel, such as LPG, natural gas, alcohol or electricity.

There are two configurations of AVF:

1. Dedicated, one fuel.
2. Non-dedicated:
   (a) Hi-fuelled,
   (b) Flexible fuelled, and
   (c) Duel fuelled.

Hi-fuelled can operate on either an alternative fuel or gasoline but not at the' same time plus they have the separate storage system.

Flexible fuelled can operate in either alternative or conventional fuel or a combination—single storage and combustion system.

Duel fuelled can burn two fuels simultaneously, stored separately and injected into the combustion chamber simultaneously. A second variation of duel fuel has now become a front runner—conventional fuel plus fuel cells (electric).

The contenders for the alternative fuel crown are known to be:

- Liquid Petroleum Gas (Propane) LPG,
- Liquid Natural Gas (methane) LNG,
- Ethanol,
- Methanol,
- Hydrogen,
- Biodiesel, and
- P-Series Fuels.

Both LPG and LNG are obtained from natural gas processing and have been the most popular alternative for many years resulting in the desire of major oil companies to become gas richer. The other five can be obtained from renewable sources, either crops/vegetable matter, sunlight, wood, or natural waste. Biodiesel, as the name suggests, is the replacement for diesel and is made primarily from vegetable oils (Soya) as well as animal waste. It can be used with existing engines, stores safely and produces a similar power output to conventional diesel engines. Several large-scale fleet tests are underway and the early reports are good, including reduced engine wear.

P-series fuel is a vegetable oil, animal plant waste sourced fuel, used as an alternative to gasoline.

Electric vehicles are three types:

1. Battery powered,
2. Fuel cell, and
3. Hybrid—gasoline plus battery or fuel cell.

Battery power still suffers from the high cost of batteries with a relatively low power range. Both hybrid and fuel cell vehicles are the fastest growing area of all alternative vehicle manufacturing.

The issues that currently affect AFV sales/production are:

- The higher initial cost of the vehicle,
- The total drive range limitation, and
- Fuel supplies—lack of a network of retailers.

All forms of AFV will have an impact on the major oil companies, either increased revenue from gas sales or reduced profits in petrol retailing. Either way the full impact is expected to be felt until 2010 when the AFV ownership will be large enough to really hurt.

Domestic Hydrocarbon Economic Environment

Structure of Indian Oil and Gas Economy

Hydrocarbon sector in the Indian Economy is to be seen in terms of its functional chain, historical and evolutionary development process. The functionality and growth of the various segments of the sector have got reflected in the institutional set up, which have grown to play the functional role and to operate the sector. Given below is a table of the segments and institutions, which together would bring out the composition of the sector. Indian domestic hydrocarbon market is no more a closed market as it used to be prior to 1997, Indian economy has consistently opened itself up by providing investment and marketing opportunities to foreign oil companies. Today, all most all oil majors and multinational oil companies are represented in India by opening their liaison office in India. Some of them have also opened one or more Indian subsidiaries, including having joint venture tie up with Indian companies. Their area of activities broadly covers the following:

- Selling and buying crude oil and other petroleum products to Indian companies. In this process, these companies in some areas have replaced Indian companies by directly dealing with the customers. Example is selling Kerosene to parallel marketers in India and selling Naphtha to Indian companies directly.
- Investing capital in Indian companies. A good example is Petronas's (National Oil Company of Malaysia) investment in LPG import at Haldia.

It is worth noting that not much foreign direct investment has materialized in hydrocarbon sector as was expected at the time of liberalizing the economy through reforms since early 90's. This has been found to be pretty glaring in the following segments:

The foreign joint venture partners in refining segment have withdrawn their interests one by one. Example, Oman Oil Company withdrew its interest from Central Indian Refinery of Bharat Petroleum Corporation, which was a green field project involving capital investment of over Rs 6,000 crore (at 1990s price level). Kuwait Petroleum Corporation has withdrawn from the refinery project of Indian Oil Corporation, which was also a green field project involving equal order of capital investment as of Central India Refinery. Not much foreign capital has been invested in downstream infrastructure projects like building tanks and pipelines. While liberalizing the hydrocarbon sector for private and foreign participation, it was expected to attract capital into this sector and augment the infrastructure base. That was one of the reasons for making Rs 2,000 crore investment a precondition for providing marketing right in the retail auto fuel segment. It can, therefore, be inferred that hydrocarbon sector has successfully attracted business interest in India from foreign companies, without associated capital investment.

Indian Oil Industry in a Growing Economy

India consumed 99.8 million tonnes of petroleum products in 2000-01. The consumption is growing at 6.2 per cent rate per annum over the last decade. Indigenous production of crude has been ranging from 27 to 35 million tonnes per year during the last decade. Import of petroleum products has been increasing at seven per cent per annum during 1991-99. These imports comprised 20 per cent of the total value of India's imports and 25 per cent of India's total exports in 1999-2000. The import dependence is projected to rise to 75 per cent of total consumption requirement in 2006. The feature of import dependence brings out mainly two issues: *first*, India's ability to buy so much oil at foreign currency at the prevailing price; and *second*, and the issue of security of oil supply at the time of exigencies like war or natural calamity. The two issues together throw up challenging tasks, like managing risk of volatile oil prices in international market, foreign exchange reserve management, managing uninterrupted supply line, optimization in logistics and inventory holding. It has been estimated that a 20 per cent increase in diesel price and 10 per cent increase in petrol price can result in 0.5 per cent reduction in GOP. Even when the oil price increase is not passed on to consumers, it has an adverse impact. Government or pool account has to finance it and that puts pressure on government budget. Government investment may go down leading to reduction in demand.

Petroleum products provided 36 per cent of total energy consumption in the country in the year 1999-2000, whereas its average share was 32 per cent for the period 1990-99.During 1999-2000, the share of petroleum products in the total energy consumed was 98.5 per cent in transport sector, 71.3 per cent in household sector, 13.6 per cent in industrial sector and 9.5 per cent in agriculture. Oil sector is a major source of revenue to the Union Government. The 12 Oil PSUs recorded profit after tax of Rs 11,825 crore against paid up capital of Rs 5,204 crore during 2000-01.

Importance of Oil & Gas for National Economy

Energy price contribute 14.2% in WPI

- 38% of ports and 7% railway traffic are comprised of petroleum sector cargo
- Total public sector capital outlay of Sixth Plan (1980-85) of 5% increased to 6.5% in Tenth Plan (2002-07)
- PSUs in O&G sector account for 38% of total revenue and 45% of dividend declared by PSUs as a whole

Oil & Gas in Meeting Energy Requirement

- 38% of India's primary energy consumption from O&G per capita consumption 117 kg compared to world average of 925 kg.
- Around 2/3rd of the requirement is through imports. This will increase to 91.6% by the year 2020 as per IEA.
- India's average oil production level for 2005 was 837,000 bbl/d and net oil imports was 1.7 million bbl/d. Future oil consumption will increase from 2.5 million bbl/d in 2005 to 3.1 million bbl/d in 2010.

Global Facet of Indian Oil Industry

Oil industry in India is moving on a dynamic course since 1991, when the country embarked upon the era of liberalization and reforms. The reform process in the oil industry has been swift, multi-pronged and its impact has been of far-reaching consequence for both the micro-management of the industry and macro-management of the economy. A peculiar feature of the reform process in oil industry is that it has a large and intimate global interface, besides the domestic aspect of liberalization, largely centering on licensing policy, pricing, restructuring and customer focus. This chapter reflects on the global aspect of the transformation of Indian Oil Industry which it is presently undergoing see change leading to certain options that we ought to exercise, keeping in view the interest of Indian consumer and that of the country at large.

It is commonly known that oil is a global commodity, in the sense that its production and consumption centers are well dispersed across the globe. While its production is concentrated only at limited potential pockets, its consumption centers are well spread out all over the world. This asymmetry in demand and supply of oil leads to widespread physical trading, which is associated with bulk intercontinental haulage, storage and multiple transactions, involving a complicated cost and pricing structure. Integration of India's Oil Industry with the international oil market, therefore, appears to be a natural process by the very logic of the trade. But bringing about seamless integration between two separate markets with their own distinct features and divergent interests is a complicated surgery involving much larger socio-political and economic process.

Reforms in Indian Economy

As in the case of most developing countries that did liberalize the economy in the last three decades of the 20th Century, India's reforms were preceded by a serious financial crisis. In 1990-91, the gross fiscal deficit of the government (Centre and States) reached 10 per cent of GDP and the annual rate of inflation peaked at nearly 17 per cent in August 1991. Fiscal imbalances, which assumed serious proportions since mid 19805, had two important facets.

First, the outpacing of the rate of growth of revenues by the expenditure growth considerably reduced the resources available for public investment in the economy.

Second; the increasing diversion of household savings to meet public consumption requirements not only resulted in expansion of public debt to unsustainable levels, but also reduced resources available for private investment.

Coupled with fiscal-imbalance, there was an unprecedented balance of payment crisis in early 1991. The Current account deficit doubled from an annual average of 2.3 billion US dollar or 1.3 per cent of GDP during the first half of the 1980s to annual average of 5.5 billion US dollar or 2.2 per cent of GDP during the second half of the 1980s. For the first time in modern history, India was faced with the prospect of defaulting on external commitments since the foreign currency reserves had fallen to a mere one billion US dollar by mid-1991.

Apart from dealing with the immediate crisis, the reforms were directed to deal with poverty and improving the wellbeing of the people. A high growth was considered essential for rapid reduction in poverty. For high growth, we needed to use resources efficiently. For efficiency, competition was considered essential. Deregulation was required to create competition. A free trading environment and competition from imports are also necessary to discipline domestic monopolists and to direct investments into activities where India has comparative advantage.

India has now gone through more than a decade of economic reforms. Beginning in 1991, the thrust of reforms was fiscal stabilization and the initiation of major structural reforms aimed at de-regulation of the economy to induce accelerated investment, growth and employment. A good number of these objectives have been achieved, though there are major challenges with respect to the sustenance of high economic growth in the years to come. For example, the reform measures had placed the economy on a higher growth path of above 6 per cent during 1992 to 2000. Though still below the long term performance of some of the newly industrialized countries of East Asia, the GDP growth rate during 1990s translated to a respectable growth rate of above four per cent in per capita terms.

Deregulation in the hydrocarbon sector is an appropriate offshoot of the reform process of the Indian economy. Oil industry being a crucial sector, the reform and liberalization process of Indian economy was largely contingent upon deregulation in oil sector and oil sector, on its part, has always been at the forefront of the national economic reform. Till 1993, the entire hydrocarbon chain in India was subjected to extensive regulation and controls. Starting from exploration and production, refining, marketing, infrastructure and investment planning, pricing till micro distribution, the whole gamut of activities were centrally planned. The philosophy behind this centralized control was: self-reliance, import substitution, strategic control, social and, distributive justice, promotion of heavy industries and state control of commanding heights of the economy. Ministry of Petroleum and Natural Gas (MOPNG) was at the helm of control and the coordination was carried out through: (a) Oil Coordination Committee (OCC) in the down stream sector, and (b) direct control in the upstream sector.

While the regulated system served the country well for a considerable length of time, it gave rise to some limitations as the politico-economic condition of the country underwent transformation. Some of the perceived limitations are enumerated below:

- APM could not generate adequate financial resources for investment in the upstream and the downstream sectors.
- Sometimes it created deficit in the oil pool account, as due to political compulsions selling prices were not revised promptly. More importantly, while waiting for the mounting receivables, Oil Companies borrowed at market rates of interest, which were higher than what they received on their outstanding.
- The subsidies and cross subsidies led to serious distortions in consumer prices and did not reflect the economic cost of petroleum products. This led to adulteration, diversion and consequent inefficient use of products.
- It is also said that assured returns on the cost-plus formula did not encourage efficiency in operations of PSUs. Since all investments and costs were reimbursed, there was no incentive to make profitable investment decisions.
- In the upstream sector, the APM had inadequate incentive to invest in risky venture.
- As long as players were PSUs, the Government could control investments and costs.

With the entry of private players in the market, the cost-plus formula would encourage ' gold plating' of the plant. This ultimately would add to the overall cost and consumers would ultimately have to bear the increase. Moreover, with the entry of private players in the market, it was becoming increasingly difficult to administer the. APM and ensure level-playing field.

Oil Securities for India: Issues and Concerns

Security measure basically means insulating a country from the shock arising from sudden and unanticipated disruption in oil supply, By definition, security measure is a defense mechanism, requiring perpetual preparedness, Security is a balancing act, it comprises making of a rational choice amongst multiple options; both short-term and long-term. Security has a cost implication. Therefore, a high degree security measure may be cost-prohibitive.

Uninterrupted supply line of fuel is a concern for all countries, developed and developing alike. It is more so for a country like India, which is dependent largely upon a war-prong source like Middle East. Diversification of crude procurement source, has been attempted, and successfully so, by private refineries and also by PSU refineries after de-canalization in April 2002. Efforts have been stepped up by Indian companies, like ONGC Videsh and Reliance, to secure crude acreage and equity in overseas oil field like Indonesia, Sudan, Sakhalin, Iraq and some other places. This is a notable step in the direction of security and self-sufficiency. Economic diplomacy and overseas commercial venture by Indian companies together would go a long way in securing India's interest in foreign soil. Augmentation of infrastructure in terms of port facilities, tankage and pipeline to handle sizeable parcel in quick operation is another necessity of the time. Creation of strategic reserves for oil is a known solution and Government in collaboration with TERI is working towards its implementation. Globalization of Indian Oil Industry is a positive step towards having security of oil and natural gas supply.

Phased Deregulation of India's Hydrocarbon Sector

The process of integrating Indian Oil Industry with world Oil market began in February 1993, when Government of India allowed private parties to import and market Kerosene and LPG at market determined price. Effective November 1993, the selling price of all lubricating oils was allowed to be fixed by the Oil Companies on commercial considerations. Around that time, licenses were granted to private companies to set up refineries and foreign companies were allowed to invest in equities of refineries.

From November 1997 till April 2002, administrative regulations on pricing, marketing, quantitative and tariff restrictions on import and export of petroleum products, including crude oil, were pruned and dismantled in a phased manner on a predetermined basis.

Thus, effective April 1998, refining sector was taken out of Administered Pricing Mechanism (APM). By implication, retention pricing concept for the refinery output and cost plus formula on refinery input (crude oil) was withdrawn. Refining licensing system was abolished. Crude oil import was made free for private and joint sector refineries. Corporation and Bongaigaon Refinery and Petrochemical Ltd. were made subsidiaries of Indian Oil Corporation. Kochi Refineries and Numaligarh Refineries were made subsidiaries of Bharat Petroleum Corporation. IBP Ltd., the stand-alone marketing PSU, was sold out to a strategic partner, namely Indian Oil Corporation, through competitive bidding by Ministry of Disinvestment.

By April 2002, quantitative restrictions on import and export of all products were gradually withdrawn by EXIM notifications from time to time. Crude oil import was decanalized for PSU refineries. APM was dismantled in phases. Oil companies were free to fix up the selling price of all products. Planning and coordination for bulk coastal supplies and inland distribution of petroleum products were left to the Oil Companies, with broad administrative guidelines. OCC was wound up. With a truncated staff, ace has been transformed to a Research and Analysis Wing of Ministry of Petroleum & Natural Gas.

From April 2002 onwards, the Union Government has allowed nine private companies to market transportation fuels, namely petrol and diesel and aviation fuel. With the entry of these firms, there has taken place a paradigm shift in the arena of retail selling. Apart from a number of incentives and customer-pulling schemes stalking the market, a cult of brand equity has entered domestic marketing.

With pricing of products made free and all stabilization funds being abolished, the maze of cross subsidization that once used to playa magic wand has gone out of scene. Subsidies are still permissible for domestic LPG (33.3 per cent) and on Kerosene (17.5 per cent) with a budgetary administered mechanism.

On the upstream sector, Indian basins have been progressively opened up and offered to private and foreign companies for investment. New Exploration licensing Policy I (NELP-I) was announced in 1997 and NELP-II was announced in 2000. NELP-I attracted 45 bids for 27 blocks. Production Sharing Contract (PSC) was signed in April 2000 for 25 blocks, of which 2 were onshore, 16 were shallow water offshore, and 7 were deep water offshore. The Government signed PSCs for 23 blocks in the second round of NELP in July 2001, of which seven were onshore, eight were shallow water offshore, and eight were deep water offshore.

Mergers and Consolidation in Indian Oil and Gas Sector

There have been structural reforms and corporate restructuring adjustments in the oil and gas sector through the process of merger and consolidation. As it has remained confined to the public sector domain, it is generally known as restructuring, carried out as a part of reform and privatization process. The objectives behind these exercises were manifold. The primes amongst these were to make the stand-alone refineries viable and to divest government shareholding in them. Chennai Petroleum Corporation Ltd (CPCL) and Bongaigaon Refinery and Petrochemicals Ltd (BRPL) were made subsidiaries of Indian Oil Corporation Ltd (IOC). Kochi Refinery Ltd (KRL) and Numaligarh Refineries Ltd (NRL) were made subsidiaries of Bharat Petroleum Corporation Ltd (BPCL). This restructuring programme was carried out by divesting the entire shareholding of the

Government in these refining companies in favour of IOC and BPCL by March 31, 2001.During 2002-03, the Aditya Birla share of MRPL refinery (26 per cent) was bought by ONGC, hitherto, a purely upstream company. By this process, ONGC made its maiden foray into refining sector and through MRPL and ONGC got into the marketing stream of HPC as a joint venture partner.

Trend and Structure of Oil and Gas Economy

Structure of Oil & Gas Economy

The petroleum industry in the private sector consists of a set of companies to undertake the following chain of activities as their main source of business:

1. Explore for and produce crude oil and natural gas; and
2. Refine and market oil products.

Some companies undertake all of the above functions; these are called integrated companies. Others undertake only one or some of them; these are usually referred to as independents. Some integrated companies are also involved in other areas of business; for example, many but not alt are producers of petrochemicals and other chemical products.

The Petro-chemical industry can then be categorized as fo1lows:

Oil Majors

Oil Majors basically comprise Large and integrated global players. Traditionally, this comprises Exxon, Royal Dutch/Shell British Petroleum (BP), Mobile Chevron and Texaco. Prior to 1984 this group also included Gulf Oil. They were known as the "Seven Sisters". Chevron acquired Gulf-Oil in 1984. To some degree, a group of slightly smaller integrated companies could be added to this list, *e.g.*, Amoco and Aero and, since their privatization, Total, Elf and ENI.

Other Integrated Companies

This group is similar to the Majors but relatively smaller in size and with lesser geographical reach. It comprises companies such as Amerada Hess, Conoco, Diamond Shamrock, Marathon, Occidental, Philips, Unocal and Ultramar.

Independents

These are yet smaller companies, most of whom specialize in a single segment. They include, for example, Anadarko, British Borneo, Enterprise, Kerr McGee, Lasmo, Ramco, Saga and Talisman. These are mostly having American operation. This categorization of the petroleum industry, thus, explicitly excludes all state-owned petroleum companies. It has only been in recent years that state-owned. Producing companies have moved outside their home countries and invested internationally, usually in the downstream. These include large state producing companies such as Saudi Aramco, Petroleos de Venezuela, and Pertamina of Indonesia from OPEC and non-OPEC state producers, such as Statoil of Norway, Petrobras of Brazil, Pemex of Mexico and Petronas of Malalaysia.

Emerging Forces for Change during the 1990s

Structure and Forces Prior to the 1990s

1. The Structure of the Private Sector Oil Industry

It remained extraordinarily stable with a few key players—the Majors prevalent from the 1920s until the late 1990s. Over this long period of time, the major private oil companies showed a remarkable degree of resilience to changing market conditions. Each company succeeded in more or less retaining its position within the private sector hierarchy, at the forefront of the private petroleum industry.

Until the demise of Gulf Oil in 1981, the private sector oil industry was characterized by a core of seven firms—the "Seven Sisters." From 1950, the Majors consistently increased their asset base. Till the first oil shock, the growth was steady, but post-1973 a new phase emerged, characterized by more erratic patterns of expansion. Most of the Majors again substantially increased their assets in the 1970s, aided by the rising oil price induced revenues. Those that conspicuously failed to replace lost Middle Eastern assets soon found themselves in trouble.

The nationalization of upstream assets in the Middle East and elsewhere were fundamental blows to the Majors, who had been the leading players in most of the Middle East and other OPEC member states. However, the Majors survived (with the eventual exception of Gulf Oil) and to some .degree prospered. They remained at the forefront of the private sector industry through the 1970s and 1980s for several reasons, such as:

1. Downstream assets were largely left intact,
2. Most majors had substantial US oil and gas production assets, and
3. The discovery and development of North Sea and Alaska created a new upstream portfolio of Strategic assets

2. Sources of Competitive Advantage

The 1990s proved to be a period when forces began to build which eventually led to important changes in the structure of the industry. The leading positions of the Majors had been reinforced for a long period by their deep-rooted sources of competitive advantage. These were reflected in a set of 'strategic assets' that advantaged the Majors relative to other private sector players. Many of these assets were inherited from the past, having been acquired and developed in earlier decades. They tended to be large, profitable, cash generating, not easily replicated and long lasting. These included:

Upstream: These were mainly large, low cost oil and gas fields. Initially they were mainly in the Middle East. They were then partially replaced by large North Sea and Alaskan fields.

Downstream: The main strategic assets are advantaged refineries and significant retail positions in key markets. Most of the industry's refining assets, at least in OECD countries, were commissioned prior to the 1980s. Capacity growth has subsequently tended to be incremental rather than in the form of green field expansions. Equally, many retail networks were also initially established in the past. Advantaged real estate and scale economies had been secured.

Petrochemicals: Strategic advantage in petrochemicals has tended to stem from technology, location and feedstock access. Again, these positions had often been initially established in the 1970s and earlier.

Corporate: In a world of imperfect and heavily regulated capital markets, financial strength proved a source of competitive advantage. Equity funding from corporate balance sheets provided the main source of finance for much of the industry, especially in countries where creditworthiness was questionable. These strategic assets were sustained by a number of key characteristics that were predominantly incorporated in the Majors. For example:

1. ***Technical skills and the ability to innovate:*** The Majors have not tended to develop and retain proprietary technologies (except in petrochemicals). However, they have remained at the forefront in their abilities to apply the best technology and innovate in new applications.
2. ***Highly effective logistical skills:*** These have been especially valuable in a business where transportation costs have been critical and ""here development projects are large and capital intensive.
3. ***Reputation and relationships:*** The Majors had critical strong relationships with home and host governments, suppliers and customers.

3. New Competitive Forces

The 1990s witnessed a build up of forces that eventually led to a restructuring of the industry through consolidation. The forces affected each business stream and introduced new sources of competition at both corporate and sectoral level. The main elements included: Natural *maturity* of previously advantaged fields. The "endowments" of the Majors, especially in the upstream began to erode. J3ig fields, such as Prudhoe Bay, Brent, Forties, Stasford, Ekofisk, etc., matured and began to decline. Equally the onshore and shallow water offshore of the Lower 48 states of the United States was also in decline. The producing assets were, in total, replaced in volume terms, but usually only by fields which were less profitable due to smaller size, higher costs and, in some cases, less favourable taxation regimes.

4. Initial Responses

The industry attempted to respond to deteriorating performance in several ways:

1. ***Cost-cutting:*** Cost reductions at corporate levels and in operating assets were the prime response. To some degree, this represented the stripping out of high cost structures that had cumulated and prevailed during the era of high oil prices from 1973-86. Head office head counts were slashed. Contracting out of non-core services became prevalent. Upstream costs were successfully reduced, often through operating and technological innovation. Technological advances included horizontal drilling, sub-sea

completions, floating production systems, seismic data processing, etc. The North Sea saw the introduction of "alliancing" between partners and contractors in order to prevent duplication and high costs. The UK government even supported cost reductions through its CRINE (Cost Reduction in the New Era) initiative from 1992.

2. ***Portfolio Restructuring:*** Non-core businesses were shed as petroleum companies went "back to basics". Most coal and minerals operations were sold. BP sold its animal feed business, BP Nutrition, Mobil sold Montgomery Ward, and Texaco sold its chemicals business, which it considered to be non-core. Arco exited almost all non-US activities and spun off its chemicals operations. Underperforming assets were also sold. For example, BP sold three US refineries—Ferndale (Washington), Marcus Hook (Delaware) and Lima (Ohio). At the same time, some companies also entered new sectors that opened in the face of deregulation. US gas marketing attracted Chevron and Shell, who purchased Tejas. In these markets they met new competitors, such as Enron (who grew mainly out of gas pipelines); power utilities such as Duke, Southern and Pacific Gas & Electric (PC & E); and innovative new players such as the internet power traders, Utility.com. Others invested in the electric power sector, mainly generation and usually IPPs. Shell bought Intergen as its vehicle. Amoco and Texaco created power divisions. In power generation, they faced competitors in the form of existing utilities, deregulated utilities anxious to invest nationally and internationally and new power sector companies. In the majority of instances these investments have either proved unrewarding or slow to generate adequate returns.
3. ***Focus on New Growth Areas:*** US companies in particular sought new business opportunities outside the core US markets. Many US upstream companies invested in the UK North Sea, *e.g.*, Amerada Hess. Most companies declared a strategic intent to invest in Asian growth markets. Few had any success. Newly opening areas, such as Azerbaijan, Russia, Kazakhstan, Angola and Yemen attracted many companies, although success proved scarce. Angola proved the most successful with Elf, Exxon and BP Amoco leading the discovery of a number of large low cost fields in the deepwater. The Former Soviet Union proved to be particularly challenging.
4. ***Financial Management:*** Shareholder returns were enhanced in several cases through share buy back schemes. Exxon consistently bought back its own shares for over a decade and rewarded shareholders despite limited earnings growth. Amoco, Mobil and Texaco also bought back shares.
5. ***Sectoral Consolidation:*** As it became progressively clear that the four strategic responses outlined above were insufficient, a number of companies began to develop and implement a new strategic response through structural change—sectoral consolidation.

Downstream oil operations in mature markets were proving to generate inadequate returns despite initiatives to cut costs and prune portfolios. The first major move was by BP and Mobil, who announced in February 1996 that they intended to merge their European oil, refining and marketing assets and lubricating oil operations. This received approval from the European Commission in August 1996. They also increased retail market shares at national and continental levels so that the BP-Mobil JV was able to compete on equal terms with Shell and Exxon who previously each had European average retail gasoline market shares of 13 per cent compared to BP's eight and Mobil's four per cent. This was a successful merger of two complementary sets of assets. This merger was followed by Shell and Texaco (plus Star, the US downstream operations of Saudi Aramco) merging in 1998 into two regional companies Equilon on the US West Coast and Motiva in the rest of the US, mainly in south and east. Dual branding (Shell and Texaco/ Star) has been retained. Ultramar and Diamond Shamrock and Ashland and Marathon also affected US downstream mergers. In the US upstream low profitability triggered a merger between the Permian Basin assets of Shell and Amoco to create 'Altura'.

A number of proposed downstream mergers fell through before implementation. Shell and Texaco failed to complete a European merger. Similarly, Philips and Ultramar Diamond Shamrock abandoned their proposed US downstream merger. It was either clear that cost savings were not easily identifiable or new management structures could not be agreed.

5. Mega Mergers: A New Era for the Petroleum Industry

These sectoral mergers, while in some cases being successful in increasing profitability at the micro level, were grossly insufficient to make any fundamental impact upon corporate level profitability and returns. The BP-Mobil European JV was an exceptional fit of assets. However, it could not be replicated either by other sets of players or in other geographical sectors. Corporate transformation, thus, required a greater response.

The first corporate level move was the merger between British Petroleum and Amoco to create BP Amoco. This was announced in August 1998 and the deal was completed with full regulatory approval on 31 December 1998. This created a new "super major" approximately equal in size to Exxon and Royal Dutch Shell. The merger had both a cost saving and strategic rationale. A cost reduction of $2 billion was promised when the deal was launched, mainly through the elimination of duplication, but also through greater contracting out of services and the introduction of a strongly performance based culture to former Amoco assets.

The BP Amoco merger was followed by a series of other deals that have further transformed the structure of the petroleum industry. Most importantly Exxon and Mobil announced in December 1998 their intention to merge. If approved by the regulatory authorities, this will create the largest petroleum company in the world, which will predictably be approximately 30 per cent larger than BP Amoco (+Arco) or Shell. The rationale is again cost-saving with the expectation that Exxon's corporate cost culture will rapidly squeeze costs out of Mobil's operations.

The French company 'Total' also responded aggressively. First, it announced in December 1998 its merging with 'Final' of Belgium. This was primarily a European downstream and chemicals merger. It was approved by the EC in March 1999. 'Total/Final' then launched a bid for French rival Elf in July 1999 which was eventually accepted by Elf after Total raised its bid by 10 per cent. The joint group will become the fourth largest Petroleum Company in the world (even after probable divestment of some of Elf's chemicals assets). Meanwhile, 'Resold' of Spain acquired 'YPF' of Argentina. Low oil prices were not a primary driver of these mergers.

The main objective was to enhance performance and profitability, whatever the external environment, and to create or access growth options. Low oil prices, nevertheless, increased the urgency to improve performance. Chevron and Texaco announced publicly in May 1999 that they were also discussing a possible merger, building on their very long standing 'Cortex' joint venture. They had previously stated that they did not feel it necessary to enter a merger. Talks broke down, reputedly because of an inability to agree management structures. Enterprise and 'Lasso', two UK based upstream independents, similarly entered into merger discussions in January 1999. These broke down by the end of March. Low oil prices had been a more important driver of this proposed deal.

6. New Drivers of Competitive Advantage

(a) Industry's Structural Changes

This set of deals has established a new petroleum industry structure. The rankings of companies in terms of market capitalization production and reserves have changed significantly. A new group of three super majors ('Exxon Mobil') the largest, followed by 'SP Amoco' (+Arco) and Royal Dutch Shell) are the largest companies with 'Total-Final/Elf' fourth in terms of market capitalization. This contrasts with the previous grouping of the six remaining sisters.

(b) Changing Industrial Boundaries

The change to the industry structure has, in fact, been more profound. Competition from players outside the industry namely those whose main business was not petroleum production, refining or marketing—was limited. The oil price rises of the 1970s had attracted some non-traditional entrants to the E&P business (e.g., ICI and RTZ in the UK North Sea). They were not, however, successful and duly exited.

There were other changes during the 1990s, which have had the effect of redefining the industry boundaries, structure and constitution. The key forces of change have been: The disintegration of the industry at an operating level.

Previously vertical integration had prevailed from the well head to burner tip or pump. Back in the *1960s* companies generally supplied their own refineries in their own ships and then provided gasoline to their own retail sites. This is no longer the normal case. Intermediate markets have now been established and deepened along the value chain. Spot, forward and futures markets have been developed. Spot crude markets initially emerged as a result of the changing membership structure of OPEC oil from the 1970s. It was accentuated by the growing availability and reduced cost of information, which lowered transaction costs and limited the value of operational integration. The net result has been that barriers to entry have fallen along all of the chain and new specialist entrants have emerged in most segments:

- Deregulation has had the effect of opening up previously closed sectors to competition. This has been particularly prevalent in the US and UK natural gas transportation and marketing businesses and the electric power sector. Deregulation is becoming an increasingly global phenomenon. The boundary between the old petroleum industry and the new deregulated gas and power industries is now indistinct. The net result is that the boundaries of the petroleum industry have now changed. The industry should now be considered to include:
- State companies, such as Saudi Aramco, PDVSA, etc., who operate commercially and on equal terms with private companies in a number of international markets,
- New refiners, such as Tosco and. Valero, who operate exclusively within the domain of the old industry, and
- Hypermarkets (such as 'Tosco' 'Carrefour'), who have attained a substantial share of a gasoline market even though gasoline retailing is only a small part of their business.

7. The "Super Major Theory"

The existence of a trio of 'Super Majors' has raised questions as to whether this group could dominate the petroleum industry. This was a concern investigated by the European Commission in its review of the Exxon-Mobil and BP Amoco/Arco acquisitions. It has been termed the "Super Major Theory". There is no unique theory, but the common theme is the assertion that the super majors will be in a position, usually at some stage in the future, to exert dominance.

The European Commission's particular concern was that there would be future collective dominance in the exploration and production sector. It was asserted that the" super majors" would dominate the non-OPEC exploration sector. As existing non-OPEC producing assets mature and decline, this would, in time, result in the super majors dominating non-OPEC production. It was then asserted that OPEC and the super majors would potentially have an alignment of interests which would result in competitive conditions conducive to active or tacit collusion between the two blocks as to crude oil output levels. In such a scenario, it was the Commission's contention that the two blocks would, through collusion made possible by the very structure of the market in the E&P sector, manipulate crude oil prices to a level which generates maximum rent for the incumbents (i.e., the OPEC states and the super majors) but which would be insufficient to sustain a number of existing oil producers or to stimulate the entry of new entrants.

BP Amoco argued strongly that this hypothesis was flawed. This was mainly because it considers that the E&P sector is competitive and that, as a result, the super majors do not have unique advantages that could generate future dominance. A number of factors were cited to support this argument:

1. The super majors do not have dominant access to technology, know-how

and skilled labor. Such knowledge is not proprietary and is available to any industry participant from oil service companies.

2. Financial resources and strength do not reside uniquely in the super majors. Capital market deregulation has made it possible for sound borrowers to access finance freely on competitive terms.
3. Resource owners—host governments—are very unlikely to permit a group of three companies to dominate development and production of their resources. Host governments regularly diversify their allocation of licenses. Most blocks are shared. Operator ship is usually spread between a numbers of different companies. 'New areas' such as the Caspian and deepwater Angola, have seen a wide allocation of awards.
4. Small E&P companies have been successful in discovering and developing oil and gas in frontier regions. Specific successes include Triton in Colombia, Hunt in Yemen, Cairn in Bangladesh and Anadarko in Algeria. Large integrated companies—but not super majors—have also been successful, *e.g.*, Elf in Angola.
5. Super majors are not and will not be in a position to control levels of oil production either now or in the future. In practice, control over both production and field abandonment is severely constrained by a number of factors as follows:
   - The companies in a vast majority of cases do not operate under exclusive, licenses—but rather as joint venture partnerships.
   - Companies are precluded from controlling production. The ultimate control of production levels lies with host governments.
6. The super majors may be the largest private petroleum companies by several measures. However, their total share of world reserves or production is still small and well below any measures of dominant shares. Even in the narrowest measure, the three super majors together only comprise 15.6 per cent of non-OPEC oil production. Other private companies and state companies in both OPEC and non-OPEC countries comprise the balance. This argument is consistent with the view that the industry is now wider than had previously been the case.

8. New Drivers of Competitive Advantage

The petroleum industry as had been known in the 1970s and 1980s and has now changed fundamentally. The petroleum players' market penetration and customers' consumer behavior have changed dramatically. While the existing players are consolidating; new players are entering. Previous endowments are eroding. There are no technological barriers to entry. Industry boundaries have shifted, widened and blurred. Some existing players are investing along the value chain into other sectors, such as gas marketing and power that had previously been effectively closed to the petroleum industry. It is also argued that, while the new 'super majors' are consolidating to improve performance, partly through cost reduction, it is wrong to presume that their size will cause them to be dominant in the petroleum industry.

The future industry structure will accordingly be determined by the competitive environment. The petroleum sector looks set to operate in increasingly open and competitive markets. Three factors seem set to influence this. First, the process of deregulation, especially in the electric power industry and to an almost similar extent in the natural gas business looks set to continue. Deregulation is deepening and widening globally. Second, host governments are progressively opening their natural resources to international investment. There have been recent openings in areas such as the Caspian, Venezuela, Brazil, Algeria and Iran. Opening is under discussion in Kuwait, Iraq and Saudi Arabia. And finally, it can reasonably be expected that the competition authorities will strive to continue to ensure that competition prevails in all stages of the industry. Consolidation has been permitted, albeit with undertakings in certain cases, but there is no evidence to indicate that the authorities intend to change the structure of the industry through competition policy.

The structure of the industry will most likely be determined by the degree to which various players establish and apply sources of competitive advantage in open markets. The analysis in section indicated that size alone is not a source of competitive advantage. Super majors will not be successful merely because they are large. Experience elsewhere implies that size is often a source of complexity and, thus, a disadvantage. In a changing industry, flexibility and speed of response is usually more valuable.

Where are the new sources of competitive advantage likely to reside? John Kay in his book entitled 'Foundations of Corporate Success' used a framework, which identified four generic dimensions that can drive competitive advantage: strategic assets; reputation; technology; and corporate architecture. This framework can be applied to the petroleum industry in the following manner:

1. *Developing Strategic Assets*

In the petroleum industry of the next decade, strategic assets can be expected to include:

- Large, low cost oil fields,
- Large, low cost gas fields with low cost access to markets
- Refineries that are advantaged by configuration, geography and costs,
- Significant retail market shares with low logistical costs and advantaged supply and a strong convenience offer, and
- Ideal sites that integrate refining and petrochemicals.

Existing players own existing strategic assets but this will not necessarily ensure that they will retain such competitive advantages. Producing assets mature and will need to be replaced by new discoveries.

New strategic assets will be created and sustained through building on three characteristics: technology; reputation; and architecture.

2. *Technology Leadership Approach*

Proprietary technology does not automatically guarantee competitive advantage in the petroleum industry today, except in the special case of petrochemicals. Nevertheless, technological skills and applications can be expected to be a source of future competitive advantage in a number of dimensions, such as:

- Innovation in the application of technology: The best examples of this have been in the upstream sector, especially in deepwater and sub-sea applications;
- Positioning for leadership in face of step changes in technology in areas such as new fuel specifications, renewable, low carbon technology, fuel cells and the hydrogen economy; and
- Application of IT to reduce operating costs, lead moves into e-commerce, nurture a learning culture and to help sculpt new corporate structures.

3. *Reputation and Goodwill*

The petroleum industry has long been one where discretionary decisions (*e.g.*, license or concessions awards) have been important. Reputation will become an increasingly important factor:

- To be a preferred partner in the development of new resources and markets that is being opened to international investment;
- To be seen by consumers, communities and governments as being environmentally sound and responsible in terms of operations and product quality;
- To be seen as ethically sound by all stakeholders; and
- To develop a strong brand that can permit the leveraging of marketing operations.

4. *Evolving new Industrial Architecture*

The successful company will develop and apply a corporate architecture or structure that nurtures consumer behavior to generate sustainable competitive advantage. From today's standpoint, such characteristics include low costs, openness, flexibility, learning orientation and empowerment. In the future, the characteristics may change: the key is to be strong in the skills that are scarce.

In short, competitive advantage can be expected to stem mostly from key competencies. Existing asset positions will be beneficial, but not a sufficient condition for future Competitive advantage. The era of change now seems well established in the petroleum industry. Change seems to be dominant precursor for future growth. Change causes a re-ranking of competitive advantage and a resulting new industry structure.

Trends of Oil and Gas Economy

Petroleum industry is now in a period of change. The seeds of change initially lay in the OPEC nationalization of the 1970s. The pressures for change accelerated during the 1990s, driven by opening markets, deregulation and low prices and margins. The pressures manifested themselves in low industry profitability.

Sectoral consolidation selectively improved profitability. Year 1998-99 then saw the emergence of the most dramatic period of consolidation and change for at least 70 years. Three new 'super majors' have emerged as the globally largest private industry players. As mergers are completed, the focus will be on the delivery of enhanced profitability, initially through cost reduction.

A new industry structure is emerging but further change is anticipated. New players with specialized skills are entering the industry. The industry boundaries have widened and blurred in the face of deregulation of gas and power and the entry of state companies into internationally competitive markets. The super majors have the potential to improve profitability but will not have unique advantages that could allow them to dominate the industry. The new petroleum industry will be increasingly competitive. Existing strategic assets will provide some advantage to the incumbents. However, longer-term competitive advantage looks set to be driven predominantly by core competencies. Skills, knowledge, flexibility and dynamism are likely to be even more important than absolute size or incumbency.

Oil and Gas economy in modern context refers to three central issues. One is globalization, another is economic development and the third is environment.

1. *Globalization*

The word 'globalization' is so commonly used in different context is that its precise meaning sometimes gets blurred. Literally it means 'to make something worldwide in scope or application. In the context of Oil and Gas economy, it is defined as "effort to create a world community, which promotes mutually beneficial interdependence, offering the chance of real prosperity to every corner of civilization". The world Oil and Gas market is increasingly becoming interconnected. The market is characterized by open market, free flowing capital, technology and labors and a healthy measure of international co-operation. Such a move towards globalization would entail fervent efforts to settle differences in various parts of the world leading to greater stability, and the promotion of trade and investments that extend help to those aspiring to improve themselves.

2. *Economic Development*

Primed with new developments in technology, international finance, information processing and communications, many regions formerly on the economic fringe have new chances to enter the mainstream of commerce. These backwaters of economic deprivation are gradually becoming relics of the past. That is not to say, of course, that the world's economic problems are solved. Especially the developing and underdeveloped nations of the world, with growing populations, have a long way to go. To allow any measure of economic growth, the world requires certain essential factors working in its favor. A crucial among them is ready, reliable source of energy. The economic dreams of the earth's billions of inhabitants can only are met by ensuring plentiful supplies of reasonably priced energy—a fact that underscores the need for 8nlightened energy policies. In contrast, policies that could significantly increase the cost of energy would make the uphill task of eradicating poverty from the world much more difficult.

There is a broad consensus among energy consumers, producers and governments that a clean environment is just as important a goal as economic development and it must receive close attention. The oil and gas industry fully recognizes this crucial need. The industry made great strides over the past several decades to reduce automotive exhaust emissions and improve the efficiency of oil. For example, emissions from the new cars of today are 95 per cent lower than the new vehicles of the 1960s. Even further reductions are anticipated with continuing improvement in new engine and fuel technologies. Both the oil and automotive industries are working hand-in-hand to meet consumers' expectations for a better environment. Faced with balancing its economic and environmental priorities, society still has to confront a thorny issue: can we have it both ways. The expert view is that yes, we can have. We do not have to choose between economic growth and a clean environment. With wise management of our natural resources and the promise of further technological advances, neither one needs to be sacrificed. In terms of workable energy policies, these three objective point to several long term policies, namely, emphasis on proven energy technologies, plentiful supplies, reasonable prices, commercial access, and full use of infrastructure currently in place.

3. *Factors that Shape Decisions of Sellers and Buyers*

While on the subject of trend and structure of oil and gas economy, we need to know the factors at work, which continue to shape decisions by sellers and buyers.

One, Psychology is winning out over real-time supply and demand; that is, market is being led by psychologically fuelled paper trading, in the face of little or no physical shortages. When US President made announcement in 1999 that 30 million barrels 'were to be withdrawn from the Strategic Petroleum Reserve, as a means of improving heating oil supplies to the Northeast, the price for a barrel of oil dropped by several dollars. Conversely, oil prices rose by several dollars in response to unguarded comments by OPEC about future supply levels. In sum, one has estimated that the psychological portion of today's oil price to be in order of $ 4 to $ 6 per barrel (Robert E. Eel, Director, Energy and National Security Center for Strategic and International Studies, Washington DC). By the way, what happened to those 30 million barrels? Because, US refineries were then operating at full capacity, the barrels withdrawn from SPR, most simply replaced imports and the displaced import barrels added to supply outside the US, to the benefit of consumers elsewhere.

Two, OPEC member countries have been faced with production limitations. Out of the eleven member countries of OPEC, probably only Saudi Arabia has the ability to substantially increase output within the range of 1 to 2 million barrels per day. All others have been producing at or close to capacity, as have oil exporters outside OPEC.

Three, The Oil Industry some time ago adopted the approach of 'just in time' in the management of inventories. Holding goods in inventories is costly, whether that good is oil or something else. To keep costs down and to increase competitiveness, working inventories are held at the bare minimum; just enough to be able to deliver the goods to the buyer 'just in time' to meet his requirements. But this approach has created a new vulnerability, as little flexibility remains in the system. A break in the supply and distribution chain, for whatever reason, will have an immediate impact on all participants.

Fourth, Current inventories of crude oil and petroleum products across the board are at unusually low levels, reflecting the 'just in time' philosophy and also consideration that oil prices will be falling in the coming months. Thus, any disruption or delay translates into higher prices, as demand temporarily at least, exceeds supply.

Fifth, unfortunately, reliable and up-to-date statistics on oil production, trade and consumption are surprisingly difficult to come by. The oil market is characterized by minimal transparency, in large part because some participants want it that way. For them, it means protecting their national interests. For others, it means enhancing their opportunities for profits.

Evolving Phases in Indian Oil Industries

1. *Indian Oil Industries—Its Global Facet*

Oil Industry in India is moving on a dynamic course since 1991, when the country embarked upon the era of liberalization and reform. The reform process in the oil industry has been swift, multi-pronged and its impact has been of far-reaching consequence for both the micro management of the Industry and macro management of the economy. A peculiar feature of the reform process in oil industry is that it has a large and intimate global interface, besides the domestic aspect of liberalization, largely centering on licensing policy, pricing, restructuring and customer focus. Let us here reflect on the global aspect of the transformation which Indian oil industry is undergoing.

2. *Reform in Oil Industry—A Historical Perspective*

Till 1993, the entire hydrocarbon chain in India was subjected to extensive regulation and controls. Starting from exploration and production, refining, marketing, infrastructure and investment planning, pricing till micro distribution, the whole gamut of activities were centrally planned. The philosophy behind this centralized control was: self-reliance, import substitution, strategic control, social and distributive justice, promotion of heavy industries and State control of commanding heights of the economy. Ministry of Petroleum and Natural Gas (MOPNG) was at the helm of control and the coordination was carried out through: (a) Oil Coordination Committee (ace) in the down-stream sector, and (b) direct control in the upstream sector.

While the regulated system served the country will for a considerable length of time, it gave rise to some limitations as the politico-economic condition of the country underwent transformation. Some of the perceived limitations are enumerated below:

- APM could not generate adequate financial resources for investment in the upstream and the downstream sectors.
- Sometimes it created deficit in the oil pool account, as due to political compulsions selling prices were not revised promptly. More importantly, while waiting for the mounting receivables, oil companies borrowed at market rates of interest, which were higher than what they received on their outstanding.
- The subsidies and cross-subsidies led to serious distortions in consumer prices and did not reflect the economic cost of petroleum products. This led to adulteration, diversion and consequent inefficient use of products.
- It is also said that assured returns on the cost-plus formula did not encourage efficiency in operations of Puss. Since all investments and costs were reimbursed, there was no incentive to make profitable investment decisions.
- In the upstream sector, the APM had inadequate incentive to invest in risky ventures.
- As long as players were Puss, the Government could control investments and costs. But with the entry of private players in the market, the cost-plus formula would encourage' gold plating' of the plant. This ultimately would add to the overall cost and consumers would ultimately have to bear the increase. Moreover, with the entry of private players in the market, it was becoming increasingly difficult to administer the APM and ensure level-playing field.

3. Phased Deregulation of India's Hydrocarbon Sector

The process of integrating Indian oil industry with world oil market began in February 1993, when Government of India allowed private parties to import and market Kerosene and LPG at market determined price. Effective November 1993, the selling price of all lubricating oils was allowed to be fixed by the oil companies on commercial considerations. Around that time, licenses were granted to private companies to set up refineries and foreign companies were allowed to invest in equities of refineries.

From November 1997 till April 2002, administrative regulations on pricing, marketing, quantitative and tariff restrictions on import and export of petroleum products including crude oil, were pruned and dismantled in a phased manner on a predetermined basis. Thus, effective April 1998, refining sector was taken out of APM. By implication, retention pricing concept for the refinery output and cost plus formula on refinery input (crude oil) was withdrawn. Refining licensing system was abolished. Crude oil import was made free for private and joint sector refineries.

On the eve of total de-regulation, a restructuring exercise of oil PSUs was carried out by March 2001. Stand-alone refineries were merged with integrated refining and marketing companies by divesting the government shareholding in these refineries. Thus, Chennai Petroleum Corporation and Bongaigaon Refinery and Petrochemical Ltd were made subsidiaries of Indian Oil Corporation. Kochi

Refineries and Numaligarh Refineries were made subsidiaries of Bharat Petroleum Corporation. IBP Ltd., the stand-alone marketing PSU was sold out to a strategic partner, namely Indian Oil Corporation, through competitive bidding by Ministry of Disinvestment.

By April 2002, quantitative restrictions on import and export of all products were gradually withdrawn in EXIM notifications from time to time. Crude oil import was decimalized for PSU refineries. APM was dismantled in phases. Oil companies were free to fix up the selling price of all products. Planning and coordination for bulk coastal supplies and inland distribution of petroleum products were left to oil companies, with broad administrative guidelines was wound up. With a truncated staff, acc has been transformed to a Research and Analysis Wing of Ministry of Petroleum and Natural Gas.

There have been gradual reductions of tariffs from the erstwhile peak level of above 50 per cent to the current peak level of 20 per cent. Duty protection available to domestic refineries by means of differential duty structure of input and output has gradually been narrowed down to the current level of 10 per cent.

From April 2002 onwards, government has allowed nine private companies to market transportation fuels: namely petrol and diesel and aviation fuel. With the entry of these firms, there has taken place a paradigm shift in the arena of retail selling. Apart from a number of incentives and customer-pulling schemes stalking the market, a cult of brand equity has entered into the domestic marketing. With pricing of products made free and all stabilization funds being abolished, the maze of cross-subsidization that once used to playa magic wand has gone out of scene. Subsidies are still permissible for domestic LPG (33.3%) and on Kerosene (17.5%) with a budgetary administered mechanism.

On the upstream sector, Indian basins have been progressively opened up and offered to private and foreign companies for investment. New Exploration licensing Policy (NELP-I) was announced in 1997 and NELP II was announced in 2000. NELP-I attracted 45 bids for 27 blocks. Production Sharing Contract (PSC) was signed in April 2000 for 25 blocks, of which two were onshore, 16 were shallow water offshore and seven were deep water offshore. The Government signed PSCs for 23 blocks in the second round of NELP in July 2001, of which seven were onshore, eight were shallow water offshore and eight were deepwater offshore.

4. *Self-Reliance*

Self-reliance in the oil sector does not necessarily mean only having right on crude oil. Exploration and production activities in the Indian basin must be promoted. The exploration of crude and extraction of crude are two separate activities having their own separate cost structure. Particularly, exploration is a risky job. Even if oil is struck in a specified field, the available geological data and techniques of measurement are inadequate to clearly define the amount of crude oil that can be extracted from any field. Hence, the assessment of the sale price of a discovery to another firm that will undertake extraction of crude oil becomes difficult. As a result, there are difficulties in the recovery of capital costs sunk into exploration. Vertical link between exploration and extraction has to be maintained through some institutional arrangements. Some models on this issue have already been worked out by Director General of Hydrocarbon. Self-reliance in oil sector also would mean developing technical capability within the country, and availability of capital and foreign exchange required for investment.

Conclusions

In this lesson, an attempt was made to provide a structural framework of world wide oil industry with linkage to Indian oil industry. The business environment in terms of demand, supply and consumption with historical base has been outlined. The likely future trend with regard to exploration, asset holding, merger and acquisitions have also been touched upon to provide a rudimentary knowledge base. The issues of current interest, like globalization, economic development and environment have also been reflected upon. The phases of deregulation of India's hydrocarbon sector have been chronicled along with the emerging issues. All these together create a compact scene on the backdrop of which a reader could get an introductory comprehension of the hydrocarbon business environment as a prelude to a study of petroleum policy and economic production of crude oil is preceded by the following four conditions:

1. One has to discover oil before it is produced.
2. Production has to mirror discovery after a time lag.
3. Currently the discovery rate is one barrel for every four barrels consumed from the inheritance of past discovery. Currently the depletion rate is about two percent a year.
4. Extraction rate is controlled by the physics of the reservoir.

REFERENCES

Alberto Clo (2004), Oil Economics & Policy. Sprigler.

Atmanand (2000), Growth and Deregulation of Indian Oil industry (Post-Reforms Analysis), Excel Books.

GAIL (2004), Natural Gas in India, GAIL-Infraline. I.Infraline.com

H.K. Abdel-AAL, B.A. Bakr. & M.A.Al Sahlawi (1992), Petroleum Economics & Engineering, Marcel Deckker Inc.

Patra, D.C. (2000), Oil Industry in India, Mittal Publications, New Delhi.

CHAPTER XIII

Geo-Politics of Oil Trading: Scanning the Global Business Scene

Fossil-fuels, such as oil and natural gas, meeting nearly 85% of the global energy demand, constitute the backbone of many petrochemical based and allied industries—prominently in energy, commercial, domestic and transport sectors. The demand for these resources is presently high from the developed economy; but the projected demand in the next decade is predicted to be higher from the developing economies, especially from BRIC's such as Brazil, Russia, India and China. The demand-supply equation has been artificially disrupted off-and-on by creating a divide across OPEC and Non-OPEC oil producing and exporting countries, which, in turn, are attributable to such factor as geo-politics, causing both trade distortions in one hand, regional and economic imbalances on the other. This chapter highlights the various aspects and dimensions of geo-politics in oil-trading in the global business scene and seeks to suggest future strategies and options to minimize the negative impact of geo-politics on the global economy by resorting to certain positive policy interventions—both at the regional as well as global levels.

Global Energy in Perspective

Anticipated worldwide economic growth in the first decade of the 21 st century will lead to concomitant increases in energy demand and carbon emissions. In the developing world in particular, the global tendencies are going to be pronounced. Over the next two decades, total world energy consumption is expected to increase by more than 50%. By 2020, energy demand in the developing world will be more than double, which will roughly equal that of industrialized nations. According to the estimates by the IEA, World Energy Outlook (2003), the prominent sources of Energy production is projected to be oil, natural gas and coal in the given order of priority during 2010-30 (Fig. 13.1).

Fig. 13.1: World Primary Energy Demand Projection

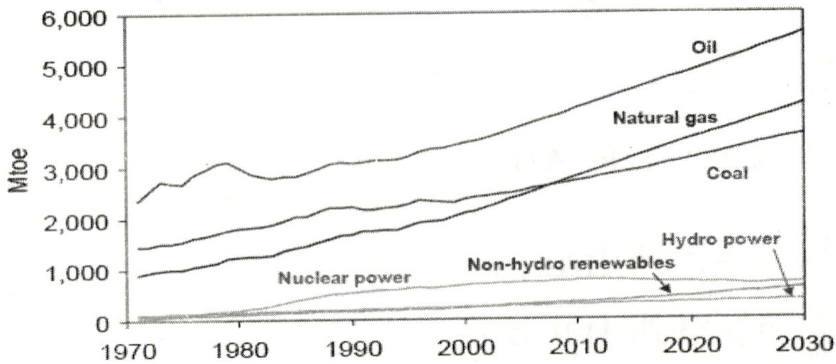

Electricity consumption forecasts, considered separately, tell an even more dramatic story. Global demand for electricity is predicted to grow by three-quarters from 1999 to 2020. In developing Asia, electricity consumption is forecast to increase by 150% over the same period. As with total energy, electricity consumption in the developing world will nearly equal that of the industrialized world by 2020. Fossil fuels (oil, gas, and coal) will continue to provide more than 85% of the world's energy for the foreseeable future. The data used to prepare the figure do not include energy generated by biomass fuels such as wood, charcoal, crop wastes, and manures. Such fuels, used especially in the developing world, may account for as much as 50 additional quads of energy each year.

Transportation is the primary driver of increased oil demand, while increased natural gas consumption will be largely for power generation and greater industrial requirements. US consumption represents roughly half of that for the industrialized world and US fuel source consumption closely mirrors world patterns. Developing Asia, Central America, and South America will see the greatest increase in requirements for natural gas; they are each expected to triple their demand over the next twenty years.

World Oil Production and Consumption

In 2004, world oil production was 83.1 MMB/D with about 48.1 MMB/D of this oil exported to various countries around the world. Exports are transported to the market using a variety of means including tankers, pipelines, trains, trucks and barges. When the crude oil reaches its destination it is processed and refined into petroleum products such as gasoline, heating oil and jet fuel. The price of crude oil is reflected in the price of these refined products. However, oil product prices are also affected by other factors, such as refining and marketing operating margins, taxes, transportation costs and local/regional market conditions and competition. In turn, oil product prices and pressures feed back into crude oil prices (OPPI, 2005). The Global proven oil reserve positions , as estimated by different international agencies, is shown in Fig 13.2. The relative position of estimated oil production by OPEC & Non-OPEC countries during 2002-2030 is depicted in Fig. 13.3. It could be noted that in years of low production of oil by OPEC countries the oil production by the Non-OPEC countries has been stepped up to meet the global demand and maintain favourable supply-demand ratio. However the projected outlook predicts that there may be spurt in production of oil by OPEC for period 2010-30 to meet the growing energy demand, especially by the BRIC nations. The regional scenario in terms of oil production is shown in Fig 13.4. The world gas reserve, sector-wise natural gas demand position and gas production region-wise are shown in Fig. 13.5, 13.6 and 13.7 respectively.

Fig. 13.2: Proven Oil Reserve Estimates

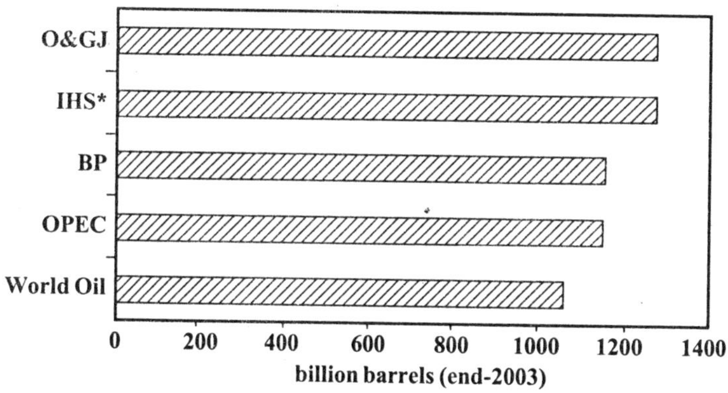

*Includes probable reserves

Source: IEA, World Energy Outlook, 2004.

Fig 13.3: OPEC vs. Non-OPEC Oil Production

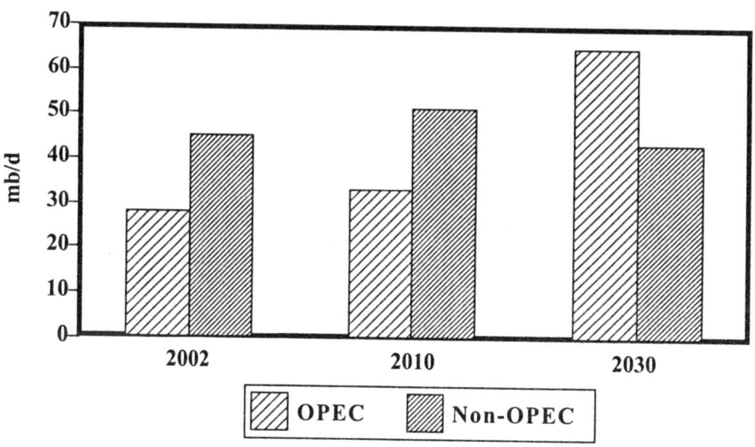

Source: IEA, World Energy Outlook, 2004.

Fig. 13.4: World Oil Production (in percentage), IEA, 2004

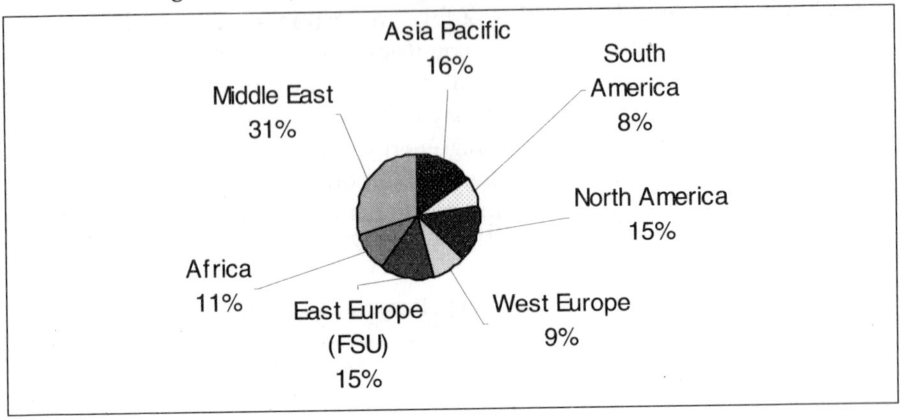

Fig. 13.5: World Gas Reserve (per centage distribution), IEA, 2004

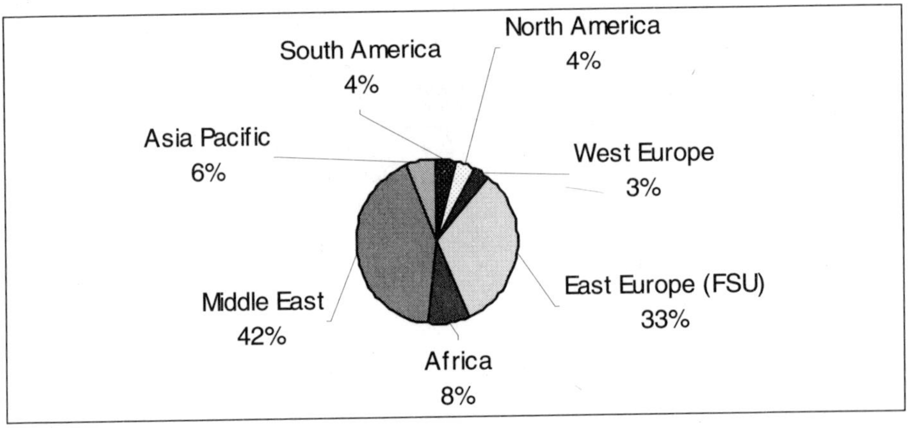

Fig. 13.6: World Natural Gas Demand

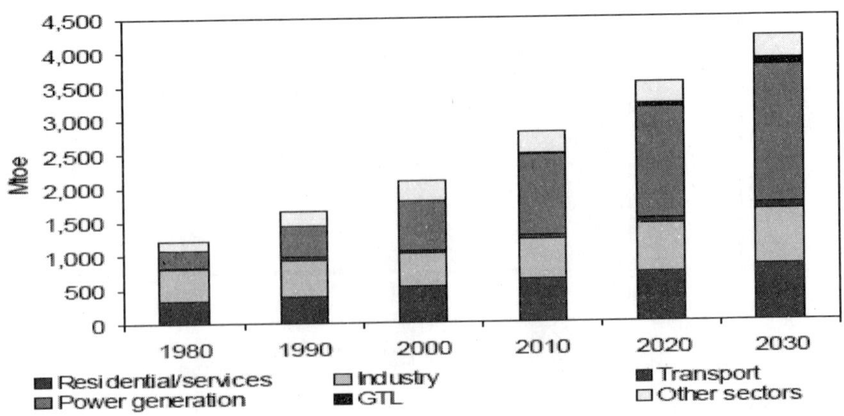

Source: IEA, World Energy Outlook, 2003.

Fig. 13.7: Gas Production by Region

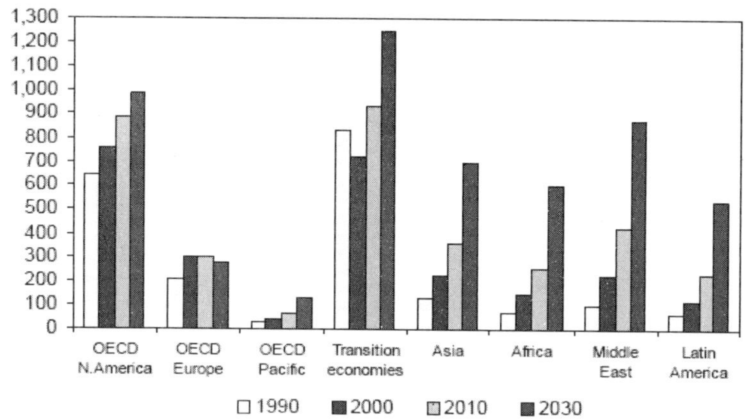

Source: IEA, World Energy Outlook, 2003.

The comparative scenario of global oil production vis-à-vis exports by major producers and exporters, representing OPEC and Non-OPEC countries during 2004, are shown in Tables 13.1 and 13.2.

OPEC and Non-OPEC Fact Sheet

Table 13.1: Top World Oil Producers, 2004

(OPEC members in italics)

	Country	Total Oil Production (million barrels per day)
(1)	*Saudi Arabia*	10.37
(2)	Russia	9.27
(3)	United States	8.69
(4)	*Iran*	4.09
(5)	Mexico	3.83
(6)	China	3.62
(7)	Norway	3.18
(8)	Canada	3.14
(9)	*Venezuela*	2.86
(10)	*United Arab Emirates*	2.76
(11)	*Kuwait*	2.51
(12)	*Nigeria*	2.51
(13)	United Kingdom	2.08
(14)	*Iraq*	2.03

Source: Energy Info. Administration (eia.doe.gov)

The main consumers of oil continue to be the industrialized countries of the Organization for Economic Cooperation and Development (OECD), particularly the US, Europe and Japan, which together consume about half of the world's

Table 13.2. Top World Oil Net Exporters, 2004

(OPEC members in italics)

	Country	Net Oil Exports (million barrels per day)
(1)	*Saudi Arabia*	8.73
(2)	Russia	6.67
(3)	Norway	2.91
(4)	*Iran*	2.55
(5)	*Venezuela*	2.36
(6)	*United Arab Emirates*	2.33
(7)	*Kuwait*	2.20
(8)	*Nigeria*	2.19
(9)	Mexico	1.80
(10)	*Algeria*	1.68
(11)	*Iraq*	1.48
(12)	*Libya*	1.34
(13)	Kazakhstan	1.06
(14)	*Qatar*	1.02

Source: Energy Info. Administration (eia.doe.gov)

annual oil output. However, consumption in emerging market regions is expanding at a faster pace (especially in China and India) as these countries grow rapidly and their use of energy in transportation, industry and residential sectors expands. The transportation sector accounts for about two-thirds of the oil consumed in the United States and around half of the oil used in the world. The petro-flows of advanced economies vis-à-vis developing economies and corresponding changes in the current account balances from 2002 to 2005 (in million $) in shown in Table 13.3.

Based on the global trend in crude oil production a long-term (50 years) crude oil production projection for the period 2000-50 with Maximum Sustainable Capacity is depicted in Fig. 13.8. The world scenario of oil consumption, region-wise as well as by the different country-groups, projected during 2003-30, may be seen from Fig. 13.9.

Table 13.3: Petro-Flows and Other Imbalances

(Billions of Dollars)

Advanced Economies	2002	2005	Δ	Developing Economies	2002	2005	Δ
United States	–475	–759	–284	Middle East	30	218	188
Euro Area	49	24	–25	China	35	116	81
Germany	46	121	75	CIS (Russia, etc.)	32	105	73
Japan	113	153	40	Latin America	–16	22	38
Other	87	131	44	Africa	–8	13	21
				Emerging Asia excl. China	37	–6	–43
				Central and Eastern Europe	–25	–56	–31

Source: International Monetary Fund, World Economic Outlook, September 2005, pp. 242, 245, 257-9

Figure 13.8: 50-year Crude Oil Scenario and Maximum Sustainable Capacity (12 MillionBarrels /Day

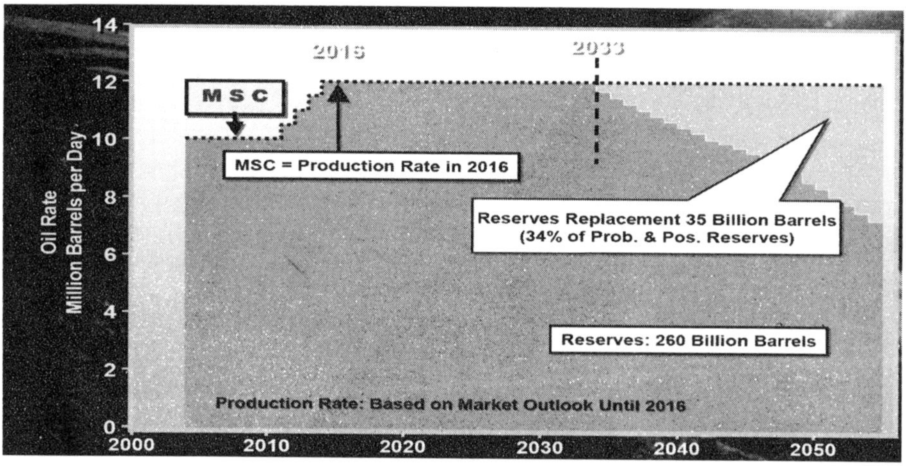

Figure 13.9: World Oil Consumption by Region and Country Group, 2003 and 2030

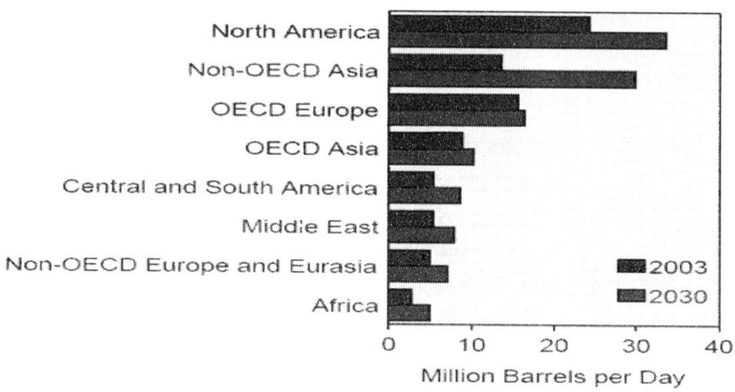

Sources: **2003:** Energy Information Administration (EIA), International Energy Annual 2003 (May-July 2005), Website www.eia.doe.gov/iea/. **2030:** EIA, System for the Analysis of Global Energy Markets (2000).

Oil Dependence and National Security

World oil consumption is expected to grow by 60% over the period 1999-2020, from 75 million to 120 million barrels per day. Much of this increased consumption will be in transportation. In the developing world, people will own more cars and trucks—China alone expects a five-fold increase in vehicles by 2020. In the US, vehicle fleet efficiency is expected to remain flat for several years.

Large increases in oil and gas consumption raise significant geopolitical issues that could intensify as competition for supplies increases, market power is accumulated in fewer places and more products is moved over longer distances. Oil supply and demand are not geographically well correlated. Despite the diversification of oil-producing regions in the past 20 years, global dependence on the Persian Gulf—which holds two-thirds of the world's proven oil reserves—will increase over the next two decades. The oil wealth of the Persian Gulf gives the region substantial geopolitical influence and constrains the ability of the US to fully exercise its strategic interests.

These effects are magnified by the concentration of excess production capacity (unused capacity that can be quickly produced when demand is high) in the Gulf. OPEC cohesion contributed to extreme oil price volatility since 1999; the high oil prices of 1999 and 2000 likely cost the US as much as 0.7 percentage points in gross domestic product (GDP). The most significant increases in oil demand will be in Asia, further enhancing the Gulf's influence. Earlier in this article we referred to the shifting web of alliance and conflict connected to oil production and consumption. The evolving reliance on Gulf oil has the potential to dramatically redefine that web.

A number of policies can be initiated or expanded whose objectives address oil and national security issues. Some of those objectives depend on investment, financial, or diplomatic actions for their realization. Examples include increasing protection against supply disruptions by expanding strategic stocks, more effectively managing oil price volatility, and encouraging expanded international production capacity. Other objectives, such as developing unconventional oil resources or affordable alternatives to oil, and using oil more efficiently are largely driven by technology.

Developing Natural Gas Resources

Geopolitical issues related to energy security are likely to emerge in connection with natural gas supply. Global demand for natural gas is growing as unevenly as it is dramatically, and the most significant increases are in those regions of the world with the fewest indigenous resources. Natural gas markets are limited by the inflexibility and expense of gas (versus liquid) transportation. Over half of the world's natural gas reserves are very far from users and it is currently not profitable to transport such "stranded" gas from these reserves to customers. Geographic disparities exist between natural gas production and consumption. These disparities highlight the need to address key technical challenges concerning natural gas: developing resources; accessing stranded resources through gas-to-liquid conversion, liquefied natural gas process improvements, and new transportation and processing infrastructures; extending the resource base using alternative fuels such as biomass or, in the long-term, methane hydrates; and using gas more efficiently in, for example, advanced turbine systems and smart buildings.

Peak-Oil: An Overview

What is Peak-Oil? No, it's not a top in energy prices. Peak-Oil, also commonly referred to as Hubbert's Peak which was named after the late Dr. M. King Hubert, a Geophysicist who made several important contributions to geophysics but is most well-known for his research on the capacities of crude oil fields and natural gas reserves, is the tendency of crude oil production to follow a bell shaped curve, steadily rising before reaching its pinnacle then entering into a permanent decline hence "Peak-Oil". Hubert's research into forecasting oil production has been stunningly accurate for predicting crude oil production peaks of various countries, such as the U.S. and Russia, many times. Initially, Hubbert's prediction in 1956 that U.S. crude oil production would peak around 1970 and decline thereafter was scoffed at then but his analysis has since proved to be extraordinarily accurate as U.S. Crude Oil production peak in the early 1970's and has steadily declined since.

Based on Hubbert's original research the potential peak in crude oil production, not just for one country, such as Saudi Arabia, but for the entire world has potentially arrived! At present, current crude oil depletion rates are running around 1.25-1.5 million barrels/day (Mbd). While Saudi Arabia, the world's largest crude oil producer, is still technically a swing producer their control over global crude oil markets, along with OPEC's, has diminished greatly and will continue to erode into the future, as Matthew Simmons, founder and Chairman of the world's largest energy investment banking company, Simmons & Co. International, points out in his new book, Twilight in the Desert. The View Hubbert's Peak, subscribe to the belief that Saudi Arabia and global crude oil production in general will soon reach an apex, after which its production will decline and the world will be confronted with an immense and potentially catastrophic oil shortage that will halt economic growth, create run away inflation, potentially destabilize the entire Middle East, and create natural resource based wars between the world's economic powers such as the United States and China (Simmons, 2008).

Developing World Energy Use

According to projections of the International Energy Agency's (IEA) *World Energy Outlook 2002*, by the year 2030 global primary energy demand will be nearly two-thirds above the levels of 2000, reaching 15.3 billion tons of oil equivalent per year by the end of the forecast period, with developing countries accounting for 62 percent of the rise. Similarly, the U.S. Energy Information Administration forecasts that by 2025, energy use in the developing world will have almost doubled. Because the emerging economies are projected to rely increasingly on coal and other fossil fuels, they will contribute much more to worldwide carbon dioxide emissions as their demand for energy quickly grows. Developing countries are forecast to account for two-thirds of the projected increase in carbon dioxide emissions, which according to many scientists contribute to global warming. Four major countries alone—Indonesia, China, India, and Brazil—will emit 2 billion tons of carbon annually by 2010, creating special challenges for international cooperation on climate issues. The United States and other industrialized nations need to engage these countries in multilateral climate initiatives such as research and development of cleaner energy technologies.

Explosive growth in Asia is expected to contribute significantly to the rise in use of energy by the developing world and have the greatest impact on world oil use, thus playing the largest role in shifting oil geopolitical trends. In developing Asian countries, where an average annual growth rate of 3 percent is projected for energy use as compared with 1.7 percent for the entire global economy, energy demand is expected to more than double in the next two decades. According to IEA projections, demand in the region will account for 69 percent of the total projected increase in developing world consumption and almost 40 percent of the increase for total world energy consumption. Asia's rapid economic growth, explosive urbanization, dramatic expansion in the transportation sector and politically important electrification programs will have a dramatic effect on the region's dependence on imported energy. Absent significant growth in renewable energy supplies and/or new energy technologies, consumption of crude oil and natural gas in Asia will rise substantially and with it significant environmental challenges. Given the inadequate resource endowment of the region and the region's already high dependence on imported oil supplies, it is anticipated that Asia will exert an increasing pull on the Middle-East and Russia in coming years.

According to *'Oil Market Intelligence, 2001'* published by the Energy Intelligence Group, an independent research service, Asia's oil use, which exceeds 20 million barrels per day (b/d), is already larger than that in the United States. By 2010, total Asian oil consumption could reach 25-30 million b/d, most of which will have to be imported from outside the region. China alone can be expected to see its oil imports rise from around 1.4 million b/d in 1999 to 3-5 million b/d by 2010. This has awakened fears in Tokyo, Seoul, and New Delhi about competition or even confrontation over energy supplies and lines of transport.

Geopolitics: The Great Unknown

Geopolitics is defined as a branch of geography that promises to explain the relationships between geographical realities and international affairs. The idea that such relationships exist was noted as early as the ancient Greeks (18,309-328). The roots of modern geopolitics spring from the work of a German geographer, Professor Friedrich Ratzel in 1897. It was Professor Ratzel who coined the phrase anthro-geographical, meaning a combination of anthropology, geography and politics. He believed that states have many of the characteristics of living organisms. He thought a state had to grow. It must expand or die. He also introduced the idea of "living frontiers" that borders were dynamic and subject to change. A Swedish Professor of geography at Gothenburg University in 1900 was the first to use the term geopolitics (in Swedish "geopolitik"). Expanding on Ratzels' earlier thoughts Professor Rudolf Kjellen is usually regarded as the founder of the science of geopolitics.

Market anxiety about access to uninterrupted supply of oil and natural gas will not disappear overnight and will persist as long as the ongoing geopolitical tensions are not eased. Signs are appearing that higher prices are beginning to impact the global economy, moderate oil demand growth and stimulate a rebound of oil industry investment worldwide, both upstream and downstream. The physical market tightness should, therefore, gradually recede but market anxiety over potential supply disruptions will persist for a while under the current geopolitical environment.

The process of adjustment to a lower more sustainable price level will take some time depending on both short-term price developments and the evolution of the ongoing geopolitical tensions (affecting the major producing countries) which, among all the forces affecting the oil market, is the most difficult to predict.

The Seven Sisters

Petroleum has for long been the object of geopolitical confrontations. The ability to fix the price and the production of oil was first established in 1928 by the Achnacarry Agreements. Among the "seven sisters", namely Major oil multinationals such as Exxon, Texaco, British Petroleum, Shell, Gulf, Standard Oil and Mobil Oil an oil oligopoly was formed to safeguard the interests of the strategically aligned oil partners. The seven sisters invested massively in extraction infrastructures, especially in the Middle-East. Several producing countries, mostly in the Third World, wanted to have a more important share of the incomes of this lucrative market.

OPEC

Venezuela, Iran, Iraq, Saudi Arabia and Kuwait founded the Organization of Petroleum Exporting Countries (OPEC) in 1960 at the Baghdad conference. Several other oil-producing nations joined thereafter the organization; viz. Qatar (1961), Indonesia (1962), Libya (1969), Algeria (1970), Nigeria (1971), Ecuador (1973-92, left the organization in order to avoid production quotas), The United Arab Emirates (1973) and Gabon (1973-94). From its foundation until the beginning of the 1970s, OPEC was unable to increase oil prices. Production was very important in non-member countries. However, there was difficulty of OPEC members to agree on a common policy with global outreach.

Context

First commercial exploitations of petroleum in the USA were in Pennsylvania in 1859. Importance of oil increased significantly in the global economy. In 1920, 95 million tons were produced annually. The number reached 500 million tonnes by 1950and a billion tonnes in 1960. Average annual production was around 3 billion tons in the 1990's. Strong growth rests for a very large part on the availability of oil resources and their low cost. Economic systems, which include industry, housing, energy generation and transportation, became dependant on cheap oil prices.

The First Major Oil-Shock

In the 1970s, OPEC countries achieved control over more than 55% of the oil supply. OPEC started to fix production quotas and established co-operation between producers in order to avoid competition that would bring the price of oil down. This was feasible in the context of a growing market demand and the dependency on only a few oil suppliers. Between 1970 and 1973, the price of the oil barrel passed from 1.80 dollars to 3.01 dollars.

The Kippur War of 1973 was fought between Israel and Egypt (and several other Arabian countries). OPEC intervened by nationalizing production facilities, reducing production by 25% and imposing export quotas. OPEC imposed quotas on countries supporting Israel. The price of oil consequently reached 11.65 dollars per barrel at the end of the same year. High oil demand, the limited capacity of developed countries to supply oil and no readily energetic substitutes gave OPEC a strategic advantage of oil trading in global market. OPEC gained the ability to control the price of oil with a market controlled by oil producers. This caused the first oil shock.

The Second Oil-Shock

In the 1970s and early 1980s the price of oil remained high but stabilized over the 1970s, around 20 dollars per barrel. Developed countries started to worry about the exhaustion of oil reserves and unreliable supply sources. This however was followed by instability in two major oil producers, Iran and Iraq. The Iranian revolution took place on 1979. Iran-Iraq War was fought in 1979-80, because Iran was trying to export the Islamic revolution to Iraq, which effected 8% removal of the world oil supply resulting in the second oil shock where the price of oil went over 35 dollars per barrel. The second oil-shock was however countervailed by resorting to the following strategies:

- Drastic, but somewhat temporary, measures to lower oil consumption;
- Relocation of energy-consuming industries;
- Consuming less energy in a more efficiently manner;
- Relying on national energy sources (petroleum, coal, natural gas, hydroelectricity, nuclear energy; and
- Substituting petroleum for other energy sources when possible.

Oil Counter-shock

A changing scene was observed at the end of the 1980s and at the beginning of the 1990s, OPEC countries lost their price-fixing power. Internal problems such as economic and geopolitical conflicts between its members vitiated the leadership status of OPEC conglomerate. New producers such as Russia, Mexico, Norway, England and Colombia combined to form alternate and new conclave which was not constrained by OPEC policies and were free to fix their own prices. Mexico surpassed Saudi Arabia in 1997 to become the second largest oil exporter to the United States, after Venezuela. Latin American countries such as Columbia and Brazil were also tried to boost their oil production to compete with OPEC nations to break he monopoly. Vietnam is exploring offshore fields, as are other Southeast Asian countries, hoping that there would be major oil reserves under the South China Sea.

Since 1982, divergences occurred within OPEC members to fix quotas and prices as competition increased. The share of OPEC dropped from 55% of all the petroleum exported in the 1970s to 41% in 1992 with all-time low of 30% in 1985. That year Saudi Arabia lowered the price of its oil to increase its market share. Oil counter-shock that lowered the price of the barrel under 20 dollars, even reaching a record of 15 dollars in 1988 was continued unabated. The oil market was again a market controlled by the demand.

During the Gulf War that followed, respecting production quotas became a major issue among OPEC members. Countries such as Kuwait started producing well above quota. This event was a motivation for the invasion of Kuwait by Iraq in 1990, which saw the price of petroleum jump to 41$. 7.8% of the world's oil production was removed (Iraq and Kuwait). Other petroleum-producing countries were quick to expand their production to replace Iraq's and Kuwait's shortfalls. The increase in oil price was however short-lived. The aftermath of the Gulf-war and the reemergence setting of OPEC may be summed-up as follows:

Aftermath of the Gulf War:

- The price of oil fell to 25 dollars per barrel by the mid 1990s.
- By 1998, the price of petroleum went under 10 dollars per barrel.
- Rendering several producing regions temporarily unprofitable.
- OPEC countries only control about 42% of the global oil production and are so in a weak position to fix prices.

Reemergence:

- At the end of the 1990s, the price of petroleum increased.
- Oil reserves are in the Middle East.
- Share of OPEC expected to climb to 48% in 2005 and 52% in 2010.

The Middle-East in the Global Oil Balance

The MENA region, through its dominance of world oil reserve ownership, occupies a central position in the global energy balance—quite apart from its substantial gas reserves, although the latter is not yet well developed. Even with the loss of ground to other energy carriers, oil (and the region) will continue to play a core role in the future of world energy (Cedoz, 2003). The prestige of Middle-Eastern countries in world energy markets stems primarily from their role in the oil market, even though the region also owns substantial reserves of natural gas. Their fortune is thus directly related to how well oil holds its share vis-à-vis other forms of energy in the evolving global energy balance. Over the years, starting with the sharp price increases of the 1970s, it has lost some ground to other fuels. The continued strength of oil in global energy stems from its dominance of the transportation sector, where it now accounts for about 96 percent of the market. It also accounts for 27 percent in the industrial sector and 9 percent in power generation—having lost ground to coal, gas, and nuclear power in these sectors. The rate of substitution away from oil is directly related to how technically feasible such changes are and to the availability of cost-effective substitutes, which explains why oil has continued to dominate the transportation sector, where efforts to introduce alternatives have so far had limited success.

In contrast to oil, the share of natural gas in total primary energy has been on the increase; it rose from 18 percent to about 23 percent between 1973 and 2001, spurred by a combination of higher oil prices, the need for energy self-sufficiency in the major consuming countries, and diversification, as well as recent environmental concerns relating to global warming and climate change. Natural gas is the least carbon-intensive of the fossil fuels, followed by oil and then coal.

The use of natural gas has also increased as a result of secular growth in the petrochemical industry, where it is the main feedstock for a wide variety of petrochemical products.

There are indications that the gas industry in the Middle East is under invested because its share of the world output (at about 14 percent) is much lower than its share of reserves (40 percent). An illustration of this can be seen from the fact that although Iran owns the world's second-largest reserves (15.3 percent of total) after Russia, it produces only about 2 percent, and indeed, imports some gas from neighboring Turkmenistan (4.9 billion cubic meters in 2002). Projections of demand for natural gas up to 2020 by the International Energy Agency (IEA, 2002) suggest continued gains for gas in the global energy balance, while oil is expected to just maintain its present share.

The Iraq Episode

There were only two credible reasons for invading Iraq: control over oil and preservation of the dollar as the world's reserve currency. Yet the government has kept silent on these factors, instead treating us to the intriguing distractions of the Hutton and Butler reports. Butler's overall finding of a "group think" failure was pure charity. Absurdities like the 45-minute claim were adopted by high-level officials and ministers because those concerned recognized the substantial reason for war—oil. WMD provided only the bureaucratic argument: the real reason was that Iraq was swimming in oil (John Chapman, 2004). It is an understatement to say the aftermath of the war in Iraq is proving to be a difficult period. World media attention is focused on anti-American demonstrations and the failure of the American military to establish civil order. Diplomats and commentators debate and opine on how, and by whom, a stable government, an orderly social system and a functioning economy should be established in Iraq; as well as what actions the United States will take regarding other Middle Eastern countries and North Korea.

For several decades, the United States, as a matter of its own enlightened self-interest, has undertaken to establish and maintain security of oil supply for all the world's economies. Any serious consideration of energy or foreign policy must recognize that now, and for the foreseeable future, oil represents the life's blood of the international economic order. The Iraq affair highlighted a coincidental development in international economics. Combined with the strike in Venezuela and political unrest in Nigeria, it showed the world's discretionary surplus oil productive capability is much less than had been previously estimated. As world economies resume normal growth with accompanying increases in oil demand, the world is likely to be faced, for the first time, with oil-supply shortages and persistent upward pressure on prices over the next several years.

Oil prices have declined since the end of the war due to the return of Iraqi and Venezuelan production and a seasonal spring demand slump, but this price drop should not induce a false complacency regarding supplies. A prolonged trend of increasing prices would severely restrain economic recovery in the United States, Europe and Japan. Oil shortages would be particularly disruptive to stability in

Asia, the area of fastest economic and oil demand growth. Japan is still in a prolonged depression and barely avoiding financial collapse. China has been an oil importer since 1993, while India has always been dependent on imports. Both are rapidly industrializing. The strike of oil workers in Venezuela, concurrent with worries about oil supplies from Iraq, revealed the lack of worldwide surplus productive capacity. It also focused attention for a short time on the deterioration of political stability in several Latin American countries.

If the United States is to develop secure, long-term and diverse supplies of oil for world economic stability, it must devote diplomatic attention to restoring relations with Russia and Latin America. As the world's largest importer, the U.S. can use oil as a tool to stabilize the political and economic systems in Russia and in several Latin American countries where potential oil reserves are large and oil production represents a large part of the economy. For the purpose, contracts should be written with Venezuela, Mexico, Argentina, Peru and Colombia (Charles Kohlhaas, 2006).

Energy Dominates Growth Debate in South Africa

Where electricity sector was previously—in the words of Thomas Edison—"a natural monopoly", it has now become a political game. The oil shocks of the Seventies resulted in governments worldwide reconsidering their energy plans—resulting in scores of nuclear power stations being built at the time. The emphasis on the growth of South Africa's energy capacity must be seen to underpin the previous policy of separate development to succeed through a healthy economy (Johan Richard, 2005).

An energy-driven economy could ensure relative peace in the labour sector. Energy self-sufficiency and labour stability was the reason for the second and third Sasols, Mossgas and the string of power stations – such as Arnot, Tutuka, Lethabo, Kendal, and the Drakensberg pumping station, Grootvlei, Hendrina, Koeberg, Majuba, Kriel and others. These projects negated the possibility of an international energy boycott and promoted economic and labour stability. The consequences of an energy shortage are today just as real as they were 30 years ago. Those consequences hold the same serious political and economic problems in the economic, social and labour spheres of today. The energy industry should lead the economic system and not be seen as an unwilling partner or subservient, economic milking cow. A country's energy certainty is related to its ability to have sufficient reserve capacity available to accommodate its economic growth rate. Economic stability usually brings political stability, and *vice-versa* (Amit Kumar, 2005).

Geo-Politics of Oil and Natural Gas

Ensuring the reliability of global energy supplies will call for policies that both encourage the use of newer, cleaner energy technologies and address the political challenges posed by the world's growing demand for oil and natural gas. Global energy policy involving high consumption of oil and natural gas as potential feedstocks seeks to encourage expansion and diversification of world energy supplies and to promote the transparency and democratic institutions that help energy-producing countries make the most productive use of their resources (Jaffe & Hayes, 2005).

Energy is the vital ingredient in the world economy. While concerted efforts are being directed towards energy efficiency and investing in to develop new energy technologies, oil and natural gas will remain critical for many years to come. Economic development around the world means global demand for oil and gas will continue growing in the near term. Most significantly, China's rapid growth and increase in overall energy demand continue to affect energy markets. Some analysts estimate that China could account for as much as one-third of the world's marginal increase in oil demand in the coming years. As a result, the world must find and develop more reliable supplies of oil and gas at prices that permit sustained economic growth. Unfortunately, it is almost an axiom in the petroleum business that oil and gas are most often found in countries with challenging political regimes or difficult physical geography.

Several ground realities shape our thinking about energy security and how we should build reliability into our energy supplies taking a cognizance of the following (Klare, 2005):

- Two-thirds of the world's known oil reserves are in the Middle-East.
- Imports supply roughly half of the oil and 15 percent of natural gas consumed by the United States, and an even greater share of the needs of some of the United State's most important allies and economic partners.
- Oil-supply shocks in any region of the world will have an impact on the U.S. economy through the instantaneous operation of international oil markets.

Geopolitics of EU Energy Supply

As one of the world's largest importers of oil, gas and coal, the EU is a major player on the international energy market. However, it remains a dwarf on the political stage as member states keep the upper hand on foreign policy. With external dependence on imports forecast to grow steadily, the EU has started to integrate energy aspects into relations with third countries (EurActiv.com, 2006). The geopolitical aspects of Europe's external energy policy remain within the competence of EU member states' foreign policies and a matter of national sovereignty. However, the progressive incorporation of previously secluded energy markets into one single, combined with the EU's exclusive competence when it comes to commercial relations with non-EU countries, is slowly driving the issue up the EU political agenda (Data Monitor, 2005).

Oil and gas reserves are unevenly distributed around the globe, and the largest reserves are situated in politically or economically insecure regions (Middle-East, Russia). North Sea oil and gas fields have already been exploited beyond their peak, leaving Europe dependent on non-EU countries for future supply. The Commission Green Paper in its deliberation on 29 November 2000 'Towards a European strategy for the security of energy supply' (http://europa.eu/scadplus/leg/en/lvb/l27037.htm) drew a sobering picture of the EU's energy situation. If no action is taken, it predicted, the EU's energy dependency will climb from 50% in 2000 to 70% in 2030. The particular situation for the main imported fossil fuels was described as follows:

Oil (i) 45% of EU oil imports originate from the Middle East;
 (ii) By 2030, 90% of EU oil consumption will have to be covered by imports
Gas (i) 40% of EU gas imports originate from Russia (30% Algeria, 25% Norway);
 (ii) By 2030, over 60% of EU gas imports are expected to come from Russia with overall dependency expected to reach 80%.
Coal (i) By 2030, 66% of EU needs is expected to be covered by imports

The Geopolitics of Oil in the Central Asia

One important geopolitical consequence of the demise of the Soviet Union was the rise of intense political and commercial competition for control of the vast energy resources of the newly independent and vulnerable states of the Caucasus and Central Asia. These energy resources and, in particular, the oil and natural gas deposits have now become the apple of discord in Central Asia introducing, according to analysts, a new chapter in the Great Game of control over Eurasia. Although the stakes involved remain the same, i.e., power, influence, security, wealth, the new playing field is further complicated by an array of problems. These include intra-regional conflict, political instability, fierce competition among multinational conglomerates, and a shortfall in commercial expertise and legal infrastructures. Moreover, the fact that the three countries which share the majority of the region as energy and resources, namely Kazakhstan, Azerbaijan and Turkmenistan, are landlocked makes them depend on their immediate neighbours for access to the Western markets.

The essence of this new geopolitical game in Central Asia is two-fold: first, control of production of the oil and gas, and second, control of the pipelines which will transfer the oil to the Western markets. From a geopolitical point of view, Central Asia has always been important. From the middle to the end of the 19th century, while the region was part of the Russian Empire, the oil-bearing areas of Baku were producing half of the world as oil supplies. In World War II, during his campaign against Russia, Hitler tried to capture Baku and the Caucasian oil fields as part of his strategy for world domination. After the war, the Soviets retained these areas as reserves, choosing to exploit oil deposits on Russian soil, in Tatarstan and Siberia.

Following the collapse of communism, the ex-Soviet republics of Central Asia, especially Azerbaijan and Kazakhstan, have been trying to exploit their natural resources, since they consider oil to be the prime means of securing their economic and political independence. According to the estimates of geologists, the oil deposits of the Caspian Sea may not be quantitatively comparable to the deposits of the Persian Gulf, but they are still considered of excellent quality and able to provide a significant alternative source of energy in the 21st century. In particular, it is estimated that the entire Caspian Sea is a basin full of oil and natural gas, starting from Azerbaijan and continuing to the opposite shore in the territory of

Kazakhstan and Turkmenistan. These deposits take on enormous importance because of the expected exhaustion of the deposits of Alaska and the North Sea by the year 2015. The US foreign policy in Central Asia is founded on the following rationale:

- The US intends to help the former Soviet republics of Kazakhstan and Azerbaijan develop their oil and natural gas industries.
- Through the development of their oil and gas industry, which will bring economic growth, the US hopes to extricate them from the Russian sphere of influence.
- The US Government is actively supporting American companies in Central Asia involved in oil development as well as in the construction of pipelines which will channel the oil to the West.
- The US will try to channel the oil coming from those countries into the international markets in order to diversify its own sources of supply and keep oil prices at low levels.
- The US Government believes that economic growth will promote regional stability and the resolution of local disputes.
- Finally, the US aims at reinforcing the role of Turkey in the region, while at the same time maintaining the policy of containment and isolation of Iran. For that reason it has actively lobbied for a pipeline which will transport oil from Baku to the Turkish port of Ceyhan.

Russia and the Caspian Basin

Russia already is an energy superpower. To achieve its full potential, Russia needs to strengthen corporate governance and the legal/regulatory framework for business, improve its foreign investment climate, allow competition in the transportation system, open the gas and oil companies Gazprom and Transneft up to reform and competition, improve its technological capabilities, and move domestic energy prices to world levels.

The Caspian Basin has tremendous potential, offering the possibility of production increases from 1.6 million barrels/day (b/d) in 2001 to 5.0 million b/d in 2010. The key issues in Caspian energy development at the moment are to: (i) complete the second pillar of the East-West Energy Corridor by developing the South Caucasus natural gas pipeline; (ii) improve the investment climate throughout the region; and (iii) bring Kazakhstan oil into the East-West corridor. Multiple pipelines that economically bring Caspian resources to the world market strengthen the sovereignty and economic viability of the new nation states in the region. U.S. efforts in the Caspian are intended to complement and not to detract from U.S. support for Russia's efforts to develop its energy export potential.

Africa

Africa is playing an increasingly important role as an energy supplier to U.S. and global markets. In 2003, both Nigeria and Angola were among the top 10 suppliers of oil to the United States. Oil production generates substantial revenue in countries such as Nigeria, Angola, Gabon, Equatorial Guinea, Republic of Congo, Chad, and Cameroon. Sao Tome and Mauritania also may become oil suppliers in the coming years. Foreign direct investment is needed to develop African energy resources as most new fields are in deepwater offshore environments that require advanced capital-intensive facilities for development. Growing oil and gas production could be a powerful engine for national economic development in these countries. However, the Niger Delta experience of 2002, in which protesters stormed oil facilities and caused their temporary shutdown, shows that oil can also be a disruptive force if a country's oil revenues are not managed in a fair and transparent manner. Nigeria has learned from its experience in the Niger Delta and is setting an example on transparency and economic reform enabled by oil revenues that the United States hopes other countries in Africa will follow.

North America

The most important and reliable sources of energy for the United States are its neighbors and we are strengthening our energy cooperation with Canada and Mexico. Senior energy experts from Canada, Mexico, and the United States recently released a North American *Energy Picture* report that, for the first time, jointly measures energy stocks, trading balances, and energy flows. What often goes unrecognized is that North American energy trade is a two-way street. Mexico is becoming an important source of U.S. oil imports. At the same time, the United States is a net natural gas exporter to Mexico, and U.S. refineries supply over 15 percent of Mexico's refined petroleum products (Work-Fall, 2005). The reliability of North American energy trade is enhanced by geographic proximity. More important than geography, however, are the rule of law and predictable investment conditions created by the North American Free-Trade Agreement (FTA), integrated pipeline networks and long-term reliable supply relationships.

Venezuela

The economic importance of oil in terms of Venezuelan-U.S. relations cannot be overstated. Venezuela is the fifth largest oil exporter in the world and the fourth largest supplier of oil to the United States after Canada, Mexico, and Saudi Arabia. Last year, Venezuela's state owned oil company, Petroleos de Venezuela (Pdvsa) accounted for 11.8% (1.52-million barrels a day) of U.S. imports.

Venezuela and the United States have enjoyed strong historical energy ties. Venezuelan oil policy, until recently, has been built upon a reputation of reliability. Unfortunately, actions and statements by parties from all sides over the last 18 months have called into question the priority Venezuelans place on their reputation as a reliable supplier. The United States will continue to work to help Venezuelans resolve their political differences. But until a constitutional, democratic, peaceful, and electoral solution is achieved, and the level of rhetoric lowered, world energy markets simply cannot view Venezuela with the same certainty that they once did (Kozloff-Coha, 2005).

Saudi Arabia and the Gulf Producers

The general thrust of Saudi economic policy has undergone a fundamental change after the oil price crash of 1986. The serious depletion of foreign assets, combined with the extensive decline in oil revenues, necessitated a revised economic policy. The depreciation of the United States dollar on international financial markets also hurt Saudi purchasing power abroad. The kingdom's external terms of trade deteriorated rapidly because oil exports were largely denominated in United States dollars, and the bulk of Saudi imports came from countries whose currencies were appreciating relative to the United States dollar. The Middle-East holds some two-thirds of proven world oil reserves. The size of its reserves, combined with its low production cost, guarantees that the Middle East will continue to play a pivotal role in the world energy market. Saudi Arabia plays a key role in global oil markets as the world's largest oil exporter. Moreover, Saudi Arabia supports international energy security by maintaining considerable excess production capacity that can be brought on line quickly in the event of a serious supply disruption anywhere in the world.

Diversifying global oil supplies should not be interpreted as diversifying "away" from Saudi Arabia or other Gulf producers. Gulf producers will continue to have an indispensable role in the world market, and the United States encourages them to increase foreign investment and steadily expand supplies. What we seek is better balance and a more flexible, resilient oil market that responds to price signals. In this regard, Gulf producers could reap greater benefits by opening their economies to more private investment so that oil and gas capacity could grow and energy supplies could respond more fully to shifts in demand. Investment in natural gas is one sector where this process is beginning. Once only for local or regional use or wasted through harmful flaring, natural gas in the form of liquefied natural gas (LNG) has become an increasingly globally traded energy source for key markets. Qatar is working with major international energy companies to become a leading LNG exporter.

Energy Scenario in South Asia

The South Asian region, which comprises Bangladesh, Bhutan, India, Maldives, Nepal, Pakistan, and Sri Lanka, is home to 1.3 billion people, close to a quarter of the world's population. The region is currently experiencing a rapid growth in energy demand, concomitant with economic growth and industrialization. Adequate energy supply is, therefore, a major challenge facing the economies in the region (Avaritopopulos, 2006).

Economic growth in South Asia averaged 5.3% a year between 1990 and 1997 with India and Pakistan recording the highest growth rate of 5.4% and 4.8%, respectively, in the same period (IEA, 1999). The total primary energy supply in South Asia, which is indicative of the total energy consumption, increased at the rate of 3.6% annually during that period. In 1997/98, the total primary energy supply in the region, including 250.7 MTOE (million tonnes of oil equivalent), renewable energy was 556.5 MTOE, of which India claimed the dominant share, accounting for about 88% of the total energy consumption. The total primary energy supply, including renewable energy, is expected to increase to 1411 MTOE in 2010/11, with biomass accounting for 28% of the total energy consumption.

While the average oil intensity in the world has declined from 0.19 TOE (tonnes of oil equivalent) for every 1000 US dollars in 1990/91 to 0.13 TOE in 1997/98, oil intensity in the region increased from 0.17 TOE to 0.19 TOE in the same period. Despite the rapid growth in energy demand, the average per capita energy consumption in the region is lowest in the world. In 1997/98, the average per capita energy consumption was 0.37 TOE compared to the world average of 1.7 TOE. Though the regional average has increased in the recent years, it has remained far below the world average; in Bangladesh and Nepal, it continues to remain far below even the regional average. A similar trend is observed in the case of per capita oil consumption, with a regional average of 0.08 TOE compared to the world average of 0.60 TOE (1997/98 figures). The regional per capita electricity consumption of 219 kWh was also far below the world average of 2258 kWh in 1997/98, illustrating the need for large-scale rural and urban electrification.

The fuel structure amongst the countries of the region varies significantly. Coal constitutes as much as 30% of the total commercial energy requirement in India. In Bangladesh, oil (53%) and natural gas (47%) are the dominant fuels (the shares refer to the total energy consumption). The pattern is similar in Pakistan (oil constitutes 46% and natural gas 38% of the total energy consumption). Sri Lanka is largely dependent on oil (87%), whereas Nepal used both oil, which is largely imported, and hydroelectricity. A significant change in the fuel structure in recent years has been the increase in the share of natural gas, because of the important gas discoveries made in India, Pakistan, and Bangladesh and the environmental considerations arising from the large quantities of coal consumed in the region. At present, gas accounts for only about eight per cent of the total energy consumption in India whereas it is the main source of energy in Bangladesh.

South Asia accounts for less than 0.5% of the world's crude oil reserves and produced 40.5 million tonnes in 1997/98. India's recoverable reserves of crude oil and natural gas have declined continuously after peaking at 806 million tonnes and 735 billion cubic metres, respectively, in 1991/92 (TERI, 1999). The current balance recoverable reserves in India are estimated at 726 million tonnes of crude oil and 692 billion cubic metres of natural gas. Most of the crude oil production in South Asia is accounted for by India, which, in 1997/98, accounted for 93% (38 million tonnes) of the total oil production in the region whereas Pakistan accounted for only 7% (3 million tonnes) in the same year. India is also the largest consumer and importer of crude oil and petroleum products. Between 1990 and 1996, the consumption of petroleum products grew at the rate of 6.7% in the region, with Nepal and Sri Lanka recording the highest growth rates of 18.9% and 9.8%, respectively. The country wise position of per capita energy and electricity consumption in South Asia is depicted below in Figure 13.10.

South Asia contains about 1.44 trillion cubic metres or about one per cent of the total gas reserves in the world. Of the total gas produced, 48% is accounted for by India, 36% by Pakistan, and 16% by Bangladesh. The countries of the region have so far been self-reliant in natural gas. However, with the demand for natural

Fig. 13.10: Per Capita Energy Consumption

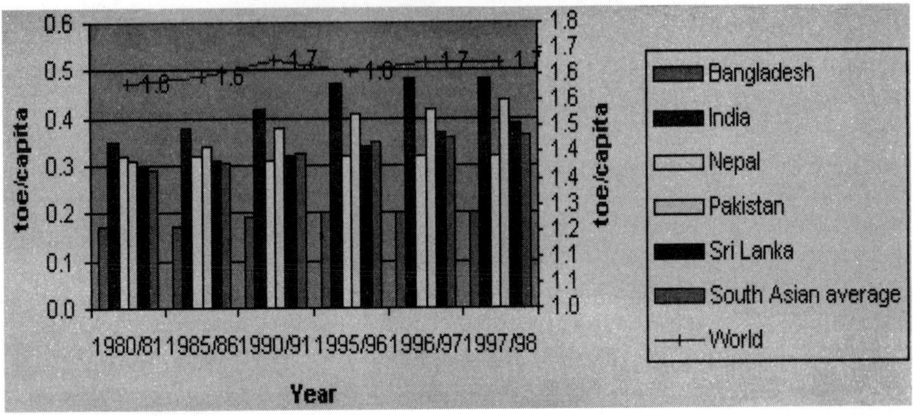

Source: TERI, 1999.

gas projected to increase to 77 billion cubic metres by 2010/11 (IEA, 1998), an increase in production and imports would be required.

The total power generation in South Asia in 1997/98 was 541 TWh, of which about 61% was coal-based, 19% was from hydroelectric plants, 10% from natural gas, 7% from oil, 2% from nuclear, and less than 1% from renewable energy sources. The share of natural gas is likely to increase in the future due to environmental concerns.

In India, the total installed capacity in 1997/98 was 89 GW, which increased to 91 GW in 1998/99, of which 73% is thermal, 24% hydel, and 3% nuclear-based. The total power generated was 463 TWh in 1997/98, which was about 30% below the demand, thereby necessitating hydro power imports of 1440 GWh in 1990/91 and 1547 GWh in 1997/98.

The World Oil Crisis: Implications for Global Security and the Middle-East

The following uses relating to the World Oil crisis are critical and have their far-reaching implications in the context of Global security in general and the Middle-East in particular (Luft, 2005):

- The global oil market environment of very strong demand and very little spare capacity offers a huge opportunity to the radical *jihadists*. The terrorists believe that the best way to hurt the global Western economy is to go after oil.
- Since the end of the major hostilities in Iraq, there have been close to 300 attacks on pipelines, refineries, and other facilities, and there have been attacks on oil installations in many other parts of the world, including Chechnya, Pakistan, India, Russia, Azerbaijan, and Nigeria.
- The cumulative impact of those attacks amounts to about 1 million barrels a day that has been taken off the market as a result of sabotage. If these million barrels a day had reached the market, oil prices would have been at least $20 a barrel lower.

- We are seeing today in essence a transfer of wealth of historic proportions from the economies of the United States, Japan, China, and Europe to the economies of the oil-producing countries. Of course, this is not a way to win a war on radical Islamic terrorism when the side that needs to defeat terrorism and radical Islam is constantly enriching the enemy.
- We are seeing the beginning of a new era in the Middle East where other players, particularly China, will move in and want to cut deals and alliances. The U.S. and Europe are trying to curb Iran's nuclear program, to stop it from developing the bomb, but the Chinese have signed a $70 billion energy deal with Iran, and it will be very difficult to get them on board at the UN Security Council.
- One of the main causes of friction between China and Japan involves access to oil and gas deposits in the East China Sea. The Chinese are also developing a strong foothold in Pakistan, where thousands of Chinese workers are building a new port in Baluchistan at Gwadar, which sits right at the entrance to the Persian Gulf.

China's Middle-East Strategy

The People's Republic of China has neither strong historical ties nor long-standing strategic interests in the Middle-East. Yet its relationship with the region is an interesting and increasingly important one. China's emphasis on modernization has required extensive financing and increasing access to oil. The Middle East has become China's fourth largest trading partner, but developing this commerce has sometimes involved China in political controversies and regional issues. Being so late in entering the region, and having less to offer in economic or technology terms than the United States, Russia, Japan, and Europe, China must go after marginal or risky markets where others cannot or will not go, supplying customers no one else will service with goods no one else will sell them. Yet while China wants to exploit and expand such links, it does not want to sacrifice too much regarding relations with the United States or incur costs in other, more important, policy areas.

By 1990, China's exports to Middle-East countries reached $1.5 billion, and more than 50,000 Chinese workers were employed in the region. By 1994, overall trade with the Gulf Cooperation Council was estimated at $2.26 billion, with China exports falling about $700 million short in covering its bills. Iran has been a special focal point. From 1990 to 1993, China-Iran trade rose from $314 to $700 million. In 1995, the two countries signed a $2 billion trade deal. China also tripled oil purchases to 60,000 barrels a day and agreed to build a joint oil refinery in China and cooperate in oil exploration. China also built power plants, cement factories, and joint shipping lines in Iran. Still, arms sales have been China's leading single field of endeavor.

By the 1990s, however, a new factor stimulated China's economic interest in the Middle East. As its rapid economic growth required more oil, China became an importer in 1993 and is becoming a major buyer, expected to require 30-50 million tons by 2000. The Middle East (Saudi Arabia, Kuwait, and Iran) and Central

Asia (whose estimated, barely tapped reserves are currently a whopping 170 billion barrels) are the best sources for these needs. In June 1997, the China National Petroleum Corporation (CNPC) outbid U.S. and other companies to win a major share in two of Kazakhstan's largest oilfields and a contract to build a 3000-kilometer pipeline from Kazakhstan to China which would also supply Iranian refineries. Chinese Premier Li Peng lobbied hard to close this $4.4 billion deal. One potential advantage of China is its lack of political baggage, since its political ambitions are more limited than the United States, Russia, Iran or Turkey. For example, Kazakhstan is using China to gain more independence from Moscow, which tried to use its political leverage while offering poor terms for an oil deal. The Chinese plan would bring Kazakhstan more money and employment opportunities. China can make better bids since it lacks alternative supplies and has a government willing to give subsidies at commercially unprofitable levels. But China is hurt by the inefficiency of its oil industry and may not be able to build the proposed pipeline. In political terms, the Kazakhstan deal will make China an even closer ally of Iran in the region. Being a late arrival on the highly competitive oil market, China must pursue more risky and marginal sources neglected by others—including Iran, Iraq and Sudan—which raise international political problems. More conventionally, China has made a $1.5 billion deal for a huge Sino-Saudi oil refinery in China and 10 million tons of Saudi oil annually for a 50-year period.

India Joins the Scramble for Oil and Natural Gas

India has recently joined the global scramble for oil and natural gas alongside other Asian states, including China, South Korea and Japan. Through diplomatic maneuvers aimed at securing transnational pipeline routes and overseas crude oil and natural gas production deals, India is seeking to lay claim to a larger share of the world's energy resources. It is also carrying out a major restructuring of the national energy industry. Though India's thirst for oil is rooted in economic imperatives, the emergence of India as a major player in foreign energy ventures will have a profound impact on world geopolitics. It takes place under conditions in which oil is already the object of the most intense competition between the US, the European Union, China, Japan and Russia. The country's international oil policy is becoming a growing point of friction with the United States. In particular, the US is determined to scuttle Indian negotiations with Iran over a pipeline to India via Pakistan. The development of closer ties between India, China and Russia, as well as India's courting of oil-rich Venezuela, are also potential threats to American interests.

In terms of global oil consumption, India is still a relatively small player. Although India is home to more than 15 percent of the world's population, it accounts for only 3 percent of world oil consumption. China, by contrast, consumes 7.6 percent of the world's oil. India's energy needs are rising sharply, however. Last year alone India's crude oil consumption increased by 10 percent. Moreover, India is highly dependent on oil imports. Some seventy percent of India's oil is imported and oil imports account for one third of the total value of all India's imports. By 2020, India is expected to have to import 80 percent of its energy needs. India has the world's fastest-growing car market, which is driving oil consumption and imports. Economic growth, rising oil prices and recent disruptions in oil supplies due to the US military interventions in Iraq and Afghanistan are propelling the Indian government to join the hunt for cheap and secure sources of oil and natural gas.

India's Energy Security Pact with Russia

India already holds a 20 percent stake in Russia's energy-rich Sakhalin-1block. ONGC Videsh Ltd. (OVL), the overseas arm of India's Oil and Natural Gas Corp. Ltd. (ONGC), has made an investment of $1.7 billion, which is expected to go up to $3.5 billion later this year. Reportedly, India is to consider investing a further $1.5 billion in the Sakhalin-3 gas field and another $1.5 billion in the joint Russian-Kazakh Kurmangazy oilfield, both in the Caspian Sea. The Russian invitation to India to join the Sakhalin-3 project is especially noteworthy, since it occurred shortly after Moscow removed a major US oil company from the same project. As one of the planned Indo-Sino joint ventures, Indian and Chinese oil firms lined up together as Asian customers for the possible purchase of the some of the assets of the Russian Yukos Oil Co., confiscated by the Putin regime in Russia. These moves are clearly aimed at establishing some sort of counterweight to American dominance over energy production. On February 14, inaugurating the third Asian gas buyers' summit in New Delhi, the Indian petroleum minister Mani Shankar Aiyer proclaimed that Asian natural gas players should come together to from an Asian gas grid. The aim of such a grid would be to enable the countries in the region to take full advantage of oil profits and thereby end the "wretched western dominance" that has prevented energy security and economic growth in Asia.

Diplomacy over Oil-bids with Iran and Pakistan

The suggestion by Iran to the previous BJP-led Indian government about the construction of a pipeline to supply oil and gas from Iran to India is once again on the table. Iran is scurrying to secure diplomatic ties with Asian powers via energy deals in order to counteract US threats of economic sanctions and military invasion. A $40 billion deal was drafted on the 7th of January with the National Iranian Oil Co. (NIOC). The deal would allow India to import natural gas over a period of 25 years, starting in 2009. NIOC would also develop two Iranian oil fields and a gas field.

Iran is the second largest crude oil producer among the Organization of the Petroleum Exporting Countries (OPEC). It owns 10 percent of the world's proven oil reserves and also has the world's second largest natural gas reserves. India perceives Iran as a viable corridor to access the natural resources and economic opportunities of Central Asia and the Middle East. During the third gas buyer's summit in February, officials of the National Iranian Gas Exports Company (NIGE Co.) began their preliminary discussions on the delivery of Iran gas via a pipeline at the India-Pakistan border, expected to be signed in Teheran soon.

The development of an Indo-Pakistani-Iranian pipeline is seen by New Delhi as a means of both helping to meet its energy needs and fostering a closer economic relationship with Pakistan. The Indian political elite calculate that this will cut across Pakistan's ability to pursue a policy of geopolitical confrontation with India and enable Indian business to dominate the Pakistani market. However, to bypass a direct agreement with Pakistan, India has proposed two separate agreements—one between India and Iran on purchasing the gas and another between Iran and Pakistan for the pipeline. During the summit the initial construction plan was revised to include plans to extend the pipeline to Southern China.

A Hemisphere of Energy Security Environment in NAFTA Region

Canada and Mexico are the top two suppliers of oil to the United States, respectively. When combined with domestic production, imports from these two continental neighbors supply more than 50 percent of total U.S. daily oil consumption. More promising still, Canada recently vaulted to the number-two spot among the world's proven reserve holders (behind Saudi Arabia) with its classification of 176 billion barrels of economically recoverable oil from massive oil sands deposits, located primarily in northern Alberta. Regardless of America's perception of Canada—and, indeed, sometimes even Canada's perception of itself—our northern neighbor is officially an energy superpower. The U.S. currently imports roughly 2 million barrels per day of Canadian crude. Of that volume, approximately 800,000 barrels come from oil sands deposits. And with oil sands production projected to increase from 1.2 million barrels daily to as much as 4 million by 2015, we will be able to count on increased supplies even amid mounting interest in Canadian oil from countries such as China. In the next decade, Canada's total daily oil production will reach close to 5 million barrels a day over half of which (more than 2.5 million barrels daily) will likely flow to the U.S. (Frederick Cedoz, 2006).

This oil trade would be more than simply an expansion of the largest commercial trading relationship in the world. Along with additional supplies of Canadian crude will come the need for American and Canadian jobs to produce the oil, and—just as important—expand the infrastructure to get that crude to market. Each barrel of oil we buy from Canada is a barrel whose profit does not end up in the hands of those who may wish us harm. And every job building a pipeline or expanding a refinery in the U.S. puts food on the table of Americans and tax revenue in our national treasury.

Mexico, on the other hand, has an uphill climb with respect to expanding its oil output, but the tools are all there. The Mexican government has allowed the nationalist sentiment that goes along with being a major oil producer to impede its ability to reliably expand production to meet domestic demand, let alone produce additional crude for export. The geology of the under-explored Mexican portions of the Gulf of Mexico is likely to be as prolific as the American waters of the Gulf have proven to be.

Transferring the World's Wealth

In 2001, oil was selling for $20 a barrel; today it sells for more than triple. This means that the Saudis, the Iranians, and all the other producers are making an extra $40 a barrel. We are seeing today in essence a transfer of wealth of historic proportions from the economies of the United States, Japan, China, and Europe to the economies of the oil-producing countries. Of course, this is not a way to win a war on radical Islamic terrorism when the side of the world that needs to defeat terrorism and radical Islam is constantly enriching the enemy. American taxpayers send their dollars and soldiers all over the world to fight for freedom and democracy. Some 77 percent of the world's oil reserves are in the hands of governments. These governments have little interest in bringing down oil prices. Unfortunately, most of the oil-producing countries are corrupt dictatorships (Luft, 2005).

How Oil Shapes Foreign Policy?

What happens when you have the United States, China, India, Europe, and Japan all competing over the same oil? We are seeing today the beginning of a new era in which the Middle East will no longer be a unipolar arena. There will be other players, particularly China, that will move in and want to cut deals and alliances (Luft, 2005). The United States and Europe are trying to curb Iran's nuclear program, to stop it from developing the bomb, but the Chinese have signed a $70 billion energy deal with Iran, and said they will veto any attempt to impose sanctions on Iran at the UN Security Council. When the Security Council tried to impose sanctions on Sudan—one of China's main oil suppliers—over the issue of Darfur, the Chinese vetoed it. These are two cases in which China's energy interest trumped their interest to be part of the international community (Baker Institute, 1999).

Currently, we are seeing a situation in which America's policy of bringing democracy to the Middle East is being constantly compromised by the fact that the United States and China are essentially competing over energy resources. This is happening all over the world, not only in the Middle East and Central Asia. It is happening in Africa and even in the Western Hemisphere, where China is moving into Venezuela and Canada. Access to energy resources will shape the world in the years to come. It will dictate the international behavior of countries as it plays an increasing role in relations between the major powers. In future, we will see new alliances forged, such as between China and Saudi Arabia.

One of the main causes of friction between China and Japan involves access to oil and gas deposits in the East China Sea. Similar occurrences are happening all over the world. The Chinese are also developing a strong foothold in Pakistan, where thousands of Chinese workers are building a new port in Baluchistan at Gwadar that sits right at the entrance to the Persian Gulf. Israel should be very sensitive to developments between the United States and China, and should be very careful in pursuing military relations with China because there will be a cost. There are a lot of things that can be done with China on many issues, but for Israel to pursue military relations with China at a time when very important parts of the U.S. defense establishment and Congress are extremely hawkish on China is a very dangerous game to play. Americans are beginning to understand that their dependence on foreign oil has doubled in the past thirty years. In 1973 America imported 30 percent of its oil. Today, it imports more than 60 percent and that will increase. Americans are beginning to understand that dependence on oil imports is America's Achilles heel and that this needs to be addressed. Oil is no longer an environmental issue. It is increasingly becoming a national security issue.

In 1973, Brazil imported 80 percent of its fuel. Today the Brazilians are on the road to energy independence because they have developed an agricultural sector that allows them to produce transportation fuel from sugar cane. Brazil today does not feel the impact of an oil crisis as other countries do. A lot of investment is going toward producing transportation fuel from coal. In South Africa, planes that fly out of Johannesburg run on synthetic jet fuel made from coal, not oil. So a country does not have to subjugate its entire foreign policy just to satisfy its need for petroleum products. Two-thirds of U.S. oil consumption is in the transportation sector. With a quarter of the world's coal reserves, America can do the same and embark on a path toward weaning itself from its oil dependence. This has already been done in the U.S. power sector—today only about 2 percent of U.S. electricity is generated from oil.

India, as a gesture of regional cooperative venture, has succeeded to tap oil and gas through pipelines from Iran. In January 2005, the Gas Authority of India Ltd. (GAIL) signed a 30-year deal with the National Iranian Gas Export Corporation for the transfer of as much as 7.5 million tons of LNG to India per year. The deal, worth an estimated $50 billion, will also entail Indian involvement in the development of Iranian gas fields. Even more noteworthy, Indian and Pakistani officials are discussing the construction of a $3 billion natural gas pipeline from Iran to India via Pakistan—an extraordinary step for two long-term adversaries. When completed, the pipeline would provide both countries with a substantial supply of gas and allow Pakistan to reap $200-$500 million per year in transit fees. The gas pipeline is a win-win proposition for Iran, India, and Pakistan (Klare, 2005).

Role of IEA

The International Energy Agency (IEA) was created in 1974 as a response to the threat posed by the first oil crisis and commemorated its 30th anniversary in 2004. While energy markets and the world have changed in many ways since then, energy security remains a fundamental goal of its member countries. However, security considerations have become more broadly defined. IEA's focus has been expanded from oil to other forms of energy, such as natural gas, of which consumption and imports are rapidly increasing, and to electricity, following several serious transmission failures in recent years. Furthermore, reliable access to energy supply needs to be compatible with other policy objectives, namely, the pursuit of greater economic efficiency in the energy sector and the mitigation of environmental consequences of energy production and use.

Recent energy market and geopolitical developments have pushed security of supply back to the top of the energy policy agenda. The events of 11th September 2001 and worsening political instability in the Arab Gulf and elsewhere have heightened the sense of vulnerability to disruptions to energy supplies. Energy installations such as nuclear power stations, gas terminals, gas pipelines, and oil installations have moved to a higher state of alert. Global cross-border energy trade has grown by almost three-quarters since 1973 and will continue to expand between now and 2030. Because of cost, geopolitical and technical factors, almost all the increase in energy production from now on will occur in non-OECD countries. As a result, the reliance of IEA members and non-IEA oil-importing developing countries on imported oil and gas will continue to grow. This will increase mutual economic interdependence, but will also intensify concerns about the world's vulnerability to a price and supply shock. These developments underline the need for IEA member countries and non-member oil and gas importing countries to take a more proactive role in dealing with the energy security risks in fossil fuel trade. Measures to deal with short-term supply emergencies or price shocks will need to be enhanced. Countries will also have to diversify their fuels as well as the geographic sources of imported fuels. Indigenous renewable energy sources will contribute to this end. Improving relations with energy suppliers will also be essential for IEA countries' security strategies. The importance of this dialogue was apparent in the effective response by producer countries to the threat of market disruption during the military action in Iraq in 2003. Better data collection and exchange for improving transparency in world markets will remain the key in this dialogue. Similarly, the importance of co-operation with other non-member countries in such fields as emergency preparedness, data exchange and energy policy reform will also grow as their shares in global energy demand and imports rise.

Long-term security of supply will depend on whether the investment needed to expand energy supply capacity will be forthcoming in a timely manner. **The 2003 *World Energy Investment Outlook*** estimates that more than $16 trillion of investment in maintaining and expanding energy supplies will be needed up to 2030. Mobilizing all this investment will require the lowering of regulatory and market barriers, and the creation of an attractive investment climate, including stable and enforceable legal and regulatory systems, is a daunting task in many developing countries and the former Soviet Union. Stamping out corruption is also essential in many countries. Good governance is crucial to extend electricity supplies to the energy-poor and give them better access to other forms of modern energy. The environmental implications for rising energy use will remain a key issue for IEA countries. Energy-related CO2 will continue to grow steadily unless tough new policies are adopted to counter this trend. The adoption of new policies in OECD and non-OECD countries, together with faster deployment of more efficient and cleaner technologies, would yield big savings in energy and promote switching to less carbon-intensive fuels. Political will and public acceptability of the economic cost of such policies will determine how far IEA countries go down this path.

New technologies will undoubtedly be a major part of the solution. Governments and the private sector should share the responsibility for RD&D of new energy technologies. While this type of involvement has declined significantly in the past decade in IEA countries, given that the energy industry's overall research efforts are undermined in new market structures, governments need to reappraise the need for renewed public commitment to energy R&D. Sharing costs and gains through international collaboration via such instruments as IEA's Technology Implementing Agreement, is one way of getting better value for the money spent on R&D. Addressing all of these policy challenges can be encompassed in how to strike the balance between the "3Es", namely, energy security, economic development and environmental protection, in a cost-effective manner. The IEA's mission is to support member countries' efforts to devise policies to this end. The IEA's operational mandate has expanded considerably over the past three decades. The concept of energy security has broadened from oil to natural gas and electricity. This trend will continue in accordance with the changes in political, technological and market framework and the emergence of new policy challenges in future.

Geopolitics of Natural Gas

Natural gas is rapidly gaining in geopolitical importance. Gas has grown from a marginal fuel consumed in regionally disconnected markets to a fuel that is transported across great distances for consumption in many different economic sectors. Increasingly, natural gas is the fuel of choice for consumers seeking its relatively low environmental impact, especially for electric power generation. As a result, world gas consumption is projected to more than double over the next three decades, rising from 23% to 28% of world total primary energy demand by 2030 and surpassing coal as the world's number two energy source and potentially overtaking oil's share in many large industrialized economies.

Gas consumption is projected to grow in nearly all world regions, with the largest absolute increases in gas use in North America and Europe and rapid growth in new markets such as China, South Asia and Latin America. It is likely that rising gas consumption in many of these markets will force an increase in imported supplies as low-cost local resources are exhausted. Three countries alone Russia, Iran, and Qatar possess 55% of current proved gas reserves. Simultaneously, falling costs for transporting gas-both by pipeline and by ship as liquefied natural gas (LNG)-will continue to improve the viability for these distant suppliers to develop markets outside their borders.

The growing importance of natural gas imports to modern economies will force new thinking about energy security. The relationships that are developing between major gas suppliers and key end use consuming countries will create new geopolitical considerations that will rise to the highest levels of economic and security policy. Already, U.S. Federal Reserve Bank Chairman Alan Greenspan has publicly discussed the implications of rising domestic gas prices and the need for LNG imports to supplement North American gas production. Security agencies have redoubled their attention to gas transportation infrastructures. With the prospect of much greater dependence on foreign supplies of natural gas, the U.S. Department of Energy in December 2003 convened a gathering of the Energy Ministers from current and future major gas exporters to the U.S. to build diplomatic ties to these important suppliers.

The Energy Forum of the James A. Baker III Institute for Public Policy and the Program on Energy and Sustainable Development at the Stanford University Institute for International Studies have begun a major effort to investigate the geopolitical consequences of a major shift to natural gas in world energy markets. A case in point of recent efforts to look at infrastructure development is the recently completed World Bank (ESMAP) study *Cross-Border Oil and Gas Pipelines: Problems and Prospects*. This study briefly examines twelve cases of cross-border energy infrastructures to identify common challenges and the best practices for mitigating these challenges. The International Energy Agency (IEA) has convened a series of workshops on cross-border gas trade, including policy makers, industry experts and academics and continues to examine issues of gas import security.

There is also a voluminous literature on hypothetical gas transport projects-lines drawn with crayon on maps that represent hundreds of proposed gas lines. Some studies such as the *Shell Global Scenarios*, have considered gas infrastructure expansion in the broadest social and geopolitical contexts. Still other efforts have focused on the specific economics of hypothetical natural gas pipeline options in particular regions. In 2000, the Asia Pacific Energy Research Center published two reports-one focused on the economics of gas pipeline options in Northeast Asia and a second on gas pipeline options for Southeast Asia. Similarly, the Baker Institute at Rice University has analyzed the pipeline and LNG options for importing gas from the Russian Far East to Japan. The International Institute for Applied Systems Analysis has also conducted a large-scale economic modeling effort to study the routing of Central Asian natural gas to European and Asian markets. Every major commercial enterprise that produces transports or sells gas across borders enlists models to explore the economics of different projects and scenarios.

The Baker Institute-Stanford University effort will expand on this existing work. In particular, the Institute shall consider the more complex issues of the international security and geopolitical consequences of emerging gas producer-consumer relationships. The Institute is currently contemplating to explore the political consequences of integrating what have historically been disconnected regional natural gas markets. The study will allow examination of whether the advent of LNG will create a truly global market for natural gas, as well as the role of likely key gas suppliers in affecting prices and security of supply in that global market. The study will also allow for systematic analysis of many questions that have long been a mainstay of the energy security debate in oil, such as the whether large gas consuming countries will compete to secure uninterrupted access to the world's most prolific natural gas resources. (Jaffee & Hayes, 2006).

Conclusions

Energy-intensive industrial sector consumes nearly 85 million barrels per day of Petroleum for economic growth. Expanded demand from the augmented capacities is being met through an optimal mix of oil and natural gas resources to support industrial and business operations worldwide at economies of scale. The projected demand of oil from China and India in near future is going to be almost two to three fold to keep pace with fast-developing economy. The potential sources to tap to meet the growing demand are going to be the Middle –east, Eastern Europe, Russia, Canada, Western and South Africa, China etc. Demand for oil and natural gas has historically maintained a striking balance until the first oil-shock experienced by the non-OPEC countries from the OPEC countries in 1974.Periodical hike in the prices of Oil and natural gas by OPEC has left little option but to diversify the production bases of the commodities by exploring alternate sources of production and supply at cheap, convenient and competitive costs. In the paper this has been suggested to be strategized in the following manner to minimize the negative impact of geo-politics of oil trading in the global scene:

(i) Creation of authentic database on country and region-wise potential reserve of oil and natural gas resources.

(ii) Optimize the production of oil and natural gas and ensure steady and uninterrupted supply of oil and natural gas at prices that are universally acceptable without hurting the interests of oil producers, exporters and consumers globally.

(iii) Discrimination between OPEC and Non-OPEC nations in matters of supply and price-fixing should be altogether dispensed with to bring in greater parity and harmony in the global marketing scene.

(iv) Considering limited life-span of oil and natural gas, there has to be greater diversification of sources to be tapped (biomass, biogas, wind hydel-thermal, geo-thermal, nuclear etc.) along with mode of feedstock to be used, especially in industrial, energy, transport, domestic and other conventional and non-conventional sectors to avoid over-exploitation in one hand and rapid depletion on the other.

(v) There is a clear need to break intra-regional monopoly and encourage inter-regional cooperation for production, supply, export and marketing of oil and natural gas in globally competitive and acceptable prices to circumvent possible negative impact of geo-politics in oil-trading.

(vi) After read through this study, a fairly stark picture of the near-to medium-term future of oil, and in fact, for the world economy, begins to emerge. Oil is such an important part of we humans to secure our lifestyles.

(vii) Increasingly, the world must rely on available energy sources which, for historical, political and even religious reasons, are at great risk. Also, it is easy to forget the balance of the 6000 oil-related items that we use every day to assure our comfort.

REFERENCES

Amit Kumar (2005), "Energy scenario in South Asia", Energy Technology News, 1st. Oct, 2005.

Amy Jaffe and M.H. Hayes (2005), "The Geopolitics of Natural Gas", The Nation, dated 4th January, 2005.

Amy Jaffe (2004), "The Growing Developing country appetite for oil & Natural Gas", Economic Perspectives, May 2004.

Arien Cohen (2006), "Reducing US dependence on Middle-eastern Oil", The Heritage Foundation, dated 7th April 2006.

Baker Institute of Study (1999), "China and Long-term energy security", Institute of Public Policy of Rice University, No. 11, April, 1999.

Charles Kohlas (2006), "After Iraq: Oil and Geopolitics, In the National Interest, After Iraq Oil and Geopolitics.htm

Constantine Arvaritopopulos (2006), "The Geopolitics of Oil in South Asia", Thesis: A journal of Foreign Policy Issues, Institute of International Relations

Data Monitor (2005), "Geopolitics of EU Energy supply" New & Trends in Europe,Vol. 10, No. 15, dated 17 August, 2005.

EurActiv.com (2006), "Geopolitics of EU energy supply", Energy, dated 19th April 2006.

Frederick Cedoz (2003), "Thinking beyond OPEC", Journal of International Security Affairs, No. 10, Spring, 2006.

Gal Luft (2005), "The World Oil Crisis: Implications for Global Security and Middle East", Jerusalem Issue Brief, 5 (7), Jerusalem Centre for Public Affairs, Dated 16 th October 2005.

Govt. of Canada (2005), "How World Oil Market Work", Office of Oil Price Information, Work-Fall, 2005.

Jaffee, A.M. & M.H. Hayes (2006), "Natural Gas and Geopolitics", Stanford University Press. USA.

James Richard (1999), "New Cohesion in OPEC's Cartel: Pricing and Politics", *MERIA Journal*, Vol. 3(2), June, 1999.

John Chapman (2004), "The real reasons Bush went for war", Guardian, London, dated 28th June, 2004.

Johan Wingard (2005), "Energy dominates growth debate in South Africa", Global Politician, dated 4th October, 2005.

Klare, Michael T. (2005), "Oil, Geopolitics and the coming war with Iran", Common Dreams News Centre, TomDispatch.com, dated 11.4.2005.

Michael T. Klare (2006), "The Geopolitics of Natural Gas", The Nation, Dated 4th January, 2005.

Nicolas Kozloff-Coha (2005), "Venezuela Chavez: Oil is a geopolitical weapon", Venezuelananalysis.com, dated 29 th March, 2005.

Okogu, B.E. (2003), "Changing Oil market: The Middle East and North Africa", IMF News, 2003.

OPPI (2005), "How World Oil Markets work-Fall 2005?", Office of the Petroleum Price Information (OPPI), Govt. of Canada.

Mathew R. Simmons (2008), Twilight in the Desert: http://www.amazon.com/Twilight-Desert-Coming-Saudi-Economy/dp/047173876X.

Commission of Green Paper (2000), Green Paper on the security of energy supply http://europa.eu/scadplus/leg/en/lvb/l27037.htm

CHAPTER XIV

E-Commerce Applications in Oil and Natural Gas Industries (Petro-Informatics)

The e-business revolution has arrived in the energy efficiency and energy services area. Companies are using e-business approaches to compete electronically, sell services and products—including energy efficiency—to new and existing customers, strengthen relationships with suppliers, contractors, and customers, and provide better customer service. Example e-businesses include the energy.corn energy marketplace superstore, utility.com—the first virtual utility, a British site that allows users to calculate savings from different energy suppliers, Web-enabled bill aggregation tools and energy audits. Another site, EDMPro.com, provides a range of energy management services targeted primarily at commercial chain accounts, including bill aggregation, load profiling, and energy efficiency analysis. Energy-efficiency services offered via the Web include home energy audits, estimation of energy costs, aggregated purchasing of energy efficiency products, and building benchmarking (Mihimester & McKelvey, 2000).

Principles of E-Business

E-business broadly covers any aspect of energy and efficiency services, including trading of oil & natural gas as well as petro-retail businesses that can take advantage of the Internet and information technology. In general, e-business goes beyond ecommerce, and encompasses four major areas:

- Branding and Reputation Management (e.g., brochureware);
- Customer Relationship Management;
- Revenue Enhancement (e.g., e-commerce); and
- Business Process Improvement (including knowledge management) and Cost Reduction.

Energy-efficiency services and products can relate to all of the above. For example, utility sties, which offer on-line home energy audits, help the utility manage their brand and reputation for caring customer services in the face of deregulation and customer choice. ECommerce (selling commodity or products over the Internet) is hut one dimension of e.business. In the energy services sector, this has been an important and highly visible dimension. However, the full e-business revolution encompasses all business processes, practices and the complete value-chain, including customers, suppliers, employees, and allies/ partners. Energy (including oil & gas) Companies have typically adopted e-business in a phased and progressive approach (http://aceepr.org/publications/ eup_pub/E_business.pdf).

In recent time, as a result of IT boom and vast expansion being taken place in e-enabled global services, in which India is a major player in the world. On the strength of this prospect, there have been a large number of e-commerce (now e-business) initiatives in the petroleum industry. In fact, the business scenario has changed dramatically over the past few years, and trend is likely to continue. Many of the initiatives in the oil patch seek to improve supply chain integration. The e-business in the petroleum industry is so-called "rig-to-pump" integration, where there is visibility throughout the value-chain from the exploration and production phase (the rig) to the end user (typified by the gasoline pump). While the petroleum industry has been a leader in business-to-business e-commerce initiatives, there are still gaps in the emerging online integration of the supply chain.

On the upstream side, there are procurement and workflow facilitators in the e-business initiatives, such as Trade-Ranger, PetroCosm, NetworkOil, and Wellogix (formerly eNersection and WellBid). On the downstream side, there are numerous petroleum product exchanges, most notably FuelQuest, EnronOnline, RedMeteor, and the American Petroleum Exchange. There are also ventures such as 'Petrovantage' looking at integrating refinery optimization with the rest of the supply chain.

The new electronic marketplaces cut costs and inefficiencies in the supply chain by creating new ways to buy and sell goods and services. E-markets can aggregate demand, which enables buyers to negotiate for more attractive prices. They improve market liquidity, by allowing numerous buyers and sellers to participate. And they provide extended market reach—buyers and sellers that were once local in operation can now do business at any time, all over the world. E-markets facilitate just-in-time inventory, alleviating the need for vast warehouses to store supplies or materials waiting to be used or sold. Thus, benefits flow to both buyers and sellers. Currently, about 600 companies are in some stage of creating an e-marketplace to capture these benefits, following the example of early leaders like Chemdex, E-Steel, and DirectAg.com, which have already proven successful in their respective industries. Chemdex, for example, created a forum for buyers and sellers of laboratory products in 1997. The company now has more than 100 corporations and educational institutions buying goods from 2,200 suppliers on its site. Pharmaceutical giants like SmithKline Beecham and Bristol-Myers Squibb buy products through Chemdex online, which helped propel the firm's revenues to $8.5 million for the fourth quarter of 1999 (http://www.eei.org/magazine/ editorial_content/nonav_stories/2000-09-01-b2b.htm).

E-Business is taking the world by storm, in Oil and Gas the use of E-business is becoming more and more prevalent. This chapter explains in a nutshell, the applications of E-business, specifically in Oil and Gas (O&G) and to overview the important operational and strategic value that E-business can deliver to the global and regional petroleum companies, to in turn to be transferred to the end-customers in the supply-chain. Today, in addition to traditional systems developments, there is an innovative idea that is transforming the business in a way the business has to be conducted. The idea is electronic business, often known as *e-business*. E-business will allow industries to create new products and services, further develop customer loyalty and eventually achieve greater market leadership. E-business brings into play an organization's resources and partners in new and innovative ways thus creating strategic advantage. The potential of e-business goes far beyond new technologies—it impacts all aspects of a business strategy, process, organization and systems—and will extend businesses beyond their own boundaries. E-business has helped enterprises to improve customer interaction, the flow and exchange of information and the reduction of costs involved in business processes.

Emerging Technology Related E-Business

A value-chain can be defined as a sequence of consecutive production activities. In the case of the energy sector, this value chain is the constellation of activities that surrounds the production of hydrocarbons, including the up stream (extraction and production of oil and gas), downstream processing (oil refining, gas processing and the production of downstream petrochemicals), auxiliary industries (financial, process chemicals, etc.), transportation (pipelines) and associated service industries. Figure 14.1 illustrates a simple value chain, applicable to the gas sector (UTC Energy Investment Series: http://www.ttutc.com/news/article/energy/value_chain.pdf).

Fig. 14.1: Hydrocarbon-Energy Value-chain

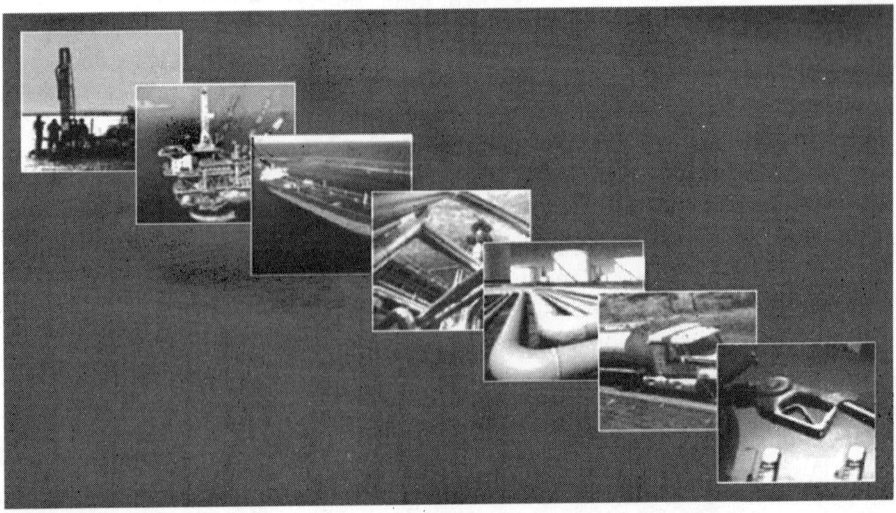

Opportunities for profitable business exist along the entire value chain, including those activities that are ancillary to the core production processes. Significant marco–economic benefits in the form of additional income, employment, technological development/technology transfer and infrastructure development also flow from an energy value chain. The more developed the value-chain, the greater the benefits that accrue to both individual firms and the economy.

The most visible activity in the oil and gas value chain is exploration and production (E&P) or upstream phase. The E&P business is reputed to be the most risk prone economically and physically, but it generates the highest returns when successful. Petroleum producing wells may yield a variety of commercial streams including oil, natural gas, condensate and natural gas liquids, which provide the company with multiple revenue streams. The business is dominated by large vertically integrated companies or firms with substantial risk capital. E&P investments also create a market for petroleum ser vices estimated at US$ 160 billion annually. These include geophysical activities, drilling and associated services, engineering and design, sub-sea engineering construction of platform, supply and maintenance of machinery and equipment. Oil and gas are produced concurrently at the E&P stage but move along separate paths thereafter.

Emerging technologies related to e-business have already made an inroad into the Oil and Gas industry, and new applications are being explored continuously. Forrester Research, Inc. found that Energy and Utilities are second only to the computing and electronic industry in their potential to do on-line business. A related Forrester study predicts that 14% of retail transactions will occur over the internet by 2006.

E-business touches on all aspects of the industry value chain and reach out to supplier networks, partners and customers. In case of Oil and Natural gas industries, as an integral part of e.enabled services, the Processes in Oil and Gas, where information is created used and stored, are illustrated below in Fig. 14.2.

Fig. 14.2: Oil and Gas Value-Chain Overview

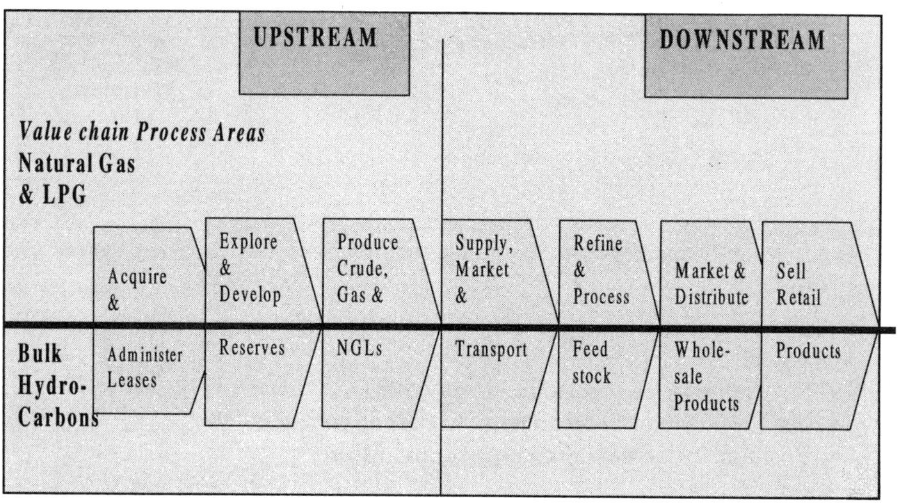

Natural gas flows continuously via pipeline from production to the final consumer, punctuated only by the need for separation and processing. Natural gas has several valuable fractions that are separated at the gas processing plant. Propane, butane and natural gasoline are removed from the gas stream for export. The LNG value chain may be structured into seven stages: gas production, pipe line transportation, processing, liquefaction, shipping, regasification, storage, distribution and sale of gas to final consumer. This is illustrated in Figure 14.3. Liquefaction is the most expensive portion of the gas value chain accounting for 30-45% of total production costs (http://www.ttutc.com/news/article/energy/value_chain.pdf).

Fig. 14.3: LNG Value-chain

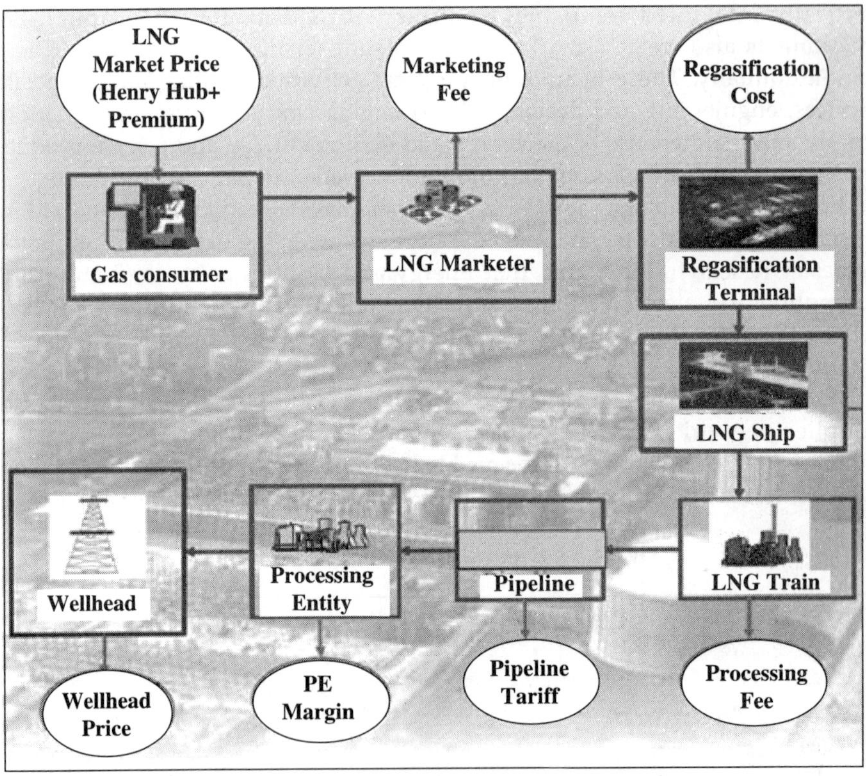

The focus of E-business for Oil and Gas companies today revolves around four basic tenets:

- Improving the management and coordination of operations around the world.
- Streamlining processes/reducing costs.
- Using information technology to best advantage.
- Position for necessary changes in the future.

The progressive stages/steps involved in case of shared and support/allied service process area is depicted below:

Shared and Support Service Process Areas

Over the years for most oil companies, especially involved with global operations, the information needs of the industry to be fed to the operational network to render customized services have become more comprehensive and complex, whilst technology, hardware and related software applications have advanced by leaps and bounds.

As figure 14.4 illustrates, the e-business applications upfront are being supported by ERP. This is done by most of the companies to increase the overall operational efficiency in the work they carry out, as also in the process be able to reduce administrative costs.

Fig. 14.4: E-business Applications across the Value Chain

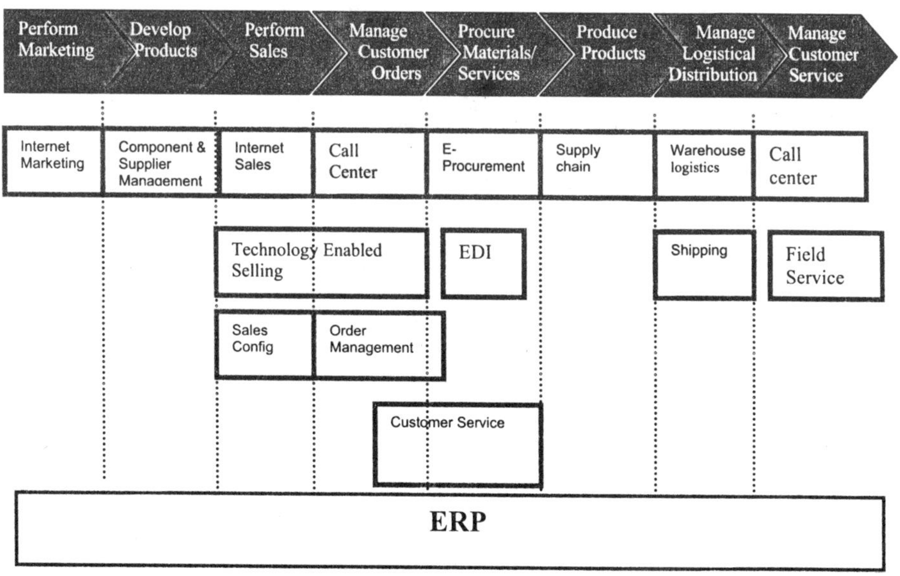

E-business can help facilitate efficiency in operations and collaboration among partners at a more efficiently and cost effectively than prior technology evolutions (e.g. Telex, Fax, EDI). In addition, E-business can allow rapid entry into new markets and industries and can allow companies to provide new products and services in a faster time period tailored to a more connected (and discerning)

wholesale or retail customer. With the Internet, customers can have better access to availability and prices of Oil and Gas commodities and at each step will require value-added service from their traditional suppliers. E-Business is one means to that end.

Direct integration of oil companies to external suppliers and third parties (engineering companies, drilling, services, governments, distributors, etc.—as illustrated in Fig. 14.5) can be enabled by internet/intranet technologies. This integration creates more seamless processes across wider reaches (nationally, regionally or globally), and in effect removes unnecessary process handoffs and overhead. The integration of oil companies with external agents for process efficiencies is at the beginning stages around the world.

Fig. 14.5: Integration Across Multiple Players Outside the Core Value Chain

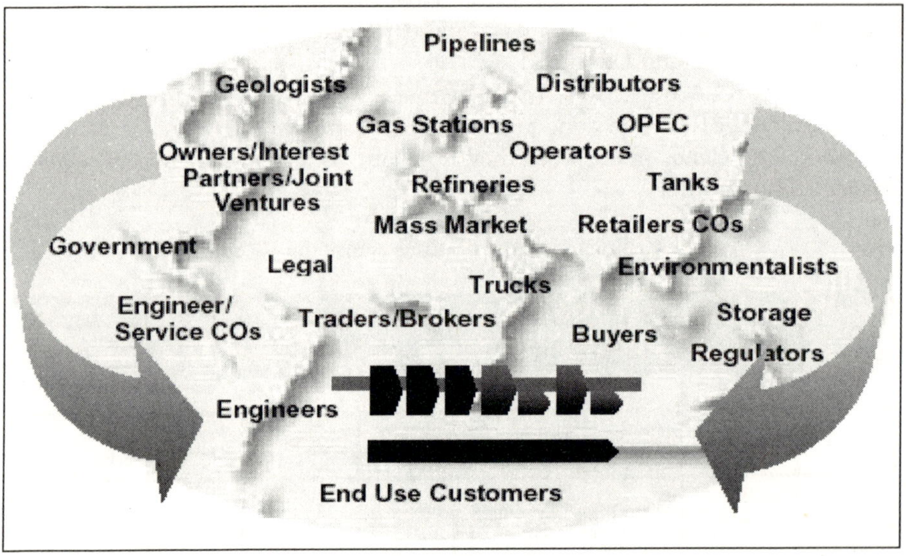

Oil and Gas companies are thinking through the ways in which E-Business can help them to be more competitive in the Internet-enabled services to help improve economy and corporate profitability. ERP system implementations were the "must do" innovations of the last two decades to get internal information, processes and transactions in order. E-business should be thought of as a necessary extension of ERP installations that in effect will allow Oil and Gas companies to "supercharge" their ERP investments to reach out and integrate seamlessly with suppliers, third parties, existing customers and new markets. In addition to extending ERP investments, E-business will speed up and facilitate the transformation of the industry through the emergence of on-line communities for purchasing and exchange of commodities. E-business will lower barriers to new entrants in areas of the Oil and Gas value chain while at the same time enabling traditional oil & gas companies to converge to other industries to offer the end use customer a more robust product offering at a higher perceived value and margin.

Model of E-business

The initiatives of E-business within the dimensions of E-Commerce outlined above (B2C, B2E, and B2B) can be categorized using tool referred to as the E-business evolution model or the 4-box Model as shown in Fig 14.6. The 4 basic steps in the4-Box Evolution Model comprise: channel enhancement, value-chain integration, industries' business transformation, and finally their convergence to help integrating as well as creating across-industries network market.

Fig. 14.6: 4-Box Evolution Model

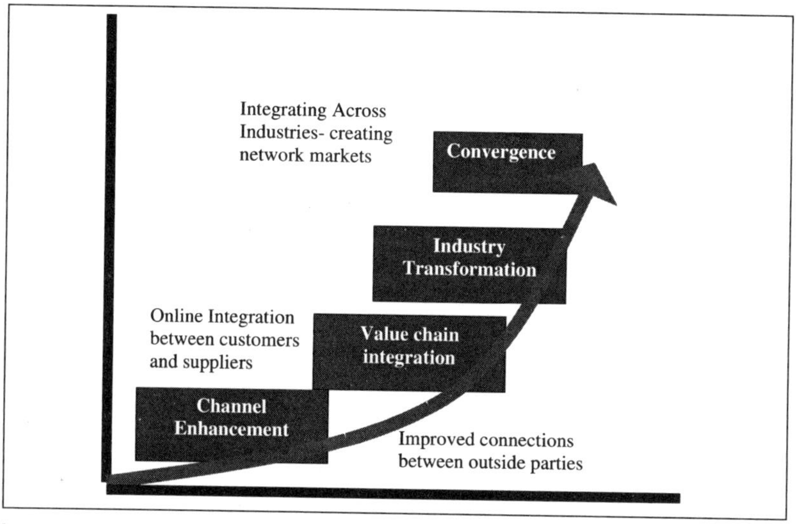

Using the 4-box model, E-business initiatives can be grouped into 4 categories along an evolutionary path—the higher up the path indicates a higher chance in organizational model required and a higher role that E-business can play. The 4 stages are not mutually exclusive for any company and do not imply that a company must evolve along a linear path—quite the contrary. New entrants to an industry or market typically enter a business transformers (boxes 3 & 4) while incumbents utilize E-business to the benefit of their internal processes and to improve their external relationships with suppliers and customers. The functions discharged by 4-stage processes are described below:

Channel Enhancement: Focuses on realizing improved connections between outside parties to the enterprise. This is accomplished with E-business through efficiencies in enterprise marketing, sales, customer service and interest sharing procedures. Opportunities for channel enhancement include: on-line catalogues, automated connections across suppliers, linked to affiliated companies to enable collaboration for spot market sales, and real time visual information sharing.

Value-chain Integration: Involves creation of seamless processes by electronically linking people, applications, departments, business units, business partners and governmental agencies-globally. Opportunities exist within the drilling proposals, drilling operations, global portfolio optimization and throughout the Oil and Gas supply chain processes.

Transformation: Involves initiatives that allow companies to more fully outsource many of their non-core activities. Outsourcing of back-office functions exists today while outsourcing of their key functions is beginning to take shape.

For example, external companies provide some exploration services, but not to the full extent possible. The advent of data visibility across organizations will enable true collaborative outsourcing. With transformation, Oil and Gas companies can focus their efforts on optimizing their portfolios to cut costs, enhance performance and create value.

Convergence: Involves the facilitation of entry into additional markets. E-business makes the viability of new business models more probable and will push companies to re-think product/market strategies and their need for future strategic partnerships. The proliferation of E-Business along with the cost efficiency that it brings, will allow a new means of reaching and supplying different products to new markets.

E-Business in Oil and Gas

A. Upstream Sector Impact and E-business Opportunity

Processes within the upstream segment of the industry are broadly outlined in the following process map Figure 14.7 that will be utilized to highlight areas that upstream companies should investigate for potential E-business opportunities. Upstream companies should consider identification and investment in activities that truly add value, that exploit process excellence, that re-bundle products/ services and that create entry barriers to others.

Fig. 14.7: Upstream Process Map

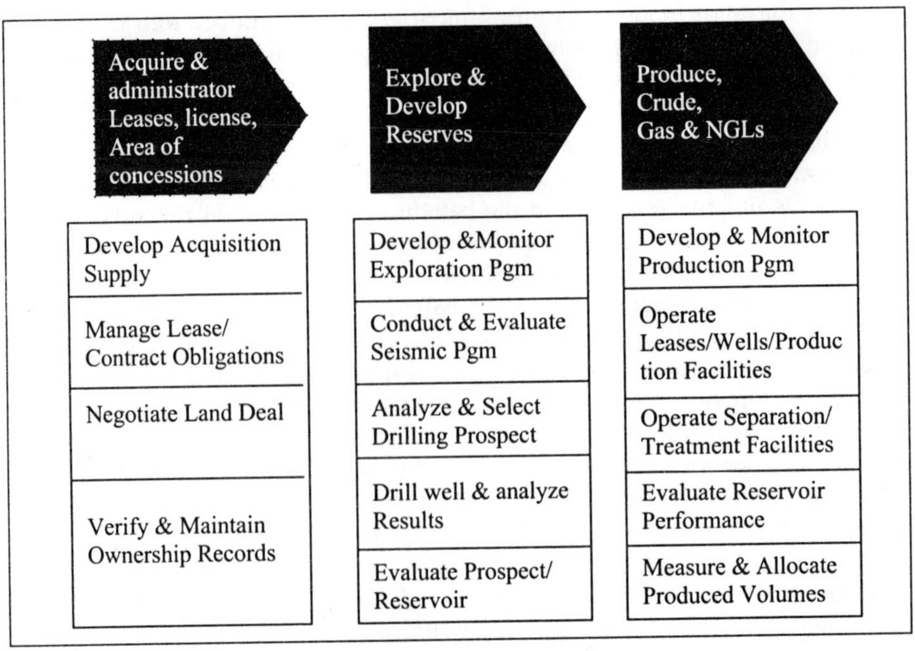

Potential applications of E-business in various E&P activities in Oil & Gas sector are outlined in the following Table 14.1.

Table 14.1: Example of Actual or Potential Use of E-business vis-à-vis E&P Activities

Process	Example of actual or potential use of E-business
Acquire & Administer Leases, License Areas or *Concessions*	(a) Internal/external data gathering for the development of acquisition or divestiture strategy can use web technology. (b) Administration of leases, contract obligation, and ownership relations with governmental organizations and third parties can be enables via web technologies.
Explore & Develop Reserves	Using web to review seismic data across organizations internal and external parties utilizing collaborative technologies will reduce cycle times, risks and costs external data may be used accessible via the internet.
Produce Crude, Gas & NGLs	(a) External data may be made accessible via the internet (b) Data can be shared amongst facilities via intranet technologies (c) Production information can be made available via the internet.

The upstream sub-sectors are not external client facing, the greatest E-business opportunities lie within linkages and collaboration inter- and intra-company (e.g. the creation of seamless process flows).

Upstream Oil and Gas companies are looking for ways to improve their exploration processes in light of the following drivers (Table 14.2):

Table 14.2

Oil Prices	Oil prices have continued to rise throughout the year, due mainly to agreement among OPEC nation's output limits. OPEC and non-OPEC Nations have discussed measures to Stabilize prices. Still prices remain near all-time lows adjusted for inflation, and companied continue to face pressure to slash budgets. Economies in the Asia Pacific and America have slowed or reversed their financial downturn, resulting in a movement toward positive economic growth.
Technology	Effective deployment of operational technology (Seismic interpretation and visualization, horizontal drilling, advanced deepwater and EOR techniques) have increased productivity and opened areas once thought to be off-limits. New computer hardware software and systems/data integration have improved business (back-office) processes and have helped reduce upstream support costs. Integration does not fully exist between geo-technical (front-office) and business (back-office) system. Dramatic improvements in IT infrastructure are occurring, leading to better global collaboration.
Globalization	Emerging economies, present opportunities for vast new markets. However, the volatile political and financial climate associated with these areas must be properly balanced.

	National Oil and Gas companies (e.g., Statoil, CNOC, Perobras, ONGC Videsh) are becoming more aggressive in areas outside of their present borders.
Environment	There are continued demand upon the petroleum industry to leave a smaller "environmental footprint." Accordingly, spending on environmental protection has increased dramatically.

Upstream companies are in the beginning stages of the use of E-business with the strongest emphasis today on integrating/transforming the value chain. In the future, an upstream company could focus on portfolio management, bringing the right outsourcers to bear as illustrated in the separation of key functions diagram (Fig. 14.8) given below:

B. Downstream Sector Impact and E-business Opportunities

Many E-business B2C and B2B opportunities exist within the downstream sector, beginning with transportation (e.g., barges), trading, through the refineries, and to the Convenience Stores where gas and other products are sold to customers. The participants in the downstream arena include suppliers, information brokers, logistics providers and the customer network. Downstream E-business Transformations of oil & gas industries take place with the outsourcing of non-core process and the entry of non-traditional players in the trading and brokering arenas as illustrated in Fig. 14.9.

Downstream E-business Convergence: Opportunities can best be illustrated by the example of a gas station meeting or interconnecting all the needs of a Customer

Fig. 14.8: Key Upstream Role Separation through Alliances, Partnerships and Outsourcing

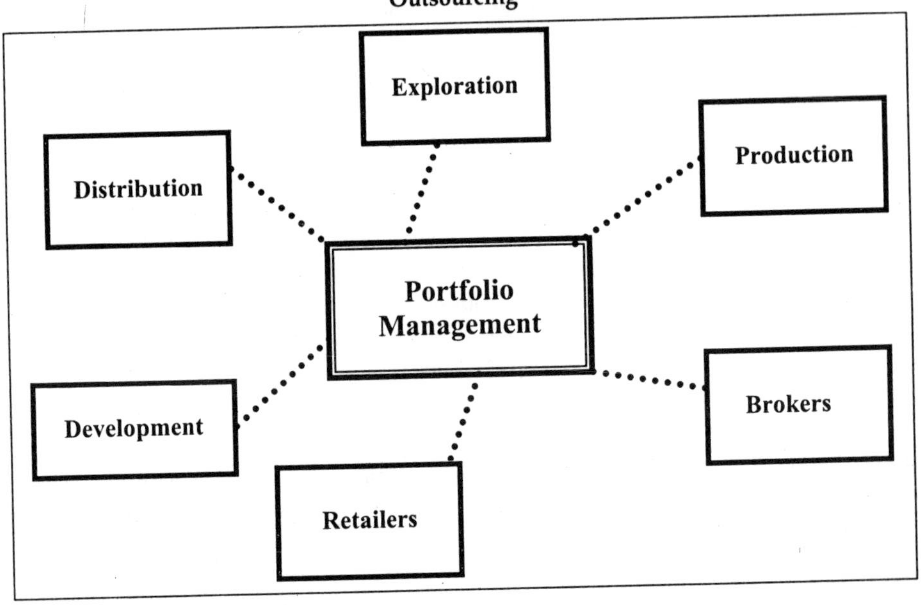

Fig. 14.9: Transformation in Downstream Oil and Gas

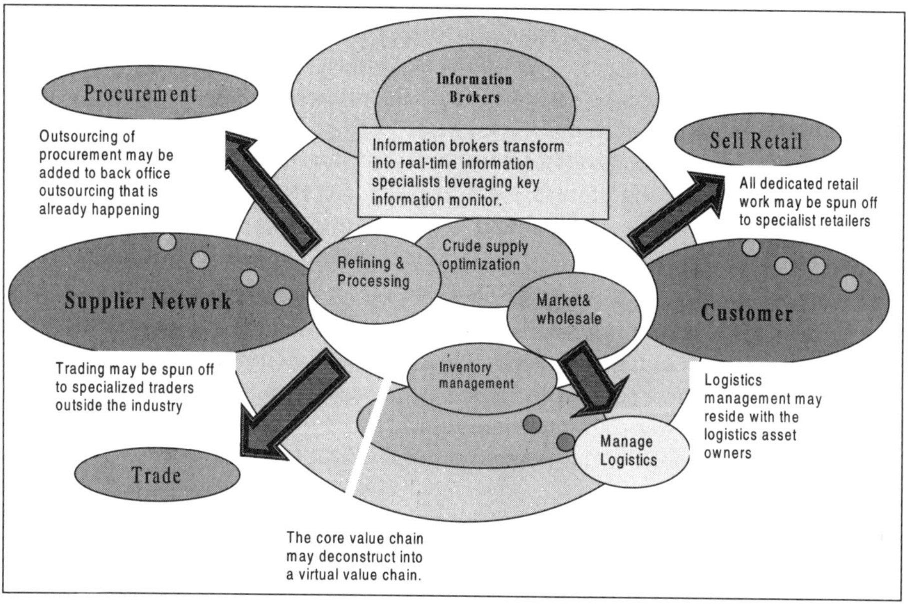

Fig. 14.10: Interconnectivity and Convergence of an Oil and Gas Service Station

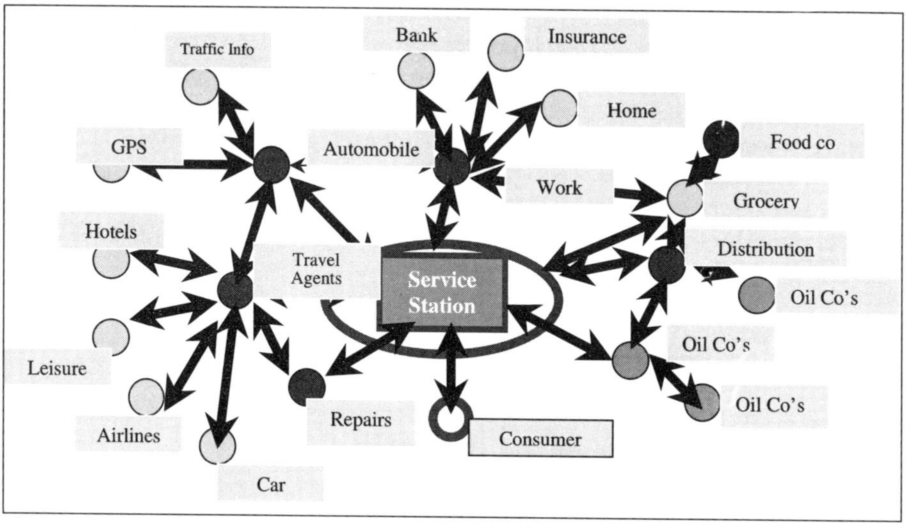

Service Stations (e.g. Petro-retail outlets) offer a complete Convenience Services to the travelers (Fig. 14.10). It may be noted here that here although the network seems to be grapevine like, but these operations are actually well integrated through convergence, taking the help of ERP approach and solutions in the Model so conceived.

E-Markets

An E-Market is an online business trading communities that focus on either indirect or specific direct goods or services. E-Markets link buyers and sellers globally by enabling them to manage, buy, sell, and trade products and services, and ultimately reduce operational expenses. E-Markets can be built around vertical (industry-specific) and horizontal (cross industry) markets. A potential evolution of E-Markets is the joining of multiple E-Markets to create Meta Markets. A Meta-Market is a portfolio of trading communities that leverage network effects and economies of scale across multiple E-Markets. E-markets and Meta-markets (Fig. 14.11):

- Will develop around existing Horizontal and Vertical Markets. Horizontal being across industries, vertical being within an industry segment
- Will provide a central platform for transaction automation, demand aggregation, improved market liquidity and extended market reach
- Will introduce new market and process efficiencies to an industry supply chain
- Will provide end-to-end procurement solutions

Forrester Research Group predicted that by 2005, $1.6 Trillion of online B-2-B trade will be conducted through E-Markets. The underlying paradigm of E-Markets is that these communities are enabling businesses to shift from optimizing an individual business to optimizing a network of businesses for competitive advantage.

E-Procurement solutions developed by Forrester Research Group (Bartel, 2007) play a key role in improving purchasing processes in enterprises through automating requisitions and purchase orders for goods and services, decentralizing buying, connecting to suppliers directly, and improving employee compliance with preferred supplier policies. Using a combination of vendor surveys, product demos, and client references, Forrester evaluated 14 leading e-Procurement solutions vendors across 118 criteria and found that Ariba, BasWare, Oracle

Fig. 14.11: The Meta-Market: A Portfolio of E-Markets

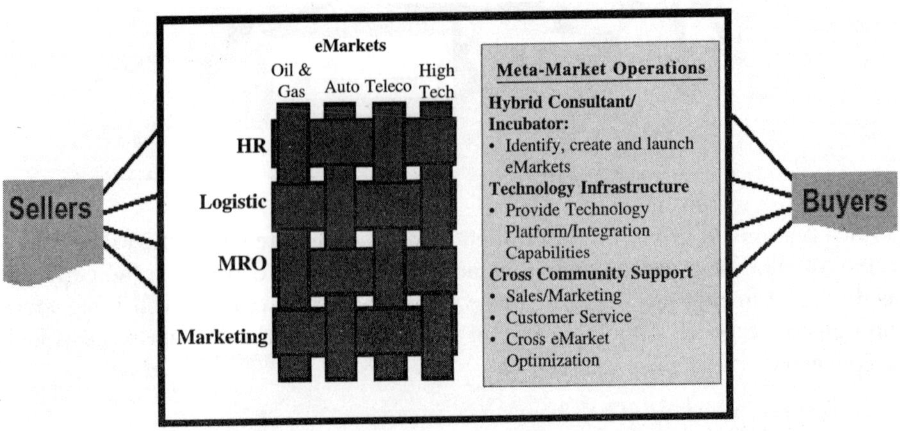

iProcurement (Oracle), Oracle PeopleSoft Enterprise eProcurement (PeopleSoft), and SAP established eProcurement leadership for overall goods and services buying and supplier support. Field glass and IQ Navigator lead in services procurement, while Ariba, BasWare, Oracle, and PeopleSoft provide good support for the buying of both services and goods. For supplier network services, Ariba was the clear Leader with SAP coming up, joined by Ketera Technologies, Perfect Commerce, and Quadrem in the Strong Performer sector with above-average scores for current offering; BasWare, cc-hubwoo, ePlus, IBX, Oracle, and PeopleSoft were not far behind. SciQuest, while appearing to score lower in the general market, does very well for its target markets of universities and research labs. E-Markets could be created by a group of buyers, a group of suppliers or by a neutral party. Industry consortium has the advantage of having participants in the e-business (http://www.oracle.com/corporate/analyst/reports/ent_apps/erp/forrester-wave-eprocurement-q2-2007.pdf).

E-Markets will significantly affect how companies gain competitive advantage. Some existing sources of competitive advantage (superior logistics, sourcing capabilities, and distribution channels) may become simply best practices, readily available to all that join an E-Market. Companies will now be able to differentiate themselves by developing the ability (culture, skills, and management processes) to work successfully with E-Markets. Those who join E-Markets early, and begin learning how to use E-Markets to their full advantage, may have a significant competitive advantage. Traditional sources of competitive advantage that may take on increasing significance are superior innovation capabilities, customer service and knowledge of customers.

E-Markets in Oil and Gas

Applications of E-Markets in the Oil and Gas industry entail the following:

(1) Buying/selling of indirect materials, and
(2) Commodity trading/exchange.

Trading/exchange concepts will be explored later in this article. Markets for buying/selling of indirect materials can be broadly categorized under the term "E-procurement", implying the automation of purchase and sell transactions electronically utilizing a marketplace. E-procurement provides significant advantages yet it is important to note that management and operation of procurement without the "e" does not go away. The value of E-procurement sites highly dependent on the local marketplace (customers) and the supplier networks (suppliers). Participants are key to cost and quality of the site. Some examples of E-Markets in the Oil and Gas arena include:

(a) **Traderanger.com**: will be an electronic marketplace with a single, standardized system for ordering and invoicing, as well as content management services. It will initially undertake all exchange activities for goods and services traded within the Oil and Gas exploration and production businesses, as well as the refining, marketing, retail and petrochemical sectors of the industry.

(b) **Sparefinders.com:** automatically links the buyers and sellers of engineering spare parts in an Internet marketplace.

(c) **Petrocosm.com** a B2B online exchange for the Oil and Gas industry linking buyers, sellers, participants and service providers to real-time product and service trading across the supply chain. Developed based on both supplier and buyer needs-requirements, PetroCosm will be a marketplace facilitating the transfer of products and services for the Oil and Gas industries worldwide.

(d) **Global Equipment Exchange** recently opened offices in South America. The Global Equipment Exchange, launched earlier this year (2000) as part of the Oil and Gas Journal Exchange (www.OGJeXchange.com). The Internet based exchange links buyer and sellers of surplus and used oil, gas and power generation industry equipment on a global scale. Global Equipment Exchange's inventory consists of a wide array of surplus and used equipment in the power generation, Oil and Gas industries.

E-Market Outlook

Because the value proposition is so powerful, e-Markets are expected to make up a significant portion of overall online business. A key success factor will be the ability to identify Value Added Communities (VACs) to probe, explore and identify the Winners as well as potential losers as per the predictions of E-Market outlook.

Winners are VAC's

- Whose buyers are the largest players in large concentrated; VACs could focus on direct materials and/or procurement.
- That evolves to own the customer relationship, the transactions, and/or both.
- Those have or are transitioning into metamarkets by expanding into multiple verticals and that technology engines that will be leveraged into metamarkets.

Losers are VAC's

- That cannot gain critical mass of buyers and/or sellers (the "chicken and egg" problem).
- Those focus on only one horizontal or small vertical category.
- With poor service capabilities or domain expertise.
- Those enter already crowded VAC markets, such as travel, technology etc.

Trade/Exchange

Trading via the Internet (or E-Trading) is more than just buying and selling of products and services among industry participants—it is a new way of doing business. The use of the Internet to automate/facilitate the traditional processes of commodity trading and risk management can be broadly categorized as E-Trading. E-Trading involves the entry of new players to the industry and the transformation of existing players. New players (e.g. newco Internet companies) have the ability to move fast and enter new industry spaces via the internet. Existing players have the advantage that they can leverage existing knowledge and relationships with industry participants.

E-Trading in Oil and Gas

External and internal trends that are pushing for E-Trading in the Oil and Gas industry include:

External trends that push E-Trading

(a) **Globalization of markets**: The Internet is allowing companies to move outside their national and regional boundaries.

(b) **24×7 market access**: With globalization, the need emerges for anytime access to the market to allow traders access to global markets during their own business day. Enabling this trend is the acceptance of after market trading, the development of electronic trading systems, and deregulation.

(c) **New E-Market models**: Online trading/exchanges, auctions, aggregators. These new on-line markets create communities. The anonymity of exchanges and auctions increases competition and brings about true market pricing. Volumes and liquidity will also rise. Development has been triggered by the success of online stock market trading companies like E-Trade, DLJ.com and Schwab.

(d) **Knowledge management**: Information is available in great abundance in the minds of individuals, within organizations, and in external sources like the Internet. Improvements in gathering, managing, and accessing this information are allowing the trading function to improve its profitability by increasing the top line (more profitable trades) and reducing the bottom line (lower administrative costs).

Internal trends that push E-Trading:

(a) **Multi-task work orientation**: much like their counterparts in the stock market;

(b) **Time sensitive and critical tasks**: deal making, execution;

(c) **Work that is driven by external data**: critical to profitable trading;

(d) **Need to leverage knowledge capital**: must be rapidly disseminated and used appropriately;

(e) **Volatile/dynamic environment**: quick reaction to constant change in Core Strategic Goals.

The enterprises that provide electronic trading services on the Internet can have varying organization frameworks—from neutral organizations to extensions of a traditional company trading departments. The Internet facilitates and automates transactions and is an excellent means for posting of availability and rapid changing prices to potential buyers.

Commodity products (i.e., gas, electricity, liquids) are the easiest to trade via the internet because they require minimal interaction between the buyer and the seller to explain product characteristics. The key processes and critical success factors (CSF's) necessary to manage & exploit the volatility via trading and risk management in the hydrocarbon supply system are listed in the Table 14.3 below:

Table 14.3: Critical Success Factors

Key Trade Processes	Trade/Risk Management Critical Success Factors
(a) Forecast demand & supply	(a) Strong relationships with producers and Consumers
(b) Crude selection & Optimization	(b) Instantaneous global access to price & changing market conditions
(c) Make document deals	(c) Understand transportation & exchange options by network
(d) Arrange transportation & Exchanges	(d) Powerful price and market analytics capability
(e) Manage risk/exposure/Position	(e) Accurate system-wide position physical and paper
(f) Settle and analyze deals	

The following Table 14.4 outlines the various mechanisms utilized on the Internet to facilitate the trading processes in the E-Market Model:

Table 14.4: Market Models

Market Model	Description
Exchanges	A market for commodity products: It fulfills last-minute buy and sell needs for industry players with preexisting business relationships
Bid Systems	A mechanism for lowering the acquisition price for products typically purchased via RFPs or RFQs: It enables a wide range of suppliers to bid competitively in real time
Aggregators	A one stop shopping venue: It streamlines purchasing by many concentrating many product catalogs for buyer groups
Auctions	A mechanism for liquidating surplus at best possible prices: It enables a wide range of potential buyers to bid competitively for products at below-market prices
Extranets	A secure invitation only site over the public web where end users buy directly from sellers.

Some electronic trading/exchange related sites are listed below. These sites typically began with a focus on a specific commodity but have expanded to offer additional value added services and have moved into offering trading support across a broader range of commodities.

- **Altranet**—Anonymous electronic trading—natural gas, crude oil, liquids, electricity
- **Enbridge**—Electronic market place for physical trading of crude oil
- **Enron Online**—Trading of Enron's natural gas, electricity, coal, weather, bandwidth, liquids, petrochemicals, pulp and paper, emission credits (not all products available on-line yet)

- **Bloomberg.com**—Wholesale power trading and emission credits
- **NYMEX**—Interactive data network for bidding, offering and trading commodity futures and options offered by NYMEX for crude oil, heating oil gasoline, natural gas, liquids, and electricity
- **TradeCapture.com**—On-line commodity trading for crude oil and refined products
- **MCX**—On-line Commodity trading for oil and refined products.

Trading Outlook

Online trading models can be local, regional or globally focused and typically feature a broad spectrum of energy-related products and services, be it for Oil, Natural Gas or Liquids. Neutral starts ups are typically local while large players seek to extend their operations on a global scale.

When reviewing electronic energy trading opportunities as whole, there is little immediate opportunity due mainly to existing business practice, market and regulatory conditions. General consensus is that the situation is poised to change due to the introduction of trading models from other parts of the world, to changes in regulations and to the trend towards globalization of the trading operations of larger industry players.

Market Trends

Today's mega trends in retailing center around branding, globalization, entertainment, and technology. The industry is heading toward convergence retailing, where the convenience center is connected to the Internet and supports services such as car washes, fast food, grocery and retail products, fuel management, kiosks, and banking. An embedded gateway is the key that connects the retail site network with external networks and the Internet. Service providers use the gateway as an access point to provide value-added services.

Sun and Cyberonix eGasStation Architecture

Sun and Cyberonix have collaborated to develop eGasStation, a Java technology-based automation and e-business solution architecture for petroleum retailers.

Sun Microsystems, Inc. and its technology partner, Cyberonix, Inc., have developed an architecture that promises to revolutionize the service station business. This solution, which is fully compliant with the Sun Open Net Environment (Sun ONE), is the eGasStation architecture. It seamlessly integrates legacy devices to help lower costs, enhance reliability, and improve customer satisfaction. The problem facing the petroleum industry is how to bring millions of devices into the digital age, without incurring the cost of a massive update and replacement program. Working with 'Cyberonix', 'Sun' developed a low-cost solution. The architecture is based on a multiyear project to apply Java technology to industrial automation and control.

With this solution, a "wrapping layer" can be added to most of the installed devices used in petroleum retail. This layer consists of hardware and Java technology-based software. An industrial controller (and optional service gateway) is added to the equipment set at the site. Java technology-based control applications run on the controller, providing connectivity to the Internet and other enterprise applications. In effect, this enables an industrial control retrofit to the existing petroleum retail equipment.

The e-GasStation Architecture

The new e-GasStation architecture allows remote access and control of retail service station operating assets, and synchronization with telematic environments. Dynamic smart services that are bundled in this unique solution empower remote monitoring and control of pump dispensers, fuel tank monitors, POS devices, car wash sensors, as well as security, HVAC, refrigeration, lighting, meters, and industrial equipment.

The e-GasStation architecture specifies a distributed services platform for real-time remote monitoring and control, data logging, and alarming of retail service station operating assets. Distilled information can be sent to a personal wireless device (in addition to e-mail, voice mail, and database logs). To Internet-enable systems such as security, energy management, and equipment monitoring, a unique solution based on Sun's Embedded Java technology was developed which is illustrated in Fig. 14.12 as follows (Sun Microsystems, 2004: http://www.sun.com/solutions/documents/solution-sheets/en_egas_ff.xml):

Fig. 14.12: The e-GasStation Architecture

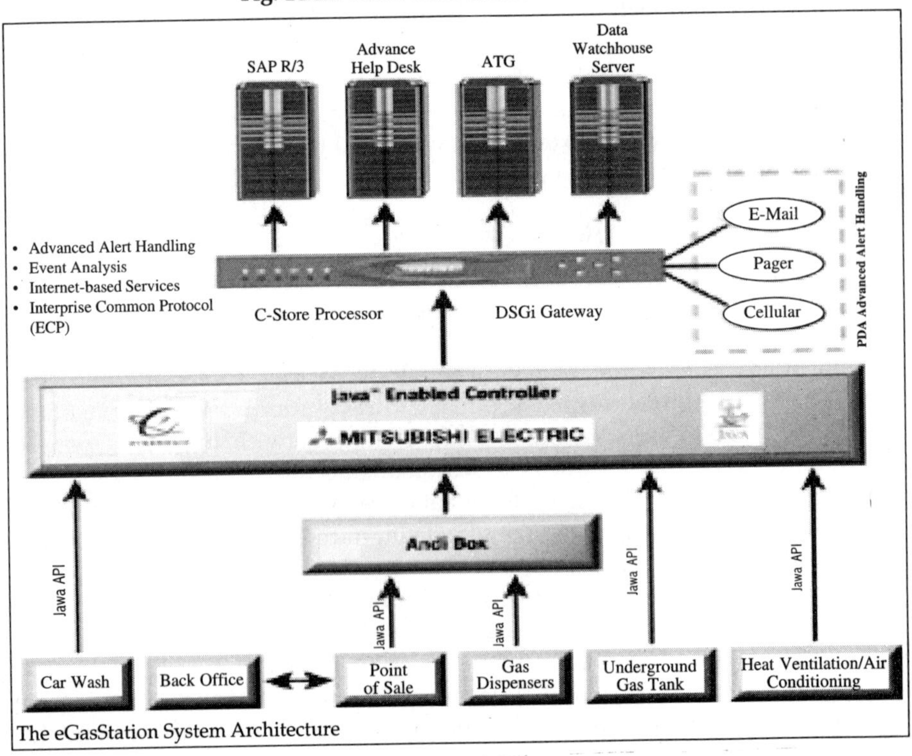

Sun's Role in e-GasStation Implementations

Sun plays two key roles in the implementation of the e-GasStation architecture:

1. Provider of the appropriate networking and back office server support infrastructure
2. Supplier of an optional service gateway device to complement the industrial controller with in-store processing and multifunction capabilities

From the workgroup to the data center, Sun servers and storage systems provide dependable solutions that enable high availability, superior scalability, flexible storage capacity, and seamless connectivity. With a solution-focused approach and an uncompromising commitment to quality and service, Sun has earned a position among the top UNIX" server vendors. Sun's service gateway, the Cobalt RAQ 4i server device, acts as a bridge between the external network and local networks based on Ethernet as well as solutions from Powerline, LANworks, Phoneline's Wireless LAN, and Bluetooth. It can reside between the industrial controller, the back office LAN, and client servers, providing a full suite of Internet and application services. As the retail petroleum industry adopts Internet technologies, Sun offers the vision and key components to ensure that these businesses thrive in the Net economy. Sun Enterprise servers are key components of integrated, tuned, and tested business solutions, developed with top-tier application providers.

Business Models/Benefits

The primary purpose for developing the e-GasStation technology is to increase profitability. Improved monitoring and maintenance of critical retail and fuel handling equipment can reduce costly failures and enhance operational efficiency. Some of the business issues currently being addressed by this technology are:

(a) **Pump Meter Drift Monitor/Control:** The e-GasStation architecture allows petroleum retailers to precisely monitor and control pump dispenser meter drift. Studies have shown an inaccuracy range of between 1.03 to 1.3 gallons dispensed for each gallon recorded under drift conditions or with improperly calibrated pumps. The ability to remotely monitor and control wet stock meters can result in significant savings.

(b) **Car Wash Monitor/Control:** Profit and customer satisfaction are enhanced by providing a more reliable car wash service. The e-GasStation architecture allows car wash sensors to be remotely monitored and controlled. Key Performance Indicators are sent to PDA devices, alerting the appropriate service representative for prompt repairs to reduce downtime and improve customer loyalty. Since most motorists pay between $4 to $7 for car wash services it is important to keep this profit center up and running.

(c) **Site Energy Management:** Using the e-GasStation architecture, knowledge gathered from site energy consumption can be used to negotiate energy contracts with reduced rates. Energy consumption trends of devices such as coolers, appliances, and HVAC systems can be used to set conservation policies. Along with these policies, remote control thermostats and lighting adjustments can save from two to 20 percent in yearly energy costs.

(d) **Shrinkage Management:** The e-GasStation solution can correlate information gathered from multiple sources such as POS transactions, tank levels, fuel leakage, and pump calibration to detect fraudulent situations and notify the appropriate representatives.

(e) **Preventive Maintenance:** Correlation between dispenser rates and POS transactions can be used to detect the reduced fuel flow rates that commonly result from clogged filters. The e-GasStation architecture uses event notification to dispatch service representatives to fix the problem before an outage occurs.

Unique Features of the e-GasStation Architecture

Remote monitoring and control of legacy operating assets:

- Legacy device capability augmented with a single Embedded Java technology-based controller;
- Common communication bus adds intelligence to legacy devices;
- Common interface to devices from different manufacturers;
- Sends and receives messages in a predictable fashion; and
- Alarm classes define diagnostic information.

The e-GasStation architecture demonstrates how low profit-margin service stations and related C-Stores can be brought into the digitally connected world, without requiring prohibitively large investments. At the same time, petroleum companies are providing the foundation for new revenue opportunities at the site, as well as stronger customer relationships.

Next-Generation Services

Once this infrastructure is in place, petroleum retailers will be in a position to offer new, Internet-based services to customers and their automobiles. As an additional revenue stream for service station operators, these should be welcome. Proposed services include:

- Video and music download to automobiles and digital radios;
- Global positioning system (GPS) mapping services;
- Local advertisers can (for a fee) send messages to customers who are waiting to fill their tanks;
- Smart chip (card, ring, key chain) integration and co branded marketing programs offer targeted, personalized services (customer relationship management activities);
- Real-time gasoline price auctions beamed to Intelligent Network Vehicles and PDA devices; and
- Automobile synchronization mechanisms that send alerts by e-mail to PDA devices, warning of potential service conditions for automobile parts.

Additional services that may be added to the e-Gas Station architecture include:

- Dynamic fuel pricing;
- Kiosk support;
- Category management and streamlined evaluation of sales data (for fuel and bar-coded, SKU items);
- Voice over Internet Protocol (VoIP) technologies to consolidate telephone lines;
- Remote software maintenance and distribution;
- Security surveillance systems; and
- Wireless technologies to help facilitate the speed and ease of deployment, while reducing costs associated with physical networks.

E-Business Applications used by Oil Giants

BRITISH PETROLEUM: A CASE STUDY

Innovation Mode: XML-enabled order exchange between British Petroleum (BP) Energy Company and Barber engineering and controls Ltd.

The first one describes about the B-2-B transaction taking place between companies.

About BP: at a Glance:

- British Petroleum is recognized as a leader in the use of e-procurement.
- Infrastructure built and experience gained to enable innovations.
- The main objective is to get hold of top 35-40 suppliers enabled for e-procurement in 2003.
- Its vision is to seamless, fully integrated automated process.

Why Buyers are pursuing e-commerce?

- To leverage the internet as a business tool.
- To reduce cycle time.
- To have a complete automated business processes.
- To have a global reach and visibility across the value chain.
- Ti improve compliance
- To gain statistical benchmarking for standard products

E-commerce hurdles for Oil and Gas Suppliers and Service Providers are:

- Multiple sales channels with unique e-procurement systems.
- General lack of IT and internet expertise.
- Cost of systems and implementation
- Transaction fees.
- Risk being reduces to a 'commodity' (downward pressure on pricing).
- Complex product and services not readily categorized in catalog
- All efficiency gains are for the buyer.

This case study showed web-based forms used both the buyer and the supplier for e-transactions. Either partner has the option to integrate this information exchange directly to their internal back-office systems. This would not affect their trading partner, because the XML transaction hub that connects them maintains the format that they us use.

CASE OF STAT-OIL

Some facts of Stat-Oil:

- Established in 1972
- Headquarters in Stavanger, Norway
- Partially privatized in 2001 through IPO process
- 16,700 employees in 23 countries
- Production/Reserves: 1 mmboepd/4.3 bn boe
- Marketing 2/3 of Norwegian gas volumes
- World's 3rd largest crude oil seller.

Why does Stat-oil need e-Business?

- Globalisation of industry.
- Reduce cost of extracting, refining and marketing oil and gas
- Maximize usage of scarce and disbursed resources.
- Take advantage of technical advances in IT and telecommunications.
- Reduce risk and mitigate best practice in operations and Health Safety and Environment (HSE).
- Offer training and consistency in information distribution throughout the Company, regardless of geography and time-zones.

Statoil's e-business Roadmap

The following table 14.5 provides Statoil's blueprint of business roadmap during the period 199-2002 in 4 stages: Foundation, Create Build & Operate and Harvest (Morten Sven Johannessen, Statoil;mosvejo@statoil.com, 2002)

Table 14.5

Foundation ..1999	Create 2000	Build and operate 2001	Harvest 2002 ..
•Implement new work-processes. •Fully integrated SAP solution. Organization change Organization readiness	•Identify opportunities •Organize and priorities •Develop skills and awareness •Launch pilots	Take ongoing and new e-business initiative "live" Measure, improve, and expand Integrate e-business into corporate and FO/RO strategy processes	Reap benefits with: •supply chain •collaboration •remote operation •borderless information management and effective knowledge sharing

What are the benefits?

- Reduction of internal transaction costs
- Reduction of external transaction costs
  ✓ *...result,* reduced costs
- Improved and simplified flow of information and data
- High speed access to information
- Standard infrastructure and standard collaboration tools
  ✓ *...result, better, quicker safer and more cost efficient information*
- Harvest further benefits from existing systems
  ✓ *...result, "operational excellence" = competitive edge*

How will this affect StatOil business?

- Increased cooperation on establishing standards and processes
- Visibility of suppliers and accessibility of suppliers on Marketplace infrastructure
- Ease of operation, faster time to market
- Ease of starting up in new locations, better utilization of existing infrastructure.

Fig 14.13. The Road to b2b e-commerce in StatOil

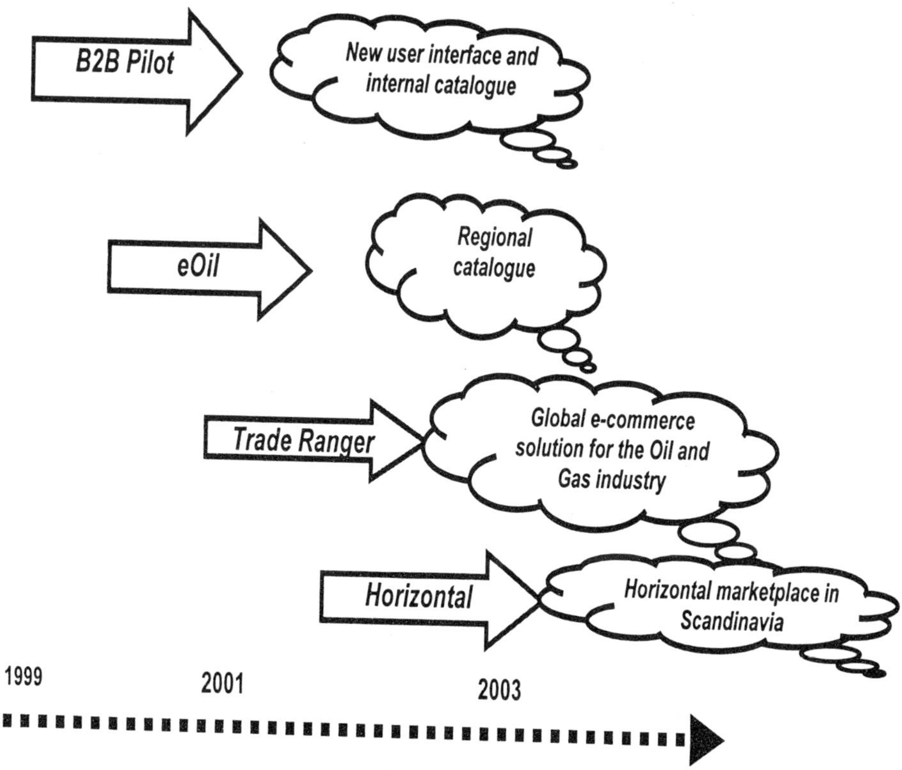

SHELL CANADA: CASE STUDY

Shell Canada Expands e-business on Secure Tivoli Software Platform

One of the largest integrated petroleum companies in Canada with approximately 3,400 employees, Shell Canada is a leading manufacturer, distributor and marketer of refined petroleum products. It is also a major producer of natural gas, natural gas liquids, bitumen and sulfur.

To retain its leadership position, Shell is deploying both business-to-consumer and business-to-business applications to provide better, faster customer service and lower operational costs. A senior staff systems analyst with Shell Canada's Shared Infrastructure group says, "e-business is very important because, among other things, it allows us to share information in a more timely fashion with customers and business partners. This saves us money and attracts customers by making Shell an easy company to deal with."(http://resources.bnet.com/topic/natural+gas+and+petroleum.html).

Challenge: Manage e-business Growth

When Shell began to develop and launch its online services, it recognized that there would be an increasing need to monitor, manage and safeguard its Web-facing applications. Security, in particular, was a concern. "On average, they were launching one new e-business application every two months," "They can't afford to deploy and manage a separate access control system for each one."As a highly satisfied, longtime user of IBM AS/400® servers running J.D. Edwards ERP applications, Shell Canada placed IBM high on its list of potential security management solution vendors. Other proposals came from Sun Microsystems and Oracle. But even more important to Shell was the fact that IBM could provide a comprehensive solution. "They looked for a stable vendor with both a breadth of product offerings and a depth of support and services to accompany those offerings," "IBM was one of the few companies that could provide all that, and its products seemed more mature compared to other security management offerings."

Solution: Single Point of Control

Shell Canada selected IBM Tivoli Access Manager for e-Business as its focal point for security authorization and administration. "Tivoli Access Manager gives us a single point from which to control and manage security for our e-business applications."

With minimal consulting from IBM Global Services, the Shared Infrastructure team completed the base installation of Tivoli Access Manager in about one day. Performing the installation themselves, with knowledge transfer from IBM, has helped the team become more self-sufficient in managing the Tivoli software. And when questions arise, they have various resources at their disposal. "The Tivoli product documentation is excellent," (IBM Tivoli Access Manager for e-business Release Notes-Version 4.1: http://publib.boulder.ibm.com/tividd/td/ITAME/SC32-1130-00/en_US/PDF/SC32-1130-00.pdf).

In the event shell systems administrators don't find what they need in the manuals, they use the Tivoli support Web site to browse product updates, or they post their questions as problems on the support site. Also, for the really tough problems, they have direct access to the developers and other technical experts within Tivoli." About a year after it installed Tivoli Access Manager, Shell implemented IBM Tivoli Monitoring with Tivoli Enterprise Console to monitor about one dozen UNIX®servers supporting its e-business environment. And now, the Shared Infrastructure team is evaluating other Tivoli performance monitoring and capacity planning tools as well.

The Centralized administration of user IDs, passwords and security policies across the company's Web servers has delivered the greatest benefit to Shell Canada. It's saving time—especially at the help desk—and improving Shell's ability to catch potential security problems. And these advantages ensure Shell can provide customers and business partners with seamless access to the information they need. In addition, Tivoli systems management solutions have enabled Shell to meet high performance expectations for its e-business applications. The company needs to be able to respond quickly to increased usage—even though usage patterns are often difficult to predict. Therefore, Shell wants to ensure that its e-business infrastructure is reliable, predictable.

Shell Manager notes that "The total cost of ownership [TCO] of the Tivoli software has decreased because of IBM improvements—based on customer feedback—in the product's ease of installation, configuration and management. IBM's resources for support and consultation also help us to lower TCO." Manager also appreciates being able to install multiple instances of Tivoli Access Manager on the same server to support multiple TCP/IP domains." They were supporting three or four different domains now:

> "It's much easier and less expensive to maintain systems when you have only one server to deal with. Another factor contributing to lower TCO is the ease with which Tivoli software integrates with other software Shell uses. For example, IBM WebSphere® Application Server is an important component of Shell's e-business infrastructure. "The integration between Tivoli Access Manager and the family of WebSphere products is improving steadily as both products develop."

BP Amoco Experience in E-Business in Oil Trading

BP Amoco—the oil giant formerly known as British Petroleum, began exploring electronic commerce more than a decade ago. Having invested billions of dollars to adapt its technology to an Internet-driven world and having completed a yearlong process emphasizing experiments with e-commerce potential, BP has progressed to what it calls "living on the Web."

These days, BP has a relatively clear picture of how e-business will transform the company and its industry, even if the timetables are in doubt. That is partly because the oil industry, with its global reach, heavy reliance on data and experience with supercomputing, has been among the most aggressive adopters of the computing and communications innovations associated with e-commerce.

But it helps that BP has become a pacesetter within the oil industry. Though its evolution is far from complete, an examination of BP's efforts sheds light on how some companies are trying to apply Internet successes, and lessons from setbacks, to their business. For example, BP had set up Getutility.com to be a brokerage for midsize gas and power utilities trading energy supplies, and then pulled back after the lack of response showed that BP had nothing unique to offer. The company is now trying to sell the site. The recent discovery phase came years after BP groups had dabbled in early forms of Web-based e-business and was complicated by the company's wave of acquisitions, including Amoco, Atlantic Richfield (ARCO) and Burmah Castrol (New York Times, 2008).

The technology groundwork for moving forward on a corporate basis had been laid by such moves as standardizing its desktop computers on Microsoft software in 1996 and, in 1999, paying MCI WorldCom $650 million over five years to create a global communications network. Most of what BP learned has been funneled into internal projects, like equipping 70 percent of its nearly 100,000 employees with laptop computers and other mobile equipment that allows them to plug into the company's intranet and the Web. The company is also loading its intranet with the data, teleconferencing packages and other services that help employees do their jobs. And it is encouraging employees to visit its Virtual Village site, where a screen depicting a downtown shopping district connects employees to Web sites that can help them with personal tasks like shopping or banking. The vendors on the Village site vary by country and city, depending on the location of the employee.

On the business-to-consumer front, BP has gone beyond providing static product information and financial data. A project in Australia allows customers of 'Wishlist'—a Melbourne-based electronic retailer, to pick up orders of consumer products at local BP service stations rather than wait at home for a delivery. Customers can also drop off products they are returning. Under a $200 million worldwide program called BP Connect, BP has begun to install Web-linked gasoline pumps at 28,000 stations so that drivers can use the time spent filling their tanks to view news headlines, check weather and traffic reports or order food at the station's convenience store. Inside the stores are Internet kiosks where drivers can send and receive e-mail and shop on the Web. (In the United States, the kiosks are being tested in Indianapolis and in Atlanta.)

Unlike in the United States, for instance, regulations in Britain currently restrict the types of information BP can put on electronic screens at the pumps. In business-to-business applications, BP was an early supporter of Internet-based exchanges to trade oil and chemicals, charter ships and buy supplies. Some of the highest-profile ventures, like Trade-Ranger, the Houston equipment-procurement exchange started a year ago by BP and 13 other petrochemical companies may never be successful.

Trade-Ranger is not only competing with traditional procurement practices but also with PetroCosm, an Internet exchange formed by Chevron, Texaco and technology vendors like Ariba and Requisite Technology. Some of its business overlaps with more focused sites like Network Oil, which auctions surplus oil field equipment, as well as private business portals where parts of BP trade directly over the Internet with a particular supplier. Similarly, BP's chemicals division is in the early days of using the World Chemical Exchange (www.chemconnect.com) or Elemica (www.elemica.com) to buy and sell chemicals. It is simultaneously developing Chemicals Choice, a private BP portal for customers who want to buy directly over the Internet from the chemicals division (New York Times, 2008).

ERP and E-Business

ERP is a structured approach to optimizing a company's internal value chain. The software, if implemented fully across an entire enterprise, connects the various components of the enterprise through a logical transmission and sharing of data. When customers and suppliers request information that have been fully integrated throughout the value chain or when executives require integrated strategies and tactics in areas such as manufacturing, inventory, procurement and accounting, ERP systems collate the data for analysis and transform the data into useful information that companies can use to support business decision-making. ERP systems, if implemented successfully, enhance and redesign business processes to eliminate non-value-added activities and allow companies to focus on core and truly value-added activities. The following are two examples where ERP systems have dramatically increased the efficiency and productivity of companies: IBM has used ERP to reduce the processing time for updating pricing data from 80 days to five minutes and Chevron has used ERP to decrease its annual purchasing cost by 15%.

E-business stands for "electronic business," which involves communications and doing business electronically through the Internet. E-business is defined as "the use of electronically enabled communication networks that allow business enterprises to transmit and receive information". It can significantly improve business performance by strengthening the linkages in the value chain between businesses (B2B) and consumers (B2C). Besides increasing efficiency in selling, marketing and purchasing, e-business achieves effectiveness through improved customer service, reduced costs and streamlined business processes. Furthermore, e-business creates a strategic, customer-focused business environment for shared business improvements, mutual benefits and joint rewards. Companies use the Internet to implement customer-relation-management (CRM) and supply-chain-management (SCM) capabilities, which enable them to link their operations seamlessly with customers and suppliers.

E-Business by a Lead Oil Company

An Oil and Gas Company with 40% growth and $70 million in annual sales revenue, sells its products through 150 distributors nationwide as well as general stores and retail outlets. By using Oracle's ERP system and e-business platform, the salespersons can track sales and promotions through the Internet, and are provided assistance and suggestions to enhance their performance. The salespersons and distributors have access to commission reports, and they can track and adjust sales orders. Through consolidating its financial, compensation, sales and depletion data into a single report, prevents out-of-stock and partial shipments. The forecasted need for 50% more labor force to handle customer service issues in the past was eradicated by integrating ERP system with e-business (Oracle, 2005: http://www.simplyhired.com/job-id/igh6uy76sr/oracle-erp-jobs/). By definitions and by their respective functions, traditional ERP systems take care of internal value chain (i.e., within a company) whereas e-businesses establish the value chain across the market and the industries. More and more companies construct their systems' architectures by integrating ERP systems with e-business. They use Web-based interface (corporate portals) with outside entities plus add-on modules such as CRM, SCM, etc. in the integration.

Future Trends

The rapid growth of the Internet will lead to a large increase in the number of ERP users. Companies are eliminating disintegrated legacy systems by replacing them with Web-enabled, integrated ERP systems. These integrated systems become part of the overall business strategy that connects an enterprise with its suppliers and customers, and transforms the entire value chain. Companies that intend to move into a net economy are beginning to emerge and focus on multi-enterprise systems integration and growth. They are forming strategic partnerships with major e-business infrastructure providers (Sun, IBM and Microsoft) to continuously integrate their ERP systems for reaching the internal and external performance target. Major ERP vendors (Oracle, SAP, BAAN, JD Edwards and are constantly updating and releasing integrated ERP/e-business suites to support an open, collaborative and competitive business environment:

- The major ERP vendors will continue to build compatible and adaptable ERP components and develop extended ERP solutions designed to address the latest market demands. For example, Oracle's Release 11 is a business application suite that consists of Supply Chain Management, Order Management and new self-service software modules. It is tied to a Customer Relationship Management application. The whole software suite works seamlessly with one another to handle everything from customer service on one end to relationship with suppliers on the other. It is all registered to run on the Web. Based on the company's vision, anyone from giant corporations to tiny dotcoms can buy a single package from Oracle to run their e-business, rather than buying software from a host of competitors and trying to stitch it all together (Outsourcing-erp.com). If it works, it will move computing from desktop PCs to huge Internet servers that run anything from Web sites to complex corporate networks. Oracle's skills and technologies are taking the center stage. JD Edwards offers its One World Software as a host service over networks. This application service is designed to be easier to deploy and adapt. It will overcome the inflexibility of the ERP system on its implementation time.
- With the convergence of the Internet and wireless technology, users can access Web-enabled ERP systems anytime and anywhere through the use of newer and easier-to-use devices, such as personal digital assistants, smart phones, in-devices and biometric tools. For example, an accounting

manager who is out of town will leverage his company's ERP with a personal digital assistant to review financial reports and give directions to his subordinates. He/she can log on to the system using his/her fingerprint or voice.

- The use of XML in B2B communications will enable a host of new relationships between companies, vendors, suppliers and customers. Exporting data from application suites and developer tools using XML will become a standardized feature. For example, IBM translates generic XML information into device-specific formats that can be used on wireless devices.
- Outsourcers, ERP vendors and e-business infrastructure providers' alliance together to provide more robust, scalable and compatible e-business platforms for the companies. PriceWaterhouseCoopers has built a strategic relationship with the Sun-Netscape Alliance (an alliance of Sun and AOL) to provide technology and services that enable companies to build business-critical e-business solutions that leverage investments in SAP R/3. Netscape Application Server for R/3 has provided a reliable infrastructure for Web solution (iPlanet) that allows customers to access PriceWaterhouseCoopers' SAP system in a secure manner.
- The future trend of ERP outsourcing is to explore into the applications service market. By the year 2007, offering ERP service over the Web will be a $2 billion business, as more than a dozen Application Service Providers (ASPs) are moving into the market. ASPs take ERP and non-ERP applications from multiple vendors and put them together into a service. Rather than selling their creations in house to corporate customers, they make their products available over the Web on a lease or rental basis. In addition, some mid-market companies are seeking to outsource their non-core business processes, such as payroll and employee benefit administration. According to a recent survey, 75 to 80% of a company's financial cost is tied up in labor or labor support. As stated by Marion (2005), any realistic attempt to reduce or manage costs in the finance and administration area has to focus not only on improved technology, but also on labor issues—the high costs of labor and the shortage of skilled labor.

Conclusions

The first and foremost driver is the constant pressure to improve processes and reduce costs to increase shareholder value. In addition to cost pressures, recent volatility in prices has pushed for strong emphasis on trading and risk management agility. A second important driver is the need to truly operate as a seamless regional or global enterprise in line with merger/acquisition and expansion plans. A third driver is the need to satisfy the more demanding needs of third parties/customers along the value chain—satisfying environment and regulatory concerns. True collaboration among internal and external entities is necessary to operate effectively in all aspects of the business.

E-business initiatives with the most immediate impact on process efficiency and cost reductions are those related to value chain integration. B-2-B initiatives, such as utilizing the Internet as a collaboration medium and participating serves in e-market-places for improving the price discovery and purchasing processes. Infomediaries portals and corporate web sites are important for public relations but have less of impacts on the bottom line. In the downstream arena, B2C initiatives are necessary to stay on par with the competition. B2C allows maximizing the use of additional sale, contact and distribution channels where brand recognition and relationships with the customer are imperative. Finally, B2E initiatives for promoting knowledge management across the enterprise boundaries can help to meet employee needs and has the potential to garner competitive advantage at all levels of the organization.

Oil and Gas companies must consider their B2B strategies carefully. Companies that do not join E-Markets may see their market power decline as networks enable consolidation of other players' influence. The choice which companies need to make early on is between being an initial sponsor of an E-Market and joining an existing E-Market. The "do nothing" option is unlikely to be viable in the long run. Companies, which are initial participants of an E-Market, have the possibility of significant benefit from the combination of greater market efficiency and profit on their investment.

As for E-business strategies in general, each company is different and has its own specific needs, issues, and goals. The specific differences must be considered carefully when outlining a corporate E-business strategy in light of company drivers and market conditions. E-business is not a passing fad, E-business strategies must be considered rapidly, carefully and coherently. Each company's decisions in regards to e-business will be different—but each company should ask all the questions necessary to respond to the challenges of e-business, to utilize e-business to its best advantage and to not be out performed by the competition. The power of the internet has proven too significantly contribute to the business strategies of any organization and all necessary questions must be asked to put a customized yet realistic e-business strategy into place as rapidly as possible. The strategy should be coherent and seamlessly integrate across an enterprises organizations, operation, technology infrastructures and geographies—be it in the America, the Middle East, the North Sea or Asia.

The fundamental benefits of E-business still hold true and especially apply to Oil and Gas Company E-business strategies. These fundamentals include:

- improvement of processes/reduction in associated costs,
- reducing cycle time/go to market for new products,
- more efficient communications in real time with internal and external groups,
- disintermediation of third parties in the supplier to end customer chain,
- ability to reach new markets more effectively and efficiently,
- Increase of customer loyalty due to desires for auto service and promoting collaboration amongst industry players and participants.

REFERENCES

Bartel, Andrews (2007), The Forrester Wave™: procurement Solutions, Q2 2007, The Forrester Wave™.

Braganza, A. *Enterprise integration: Creating competitive capabilities,* Integrated Manufacturing Systems.

Buckhout, S., Frey, E. and Nemec, J., Jr. Making ERP succeed: Turning fear into promise. *IEEE Engineering Management Review.*

Callaway, E. (2000), *Enterprise Resource Planning—Integrating Application and Business Processes Across the Enterprise.* Computer Technology Research Corporation.

Chartwell, Inc. (2000), *Chat/well's Guide to e-commerce in the Energy Industry.* Atlanta, Ga.: Chartwell.

Chason, I., E-marketing Strategy, McGraw-Hill Professional Book Group, Maidenhead, Berkshire, UK.

Chris Skrebowski (2002), Petroleum Review, Energy Institute, *Is 'Sweating the Asset' the right business strategy?*

Chris Skrebowski (2004), Petroleum Review, Energy Institute, *Business Management IT.*

Corporate portals and e-business integration: A managers Guides. Davydov, M.M. McGraw-Hill Professional Book Group.

Cranfield MSc Thesis, *Electronic Marketplaces: Supplier Perspectives of Participation and Implementation,* Cranfield Univeristy, 2000.

Doing E-business: Strategies for thriving in an electronic market place—page 226 by David Taylor, Alyse D. Terhune.

E-business 2.0: Roadmap for Success—page 317 by Ravi Kalakota, Marcia Robinson

E-business opportunities in the petroleum industry by Yankee Group

Energy Management Handbook, page 590 by C. Turner Wayne, Wayne C Turner

Erlikh, L. (2000), Leveraging Legacy System Dollars for e-business. *IT Professional.*

Fellenstein, C. and Wood, R. (2000), *Exploring E-Commerce, Global E-Business, and E-Societies.* Prentice Hall.

Fingar, P., Kumar, H. and Tarun, S. (2000), *Enterprise E-Commerce: The Software Component Breakthrough for Business-to-Business Commerce.* Meghan-Kiffer Press.

Global Electronic Business Research: Opportunities and Directions—page 287 by Nabeel A.Y. Al-Qirim

Hsieh, C., Yang, H. & Lin, B., *Roles of knowledge management in online process.* Industrial management and data systems.

IBM (1999), *Beyond ERP: Achieving Greater Return on ERP Investments.*

IBM Tivoli Access Manager for e-business Release Notes-Version 4.1: http://publib.boulder.ibm.com/tividd/td/ITAME/SC32-1130-00/en_US/PDF/SC32-1130-00.pdf

iPlanet (2000), *Sun-Netscape Alliance's Vision for Net Economy Integration Amasses Global Support from Industry Leaders, Customers.*

Iyer, G. *Strategic decision making in industrial procurement: implications for buying decisions approaches and buyer-seller relationships.* Journal of business and Industrial Marketing.

Kalakota. R. and Robinson, M., *E-business: Roadmap for Success.*

Kosiur, D., Understanding electronic commerce. Microsoft Press.

Morten Sven Johannessen, Statoil;mosvejo@statoil.com, (2002), StatOil: e-Business in an international oil company: Presentation in a WTO Seminar on "e-Business" at Geneva on 22.4.2004.

New York Times (2008), Business to-Business: One Oil Company (BP) takes a big dip, Sept 21, 2008.

Norris, G., Hurley, J.R., Hartley, K.M., Dunleavy, J.R., and Balls, J.D. (2000), *E-Business and*

ERP-Transforming the Enterprise. PriceWatehouseCoopers.

Oracle, 2005: http://www.simplyhired.com/job-id/igh6uy76sr/oracle-erp-jobs/

Outsourcing-erp.com. (2000), *Big ERP Solutions for Mid-Market Companies.*

Philip E. Mihimester, Michael McKelvey (2000), The E-Business Revolution in Energy Services: http://aceepr.org/publications/eup_pub/E_business.

PriceWaterhouseCoopers (1999), E-Business Technology Forecast.

Strategies for Generating E-business Returns on Investment—page 167 edited by Namchul Shin.

Sun Microsystems, 2004: http://www.sun.com/solutions/documents/solution-sheets/en_egas_ff.xml

The New Economy of Oil: Impacts on Business, Geopolitics and Society, page 88 by John V Mitchell. Norman Selly.

Wilson, T. (1999), Oracle suite integrates ERP, e-business apps, *InternetWeek,*

Wilson, T. (2000), Handing off the burden, *InternetWeek,* January, 13 (Masterfile) on World Wide Web.

Websites

www.sap.com/industries/ oil-gas/pdf/oilandgas_overview.pdf

www.idea-group.com/downloads/excerpts/IRM1931777063.pdf

www.edms.com.my/pdf/c_oil.pdf

www.managingautomation.com/maonline/directory/browse/CRMModulesforERP-144?page=6

www.icma.com/info/f2b1201.htm

www.mindbranch.com/products/R388-1249.html

committees.api.org/business/ pidx/docs/PIDX_Europe_flier_final0205.pdf

www.ibm.com/industries/chemicalspetroleum/doc/content/bin/Linux_in_Petroleum.pdf

www.sun.com/products-n-solutions/ markets/features/egasarchitecture.pdf

www-03.ibm.com/industries/chemicalspetroleum/doc/content/bin/GSE.pdf

committees.api.org/business/pidx/docs/bulletinsandwhitepapers/ThePetroleumIndustryandXML.pdf

www.ofs-portal.com/NR/rdonlyres/74FE7328-974B-4B00-8F020E8C977B6314/0/OFSP_EnergyNetwork_04232002.pdf

www.gilat.com/post/GigaXtand.pdf

www.sap.com/industries/oil-gas/pdf/Bharat_Petroleum.pdf

www.worldenergy.org/wecgeis/publications/default/tech_papers/18th_Congress/downloads/rt/rt8/rt8_hodges.pdf

www.cisco.com/web/about/ac79/docs/wp/Santos_CS_1104.pdf

www.scala.net/downloads/whitepapers/ iscala_whitepaper_0205.pdf

csrc.lse.ac.uk/asp/aspecis/20010035.pdf

www.energyinst.org.uk/index.cfm?PageID=650

www.wpc2002.com/preindexview.htm-editionsectionid=61&user=reader.htm

www.icfconsultancy/papers/e-businessrevolution.pdf

http://aceepr.org/publications/eup_pub/E_business.pdf

http://www.eei.org/magazine/editorial_content/nonav_stories/2000-09-01-b2b.htm

http://www.oracle.com/corporate/analyst/reports/ent_apps/erp/forrester-wave-eprocurement-q2-2007.pdf

http://query.nytimes.com/gst/fullpage.html?res=9C06EEDF133EF93BA25757C0A9679C8B63&sec=&spon=&pagewanted=all

Index

A

A.T. Kearney Report:
  Findings of, 347
Abu Dhabi National Oil Company (ADNOC) 209
Accounting Concepts:
  The Basic Elements, 364
Accounting for International Operations, 396
Accounting Methods
  Historical Development of, 376
Accounting Systems:
  Comparison of, 370
Accounting Treatment of these Costs under SE Compared to FC, 375
Accounts:
  Payable, 426
  Receivable, 426
Acreage Valuation, 143
Administrative Pricing Mechanism (APM) 281, 301
Advanced Recycle Technologies, 247
Africa, 476
Agencies According Approval, 162
Ancillary Services, 343
Asia's Natural Gas Supply and Demand, 316
Asian Gas Market Overview, 316
Asian Tiger Export Demand Driven Adjustment to Oil-Shock, 49
Asset Life-cycle, 123
  Importance of Phases, Objectives and Decisions in, 124
Asset Management:
  Key Tools used in, 125
  Knowledge Management Perspective of, 135
  Role of Technology in, 135
  Scope of, 119
  Objectives, 120
    What are Asset Management Objectives?, 120
    Why are they Important?, 120
    Why must we Balance Internal and External Factors in Setting Objectives?, 120
    What are the Consequences of not Setting Asset Management Objectives?, 121
  Processes, 122
  Preparation of, Plans, 122
Association Surface Equipment, 23
Atmospheric Distillation, 237
Auto-Fuel, 427
  Policy, 269

B

Backward and Forward Integration, 290
Barauni Refinery, IOCL, 263
Bharat Petroleum Corporation Ltd. (BPCL), 266
Bill of Lading, 194
Bombay High (BH), 275
Bongaigaon Refinery & Petrochemicals Ltd. (BRPL), 30, 267
Book Value and Book Value Multiple, 144
Book Value Multiples, 149
Book Value, Sec Value and Market Value of Reserves, 369
Booz Allen Performance Wheel, 31
BP:
  at a Glance, 513
BPCL's Additional Value Propositions, 353
Brand and Product:
  Basic Difference Between, 340
Brand Building Processes, 348
Brand Name, Brand Personality and Brand Image
  Differences amongst, 340
Brand Personality and Brand Image:
  Importance of, 339
Build the Offer, 351
Building the Brand Equity, 340
Bulk Terminal Management, 426
Business Models/Benefits, 511
Business Unit:
  Decision-making by the, 127

C

Cairn India Initiative in Rajasthan-Gujarat Pipeline, 159
Calculated Risk Profile of Portfolio with Different Proportions of Prospects A and B, 134
Calculation:
  Bases of, 378
Capacity Issues, 60
Capital Resources and Liquidity, 390
Carbon Emissions Information, 45
Cash-Flow and Operating Profit Multiples, 144

Cash-Flow Multiple, 142, 149
Catalysts, 254
Catalytic Reforming:
Process, 256
Reactions in, 244
Cauvery Basin Refinery-CPCL, 267
CDU Process Objective, 238
Ceiling Test, 369
Central Asia:
Geopolitics of Oil in the, 475
Challenge: Manage e-business Growth, 516
Changing Patterns of Demand and Consumption, 234
Chemical Methods, 102
Chennai Petroleum Corporation Ltd. (CPCL), 28
Chicago Board of Trade (CBOT) 326
Chicago Mercantile Exchange (CME), 325, 326
China's Middle-East Strategy, 481
Clearances Required, 162
CNG Marketing, 199
Coal Production and Consumption in India, 43
Coal Supply, 54
Coal, 43
Coal-Bed Methane, 116
Combined-Cycle Gas Turbine (CCGT), 171
Commodity Futures and Options, 323
Commodity Futures Exchanges, 325
Commodity Futures Trading Commission (CFTC) 327
Commodity vs. Brand Retailing, 338
Company Start-up Results under FC&SE Accounting, 371
Comparable Sales, 145
Comparing Financial Statements, 404
Comparison of Forward and Futures Contracts, 325
Comparison of IEO2007 and IEA World Energy:
Consumption Growth Rates, 36
by Fuel, 36, 37
Comparison of the Real Demand Growth Trend Rate and Official Forecasts, 52
Competitive Market Position, 58
Components of Gross Refining Margin, 394
Components of Producer Price, 414
Components of the Gross Refining Margin and Average Refined Product Revenues for FRS Companies, 394
Computer Assisted Exploration, 94
Consumer Experience-based Differentiation, 356
Consumer Price, 414, 415
Consumer Segmentation Pattern of US Petroleum Buyers, 349
Contour Maps, 100
Contracts and Markets, 323
Contractual Systems, 397
Control Functions, 260
Control of Parameters, 261
Convenience Stores, 343
Conventional Testing, 20
Conversion for Upgradation of Product Quality, 242
Conversion Process, 242
Conversion: Cracking and Rearranging Molecules to Add Value, 205
Cores, 98
Corrosion Monitoring, 176
Cost Depletion and Percentage Depletion, 372
Cost of Service, 148
Cost Recovery, 400
Country Risk Factor, 150
Critical Success Factors, 508
Cross-Border Pipelines:
Future Role of, 169
Problems of, 172
Size of Gas Reserves, 170
Problems of Negotiating Export Contracts, 170
Security of Supply, 170
Problems of Long-distance Transportation, 171
Cross-sectional view of LNG Ship's Hull and Containment System, 195
Crude and Product Prices:
Prevailing in International Market, 287
Crude Benchmark, 214
Crude Costs:
Elements of, 276-277
Crude Distilation Unit (CDU), 285
Process Schematic, 239
Crude Freight Cost, 278
Crude Oil and Operating Costs:
Break-up of, 277
Crude Oil, 186, 210, 211, 217, 233
is a Composite Product, 203
is Quality-Specific, 204
How is converted in the Refinery Process?, 204
and Gas Shipping, 187
as an Input Cost to Refiners, 388
Desalting System, 13
Evaluation, 215
Exchanges, 386
Imports from Middle-East 280
other Countries, 280
Marketing, 296
of Indian Origin, 228
Pipelines in India, 275
Pricing and Evaluation, 208
Pricing, 387
Quality, 18
Reserves, 108
Storage, 21
Economics of, 203
Types of, according to the U.S. Environmental Protection Agency, 5

Value of, 215
Price of, 215
50-year Scenario and Maximum Sustainable Capacity, 465
Crude Processing Unit (CDU) 285
Crude:
Landed Cost of, 216
C-Store Purchases/Price Book, 426
Current Price Build-up of Domestic Gas, 416

D

Decision Check Points and Decision Criteria, 124
Strategic Fit, 124
Economic Fit, 125
Work Quality, 125
Technology, 125
Reality Check, 125
Financial Considerations, 125
Risks, 125
Deferred Taxes and the Cost of Capital, 148
Deisopentanizer, 247
Demand for Commercial Energy for Final Consumption, 56
Demand Profile, 309
Demand Shock can Trigger Price Hike, 51
Demand-Driven Revenue Curve, 348
Demographic Rate of Oil Demand 50
Depleting Global Reserves, 58
Depreciation, Depletion and Amortization, 372
Deregulation Overview of Petro-retail Business, 346
Design Optimization, 161
Developing Strategic Assets, 451
Developing World Energy Use, 467
Digboi Refinery, 265
Diplomacy over Oil-bids with Iran and Pakistan, 483
Discount Rate Components, 140
Discounted Cash Flow (DCF), 141
Analysis, 139
Domestic Hydrocarbon Economic Environment, 436
Domestic Price Structure of Natural Gas, 414
Downstream Processing, 17
Downstream Sector Impact and E-business Opportunities, 502
Downward Pressure on LNG Prices:
A Feature of the Next Decade?, 318
Drill Mud Circulation System, 85
Drill Stem Test (DST), 20, 99
Drill:
Preparing to, 83
Drilling Costs, 378
Development, 380
Drilling for Oil, 82
Drilling Operation, 86
Drivers of Change, 29
Drivers of High Refining Margin, 216
Dry Natural Gas Production and Consumption in India, 43
Dry Trade, 191
Duplication and Economies of Scale, 146

E

E-business :
Applications across the Value Chain, 497
Applications used by Oil Giants, 513
Applications in Oil and Natural Gas Industries, 492
by a Lead Oil Company, 519
ERP and, 519
in Oil and Gas, 500
Emerging Technology Related, 494
Hurdles for Oil and Gas Suppliers and Service Providers are, 513
Potential Use of, 501
Principles of, 492
The Impact on Both Upstream and Down Stream Industries, 432
Economic Consequences, 333
Effort/Impact Matrix, 423
Electric Logs, 99
Electrical Dehydration, 13
Electrical Energy Supply, 56
Electricity Generation and Consumption in India, 44
Electricity, 43
Electronic Trading, 327, 435
E-Market Outlook, 506
E-Markets, 504
Emulsion and Contaminants:
Treatment of, 13
Energy and Hydrocarbon Loss, 292
Energy Distribution between Developed and Developing Countries, 53, 54
Energy Dominates Growth Debate in South Africa, 473
Energy Futures Contracts Trading, 322
Energy Loss:
Reduction in, 292
Energy Needs of Growing Indian Economy, 56
Energy Options Contracts Trading, 322
Energy Savings Measure, 359
Energy Sector:
Expenditure towards, 57
Energy Security Environment:
in NAFTA Region, 484
Energy Supply Scenario, 54
Enhanced Oil Recovery (EOR), 101
Enhancing Oil and Gas Production, 114
Environmental Issues, 435
EOR Production by Country, 102
EOR/IOR:
Artificial Lift, 21

Equivalent Distillation Capacity (EDC), 291
EU Energy Supply:
Geopolitics of, 474
Evaluation Methodology, 216
Evolving New Industrial Architecture, 452
Existing Refineries:
Expansion of, 268
Exploration and Development:
Indian Scene, 90
Exploration and Production Sector, 70, 79
Exploration Techniques for Petroleum, 96
Exploratory Drilling Costs, 379
Exploring Alternative Fuels, 435
External Factors, 393
External trends that push E-Trading, 507

F

Factors Affecting Asset Value, 123
Fear of Shortage, 59
Feed Naphtha Quality and Pre-treatment, 243
Final Energy Consumption:
Projected Demand of, 56
Final Product Pattern, 287
Financial Accounting Issues, 403
Financial Accounting vs. Contract Accounting, 403
Financial and Accounting Systems for Oil and Natural Gas, 363
Financial Modules, 425
Financial Statements, 375
Finding Costs Ratios, 406
Finding Oil:
Increasing Role of Technology in, 91
First Major Oil-Shock, 469
Fixation of Retention Price per ton of Crude 284
Fluid Catalytic Cracking Unit, 250
Fluid Separation and Treatment, 12, 14
Fluidic Catalytic Cracking Process (FCC), 248
Schematic diagram of, 249
Food Services, 343
Foreign Direct Investment, 328
Foreign Exchange Laws, 151
Foreign Oil and Gas Reserves:
Valuation of, 150
Foreign Operations, 150
Formation Evaluation, 101
Formula for Unit of Production Method, 373
Formula Price, 213
Fossil Fuel-related CO_2 Emissions in India, 45
Fossil Fuels, 45
Fractionation Section, 251
Franchising Models in the Petroleum Industry, 335
Freight Market, 193
Fuel-based Differentiation, 351
Full-cost Accounting, 370, 382
Full-Cost Accounting:
Introduction to, 378
Full-Cost and Successful Efforts Accounting, 368
Full-Cost Overview, 379
Furnace Oil (FO) 200
Future Outlook, 89
Future Supply vs. Demand of Conventional Oil, 57
Future Trends, 520
Future Vision and Strategy, 114
Futures and Options Contracts and Markets, 321

G

Gap Analysis, 421
Gas Authority of India Ltd (GAIL) 201, 302
All India Region-wise and Sector-wise Gas Supply by, 65
Gas Costs:
Increase in, 418
Gas Measurement and Sale, 384
Gas Pipeline Accounting, 409
Gas Pool Account, 415
Gas Production by Region, 463
Gas Purchase from JVCs, 414
Gas Sale Agreement (GSA) 194
Gas Station Canopy, 358
Gas Well, 23
Gases, 233
Gas-to-Liquid (GTL) 58
General Regulations, 409
Generally Accepted Accounting Principles, 363
Generic Process of Oil Refining-Schematic 237
Genesis and Technology Options of Oil
Exploration, 1
Genesis, 1
Reserves and Resources, 1
Geochemical Surveys, 100
Geologic Maps, 100
Geophysical Surveys, 99
Geo-Politics and Oil, 62
Geo-Politics of Oil Trading: Scanning the Global Business Scene, 459
Geopolitics: The Great Unknown, 468
Global and Regional LNG Supplies Continue to Expand, 317
Global Economy Growth is Vital for Future Oil Production, 49
Global Energy Demand Outlook, 39
Global Energy Demand
IEA Projections of, 38
Perspective, 38
Global Energy in Perspective, 459
Global Energy Supply, 39
Demand Scenario, 39
Global Facet of Indian Oil Industry, 438
Global Oil Consumption Pattern:
Country Profile in, 431
Global Oil Consumption, 431
Global Oil Production, 430
Goldman Sachs Picks, 104

Governance Issues, 162
Government Involvement in Operations, 398
Government Participation, 400
Gross Product Worth (GPW), 216, 283
Gross Refinery Margin (GRM), 216
Gross Refining Margin, 393
Growth in LPG Marketing in India, 311
Guidelines for Laying Petroleum Product Pipelines, 269
Guwahati Refinery, 263

H

Haldia Refinery, 265
Handling at Ports, 187
Hexorb, 248
Higher Oil Prices Change vs. Future Demand Trends, 51
Historic Oil Production, 27
Historic Refining Capacity, 28
Historical Cost Accounting Methods, 373
Historical Development of Accounting Standards on Deferred Tax, 377
How Oil Shapes Foreign Policy?, 485
How to Create Product/brand Differentiation in c-Store Businesses, 354
How will this affect StatOil business?, 515
Human Resource Development, 290
Hydrate:
  Prevention of, 15
Hydro, 46
Hydrocarbon Sector:
  Objectives for the, 69
Hydrocarbon Vision-2025, 69
Hydrocarbon-Energy Value-chain, 494
Hydro-Cracking Unit:
  Schematic Presentation of a, 255
Hydrocracking, 252
Hydro-Power Supply, 56

I

IEO, 62
Import Through Pipelines:
  pros and cons, 169, 201
Importance of Oil & Gas for National Economy, 438
Imports/Exports of Crude Oil and Petroleum Products, 307
Improved Oil Recovery/Enhanced Oil Recovery Projects, 115
Independents, 443
India Joins the Scramble for Oil and Natural Gas, 482
India Petroleum Industry:
  Commodity Balance Scenario of, 183
India:
  Availability and Utilization of Natural Gas in, 63
  Dependence on Crude in the Refining Industry, 273
  Growth of Franchisee-based Petro-Retail Market in, 335
  Investment and Technical Specifications of Major Crude-Oil and Petroleum Products Pipelines in, 174
  Marketing of Transportation Fuels in, 200
  Natural Gas Pipelines in, 196
  Performance of Existing Natural Gas Pipelines in, 197
  Pipelines and their Use Pattern in, 197
  Petroleum Pipelines under Operation in, 166
  Break-up of Existing Petroleum Products Pipeline in, 168
  Pipeline Network in, 276
  Refineries in. 271
  State and Basin-wise Oil and Gas Fields in, 106
  State-wise Gross and Net Production of Natural Gas in, 106
  Overview of Oil and Gas Sector, 40
  Overall Production, Consumption and
  Projected Demand of Energy, 40
  Policy Direction for, 227
  Primary Energy Requirements Scenario, 42
  TPEP and TPEC, 41
  The Petroleum Shopper in, 349
India's Energy Security Pact with Russia, 483
India's OPEC Policy, 225
India's Position in Global Primary Energy Consumption, 53
Indian Downstream Major, 28
Indian Energy Scenario, 53
Indian Experience in Petro-Retailing, 344
Indian Oil and Gas Economy:
  Structure of, 436
Indian Oil and Gas Sector:
  Industry Report, 298
  Mergers and Consolidation in, 442
Indian Oil Corporation Limited (IOCL), 28, 266
Indian Oil Industries:
  Evolving Phases in, 455
  in a Growing Economy, 437
  Its Global Facet, 455
  Liberalization in, 272
Indian Oil's Initiatives, 356
Indian Pipeline Systems Development:
  Perspectives in, 159
Indian Refineries:
  Areas of Action for, 227
Indian Tonnage, 190
Individual Refinery:
  How to Run an, 293
Industry-wise Off-take of Natural Gas in India, 310
Initial Responses, 445
Installed Capacity and Refinery Crude Throughputs, 264
Installed Electricity Generation Capacity in India, 44

Integrated Transport Operation, 184
Integration Across Multiple Players Outside the Core Value Chain, 498
Interconnectivity and Convergence of an Oil and Gas Service Station, 503
Internal Factors, 393
Internal Rate of Return/Return on Investment, 420
Internal Trends that Push E-Trading, 507
International Accounting Standards, 403
International Energy Agency (IEA), 32
 Role of, 486
International Energy Outlook, 38
International Gas Prices of Representative Countries, 419
International Hydrocarbon Economic Environment, 430
International Petroleum Exchange (IPE), 5
Iraq Episode, 472
ISI-Developed Integrated Oil and Gas Accounting Software, 385
Isomerization Process:
 Objective, 245
 Schematic Diagram of, 246

J

Joint Operating Agreements, 402
Joint Venture Companies (JVCs) 329

K

Kelkar Committee on Price Structure and Pricing Policy, 411
Key Terms:
 Definition of, 283
Know your Consumer, 347
Knowledge Management (KM) 154
Kochi Refineries Limited (KRL), 267
Koyali Refinery-IOCL, 263
Kuwait Petroleum Corporation (KPC) 209

L

Light Gasoline, 233
Linked Retailing, 343
Liquefied Natural Gas (LNG), 67, 169, 201, 302
 Imports to India, 67
 Gas Pricing, 68
Liquefied Petroleum Gas (LPG), 17, 200, 205
Liquid Level Controller (LLC) 14
LNG Carriage Cost:
 Indian Flag vs. Foreign Flag, 314
LNG Price, 418
 Benchmarking of, 419
LNG Trade:
 Profile of 196
 in 2002 in Major Destination Countries, 196
LNG Transportation Policy of GOI, 313-14
LNG Value-chain, 496
Local Distribution Companies (LDC) 305
London Clearing House (LCH) 327
Long-term Outlook, 62
Losers are VAC's, 506
LPG Import Infrastructure, 198
LPG Marketing by Public Sector Oil Marketing Companies (OMCs), 303
LPG Pipeline throughput, 199
LPG Transportation by Road and Rail, 198
Lube Oil Manufacture, 256

M

Main Reactions, 246
Mainline Maintenance, 176
Major Oilfield-wise Indian Crude oil Production, 228
Management and Evaluation of Upstream Assets, 119
Manali Refinery:
 Chennai Petroleum Corporation Ltd. (CPCL), 266
Mangalore Refineries and Petrochemical Ltd. (MRPL) 201, 268
Maps and Cross-Sections, 100
Market Determined Pricing Mechanism (MDPM), 281
Market Intelligence (MI), 335
Market Models, 508
Market Segments and Transportation Legs, 199
Market Share and Infrastructure, 271
Market Trends, 509
Marketing of Mini-LPG Cylinders by OMCs, 303
Marketing of Petroleum Products by Oil Companies, 310
Marketing of Transportation Fuels, 304
Master Limited Partnerships, 143
Mathura Refinery, 265
Mega Mergers:
 A New Era for the Petroleum Industry, 447
Meta-Market: A Portfolio of E-Markets, 504
Methods of Computation, 377
 The Deferral Method, 377
 The Liability Method, 378
Middle Distillates, 234
Middle East: Expansions at Qatar, Abu Dhabi, and Oman Greenfield Project in Yemen, 318
Middle-East in the Global Oil Balance, 471
Ministry of Petroleum and Natural Gas (MOP&NG) 69
Model of E-business, 499
Model Production Sharing Contract (MPSC), 73
Modes of Transportation, 185
Mud Circulation in the Hole, 85
Mumbai Refinery (HPCL), 266

N

Naphtha Hydro Treatment:
 Chemistry of, 243
Naphtha, 233
National Futures Association (NFA), 327
National Oil Companies (NOCs), 73, 209

Creation of, 25
Evolution of, 25
Development of, in Second Half of 12th Century, 26
Natural Gas Allocation and Supply Scenario, 64
Natural Gas Futures Market:
A Case Study, 329
Natural Gas in Asia's Energy Supply Chain:
Importance of, 316
Natural Gas Marketing, 302
Natural Gas Processing, 391
Natural Gas Resources:
Developing, 466
Natural Gas Supply, 55
Natural Gas through Transnational Pipelines:
Import of, 65
Iran-Pakistan-India (IPI) Pipeline Project, 65
Myanmar-Bangladesh-India Gas Pipeline Project, 66
Turkmenistan-Afghanistan-Pakistan (TAP) Pipeline, 67
Natural Gas Trading:
Strategy for Petroleum and, 296
Natural Gas Treatment, 15
Natural Gas, 42, 71
Dehydration of, 15
Geopolitics of, 488
Global Scenario in, 63
Objectives, 71
The Fuel of the 21st Century, 23
Navigating the Natural Gas Futures Market, 330
Nelson Complexity Indices, 145
Net Back Margin
Need and Importance of, 288
Net Back Margin, 283
Net Back Margin:
Methodology of Evaluation of, 284
Net Back Value, 284
Net Margin, 394
New Competitive Forces, 445
New Drivers of Competitive Advantage, 448, 450
New Exploration Licensing Policy (NELP), 64, 114, 115
The Backdrop, 73
Why?, 73
Salient Achievement under, 74
New Industrial Countries (NICs) 49
New Pipeline Project Implementation, 177
New Retail Outlet:
Establishing a, 334
New York Mercantile Exchange (NYMEX) 5, 325
Next-Generation Services, 512
No Income Taxes or G&A Costs Considered, 372
Non-conventional Renewable, 46
Non-Fossil Fuels, 46
North America, 477
Nuclear Power Supply, 56
Nuclear, 46
Numaligarh Refinery Limited, 267
Number of Wells and Metreage Drilled, 109

O

Ocean Transportation, 186
Off-shore Drilling Operations, 81
Offshore Seismic Exploration, 93
Offshore Terminals, 176
Oil & Gas Economy:
Structure of, 443
Oil & Gas in Meeting Energy Requirement, 438
Oil & Natural Gas Corporation (ONGC), 64, 105, 154, 201, 304
Oil and Gas Demand Supply Scenario, 114
Oil and Gas Economy:
Trends of, 443, 452
Globalization, 453
Economic Development, 453
Factors that Shape Decisions of Sellers and Buyers, 454
Structure of, 443
Oil and Gas from Abroad, 116
Oil and Gas Industry:
Brief History of, 6
Oil and Gas Properties, 136
Oil and Gas Revenue: A Case of ATP Oil and Gas Corporation, 388
Oil and Gas
Allocation of, 392
Alternate Sources of, 116
E-Markets in, 505
E-Trading in, 507
Measurement and Sale of, 384
Measurement of, 15
Value-Chain Overview, 495
Well Operating Costs, 139
Oil and Natural Gas Accounting:
Broad Principles, 373
Oil and Natural Gas:
Contribution of, 35
Exploration, Drilling and Production, 77
Geo-Politics of, 473
Global Energy Scene, 35
Introduction to, 1
Transportation of, 179
Supply Plan Management in Oil Industry, 181
Transportation of Petroleum Products, 183
Oil Companies:
A Brief History of, 24
Oil Coordination Committee (OCC), 182, 282
Oil Cost Review Committee (OCRC) 283
Oil Counter-shock, 470
Oil Demand is Driven by Higher Prices: Demand Shock, 50

Oil Demand Shock and World Oil Price Trend, 47
Oil Dependence and National Security, 465
Oil India Ltd (OIL) 201
Oil Industrial Structure in India, 346
Oil Industry Development Board (OIDB) 70
Oil Industry Supply Chain Management, 181
Oil Industry, Reform in:
A Historical Perspective, 455
Oil Industry:
Historical Perspective in Indian Context, 104
New Paradigm in, 30
Structure, 346
Oil Majors, 443
Oil Market Report 51
Oil Marketing Companies (OMCs) 300-303
Oil Measurement and Sale, 384
Oil Prices:
Demographic Demand and, 47
History of, 8
The Real Impact of Higher, 48
Oil Production:
History of, 3, 27
Target and Strategy for, 113
Oil Rig:
Anatomy of, 84
Oil Securities for India: Issues and Concerns, 441
Oil Seeps, 98
Oil Shocks on Demographic Demand:
Impact of, 48
Oil Supply Security, 63
Oil Trade:
BP Amoco Experience in E-Business in, 517
The Balancing Flow, 217
Oil:
Classification of, 5
Future of, 103, 432
Origin of, 2
*Biogenic Theory, 2
*Abiogenic Theory of Origin of Oil, 3
Online Inspection, 177
Onshore Seismic Exploration, 93
OPEC Crude Oil Production vs. Quota, 224
OPEC Policy:
Impacts of, 224
OPEC vs. Non-OPEC Oil Production, 461
Open General License (OGL) 68
Operating Cost Elements, 278
Operating Cost of the Refinery, 393
Operating Cost, 138, 292
Optimising Existing Operations, 288
Optimization of Refinery Configuration, 290
Optimization of Upstream Technologies for Upgrading and Implementation, 151
Optimizing Crude Cost:
Summing-up, 291
Optimizing Crude FOB Cost, 289
Order Entry/Inventory Control, 427
Organization of Petroleum Exporting Countries (OPEC), 7, 39, 61, 170, 207, 219, 278, 323, 469
and Non-OPEC Fact Sheet, 463
Oil Policy, 221
Production Cut and Compliance, 223
Reserves, 221
Role in International Oil Trading, 297
Role in Price Structuring, 219
World Oil Market, 219
OSP of NOCs, 214
OTC Energy and Oil Derivative Markets, 319
OTC Oil Derivatives Market, 320

P

PAMS Module, 425
Panipat Refinery:
IOCL, 265
Panna-Mukta and Tapti, 417
Paper Market, 211
Paradigm Shift in Business Process, 274
Parallel Marketing of LPG, 304
Payment of Royalties, 399
Peak-Oil:
An Overview, 466
Pecking Order, 217
Per Capita Energy Consumption, 480
Performance Indicators, 291
Permeability, 10
Petro-Flows, 464
Petroleum Accounting Management System (PAMS), 425
Petroleum and Processes of Extraction
Origin of, 8
Fault trap, 9
Anticline, 9
Salt dome, 9
Petroleum Fiscal Systems, 396
Petroleum India International (PII) 227
Petroleum Operations:
Profile of, 11
Petroleum Production and Consumption in India, 42
Petroleum Products, 186
Sectoral Use of, 199
Self-sufficiency in, 279
Petroleum Supply Chain Economics, 203
Petroleum Tariff as percentage of Railway Revenues, 185
Petroleum Transportation:
Players in, 184
Petroleum:
Import and Export of, 306
Petronet Initiative, 160
Petro-retail:
Special Nature of, 341
Petro-retailing, 331

A chronology of the Evolution of Concept, 345
A.T. Kearney Report on, 342
Phased Deregulation of India's Hydrocarbon Sector, 441, 456
Physical Market, 208
Fundaments of, 211
Players in the, 209
Pipeline Economics, 313
Pipeline Maintenance, 176
Pipeline Materials Management, 177
Pipeline Repairs and Rehabilitation, 177
Pipeline Route Selection, 161
Pipeline Transportation, 164, 197
Pipelines and Natural Gas, 146
Pipelines Operations, 175
Pipelines:
Oil and Gas: Comparison, 164
Transportation Operations, 165
Configuration of Cross-Country, 165
Mid-Stream Sector, 158
Transportation, 158
Planning and Measuring Financial Performance, 420, **422**
Planning for Economics of Scale, 290
Plan-wise Outlay, 57
Platforming Process, 244
Platts and Argus, 217
POL Cargo Handled in Majors Ports, 187
Policies and Procedures, 329
Pooling Mechanism, 282
Porosity, 10
Portfolio Matrix:
Limitations to and Way to Overcome, 134
Portfolio Optimization Matrix, 133
Positive Displacement Pumps, 22
Post-Auditing:
Continuous Improvement through, 155
Pre-Process Disposition of the Pre-treatment Process, 244
Prestige Seeker, 350
Price Applicable for Gas Produced under
Price Applicable for Gas Produced under:
NELP Blocks, 418
pre-NELP Exploratory Fields, 417
Price Build-up for End Consumers, 415
Price Build-up for Gas Transporter, 415
Price of Products, 216
Price-based Differentiation, 355
Pricing of Physical Crude Oil Trades, 388
Pricing, 208
Primary Energy and Electricity Resources, 46
Primary Energy Consumption by Fuel, 54
Primary Process Technique, 256
Primary Separation, 236
Primary Separation: Atmospheric and Vacuum Distillation Cuts, 242
Process Configurations, 253
Process Control Basics, 260
Process Control, 261
Process Definition, 260
Process Objective, 252, 256
Process Parameters, 260
Process Principles, 252
Process Steps, 256
Processing Facilities Required at the Oil Field for Oil, 163
Well Treatment, 163
Gathering Systems, 163
Gas-Plant Processing, 163
Producer Price of Gas, 414
Product in a System:
Basic Element of a, 12
Product Lines, 233
Product Pipelines, 275
Product Specifications, 258
Product Tankers, 178
Production and Sales, 89
Production Logging, 20
Production of Petroleum Products in India, 110
Production Sharing Contracts (PSC), 115
Production Sharing Contracts, 398
Production Tests, 19
Products, 275
Profit Oil, 401
Project Overview, 359
Projected Petroleum Products, 113
Projection of Global Energy Demand:
IEA vs. IEO, 35
Promoting LPG as Auto-Fuel, 303
Proven Oil Reserve Estimates, 461
Proven Reserves of Fossil Fuels and R/P Ratio, 78
Public Sector Oil Companies (PSUs) 274
Public Utility Commission (PUC) 305
Pump Stations, 176
Purchase Orders, 427

Q

Quality Assurance Checks, 129
during Life-cycle, 129
Quality Assurance Criteria, 128
Quality Assurance, 126
Quantum of Oil Import vis-à-vis the Cash Outflow, 55
Quarterly Required Distributions (QRD) 143

R

Rate Base, 148
Rate Design, 149
Rate Determination, 147
Rationale for FOB, 314
Ravva, 417
Reaction Chemistry, 254, 257
Reactor, 249
Reactor-Regenerator Section, 248

Reactor-Riser, 248
Recording Gas Revenue, 391
Recording Oil Revenue, 385
Recoverable vs. Non-recoverable Costs, 402
Recovery Processes, 88
Reduced Crude Oil (RCO), 285
Refined and Petro-chemical Product Marketing, 305
Refinery:
  Company-wise Locations and Capacity of the, 263
  Comparison, 146
  Economics, 230
  Financial Analysis and Evaluation of, 144
  Measures for Improving Profitability, 288
Refinery Cost Elements, 276
  Cost Implications and Break-up of, 277
Refinery Energy and Losses:
  Reduction in, 289
Refinery Gate Value, 283
Refinery Industry:
  Growth of, 261
Refinery Inputs:
  Other, 19
Refinery Operation Costs:
  Reduction in, 289
Refinery Process and Technology, 236
Refinery Profitability I Margins under Free Market Scenario, 283
Refinery Profitability/Margins, 281
Refining and Marketing:
  Downstream Industry, 435
Refining Capacity Addition:
  during 10th Plan, 270
  during 11th Plan, 270
  during 12th Plan, 270
Refining Capacity and Capacity Utilisation, 268
Refining Capacity, Actual Crude Throughput and Capacity Utilization, 268
Refining Capacity:
  Historic, 28
Refining Cost:
  Elements of, 281
Refining Margin:
  Need and Importance of, 282
Refining Profitability under APM, 282
Refining Strategy and Operations, 292
Refining Techniques and Processes, 232
Refining:
  Historic Backdrop of, 232
Reforms in Indian Economy, 439
Reformulated Gasoline 19
Regenerator, 251
Regional Oil Well Operating Costs, 139
Regulated Industry, 78
Regulations, 327
Regulatory Framework of Gas Industry, 69
Reliance Petroleum Limited (RPL) Private Sector Jamnagar, 201, 268
Reputation and Goodwill, 452
Research Findings, 342
Research:
  Key Finding of, 342
Reserve Cost Ratios, 406
Reserve Ratios, 405
Reserve Recognition Accounting, 367
Reserve Replacement Ratio, 405
Reserve Value Ratios, 407
Residual Fuel Oils, 234
Results of Operations, 389
Retail Function Involves, 333
Retail Modules, 426
Retail Outlets:
  Ancillary Services by, 344
Retailing Concept, 332
Retailing is Selling, 333
Retailing:
  Explains the Various Stages of the Wheel of, 338
  The Effect of, 333
  The Wheel of, 338
Return on Investment Computation for a Retail Outlet, 420
Revenue Accounting, 411
Revenue from Oil, 392
Revenue Requirement, 147
Rigs:
  Types of, 82
    Mobile Rigs, 82
    Desert Rigs, 82
    Heli Rigs, 82
    TBA Rigs, 83
    Off-Shore Rigs, 83
  Setting the, 83
Risk Profile of Portfolio, 134
Routine Chore Doer, 349
Russia and the Caspian Basin, 476

S

Safety Systems in Oil, 23
Sale and Purchase Agreement (SPA), 194
Sales Maximization vs. Profit Maximization, 424
Sales Performance of Petroleum Products in Public and Private Sectors, 308
Sankar Committee on Gas Pricing, 413
Saudi Arabia and the Gulf Producers, 478
Scenario of Global Oil Production by the Major Oil-Producing Countries, 431
Schedule for Introducing Improved Quality Fuels as per Auto Fuel Policy, 269
Schematic Diagram of a Petroleum Trap, 86
Schematic Presentation of the Catalytic Reforming Process, 257

SE vs. FC, 374
Second Oil-Shock, 470
Secretariat for Industrial Approvals (SIA), 329
Sector-wise Energy Consumption, 57
Seismic Exploration, 91
Self-Reliance, 457
Self-sufficiency in Petroleum Products, 279
Separation: Heavy on the Bottom, Light on the Top, 205
Service Contracts, 401
Share of POL Traffic in Total Traffic handled at Major Ports, 187
Shared and Support Service Process Areas, 497
Shell Canada Expands e-business on Secure Tivoli Software Platform, 516
Ship:
  Types of, 191
Shipping Cost:
  Reduction in, 289, 291
Shipping Fleet for LPG in India, 198
Shipping, 190
  of Liquefied Natural Gas, 194
Short-Term Oil Market, 61
Signature and Production Bonuses, 399
Simple Distillation, 17
Site Selection Criteria, 334
Slant-hole and Horizontal Wells, 87
Sliding Scale Royalty, 400
SMC Reports: Natural Gas Price Forecasting and Advisory Services, 330
Social Consequences, 333
Solution: Single Point of Control, 516
Solvent Flooding, 102
Some facts of Stat-Oil, 514
Sour Water Stripping, 258
Sources and Availability, 206
Sources of India's Imported Crude, 225
South Asia:
  Energy Scenario in, 478
Special Products, 283
Start-up Company:
  Comparison of Accounting Impact for a, 371
Stations Maintenance, 176
Statoil's e-business Roadmap, 514
Strategy of 10th Plan for E&P Activities, 112
Stratigraphic 'Test Wells', 381
Strength of Retailing, 332
Strong Brands Drive Revenue Growth, 347
Structural Shifts Envisaged in Transportation of Petroleum Products, 201
Structure of the Private Sector Oil Industry, 444
Subsurface Controlled Subsurface Safety Valves (SCSSV), 23
Successful Efforts Accounting, 368
Sulfur Removal, 164
Sulphur Recovery Unit, 257
Sun and Cyberonix eGasStation Architecture, 509
Sun's Role in e-GasStation Implementations, 511
Super Major Theory, 449
Superior Kerosene Oil (SKO), 200
Supply Plan Management, 182
Supply Strategy, 308
Surface Data, 97
Surface Geology, 96
Surface Safety Systems Surface Safety Valve, 23

T

Tank Farms, 176
Tank Trucks, 178
Tank Wagons, 178
Tanker Chartering, 192
  A view of, 192
    Voyage Charter, 192
    Time Charter, 192
    Bareboat Charter, 192
    Trip-Time Charter, 193
    Contract of Affreightment (COA), 193
Tanker, 146
  The Most Economic Transport Mode, 218
Tapping Non-conventional Oil Resources, 58
Targets in Respect of Major Activities, 108
Tatipaka Refinery-ONGC, 268
Taxation, 218
Techno-Commercial Working Committee (TCWC) 66
Technological Upgradations, 290
Technology Leadership Approach, 451
TERI Report, 315
Terminal Automation, 189
Terminal Facilities:
  An Overall view of, 188
Terminal Management, 187
Terminal:
  Benefits of Automation for, 189
  View of Storage Facility in a, 188
  View of a Tanker Loading Operation in a, 189
The e-GasStation Architecture, 510
The Seven Sisters, 469
The Upstream Industry, 433
  Future of the North Sea, 433
  Western Investment in Middle-East, 433
  US Independents Prefer to Explore Overseas, 433
  Republic of China, 433
  Asia-Pacific Region, 434
  Libya, 434
  Africa, 434
Thermal Methods, 102
Time Poor, 349
Timing of Revenue Recognition, 392
Tonnage, 191
Top World Oil Exporters, 221
Top World Oil Net Exporters, 464

Top World Oil Producers, 221, 463
Total Asia Gas Demand Profile, 317
Total Primary Commercial Energy Supply (TPCES) 114
Tracking of Sales, 421
Tradable and non-tradable Crude, 212
Trade and Transportation, 217
Trade in LNG, 194
Trade/Exchange, 506
Trading of Oil and Natural Gas, 305
Trading Outlook, 509
Trading Petroleum Products, 298
Transferring the World's Wealth, 484
Transformation in Downstream Oil and Gas, 503
Transmission Charges, 416
Transportation:
- by Railways, 185
- by Roads, 186

Transportation in Oil Industry:
- A Multi-Modal Operation, 184

Transportation Legs in Petroleum Transportation System, 200
Transportation Mechanism of Pipeline Nominations, 311
Transportation of LPG by Pipeline: Jamnaar-Loni Pipeline, 199
Transportation of Petroleum Products by Multiple Operators/Agencies, 184
Transportation Services, 410
Traps:
- Types of, 10

Treatment Processes, 13
Trust Seeker, 349
Types of Process Configurations, 245
Typical Asset Lives for Depreciation and Amortization, 372
Typical Drilling and Completion Costs and their Accounting Treatment under SE, 381
Typical Product Pattern of a Modern Refinery, 285

U

Ultra Large Crude Carriers (ULCCs) 146
Uncertainty and Price, 60
Underground Coal Specification (UCS) 113
Understanding Petroleum Retail Business, 331
Unique Features of e-GasStation Architecture, 512
Upstream Assts Management (UAM) 119
Upstream Process Map, 500
Upstream Sector Impact and E-business Opportunity, 500
USA:
- Brand Image to Promote the Sales of Premium Grade Petro-Products in, 352
- Production Cost and Fiscal Structure, 141
- Summary of Oil Well Production Statistics, 138
- Summary of Gas Well Production Statistics (GAS WELL), 138

Utilization of Natural Gas, 64

V

Vaccum Distilation Unit (VDU), 285
- Process Schematic, 240

Valuation of Undeveloped Reserves, 142
Valuation, 144
Value Improving Practices (VIPs) 126
Value-added Products and Services-based Differentiation, 352
Venezuela, 477
Vessels:
- Size of, 190

Visakh Refinery (HPCL), 266

W

WACC 141
Well Completion, 12
Well Cuttings, 98
Wells:
- Classification of, 22
- Types of, 87

West Texas Intermediate (WTI) 5, 214
Wet Trade, 191
Wholesale Marketing, 427
Wholesale Modules, 426
Why Buyers are pursuing e-commerce?, 513
Why does Stat-oil need e-Business?, 514
Winners are VAC's, 506
Work Accomplishment between Major Decisions, 127
World Demand Supply Balance 224
World Energy Investment Outlook 49
World EOR Production by Method, 102
World Gas Reserve, IEA, 462
World Natural Gas Demand, 462
World Oil Consumption by Region and Country Group, 465
World Oil Crisis: Implications for Global Security and the Middle-East, 480
World Oil Production and Consumption, 460
World Oil Production and Exportable Surplus, 220
World Oil Production, 462
World Primary Energy Demand Projection, 460
World Scale, 194